W9-BCN-225

AN ANNOTATED INDEX OF MEDIEVAL WOMEN

The photographs on the cover
are reproduced courtesy of the following sources:

Bayerische Staatsbibliothek
British Library
Bibliothèque Nationale
Österreichische Nationalbibliothek

AN ANNOTATED INDEX OF MEDIEVAL WOMEN

BY

ANNE ECHOLS

AND

MARTY WILLIAMS

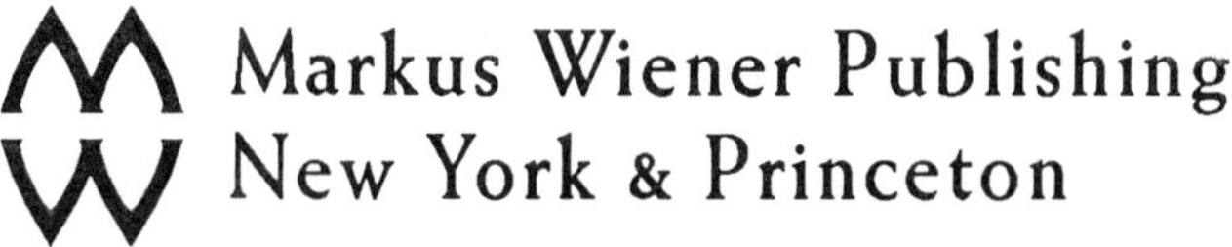

Berg Publishers
Oxford, England

For information write to:

Markus Wiener Publishing, Inc.
114 Jefferson Road, Princeton, NJ 08540

For the United Kingdom and Continental Europe write to:

Berg Publishers Ltd.
150 Cowley Road, Oxford OX4 1JJ, U.K.

LIBRARY OF CONGRESS CATALOGING-IN-PUBLICATION DATA

The Annotated Index of Medieval Women / edited by Anne Echols and Marty Williams

ISBN 0-910129-27-4

1. Women—Europe—Biography—Dictionaries.
2. Women—History—Middle Ages, 500–1500—Dictionaries.
3. Prosopography—Europe.

I. Echols, Anne. II. Williams, Marty.

CT3220.A56 1990 90-39810 CIP

920.72'094—dc20

CIP CATALOGUE DATA IS ALSO AVAILABLE FROM THE BRITISH LIBRARY.

Printed in the United States of America on acid-free paper

Acknowledgments

Many people have offered valuable suggestions throughout the writing of the ***Annotated Index.***

We are especially grateful to Inge Neske of Munich, Germany, for her encouragement at the beginning of the project. Michael Sheehan of the Pontifical Institute of Medieval Studies in Toronto, Canada, read a later draft of the manuscript and provided us with many useful insights, as did Margaret Schaus, reference librarian at Haverford College, Pennsylvania. We would also like to thank the librarians at the Spartanburg County Public Library (Spartanburg, South Carolina) for their research help. The reference librarians at the Woodruff Library of Emory University (Atlanta, Georgia) were also very helpful, with special thanks to Eric Nitschke.

As a final note, this book would not have been possible without the use of computers. We would like to thank our friends Susan Hollingshead and Robert Gordon for their support and advice on how to use various software packages effectively.

TABLE OF CONTENTS

INTRODUCTION

The ***Annotated Index of Medieval Women*** was born of our frustration in researching medieval women for our forth-coming book, ***Between Pit and Pedestal***. Although there are a number of reference tools and textbooks which help identify medieval men, we found no such works available solely on the subject of medieval women. Instead we often had to research females by combing through biographical sources on their fathers or husbands.* Information gleaned in this fashion tended to be sketchy, merely stating the names of male relatives rather than presenting facts about the women themselves. Vague or confusing information was even worse; for example, women were frequently identified merely as "the heiress of X" or "the countess of Y." To obtain a complete and accurate account of a woman's genealogy and accomplishments, we had to consult many different types of published sources and sort out much conflicting data. As a result of this research, we have created brief life stories (when possible) which present these females not as one-dimensional, genealogical appendages to males, but rather as flesh and blood women who participated in many aspects of medieval society.

Everyone who has read this ***Index*** in manuscript form has been very complimentary. On the other hand, each person has also made suggestions for improvements. Some want us to include earlier women—those from the fifth through the eight centuries. Others want more German, Italian, or Spanish sources. One reader advised us to add several biographical categories. Yet another

---

* During the past twenty years, a vast body of research has begun to remedy the omission of women from medieval history. For a good explanation of current work and the changes in historiography, see Susan M. Stuard (ed.), *Women in Medieval History and Historiography* (Philadelphia, 1987).

wants us to drop all older or non-scholarly sources. We have acted on some of these suggestions, but could not implement them all.

Undoubtedly, we could make this ***Index*** even more complete if we worked at it for another twenty years, since there is a vast amount of ongoing research in this field. We feel, however, that it is important to make this work available in a timely manner; in its present form this ***Index*** should be a valuable research tool.

Though we could not include everything that our readers suggested, what ***The Annotated Index of Medieval Women*** does contain is some 1,500 entries which present a cross-section of women from a span of seven centuries (beginning with the year A.D. 800), nearly thirty countries, and a wide variety of social classes and spheres of influence. The largest groups of women are from the thirteenth and fourteenth centuries, from England and France, and from the upper echelons of society. This focus was partly created by the availability of published sources from those centuries and geographical areas. On the other hand, in addition to such famous individuals as Eleanor of Aquitaine and Joan of Arc, we have included numerous obscure women—like a Parisian molecatcher, a Dutch tennis champion, and a Spanish poet. This diversity helps to give a sense of the often unnoticed participation of women in many aspects of the medieval world. It will also allow historians to use this index to study peasants and townswomen. To facilitate this function, we have compiled cross reference categories for each entry. They will enable the reader to find only thirteenth-century English alewives, for example, by comparing the list of thirteenth-century women with the list of women from England and the list of alewives.

In fact, this index can be used in a number of ways. The most complete information can be obtained by browsing through the ***Main Listings***. (In the *Main Listings*, a dagger (†) at the beginning of a woman's name indicates that she has her own entry.) The ***Cross Reference Listings*** which follow the *Main Listings* section are valuable for finding specific groups of individuals—like those thirteenth-century English alewives. The ***Biographical Categories*** comprise the largest section of the *Cross References*. For each main entry we have attempted to include the greatest number of categories. To understand our entire cross reference system, please refer to the *Reader's Guide to Using the Index* beginning on page xiii.

Our sources are identified very briefly in the *Main Listings*, but are cited in full in the ***Complete Bibliography*** at the end of the book. We have not attempted to name every source for each woman. Where possible, however, we have tried to include a wide range of sources. Thus the student who is unable to find one particular book should be able to use one of the other sources listed. Moreover, each work listed frequently gives different facts or interpretations about the woman. Some of our sources (usually general medieval histories) contain errors about genealogy and/or confuse one woman with another (such as a mother with her daughter). We have tried to avoid these pitfalls by confirming our information from several sources. In the event of conflicting data, we present a balanced view of the existing sources, as well as our own interpretation.

Our bibliography includes general medieval texts, printed primary sources from England and France (very few from the rest of Europe), largely English-language articles or monographs which deal with women, family, and social history (most of these have been written since 1970), and even some works of popular history. A few such titles are included in the hope that this ***Index*** will be helpful even to the non-scholarly community or to anyone who has little access to the most fully-equipped library facilities. Moreover, older—and by current standards less-scholarly—works have often proved to be the best places to find references to women who are not well-known. We have frequently discovered a woman's name in such a source and then proceeded to find other references to her through searching out information on her region, husband, sons, father, religious donations or community, etc. We have read most of the sources listed in our bibliography. In a few cases, however, we have taken another scholar's advice on a source that we have not personally seen. Occasionally we have searched a book's index for a specific woman rather than reading the entire work. We have tried to make the bibliography as broad as possible, but do not pretend to have cited every worthwhile source.

To help readers/students/historians use this ***Index***, we have attempted to include everything that we would want in such a reference tool; for example, a listing for a woman who appears to be relatively unimportant herself may be included because she is often confused with another female with the same, or a similar, name.

We realize, however, that as work on the subject of medieval women progresses, more entries and biographical categories could be added to our pioneering effort. Moreover, as research continues, new facts and interpretations come to light. Thus many of our entries are probably not complete pictures, but merely starting points for the study of medieval history and women's studies.

READER'S GUIDE TO USING THE INDEX

How to Use Main Listings to Find Women by Name

Women are listed alphabetically by first names—except where the given names are unclear (for example, lady de Coucy can be found under Coucy, lady de). In the Main Listings are: names, dates, countries, brief summaries of available biographical information, categories under which the women are cross referenced, and short bibliographic references.

Since many women's names have variant spellings, we have tried to put the variations under one spelling, for instance, Catarina and Katharine are both forms of the name Catherine, and can be found under *Catherine* in the C's. Similarly, all variations of *Jean* (Joan, Jeanne, Joanna, etc.) are listed as if each were spelled Jean. A sample order might be: Joan of Arc, Jeanne de Bourbon, Joanna of Naples. We have, however, listed variations in brackets after a woman's name.

A sample listing might read:

ADELE OF CHAMPAGNE, queen of France
[Adela; Alix; Adele of Blois]

(Adele would be listed alphabetically as if her name were Adele Champagne.)

The following is a list of the names with variant spellings which have been included together under the first name variation:

Aaeles; Aales; Aalis; Aaliz
See ALICE

ADELAIDE [Adelais; Adelheid; Alazais; Azalais]
Also see: ALICE

ADELE
[Adela; Adelie; Adella]
Adelheid See ADELAIDE
Aelis See ALICE
AGNES [Agnese]
Alaiz See ALICE
Alazais See ADELAIDE
ALESSANDRA
[Alesandra; Alexandra]
ALIANORE; ALIÉNOR
See ELEANOR
ALICE
[Aaeles; Aales; Aalis; Aaliz; Aelis; Alaiz; Alix; Alys]
Also see: ADELAIDE
AMICIA
[Amica; Amice; Amicie; Amitia]
Ana See ANNE
ANASTASIA
[Anastacia; Anastaise]
Anès See ANNE
ANGELA [Angele]
ANNE
[Ana; Anees; Anès; Ann; Anna]
Azalais See ADELAIDE

BEATRICE [Beatrix; Beatriz; Bietrix]
BERTHA [Berthe]
Bietrix See BEATRICE
BONA [Bonne]

Caecelia See CECILIA
CATHERINE / KATHERINE
[Caterina; Catharina; Catharine; Katerine; Katharine]
CECILIA [Caecelia; Cecile; Cecily]
Christiane See CRISTIANA
CHRISTINE
[Christina; Cristina; Cristine; Crystene]
CLARE [Clair; Clara]
CLARICIA [Clarice; Clarissa]
CONSTANCE
[Constantia; Costanza]
Costanza See CONSTANCE
Cristina; Cristine; Crystene
See CHRISTINE
CUNIGUNDE (A) / KUNIGUNDE

DENISE [Denyse]
DIEMUD
[Diemudis; Diemuod]
DIONYSIA
[Dionisia; Dyonisia]
DOROTHY
[Dorotea; Dorothea]
Dulce See DOUCE
Dyonisia See DIONYSIA

EDITH Also see: EADGYTH
ELEANOR / ALIANORE / LEONOR [Aliénor; Eleanora; Elinor; Leonora]
ELIZABETH
[Elisabeth; Elizabetta]
ELLEN [Elen]
EUDOCIA [Eudoxia]
EUPHEMIA [Eufimia; Evfimia]

GIOVANNA See JEAN/JOAN
GISELA [Gisel; Gisèle; Gisle]

HELEN [Helena; Helene]

INGEBORG
[Ingebjorg; Ingibiorg]
ISABELLE
[Isabeau; Isabel; Isabella; Isabiau]
Also see: YSABEL

JEAN/JOAN
[Giovanna; Jeanne; Jehanne; Joanna; Johanna; Juana]
JEANNETTE [Jehannette]
Joanna; Johanna
See JEAN/JOAN
Juana See JEAN/JOAN
Jehannette See JEANNETTE

KATHERINE
[Katerine; Katharine]
See CATHERINE
KUNIGUNDE
[Kunegunde; Kunigunda]
See CUNEGUNDE

LEONOR [Leonora]
See ELEANOR
LIUTGARD
[Lutgard; Liutgarde; Liudgard]

MABEL
[Mabil; Mabille; Mabile; Mabella]
MADELEINE
[Maddalena; Magdelena]
Magdelena See MADELEINE
MAHAUT [Maheut]
MARGARET
[Margaretha; Margarida; Margarita; Margherita; Marguerite]
MARGERY
[Margerie; Marjery; Marjorie; Marjory]
Margherita See MARGARET
Maria; Marie See MARY
Marjery; Marjorie; Marjory
See MARGERY
Marguerite See MARGARET
MARTHA
[Marthe; Mata; Matha]
MARY [Maria; Marie]
MATILDA / MAUD
Maud See MATILDA/MAUD

NICHOLE [Nicole; Nicola]

PERRETTE
[Peretta; Perette; Perrotte]
PERRONELLE
[Péronelle; Peronnelle; Perrenelle; Perronnele; Perronnelle]
PHILIPPA [Phelippe; Phillippia]

SANCIA
[Sancha; Sanche; Sanchia]
SARAH [Sara; Sarra; Sarre]
SIBYL
[Sibila; Sibilia; Sibylla;

Sibylle; Sybil; Sybilla; Sybille]

Sybil; Sybilla; Sybille
See SIBYL

THERESA [Teresa]

TIFFANIA
[Thyphainne; Tiphaine; Tyfaine; Tyfainne; Typhainne]

YSABEL
[Ysabelle; Ysabiau]
Also see: ISABEL

How to Find Women by Date

These lists are organized by first dates; where several women have the same date, they are arranged alphabetically. Where only one known date exists, we have had to use that as our first date, even though it may well be the date of death. A woman who lived from 1196 until 1250 will be listed in the 1100s. Where necessary we have used the following abbreviations: b for date of birth; m for married; d for died; and fl for floruit. If there is only one date with no abbreviation beside it, then it is the only date available for that particular woman.

Dates are divided into the following lists:

800–900
901–1000
1001–1100
1101–1200
1201–1300
1301–1400
1401–1500

How to Find Women by Country

We have tried to list women under the largest possible number of countries. Therefore, a woman may be listed under her country of birth, the countries she moved to when she married, retired, was exiled, and so on. Moreover, if a man was king of two countries we have listed his wife under both—even though she may have lived primarily in one of the two. Most of these countries are modern national designations, but there are a few exceptions—such as Bohemia, Byzantium, and Flanders. In most cases, we have chosen to use modern American spellings. For example, Luxembourg is more often seen in medieval names as "Luxemburg," but we have spelled it the modern American way.

NOTE: Women are listed alphabetically by country; if a woman has a name enclosed in brackets after her name, for instance:

Katherine Swynford [Catherine]

she will be found in the Main Listings under the name in brackets.

The following are the countries included in this index:

Austria	France	Netherlands
Belgium	Germany	Norway
Bohemia	Greenland	Poland
Bulgaria	Hungary	Portugal
Byzantium	Iceland	Russia
China	Ireland	Scotland
Cyprus	Israel	Spain
Czechoslovakia	Italy	Sweden
Denmark	Lebanon	Switzerland
England	Luxembourg	Turkey
Flanders		Wales

How to Find Women by Biographical Category

We have tried to make this section as useful as possible, but we have not included every possibile classification. Some of our categories include hundreds of women while others have only two representatives. In some cases we have used words which were not part of the terminology of the Middle Ages. In other cases, we have utilized catch-all terms. For instance, we use the category "religieuses" as a short term to describe those women who lived the religious life but were not professed nuns, anchoresses, etc.

In order to more precisely explain women's roles, still other cross reference categories have been defined in narrower terms than their usual meanings. Thus "queens" generally denotes consorts or women who ruled in name only, while "rulers" and "regents" both denote women who actively participated in medieval governments. The explanation of exactly what each category includes can be found in the "Biographical Categories" section which begins on page 461.

NOTE: A woman listed as:

Alix of France [Alice]

can be found under the variation of her name that is enclosed in brackets.

The following is a list of the categories used:

ABBESSES

ABDUCTION

ADULTERY
Also see: MISTRESSES. WOMEN OF EASY VIRTUE.

ALEWIVES
Also see: MERCHANTS. OCCUPATIONS. TAVERNERS.

Alms see: CHARITY.

ANCHORESSES

ANTINOMIAN
Also see: HERETICS.

APOTHECARIES
Also see: MEDICINE.

APPAREL
Also see: CLOTHWORKERS. OCCUPATIONS. SILKWORK.

APPRENTICES
Also see: EMPLOYERS. OCCUPATIONS.

Architecture see: BUILDERS.

ART PATRONS
Also see: PATRONS OF LITERATURE.

ARTISTIC CLOTHWORK
Also see: CLOTHWORKERS. SILKWORK.

ARTISTS

ASTRONOMY

Bakers see: PROVISIONING.

BANKING

BARBERS
Also see: MEDICINE.

BATHHOUSE
Also see: OCCUPATIONS.

BEGUINES

BEQUESTS
Also see: ESTATE.

Bigamy see: ADULTERY

BOOK OWNERS
Also see: PATRONS OF LITERATURE. WRITERS.

BOOKMAKING
Also see: ARTISTS. OCCUPATIONS. WRITERS.

BUILDERS
Also see: MERCHANTS. OCCUPATIONS.

Butchers see: PROVISIONING.

CANDLE MAKERS

Canonesses see: NUNS.

Carpenters see: BUILDERS.

CATHARS
Also see: HERETICS.

CHARITY
Also see: RELIGIOUS PATRONS.

Chess see: GAMES.

CHILDBIRTH
Also see: MEDICINE. MIDWIVES.

CHILDCARE
Also see: SERVANTS.

CLOTHWORKERS
Also see: APPAREL. ARTISTIC CLOTHWORK. OCCUPATIONS. SILKWORK.

Courts see:
ECCLESIASTICAL COURTS. LEGAL ACTIVITY. MANORS. ORDEALS.
Crafts see: OCCUPATIONS.
CRUSADES
Also see: SOLDIERS.

DANCE
DIVORCE
DOCTORS/EMPIRICS
For specialized practices see: MEDICINE.
DOWRY/DOWER
DRAMA
Dressmakers see: APPAREL.
DWARVES

ECCLESIASTICAL COURTS
EDUCATED
Also see: SCHOLARS.
Embroiderers see: ARTISTIC CLOTHWORK.
EMPLOYERS
Also see: APPRENTICES. OCCUPATIONS. RECOMANDRESSES.
Envoys see: NEGOTIATORS.
ESTATE
Also see: LAND/ PROPERTY. MANAGERS.
Estate administrators see: MANAGERS.
Executions see: PUNISHMENTS.

Fishmongers see: PROVISIONING.

GAMES
Also see: HUNTING.
GEMS/JEWELRY
Also see: GOLDSMITHS.
GENEALOGY
GOLDSMITHS
Also see: GEMS/JEWELRY. OCCUPATIONS.
Governesses see: TEACHERS.

HANDICAPPED
Also see: MEDICINE.
Hat makers see: APPAREL.
Hawking see: HUNTING.
Herbwives see: APOTHECARIES.
HERETICS
Also see: ANTINOMIANISM. CATHARS. HUSSITES. LOLLARDS. WALDENSIANS. WITCHCRAFT.
Hucksters see: MERCHANTS.
HUNTING
HUSSITES
Also see: HERETICS.

ILLEGITIMACY
Illuminators see: ARTISTS.
INNKEEPERS
Also see: OCCUPATIONS.
Inquisition see: ECCLESIASTICAL COURTS.

singly see: ALEWIVES. APPAREL. APPRENTICES. BANKING. BATHHOUSE. BOOKMAKING. BUILDERS. CANDLE MAKERS. CLOTHWORKERS. EMPLOYERS. GEMS/ JEWELRY. GOLDSMITHS. INNKEEPERS. LAUNDRESSES. MINING. POTTERS. PROVISIONING. RECOMANDRESSES. SERVANTS. SHIPPING. SILKWORK. TANNERS. TAVERNERS.

ORDEALS
Also see: COURTS.

ORPHANS

Painters see: ARTISTS.

PATRONS OF LITERATURE
Also see: BOOK OWNERS.

PAWNS

Peasants
see: MANORS.

PILGRIMS

PLAGUE
Also see: MEDICINE.

Playwrights
see: DRAMA.

POETS/TROUBADOURS
Also see: WRITERS.

POLITICS
Also see: NEGOTIATORS. REGENTS. RULERS.

POPES

POTTERS
Also see: OCCUPATIONS.

Poulterers see: PROVISIONING.

PREACHERS

Prioresses see: ABBESSES.

PRISONS
Also see: PUNISHMENTS.

PROSTITUTES
Also see: ADULTERY. MISTRESSES. WOMEN OF EASY VIRTUE.

PROVISIONING
Also see: ALEWIVES. INNKEEPERS. OCCUPATIONS. TAVERNERS.

PUNISHMENTS
Also see: PRISONS.

QUEENS
Also see: REGENTS. RULERS.

RAPE

REBELLIONS
Also see: SQUABBLES.

Recluses
see: ANCHORESSES.

RECOMMANDRESSES
Also see: OCCUPATIONS.

REGENTS
Also see: POLITICS. QUEENS. RULERS.

RELICS
Also see: RELIGIOUS PATRONS. SAINTS.

RELIGIEUSES
Also see: ABBESSES. ANCHORESSES. BEGUINES. NUNS.

How to Find Women by Last Names, Titles, Regions, and Cities

In this section women are listed according to their last names, cities, titles, estates, and/or regions (and those of their husbands and families).

For example:

Abella of Salerno can be found under *Italy* in the Cross-Reference by Country listings; she is found under *Salerno* in the Index of Names, Titles, Regions, and Cities.

Adelaide of Anjou's country is *France*; she is listed under *Anjou, Gévaudun*, and *Arles* in the Index of Names, Titles, Regions, and Cities. These lists will help readers identify particularly confusing women, such as the multiple "Elizabeth de Burghs."

Note that queens are frequently not listed under these categories—only in the lists of countries.

Once again, we have tried to list women under the broadest range of possibilities, and have arranged the last names, cities, and so forth in alphabetical order. Some categories will include many women, while other will have only one. Where possible we have checked current reference materials for modern American spellings.

NOTE: When a woman has a name in brackets after her name:

Maud de Braose [Matilda]

look for her in the Main Listings under the name in brackets.

How to Use the Complete Bibliography

Our bibliography serves largely as a beginning point for those wishing to do further research on the women of this time period. There are, of course, many sources that we have not cited, and numerous books—such as the Parisian tax survey from the year 1292—list more women than we have included in this index.

At the end of each woman's entry in the Main Listings there are shortened bibliographic references with page numbers. Note that a series of dots between source page numbers (i.e., Bynum, *Holy...*, pp. 24, 27, 86, 140, 141–2 ... 395 n.11, 401 n.84.) indicates that the woman is mentioned so often between those pages that we can not list the pages separately.

To find the full citations, turn to the "Complete Bibliography." Most sources will be found in the large list of "Sources with Authors"—listed alphabetically by the author's last name.

Example: in the Main Listing you might see:

Hanawalt, "Fur...";

turning to Hanawalt in the "Complete Bibliography," you would find:

Hanawalt, Barbara A. "Fur Collar Crime: The Pattern of Crime among the Fourteenth Century English Nobility." *Journal of Social History*. 8 (Summer 1975): 1–17.

Sources with no author (such as *St. Catherine...Letters*), will be found listed alphabetically by the first word in the List of Sources without Authors.

There is also a very short List of Abbreviations which contains such sources as *Acta Sanctorum*—which we have abbreviated *A.S.* throughout the Main Listings.

— A —

AASE

See—ASA.

AASTA GRÖNSKE **[Åsta]**

c. 970s–1020 Norway

Wife of Harold Grönske, king of Vestfold. Aasta bore his posthumous son (c.990), Olaf II Haraldsson (St. Olaf), later king of Norway. Her second husband was Sigurd Syr, king of Ringerike. They had several sons including Harold Sigurdsson, later King Harold III Hardrada of Norway. Aasta and Sigurd Syr helped put Olaf on the throne.

♦ **Models. Politics. Queens.** ♦

Boyesen, *Story...*, pp. 182, 186–188, 199–200, 240. Bukdahl, *Scandinavaia...*, v.1, p. 316. Larsen, *History...*, p. 98.

ABELLA OF SALERNO

fl.c. 1200s Italy

Author of medical treatise on "black bile" or madness (*De atra bile*), and one on childbirth (*De natura seminis*). Abella taught both subjects at Salerno.

♦ **Insanity. Medicine. Teachers. University. Writers.** ♦

Hughes, *Women...*, p. 147. Hurd-Mead, *History...*, pp. 225 & 308. Lipinska, *Histoire...*, p. 99. Mozans, *Woman...*, p. 286.

ADA OF SCOTLAND, countess of Holland

fl.c. 1140s–1160s Netherlands; Scotland

See—ADA OF WARENNE.

♦ **Genealogy.** ♦

ADA OF WARENNE **[Adelina of Warrenne]**

c. 1130s–d. 1178 Scotland

Daughter of †Isabel (Elizabeth) of Vermandois and her second husband, William de Warenne. Married Henry of Scotland, earl of Northumberland and Huntingdon (1114–1152). Their sons were: Malcolm IV, William, and David. Their daughter, †Ada of Scotland, married Florent III, count of Holland, in 1162.

♦ **Dowry/dower. Regents. Widows.** ♦

Barlow, *Feudal...*, pp. 212–213. Barrow, *Feudal...*, pp. 243, 420. *DNB,* v.9, p. 546. Duncan, *Scotland...*, pp. 137, 174, 204, 221. Mackie, *History...*, pp. 47 & 48. Warren, *Henry...*, pp. 175, 176.

ADELAIDE [Adelais; Adelheid; Alazais; Azalais]

Also see: ALICE.

ADELAIDE OF ANJOU

c. 949–d.c. 1020 France

Daughter of Foulques II the Good of Anjou (d.960); married Stephen, count of Gévaudan. After his death (c.979), thirty-year-old Adelaide was forced into a political marriage with the future Louis V, the sixteen-year-old son of Lothar, king of France. This union was a dismal failure. In 984, the wealthy Adelaide left Louis, who was then virtually penniless. Adelaide soon married William II of Arles; they were the parents of †Constance of Arles.

♦ **Divorce. Estate. Pawns.** ♦

DBF, v.2, p. 61. Fawtier, *Capetian...*, pp. 55–56. McKitterick, *Frankish...*, pp. 322, 323, Table 9. Stafford, *Queens...*, pp. 4 & 50–51.

ADELAIDE, queen of Burgundy and Provence

See—EADGIFU OF ENGLAND, queen of Burgundy and Provence.

ADELHEID OF BURGUNDY, Holy Roman Empress [Empress Adelaide]

c. 933–d.c. 999 Germany; Italy

Daughter of †Bertha of Swabia and Rudolph II of Burgundy. Married Lothar, king of Italy. When he died, Berengar II, count of Ivrea, kidnapped Adelheid because she refused to marry his son. She escaped and appealed to the Saxon king, Otto I (the Great). In 951, he marched into Italy, subdued Berengar, and married the young widow. The couple returned to Italy in 962, and were crowned by Pope John XII. Adelheid founded the monastery of San Salvatore in Pavia (c.971); she sometimes served as a regent for her male relatives.

♦ **Abduction. Politics. Popes. Prisons. Regents. Religious patrons. Saints.** ♦

Barraclough, *Origins...*, pp. 50–53. Bryce, *Holy...*, pp. 84 & 88. *Cambridge...*, III, pp. 140, 141, 143n., 156, 158, 159, 162, 168, 171, 174, 194, 195, 205 & n., 207, 209–211. *DBF,* v.1, pp. 513–514. Duckett, *Death...*, pp. 79, 81f, 98, 103, 106ff, 209, & 211f. Ennen, *Medieval...*, pp. 61–2, 63, 64, 66. Jourdain, "Memoire...," p. 148. McKitterick, *Frankish...*, pp. 265, 283, 284, & Table 5. Pinnow, *History...*, pp. 33 & 37. Stafford, *Queens...*, pp. 6–12, 25, 45, 53–56, 102–116, 121–124, 138–150, 160–161, 167–190, 206, & 210. Stubbs, *Germany...*, pp. 102, 107, 113, 116, 117–8. Wright, *Works...*, p. 152.

ADELAIDE (Capet), queen of France **[Adelaide of Aquitaine]**

c. 960s–1000s France

Wife of Hugh Capet; mother of Robert II. Adelaide was especially active during the early years of Robert's reign, and she helped to provide stability for the transition from Hugh's reign to that of Robert. She also met personally with †Empress Theophano to secure a treaty of alliance. Adelaide's active participation can be inferred from the number of charters bearing her name. She founded Notre Dame of Argentueil.

♦ **Negotiators. Religious patrons. Rulers. Widows.** ♦

Decaux, *Histoire...*, p. 188. Duckett, *Death...*, p. 123. Facinger, "Study...," pp. 21, 24–25, & 40–41. Stafford, *Queens...*, pp. 41, 77, 88, 107, 111, 141, & 178.

ADELAIDE, queen of FRANCE

fl. 870s France

Around 875, King Charles the Bald forced his son Louis II the Stammerer to repudiate his wife, †Ansgard, and marry the politically well-connected Adelaide. (Her brother was Wilfrid, abbot of Flavigny, and she was also related to Audran II, count of Troyes.) In 879, she bore Louis a posthumous son, Charles the Simple. Adelaide and Ansgard then fought each other for their sons' rights. Ansgard's sons, Louis III and Carloman III, ruled from 879 until 884, while Adelaide's son ruled as Charles III from 893 until 923.

♦ **Pawns. Politics. Squabbles. Widows.** ♦

DBF, v.1, pp. 515–516. McNamara and Wemple, "Marriage...," p. 112. Riché, *Les Carolingiens...*, p. 205. Stafford, *Queens...*, pp. 2, 75, 160, & 199. Wemple, *Women...*, p. 84.

ADELHEID OF GERMANY **[Adelaide of Quedlinburg]**

977–1045 Germany

Daughter of †Theophano of Byzantium and Emperor Otto II. Adelheid was abbess of several important religious foundations. In 984 she was abducted as a political pawn for Henry the Quarrelsome of Bavaria. After Adelheid was released, Henry "repaid" her by giving her the monastery of Vreden.

♦ **Abbesses. Abduction. Managers. Pawns. Politics.** ♦

Cambridge..., III, pp. 276, 290. Ennen, *Medieval...*, pp. 82 & 83. Leyser, *Rule...*, pp. 12, 54, 69, 89, 94.

ADELHEID OF KIEV

See—EUPRAXIA OF KIEV.

ADELAIDE OF LOUVAIN

See—ADELICIA.

ADELAIDE OF MAURIENNE, queen of France

m. 1115–d. 1154 France

Daughter of Count Humbert II of Maurienne. Queen consort of King Louis VI of France, and his partner in government. In fact, many chroniclers and later historians asserted that the mediocre Louis was lucky to have had such an intelligent and active wife. She made benefactions, donations, and appointments. Adelaide also signed charters, settled legal suits, and helped in policy-making decisions. She founded the abbey of Montmartre and was its benefactress. After Louis died in 1137, she married Mathieu de Montmorency. Toward the end of her life, she retired to Montmartre.

♦ **Legal activity. Religieuses. Religious patrons. Rulers.** ♦

Bedos Rezak, "*Women...*," pp. 63–64. *DBF,* v.1, p. 516. Facinger, "Study...", pp. 7, 22, 27, 28–29, 30, 31, 32, & 44. Fawtier, *Capetian...*, pp. 19, 27. Hollister, *Medieval Europe...*, p. 250.

ADELAIDE DE PORCAIRQUES **[Azalais]**

c. 1140–d.c. 1170 France

Troubadour from Montpellier. An accomplished and learned noblewoman, she composed a number of chansons in honor of her "true love," Gui Guerrejat.

♦ **Educated. Poets/troubadours.** ♦

Bogin, *Women...*, pp. 94–97 & 166–167. Boutière and Schutz, *Biographies des...*, p. 341. *DBF,* v.1, pp. 523–524. Egan, *Vidas...*, p. 10.

AZALAIS DE ROCAMARTINA [Alazais; Adelaide of Roquemartine]

fl. 1170s–d.c. 1201 France

First wife of Barral, lord of Marseilles. He repudiated her around 1190. A supporter of troubadours, she also figures in some poetry, especially that of Peire Vidal.

♦ **Divorce. Models. Patrons of literature. Poets/troubadours.** ♦

Bonner (ed.), *Songs...*, pp. 164–165, 288, 290, 292. Boutière and Schutz, *Biographies des...*, pp. 356–360 & 461 n6. Decaux, *Histoire...*, p. 249. Lejeune, "*La Femme...*," p. 208. Marks, *Pilgrims...*, pp. 228, 231, 248.

ADELAIDE OF ROMAINMOUTIER **[Adelaide of Burgundy]**

fl. 880s–920s France

Sister of Rudolph I, king of Burgundy, who gave her the abbey of Romainmoutier. Adelaide married Richard the Justiciar, duke of Burgundy, and was mother of Raoul, king of France (crowned 923). After her husband died in 921, Adelaide retired to her convent but retained her secular title.

♦ **Abbesses. Estate. Managers. Religious patrons.** ♦

DBF, v.1, p. 515. Poupardin, *Le Royaume...*, pp. 13, 15, 205, 351. Riché, *Les Carolingiens...*, p. 227.

ADELAIDE OF SAVONA, countess of Sicily, queen of Jerusalem

m. 1089–d. 1118 Israel; Italy

Daughter of the marquis of Savona. In 1089 she became the third wife of Roger I, Great Count of Sicily. After his death (1101), although young and inexperienced, Adelaide proved to be an able regent for her son, Roger II (b.1095). In 1113, she married Baldwin I of Boulogne, king of Jerusalem, but she soon returned to Sicily. Adelaide founded the Greek monastery of S. Maria del Patirion.

♦ **Divorce. Dowry/dower. Queens. Regents. Religious patrons. Religieuses.**♦

DBF, v.5, p. 871. Douglas, *Norman...*, pp. 33–38, 55, 56, 107, 163, 190, 196. Finucane, *Soldiers...*, p. 54. Hamilton, "Women...," pp. 145–146. Haskins, *Normans...*, p. 210. Norwich, *Kingdom...*, pp. 35, 92, 125, 234, 404–405. Norwich, *Normans...*, pp. 54, 280–284, 286–290, 304. Smith, *Sicily...*, p. 24.

ADELHEID OF SAVOY **[Adelaide of Turin, of Susa]**

c. 1030s–d. 1091 France; Germany; Italy

Daughter and heiress of Manfred of Susa (d.1035); married (1) Hermann of Swabia, count of Turin (d.1038) and (2) Otto of Savoy. Adelheid was regent of their extensive estates (including Turin, Maurienne, and Tarantaise) for their young son. An exceptionally able ruler, she continued this role even after their son was grown. Her daughter, †Bertha of Susa, married Henry IV of Germany in 1066. Because Adelheid was a friend of †Matilda of Tuscany, and an admirer of Pope Gregory VII, she took her son-in-law's investiture case to the pontiff. She later accompanied Henry and Bertha to Canossa where she was one of Henry's sponsors, witnessing and confirming his promises to the pope.

♦ **Negotiators. Politics. Popes. Regents. Rulers. Widows.** ♦

Duff, *Matilda...*, pp. 87, 114, 145–148, 152, 153, 158, 161, 212, & 291. Fuhrmann, *Germany...*, pp. 65, 66. Haverkamp, *Medieval...*, p. 121. Leyser, *Rule...*, p. 152. Pinnow, *History...*, p. 71. Robinson, *Readings...*, pp. 268 & 283.

ADELAIDE OF TOULOUSE, viscountess of Albi, countess of Burlatz

m. 1171–d.c. 1199 France

Daughter of †Constance of France and Raymond V, count of Toulouse. Wife of Roger II, viscount of Albi, Béziers, and Carcassonne. Like most of her family, Adelaide was an avid Cathar. She also supported poets.

♦ **Cathars. Models. Patrons of literature. Poets/troubadours. Popes.** ♦

Bonner (ed.), *Songs...*, pp. 133, 239, 272–273. Boutière and Schutz, *Biographies des...*, pp. 392–403. *DBF,* v.1, p. 519. Lejeune, "La Femme...," p. 207.

ADELAIDE OF TOURS **[Aelis of Auxerre]**

m.c. 830s–860s France

Daughter of Hugh, count of Tours. Married Conrad II of Auxerre and Artois (d.c.863). They built a church at the abbey of St. Germain d'Auxerre. There is some confusion over whether or not Adelaide remarried after Conrad's death. Her second husband is sometimes reported to have been Robert the Strong of France (and count of Anjou). Robert and his wife were the ancestors of the Capetian line. After Conrad died, however, Adelaide may well have been too old to have children. Another possibility is that Conrad and Adelaide had a daughter named Adelaide who did marry Robert the Strong.

♦ **Genealogy. Religious patrons.** ♦

Anselme, *Histoire...*, v.1, pp. 67–68. *DBF,* v.1, pp. 516–517. Riché, *Les Carolingiens...*, p. 330. Wemple, *Women...*, p. 92.

ADELHEID OF VOHBURG

divorced 1153 Germany

First wife of Frederick I Barbarossa of Germany. He divorced her on the grounds of consanguinity.

♦ **Divorce. Pawns.** ♦

Cambridge..., V, p. 390. Fuhrmann, *Germany...*, p. 142. Richardson, "Marriage...," p. 293. Stubbs, *Germany...*, p. 209.

ADELASIA OF TORRES, queen of Sardinia

1220s–1240s Italy

Heiress of Torres. As a widow in 1238, Adelasia was married to young Enzio—an illegitimate son of Emperor Frederick II. The marriage was annulled in 1243.

♦ **Divorce. Estate. Popes. Queens.** ♦

Cambridge..., VI, pp. 152, 154, 157. Haverkamp, *Medieval...*, p. 255. Kantorowicz, *Frederick...*, p. 470.

ADELE [Adela; Adelie; Adella]

ADELE, countess of BLOIS and Chartres **[Adela of Normandy]**

c. 1062–1138 France

Youngest daughter †Matilda of Flanders and William the Conqueror. In 1081 Adele married Stephen (Étienne), count of Blois, Tours, Chartres, and Champagne. They were parents of King Stephen of England and Thibaut II of Champagne (sometimes numbered Thibaut IV). Well-educated, Adele received and wrote many letters. A variety of books were dedicated to her because she was a patroness of authors and poets. While her husband was on Crusade, Adele was regent of their lands.

She also arranged Bohemund of Antioch's marriage to †Constance of France (widow of the count of Champagne). Adele later retired to the convent of Marcigny.

♦ **Educated. Models. Negotiators. Patrons of literature. Regents. Religieuses.** ♦

Barlow, *Feudal...*, pp. 180, 183, 195, 253. Bridge, *Crusades...*, pp. 70–71, 76, 92, 95, 140. *Chronicles...*, pp. 72–74, 78–81, 97. Decaux, *Histoire...*, pp. 213 & 224. Farmer, "Persuasive...," pp. 522–523, 524–525, 526, 533, 541. Gardiner, *English...*, pp. 54–55. Green, *Letters...*, p. 7–8. Heinrich, *Canonesses...*, pp. 196–199. Pernoud, *La femme...*, pp. 217–225. Ritchie, "Bohemund...," p. 301. Robinson, *Readings...*, pp. 321–325. Thompson, *Literacy...*, p. 168.

ADELE OF CHAMPAGNE, queen of France

[Adela; Alix; Adele of Blois]

b. 1145–d. 1206 France

Daughter of Thibaut II of Champagne (see above); became third wife of Louis VII of France in 1160; mother of Philip II Augustus of France (b.1165). While Philip was on Crusade in 1190, Adele was named co-regent. Her energy and authority made her an excellent ruler.

♦ **Dowry/dower. Popes. Regents. Soldiers. Squabbles. Writers.** ♦

Baldwin, *Government...*, pp. 6, 14–17, 44, 69, 102, 103, 368, 466 n37, 528 n109. Barlow, *Feudal...*, p. 289. Bréquigny, *Lettres de rois...*, I, pp. 6–7. *DBF*, v.1, p. 528. Facinger, "Study...," pp. 8–9, 14, 17, 37–38, & 44. Fawtier, *Capetian...*, pp. 27–8, 51, 56, 77, 85, 113, 126, 177. Kelly, *Eleanor...*, pp. 110–111, 126, 127, 140, 160, 202, & 227 Warren, *Henry...*, pp. 88, 90, 104, 148.

ADELIE (l'erbière)

1292 France

In the Parisian tax survey of 1292, Dame Adelie was listed as an *erbière* (seller of medicinal and kitchen herbs). She was taxed 3s.

♦ **Apothecaries. Less-affluent.** ♦

Géraud, *Paris sous...*, p. 149.

ADELA OF FLANDERS, queen of Denmark

m.c. 1072–d.c. 1118 Denmark; Flanders

Daughter of †Gertrude of Saxony and Robert I the Frisian, count of Flanders. Adela married Canute IV of Denmark (sometimes called Canute II or III). He was named a holy martyr and saint after his murder (c.1085). Adela later married Roger de Poville, duke of Calabria. Charles of Denmark, her son by Canute, became count of Flanders after her death.

♦ **Estate. Murder. Queens. Saints.** ♦

Anselme, *Histoire...*, v.2, pp. 718–719. Barlow, *Feudal...*, p. 140. Pirenne, *Histoire...*, v.1, p. 109. Warlop, *Flemish...*, v.2, pt.1, n222.

ADELA OF FRANCE, countess of Flanders

c. 1030 Flanders; France

See—JUDITH OF FLANDERS and MATILDA OF FLANDERS, queen of England

♦ **Genealogy** ♦

ADELA OF FRANCE, countess of Vermandois **[Hildebrante]**

fl. 910s–940s France

Daughter of King Robert I of France (d.923) and his first wife Beatrice; married Herbert II, count of Vermandois and Soissons. The marriage was a bargain for Herbert; he not only elevated his social/political status, but also got control of her dowry—the county of Meaux.

♦ **Dowry/dower. Genealogy.** ♦

Anselme, *Histoire...*, v.1, pp. 49 & 68 (calls her Hildebrante). Dunbabin, *France...*, pp. 95 & 102. McKitterick, *Frankish...*, p. 7. Sassier, *Hugues...*, p. 95.

ADELHEID

See—ADELAIDE.

ADELICIA OF LOUVAIN, queen of England
[Adela; Adelaide; Adeliza; Aelis; Alice]

b. 1103–d. 1151 Belgium; England; France

Daughter of Godfrey, count of Louvain (and marquis of Antwerp). In 1121, Adelicia became the second wife of King Henry I of England. She was particularly interested in the growth of literature in the French vernacular; patroness of troubadours like Geoffrey Gaimar and David the Trouvère. In 1138, the widowed Adelicia married William d'Aubigny, who became earl of Arundel. They had several children.

♦ **Educated. Estate. Patrons of literature. Queens. Widows.** ♦

Barlow, *Feudal...*, pp. 197, 214, 216, 251. *DNB,* v.1, pp. 137–138, 233–234; v.9, p. 447. Fox, *Literary...*, p. 36. Gardiner, *English...*, p. 56. Jourdain, "Memoire...," p. 476. Lejeune, "La Femme...," p. 205. Morson, "English...," p. 147. Thompson, *Literacy...*, p. 171.

ADELINA OF WARRENNE

See—ADA OF WARENNE.

ADELMODIE

See—ALMODIS.

ADRIANA DEL MILA

fl. 1460s–1500 Italy

Wife of Lodovico Orsini, lord of Bassanello. Spanish cousin of Rodrigo Borgia (later Pope Alexander VI). Adriana was an intelligent, literate woman; Rodrigo entrusted several of his children to her for education and introduction into society. Under her tutelage, †Lucrezia Borgia became a poet, learned a number of languages, and developed into a fascinating conversationalist. For years, the two women remained friends and constant companions.

♦ **Childcare. Educated. Popes. Teachers. Widows.** ♦

Chamberlin, *Fall...*, pp. 39, 40, 42, 98–99, 103, 105, 132–133, 263. Cloulas, *Borgias...*, pp. 53, 60, 75, 95, 98, 206, 208, 209. Collison-Morley, *Borgias...*, pp. 30, 32, 52, 59, & 179. Fusero, *Borgias...*, pp. 142, 170–171, 172, 173–176, etc. Johnson, *Borgias...*, pp. 8–9, 82, 93, 98–99, 102, 103, 105.

AELFGIFU

c. 940s–d.c. 970 England

Wife of Eadwig (Edwy), Anglo-Saxon king of England. In the 950s, Dunstan, archbishop of Canterbury, insisted that the couple part because of consanguinity. This was probably a political move against Eadwig; he and Aelfgifu retaliated by forcing Dunstan into exile. She was almost certainly the same Aelfgifu whose extant will was written around the year 970.

♦ **Bequests. Charity. Divorce. Politics.** ♦

DNB, v.1, pp. 149–150. Fell, *Women...*, p. 96. Stafford, *Queens...*, pp. 16, 75, 108, 126, & 189. Whitelock, *Anglo-Saxon...*, pp. 21–23.

AELFGIFU OF NORTHAMPTON **[Alfifa]**

c. 1000–c. 1040 England; Norway

Presumably the daughter of Wulfrun and Earl Aelfhelm of Northampton. Mistress/wife of Canute II of Denmark, king of England; their marriage was never recognized by the church. Nevertheless, Canute's "legitimate" wife, †Emma of Normandy, supposedly hated Aelfgifu. Around 1030, Canute sent Aelfgifu and their young son Sweyn to govern Norway. Probably most of her unpopular measures in that country were undertaken on Canute's orders. Their government was overthrown and Aelfgifu fled the country around 1036. Her other son by Canute, Harold Harefoot, became king of England for a short time.

♦ **Adultery. Regents. Squabbles.** ♦

Barlow, *Edward...*, pp. 37–9, 42, 43n, 44. Blair, *Anglo-Saxon...*, pp. 100 & 104. Boyesen, *Story...*, pp. 225–229. Campbell, *Anglo-Saxons...*, pp. 214, 215, & 216. Campbell, "Queen...," pp. 66–79. Derry, *History...*, pp. 39–40. Jones, *Vikings...*, pp. 372, 383, 385, 398. Larsen, *History...*, pp. 104, 105, & 110. Stafford, *Queens...*, pp. 4, 31, 40, 72, 140, & 163.

AELFLAED **[Aelfflaed]**

m. 901 England

Second wife of Edward the Elder, Anglo-Saxon king of England. Commissioned the making of a lavish embroidered stole for the church.

After Edward divorced Aelflaed, she retired to the convent of Wilton with her daughters.

♦ **Art patrons. Artistic clothwork. Divorce. Religieuses. Religious patrons.** ♦

DNB, v.6, p. 423. Hinton, *Alfred's...,* p. 93. Lucas, *Women...,* p. 44. Page, *Life in...,* p. 76. Stafford, *Queens...,* pp. 43, 70, 74, 90, 107, 179, 190.

AELFTHRYTH **[Aethelthryth; Elfreda]**

c. 950s–d.c. 1002 England

She was presumably the widow of Aethelwold of East Anglia in 964 when she became the third wife of King Edgar of England. (Some sources indicate that Edgar never married †Wulfthryth, so Aelfthryth would be his second legitimate wife.) Aelfthryth was the mother of Edgar's son Ethelred II the Unready. She acquired lands from Edgar and she interceded with him to elevate the position of her ally, Aethelwold, bishop of Winchester. Dunstan, archbishop of Canterbury, accused Aelfthryth of committing adultery with Edgar (possibly because third marriages were uncanonical at the time). When Edgar died in 975, Aelfthryth fought Dunstan for her son's succession to the crown. Chronicles written after her death accused her of conspiracy in the murder of the heir Edward the Martyr (979). After Edward's death, Ethelred did succeed to the throne and Aelfthryth had some power in his government. At the end of her life, she retired to Wherwell.

♦ **Adultery. Childcare. Models. Murder. Politics. Religieuses. Religious patrons. Rulers. Widows.** ♦

Barlow, *Edward...,* pp. 32, 34. Farmer, *Oxford...,* p. 125. Fell, *Women...,* pp. 104 & 127. Lucas, *Women...,* p. 45. McNamara and Wemple, "The Power...," p. 91. Schulenburg, "Women's...," p. 227. Stafford, *Queens...,* pp. 16, 21–22, 79, 85, 91, 98, 103, 110–112, 124–127, 133, 141–143, 151, 156, 160–165, & 178. Stafford, "Sons...," pp. 79–80, 86, & 91. Whitelock, *Anglo-Saxon...,* p. 7. Wright, *Cultivation...,* pp. 55, 63, 74, 77, 115, 146–154, 157–162, 165–170.

AELFTHRYTH OF WESSEX

c. 880s–920s England; Flanders

Daughter of Alfred the Great of England. In the middle of the 890s, her father gave her in marriage to Baldwin II, count of Flanders, as part of an alliance treaty. Aelfthryth gave some of her English lands to a religious foundation in Ghent.

♦ **Dowry/dower. Pawns. Religious patrons.** ♦

DNB, v.1, pp. 156–157. Hodgkin, *History...,* II, p. 634. Page, *Life in...,* p. 23. Stenton, *Anglo-Saxon...,* p. 340.

AELIPS DE BEAUCHAMP

fl. 1410–1420 France

Became lady of le Plouy-Domquer in 1410. This estate included a chateau fortified with earthen ramparts. In 1417, Aelips inherited the seigneurie of Beauchamp which then passed to her husband, Hue Bournel, lord of Thièmbronne. In 1420, Aelips also received Lambercourt, where she had the right of "cullage," meaning that village grooms had to pay her to obtain the right to sleep with their new brides. In reality, this was merely a tax—the price was set at a certain measure of white flour and wine.

♦ **Estate. Legal activity.** ♦

Belleval, *Les fiefs...*, pp. 29, 191–192, & 258–259.

AÉNOR OF CHÂTELLERAULT

c. 1120 France

See—PETRONILLA OF ACQUITAINE and ELEANOR OF ACQUITAINE, queen of France, queen of England

♦ **Genealogy.** ♦

AETHELFLAED OF DAMERHAM

m.c. 945–c. 980 England

Daughter of an ealdorman named Aelfgar; second wife of King Edmund I who was murdered in 946. Aethelflaed willed much of her property to her sister Aelfflaed and brother-in-law Brihtnoth.

♦ **Bequests. Estate. Queens. Religious patrons. Widows.** ♦

Fell, *Women...*, pp. 96–7. Lucas, *Women...*, p. 45. Stafford, "*Queens...*," pp. 143 & 166. Whitelock, *Anglo-Saxon...*, pp. 35–37.

AETHELFLAED, lady of the MERCIANS

[Ethelflaed; Aethelfleda of Wessex and Mercia]

c. 872–d. 918 England

Daughter of Alfred the Great. Around 890 her father achieved an alliance with English Mercia (against the "Danes") by marrying her to Aethelred, ealdorman of Mercia (d.911). Aethelflaed—sometimes acting in concert with her brother Edward the Elder—subdued and fortified the frontiers of Mercia. She very nearly completed her fortifications, and she took one of the last Viking strongholds, Leicester, shortly before her death in 918. Her efforts helped Edward the Elder bring most of England under his rule. The Anglo-Saxon poem *Judith* is modeled on her. Aethelflaed was also instrumental in getting St. Oswald of Northumbria's bones moved to Mercia.

♦ **Models. Negotiators. Relics. Religious patrons. Rulers. Soldiers. Widows.** ♦

Blair, *Anglo-Saxon...*, pp. 78 & 80–81. Brooke, *From Alfred...*, pp. 43, 50–52. Campbell, *Anglo-Saxons...*, pp. 155 & 161. Fell, *Women...*, pp. 9,

12, 82, 91–93, & 99. Jones, *Vikings...*, pp. 226, 233, 234, 235. Stafford, *Queens...*, pp. 26, 112, 118, 121, 140–141, & 173. Stenton, *Anglo-Saxon...*, pp. 257, 320, 322–326, 329, 521–2, 528. Wainwright, "Aethelflaed...," pp. 53–69.

AETHELSWITH OF WESSEX, queen of Mercia

m. 853–d.c. 888 England

Daughter of Osburga and Aethelwulf of Wessex; sister of Alfred the Great. In 853, she was forced to contract a political marriage with King Burgred of Mercia to seal the alliance of the two warring kingdoms (Mercia and Wessex) against the Vikings and the Welsh. In many aspects of government, Aethelswith ruled with her husband; she signed charters, granted lands, etc.

♦ **Pawns. Religious patrons. Rulers.** ♦

Campbell, *Anglo-Saxons*, pp. 138 & 139. Fell, *Women...* , pp. 93–94. Hinton, *Alfred's...*, pp. 52 & 193. Page, *Life in...*, pp. 48 & 67. Stafford, *Queens...*, pp. 18, 48, 129, & 140.

AFFRECA OF MAN, countess of Ulster **[Affrica]**

m.c. 1180–1220s Ireland; Scotland

Daughter of Gottred (Godred), king of Man. Married John de Courcy, who was earl of Ulster for a time.

♦ **Dowry/dower. Pawns. Religious patrons. Widows.** ♦

Barlow, *Feudal...*, p. 348. Curtis, *Ireland...*, p. 62. Orpen, *Ireland...*, II, pp. 19, 21–2, 144.

AGATHA (of Hungary)

c. 1040 Hungary; Scotland

See—CHRISTINA (of Hungary) and (St.) MARGARET, queen of Scotland

♦ **Genealogy.** ♦

AGELTRUDIS (of Spoleto) **[Empress Agiltrude of Benevento]**

c. 870s–900s Italy

Ambitious and fiery wife of Guy III of Spoleto (d.894). She was a military and political power during both her husband's reign and that of their son, Lambert (d.898). During the 890s she served as Lambert's regent, defended Rome for him, convened councils, and rendered legal decisions in his name.

♦ **Legal activity. Popes. Queens. Regents. Soldiers. Widows.** ♦

Brusher, *Popes...*, p. 228. *Cambridge...*, III, pp. 65–67, 149, 454. Duckett, *Death...*, pp. 27–28 & 30. Ernouf, *Histoire...*, pp. 462–464. Partner, *Lands...*, pp. 75–77. Stafford, *Queens...*, pp. 24, 102, 118, 120, 136, 140, & 151.

AGNES [Agnese]

AGNES, countess of AIX

c. 1080s–c. 1120s France; Spain

After her marriage to Alard Guillebaud was declared null due to consanguinity, Agnes retired to Fontevrault. She was a major force in establishing several other houses dependant on Fontevrault.

♦ **Abbesses. Divorce. Nurses. Religious patrons.** ♦

DBF, v. 1, pp. 736–737. Hurd-Mead, *History...,* p. 176. Pernoud, *La femme...,* pp. 134–135.

AGNES OF ANJOU [Agnes of Burgundy, countess of Poitou]

m. 1019–d. 1068 France

Daughter of Otte Guillaume, duke of Burgundy. Married (1) William V of Aquitaine; (2) Geoffrey Martel of Anjou (c.1040–1060) whom she later divorced. Agnes served as a regent in Aquitaine for her son, William VII (who succeeded his half-brother William VI in 1038). She was well-educated and was an influential patroness of the church. Agnes paid a huge sum for a copy of a collection of the sermons of Haime of Halberstadt.

♦ **Book owners. Educated. Divorce. Negotiators. Popes. Regents. Religious patrons. Widows.** ♦

DBF, v.1, pp. 741–745; v.17, p. 144. Dunbabin, *France...,* pp. 176, 188, & 239. Johnson, *Prayer...,* pp. 8, 11–14, 16, 17, 32, 33, 53–5, 70, 71, 76, 77, 104, 105, 108, 150, 185, 186. Jourdain, "Memoire...," p. 474. Marks, *Pilgrims...,* pp. 29–30. Thompson, *Literacy...,* p. 129. Verdon, "Recherches...," pp. 121–122.

AGNESE ARIZONELLI

1432 Italy

Wife of Giacomo Arizonelli. In 1432, she "confessed" to the Inquisitor of Lombardy that she had conjured and worshipped the Devil, described as a black goat. She supposedly also used the Devil's help to destroy crops by causing storms.

♦ **Ecclesiastical courts–Inquisition. Witchcraft.** ♦

Lea, *Materials...,* pp. 232–233. Summers, *Geography...,* p. 548.

AGNES ASSER

fl. 1470s–1490s England

The only woman listed among thirty London coopers who had their own trade marks in the late 1400s.

♦ **Merchants–coopers.** ♦

Calendar of Letter..., L, p. 1.

AGNES AVESOT

fl. 1322 France

In 1322, this chambermaid was accused along with her mistress, †Jeanne Clarisse, of illegally practicing medicine.

♦ **Doctors/empirics. Miscreants. Servants–maids.** ♦

Hughes, *Women...*, p. 144. Wickersheimer, *Dictionnaire...*, v.1, p. 10.

AGNES BERNAUER

d. 1435 Austria; Germany

Married Albert of Bavaria. Albert's father, the duke of Bavaria, wished to remove Agnes so that his son would be free to contract a more financially and socially profitable match. While Albert was away, his father arrested Agnes for practicing witchcraft. Although she was probably innocent of all charges, the duke managed to have her tried, convicted, and executed by drowning—all before Albert could return home.

♦ **Punishments-executed. Witchcraft.** ♦

Harksen, *Women...*, p. 38. Kieckhefer, *European...*, p. 124. Schoenfeld, *Women...*, p. 197 (a chatty, not very scholarly, older source).

AGNES OF BOHEMIA **[Blessed Agnes]**

c. 1205–d.c. 1282 Bohemia

Daughter of †Constance (of Hungary) and King Premysl Ottokar I of Bohemia. Agnes refused to marry; she instead persuaded Pope Gregory IX to allow her to become a Poor Clare and found a convent at Prague. She also helped establish a hospital in 1253. Agnes performed all types of work, from menial jobs to nursing the patients. A friend of St. Francis of Assisi and of †Clare of Assisi.

♦ **Nuns. Nurses. Popes. Religious patrons. Unmarried.** ♦

Attwater, *Dictionary...*, p. 7. Bynum, *Holy...*, pp. 86 & 100. Eckenstein, *Woman...*, pp. 295–297. Harrsen, *Cursus...*, pp. 4, 7–8, 17–21, 23, 29, 44, 49–56. Power, *Nunneries...*, p. 500.

AGNES BRID

fl. 1281 England

Bondswoman of the manor of Hales. After her husband Thomas died, she gave her land to her grown son Thomas because she was unable to work it or provide the necessary services to the lord. An agreement was witnessed in the manor court in 1281 which stated that Thomas would build a cottage for Agnes (including three doors and two windows) and would yearly provide her with specified amounts of coal, peas, oats, and wheat.

♦ **Land/property. Legal activity. Manors. Widows.** ♦

Bennett, *Life...*, p. 253. Labarge, *Small Sound...*, p. 166.

AGNES DE BROUGHTON

fl. 1297–1332 England

Member of important peasant family in the village of Broughton; wife of John de Broughton. Most of her numerous fines in the village court were fees for her brewing activities. In addition, Agnes was cited in 1297 for making a concord without license to do so, and in 1322 she was charged with receiving a banished woman. In the lay subsidy roll of 1327, Agnes was taxed 6d, and in 1332 her tax had increased to 20d.

♦ **Alewives. Land/property. Manors. Miscreants.** ♦

Britton, *Community...*, pp. 33, 72, 197, & 247 n57.

AGNES BROUMATTIN

fl. 1440s–1450s France; Germany

The records of Strasbourg from the years 1445 through 1453 list Agnes among those who were licensed during that time to practice her trade as a waggoner.

♦ **Merchants–waggoners.** ♦

O'Faolain, *Not in...*, p. 154.

AGNES BRUNDYSSCH

1400s England

See—ALICE SEFORD.

♦ **Apprentices–mistresses. Bequests. Silkwork.** ♦

AGNES OF BURGUNDY, duchess of Bourbon

c. 1410–d. 1476 France

Daughter of †Margaret of Hainault (of Bavaria) and John the Fearless, duke of Burgundy. Married Duke Charles of Bourbon in 1425. After he died (1456), Agnes commissioned artwork on his mausoleum and then recommended the sculptor to her brother, Philip the Good, duke of Burgundy. In addition to art, she was interested in a variety of intellectual and cultural fields.

♦ **Art patrons. Educated. Models. Widows.** ♦

Anselme, *Histoire...*, v.1, pp. 305 & 308. Calmette, *Golden...*, p. 111. Cartellieri, *Court...*, pp. 170 & 214. Commynes, *Memoirs...*, p. 98. Vaughan, *John...*, pp. 114, 245, 247n., 248.

AGNES OF BURGUNDY, countess of Poitou

See—AGNES OF ANJOU.

AGNES DE BURY

1344 England

Wife of William de Bury. In November of 1344, a London court convicted Agnes on charges of buying second-hand, light furs, having them dyed black, and then selling them as good, new, dark furs. She was sentenced to a prison term.

♦ **Legal activity. Merchants–fur dealers. Miscreants. Prisons.** ♦

Calendar of Plea..., I, p. 213.

AGNES BUTLER

fl. 1460s–1480s England

A nun of St. Michael's, Stamford, who had trouble keeping her vow of chastity. Agnes first went off with an Austin friar. She later ran away with a wandering harp-player. Agnes only returned to her convent after she had lived with him for about eighteen months.

♦ **Music. Nuns. Virginity. Women of easy virtue.** ♦

Kendall, *Yorkist...*, p. 270. Power, *Nunneries...*, pp. 449.

AGNES CHAUCER

fl. 1320s–1360s England

Daughter of John of Copton. Married (1) Henry Northwell, (2) John Chaucer, vintner of London (c. 1340), and (3) Bartholomew Attechapel (c.1367). Mother of Geoffrey Chaucer.

♦ **Genealogy. Merchants.** ♦

Braddy, "Chaucer and...," pp. 224–225. *DNB,* v.4, p. 155. Gardner, *Life...*, pp. 23, 32–33, 153.

AGNES COMYN

See—countess of STRATHERN.

AGNES DE CONDET

d.c. 1223 England

Wife of Walter Clifford. Her will was unusual because it was written while her husband was still alive. Agnes left money to the building funds of six churches. In addition, she bequeathed money to some fifty-five people and institutions, and also left eleven bequests of chattels.

♦ **Bequests. Charity. Religious patrons.** ♦

Sheehan, *The Will...*, pp. 261, 265, 286 n.260, 309.

AGNES COOK **[Agnes Cok]**

fl. 1376 England

Apprenticed to Johanna and William Kaly. In 1376 they agreed to release her from the contract, if she wished.

♦ **Apprentices. Unmarried.** ♦

Calendar of Plea..., II, p. 219. Power, *Women...*, p. 59.

AGNES COOK **[Agnes le Keu]**

fl. 1313 England

Daughter of Katherine and Robert Cook. In her father's will (proved 1313), she was left a dowry of twenty marks, as well as a featherbed, coverlets, and linens.

♦ **Bequests–personal items. Dowry/dower.** ♦

Calendar of Wills..., I, p. 243.

AGNES OF COURTENAY

c. 1135–d.c. 1185 Israel; Turkey

Daughter of Jocelyn II of Edessa. Married (1) Reynald of Marasch; (2) Amalric of Jerusalem (annuled)—their son was Baldwin IV of Jerusalem; (3) Hugh of Ramleh (d.1169); and (4) Reynald of Sidon. Agnes acquired (and ruled) lands, was a political force, and negotiated marriages.

♦ **Divorce. Leprosy. Managers. Negotiators. Politics. Widows.** ♦

Anselme, *Histoire...*, v.1, p. 529. *DBF*, v.5, p. 873. Hamilton, "Women...," pp. 159–160, 163–165, 166–170. Payne, *Dream...*, p. 177.

AGNES OF DEDO

c. 1170 Austria; Germany

See—AGNES OF MERAN, GERTRUDE OF MERAN, and (St.) HEDWIG OF SILESIA

♦ **Genealogy.** ♦

AGNES DESJARDINS

c. 1438–d. 1461 France

Became abbess of Montmartre in December of 1438. During her tenure, the once rich abbey continued to decline. Eventually the nuns had to hawk wine in the streets of Paris and run a tavern at the abbey to make enough money to live. Agnes seems to have led the way by allowing men to dine and drink with her.

♦ **Abbesses. Models. Taverners. Women of easy virtue.** ♦

Champion, *François...*, I, p. 317.

AGNES DEYNTEE

fl. 1460s England

A London court convicted Agnes of selling old, spoiled butter. She was sentenced to several hours in the pillory with the offending product hanging from her neck. Agnes was then obliged to quit the town.

♦ **Less-affluent. Miscreants. Provisioning–dairy. Punishments.** ♦

Calendar of Letter..., L, p. 141. Kendall, *Yorkist...*, p. 62.

AGNES, countess of DUNBAR [Black Agnes, countess of March]
fl. 1338 Scotland

Daughter of Randolph, earl of Moray. For nearly five months of the year 1338, she and her ladies held Dunbar Castle for King David II, against the English.

♦ **Managers. Soldiers.** ♦

Brown, *History...*, p. 174. Bryant, *Age...*, pp. 280–281. Glover, *Story...*, p. 89. Hallam (ed.), *Four...*, p. 264. Mackie, *History...*, p. 86. Mackie, *Short...*, p. 76. Power, *Women...*, p. 45.

AGNES D'ÉVREUX, countess of Montfort
fl. 1060–1080 France

Daughter of Richard, count of Évreux. Third wife of Simon de Montfort; their daughter was †Bertrade de Montfort, countess of Anjou and queen of France.

♦ **Genealogy.** ♦

DBF, v.6, p. 259. Vitalis, *Ecclesiastical...*, v.3, p. 128; v.4, pp. 113, 215, 216.

AGNES FITZJOHN [Agnes de Munchanesi]
d. 1224 England

Daughter of †Sybil de Lacy and Payn FitzJohn. Married Warine (I) de Munchanesi. Her dowry included various Lacy holdings. She donated some of her land to the Templars. Three sons: Hubert, Ralph, and William.

♦ **Dowry/dower. Religious patrons.** ♦

DNB, vol. 13, p. 1187. Wrightman, *Lacy...*, pp. 177 & 207.

AGNES FORSTER
c. 1430s–d.c. 1484 England

Wife of wealthy fishmonger/former mayor of London; mother of Robert Forster, grocer of London. As a widow, Agnes constructed an addition to Lud Gate Prison, and enacted reforms for that institution. This earned her the job of keeping French prisoners of war; their ransoms were worth more than 30,000 gold crowns. Agnes owned a number of books which she would only lend on condition that the borrower sign a contract for the book's return.

♦ **Book owners. Charity. Educated. Land/property. Legal activity. Prisons. Widows.** ♦

Calendar of Letter..., L, pp. 40–43. *Calendar of Plea...*, VI, pp. 106, 114–116, 174, 176. Kendall, *Yorkist...*, pp. 428–430. Thrupp, *Merchant...*, pp. 173, 341.

AGNES OF FRANCE **[Empress Anna of Byzantium]**
c. 1171–d. 1220 Byzantium; France; Turkey

Daughter of †Adele of Champagne and Louis VII of France. Agnes changed her name to Anna in 1180 when she married twelve-year-old Alexius (II) Comnenus, emperor of Byzantium. After Andronicus Comnenus deposed and killed the boy emperor, he married Agnes (1182). Two years later she fled Constantinople with him. When they were caught and Andronicus was killed, she returned to the palace. By 1190 she was having an affair with a courtier, Theodore Branas. Once Constantinople became a Latin province, she urged Theodore to join the new government. She was then allowed to keep her dowry and marry Theodore. In 1206 they were appointed to govern Adrianople and Didymoticus.

♦ **Adultery. Dowry/dower. Pawns. Queens. Rebellions. Rulers. Widows.** ♦

Cambridge..., IV, pp. 379, 382; VI, p. 286. *DBF,* v.1, pp. 747–749. Diehl, *Byzantine...*, pp. 244–258. Norwich, *Kingdom...*, pp. 330 & 340–341.

AGNES OF FRANCE, duchess of Burgundy
m. 1279–d. 1325 France

Daughter of †Marguerite of Provence and Louis IX of France. Married Robert II, duke of Burgundy; mother of his nine children. After her husband died in 1306, Agnes was regent of Burgundy for their son Hugh V.

♦ **Crusades. Regents. Widows.** ♦

Calmette, Golden..., p. 14. *DBF,* v.1, pp. 749–750.

AGNES FRANCOU
1321 France

Nurse in Montaillou for Waldensian heretic, Raymond de la Coste.

♦ **Ecclesiastical courts–Inquisition. Heretics. Nurses. Waldensians.** ♦

Duvernoy, *Inquisition à Pamiers...*, pp. 123–127. Ladurie, *Montaillou...*, p. 208 n.1.

AGNES OF GERMANY **[Agnes of Franconia; of Swabia]**
c. 1070s–c. 1120s Austria; Germany

Daughter of †Bertha of Susa and Henry IV of Germany. Married (1) Frederick Hohenstaufen, duke of Swabia (d.1105), and (2) Leopold III, margrave of Austria. Mother of Frederick II of Swabia and Otto of Freising—an important chronicler of twelfth-century Germany.

♦ **Estate. Genealogy. Pawns.** ♦

Cambridge..., V, pp. 140, 153, 154 & n, 351. Fuhrmann, *Germany...*, pp. 117, 136. Haverkamp, *Medieval...*, pp. 95, 116, 125, 137. Stephenson, *Mediaeval...*, pp. 383 & 402.

AGNES OF HAPSBURG, queen of Hungary

c. 1280–1351 Austria; Germany; Hungary; Italy

Daughter of Albert, king of the Romans (Albert I, king of Germany, and uncrowned Holy Roman Emperor); married Andrew III of Hungary. As a widow, Agnes became abbess of her mother Elizabeth's foundation of Konigsfeld. Pious, educated, and charitable, Agnes lived at her convent for some fifty years. She also became a renowned negotiator, and was especially effective at concluding peace treaties.

♦ **Abbesses. Charity. Educated. Models. Negotiators. Politics. Widows.** ♦

Cambridge..., VII, pp. 92, 192. Heer, *Holy...*, p. 106. Stubbs, *Later...*, p. 93.

AGNES D'HARCOURT

c. 1250s–d.c. 1290 France

Lady-of-honor to †Princess Isabelle of France (sister of St. Louis IX of France). Nun, and later abbess, at Longchamp, Agnes wrote Blessed Isabelle's biography.

♦ **Abbesses. Servants–ladies. Writers–biography.** ♦

DBF, v.1, p. 750. Jordan, Louis..., pp. 9n, 10, 11n. Jourdain, "Memoire...," p. 484. McDonnell, *Beguines...*, pp. 97n, 375, & 401. Thompson, *Literacy...*, p. 146.

AGNES (of Holbourne)

1338 England

In a London court of March 1338, Agnes and her sister Juliana (who rented a house in Holbourne together) were presented as being prostitutes, and were accused of associating with men of ill fame.

♦ **Less-affluent. Prostitutes. Unmarried.** ♦

Calendar of Plea..., I, p. 188.

AGNES ATTE HOLTE

1354/5 England

Orphaned daughter of Stephen atte Holte; ward of John de Bergholte, carpenter of London. In 1354, Richard and †Alice Stanford were accused of abducting Agnes. They were acquitted, but the case evidently caused the mayor and aldermen to examine Agnes' situation since she soon received a new guardian.

♦ **Abduction. Orphans.** ♦

Calendar of Plea..., I, p. 242.

AGNES OF HUNTINGDON **[Agnes la medica]**

fl. 1270s England

She was called a "doctor" and was regarded as skillful by her neighbors at Stanground, Huntingdonshire.

♦ **Doctors/empirics. Land/property.** ♦

Labarge, *Small Sound...*, p. 174. Rubin, *Medieval...*, pp. 186–187. Talbot and Hammond, *Medical...*, p. 10.

AGNES IRLOND

1364 England

In September of 1364, Agnes and her husband John, Joan and John Cotyller, and Isabel Hemyng were all charged in a London court with disturbing the peace. The jury not only found them guilty but further stated that Agnes, Joan, and Isabel were common scolds and brawlers. All three women were sentenced to Newgate prison.

♦ **Miscreants. Prisons.** ♦

Calendar of Plea..., I, p. 277.

AGNES KATELINE **[Agnes Cateline]**

fl. 1297–1332 England

Paid brewing fines (fees) in Broughton village several times between 1297 and 1332. As a widow, she kept control of some lands and at least one tenement, even though her son John was grown by that time (c.1300). For instance, in 1309, she was fined as sole owner for not keeping her ditches repaired.

♦ **Alewives. Land/property. Manors. Widows.** ♦

Britton, *Community...*, pp. 21–22, 209, 245 n29, & 247 n60.

AGNES KNETCHUR

1397 England

Servant of a Herefordshire vicar. In 1397, an ecclesiastical court accused her of causing a scandal by ringing the church bells, having sex with the vicar, and engaging in a variety of other prohibited activities.

♦ **Ecclesiastical courts. Servants. Women of easy virtue.** ♦

Hair, *Bawdy...*, p. 81 (#151).

AGNES DE LAUNCREONA

m.c. 1387 Bohemia; England

Bohemian attendant of †Anne of Bohemia, queen of Richard II of England. In her new homeland, Agnes caused a scandal when Robert de Vere, earl of Oxford, fell in love with her. He even divorced King Edward III's granddaughter, †Philippa de Coucy, in order to marry Agnes.

♦ **Models. Servants–ladies. Women of easy virtue.** ♦

DNB, v.20, p. 245. Froissart, *Chronicles...*, I, pp. 407 & 417. Somerset, *Ladies...*, p. 7. Tuck, *Richard...*, pp. 78, 114.

AGNESE DEL MAINO **[di Maino]**

c. 1410–c. 1450 Italy

Mistress of Filippo Maria Visconti, duke of Milan, and mother of his only child, †Bianca Maria Visconti. When Filippo Maria died, Agnese managed to acquire the independent city of Pavia for Bianca's husband, Francesco Sforza, and thereby helped him become duke of Milan.

♦ **Mistresses. Politics.** ♦

Cartwright, *Beatrice...*, p. 16. Collison-Morley, *Sforzas...*, pp. 33 & 60. Norwich, *History...*, p. 297. Pasolini, *Catherine...*, pp. 11 & 13.

AGNES, countess of MARCH

See—AGNES, countess of DUNBAR.

AGNES OF MEISSEN **[Agnes of Quedlinburg]**

1184–1203 Germany

A writer and a weaver, Agnes helped produce the famous Quedlinburg tapestries.

♦ **Abbesses. Artistic clothwork. Artists. Writers.** ♦

Anderson and Zinsser, *A History of...*, p. 201. Greer, *Obstacle...*, p. 159. Heinrich, *Canonesses...*, pp. 189–190. Munsterberg, *History...*, p. 16. Pernoud, *La femme...*, p. 69.

AGNES OF MERAN

c. 1180s–d. 1201 Austria; France; Italy

Daughter of †Agnes of Dedo and Berthold IV, count of Meran and Andrechs (in the Tyrol). Philip II of France repudiated his second wife, †Ingeborg of Denmark, and later married Agnes of Meran (1196). Philip was finally forced by the pope and Ingeborg to renounce his "marriage" to Agnes, but her son Philip Hurepel was later legitimized.

♦ **Adultery. Childbirth. Divorce. Popes.** ♦

Appleby, *John...*, pp. 96, 101, 177. Baldwin, *Government...*, pp. 84–86, 165, 269, 357–358. Barlow, *Feudal...*, p. 416. Decaux, *Histoire...* , pp. 278–285. Kelly, *Eleanor...*, pp. 337, 367, 370. Pernoud, *Eleanor...*, pp. 255, 257, 261.

AGNES MOLTON **[Moltone; Malleton; Multone]**

fl. 1284–d.c. 1308 England

She and her husband Robert de Moltone owned property and conducted business together in London. In 1308, the widowed Agnes willed a workshop, tenements, rents, etc. to her children, and she had enough money left to establish a chantry.

♦ **Bequests. Land/property. Legal activity. Religious patrons.** ♦

Calendar of Letter..., A, pp. 83 & 167. *Calendar of Wills...*, I, p. 198. *Nuisance...*, pp. 2–3, 4, 10.

AGNES DE MONCEAUX

fl. 1265–1290s England

During the years 1265 through 1293, Agnes was chief lady-in-waiting to †Isabella de Fortibus, countess of Aumale. Agnes was generously rewarded; not only did Isabella give her manors in Dorset worth £80 a year, but Agnes also later received an annuity.

♦ **Estate. Servants–ladies.** ♦

Denholm-Young, "Yorkshire...," p. 392. Labarge, *Small Sound...*, p. 84.

(St.) AGNES DA MONTEPULCIANO **[Saint Agnese]**

1268–1317 Italy

An enthusiastic participant in the humanistic trend of viewing Christ as more man-like. Abbess of Procena before returning to Montepulciano. Known for healing and prophetic gifts, as well as for her visions of the Baby Jesus.

♦ **Abbesses. Medicine. Models. Mystics. Saints.** ♦

A.S., Ap v.3, pp. 911, 943–4. Attwater, *Dictionary...*, p. 7. Bynum, *Holy...*, pp. 74, 140, 145, 166, 169, 170, 186, 211, 234, 241, 243, 246, 273, 274...etc. Herlihy, "Children...," pp. 126–127.

AGNES DE MUNCHANESI

See—AGNES FITZJOHN.

AGNES MUNDENE

1350 England

Wife of Osbert de Mundene. In the Pleas before the Mayor of London in May, 1350, Joan Taylour and Agnes were the only two women in a group of eleven citizens accused of forestalling tannery, tiles, and poultry. Agnes admitted the crime and was sent to prison, but Joan denied the charge and put herself on the mercy of her country.

♦ **Merchants. Miscreants. Prisons.** ♦

Calendar of Plea..., I, pp. 232–233.

AGNES OF NAVARRE, countess of Foix **[Agnes d'Évreux]**

c. 1330–1380s France; Spain

Daughter of †Jeanne of France and Philip d'Évreux, rulers of Navarre; sister of Charles II the Bad, king of Navarre. In 1349, Agnes married Gaston Phoebus, count of Foix. The couple separated around 1363. Her fifteen-year-old son Gaston was killed by his father in a freak accident set up by Charles the Bad.

♦ **Divorce. Models. Pawns. Politics.** ♦

DBF, v.1, pp. 754–755. Froissart, *Chronicles...*, I, pp. 312 & 315–319. Jamison, *Life...*, II, pp. 29–35. Leroy, *La Navarre...*, p. 129. Moulin, *La Poesie...*, I, p. 89. Tuchman, *Distant...*, pp. 220 & 360.

AGNES (of Norfolk)

1209 England

See—GALIENA (of Norfolk).

♦ **Ordeals. Witchcraft.** ♦

AGNES PAGE

fl. 1294–1325 England

In 1294, she was cited in court of Broughton for making a concord without license, but the fine was dismissed due to her poverty. In 1314, Agnes was fined for breaking and entering Cristina la Coupere's house.

♦ **Manors. Miscreants.** ♦

Britton, *Community...*, pp. 33, 213, 247 n57, & 268 n45.

AGNES PASTON **[Agnes Berry]**

c. 1410s–1460s England

Married William Paston (who later became a judge) in the early 1400s. They had a son, John (married †Margaret (Mauteby) Paston c.1440), and a daughter, †Elizabeth (married, age 30, to Robert Poynings in 1459). Agnes treated neither child with much affection; she advised John's tutor to thrash him and she herself beat Elizabeth regularly. Agnes did, however, join her daughter-in-law on a pilgrimage to effect a cure for John's "great disease."

♦ **Childcare. Educated. Estate. Managers. Pilgrims.** ♦

Barron, "Lords of...," pp. 105 & 112. Gardiner, *English...*, p. 116. Gies, *Women...*, pp. 210–212, 217, 225–226. Haskell, "Paston...," p. 470. Kendall, *Yorkist...*, pp. 43, 206, 378–380, & 411–412. McFarlane, *Nobility...*, p.239. *Paston...*

AGNES PICKERELL

d.c. 1373 England

Her will, proved in 1373, left bequests to a number of the charitable fraternities of London.

♦ **Bequests. Charity.** ♦

Calendar of Wills..., II, p. 154. Robertson, *Chaucer's...*, p. 83.

AGNES OF POITOU, Holy Roman Empress
[Agnes of Guienne, Bavaria, Germany]

c. 1030s–d. 1077 France; Germany; Italy

Daughter of †Agnes of Anjou and William V of Aquitaine. Literate; patroness of arts and literature; and an influential supporter of the Cluniacs. Second wife of Henry III, king of Germany (m.1043); crowned Empress by Pope Clement II in 1046. Her husband gave her the province of Bavaria. When he died in 1056, she became regent of Germany for their son, six-year-old Henry IV. Agnes was never in full control of either the country or her son. Finally the young Henry was kidnapped by the archbishop of Cologne. Agnes then relinquished her governmental duties in favor of being a pilgrim, papal supporter, and penitent in Italy. In 1070, she entered a Roman convent.

♦ **Educated. Patrons of literature. Pilgrims. Popes. Regents. Religieuses. Widows.** ♦

Barraclough, *Origins...*, pp. 93, 94, & 104. *DBF*, v.1, pp. 755–758. Fuhrmann, *Germany...*, pp. 39, 40, 41, 44, 52, 57, 59, 61, 62. Hampe, *Germany...*, pp. 4, 48, 49, 60, 64. Haverkamp, *Medieval...*, pp. 1, 102, 105, 106, 107. Henderson, *Short...*, pp. 58 & 60. Johnson, *Prayer...*, pp. 13, 149–150. Norwich, *Normans...*, pp. 74, 120, 122, 159, 201, & 205. Osborne, *Greatest...*, pp. 164, 299, 316. Pinnow, *History...*, pp. 45 & 64–65. Stafford, *Queens...*, pp. 88, 161, & 210. Stubbs, *Germany...*, pp. 149, 157, 161–164. Thompson, *Feudal...*, I, pp. 94, 100, 115, 128. Thompson, *Literacy...*, p. 89.

AGNES OF QUEDLINBURG

See—AGNES OF MEISSEN.

AGNES ROKINGEHAM

fl. 1275 England

Daughter of Hugh de Rokingeham of London. From his will (1275), Agnes and her mother, Hugh's widow, †Cristina, inherited a tavern.

♦ **Bequests. Less-affluent. Taverners.** ♦

Calendar of Wills..., I, pp. 25–26.

AGNES RUSSELL

1305 England

Daughter of Elyas and Juliana Russell. In her mother's will (1305), Agnes was left certain rents and a variety of personal items, including: a green robe with three garnitures and a matching furred mantle; two tapestries; two feather beds; a number of brass and silver implements; a chest; and some linens.

♦ **Bequests–personal items. Land/property.** ♦

Calendar of Wills..., I, pp. 173–174.

AGNES OF SAARBRÜCKEN

fl. 1120s Germany

Daughter of Count Frederick of Saarbrücken; second wife of Frederick II, duke of Swabia. For nearly a year (1129/30), Agnes defended the city of Spires for her husband—against combined Bavarian and Saxon forces.

♦ **Negotiators. Soldiers.** ♦

Cambridge..., V, p. 339. Haverkamp, *Medieval...*, p. 141.

AGNES SADLER

1386 England

One of the leaders of a peasant revolt at Romley (Ramsley) in 1386.

♦ **Manors. Punishments. Rebellions.** ♦

Hilton, *English...*, pp. 105–106. Labarge, *Small Sound...*, p. 158. Razi, "Family...," p. 19. Shahar, *Fourth...*, p. 221.

AGNES DE SECHELLES

1371 France

She lived in the castle of Mareuil in 1371, while her husband, Hugues de Châtillon (leader of the French crossbow troops), was a prisoner in England. She also kept the English knight, Simon de Burleigh, as a prisoner at Mareuil in the same year, but he later escaped from the castle.

♦ **Managers. Prisons–jailers.** ♦

Belleval, *Les fiefs...*, pp. 212–213.

AGNES SIGILY

1338 England

In February of 1338 a London court acquitted Agnes but found her fellow huckster, Anabilla le Hokester, guilty of forestalling the corn market.

♦ **Less-affluent. Merchants.** ♦

Calendar of Plea..., I, p. 166.

AGNES SOREL **[dame de Beauté]**

1420s–1450 France

Daughter of Catherine de Maignelais and Jean Soreau, lord of Coudun. Agnes became the mistress of Charles VII of France around the year 1435; their children were: †Charlotte, Jeanne, and Marie (de Valois). Agnes was said to be a political asset to Charles. More so than his queen, †Marie of Anjou, Agnes set the fashions, lived in high estate, held audiences, spoke up for those in trouble, and attracted able advisors to Charles. For years after her death in 1450, conventional French depictions of the Madonna featured Agnes' face and figure.

♦ **Childbirth. Estate. Mistresses. Models. Murder. Politics. Tournaments.** ♦

Cartellieri, *Court...*, pp. 114–115. Champion, *Louis XI*, pp. 91, 108, 113, 121, & 241. Cleugh, *Chant...*, pp. 44, 49, 70–71, 76–85, 90–94... Decaux, *Histoire...*, pp. 436–440, 444, 446. Gies, *Merchants...*, pp. 233–235. Leveque, *Agnes...* (a readable but not especially scholarly biography). Lewis, *King...*, pp. 116 & 222. Philippe, *Agnes...* Vale, *Charles...*, pp. 5, 91–3, 95, 100, 102, 108–9, 113, 129, 131, 133, 135–6, 139, 232.

AGNES VON STAUFEN

m. 1193 Germany

Daughter of Conrad von Staufen, count palatine of the Rhine. Although there had been talk of a marriage with Philip II of France, Agnes actually wed Henry (the oldest son of Henry the Lion of Bavaria and Saxony). This was reputedly a love match between the bride and groom.

♦ **Dowry/dower. Models.** ♦

Cambridge..., V, p. 469. Fuhrmann, *Germany...*, p. 182. Haverkamp, *Medieval...*, p. 236.

AGNES THOMAS

1290 England

At the Newton manor court in July of 1290, Agnes was fined for allowing her geese to trespass on the manor lord's pasture.

♦ **Manor. Miscreants.** ♦

Ault, *Open Field...*, p. 151.

AGNES WOMBE

1349 England

In London court of 1349, Agnes Wombe of Bedford and Joan de Sloghteford were accused of enticing †Joan la Whycchere, servant of Thomas de Shene, away from Thomas before her contract legally ended.

♦ **Employers. Miscreants.** ♦

Calendar of Plea..., I, p. 231.

AGRIPPINA OF MOSCOW, grand duchess of Riasan

[Anna of Moscow]

c. 1450s–1500s Russia

Sister of Ivan III of Moscow. In 1465 he married her to seventeen-year-old Vasili, grand duke of Riasan (died 1483). Agrippina became regent for her grandson, Ivan VI, in 1500. Through her efforts the grand duchy of Riasan became a part of greater Russia under the rule of her brother.

♦ **Politics. Regents.** ♦

Pares, *History...*, p. 93. Vernadsky, *Russia...*, p. 99.

ALAZAIS

See—ADELAIDE.

ALBERADA OF BUONALBERGO **[Auberea]**

fl. 1049–1122 Italy

First wife of Robert Guiscard, later duke of Apulia; son Bohemund of Antioch (b.1055). After Robert repudiated her (on grounds of consanguinity) in 1058, Alberada married two more times. In 1122, she helped endow a Benedictine house near Salerno.

♦ **Divorce. Religious patrons.** ♦

Cambridge..., V, p. 174. Norwich, *Kingdom...*, pp. 113 & 395. Norwich, *Normans...*, pp. 78–9, 116, 118, 195, 227 & 247. Ritchie, "Bohemund...," p. 293.

ALDA OF ARLES

m. 936 Italy

The only legitimate daughter of Hugh of Arles by his wife Willa. Alda married Alberic of Rome (the son of †Marozia of Rome). He died in 954.

♦ **Estate. Genealogy. Pawns.** ♦

Brusher, *Popes...*, p. 254. *Cambridge...*, III, p. 155. Ernouf, *Histoire...*, pp. 328, 357, 473 (an old, not very scholarly source).

ALESSANDRA [Alesandra; Alexandra]

ALEXANDRA CROWE

fl. 1370s England

Wife of John Crowe, clerk of the Chapel in the entourage of John of Gaunt. John and Alexandra each received pensions from Gaunt, despite the fact that clerical marriages were proclaimed illegal by the church.

♦ **Adultery–clerical wives. Miscreants. Servants.** ♦

Armitage-Smith, *John...*, p. 177.

ALESANDRA GILANI

fl. 1313–d.c. 1326 Italy

At the University of Bologna, she was a "prosecutor" for Mundinus de Luzzi, an early teacher of dissection. She prepared the bodies—doing such pre-class work as cleaning veins and filling them with colored liquids. After Alesandra died, a memorial tablet was placed at the hospital of Santa Maria de Mereto in her honor.

♦ **Medicine. Models. Teachers. University.** ♦

Boulding, *Underside...*, p. 474. Hughes, *Women...*, pp. 74 & 86–87. Hurd-Mead, *History...*, pp. 225 & 277.

ALESSANDRA STROZZI [Alessandra Macinghi]

b. 1407–d. 1471 Italy

Well-off Florentine woman; married Matteo di Simone Strozzi in 1422. After he died in 1436, Alessandra single-handedly ran the family estates and kept their fortune intact. A number of letters which passed between Alessandra and her exiled sons detail the intelligence and industriousness of this Florentine widow.

♦ **Educated. Land/property. Managers. Merchants. Widows. Writers.** ♦

Macinghi negli Strozzi, *Lettere...* Maguire, *Women...*, pp. 4, 23, 40. Martines, "A Way of...," pp. 15–28. Ronciere, "Tuscan Notables...," pp. 247, 293, 304. Sachs, *Renaissance...*, pp. 15–16. Uitz, *Legend...*, pp. 43, 145–147, 151.

ALFONSINA ORSINI

b. 1472–d. 1520 Italy

Daughter of Roberto Orsini. Hand-picked by future mother-in-law, †Clarissa Orsini, to marry Pietro de'Medici (d.1503). Haughty and very capable, Alfonsina yet failed at her assigned task; she could not control Pietro nor stop his loose-living ways. Alfonsina sometimes dominated her son Lorenzo di Pietro de'Medici. Her advice that he institute absolute rule was vigorously opposed by Florentine citizenry.

♦ **Pawns. Politics.** ♦

Brion, *Medici*, pp. 128 & 205. Cleugh, *Medici...*, pp. 159, 161, 194, 196, 238, 240. Hook, *Lorenzo...*, pp. 169, 178. Maguire, *Women...*, pp. 5, 170, 174, 184, 186, 188–189, 195.

ALIANORE [Alianora; Aliénor]

See—ELEANOR.

ALICE [Aaeles; Aales; Aalis; Aaliz; Aelis; Alaiz; Alix; Alys]

Also see: ADELAIDE

ALICE, princess of ANTIOCH

See—ALICE OF JERUSALEM.

AELIS (of Auxerre)

See—ADELAIDE OF TOURS.

AALIS (la barbière)

1292 France

Practiced as a barber in the Parisian parish of Saint Severin de Petit Point. In 1292 she was taxed at a rate of 8s.

♦ **Barbers.** ♦

Géraud, *Paris sous...*, p. 150. Hughes, *Women...*, p. 140.

ALICE BARLEY

1324 England

In the manor court of Foxton, Cambridgeshire, in 1324, Alice was fined 3s 4d for not releasing a lamb to the lady of the manor's bailiff. Furthermore, Alice's brother, Robert, was fined—as "the responsible male"—for not making her give up the lamb.

♦ **Manors. Miscreants.** ♦

Muir, *English...*, p. 68.

ALICE BOKEREL

fl. 1282–1284 England

After her husband, William Bokerel, died in 1282, Alice married John le Branchesle, a taverner of London. For the next several years she owned property and conducted business both on her own and with her new husband.

♦ **Land/property. Merchants. Taverners.** ♦

Calendar of Letter..., A, pp. 52, 83, & 86.

ALIX LA BOURGOLLE **[Alix la Bourgotte]**

c. 1410s–d. 1466 France

A well-known recluse of Paris. Alix lived in a cell attached to the Church of the Innocents; she attended Mass by means of a small, latticed window in her cell.

♦ **Anchoresses. Models. Unmarried.** ♦

Champion, *François...*, I, p. 304. *DBF,* v.2, p. 66.

ALICE BROTHERTON

See—ALICE MONTACUTE.

ALIX OF BRITTANY

b. 1199–c. 1230s France

Daughter and heiress of †Constance of Brittany by her third husband, Guy de Thouars of Poitou. In 1212, Alix married Peter de Dreux (Peter Mauclerc). Their son and heir was John I, count of Brittany.

♦ **Estate. Genealogy.** ♦

Baldwin, *Government...*, pp. 198, 217, 271. Borderie, *Histoire...*, III, pp. 288, 292, 296, 297–8, 413 n3; IV, pp. 357 n2, 387. Fawtier, *Capetian...*, pp. 134–5, 150. Le Patourel, *Feudal...*, XV, p. 163. Powicke, *Thirteenth...*, p. 92 & n.

ALIX OF BRITTANY, countess of Blois **[Alice de Bretagne]**

b. 1243–d. 1288 France

Daughter of Blanche of Champagne and John I, count of Brittany. In 1254, Alix married Jean de Châtillon, count of Blois.

♦ **Medicine. Writers–letters.** ♦

Borderie, *Histoire...*, v.3, p. 357. Bréquigny, *Lettres de rois...*, pp. 178–179 & 275–276.

ALICE DE BRYENE

c. 1350s–d.c. 1415 England

Daughter of Robert de Bures (d.1361); married Sir Guy de Bryene the younger (d.1386). They had two daughters, Philippa (b.c. 1378) and †Elizabeth (b.c. 1380), who were the co-heirs of their grandfather, Guy de Bryene the elder. Alice lived at her manor house of Acton in Suffolk. Her extant household account book of the years 1412 and

1413 illustrates the details of running a lady's household. The accounts include the numbers of guests, what they ate, the remaining provisions, purchases made, etc. Although she had many servants, her household book makes it clear that Alice herself worked hard at managing her estate.

♦ **Estate. Legal activity. Managers. Widows.** ♦

C.P., v.2, p. 362. *Household Book of Dame Alice...*

ALICE BURLE

1489 England

Kidnapped from her parents' London home in 1489 by a pimp named Peter Manyfeld. Soon after he raped her, he tired of Alice and sold her. At his trial, Peter admitted his guilt, but he escaped before sentencing.

♦ **Abduction. Rape. Unmarried.** ♦

Hair, *Bawdy...*, p. 205 (#533).

ALICE CANTEBRUGGE

1350 England

Wife of Thomas de Cantebrugge. As a *femme sole* merchant she reported the theft of her armor and other goods worth £200.

♦ **Legal activity. Merchants.** ♦

Abram, "*Women...*," p. 280. *Liber Albus*, Bk. III, pt. III, pp. 436–437.

ALIX OF CHAMPAGNE, queen of Cyprus **[Adelaide of Cyprus]**

c. 1195–1246 Cyprus; France

Daughter of †Isabella of Jerusalem and Henry II, count of Champagne. Married Hugh of Lusignan, king of Cyprus (d.1218). They had two daughters: Marie, countess of Jaffa, and Isabeau, princess of Antioch. After Hugh died, Alix married Ralph of Soissons, lord of Coeuvres. Alix challenged Thibaut of Champagne's right to his county; †Blanche of Castile and Louis IX of France eventually helped Thibaut buy the claim from Alix.

♦ **Estate. Queens. Regents. Soldiers. Squabbles.** ♦

Anselme, *Histoire...*, v.2, p. 842. *Cambridge...*, V, p. 315 & n; VI, p. 342 n. *Chronicles...*, p. 254. Fawtier, *Capetian...*, p. 127. Robinson, *Readings...*, pp. 178–179.

ALIX OF CHAMPAGNE

See—ADELE OF CHAMPAGNE, queen of France.

AALES (la chandelière)

1292 France

In the 1292 tax rolls of Paris, Aales was listed as a tallow candle maker and was taxed 6s on her business.

♦ **Candle makers–tallow.** ♦

Géraud, *Paris sous...*, p. 35.

ALICE CHAUCER, duchess of Suffolk **[countess of Salisbury]**

c. 1400–d.c 1475 England

Granddaughter of Geoffrey Chaucer; she was the only child of Matilda Burghersh and Thomas Chaucer. Alice married (1) Sir John Philip (d. 1415); (2) Thomas de Montacute, fourth earl of Salisbury (d.1428); and (3) (c.1430) William de la Pole, duke of Suffolk. After his death in 1450, Alice was indicted for treason in Jack Cade's rebellion, but by 1451 she had made peace with her opponent, the duke of York. Wealthy, educated, and strong-willed, Alice controlled much of Suffolk and the city of Norwich during the 1460s. Despite a long-running feud over ownership of the manor of Cotton, she declared that it belonged to her and proceeded to hold a manor court there (c.1465). Alice's tomb at Ewelme (including her alabaster effigy) was a good example of late medieval sculptural art.

♦ **Book owners. Educated. Legal activity. Managers. Models. Politics. Rebellions. Widows.** ♦

Boase, "Mortality...," p. 240. Champion, *Louis...*, p. 101. Clive, Sun..., pp. xxxii, 187, 228. *DNB*, vol. 13, p. 655. Goodman, *Wars...*, pp. 45, 105. Johnson, *Duke...*, pp. 90n, 91, 128n. Kendall, *Yorkist...*, pp. 213, 216, & 217. *Oxford...Prose*, p. 431. *Paston...*, I, pp. 135, 256, 279, 310–311, 323, 330, 338, 446, 527, 570, 584; II, pp. 13, 151–2, 182, 210, 213, 237, 257, 374, 383, 388, 391, 400, 581–2. *Stonor...*, v.1, pp. 91, 113–114, 116, 120, 151, 154; v.2, pp. 128, 168.

ALICE CHESTER

fl. 1450s–d. 1485 England

Widow of Henry Chester of London. She became a wealthy trader with Spain, Portugal, and Flanders. Alice paid the large sum of £41 to obtain the use of a crane to unload iron she had received from a Spanish shipping venture.

♦ **Merchants. Religious patrons. Shipping. Widows.** ♦

Anderson and Zinsser, *A History of...*, p. 427. Carus-Wilson, "Overseas...," p. 243. Hindley, *England...*, pp. 157, 158.

ALICE DE CLARE **[Adeliza FitzGilbert]**

c. 1080–1130 England; France

Daughter of Richard FitzGilbert. Married Walter Tirel. After the accident which killed William II of England, Walter (and probably Alice) quickly took ship for France—leaving many doubts about his possible involvement in the king's death. Hugh, lord of Poix, was the son of Walter and Alice. As a widow, Alice retired to Conflans.

♦ **Murder. Religieuses. Widows.** ♦

Chambers, *Norman...*, pp. 123–125. *DNB*, v.19, pp. 894–895.

ALICE DENECOUMBE

1340 England

Widow of Henry de Denecoumbe of London. In January 1340, Alice asked for an investigation, claiming that she had been abducted by robbers who also stole 100s and a variety of goods, gold bracelets, etc.

♦ **Abduction. Legal activity. Widows.** ♦

Calendar of Plea..., I, p. 120.

ALICE DEXTER

1389 England

Alice and her husband Roger were suspected of being Lollard leaders in Leicester.

♦ **Lollards.** ♦

Anderson and Zinsser, *A History of...*, p. 235. Cross, "Great...," p. 360.

ALICE DONBELY

1338 England

In London court, July 1338, Robert de Stratford, cordwainer, was accused of harboring several prostitutes including Alice Donbely and †Alice Tredewedowe.

♦ **Prostitutes.** ♦

Calendar of Plea..., I, p. 173.

ALICE DRAYTON

fl. 1410–d. 1468 England

Heiress of lands at Horton, etc. Married (1) Thomas Stonor (d.1431) and (2) Richard Drayton of Oxfordshire.

♦ **Estate. Models. Teachers. Writers–letters.** ♦

Stonor..., xxi, xxii, xli; v.1, pp. 42, 49–51, 95, 97, 101, 104–105; v.2, pp. 174 & 181.

ALIX OF FRANCE, countess of Blois and Chartres **[Aelith]**

c. 1149–1190s France

Daughter of †Eleanor of Aquitaine and Louis VII of France. Married Thibaut V of Blois and Chartres in 1164. He died in Acre in 1191. They had at least five children.

♦ **Crusades. Patrons of literature. Religious patrons.** ♦

DBF, v.2, p. 2; v.6, p. 686. Kelly, *Eleanor...*, pp. 74, 80, 126, 159. Pernoud, *Eleanor...*, pp. 78, 96, 120, 123, 152, 158, 253. Tierney, *Western...*, pp. 330, 452. Warren, *Henry...*, pp. 78n, 90, 109.

ALYS OF FRANCE

c. 1160–1200s England; France

Daughter of †Constance of Castile and Louis VII of France. Betrothed to Richard (later Richard I) of England. After his father King Henry II died, Richard repudiated Alys, supposedly because of rumors that she had been his father's mistress. There is no evidence that this accusation had any basis in fact; Richard may have invented it as a pretext for refusing to marry Alys. She was eventually returned to France. At the age of thirty, and with a tarnished reputation, the marriage market was nearly closed to Alys. She had to be content with a less socially prominent husband, William II, count of Ponthieu (m.1195).

♦ **Adultery. Divorce–betrothal. Models. Pawns.** ♦

Appleby, *John...*, pp. 37–9, 60, 63–4. Baldwin, *Government...*, pp. 19–20, 21, 78, 89, 269. Barlow, *Feudal...*, pp. 331, 350, 351, 352, 357. Bingham, *Crowned...*, pp. 74, 89, & 102. *DBF*, v.2, pp. 64–65. Gillingham, *Richard...*, pp. 54, 57, 76, 100, 102–105, 110, 120, 122, 127, 139, 140, 159, 160, 179, 220, 227, 256–8, 261, 296. Kelly, *Eleanor...*, pp. 136, 159, 184...337, 338, 385. Lloyd, *Maligned...*, pp. 31, 33–4, 54, 61, 67. Pernoud, *Eleanor...*, pp. 172, 185, 186, 191, 197, 208, 212, 224, 229. Richardson, "Marriage...," pp. 311–312. Warren, *Henry...*, pp. 109, 119 & n, 145 & n2, 222 n4, 598, 611 & n2, 612, 617, 622, 623, 625.

ALICE ATTE HARPE

1355 England

A London court of 1355 committed Alice (along with Margery atte Cocke and Englesia la Huxtere) to prison for selling beer against the law.

♦ **Alewives. Miscreants. Prisons.** ♦

Calendar of Plea..., I, p. 255.

ALICE HENLEY **[Dame Alice de Henley]**

fl. 1445–1451 England

Alice was elected prioress of Godstow, a Benedictine abbey near Oxford, in 1445. She was responsible for having a cartulary of Godstow produced.

♦ **Abbesses. Educated. Patrons of literature.** ♦

Bullough and Storey, *Study...*, p. 146. Davis, *Medieval Cartularies...*, p. 52 #'s 462 & 463. Rowland, *Medieval...*, p. 12.

ALICE HORSFORD

1370 England

Widow of John de Horsford. In 1370, at the Gildhall of London, Alice claimed ownership of half of a ship called the *Saynte Mariebot.*

♦ **Shipping–ship owners. Widows.** ♦

Calendar of Plea..., II, p. 114. Power, *Women...*, p. 56.

ALICE HULLE

fl. 1250s England

Tenant of Bertone, a manor belonging to the Hereford Bishopric in the mid-1200s. In the tenant lists, Alice is reported as the widow of William

Hulle of Welyntone. She held two virgates of land by herself, for which she owed a variety of rents and services.

♦ **Land/property. Manors. Widows.** ♦

Bannister (ed.), *Red Book...*, p. 2.

ALICE OF JERUSALEM, princess of Antioch

m.c. 1126 Israel; Turkey

Daughter of †Morphia of Melitene and Baldwin II of Jerusalem; married Bohemund II of Antioch. Alice was regent for their daughter †Constance of Antioch. Alice later tried several unsuccessful ploys to retain her power.

♦ **Crusades. Politics. Regents. Widows.** ♦

Bridge, *Crusades...*, pp. 145 & 147. *Cambridge...*, V, pp. 301, 305. *DBF*, v.5, p. 873. Douglas, *Norman...*, p. 190 & Table 3. Hamilton, "Women...," pp. 147 & 151. Payne, *Dream...*, pp. 133–5, 138, 140. Pernoud, *Eleanor...*, pp. 68, 69, 70.

ALICE KNYVET

1461 England

Wife of John Knyvet. In 1461, when King Edward IV tried to take the castle of Bokenham, Alice held it in defiance of him and the royal commissioners. She vowed to keep the castle, as her husband had charged her to do. Assisted by some fifty defenders armed with swords, and bows and arrows, Alice kept her word until the king's troops finally left her in peace.

♦ **Managers. Soldiers.** ♦

Ide, *Women...*, A, p. 114. Kendall, Yorkist..., p. 414. Power, *Women...*, pp. 45–46.

ALICE KYTELER

c. 1290s–1320s Ireland

Lady Alice married: William Outlawe; Adam le Blund; Richard de Valle; and Sir John le Poer. After Sir John's death, she and his eldest son inherited the whole estate. Partially in an effort to break the will, Sir John's other children had Lady Alice accused of practicing witchcraft. The case was long and involved, making it difficult to judge the truth of the charges. Eventually a number of other people were named in the case. Only one, †Petronella Meath, was burned at the stake. Several others, like †Helen and †Syssoh Galrussyn, †Eva de Brounestoun, and †Annota Lange, were whipped, banished, and/or excommunicated. Lady Alice and †Sarah Meath simply ran away before the trial.

♦ **Ecclesiastical courts. Estate. Squabbles. Widows. Witchcraft.** ♦

Ewen, *Witchcraft...*, pp. 29–33. Kieckhefer, *European...*, p. 111. Kittredge, *Witchcraft...*, pp. 77f. Lea, *Materials...*, III, pp. 456–458. McCall, *Medieval...*, pp. 250–251. Robbins, *Encyclopedia...*, pp. 275 & 294–5. Russell, *History...*, pp. 90–91. Russell, *Witchcraft...*, p. 189. Summers, *Geography...*, pp. 85–91. Wright, *Contemporary...*

ALICE LACY

[Alice de Lacy; Aleysa de Lascy; countess of Lancaster/Lincoln]

c. 1280–d. 1348 England

Daughter of Margaret, heiress of the earldom of Salisbury, and Henry Lacy, earl of Lincoln. In 1294, Alice married Thomas of Lancaster. A private feud between the great earldoms of Lancaster and Surrey began when John de Warenne "abducted" Alice by her own choice in 1317. She eventually outlived three husbands—including Hugh la Freyne, who presumably abducted and seduced her after she had taken a vow of chastity.

♦ **Abduction. Dowry/dower. Estate. Models. Politics. Prisons. Squabbles. Virginity–chastity vows. Widows.** ♦

DNB, v.11, p. 375. Fryde, *Tyranny...,* pp. 25, 35, 64, 79, 83, 106, 113, 183, 230. Gransden, "Alleged Rape...," p. 336. Holmes, *Later...,* pp. 112–115. McFarlane, *Nobility...,* pp. 263–264. Rosenthal, *Nobles...,* p. 184. Warren, *Anchorites...,* p. 174.

ALICE DE LINCOLN

1338 England

At a London inquest of evil-doers in March of 1338, Alice was accused of keeping a disorderly house in Hosierlane.

♦ **Land/property. Miscreants. Prostitutes.** ♦

Calendar of Plea..., I, p. 188.

ALICE DE LYE

1370s/1380s England

A merchant in Shrewsbury, Alice was recognized as a weaver during the 1370s and 1380s. In 1383, she was also cited as a brewer.

♦ **Alewives. Clothworkers–weaving. Miscreants.** ♦

Hutton, "Women in...," p. 91.

ALIX DE MÂCON **[Countess Alix of Mâcon]**

c. 1220s–c. 1260s France

Daughter of Girard II, count of Vienne; married Jean de Dreux. She later ceded Mâcon to King Louis IX, and retired to the abbey of Maubisson. Alix became abbess of the convent of Notre Dame du Lys, near Melun, which was founded by Blanche of Castile, queen of France. After Blanche died, Alix carried her heart to the convent for enshrinement.

♦ **Abbesses. Estate. Relics. Widows.** ♦

Butler, *Women...,* pp. 200 & 218 (old, but fairly reliable). *DBF,* v.2, p. 47.

ALICE ATTE MARCH

b. 1335 England

Orphaned daughter of Juliana and John atte March. Henry de Suttone abducted Alice and appointed himself guardian of the child and her property—valued at around 50s per year. A complaint against this situation was made in London court (August, 1342). While the case was pending, Henry married the seven-year-old girl to a tailor named Thomas de Staunesby. Henry was imprisoned for not producing the girl in court, and because his accounts were in arrears (he owed Alice £4). There are no details of what happened to this child-bride.

♦ **Abduction. Land/property. Orphans.** ♦

Calendar of Plea..., I, pp. 205–206.

ALICE MONTACUTE **[Montagu; Alice Brotherton]**

1338 England

Daughter and co-heiress of Thomas Brotherton (younger son of King Edward I), earl of Norfolk. Wife of Sir Edward de Monte Acuto (Montagu). In 1338, after her father died, the estate was split between Alice and her older sister, †Margaret Marshall (wife of John de Segrave).

♦ **Estate.** ♦

Calendar of Plea..., I, pp. 174 & 185–186. *C.P.*, v.9, p. 600. *DNB,* v.19, p. 633.

ALICE MONTAGU, countess of Salisbury **[Alice de Montacute]**

c. 1400s–d.c. 1464 England

Daughter and heiress of Thomas de Montacute, earl of Salisbury. In 1428, Alice inherited Thomas's estate; her husband, Richard Neville, became earl of Salisbury in her right. Mother of Richard Neville (called "Warwick the kingmaker").

♦ **Estate. Genealogy. Rebellions.** ♦

Clive, *Sun...*, pp. 11 & 17. Jacob, *Fifteenth...*, pp. 322, 464. Johnson, *Duke...*, p. 186. *Letters of Queen...*, pp. 90–91. McFarlane, *Nobility...*, p. 271. Ross, *Wars...*, p. 31. Scofield, *Life...*, I, p. 5.

ALICE DE MONTFORT **[Aelis; Helis]**

fl.c. 1200s–1230s France

Oldest daughter of †Petronille of Comminges, countess of Bigorre, and Guy de Montfort (second son of Simon the Crusader de Montfort). Alice married Pernel de Comminges in 1216; their daughters were Alice and Perrette. Alice de Montfort became embroiled in an inheritance fight. One troubadour extolled her virtue, while another lauded her quick wit.

♦ **Estate. Models. Poets/troubadours. Squabbles.** ♦

Bonner (ed.), *Songs...*, pp. 141, 142, 185, 276, 296. Colomez, *Histoire...*, pp. 43–73 passim. *C.P.*, v.7, p. 541. Labarge, *Simon...*, pp. 131 & 133.

ALICE DE MONTMORENCY **[Alice de Montfort]**

c. 1180–d. 1221 France

Daughter of Laurence (Laura) of Hainault and Bouchard IV de Montmorency. Alice married Simon the Crusader de Montfort in 1190. Their sons included Amauri de Montfort and Simon de Montfort, earl of

Leicester. After her first husband died, Alice married William des Barres the younger.

♦ **Crusades–Albigensian. Estate. Soldiers.** ♦

Anselme, *Histoire...*, v.3, p. 569. *C.P.*, v.7, p. 540. Powicke, "Loretta...," p. 167. Sumption, *Albigensian...*, pp. 146, 192, 196.

ALICE PERRERS

c. 1349–d.c. 1400 England

Wife of knight, William of Windsor. Lady-in-waiting to Edward III's queen, †Philippa of Hainault (c.1366); then mistress to Edward III. Alice has most often been denounced as greedy and unscrupulous, but she was apparently also bright and loyal. In 1371, the king gave Alice the manor of Wendover, and in 1373, he gave her more land, money, an annuity, and most of the late queen's jewels. In 1375, a tournament was held in honor of Alice. She attended the event as "the Lady of the Sun," dressed in ermine, pearls, and cloth of gold. Many of the king's counsellors did not like the amount of wealth lavished on Alice or her influence over Edward III. Sermons were preached against her and many influential nobles claimed that she had a hand in policy making and financial considerations. She probably helped Geoffrey Chaucer, and even the pope once appealed to her for help in dealing with Edward. In 1376, the "Good Parliament" accused her of dominating the king, interfering with justice, and enriching herself at the cost of the realm. In fact, Alice was so unpopular that she was accused of practicing love magic/witchcraft. Although she was banished and her property confiscated, she was later allowed to return to her position at court and her wealth was restored.

♦ **Banking. Estate. Gems/jewelry. Legal activity. Mistresses. Models. Patrons of literature. Politics. Popes. Tournaments. Witchcraft.** ♦

Armitage-Smith, *John...*, pp. 122, 129, 131, 185, & 194. Braddy, "Chaucer, Alice...," and "Chaucer and...". Brewer, *Chaucer...*, pp. 43–45. Bryant, *Age...*, pp. 444, 452, 454 & 455. Butt, *History...*, pp. 330, 346, 347, 348, 352, 362. *Calendar of Plea...*, II, pp. 11, 36, 232. Gardner, *Life...*, pp. 33, 35, 113, 115, 155, 161, 173, 178–190, 206, 219, 226, 230, 250, 271. Given-Wilson, *English...*, pp. 129, 169. Hardy, Philippa..., pp. 294–5, 302–3, 305–7. Holmes, *Later...*, pp. 162, 163, & 182–184. Kay, *Lady...* (a popular biography). Kittredge, *Witchcraft...*, pp. 78 & 105. Somerset, *Ladies...*, pp. 6 & 10. Tuchman, *Distant...*, 297–298, 301, 308–309, 313, 318.

AELIS (la poissonière)

1292 France

Dame Aelis sold fish in Paris; she was taxed 10s in 1292.

♦ **Merchants. Provisioning–fishmongers.** ♦

Géraud, *Paris sous...*, p. 108.

ALICE (Poplar)

1413/1414 England

The account books of Edmund Mortimer, earl of March (age 23 at the time), show a number of large payments to "Alice at Poplar." Since these payments are sandwiched in among his other entertainment expenditures (harpstrings, books, gambling debts, etc.), it appears that Alice was another "luxury item."

♦ **Women of easy virtue.** ♦

McFarlane, *Nobility...*, p. 246.

ALICE OF RALLINGBURY

1303 England

Widow of Gilbert Edward. Brought suit in Barnet manor court in 1303 against Richard Snouh for illegally holding her lands. Alice had been publicly endowed with the property at the church door before her marriage and had paid the proper entry fee; therefore the court ruled in her favor.

♦ **Land/property. Legal activity. Manors. Squabbles. Widows.** ♦

Homans, *English...*, p. 179.

ALICE ROMAYN

1313 England

Daughter of †Juliana Hauteyn and Thomas Romayn, late alderman, pepperer, sheriff, and mayor of London. Alice and her sister Johanna were nuns at Halywell. Her father willed them both certain rents and tenements (1313).

♦ **Bequests. Nuns.** ♦

Calendar of Wills..., I, p. 238.

ALICE SEFORD

fl. 1400s England

Apprenticed to †Agnes Brundyssch of London to learn silkworking trade. In her will, Agnes remitted Alice's apprenticeship terms.

♦ **Apprentices. Bequests. Silkwork.** ♦

Dale, "London...," pp. 326–327. Hindley, *England...*, p. 156.

ALICE SHEDYNGTON **[Shevyngton]**

c. 1400 England

As a young woman she was the servant of a rich family. Later she became a lay healer, traveling the countryside as an eye doctor. She also gained a reputation for curing smallpox and for preventing pitting from that disease by the application of red cloths (a treatment advocated by the best physicians).

♦ **Doctors/empirics–eye doctors. Legal activity. Servants.** ♦

Hurd-Mead, *History...*, p. 265. (She is presumably the same woman whose exploits are discussed in Lacey, "Women...," pp. 48–49.)

ALICE SHETHER

1375 England

Charged in London court with being a malicious scold, and a sower of discord in the community. Sentenced to the thews (stocks for women) for an hour.

♦ **Miscreants. Punishments.** ♦

Robertson, *Chaucer's...*, pp. 104–105 from Riley, *Memorials...*, pp. 385–386. Labarge, *Small Sound...*, p. 155.

ALICE STANFORD

1354/1355 England

See—AGNES ATTE HOLTE.

♦ **Abduction–abductors.** ♦

ALICE STAUNDON

1330 England

Her father, Peter de Staundon (London will, 1330), left a bakehouse for Alice and her mother Margaret to work.

♦ **Bequests. Less-affluent. Provisioning–bakers.** ♦

Calendar of Wills..., I, p. 358.

ALICE (of Stratford)

1251/1252 England

Ropemaker of 1250s in town of Stratford.

♦ **Less-affluent. Merchants–rope makers.** ♦

Mackenney, "Towns...," pp. 126–127.

AAELES (la tapicière)

1292 France

In the 1292 Paris tax lists Aaeles was recorded doing business on the rue de Vernueil. She was taxed 19s for her rug and tapestry making craft.

♦ **Artistic clothwork. Clothworkers. Land/property.** ♦

Géraud, *Paris sous...*, p. 41.

ALICE TREDEWEDOWE

1338 England

See—ALICE DONBELY.

♦ **Prostitutes.** ♦

ALIX DE VERGY, duchess of Burgundy

m. 1199–d. 1251 France

Daughter of Hugues de Vergy; in 1199 Alix married Eudes III, duke of Burgundy. When he died in 1218, she became regent for their young son. Alix recouped the area's financial position; confirmed town charters; concluded an alliance with Thibaut of Champagne; and founded a Dominican convent.

♦ **Negotiators. Regents. Religious patrons. Widows.** ♦

Baldwin, *Government...*, p. 271. *DBF*, v.2, p. 71. Decaux, *Histoire...*, p. 214. Heer, *Medieval...*, p. 262. Lehmann, *Rôle de la...*, p. 213. Valous, *Patriciat...*, p. 170.

ALICE DE WYLESDONE

d.c. 1305 England

In her will (proved London, 1305), Alice left her servant Cristina a tenement. Among other bequests, she also left 3s for the upkeep/repair of London Bridge.

♦ **Bequests. Charity–bridges. Employers.** ♦

Calendar of Wills..., I, p. 175

ALICE LA WYMPLERE **[le Wimpler]**

1281–1309 England

Probably the widow of Henry le Wimpler of London. Evidently she was also a wimple-maker during the years 1281 and 1282 when she acknowledged debts for yarn and other supplies. In her will, 1309, she left shops, rents, etc., mostly to her daughter †Avice who was also named custodian for Alice's wards William Gratefige and his wife Johanna.

♦ **Apparel–wimplers. Bequests. Childcare. Land/property.** ♦

Calendar of Letter..., A, p. 45. *Calendar of Wills...*, I, p. 208.

AALIS (l'ymaginière)

1292 France

Painter and/or sculptor, taxed 12d for her work in the 1292 Paris survey.

♦ **Artists. Less-affluent.** ♦

Géraud, *Paris sous...*, p. 169.

ALISON DUMAY

d.c. 1431 France

Presumably a low-born woman of the town of Nancy. Charles, duke of Lorraine, deserted his wife, †Margaret of Bavaria, for Alison. She had five children by Charles. Alison was extremely unpopular because she abused the power this illicit relationship gave her. After Charles died, the populace of Lorraine rebelled, causing her death (in unspecified manner).

♦ **Illegitimacy. Mistresses. Murder. Rebellions.** ♦

DBF, v. 2, p. 45. Pernoud, *Retrial...,* p. 95.

ALISON LA JOURDAIN

fl. 1415 France

She had had a varied career by 1415 when a weaving guild of Paris attempted to have her removed from the craft. Alison had left her husband to become a hatmaker, and later a weaver. So many men frequented her home that she was accused of running a whorehouse. It is possible, however, as some of her friends testitfied, that Alison was no "madam," she was just "good company."

♦ **Apparel–hatmakers. Clothworkers. Divorce. Land/property. Prostitutes.**♦

O'Faolain, *Not In...,* pp. 158–159.

ALISON LA MÉTAILLE **[Alipson; Alixon]**

fl. 1420s France

A potter in Paris; she specialized in making pewterware in her shop, the second house by the Notre Dame bridge, from at least 1425 until 1428.

♦ **Land/property. Potters.** ♦

Comptes du..., pp. 39, 85, 130, 162.

ALISON (la nourrice)

1292 France

In 1292 tax rolls of Paris, Alison was listed as a nurse to a cordwaner on the rue Andri-Malet; she paid a tax of 12d.

♦ **Less-affluent. Nurses.** ♦

Géraud, *Paris sous...,* p. 121. Hughes, *Women...,* p. 147.

ALISON (of Port-Royal)

fl. 1460 France

A young nun at the abbey of Port-Royal (called "Pourras"). The abbess, †Huguette du Hamel, tried to force Alison to bathe with a male friend, but Alison refused to be seduced. The infuriated Huguette threw Alison's clothing into the bath, and later sold the recalcitrant novice to an abbot. Both women were mentioned by the poet François Villon.

♦ **Models. Nuns. Virginity.** ♦

Bonner, *Complete...,* p. 206. Champion, *François...,* II, p. 14. Lewis, *François...,* p. 117.

ALMODIS (I) OF LIMOGES **[Adelmodie]**

c. 1000s France

Sister of Guy, viscount of Limoges. Married Adalbert I, count of La Marche. Almodis was the mother of Bernard I, count of La Marche; grandmother of †Almodis (II) and great-grandmother of †Almodis (III) and †(IV)—see below.

♦ **Genealogy.** ♦

Anselme, *Histoire...*, v.3, p. 69. Lewis, *Development...*, p. 346.

NOTE: We have numbered these four women named Almodis because they were all related to one another and they are sometimes confused with each other.

ALMODIS (II) DE LA MARCHE, countess of Barcelona

d. 1071 France

Daughter of Amelie and Bernard I, count of La Marche. Almodis married: (1) Hugh V of Lusignan; (2) William III, count of Arles and Provence; (3) Pons III, count of Toulouse—their daughter was †Almodis (III)—see below; and (4) in1052, Ramon Berenguer I, count of Barcelona. She ruled with Ramon and also helped him produce a law code, the *Usages of Barcelona.* Almodis was supposedly murdered in 1071 by her stepson (Ramon Berenguer's son by his first wife, Elizabeth of Narbonne).

♦ **Divorce. Estate. Legal activity. Murder. Religious patrons. Rulers. Writers.** ♦

Anselme, *Histoire...*, v.2, pp. 684–685. Bisson, *Medieval Crown...*, pp. 25–26. *DBF,* v.2, p. 275. Farreras et al, *Histoire...*, pp. 255–256, 260, 264. Lewis, *Development...*, pp. 275, 346, 351, 366, 392 & n. McNamara and Wemple, "Sanctity...," p. 109. Payne, *Dream...*, p. 49. Pernoud, *La femme...*, p. 181. Shneidman, *Rise...*, pp. 190, 294, 296, 304.

ALMODIS (III) OF TOULOUSE

m.c. 1063–d.c. 1135 France

Daughter of †Almodis (II) de La Marche and her third husband, Pons III, count of Toulouse. Almodis (III) married Pierre, count of Substantion and Melgeuil. After Pierre died in 1086, she served as regent for her son Raymond IV, count of Toulouse. Still later, Almodis became regent for her grandson Bernard.

♦ **Estate. Regents. Widows.** ♦

Anselme, *Histoire...*, v.2, p. 684. *DBF,* v.2, pp. 276–277.

ALMODIS (IV), countess of LA MARCHE

fl. 1080s–d. 1129 France

Daughter of Ponce and Adalbert II of La Marche. Niece of †Almodis (II). Almodis (IV) inherited the county of La Marche from her brother Boson III, who died in 1091. Before 1098, she married Roger of Montgomery (son of Roger and †Mabel of Bellême). Their sons were Adalbert, Boson, and Eudes; they also had a daughter named Ponce.

♦ **Estate. Legal activity. Managers. Religious patrons. Squabbles.** ♦

Anselme, *Histoire...*, v.3, p. 70. *DBF,* v.11, p. 275.

ALMUCS DE CASTELNAU **[Almodis de Châteauneuf]**

c. 1147–m.c. 1155 France

Noblewoman of Provence; married Guiraut I de Simiane (or Guigne de Châteauneuf); she sometimes served as her husband's regent. Almucs was a patron of troubadours, and was also a poet herself. She may have exchanged verses with other troubadours. Almucs was mentioned in a work by †Castelloza—another female troubadour.

♦ **Models. Patrons of literature. Poets/troubadours. Regents.** ♦

Bogin, *Women...*, pp. 35, 92–93, & 165–166. Boutière and Schutz, *Biographies des...*, pp. 422–424. *DBF*, v.2, p. 277. Dronke, *Women...*, pp. 100–101, & 300. Egan, *Vidas...*, pp. 6–7.

ALSON POTKYN

1468 England

Wife of farmer, Custans Pothyn. Among the items she received from his will (1468) were: a cow, sheep, pillows and a mattress, a variety of linens and covers for the bed, and six candlesticks.

♦ **Bequests–personal items. Manors.** ♦

Coulton, *Life...*, III, pp. 147–148.

AMALBERGA

c. 833–d. 861 Italy

She was abbess of S. Salvatore (in Brescia) for nearly thirty years. Emperor Lothar I gave her judicial rights on these monastery lands. She also received charters freeing her convent from various taxes.

♦ **Abbesses. Legal activity. Managers.** ♦

Wemple, "S. Salvatore...," pp. 90–91.

AMBROISE DE LORE

c. 1440–d. 1468 France

Daughter of Baron d'Ivry. Robert d'Estouteville, Provost of Paris, supposedly won her as his bride in a tournament. François Villon wrote a poem for Robert in which Ambroise's name is spelled by the first letters of each line. Robert and Ambroise lived on the rue de Jouy until she died in 1468 of an epidemic—probably plague.

♦ **Models. Plague. Tournaments.** ♦

Bonner (ed.), *Complete...*, p. 210. Champion, *François...*, I, pp. 177, 180, 181, & 282; II, pp. 56, 161, & 183. Lewis, *François...*, pp. 67 & 292.

AMELINE (la bourchière)

1292 France

In the Parisian tax survey of 1292, she was listed as a butcher on the rue Renier-Bourdon; taxed 12d.

♦ **Less-affluent. Provisioning–butchers.** ♦

Géraud, *Paris sous...*, p. 17.

AMELINE (la cordoanière)
1292 France
Taxed 12s in 1292 Paris for her leather shoemaking business.
♦ **Apparel–shoemakers. Merchants.** ♦
Géraud, *Paris sous...*, p. 47.

AMELINE (la couturière)
1292 France
Ameline was a dressmaker living on the rue de Froit-Mantel. She paid a tax of 3s in 1292 Paris.
♦ **Apparel–dressmakers. Less-affluent.** ♦
Géraud, *Paris sous...*, p. 10.

AMELINE (la miresse)
fl. 1313–1325 France
Doctor practicing in Paris in 1313 on the rue Guillaume Porée. In later years, 1324/5, she was charged with illegally practicing medicine.
♦ **Doctors/empirics. Miscreants.** ♦
Hughes, *Women...*, pp. 141 & 145. Wickersheimer, *Dictionnaire...*, v. 1, p. 21.

AMICIA [Amica; Amice; Amicie; Amitia]

AMICE DE CLARE
c. 1220–d. 1284 England
Daughter of †Isabella Marshall and Gilbert de Clare; wife of Baldwin de Redvers, earl of Devon; mother of †Isabella de Fortibus. Part owner with Isabella of the manor of Holderness (1260). Later problems were caused by the fact that Amice was a royal supporter while Isabella was on the side of Simon and †Eleanor de Montfort (and the associated barons). Mother and daughter were reconciled in 1274.
♦ **Estate. Politics. Squabbles. Widows.** ♦
Denholm-Young, "Yorkshire...," pp. 410–415. *DNB*, v.4, p. 378. Labarge, *Small Sound...*, p. 83.

AMICIA DE GAEL, countess of Leicester
fl. 1120s England; France
See her grandmother's entry—EMMA FITZOSBERN, countess of Norfolk.
♦ **Estate. Genealogy.** ♦
C.P., v.7, pp. 529–530. Elkins, *Holy...*, pp. 57 & 63. Le Patourel, *Feudal...*, VI, pp. 6, 9, 15.

AMICIA OF GLOUCESTER

m.c. 1175 England

Daughter and co-heiress of William, earl of Gloucester. Married Richard, sixth earl of Clare (later earl of Hertford). Their son and heir was Gilbert de Clare.

♦ **Estate. Genealogy.** ♦

Appleby, *John...*, pp. 19 & 228. Barrow, *Feudal...*, p. 216. *DNB,* v.4, p. 378.

AMICIA OF LEICESTER **[Amicia de Beaumont; de Montfort]**

c. 1160s–1210s England

Granddaughter of †Amicia de Gael; older daughter of †Petronilla of Grandmesnil and Robert III de Beaumont, earl of Leicester. When Amicia's brother, Robert IV, earl of Leicester, died, she and her sister †Margaret of Leicester (wife of Saer de Quincy, earl of Winchester), split the large inheritance. Amicia's husband, Simon de Montfort, became earl of Leicester in her right. Her second husband was William de Barres, count of Rochefort.

♦ **Estate. Genealogy.** ♦

Baldwin, *Government...*, p. 114. *C.P.*, v.7, p. 520. *DNB,* vol.13, p. 731; v.16, pp. 556–557. Labarge, *Simon...*, pp. 17 & 35. Powicke, "Loretta...," pp. 152, 154.

AMICE LA PLOMERE

d.c. 1290 England

Her will (1290 London) showed that she had little to leave; but evidently her business as a feathermonger was profitable enough for her to have a free tenement. [Plomere = feathermonger]

♦ **Less-affluent. Merchants–feather dealers.** ♦

Calendar of Wills..., I, p. 95.

ANASTASIA [Anastacia; Anastaise]

ANASTASIA OF KIEV

fl. 1030s–1060s Austria; Hungary; Russia

Daughter of †Ingegarde of Sweden and Yaroslav I, prince of Kiev (r.1019–1054). Anastasia married King Andrew I of Hungary around 1050. In the midst of a fight for control of Hungary, they tried to escape to Austria. Anastasia and her son carried the royal treasury to a monastery at Melk where they found refuge.

♦ **Banking. Gems/jewelry. Queens. Rebellions.** ♦

Cambridge..., IV, p. 577. Pares, *History...*, p. 35. Pernoud, *La femme...*, p. 229. Thompson, *Feudal...*, II, p. 601.

ANASTAISE (of Paris)

fl. 1390s–1420s France

Professional illuminator working in Paris in the early fifteenth century.

♦ **Artists. Bookmaking. Models.** ♦

Greer, *Obstacle...*, p. 161. Pisan, *City...*, p. 85.

ANASTASIA SPYCHEFAT

1312 England

In 1312 in St. Albans court, Anastasia accused Richard de Capele of murdering her husband. Richard pointed out several small discrepancies between her appeal and her formal writ (different name spellings, etc.); he evaded justice on this technicality.

♦ **Legal activity. Murder.** ♦

Bellamy, *Crime...*, p. 126.

ANASTASO OF BYZANTIUM

See—THEOPHANO, empress of BYZANTIUM

ANGELA [Angele]

ANGELE DE LA BARTHE

d. 1275 France

On trial in Toulouse, fifty-six-year-old Angele "confessed" that she had fornicated with an incubus. She had then borne a child which was part wolf and part snake. For two years the creature had eaten small children from the neighborhood before disappearing. Angele was convicted of practicing witchcraft and was burned.

♦ **Childcare. Ecclesiastical courts. Insanity. Punishments. Unmarried. Witchcraft.** ♦

Cohn, *Europe's...*, pp. 127–128. Robbins, *Encyclopedia...*, p. 208, 516, 517. Russell, *Witchcraft...*, p. 164. Summers, *Geography...*, pp. 362 & 524.

ANGELA BORGIA **[Angela Lanzol]**

c. 1480s–1510s Italy

Cousin, friend, and favorite lady-in-waiting to †Lucrezia Borgia. She caused problems in Ferrara when two men fell in love with her.

♦ **Servants. Unmarried. Women of easy virtue.** ♦

Chamberlin, *Fall...*, pp. 253 & 263. Cloulas, *Borgias...*, pp. 202, 215, 274, 279, 288, 289, 290. Fusero, *Borgias...*, p. 287. Johnson, *Borgias...*, pp. 197 & 202. Prescott, *Princes...*, pp. 224 & 225.

ANGELA OF FOLIGNO **[Blessed Angela]**

1250–1309 Italy

After her mother, sons, and husband all died, Angela gave away her property in order to follow a more pious calling. She went on pilgrimages, suffered two years of pain, and then began to have visions. She wrote several treatises, like her *Instructions*, showing the way to build character through prayer and serious training. She also taught that poverty, humility, and love were the way to find God. She was called "Mistress of Theology."

♦ **Mystics. Pilgrims. Religieuses. Widows. Writers–theology.** ♦

Book of the Divine... Bynum, *Holy...*, pp. 24, 27, 86, 140, 141–2 ... 395 n.11, 401 n84. Cruikshank (ed.), *The Book of the Visions....* Dronke, *Women...*, pp. 209, 215–217, 318. Ferré, "Les principales...," pp. 21–34. Ferré, La spiritualité... Lagorio, "Continental...," pp. 178–181. Leff, *Heresy...*, v.1, p. 32. Petroff, *Medieval...*, pp. 254–262.

(St.) ANGELA MERICI

1474–1540 Italy

She became the founder of the Order of Ursuline nuns when she and a group of followers devoted themselves to teaching poor girls. Angela and her women were not enclosed, nor did they take regular vows.

♦ **Orphans. Religieuses. Religious patrons. Teachers.** ♦

Attwater, *Dictionary...*, p. 20. Caraman, *St. Angela.* Farmer, *Oxford...*, p. 17. Monica, *Angela...*

ANGELA NOGAROLA

c. 1390s–1420s Italy

Well-educated; aunt of †Ginevra and †Isotta Nogarola. Wrote Latin poetry using many classical quotations.

♦ **Scholars. Writers.** ♦

Kristeller, "Learned...," p. 96. Robathan, "Bluestocking...," p. 106.

ANGELBERGA **[Engelberga; Engelbertha; Ingelberg]**

c. 840–890 France; Germany; Italy; Switzerland

Married Louis II, Holy Roman Emperor. In the middle of the 800s, Angelberga ruled with Louis, signing charters and minting coins in both their names. She also fought with her husband in central and southern Italy and then continued to fight as his regent in northern Italy. In 872, Louis divorced her because she had alienated so many important central Italians. He then proceeded to marry a noblewoman of that area, but Angelberga and Louis were back together before his death in 875. She continued to be such a potent political force that Charles the Fat (Charles II of France, Emperor Charles III) exiled her to a Swiss nunnery in an attempt to nullify her power. However, it was not until 888 that she actually retired to a convent, her own foundation of St. Sixtus at Piacenza. Angelberga's pious activities also included supporting the bishop of Ravenna against more than one pope, and transporting the relics of St. Germanus to her monastery of St. Sixtus.

♦ **Adultery. Banking. Divorce. Dowry/dower. Negotiators. Popes. Regents. Relics. Religieuses. Religious patrons. Rulers. Soldiers. Widows.** ♦

Cambridge..., III, pp. 44, 46, 47, 56. Jenkins, *Byzantium...*, pp. 180 & 181. McKitterick, *Frankish...*, pp. 261, 318, Table 3. Odegaard, "The Empress...," pp. 77–103. Riché, *Les Carolingiens...*, p. 178. Stafford, *Queens...*, pp. 17, 23–24, 38, 70, 75, 101–102, 118, 121, 134–139, 166–182, 201–210. Wemple, *Women...*, pp. 91 & 171.

ANGELICA DEL LAMA

1481 Italy

Widow of Gasparre del Lama. In Florence in 1481, in order to transact legal business, she had a *mundualdus* (responsible male) appointed for herself.

♦ **Legal activity. Widows.** ♦

Kuehn, "Cum Consensu...," p. 309.

ANKARETTE TWYNYHO

d. 1477 England

Servant of †Isabel Neville and her husband George, duke of Clarence. In 1477, Clarence had her dragged from her home in Somerset, charging that she had caused Isabel's death by poison. Ankarette was quickly tried and hanged for this fictitious crime. The duke was later found guilty of *embracery* (threatening, bribing, etc., the jurors) in this case.

♦ **Punishments. Murder. Servants.** ♦

Bellamy, *Crime...*, pp. 57–58. Butt, *History...*, pp. 608–609. Clive, *Sun...*, pp. 234–7, 239. Scofield, *Life...*, II, pp. 186–187.

ANNABELLA DRUMMOND, queen of Scotland [Anabil de Drummond]

c. 1370s–d. 1401 Scotland

Niece of Queen †Margaret of Logy. Annabella married John, earl of Carrick, who later became King Robert III of Scotland. Their son, James I, king of Scotland, was born c. 1394. She was crowned queen at Scone in 1390. Annabella died in 1401, probably of the pestilence.

♦ **Plague. Queens.** ♦

Allan, "Historical...," p. 343. Brown, *History...*, I, p. 195. Tuck, *Richard...*, p. 164. Williamson, *Kings...*, p. 229, Table 18.

ANNE [Ana; Anees; Anès; Ann; Anna]

ANNE OF ANTIOCH

See—ANNE DE CHATILLON.

ANNE BEAUCHAMP, countess of Warwick

c. 1422–d. 1492 England

Daughter of †Elizabeth Berkeley and Richard Beauchamp, earl of Warwick. Married Richard Neville (later called "the kingmaker") in 1434; he became earl of Warwick in her right. They had two daughters: †Anne Neville, duchess of Gloucester (later queen of England), and †Isabel Neville, duchess of Clarence. After her husband's defeat and death (1471), Anne's lands were confiscated and divided between her sons-in-law.

♦ **Educated. Estate. Politics. Rebellions. Widows. Writer–letters.** ♦

Butt, *History...*, pp. 548, 601–602. Clive, *Sun...*, pp. xl, 152, 154, 174, 198–9. Green, *Letters...*, pp. 100–104. Jacob, *Fifteenth...*, pp. 336, 464, 568, 581. McFarlane, *Nobility...*, pp. 155 & 187. Scofield, *Life...*, I, pp. 6, 558, & 583; II, pp. 27, 59–60, & 93. Warren, *Anchorites...*, p. 206.

ANNE OF BEAUJEU [Anne of France]

c. 1460–d. 1522 France

Daughter of †Charlotte of Savoy and Louis XI of France; married Pierre of Bourbon, lord of Beaujeu. In 1483, Anne's dying father appointed her co-regent of France because the heir, Charles VIII, was a minor. Despite some opposition, especially from Louis of Orleans, she proved to be an excellent, strong-minded ruler. Anne quelled rebellious barons, and she secured Brittany by a marriage contract between Charles and †Anne, heiress of Brittany. When Charles began to rule in 1492, he proved to be much less able than his sister.

♦ **Estate. Models. Negotiators. Regents.** ♦

Cleugh, *Chant...*, pp. 130, 160, 193, 196, 284 & 289. Commynes, *Memoirs...*, I, pp. 13, 120n, 347n; II, 413, 417, 421, 439, 440, & 455. Coryn, *House...*, pp. 270, 273, 275, 279, 280, 286–295, 297–303, 306, 308, 311–314, 327, 348. Decaux, *Histoire...*, pp. 447–450, 455–459, 464, 477. Griffiths and Thomas, *Making...*, pp. 118–121 & 170–172. Ide, *Women...*, p. 142. Pelicier, *Essai sur...* Valous, *Patriciat...*, p. 148.

ANNE, princess of BOHEMIA

c. 1210s–1250s Bohemia; Germany; Poland

Daughter of †Constance (of Hungary) and King Premysl Ottokar I of Bohemia. Married Heinrich of Silesia and Poland. Like her mother-in-law (St.) Hedwig, Anne was very pious and interested in the care of the sick. Her nursing specialties were children (particularly orphans) and those with fevers. In 1253 she founded a hospital and nunnery at Kreuzberg and another at Neumarkt.

♦ **Childcare. Medicine–hospitals. Nurses. Orphans. Religious patrons.** ♦

Goodich, "Contours...," p. 23. Harrsen, *Cursus...*, pp. 18–20, 49, 50, 54. Hughes, *Women...*, p. 132. Hurd-Mead, *History...*, p. 220.

ANNE OF BOHEMIA, queen of England

1366–1394 Bohemia; England

Daughter of Charles of Bohemia (Charles IV, Holy Roman Emperor) and his fourth wife, †Elizabeth of Pomerania. In 1382, Anne married Richard II, king of England. She was a patroness of several writers, presumably including Geoffrey Chaucer. Despite much anti-Bohemian feeling in her new country, hers was a very happy marriage. In fact, her death in 1394 caused Richard such grief that a supposed insult to her memory induced the king to knock down the earl of Arundel at Anne's funeral. Richard also destroyed their favorite palace.

♦ **Book owners. Clothworkers. Models. Patrons of literature. Plague. Soldiers. Tournaments.** ♦

Brewer, *Chaucer...*, pp. 58–59. Butt, *History...*, pp. 380, 413, 421. Froissart, *Chronicles...*, I, pp. 175, 195, 236–237, 289, 410, 411, 418; II, pp. 75–76, 89, 116–117, 127. Gardner, *Life...*, pp. 118, 217–218, 247–248, 257, 258, 261, 263, 266, 271–272, 296, 312. Holmes, *Later...*, pp. 186 & 189–190. Hutchison, *King...*, pp. 76, 135, 201. *Oxford...Prose*, p. 450. Somerset, *Ladies...*, p. 7. Tuchman, *Distant...*, pp. 374, 436, 561, & 563.

ANNE OF BRITTANY, queen of France

1477–1514 France

Daughter and heiress of Francis, duke of Brittany. To ensure that her duchy would revert to France, her marriage contract stipulated that if Charles VIII died, she was to marry the next heir, Louis of Orleans. She married Charles VIII in 1491 and he died in 1498. Louis then divorced his wife, †Jeanne of France, and married Anne. She and Louis had a daughter named Claude who later became queen of France; their other daughter, Renee, later became duchess of Ferrara. Anne was literate and owned a number of books, mostly breviaries, Books of Hours, and similar religious works. As her reading matter indicates, she was conservative, pious, and serious-minded. Anne was also conscious of her rights and her importance. She supposedly made it quite clear to both her royal husbands that she would not be shouldered aside or mistreated.

♦ **Book owners. Educated. Estate. Patrons of literature. Pawns. Politics.** ♦

Bell, "Medieval...," p. 155. Chamberlin, *Fall...*, pp. 161 & 173–174. Commynes, *Memoirs...*, I, p. 76n; II, pp. 384n, 449, 450, 566, & 590. Coryn, *House...*, pp. 287, 289, 298, 299, 304, 308–311, 314–317, 320, 344, & 346. Decaux, *Histoire...*, pp. 459–464 & 472–477. Griffiths and Thomas,

Making..., pp. 105 & 171–172. Putnam, *Marguerite...*, pp. 3–4, 11–12, 23, 29–31, 68–70, 80–82, 100, 109, 217 & 320. Sanborn, *Anne....*

ANNE OF BURGUNDY, duchess of Bedford

b. 1402–d. 1432 France

Daughter of †Margaret of Hainault and John the Fearless, duke of Burgundy. In 1423, Anne married John, duke of Bedford. Kind and pious, Anne was notable for her charitable donations, and was loved by the poor of Paris. She had †Joan of Arc examined for virginity and then forbade the guards to touch the future saint. Anne died of the plague, which she caught while visiting other victims of the disease.

♦ **Charity. Negotiators. Pawns. Plague. Religious patrons. Virginity.** ♦

Calmette, *Golden...*, pp. 111, 140, 145, 147, 316, 317. Cartellieri, *Court...*, pp. 60–61. Champion, *François...*, pp. 18, 162 & 291. Commynes, *Memoirs...*, I, p. 122. Huizinga, *Waning...*, pp. 162–163. Jacob, *Fifteenth...*, pp. 207, 225. Pernoud, *Retrial...*, pp. 162 & 177. Seward, *Hundred...*, pp. 196, 202, 225.

ANNE, princess of Byzantium

c. 963–d. 1011 Byzantium; Russia

Daughter of †Theophano and Romanus II of Byzantium. In 989 her brothers, the co-emperors Basil II and Constantine VIII, married her to Vladimir I, prince of Kiev, as part of a peace treaty. He became a Christian immediately before the wedding. Anne was none too happy about sacrificing herself for politics and religion—in fact, she became so ill upon arriving in Kiev that it supposedly took a miracle to save her.

♦ **Dowry/dower. Pawns. Religious patrons. Superstitions–miracles.** ♦

Bridge, *Crusades...*, p. 34. *Cambridge...*, IV, pp. 68, 90, 209. Daniel-Rops, *Church...*, p. 512. Jenkins, *Byzantium...*, pp. 270, 308, & 311. Pares, *History...*, pp. 31–32. Tierney, *Western...*, p. 219. Vernadsky, *Kievan...*, pp. 63, 65, & 75.

ANNA, empress of Byzantium

See—AGNES OF FRANCE.

See—CONSTANCE OF HOHENSTAUFEN.

ANNE OF CAUX **[of Normandy]**

1474 France; England

French nurse of Edward of York. In 1474, as King Edward IV of England, he gave her a generous pension of £20 per year.

♦ **Childcare. Nurses–wetnurses. Servants.** ♦

Clive, *Sun...*, p. xxvii. Scofield, *Life...*, I, p. 2.

ANÈS (la cervoisière)

1292 France

In 1292 survey of Paris, Dame Anès was listed as a brewer. She evidently had a thriving business on the rue St. Martin since she paid 48s in taxes.

♦ **Alewives. Land/property.** ♦

Géraud, *Paris sous...*, p. 61.

ANNE DE CHÂTILLON **[Anne of Antioch]**

1154–1184 France; Hungary; Turkey

Daughter of †Constance of Antioch and Renaud de Châtillon. First wife of King Béla III of Hungary; mother of King Andrew II of Hungary. Anne brought French culture into her new homeland.

♦ **Art patrons. Banking. Queens.** ♦

DBF, v.2, p. 1331. Pamlényi, *History...*, pp. 60 & 608. Runciman, *Sicilian...*, Table VI.

ANNA COMNENA, princess of Byzantium

b. 1083–d. 1148 Byzantium

Daughter of †Irene Ducas and Emperor Alexius Comnenus; married Nicephorus Bryennius in 1097. Educated, ambitious, and haughty, both before and after her father's death (1118), Anna masterminded several plots to gain the Byzantine throne for herself and her husband. Since all of these coups failed, Anna embarked on a more successful hobby—she wrote the *Alexiad*, a history of her father and his reign. She included descriptions of many of the Norman knights of Sicily and the Western European Crusaders—most of whom she considered barbarians. Anna was not an objective writer, but her history is unique and informative about both Byzantium and her own life.

♦ **Educated. Medicine. Politics. Rebellions. Religieuses. Widows. Writers.** ♦

Buckler, *Anna....* *Cambridge...*, IV, pp. 346 & 351. *Chronicles...*, pp. 52, 61, 66–8, 69–72, 108. Comnena, *Alexiad.* Diehl, *Byzantine...*, pp. 174–197. Hughes, *Women...*, pp. 37–39, 41, 46, 50, 58, 114n. Hurd-Mead, *History...*, pp. 113, 116, 167, 168, & 176. Norwich, *Normans...*, pp. 69–78, 117, 223–236, 231–232, 244–245, & 248. Thièbaux, *The Writings...*, pp. 91–104.

ANNA DALASSENA

c. 1040s–d.c. 1105 Byzantium

Wife of John Comnenus (d.1067); mother of Alexius Comnenus; grandmother of †Anna Comnena. While Alexius was with the army, she served as his regent. Exceptionally influential for years, she later lost favor and finally left the Byzantine court to live at the monastery of Pantepoptes.

♦ **Banking. Models. Negotiators. Popes. Regents. Religieuses. Widows.** ♦

Cambridge..., IV, pp. 326, 328, 332, 346. *Chronicles...*, p. 32. Comnena, *Alexiad*, pp. 83, 116, 119–122, 195. Diehl, *Byzantine...*, pp. 199, 200, & 204.

ANNE DEVEREUX, countess of Pembroke

c. 1450s–1480s England

Daughter of William Devereaux, lord Ferrers of Chartley. Married William Herbert who became earl of Pembroke when he took Pembroke Castle and obtained custody of four-year-old Henry Tudor (later Henry VII). Anne brought up the future king with her own children at Raglan Castle. After Herbert died (1469), Henry was in some danger, but Anne protected him until he could join his uncle, Jasper Tudor. Henry retained affection for her even after he became king.

♦ **Childcare. Managers. Widows.** ♦

DNB, vol. 9, p. 671. Griffiths and Thomas, *Making...*, pp. 58–59, 68 & 71. Kendall, *Yorkist...*, p. 373. Rees, *Son...*, pp. 71 & 76.

ANNE OF FRANCE

See—ANNE OF BEAUJEU.

ANÈS (la gueinnière)

1292 France

In 1292 Parisian tax poll, Anès was listed as a sheath and scabbard maker at la Saunerie, and was taxed 40s.

♦ **Merchants–sheath/scabbard.** ♦

Géraud, *Paris sous...*, p. 31.

ANNA HARBATOVA

fl.c. 1390s Bohemia; Czechoslovakia

See—DOROTHY OF STRYGL.

♦ **Banking. Prostitutes.** ♦

ANNE HOLLAND

m.c. 1465–d.c. 1471 England

Daughter and heiress of Henry Holland and †Anne of York, duke and duchess of Exeter. Although betrothed to Warwick the kingmaker's nephew, after her father was exiled, Anne became the bride of Sir Thomas Grey, †Elizabeth Woodville's son. This about-face was due to a large bribe by the queen to Anne's mother.

♦ **Divorce–betrothal. Estate. Pawns.** ♦

Clive, *Sun...*, pp. 99, 114, 146. *DNB,* v.8, p. 645. Scofield, *Life...*, I, p. 397. St. Aubyn, *Year...*, p. 53.

ANNE OF KIEV, queen of France **[Anne of Russia; Agnes]**
b. 1024–d.c. 1080 France; Russia

Daughter of †Ingegarde of Sweden and Yaroslav I, prince of Kiev; married Henry I, king of France in 1051. When Henry died in 1060, their son Philip was only eight years old; Anne had a part in his regency administration. In 1061, she married Raoul de Crépy, count of Valois (d. 1074). She remained devout, known for charity and for land grants to French churches and monasteries. Although she had been brought up in the Eastern church, during conflict between the Eastern and Western churches in 1054, she sided with her new country and the Roman church. At that time she received a new name, Agnes. Anne was also interested in learning and could write a little.

♦ **Charity. Educated. Popes. Regents. Religious patrons.** ♦

Decaux, *Histoire...*, pp. 191–192. Dunbabin, *France...*, pp. 136, 216. Ennen, *Medieval...*, pp. 74–75. Facinger, "Study...," pp. 13, 22, 36 & 41. Pares, *History...*, p. 35. Pernoud, *La femme...*, pp. 136, 229–236. Stafford, *Queens...*, pp. 42, 54, 134, 170–171. Vernadsky, *Kievan...*, pp. 278, 342, 343.

ANNE DE LUSIGNAN, duchess of Savoy **[Anne of Savoy]**
c. 1420s–1460s Cyprus; France; Italy; Switzerland

Daughter of the king of Cyprus. Married Louis, duke of Savoy; mother of †Charlotte of Savoy, queen of France. Her husband left most of the governing responsibilities to her (from 1439), since she was much stronger and more energetic than he. By 1450, Anne controlled a large amount of territory.

♦ **Negotiators. Politics. Rulers.** ♦

Anselme, *Histoire...*, v.1, p. 122. *Cambridge...*, IV, p. 181. Cleugh, *Chant...*, pp. 100, 101, 109, 116–118. Jose, *La Maison...*, I, pp. 65, 74, 347, 404, 415–433; II, pp. 85, 92, 131, 133, 261, 277.

ANNE DE MANY, countess of Pembroke
m.c. 1369–1390s England

Daughter of Walter de Many and †Margaret Marshall (later countess of Norfolk). Around 1369 she married John de Hastings, earl of Pembroke, without the proper dispensation; the couple were required to pay 1,000 gold florins to receive that legitimization of their union. After John died in 1375, Anne had to fight to obtain her dower rights. She was finally granted this on condition that she not remarry without the king's permission. Her son John (b.1372) died in 1389.

♦ **Dowry/dower. Ecclesiastical courts. Religious patrons. Widows.** ♦

DNB, v.9, p. 132. Given-Wilson, *English...*, p. 146. Rosenthal, *Nobles...*, pp. 139–140 & 174.

ANNA OF MOCHOV

fl. 1400–1420s Bohemia

An attendant in Queen †Sophia of Bohemia's court, Anna was an early noble patroness of Hus and his clerical reforms.

♦ **Hussites. Models. Servants–ladies.** ♦

Klassen, *Nobility...*, pp. 90, 112, 116. Lutzow, *Hussite...*, p. 3.

ANNE MORTIMER

c. 1395–c. 1410s England; Ireland

Daughter of Eleanor and Roger Mortimer VI, earl of March; sister and heiress of Edmund, earl of March. Married Richard, earl of Cambridge; mother of Richard, duke of York (b.1411). Anne was the granddaughter of Lionel, duke of Clarence, and was grandmother of kings Edward IV and Richard III.

♦ **Estate. Genealogy.** ♦

Butt, *History...*, p. 490. Curtis, *Ireland...*, pp. 129 & 133. *DNB,* v.16, p. 1016. Hardy, *Philippa...*, p. 309. Johnson, *Duke...*, pp. 1 & 12. St. Aubyn, *Year...*, p. 62.

ANNA OF MOSCOW

See—AGRIPPINA OF MOSCOW.

ANNE MOWBRAY

b. 1471–d. 1481 England

Daughter of †Elizabeth Talbot and John (III) Mowbray, duke of Norfolk. In 1478, Anne was married at age six to four-year-old Richard, duke of York, the second son of King Edward IV. She soon died, not long before her child-groom disappeared in the Tower of London.

♦ **Models. Pawns. Tournaments.** ♦

Cely..., p. 79. Clive, *Sun...*, pp. 243–245. Kendall, *Yorkist...*, p. 365. McFarlane, *Nobility...*, p. 155. Scofield, *Life...*, II, pp. 203–5 & 323. St. Aubyn, *Year...*, pp. 39 & 40.

ANNE NEVILLE, duchess of Buckingham

c. 1400s–d.c. 1480 England

Daughter of †Joan Beaufort and Ralph Neville, earl of Westmoreland. Anne married Humphrey Stafford, duke of Buckingham; her second husband was Walter Blount, baron Mountjoy. Chosen as envoy by London citizens to meet with †Margaret of Anjou and obtain favorable terms for the city.

♦ **Bequests. Negotiators.** ♦

Clive, *Sun...*, pp. 5 & 41. *Coronation...*, p. 40. McFarlane, *Nobility...*, pp. 66, 107, 205. Mertes, *English...*, pp. 54, 105, 109, 210. Rawcliffe, *Staffords...*, pp. 20, 54–56, 67, 71. Rosenthal, *Nobles...*, p. 141. Scofield, *Life...*, I, pp. 6, 145–6, 545 n5. Warren, *Anchorites...*, pp. 198, 199, 207.

ANNE NEVILLE, queen of England

b. 1456–d. 1485 England

Daughter of †Anne Beauchamp, countess of Warwick, and Richard Neville (Warwick the kingmaker). When her father changed sides and threw his support to †Margaret of Anjou and King Henry VI of England, Anne was betrothed to their son, Edward, prince of Wales. After he died in 1471, Anne married Richard, duke of Gloucester (later King Richard III), in 1472. She died shortly before her husband was killed at Bosworth field.

♦ **Dance. Drama. Models. Pawns. Queens. Tournaments.** ♦

Commynes, *Memoirs...,* I, pp. 214, 365, 368. Clive, *Sun...,* pp. 98, 152–4, 174, 181, 198–200, 262, 290–1, 294, 298. Kelly, "Canonical...," pp. 271 & 272. Jacob, *Fifteenth...,* pp. 564, 571, 621, 636. Ross, *Wars...,* pp. 33, 68, 85, 94, 95, 159. Scofield, *Life...,* I, pp. 529–531, 558, 582–585; II, 6–7 & 26–27. St. Aubyn, *Year...,* pp. 55, 58, 118, 166–170, 172, 184–185, 201–202.

ANNA PALMER

1393 England

Anchoress in Northampton. In 1393, while being questioned as a possible Lollard, Anna called the bishop of Lincoln the "AntiChrist" and denied any heretical leanings. She was imprisoned and then sent to London for further questioning.

♦ **Anchoresses. Ecclesiastical courts. Lollards. Prisons.** ♦

Cross, "Great...," p. 361. Warren, *Anchorites...,* p. 81.

ANNE PASTON

fl. 1460–1480s England

Daughter of †Margaret and John (I) Paston. She fell in love with a clerk, John Pampyng, but her parents forbid her to marry him and instead forced her to wed William Yelverton.

♦ **Pawns. Writers–letters.** ♦

Barron, "Lords of...," p. 111. Haskell, "Paston...," p. 461. Kendall, *Yorkist...,* p. 315. *Paston...,* I, pp. 337, 339, 348, 365, 386–7, 389, 451, 472–3, 492, 496, 529, 536, 540, 574, 577, 599, 605, 621, 639, 647, 654, & 669.

ANEES DE QUINKERE

1383 Belgium; Flanders

Wife of Jan Moens. In 1383, as a widow, Anees was a member of the blue dyers guild in Ghent.

♦ **Clothworkers. Widows.** ♦

Nicholas, *Domestic Life...,* p. 101.

ANNE OF RUSSIA, queen of France

See—ANNE OF KIEV.

ANNE OF SAVOY, empress of Byzantium **[Anna]**

c. 1320–1353 Byzantium; Italy

Daughter of Amadeus V of Savoy. Married Byzantine Emperor Andronicus III in 1326. When he died in 1341, Anne served as regent for their son, John V Paleologus. Fearful that her son was about to lose his realm, Anne sent emissaries to Pope Clement VI in 1343. Her efforts to effect a union of the Eastern and Western churches were in vain and only added to her unpopularity with the Greeks. In 1347 she was overthrown by John Cantacuzene.

♦ **Popes. Rebellions. Regents. Widows.** ♦

Boulding, *Underside...*, pp. 442–443. *Cambridge...*, IV, pp. 541, 543, 615. Diehl, *Byzantine...*, pp. 287–308. Tuchman, *Distant...*, p. 573.

ANNE OF SAVOY

See—ANNE DE LUSIGNAN.

ANNA SFORZA

b. 1473–d. 1497 Italy

Daughter of †Bona of Savoy and Galeazzo Maria Sforza, duke of Milan; she married Alfonso d'Este of Ferrara in 1497. Anna died giving birth to a stillborn baby.

♦ **Book owners. Childbirth. Dowry/dower. Slaves.** ♦

Bell, "Medieval...," p. 176. Cartwright, *Beatrice...*, pp. 8, 45, 48, 70, 78, 186, 190–200, 253, 259 & 323. Cloulas, *Borgias...*, pp. 76, 205, 271. Fusero, *Borgias...*, p. 162. Johnson, *Borgias...*, p. 196. Prescott, *Princes...*, pp. 114, 133, 167, 216. Sizeranne, *Beatrice...*, p. 259.

ANNE SHIRLEY

fl.c. 1450s England

One of several gentlewomen who signed the Findern Anthology. This collection of poems was selected, transcribed, and possibly written by these women. The extant copies bear the signatures of Anne Shirley, Frances Crucken, Elizabeth Coton, and Elizabeth Francis.

♦ **Book owners. Educated. Patrons of literature. Writers.** ♦

Hanson-Smith, "Woman's...," p. 179.

ANNE STAFFORD

c. 1480s–1544 England; Wales

Daughter of †Katherine Woodville and Henry Stafford, duke of Buckingham. Married Sir Walter Herbert, a powerful lord of southern Wales. Around 1509, Anne married her second husband, George Hastings, earl of Huntingdon.

♦ **Genealogy. Rebellions.** ♦

DNB, v.18, p. 858. Griffiths and Thomas, *Making...*, p. 129. Rawcliffe, *Staffords...*, pp. 39–40, 173–174.

ANÈS (la taupière)

1292 France

Anès and her daughter, Erembourc, practiced a rare occupation in 1292 Paris—as mole catchers. The two women were taxed 4s.

♦ **Less-affluent. Mole catchers.** ♦

Géraud, *Paris sous...*, p. 41.

ANNE OF WOODSTOCK, countess of Stafford

b. 1370s–d. 1438 England

Daughter of †Eleanor de Bohun and Thomas of Woodstock, duke of Gloucester. In 1391, she married Thomas, earl of Stafford (d. 1392). Around 1398, Anne married Thomas's younger brother (and eventual successor), Edmund, who died in 1403. Shortly thereafter, Anne married, Sir William Bourchier (later created count of Eu). From the time of his death (1420) until her own, the widowed countess controlled a vast amount of land which was hers by right of inheritance and by dowers accumulated mostly from her two Stafford husbands. Anne also inherited illuminated books from her mother in 1399.

♦ **Book owners. Estate. Widows.** ♦

DNB, v. 19, p. 637. Johnson, *Duke...*, p. 68. McFarlane, *Nobility...*, pp. 66, 204–5, 236 & 241. Rawcliffe, *Staffords...*, pp. 12–19, 37, 45, 70, 84, 95, 104, 106–110, 157, 159, 192–3.

ANNE OF YORK

b. 1475–d.c. 1510 England

Daughter of †Elizabeth Woodville and King Edward IV of England. In 1495, Anne married Thomas Howard, son of the earl of Surrey.

♦ **Genealogy.** ♦

Clive, *Sun...*, pp. 240, 243, 306. McFarlane, *Nobility...*, p. 81. Scofield, *Life...*, II, pp. 163 & 267. Williamson, *Kings...*, p. 96.

ANNE OF YORK, duchess of Exeter

b. 1439–d. 1476 England

Daughter of †Cicely Neville and Richard, duke of York. Married 1447 to Henry Holland, duke of Exeter. They had a daughter, †Anne Holland, who married †Elizabeth Woodville's son, Sir Thomas Grey. Anne of York's brother, King Edward IV, granted her the castle of Thorpe Waterfield. When her husband was exiled she experienced financial difficulties. After her husband was released from captivity, Anne divorced him and married Thomas St. Leger in 1472—he was presumably already her lover. They had one daughter, Anne St. Leger.

♦ **Adultery. Divorce. Estate. Negotiators.** ♦

Clive, *Sun...*, pp. xli, 65, 93, 107, 121, 204, 296. *DNB*, vol. 16, pp. 1062 & 1070. Johnson, *Duke...*, p. 68. Rosenthal, *Nobles...*, pp. 171–173. Scofield, *Life...*, I, pp. 2, 78, 159, 397; II, pp. 22–23, 150, & 151. St. Aubyn, *Year...*, pp. 62–63.

ANNE-MARIE DE GEORGEL

c. 1300–d. 1335 France

At Toulouse in 1335, this middle-aged woman "confessed" that she had engaged in carnal relations with the Devil—an awesome black man. He supposedly also taught her to make diabolical potions, and perform a variety of evil/magical deeds. She was burned at the stake as a witch.

♦ **Adultery. Punishments. Witchcraft.** ♦

Cohn, *Europe's...*, pp. 129–130, 132, 137–138. Lea, *Materials...*, p. 231. Russell, *Witchcraft...*, pp. 184–185. Summers, *Geography...*, pp. 378–379.

ANNORA DE BRAOSE **[de Briouze]**

c. 1190s–d. 1241 England

Daughter of Maud (of St. Valery) and William de Braose; married Hugh de Mortimer. After his death in 1227, Annora became a recluse at Iffley (c.1230).

♦ **Anchoresses. Estate. Prisons. Religious patrons. Widows.** ♦

Clark and Williams, "Impact...," p. 163. Labarge, *Small Sound...*, pp. 124, 126, 127. Powicke, "Loretta...," pp. 148, 149, 156, 158, 162–163, 165. Warren, *Anchorites...*, p. 25.

ANNOTA LANGE

1320s Ireland

See—ALICE KYTELER.

♦ **Witchcraft.** ♦

ANSGARD (of France)

divorced 875 France

See—ADELAIDE, queen of FRANCE.

♦ **Divorce. Squabbles.** ♦

Cambridge..., III, pp. 57, 77n. Riché, *Les Carolingiens...*, p. 205. Sismondi, *French...*, p. 357. Stafford, *Queens...*, pp. 75 & 160. Wemple, *Women...*, p. 84.

ANTIGONE (of Gloucester)

c. 1430s–1460s England; France

Natural daughter of Humphrey, duke of Gloucester. Antigone married Henry Grey, lord Powys, earl of Tankerville. After his death in 1450, she married Jean d'Amancier.

♦ **Illegitimacy. Pawns. Widows.** ♦

C.P., v.5, p. 736; v.6, p. 139. Jacob, *Fifteenth...*, p. 486.

ANTOINETTE DE BELLEGARDE

1360 France

In 1360, she was accused of practicing medicine illegally and was fined 25s. She was later fined 10s for practicing surgery without license.

♦ **Doctors/empirics. Miscreants. Surgeons.** ♦

Hughes, *Women...*, p. 145. Wickersheimer, *Dictionnaire...*, v.1, p. 39.

ANTOINETTE DE VILLEQUIER **[Antoinette de Maignelais]**

fl. 1450s–1460s France

Wife of Andre de Villequier; relative of †Agnes Sorel. Mistress of Charles VII of France in his later years. By 1460 she had left the king to become the paramour of the duke of Brittany. The dauphin (Louis XI) corresponded with Antoinette; she kept him informed on affairs at the French court while he was in exile at the court of Burgundy. She reputedly procured other young girls for Charles VII.

♦ **Educated. Mistresses. Models. Politics. Spies.** ♦

Champion, *Louis...*, pp. 137 & 138. Cleugh, *Chant...*, pp. 134, 136, 137. Decaux, *Histoire...*, p. 446. Lewis, *King...*, p. 222. Vale, *Charles...*, pp. 135–6 & 188–9.

ANTONIA DANIELLO **[Maestra Antonia of Florence]**

c. 1370s–1408 Italy

Possibly studied at the medical school in Florence. She was given a degree or license to practice medicine in that city around the year 1386.

♦ **Doctors/empirics. Educated. Jews. University.** ♦

Herlihy, *Opera...*, p. 160. Hughes, *Women...*, pp. 62 & 142. Hurd-Mead, *History...*, p. 276. Lipinska, *Histoire...*, p. 149.

ANTONIA UCCELLO

1456–1491 Italy

Daughter of artist Paolo Uccello, Antonia was also a painter herself. Her work included painting for her Carmelite house.

♦ **Artists. Religieuses. Unmarried.** ♦

Anderson and Zinsser, *A History of...*, p. 412. Greer, *Obstacle...*, p. 15. Petersen and Wilson, *Women...*, p. 28.

AOIFE, countess of LEINSTER

See—EVA.

AREMBURGE D'URGEL

See—AUREMBAIX, countess of URGEL.

ARLETTE (of Normandy) **[Herleve of Falaise]**

fl. 1010s–1040s France

Mistress of Robert I of Normandy; mother of William the Conqueror of England. She married Herluin of Conteville; their sons were Odo, bishop of Bayeux, and Robert, count of Mortain.

♦ **Genealogy. Mistresses.** ♦

Barlow, *Feudal...*, p. 65. Bates, *Normandy...*, p. 151. Brown, *Normans...*, pp. 37, 57. Decaux, *Histoire...*, p. 209. Douglas, *William...*, pp. 15, 31,

112, 379–82, Table 6. Haskins, *Normans...*, pp. 53 & 166. Vitalis, *Ecclesiastical...*, v.4, pp. 98 & 116. Williamson, *Kings...*, p. 43. Wood, *Search...*, p. 206.

ARMANDE ROBERT

fl. 1335 France

In 1335 trial, †Paule Viguier, Armande Robert, †Matheline Faure, and †Pierrille Roland "confessed" that they had attended witch meetings.

♦ **Witchcraft.** ♦

Lea, *Materials...*, p. 230. Russell, *Witchcraft...*, p. 182. Summers, *Geography...*, pp. 378–379.

ASA, queen of Agdir **[Aase]**

c. 800s–850s Norway

The details of her life come from Scandinavian sagas, and are possibly more romantic than accurate. She was presumably the daughter of King Harald Red-beard of Agdir. She was abducted by Gudrod the Hunting-king of Vestfold (Norway), who also killed her father and brother in order to marry Asa. After Gudrod and Asa had a baby, Halfdan the Swart, she supposedly avenged her father's death by killing Gudrod. Asa then took baby Halfdan back to Agdir where she ruled on his behalf. Asa was the grandmother of the famous Viking chief, Harold I Fair-hair of Norway. One of the bodies found in the burial ship called the *Oseberg Mound* may be that of Queen Asa. The boat contains all the things a royal lady needed to take with her to the afterworld: food, animals, a slave, tools for weaving and embroidering the beautiful tapestries she liked to make, and a variety of other items.

♦ **Abduction. Artistic clothwork. Models. Murder. Regents. Shipping.** ♦

Bukdahl, *Scandinavia...*, v.1, p. 110. Jones, *Vikings...*, pp. 84–5. Larsen, *History...*, pp. 71 & 81.

ASCELINNE (la deicière)

1292 France

In the Paris records of 1292 she was taxed 2s on her business—making thimbles—on the rue de Mau-Conseil.

♦ **Less-affluent. Merchants–thimbles.** ♦

Géraud, *Paris sous...*, p. 43.

ÅSTA (of Norway)

See—AASTA GRÖNSKE.

ASTRID (of Denmark) **[Aastrid]**

c. 990s–1000s Denmark

According to romantic legend recorded in sagas, Astrid secretly warned King Olaf Tryggvesson of Norway of a treacherous plot against him by her husband Earl Sigvalde. One saga even reported that Olaf did not die during the ensuing battle at sea but was picked up by the boat Astrid sent to rescue him.

♦ **Models. Politics. Spies.** ♦

Boyesen, *Story...*, pp. 163 & 171. Jones, *Vikings...*, p. 138.

ASTRID OF NORWAY

c. 950s–980s — Norway; Russia

Daughter of Erik of Ofrestad; wife of Tryggve of Vik, who was killed around 968. Their son Olaf I Tryggvesson had a good claim to the Norwegian throne, so King Harold II Gray-pelt's mother, †Gunhild, tried to find and kill Astrid and Olaf. According to the sagas, after many vicissitudes of fate, Astrid and Olaf were taken captive and sold separately as slaves. Astrid finally returned to Norway as the wife of a rich merchant. Olaf eventually did become king of Norway (995–1000).

♦ **Childcare. Models. Slaves. Widows.** ♦

Boyesen, *Story...*, pp. 108, 109, 134, 135. Jones, *Vikings...*, p. 136. Larsen, *History...*, pp. 94–95.

ASTRID OF SWEDEN

fl. 1000s–1030s — Sweden; Norway

Daughter of King Olaf of Sweden. Married King Olaf II Haroldsson (St. Olaf), who died in battle trying to take Norway back from Canute of Denmark in 1030. Astrid used Swedish relatives and allies to help her son, Magnus Olafsson, gain the throne of Norway.

♦ **Negotiators. Pawns. Politics. Widows.** ♦

Boyesen, *Story...*, pp. 197–8 & 218. Jones, *Vikings...*, p. 379. Larsen, *History...*, pp. 103–4 & 111.

AUBRÉE D'IVRY, countess of Bayeux

fl. 1050 — France

Aubrée supposedly hired the famous architect Lanfroi to build the virtually impregnable tower of Ivry, and then murdered him to protect the castle's secrets. She was later murdered herself, by her husband Ralph of Ivry (Raoul, count of Ivry), because she had tried to take over the tower and keep him out of it.

♦ **Builders. Models. Murder. Soldiers. Squabbles.** ♦

Brown, *Normans...*, p. 44 n134. Decaux, *Histoire...*, p. 211. *DBF,* v.4, pp. 226–227. Vitalis, *Ecclesiastical...*, v.4, pp. 114, 199, & 290.

AUD "the Deep-Minded" — **[Unnr]**

c. 870s–d.c. 900 — Iceland; Ireland; Scotland

Daughter of Ketill Flat-nose, a Viking chief in the Western Islands. Wife of Olaf the White, a Viking chief who lived in Ireland. After Olaf died, the widowed Aud led her family and dependents by way of the Orkneys to Iceland. There she took over a large amount of land and assumed the head of household duties: providing for her family, servants, etc., and meeting with the Viking lawmaking/political body. Aud is mentioned in Icelandic sagas.

♦ **Legal activity. Managers. Models. Politics. Shipping. Widows.** ♦

Byock, *Medieval Iceland...*, p. 56. *Cambridge...*, III, pp. 325, 331. Jones, *Vikings...*, p. 277. Larsen, *History...*, pp. 29 & 76.

AURORA OF CORDOBA

See—SUBH OF CORDOBA.

AUREMBAIX, countess of URGEL [Arembaud; Aremburge d'Urgel]

d. 1231 Portugal; Spain

Daughter and eventual heiress of Ermingaud VII of Urgel; married Ponce de Cabrera. As a widow, Aurembaix sought military aid from Jaime I of Aragon, and she became his mistress. Eventually, the nobles of Urgel agreed to acknowledge her as ruler of Urgel on condition that she marry Pedro, prince of Portugal. They were married in 1229. After she died, a civil war broke out over the succession of Urgel.

♦ **Estate. Mistresses. Rulers. Squabbles. Widows.** ♦

Anselme, *Histoire...*, v.1, p. 576. Bisson, *Medieval Crown...*, pp. 49, 60, 62–3, 65. Ferraras et al, *Histoire...*, pp. 294, 296–297. Shneidman, *Rise...*, pp. 12, 13, 17, 129, 132, 154, 173, 174, 179, 309, 404, & 486.

AVA OF MELK

d. 1127 Austria

With her sons serving as scribes, Ava wrote religious poetry and hagiography. Five of her poems are extant.

♦ **Religieuses. Widows. Writers–poetry and hagiography.** ♦

Dronke, *Women...*, p. 84. Fredericksen, *Women...*, pp. 19–20. Harksen, *Women...*, p. 50. Schoenfeld, *Women...*, p. 135 (an older, but still informative work). Sparrow, "Women...," p. 22. Also see–*Dichtungen der Frau Ava.*

AVELINE (la barbière)

1292–1313 France

From 1292 until 1313 (at least), Aveline of the rue aux Ours was listed in tax records of Paris as a barber.

♦ **Barbers.** ♦

Géraud, *Paris sous...*, p. 53. Hughes, *Women...*, p. 140. Wickersheimer, *Dictionnaire...*, v.1, p. 56.

AVELINE (la chapelière)

1292 France

Aveline was recorded in 1292 Paris as a *chapelière de feutre*—she made felt hats. Business must have been booming; she was taxed 30s.

♦ **Apparel–hatmakers. Merchants.** ♦

Géraud, *Paris sous...*, p. 95.

AVELINE (l'estuverresse)

1292 France

In 1292 Paris tax summary, Aveline was listed as owner/operator of a bathhouse on the rue St. Denys.

♦ **Bathhouse.** ♦

Géraud, *Paris sous...*, p. 622. Hughes, *Women...*, p. 290.

AVELINE DE FORZ, countess of Aumale

m. 1270–d. 1274 England

Daughter and heiress of William, earl of Albemarle (Aumale) and Isabella de Redvers (†Isabella de Fortibus). First wife of Edmund, earl of Lancaster (son of Henry III of England). They were married in 1270, but Aveline died childless in 1274. Much of her estate was then seized by Edward I.

♦ **Estate. Pawns.** ♦

Denholm-Young, "Yorkshire...," pp. 396 & 409. McFarlane, *Nobility...*, pp. 256–257. Prestwich, *Edward...*, pp. 103, 296, 352. Williamson, *Kings...*, p. 69.

AVICE GARDEBOIS

1280 England

In London court of 1280, her husband John Gardebois appointed Avice his attorney to receive the 48 marks owed him by another citizen.

♦ **Banking. Legal activity–attorneys.** ♦

Calendar of Letter..., A, p. 31.

AVICE LA WYMPLERE

1309 England

See—ALICE LA WYMPLERE.

♦ **Bequests. Childcare.** ♦

AVIS WADE

fl. 1310s England

Married John Wade in Belper, Derbyshire (c.1310). In 1312, John complained that he had not received the promised dowry. Avis's father, Richard, then agreed to immediately turn over to John 22s worth of goods and animals—a cow with calf, a surcoat, and three sheep.

♦ **Dowry/dower. Land/property. Manors.** ♦

Homans, *English...*, pp. 140–141.

AZALAIS

See—ADELAIDE.

Lady BADDLESMERE

1321 — England

In charge of the castle of Leeds during her husband's absence, Lady Baddlesmere refused to allow Queen †Isabella access to the fortress. Her refusal provided a welcome pretext for Edward II, who was searching for an excuse to act against Lord Baddlesmere. The king besieged the castle and sent Lady Baddlesmere to the Tower of London. Most sources do not give her name; it seems likely, however, that she was Margaret de Clare, the co-heir with her sister Maud (who married Robert de Welle) of Richard de Clare (d.1318). Margaret was the wife of Bartholomew de Badlesmere.

♦ **Estate. Managers. Prisons. Soldiers.** ♦

Bryant, *Age...*, p. 217. *Calendar of Close...*, 1318–1322, pp. 504–5. *Cambridge...*, VII, p. 423. *C.P.*, v.3, p. 247 ftn.C. *DNB*, v.10, p. 502. Fryde, *Tyranny...*, pp. 50–1.

BARBARA ARRENTI

fl. 1400s — Italy

A teacher and writer presumably affiliated with the University of Bologna; her subjects were law and philosophy.

♦ **Legal activity. Scholars. Teachers. University. Writers.** ♦

Greer, *Obstacle...*, p. 209. Ragg, *Women...*, p. 196.

BARBARA VON BRANDENBURG — **[Barbara Hohenzollern]**

1422–1481 — Germany; Italy

Became marchioness of Mantua as wife of Lodovico Gonzaga (d.1478). They were the parents of Federigo Gonzaga. Barbara was a friend of Rodrigo Borgia (Pope Alexander VI); they shared a love of hunting. Barbara kept slaves, at least one female dwarf, and a zoo. She was widely known as a cultured, educated, and capable woman.

♦ **Dwarves. Educated. Hunting. Models. Negotiators. Popes. Slaves.** ♦

Chamberlin, *World...*, pp. 166 & 290. Fusero, *Borgias....*, p. 124. Johnson, *Borgias...*, pp. 62 & 65. Simon, *Tapestry...*, pp. 10, 11, 30, 33, 37, 41, 46, 50, 51, 106–7, 146, 194. Verheyen, *Paintings...*, p. 1 n.3.

BARBARA OF CILLY, Holy Roman Empress

m.c. 1405–1440s Bohemia; Germany; Hungary

Daughter of Count Arminius of Cilli. Second wife of Sigismund, king of Bohemia and Hungary—who became Holy Roman Emperor. Apparently, Barbara was a supporter of the Hussite movement (and Catholic authors have tended to write about her as an evil influence). After Sigismund died in 1437, she conspired with Ladislas III of Poland to join the crowns of Hungary and Poland through their marriage. Presumably these negotiations fell through.

♦ **Hussites. Models. Politics. Prisons. Rulers. Widows.** ♦

Cartwright, *Beatrice...*, p. 218. Stubbs, *Later...*, pp. 166, 175, 176. Vambéry, *Hungary...*, pp. 186–7, 189, 190, 193.

BARBARA GWICHTMACHERIN

fl. 1450s–1470s Germany

Nun at St. Catherine's convent at Nuremberg; in the 1450s she painted the illuminations in breviaries copied by †Margaretha Cartheuserin.

♦ **Artists. Bookmaking. Nuns.** ♦

Carr, "Women...," p. 8. Harksen, *Women...*, p. 46. Greer, *Obstacle...*, pp. 161–162.

BARBERA RAGNONI

fl. 1480s Italy

Worked on a painting known as the *Adoration of the Shepherds*, but there is some controversy over whether she was the original artist, or whether Barbera "ruined" an unknown male painter's work.

♦ **Artists.** ♦

Greer, *Obstacle...*, pp. 178–179. Petersen and Wilson, *Women...*, p. 23. Sparrow, "Women...," pp. 23 & 35.

BASILIA DE CLARE

1170s England; Ireland; Wales

Sister of Richard de Clare ("Strongbow"). She married (1) Robert de Quenci, and (2) Raymond FitzGerald. The purpose of her second marriage was to achieve a Welsh alliance for her brother—but relations between Basilia and Strongbow were not entirely cordial.

♦ **Dowry/dower. Pawns. Politics.** ♦

DNB, v. 4, p. 392. Orpen, *Ireland...*, I, pp. 323, 334, 336, 356, 387; II, p. 211 n.

BASILIA MADERMAN

1313 England

Her husband, Robert le Maderman, willed her a tenement and five shops for life (1313). Basilia then went to London court and reclaimed a freehold lease on the shops by proving joint ownership of the property.

♦ **Bequests. Land/property. Legal activity. Merchants.** ♦

Calendar of Wills..., I, p. 243.

BATTISTA DA MONTEFELTRO **[Malatesta]**

1383–1450 Italy

Daughter of Count Antonio of Urbino; 1405, married Galeazzo Malatesta, lord of Pesaro. A scholar; interested in classical Latin. In 1405, humanist Leonardo Bruni wrote to her. After her husband was assassinated in 1431, Battista returned to Urbino were she helped educate her granddaughter, †Costanza Varano. In 1433, Battista delivered an oration to Emperor Sigismund in an effort to save her son-in-law, Pier Gentile Varano, and to get Pesaro restored to her family. She later became a member of the order of St. Clare.

♦ **Politics. Religieuses. Scholars. Teachers. Widows.** ♦

Franceschini, "Battista...". Kelly-Gadol, "Did Women...," p. 152. King and Rabil, *Her Immaculate...*, pp. 13–15, 16, 18, 26, 35–38, 39, 43, & 135. Kristeller, "Learned...," pp. 93–94 & 96. Robathan, "Bluestocking...," p. 106.

BATTISTA SFORZA

1446–1472 Italy

Daughter of †Costanza Varano and Alessandro Sforza, lord of Pesaro. Married at age thirteen to thirty-eight-year-old Federigo da Montefeltro of Urbino (his second wife). A patron and friend of humanist scholars, Battista was famed for her Latin orations. She also served as her husband's partner and his regent when he was absent.

♦ **Models. Patrons of literature. Regents. Scholars.** ♦

Chamberlin, *World...*, p. 198. King and Rabil, *Her Immaculate...*, pp. 18 & 23. Kristeller, "Learned...," p. 94. Prescott, *Princes...*, p. 251.

BAYALUN

fl. 1330s Byzantium; China; Russia

Daughter of Byzantine emperor Andronicus III who gave her in marriage to the Khan of the Golden Horde, Ozbeg (Uzbek). (She was Ozbeg's third wife; his first—or most important—wife at the time was Taidoghli.) In 1334, Bayalun traveled in great state to Constantinople to visit her father, and give birth to her baby. It is not clear whether she ever returned to Ozbeg.

♦ **Pawns. Queens. Slaves–owners.** ♦

Spuler, *History...*, pp. 186, 190, 193, 196–7, 200. Vernadsky, *Mongols...*, p. 196.

BEATRICE [Béatrix, Beatriz, Bietrix]

BEATRICE OF ARAGON, queen of Hungary [Beatrice of Naples]
c. 1450s–1490s Hungary; Italy; Spain

Daughter of Ferrante I of Aragon, king of Naples. Beatrice became the second wife of Mathias Corvinus of Hungary around the year 1476. After his death, Beatrice married Ladislaus II, king of Hungary (and Bohemia).

♦ **Educated. Queens.** ♦

Berzeviczy, *Béatrice....* Cloulas, *Borgias...*, pp. 81–2. Commynes, *Memoirs...*, II, p. 476. Fusero, *Borgias...*, p. 159. Kristeller, "Learned...," p. 93. Pamlényi, *History...*, pp. 100 & 622. Sizeranne, *Beatrice...*, p. 260.

BEATRICE BASSETT
1364 England

Arrested for defaming a London alderman who had demanded that she quit dumping refuse on the streets.

♦ **Less-affluent. Miscreants.** ♦

Calendar of Plea..., II, p. 6.

BEATRICE BROUNYING
1297–1306 England

Resident of the village of Broughton where she was frequently cited as an alewife. In 1301, William Hobbe was fined for committing adultery with her (a baby was born of this indiscretion).

♦ **Adultery. Alewives. Manors.** ♦

Britton, *Community...*, pp. 34 table 6, 235, & 250 n.36.

BÉATRIZ (la buffretière)
1292 France

In 1292 Paris survey, she was taxed 2s for her business as a winemonger.

♦ **Alewives–wine. Less-affluent.** ♦

Géraud, *Paris sous...*, p. 162.

BEATRICE OF BURGUNDY, Holy Roman Empress
1140–1184 France; Germany

Daughter of Rainald, count of Burgundy. Second wife of Frederick I "Barbarossa" (married in 1156); crowned Empress by Pope Paschal III in 1167 at Rome. She was a wealthy heiress, bringing Barbarossa parts of Burgundy and Provence through their marriage. Beatrice was also well-educated; she studied poetry and wrote her own epitaph of eight Latin verses. Gautier d'Arras dedicated his *Ille et Galeron* to Beatrice. She traveled with her husband, had an active influence on his court, and bore him at least ten children.

♦ **Dowry/dower. Educated. Patrons of literature. Prisons. Writers.** ♦

Barraclough, *Origins...*, p. 173. *Cambridge...*, V, pp. 389, 390, 422. Ennen, *Medieval...*, pp. 144, 145–146. Fuhrmann, *Germany...*, pp. 21, 150, 159, 163, 179, 186. Haverkamp, *Medieval...*, pp. 223, 234, 265. Lejeune, "La Femme...," p. 207. Norwich, *Kingdom...*, pp. 203–204, 272, & 311n. Pinnow, *History...*, p. 108. Thièbaux, *The Writings...*, p. xi. Thompson, *Literacy...*, p. 139.

BEATRICE CANDIA **[Candida]**
c. 1300 Italy

Widow of Gherardo di Candia. Famous in Venice as an excellent doctor.

♦ **Doctors/empirics. Widows.** ♦

Hughes, *Women...*, p. 142. Hurd-Mead, *History...*, pp. 226 & 278. Lipinska, *Histoire...*, p. 148.

BEATRICE OF CASTILE
b. 1353–d. 1368 Spain

Oldest daughter of exiled king of Castile, Pedro I the Cruel; in 1366, she entered a convent.

♦ **Illegitimacy. Nuns.** ♦

Armitage-Smith, *John...*, p. 92. Jamison, *Life...*, I, p. 285.

BEATRICE OF CASTILE, queen of Portugal
c. 1310s–1350s Portugal; Spain

See—LEONOR (Eleanor) OF PORTUGAL, queen of Aragon, and MARIA (Mary) OF PORTUGAL, queen of Castile.

Also see—INES DE CASTRO.

♦ **Genealogy.** ♦

BEATRICE DI CORREGGIO **[Beatrice d'Este, the elder]**
c. 1427–d. 1497 Italy

Daughter of Niccolo III d'Este; sister of Ercole I d'Este; aunt of the more famous †Beatrice d'Este. Supposedly beautiful, charming, and a talented dancer, Beatrice was known as the "Queen of Festivals" at the court of Ferrara. She presumably married Borso (or Niccolo) da Correggio, and later Tristan Sforza.

♦ **Dance. Educated. Models.** ♦

Cartwright, *Beatrice...*, pp. 4–5, 22, 115, 148, 169, & 323. Gardner, *Dukes...*, pp. 39 & 55n.

BEATRICE DE DIA **[Béatritz, countess of Die]**

c. 1130s–c. 1170s France

Daughter of Marguerite de Bourgogne-Compte (d.1163) and Guigues IV, count of Albon (d.1142). Married Guillem of Poitiers. One of the best known Provençal female troubadours; five of her poems are extant—one complete with musical score. She wrote of her own courtly romance with Raimbaut of Orange.

♦ **Music. Poets/troubadours.** ♦

Bogin, *Women...*, pp. 16, 82–91, & 163. Bonner (ed.), *Songs...*, pp. 111–113, 266–267. Boutière and Schutz, *Biographies des...*, pp. 445–446. Drinker, *Music...*, pp. 210–212. Dronke, *Women...*, pp. 103–106, 109. Egan, *Vidas...*, pp. 28–29. Harksen, *Women...*, p. 52. Morrall, *Imprint...*, p. 109. Moulin, *La Poésie...*, pp. 76–78. Santy, *La Comtesse....*

BEATRICE OF ENGLAND

1242–1275 England; France

Daughter of †Eleanor of Provence and Henry III, king of England. In 1260, Beatrice married John (II), later duke of Brittany. Their son Arthur (II) of Brittany was born in 1262. Their youngest son John became earl of Richmond in 1306.

♦ **Genealogy. Writers–letters.** ♦

Anselme, *Histoire...*, I, p. 448. Bréquigny, *Lettres de rois...*, I, p. 153. *Calendar of Plea...*, I, p. 38. Labarge, *Simon...*, pp. 180–181. Powicke, *Thirteenth...*, pp. 97, 159, 235. Williamson, *Kings...*, p. 69.

BEATRICE D'ESTE THE ELDER

See—BEATRICE di CORREGGIO.

BEATRICE D'ESTE

b. 1475–d. 1497 Italy

Daughter of †Leonora of Aragon and Ercole I d'Este. Married in 1491 to forty-year-old Ludovic ("the Moor") Sforza, duke of Bari, and regent of Milan for his weak nephew Giangaleazzo Sforza. Ludovic became duke of Milan in 1494. As a young bride, Beatrice had a huge wardrobe containing hundreds of dresses and many expensive jewels. She also loved dancing, hunting, music, and literature. Both she and her husband were art patrons. Leonardo da Vinci fashioned some of her cupboards. Beatrice often held literary and music courts at which the best poets gathered. Beatrice was a very strong-willed woman; she supposedly made Ludovic give up one of his mistresses, and she fought her rival †Isabella of Aragon, duchess of Milan, for the position of first lady of the court. She served her husband well as an envoy to Venice, and also proved her mettle by defending the Castello when Milan was threatened. In fact, Ludovic considered her so important to his success that, when she died giving birth to her still-born third son, he felt his "lucky charm" was gone and he began to fail.

♦ **Art patrons. Childbirth. Dance. Educated. Hunting. Music. Negotiators. Patrons of literature. Politics. Soldiers. Superstitions.** ♦

Bellonci, "Beatrice...," pp. 285–295 passim. Cartwright, *Beatrice....* Chamberlin, *World...*, pp. 182, 199, & 269–270. Chamberlin, *Fall...*, pp. 112, 121–123, 258. Collison-Morley, *Sforzas...*, pp. 149–158. Prescott, *Princes...*, pp. 12–13, 28, 80, 132–8, 142, 143, 169, 205, 209. Simon, *Tapestry...*, pp. 74, 75, 93, 95–6, 114, 140, 157. Sizeranne, *Beatrice....* Trevelyan, *Short...*, pp. 187, 189, & 199.

BEATRICE D'ESTELLIN **[Béatrix]**

c. 1370s–1450 France

Godmother of †Joan of Arc. This widow testified for Joan's character at the retrial in her hometown of Domremy.

♦ **Ecclesiastical courts–Inquisition. Legal activity. Manors. Widows.** ♦

Barstow, *Joan...*, p. 51. *DBF*, v.1, p. 738. Pernoud, *Retrial...*, pp. 57–58.

BEATRICE OF FALKENSTEIN **[Beatrice of Falkenburg]**

m. 1268 England; Germany

Daughter of Philip of Falkenstein; reputedly very beautiful. Third wife of Richard of Cornwall, titular king of the Romans. She returned with him to England, where he died in 1272.

♦ **Pawns. Queens.** ♦

Cambridge..., VI, p. 126. Lewis, "Beatrice...," pp. 279–282. Prestwich, *Edward...*, p. 63. Stubbs, *Later...*, p. 59.

BEATRICE (of France), duchess of Haute-Lorraine

b. 938–d. 1005 France; Germany

Daughter of †Hathui (Hedwig) and Hugh the Great count of Paris. Married Frederick I, duke of Haute-Lorraine in 954. After his death, Beatrice was regent for son Thierry for ten years. Reluctant to relinquish her power, she fought to retain her position and was imprisoned by her son. In 987 she served as Empress †Adelheid's envoy at Compiegne, thereby helping her brother (Hugh Capet) become king of France.

♦ **Negotiators. Prisons. Regents. Soldiers. Squabbles. Widows.** ♦

Anselme, *Histoire...*, v.1, p. 69. *DBF*, v.5, pp. 1038–1039. Sismondi, *French...*, p. 454.

BEATRIZ GALINDO **[Beatrix de Galindo]**

c. 1470–1500s Italy; Spain

Educated in Italy; hired by Queen †Isabella of Castile as a Latin tutor. Beatriz remained at court to teach the Spanish princesses. Taught several subjects at the University of Salamanca; founded a hospital in Madrid.

♦ **Medicine. Religious patrons. Servants. Teachers. University.** ♦
Altamira, *Spain...*, p. 308. Gardiner, *English...*, pp. 151–153. Hurd-Mead, *History...*, pp. 300, 311, & 352. Lipinska, *Histoire...*, p. 158. Miller, *Castles...*, p. 158.

BEATRICE DE GUZMAN **[Beatrix of Castile]**
fl. 1240–d. 1304 Portugal; Spain

Natural daughter of Alfonso X of Castile and Maria de Guzman-Villena. Possibly mistress of Alfonso III of Portugal before she became his wife. Alfonso divorced his wife, †Matilda of Boulogne, to marry Beatrice (1249), and Pope Urban IV eventually legalized their union. Alfonso and Beatrice's son, Diniz, thereby became the legitimate heir to the Portugese throne.

♦ **Adultery. Illegitimacy. Politics. Popes.** ♦
Anselme, *Histoire...*, v.1, p. 582. McNabb, *St. Elizabeth...*, pp. 23–24. Stephens, *Story...*, p. 81.

BEATRICE DE LAGLEIZE
See—BEATRICE OF PLANISOLLES.

BIETRIX (la metresse)
1292 France

Taxed 3s in 1292 Paris survey; she was probably a private tutor.

♦ **Less-affluent. Teachers.** ♦
Géraud, *Paris sous...*, p. 109.

BEATRICE OF MONYONS
1430 France

Nun at convent of Perpignan; became violent and attacked other nuns.

♦ **Insanity. Nuns.** ♦
Otis, "Prostitution...," pp. 152–157.

BEATRICE OF NAZARETH **[Beatrice of Tirlemont]**
d. 1268 Belgium; Flanders; Netherlands

Educated as a child by Beguines. Professed as a Cistercian at age sixteen. Prioress at Nazareth (in Brabant) for over thirty years. Beatrice wrote a record of her spiritual growth in *Seven Manieren van Minne* (Seven Ways of Loving). She wrote in Flemish, but her work was later translated into Latin.

♦ **Abbesses. Beguines. Educated. Mystics. Writers–theology.** ♦
A.S., Feb. v.3, p. 724. Bynum, *Holy...*, pp. 86, 115, 123, 152, 161–3, 164, 171, 186, 200, 203, 204, 209, 214, 246, 256, 261, 273, 275. Colledge, *Netherlands...*, pp. 8–9, 19–29. Lagorio, "Continental...," pp. 175–176. McDonnell, *Beguines...*, pp. 28–29, 98, 152, 272, 332, 365, 386–387, 392–393, 395, 396, 447n., 494, 495. Zum Brunn and Epiney-Burgard, *Women...*, pp. 71–94.

BEATRICE OF PLANISOLLES **[Béatrice de Lagleize]**
fl. 1310s–1320s France

Heretic of Montaillou; also accused of dallying with a lover while her maid kept a look-out.

♦ **Employers. Heretics. Ecclesiastical courts–Inquisition. Women of easy virtue.** ♦

Decaux, *Histoire...*, pp. 246 & 296. Dronke, *Women...*, pp. 212–213, 305, 317 (she is called Beatrice de Lagleize here). Duvernoy, *Inquisition à Pamiers...*, pp. 255–256; on p. 215 (called Beatrice of Lagleize). Ladurie, *Montaillou...*, pp. 11, 16, 32, 39, 64, 131, 150, 153, 161, 166–168.

BEATRICE PORTINARI
1266–1290 Italy

Daughter of Florentine noble, Folco Portinari. Married Simone dei Bardi. Inspired Dante to write sonnets of the *Vita Nuova*; she is found in "Heaven" in his *Divine Comedy.*

♦ **Educated. Models.** ♦

Bernardo, "Petrarch's...," p. 66. Chubb, *Dante...*, pp. 9, 17, 89, 130–200.....716, 733–46, 749, 751. Effinger, *Women...*, pp. 87–90. Holmes, *Florence...*, pp. 59, 92, 110, 114, 117–20, 234, 250–3, 255–6, 258. Stephenson, *Mediaeval...*, p. 478. Wimsatt, "Beatrice as...," pp. 402–414.

BEATRIX OF PORTUGAL, queen of Castile **[Brites]**
b. 1371–1390s Portugal; Spain

Daughter of King Fernando I of Portugal and his mistress/wife, †Leonor Teles. She was Fernando's heir and was legitimized so that she could inherit and serve as a useful marital pawn. As a child, Beatrix was betrothed many times; in 1383 she finally married John I, king of Castile (d.1390). Although she fought to retain the crown of Portugal, Beatrice never succeeded to the throne because the Portugese wanted to remain independent of Castile. They instead chose to recognize an illegitimate half-brother of the late King Fernando; he became King John I of Portugal.

♦ **Dowry/dower. Illegitimacy. Pawns. Politics.** ♦

Armitage-Smith, *John...*, pp. 264, 267, & 273. Dos Passos, *Portugal...*, pp. 54 & 55. Froissart, *Chronicles...*, I, pp. 234, 244, 324, 325, 338, 340–344, 350, 351. Leroy, *La Navarre...*, p. 142 [some confusion in this source]. Livermore, *History...*, pp. 164–165. Nowell, *History...*, pp. 17–18. Stephens, *Story...*, pp. 106 & 107.

BEATRICE OF PORTUGAL **[Brites; Beatrix]**
c. 1380s–d. 1439 England; Portugal

Illegitimate daughter of John I of Portugal and Inez Peres. In 1404, her father's legitimate wife, †Philippa of Lancaster, arranged for Beatrice to marry Thomas, earl of Arundel and Warenne. Not long after Thomas died (1415), Beatrice married John Holland, earl of Huntingdon (and later duke of Exeter).

♦ **Dowry/dower. Illegitimacy.** ♦

C.P., v. 1, p. 246. Livermore, *New...*, p. 107. Roche, *Dona...*, pp. 56, 78.

BEATRICE OF PROVENCE

m. 1246–d. 1267 France; Italy

Youngest daughter of †Beatrice of Savoy and Raymond Berengar, count of Provence. She inherited Provence, which she passed to her husband, Charles I of Anjou, later king of Sicily and Naples. Beatrice pawned her gems to provide a war chest for Charles's foray into Italy. Their son was Charles II of Anjou (r.1285–1309).

♦ **Estate. Gems/jewelry. Pawns. Queens.** ♦

Altamira, *Spain...*, p. 242. Armitage-Smith, *John...*, p. 90. Commynes, *Memoirs...*, pp. 440 & 600. *DBF*, v.5, pp. 1040–1041. Jordan, *Louis...*, pp. 18–19, 31. Labarge, *Simon...*, p. 68. Powicke, *Thirteenth...*, pp. 119, 234. Runciman, *Sicilian...*, pp. 59–60, 70–3, 86, 90, 95, 101, 117, 138. Stephenson, *Mediaeval...*, p. 445. Trevelyan, *Short...*, p. 112.

BEATRICE PUTTOCK

fl. 1299–1320 England

A constant trouble-maker in the village of Warboys. In 1299, she became pregnant out-of-wedlock, and two years later she married without license. Between 1300 and 1320, Beatrice was cited for numerous misdeeds like stealing geese, wrongly raising the hue and cry, and (1309) assaulting Thomas Raven. Finally she was prohibited the vill (ousted from her village).

♦ **Adultery. Manors. Miscreants. Punishments.** ♦

Hogan, "Medieval Villainy...," pp. 140, 144, 145, & 193.

BEATRICE OF RETHEL, queen of Sicily

m.c. 1152 Italy

Daughter of the count of Rethel; third wife of Roger II of Sicily. He died less than two years after their marriage. Beatrice died bearing his posthumous daughter and eventual heiress, †Constance of Sicily.

♦ **Childbirth. Genealogy. Queens.** ♦

Cambridge..., V, p. 191n. Curtis, *Roger...*, pp. 293–294. Douglas, *Norman...*, Table 2. Norwich, *Kingdom...*, pp. 89n., 149, & 163.

BEATRICE OF SAVOY, countess of Provence

c. 1220s–d. 1266 France

Daughter of Beatrix de Genève and Thomas I, count of Savoy. Wife of Raymond Berengar of Provence (d.1245)—sources differ on whether he should be numbered Raymond Berengar IV, V, or VI. Mother of four daughters: †Marguerite, †Eleanor, †Sancia, and †Beatrice. She helped arrange their marriages, thus allying Savoy with the kings of England, France, and Naples. She was also interested in the study of medicine. Beatrice commissioned Aldobrandino of Siena to write an encyclopedia for her. This *Regime du Corps*, was especially useful to women because it included information on hygiene, gynecology, and skin care.

♦ **Medicine. Negotiators. Patrons of literature. Politics. Squabbles.** ♦

Cox, *Eagles...*, pp. 5, 9, 20–22, 44.....257, 281–2, 311, 314–315. *DBF,* v.5, pp. 1041–1042. Hallam (ed.), *Four...*, pp. 56 & 78. Hurd-Mead, *History...*, pp. 217–218. Labarge, *Simon...*, pp. 69–70. Paris, *Chronicles...*, p. 130. Powicke, *Thirteenth...*, pp. 74, 107, 119. Runciman, *Sicilian...*, pp. 59–60, 72–5.

BEATRICE SHARPE

1435 England

In Durham in 1435, Beatrice was whipped three times around the church for committing adultery with John West (he simply fled the town).

♦ **Adultery. Ecclesiastical courts. Punishments.** ♦

Hair, *Bawdy...*, p. 183 (#466).

BEATRICE OF SWABIA, queen of Castile
[Beatrix Hohenstaufen of Saxony; the Younger]

m. 1219 Germany; Spain

Daughter of †Irene Angela and Philip of Swabia. Married Ferdinand III, king of Castile in 1219. They had ten children. Their son Alfonso X attempted to claim the duchy of Swabia in her right. She is known as Beatrice the Younger because Philip also had an older daughter named Beatrix. The older girl married Otto IV in 1212 and died a few weeks later.

♦ **Genealogy. Queens.** ♦

Altamira, *Spain...*, pp. 230 & 231. *Cambridge...*, VI, p. 116; VII, p. 570. Livermore, *History...*, p. 128. Miron, *Queens...*, p. 36. Shneidman, *Rise...*, p. 327. Smith, *Spain...*, pp. 63–64.

BEATRICE OF TIRLEMONT

See—BEATRICE OF NAZARETH.

BEATRICE, marchioness of TUSCANY

fl. 1030–d. 1076 Italy

Daughter of Frederick, duke of Upper Lorraine. Around 1040, Beatrice married Boniface II, count of Tuscany; daughter †Matilda of Tuscany born in 1046. Boniface was murdered in 1052; Beatrice later married Godfrey IV "the Bearded" of Lorraine (d. 1069). Along with her daughter, Beatrice supported Pope Gregory VII in his conflict with the western emperor, Henry IV.

♦ **Estate. Managers. Pawns. Popes. Prisons. Widows.** ♦

Cambridge..., V, pp. 23, 31, 45, 59, 64, 112, 146. Ennen, *Medieval...*, pp. 69 & 70. Fuhrmann, *Germany...*, pp. 41, 65. Hampe, *Germany...*, pp. 58 & 59. Haverkamp, *Medieval...*, pp. 96, 102, 111, 114. McNamara and

Wemple, "Sanctity...," p. 111. McNamara and Wemple, "The Power...," p. 95. Norwich, *Normans...*, pp. 121 & 202. Partner, *Lands...*, pp. 116, 126n., 127.

BEATRICE DE VESCI

fl. 1100s–1130s England

Daughter and heiress of Ivo de Vesci. Married Eustace FitzJohn. Their son William de Vesci took his mother's name when he became heir to her honour of Alnwick.

♦ **Childbirth. Estate.** ♦

DNB, v.7, p. 184. Wrightman, *Lacy...*, p. 246.

BEATRICE OF VIENNOIS, countess of Albon

c. 1170s–d. 1228 France; Germany

Her first husband was William Taillefer of Toulouse. Around 1184, Beatrice married Hugh III, duke of Burgundy (d.1193). (He repudiated his wife, Alix of Lorraine—daughter of Mathew I of Lorraine and †Bertha of Swabia—in 1183, but their son Eudes III remained Hugh's heir.)

♦ **Dowry/dower. Estate.** ♦

Anselme, *Histoire...*, v.1, p. 541. *DBF,* v.6, p. 1492. Le Patourel, *Feudal...*, XV, p. 176.

BEATRICE DE WARENNE

fl. 1200–d. 1214 England

Daughter and heiress of William de Warenne, lord of Wormegay (Norfolk). Married Doon Bardolf; they had son William. After Doon died, (c.1211), Beatrice married Hubert de Burgh (later justiciar of England).

♦ **Dowry/dower. Estate. Legal activity.** ♦

DNB, v.20, p. 832. Weiss, "Castellan...," p. 247.

BEATRICE LA WELSSHE

1338 England

Accused of keeping such a disorderly house (in Holbourne, London) that she posed a danger to the community.

♦ **Land/property. Miscreants.** ♦

Calendar of Plea..., I, pp. 188–189.

Madame de BEAUGRANT

1468 France

Duchess †Marie of Burgundy's dwarf. Dressed as a shepherdess, Madame de Beaugrant entertained at the wedding festivities in honor of †Margaret of York and Charles the Bold, duke of Burgundy. Marie then gave Madame to Margaret, her new stepmother.

♦ **Dance. Dwarves.** ♦

Cartellieri, *Court...*, p. 162. Huizinga, *Waning...*, p. 17.

BELOTA (the Jew) **[Johanna Belota]**
1320s France

Doctor in Paris; arrested for practicing illegally and prohibited from further practice.

♦ **Doctors/empirics. Jews. Punishments.** ♦

Hughes, *Women...*, p. 144. Power, *Women...*, p. 88. Uitz, *Legend...*, p. 67. Wickersheimer, *Dictionnaire...*, v.1, p. 66.

BERENGARIA OF CASTILE

See—BERENGUELA OF CASTILE.

BERENGARIA OF NAVARRE, queen of England
b. 1163–d.c. 1230 England; France; Spain

Daughter of Beatrice (Sanchia) of Castile and Sancho VI of Navarre. Berengaria married Richard I of England in 1191. As a widow, she founded an abbey at Le Mans. She retired to this establishment, and presumably died there in 1230.

♦ **Crusades. Dowry/dower. Popes. Queens. Religieuses. Religious patrons. Widows.** ♦

Appleby, *John...*, pp. 52, 60, 83, 112, 160, 265–7. Baldwin, *Government...*, pp. 78, 249, 296, 301, 525 n66. *DNB,* v.2, pp. 325–326; v.16, p. 1027. Gillingham, *Richard...*, pp. 139, 141, 154, 158–166, 193, 218, 220, 249, 271, 283, 297. Green, *Letters...*, pp. 30–34. Kelly, *Eleanor...*, pp. 262–4, 266, 267, 271, 283, 288, 300–301, 323, 329, 342, 345–6, 349, 352, 361. Lloyd, *Maligned...*, pp. 54–61, 100–101, 111, 148, 364–5. Norwich, *Kingdom...*, pp. 371–373 & 380. Pernoud, *Eleanor...*, pp. 211–2, 215–6, 222, 237, 243, 245, 256, 257.

BERENGUELA OF CASTILE **[Berengaria of Castile]**
m. 1197–d. 1246 Spain

Daughter of †Eleanor (Leonor) of England and Alfonso VIII of Castile. Married (1197) Alfonso IX of Leon. The pope later separated the couple due to consanguinity, but not before they had a son, Ferdinand III (St. Ferdinand—San Fernando Rey). Berenguela served as her brother Henry I's regent from 1214 until his death in 1217, when she inherited Castile. She passed this kingdom on to her son Ferdinand, and then helped him inherit Leon from his father. She influenced Ferdinand's political and military ventures, and in 1219 she arranged his marriage to †Beatrice of Swabia.

♦ **Divorce. Negotiators. Politics. Regents. Soldiers.** ♦

Altamira, *Spain...*, pp. 167–168. *Cambridge...*, VI, pp. 30, 408, 410. Effinger, *Women...*, pp. 284–292. Kelly, *Eleanor...*, p. 359. Livermore, *History...*, pp. 117 & 118. Pernoud, *Eleanor...*, p. 259. Smith, *Spain...*, pp. 59 & 62–63.

Duchess of BERRY

See—JEANNE DE BOULOGNE, duchess of Berry.

BERTE [la tartrière]

1292 France

She was taxed 5s for her pastry-selling business in 1292 Paris.

♦ **Provisioning–pastry.** ♦

Géraud, *Paris sous...*, p. 97.

BERTHA [Berthe]

BERTHA

fl. 780s–810s France

Daughter of Charlemagne and †Hildegard. She fell in love with cleric/poet Angilbert of St. Riquier. After their second child was born, Charlemagne finally agreed to allow the couple to marry. One of their children was historian Nithard. Bertha presumably took the veil in 814.

♦ **Genealogy. Mistresses. Models. Nuns.** ♦

Carolingian..., pp. 22, 172, 200. Decaux, *Histoire...*, p. 163. Ennen, *Medieval...*, p. 53. Ganshof, *Carolingians...*, p. 170. Riché, *Les Carolingiens...*, p. 140. Wemple, *Women...*, pp. xv and 79.

BERTHA OF AVENAY

fl. 840s France; Italy

Daughter of Emperor Lothar I; abbess of Avenay. In the 840s, Bertha had a running feud with Archbishop Hincmar of Reims over lands and rights.

♦ **Abbesses. Managers. Squabbles. Writers–letters.** ♦

Duckett, *Carolingian...*, pp. 209–210. Wemple, *Women...*, p. xiv.

BERTHA OF CHARTRES **[Bertha of Burgundy; Blois; Arles]**

b. 964–d.c. 1025 France

Daughter of Conrad, king of Burgundy (Arles), and †Matilda of France. Bertha was the widow of Eudes I (or Odo I), count of Blois, when she became the second wife of King Robert II of France. Since they were distantly related, the pope demanded that Robert give her up. He refused to do so until around 1002 when he finally repudiated Bertha, and married †Constance of Arles (sometimes known as Constance of Toulouse). Bertha followed Robert to the Holy Land and attempted a reunion, but their marriage was never recognized.

♦ **Divorce. Popes. Queens.** ♦

Cambridge..., III, pp. 103, 104, 116n., 143n., 256. *DBF,* v.6, p. 186. Decaux, *Histoire...*, pp. 188–190. Duby, *Medieval...*, pp. 46–49. Duckett, *Death...*, pp. 122, 130, & 304. Dunbabin, *France...*, pp. 136 & 191. Ennen, *Medieval...*, pp. 73–74. Facinger, "Study...," pp. 5 & 35–36. Fawtier, *Capetian...*, pp. 50–1. Pernoud, *La femme...*, pp. 178–9. Stafford, *Queens...*, pp. 32–33, 42, 50, 72, 74, 77–78, 81, 83, & 84.

BERTHA OF HOLLAND **[Bertha de Frise]**
m. 1072–d. 1094 France; Netherlands

Daughter of Florent I, count of Holland. First wife of King Philip I of France. He attempted to repudiate Bertha in 1092 so that he could marry †Bertrade de Montfort. Before the issue was settled, Bertha died. Although Philip did manage to make Bertrade his queen, he refused to dispossess Bertha's son, Louis (VI).

♦ **Divorce. Queens.** ♦

Barlow, *Feudal...*, pp. 140, 159. Decaux, *Histoire...*, p. 245. Facinger, "Study...," pp. 10, 22, & 25. Fuhrmann, *Germany...*, p. 82.

BERTHA OF ITALY
915 Italy

Daughter of Berengar of Italy; abbess of S. Salvatore. Her father granted her the right to fortify the convent against Magyar invaders.

♦ **Abbesses. Soldiers.** ♦

Wemple, "S. Salvatore...," p. 93.

BERTHA DE SENS, countess of Vienne **[Berthe de Roussillon]**
c. 830s–860s France

Daughter of Hugues, count of Sens and Tours. Married Géraud de Roussillon, count of Vienne. Bertha helped him maintain his power against the claims of Charles of Provence. She even took personal charge of the defenses of the capital, Vienne. However, Bertha was finally forced to surrender to Charles (who had bribed some of the defenders).

♦ **Artistic clothwork. Religious patrons. Rulers. Soldiers.** ♦

DBF, v.6, pp. 184–185. Decaux, *Histoire...*, p. 174. Jourdain, "Memoire...," p. 473. Lehmann, *Rôle de la...*, p. 137. Riché, *Les Carolingiens...*, p. 197. Wemple, *Women...*, p. 92.

BERTHA OF SULZBACH **[Empress Irene of Byzantium]**
m. 1146–d.c. 1160 Byzantium; Germany

Bertha took the more Byzantine name of Irene when she married Emperor Manuel Comnenus in 1146 as part of an alliance treaty with her brother, Holy Roman Emperor Conrad III. Bertha was the mother of †Maria Comnena, princess of Byzantium. Her husband supposedly neglected Bertha because she was more interested in virtue and piety than in fashion and gaiety. Bertha concentrated on charity—founding a hospital and a medical school (both benefitted the western Crusaders)—and on literature—the grammarian Tzetzes dedicated his first edition of *Chiliades* to Bertha. She befriended the Crusaders and kept amicable relations existing between Manuel and Conrad III. She became a valuable advisor to her husband, and even uncovered a plot against his life.

♦ **Crusades. Educated. Medicine. Patrons of literature. Pawns. Politics. Religious patrons. University.** ♦

Cambridge..., IV, pp. 360, 365; V, p. 356. *Chronicles...*, pp. 138, 139–40. Diehl, *Byzantine...*, pp. 226–243. Fuhrmann, *Germany...*, p. 128. Haverkamp, *Medieval...*, pp. 143. Hurd-Mead, *History...*, pp. 168 & 176. Norwich, *Kingdom...*, pp. 114–115, 135–138, & 270. Pernoud, *Eleanor...*, p. 59.

BERTHA OF SUSA **[Bertha of Turin; Savoy]**

m. 1066–d. 1087 Germany; Italy

Daughter of †Adelheid (of Susa) and Otto of Savoy, count of Turin, Maurienne, and Tarantaise. Married the king of Germany, Henry IV, at Tribur in 1066. When she accompanied him to his penance at Canossa in 1077, their son (later Henry V) was about two years old. She was crowned Holy Roman Empress by Pope Clement III in 1084.

♦ **Divorce. Pawns. Popes. Queens.** ♦

Cambridge..., V, pp. 34, 69, 79, 116, 117, 127, 145. Duff, *Matilda...*, pp. 42, 114–116, 145–148, 153, 175, & 212. Fuhrmann, *Germany...*, pp. 52, 61, 65, 68. Haverkamp, *Medieval...*, pp. 107, 121. Norwich, *Normans...*, pp. 238–239. Pinnow, *History...*, p. 71. Robinson, *Readings...*, I, p. 268.

BERTHA OF SWABIA

fl. 920s–940s France; Germany

Daughter of Burchard II of Swabia. Married Rudolph II of Burgundy; mother of Empress †Adelheid. Rudolph's death in 937 left Bertha with three small children, so she became the wife of Hugh of Arles—possibly because he abducted her. Hugh later repudiated Bertha and she returned to a nunnery in Burgundy where her son Conrad had become ruler.

♦ **Abduction. Divorce. Estate. Religieuses. Widows.** ♦

DBF, v.9, pp. 480–481. Duckett, *Death...*, pp. 70, 166, & 208. Ernouf, *Histoire...*, pp. 240–242 & 289. McKitterick, *Frankish...*, p. 265. Riché, *Les Carolingiens...*, pp. 221, 247–248. Stafford, *Queens...*, pp. 21, 53, 169 & 176. Wright, *Works...*, pp. 97–8, 152.

BERTHA OF SWABIA, duchess of Lorraine **[Berthe]**

c. 1130s–d. 1195 France; Germany

Daughter of †Judith of Bavaria and Frederick II, duke of Swabia. Married Mathew I of Upper Lorraine (d.1176). She governed Lorraine for her sons, and even minted coins for the area. Bertha was a good regent, but she later refused to relinquish control to her oldest son Simon. Instead, Bertha led a younger sibling, Ferry, in a rebellion against Simon. Unable to win, toward the end of her life, Bertha made peace between her two sons.

♦ **Banking. Negotiators. Rebellions. Regents. Squabbles. Widows.** ♦

DBF, v.6, p. 185; v.13, p. 1161. Haverkamp, *Medieval...,* p. 221. Lesourd, *La Lorraine...,* p. 65.

BERTHA OF TUSCANY **[Bertha of Arles]**

c. 860s–890s France; Italy

Daughter of †Waldrada and Lothar II of Lotharingia. Married Thibaut, count of Arles; their son was Hugh of Arles. Her second husband was Adalbert II, marquis of Tuscany. Intelligent and ambitious, Bertha encouraged her husband to struggle for the crown of Italy, married her daughter †Ermengarde to Adalbert of Ivrea for political reasons, and set up what amounted to a secret police/spy force in various Italian states. After Adalbert's death, she acted as regent, gaining support for herself and her son through gifts and intrigues.

♦ **Illegitimacy. Negotiators. Politics. Regents. Spies. Widows.** ♦

DBF, v.6, pp. 185–186. Duckett, *Death...,* p. 56. Ernouf, *Histoire...,* pp. 48, 77, 80–82, 111, 123–135, 162–163, 170, 192–195, 205–206, 211, 220, 222, 226, 251–254. Leyser, *Medieval...,* pp. 110, 111–2. Riché, *Les Carolingiens...,* p. 417. Stafford, *Queens...,* pp. 20–21, 24, & 138. Wright, *Works...,* pp. 58, 96, 117.

BERTHA OF TUSCANY **[Berta]**

fl. 930s–950s France; Italy

Daughter of †Willa and Boson, marquis of Tuscany. Married Boson, count of Arles and Provence. After his death, she married (c.949) Raymond, count of Toulouse. By Raymond she had sons Raymond, Pons, and Hughes.

♦ **Genealogy.** ♦

Anselme, *Histoire...,* II, pp. 682–683. Wright, *Works...,* pp. 150, 199.

BERTHEIDA

fl. 960s–990s Germany

After her mother, Bertha of Munster, died, Bertheida claimed the nunnery of Borghorst as her own inheritance. She went to Otto III's court to plead her case; she won in 989, despite the opposition of the archbishop and of the nuns of Borghorst themselves.

♦ **Legal activity. Religious patrons. Squabbles.** ♦

Leyser, *Rule...,* p. 66.

BERTILLA

c. 870s–910s Italy

Member of important Supponide clan; married Berengar I of Italy. A palace coup resulted (c.911–915), and her brothers were ousted from power. Berengar presumably murdered Bertilla because of her infidelity.

♦ **Murder. Pawns. Rebellions. Women of easy virtue.** ♦

Ernouf, *Histoire...*, pp. 206 & 455–456. Stafford, *Queens...*, pp. 39–41, 188, & 203.

BERTRADE DE MONTFORT, countess of Anjou, queen of France

b. 1075–d. 1119 France

Daughter of †Agnes d'Évreux and Simon de Montfort. At age sixteen, Bertrade was forced to wed fifty-year-old Foulques IV le Rechin, the often-married count of Anjou. When the young king of France, Philip I, visited the couple, he fell in love with Bertrade. She and Philip obtained quasi-legitimate divorces from their respective spouses, and then got married. This caused years of legal and ecclesiastical hardship for the king and all of France. Bertrade was finally recognized as queen, but her machinations to have her own son supersede Philip's heir, Louis VI, failed. Toward the end of her life, Bertrade retired to Fontevrault.

♦ **Divorce. Models. Politics. Popes. Religieuses. Squabbles.** ♦

Barlow, *Feudal...*, pp. 167, 193–5. Butler, *Women...*, pp. 46–52. *DBF*, v.2, pp. 1268 & 1269. Duby, *Knight...*, pp. 3–22. Facinger, "Study...," pp. 6–7, 27–28, 36, & 42. Hallam (ed.), *Plantagenet...*, pp. 36 & 37. Pernoud, *Eleanor...*, pp. 28 & 93. Pernoud, *La femme...*, pp. 136–143. Vitalis, *Ecclesiastical...*, IV, pp. xxiv, 184–187, 260–263, 288 n6.

BERTRANDE OF AVIGNON

1463 France

Doctor on the rue Calade in Avignon. In 1463 she was paid 2s for medicating a patient at l'Hopital de Cor-Sant.

♦ **Doctors/empirics. Medicine–hospitals.** ♦

Hughes, *Women...*, p. 142. Wickersheimer, *Dictionnaire...*, p. 84.

BETHLEM OF GRECI

c. 1121–c. 1175 Italy

Daughter of Géraud, count of Greci. In 1121 she was elected abbess of S. Maria di Porta Somma, a Benedictine convent at Benevento. Very energetic and assertive, she used family wealth and connections, courts of law, etc., to benefit her abbey politically and financially.

♦ **Abbesses. Legal activity. Managers.** ♦

Jamison, "Bethlem...".

BETHOC OF SCOTLAND

fl. 1000–1030s Scotland

Middle daughter, and eventually heiress, of Malcolm II, king of Scotland (d.1034). Married Crinan, abbot of Dunkeld; son, Duncan I (r. 1034–1040); grandson, Malcolm III.

♦ **Estate. Genealogy.** ♦

Cambridge..., VII, pp. 553, 554 n2. *DNB*, v.12, p. 844. Duncan, *Scotland...*, pp. 99 & 100. Mackie, *History...*, p. 46. Williamson, *Kings...*, p. 228, Table 18.

BEZOLE **[Perzola]**

fl. 930s France

Mistress of Hugh of Arles; mother of his illegitimate daughter Bertha. Although Bezole was low-born, her imperious manner led to her being nicknamed "Juno."

♦ **Mistresses. Models.** ♦

Cambridge..., IV, p. 64. Ernouf, *Histoire...*, pp. 309–310. Stafford, *Queens...*, p. 53. Wright, *Works...*, pp. 152, 189.

BIANCA GIOVANNA SFORZA

1482–1496 Italy

Illegitimate daughter of Ludovic "the Moor" Sforza and Bernardina de Corradis. In 1490, at the age of eight, her father married her to Galeazzo de San Severino.

♦ **Illegitimacy. Models. Pawns.** ♦

Ady, *History...*, pp. 162 & 286. Prescott, *Princes...*, pp. 12, 134, 137. Sizeranne, *Beatrice...*, pp. 160, 165, 168, 170, & 259.

BIANCA MARIA SFORZA, Holy Roman Empress

1472–1510 Austria; Germany; Italy

Daughter of †Bona of Savoy and Galeazzo Maria Sforza. In 1493, she married Maximilian of Austria who needed her huge dowry of 400,000 ducats. Maximilian virtually ignored his second wife, accusing her of being light-headed, a spendthrift, and gluttonous. Bianca was also very kind-hearted. She tried to help her mother and, later, Ludovic the Moor. After the latter's downfall, she cared for his two sons by †Beatrice d'Este.

♦ **Childcare. Dowry/dower. Pawns.** ♦

Cartwright, *Beatrice...*, pp. 43, 70, 106, 121, 160, 179, 208–222, 252, 339, & 377. Commynes, *Memoirs...*, p. 450. Prescott, *Princes...*, pp. 114, & 139. Simon, *Tapestry...*, p. 95. Sizeranne, *Beatrice...*, pp. 192, 194, 202–204, 228–229, 232–235, 239, 246–247, & 252. Trevelyan, *Short...*, p. 191.

BIANCA MARIA VISCONTI

1424–1468 Italy

Daughter and heiress of Filippo Maria Visconti, duke of Milan, and †Agnese del Maino. In 1441, Bianca was married to Francesco Sforza for political reasons. In addition to caring for their eight children, she served her husband as an advisor and a military leader. After Francesco died in 1466, Bianca proved to be a wise regent for their son Galeazzo Maria. Pious and charitable, Bianca was also a patron of artists and humanists.

♦ **Art patrons. Charity. Educated. Estate. Illegitimacy. Politics. Regents. Soldiers. Teachers. Widows.** ♦

Cartwright, *Beatrice...*, pp. 14–18. Cleugh, *Medici...*, pp. 67, 72, 77, 82, 90. Collison-Morley, *Sforzas...*, pp. 33, 44–46, 60, & 97. Commynes, *Memoirs...*, pp. 451 & 460n. King and Rabil, *Her Immaculate...*, pp. 20, 39–41, 44–47. Norwich, *History...*, pp. 319–321. Pasolini, *Catherine...*, pp. 11–13, & 16. Prescott, *Princes...*, pp. 96–7, 101, 104–5, 111.

BIANCA OF SAVOY **[Blanche]**

c. 1340s–1370s Italy

Sister of Amadeus VI of Savoy. Married Galeazzo (II) Visconti (d.1378); mother of Giangaleazzo and †Violante. Although usually not a political force, she came out of retirement to support her son against his uncle, Bernabo.

♦ **Negotiators. Politics. Widows.** ♦

Cambridge..., VII, p. 59. Chamberlin, *Count...*, pp. 23, 41, 58, 114, & 115. Hardy, *Philippa...*, pp. 96–7, 101, 104–5, 111. José, *La Maison...*, pp. 58, 88, 134, 135, 136, 160 n1, 162, 202, 208, 214, 218, 272, 304, 307. Tuchman, *Distant...*, pp. 225, 267, 269, 270.

BIRGITTA

See—BRIDGET.

BLANCHE OF ANJOU, queen of Aragon **[Blanche of Naples]**

b. 1283–d. 1310 Italy; Spain

Daughter of Marie of Hungary and Charles II of Anjou, king of Sicily. Blanche was the first wife of Jaime II of Aragon. She assisted her husband in negotiating treaties and was an influential supporter of the Franciscans.

♦ **Dowry/dower. Negotiators. Politics. Religious patrons.** ♦

Bisson, *Medieval Crown...*, pp. 92 & 96. *Cambridge...*, VII, pp. 6, 586, & 587. Hillgarth, *Pere...*, pp. 3, 134, 136, 168 n91, 232, 405 n23. Miron, *Queens...*, pp. 141–147. Shneidman, *Rise...*, pp. 63, 77, 343, 344, 402.

BLANCHE OF ARAGON **[Blanca of Navarre]**

b. 1424–d. 1460s Spain

Daughter of †Blanche of Navarre and John II of Aragon. Married Henry IV of Castile (later known as Henry the Impotent). They had no children, so he divorced Blanche in 1453. She was surrendered in 1462 by her father as part of a treaty which specified her sister †Leonor of Aragon as heiress of Navarre. Blanche was imprisoned, and reputedly murdered, by her sister.

♦ **Divorce. Murder. Pawns. Prisons.** ♦

Bisson, *Medieval Crown...*, p. 150. Dezert, *Don Carlos...*, pp. 110 & 125. Hillgarth, *Spanish...*, pp. 283 & 329. Livermore, *History...*, pp. 113, 158, 170, 179 [he confuses her with her mother]. Miller, *Castles...*, p. 28 [also a confusion of names].

BLANCHE OF ARTOIS

m. 1269–d. 1302 England; France; Spain

Daughter of †Mahaut de Brabant and Robert I, count of Artois. In 1269 she married Henry III, count of Champagne, king of Navarre. After he died in 1274, Blanche held his domains for their daughter/heiress, †Jeanne of Navarre. In 1275, Blanche concluded the Treaty of Orleans with Philip III of France. To seal this bargain, Jeanne was to marry Philip's son (later King Philip IV the Fair). In that same year, Blanche married her second husband, Edmund of Lancaster.

♦ **Estate. Negotiators. Regents.** ♦

Armitage-Smith, *John...*, p. 197. Benton, "Philip...," pp. 283–284. *Cambridge...*, VII, pp. 306, 307, 403. *DBF*, v.3, p. 1214 & v.6, p. 615. Evergates, "Chancery...," p. 172. Fawtier, *Capetian...*, pp. 127, 128–9. Leroy, *La Navarre...*, pp. 44 & 45. Powicke, *Thirteenth...*, pp. 236, 238–241. Shneidman, *Rise...*, pp. 299, 300, 311.

BLANCHE OF BOURBON

b. 1338–d. 1361 France; Spain

Daughter of Pierre I, duke of Bourbon and †Isabel of Savoy (daughter of Mahaut de Chatillon and Charles of France, count of Valois). Blanche was forced into a political marriage with Pedro I the Cruel, king of Castile, in 1352. The next day, Pedro repudiated her, claiming that he was already married to his mistress, †Maria de Padilla. He then imprisoned Blanche and refused to return her huge dowry. This caused a French alliance with Aragon to oust Pedro. Blanche died in 1361 before this squabble was settled.

♦ **Divorce. Dowry/dower. Pawns. Prisons.** ♦

Anselme, *Histoire...*, v.1, pp. 299–300. Armitage-Smith, *John...*, p. 37. *Cambridge...*, VII, pp. 361, 575, 576, & 579. Hardy, *Philippa...*, pp. 199 & 284. Jamison, *Life...*, I, pp. 249, 251, 253, & 267. Smith, *Spain...*, pp. 72–73. Tuchman, *Distant...*, p. 249.

BLANCHE OF BURGUNDY **[Blanche of Artois]**

b. 1295–1326 France

Daughter of Othon of Burgundy and †Mahaut, countess of Artois. Married Charles, count of La Marche (later Charles IV of France). She became involved in an adultery scandal and was forced to retire to a nunnery, where she died young.

♦ **Adultery. Divorce. Models. Religieuses.** ♦

Butler, *Women...*, pp. 257–262. *Cambridge...*, VII, p. 338. *DBF*, v.6, pp. 615–616. Decaux, *Histoire...*, p. 365. Fawtier, *Capetian...*, p. 53. Jamison, *Life...*, I, p. 38.

BLANCHE OF CASTILE, queen of France

b. 1188–d. 1252 France; Spain

Daughter of †Eleanor (Leonor) of England and Alfonso VIII, king of Castile. In 1200, married Louis (later Louis VIII) of France as part of a treaty; sons: (St.) Louis IX, Robert of Artois, Alphonse of Poitiers, and Charles of Anjou. When her husband died (c.1226), he appointed Blanche as regent for Louis IX. She proved an excellent ruler; she quelled rebellious nobles, dealt fairly with her Jewish subjects, negotiated treaties, established equitable laws and an efficient bureaucracy, and even chose Louis's bride. Blanche taught her son to lead armies, but she also instilled piety and an appreciation of learning in Louis. Her influence was so great that she remained virtually a co-ruler until her death.

♦ **Banking. Educated. Jews. Models. Negotiators. Popes. Regents. Religious patrons. Rulers. Soldiers. Teachers. Widows.** ♦

Appleby, *John...*, pp. 95–7, 102, 116, 260, 263. Bertrand, *La France....* Bréquigny, *Lettres de rois...*, p. 83. Brion, *Blanche....* Fawtier, *Capetian...*, pp. 27–9, 30, 34, 57, 63, 115, 116, 122, 123, 127, 135, 146, 164, 218, 219. Heer, *Medieval...*, pp. 109, 262, 263. Jordan, *Louis...*, pp. 4–9, 12–14, 30, 41, 42, 47, 54, 70, 80, 91–2, 104, 110–125, 145, 178, 185, 191, 206n. Lehmann, *Rôle de la...*, pp. 328–333, 339, 341, & 346. Lloyd, *Maligned...*, pp. 96–7, 148, 339. McCall, *Medieval...*, pp. 157–158. Paris, *Chronicles...*, pp. 111, 131, 180, 201, 212, 256. Pernoud, *Blanche....* Robinson, *Readings...*, I, pp. 213–217. Stephenson, *Mediaeval...*, pp. 444–446.

BLANCHE, princess of ENGLAND

b. 1392–d.c. 1407 England; Germany

Daughter of †Mary de Bohun and the future King Henry IV of England. Received good education at home until, at age ten, she was married to Ludwig of Bavaria (Lewis, count Palatine). They had one son named Rupert.

♦ **Educated. Pawns.** ♦

Hohler, "Court...," p. 156. Jacob, *Fifteenth...*, p. 68. McFarlane, *Nobility...*, p. 244. Williamson, *Kings...*, p. 86.

BLANCHE D'ÉVREUX

See—BLANCHE OF NAVARRE, queen of France.

BLANCHE OF FRANCE

b. 1252–d. 1320 France; Spain

Daughter of †Marguerite of Provence and King Louis IX of France. In 1269, Blanche married Ferdinand de la Cerda, the heir to the throne of Castile. After Ferdinand died in 1275, their sons Ferdinand and Alfonso should have been next in line for the throne. However, Blanche's father-in-law, Alfonso X, named his younger son Sancho (IV) as his heir. Blanche and her two sons fled to Aragon where she intrigued and pleaded for their rights.

♦ **Art patrons. Politics. Religieuses. Religious patrons. Widows.** ♦

Anselme, *Histoire...*, v.1, pp. 86–7. *Cambridge...*, VII, pp. 308, 320, & 571. Jordan, *Louis...*, p. 188. Runciman, *Sicilian...*, p. 204. Shneidman, *Rise...*, p. 323.

BLANCHE OF FRANCE **[Margaret de Valois]**

b. 1316–d. 1348 Bohemia; France

Daughter of †Mahaut de Châtillon (of Saint Pol) and Charles de Valois. Blanche became the first wife of Wenceslas of Luxembourg, king of Bohemia, in 1325 (he later became Emperor Charles IV). She introduced French customs and learning in her new country. (Margaret was her baptismal name.)

♦ **Educated. Queens.** ♦

Anselme, *Histoire...*, v.1, p. 102. *DBF*, v.6, p. 618; and v.8, p. 554. Leuschner, *Germany...*, p. 152.

BLANCHE OF LANCASTER

[Blanche of Richmond, duchess of Lancaster]

b. 1341–d. 1369 England

Daughter/heiress of †Isabel Beaumont and Henry, duke of Lancaster. Married John of Gaunt in 1359. Their son Henry became King Henry IV of England in 1399. Blanche and John also had two daughters, †Elizabeth and †Philippa (of Lancaster). Blanche was known as a kind and charming woman; Gaunt evidently loved her, and Chaucer wrote *The Book of the Duchesse* in her honor.

♦ **Educated. Estate. Models. Plague.** ♦

Armitage-Smith, *John...*, pp. 10–14, 20, 75, 77, 227, 390, & 461. Anderson, "Blanche...," pp. 152–159. Butt, *History...*, pp. 324, 330. Froissart, *Chronicles...*, I, p. 138. Gardner, *Life...*, pp. 43, 107, 109, 113, 116–118, 127, 135, 136, 139, 144, 158, 174–176, 216, 230, 271, 279. Hardy, *Philippa...*, pp. 151, 225, 253, 256–7, 262, 264–5, 270, 272, 301, 303–4, 309. Lewis, "Anniversary...". Roche, *Dona...*, pp. 1, 5, 7–9, 13, 16, 20, 45, 51, 57, 66, 71, 73.

BLANCHE OF LAURAC

fl. 1180s–1190s France

Noblewoman of the family which held castle Laurac where Cathar community flourished. Her sons and daughters were brought up to be firm Cathars.

♦ **Cathars. Childcare. Managers.** ♦

Abels and Harrison, "Participation...," p. 232. Heer, *Medieval...*, p. 168. Lambert, *Medieval...*, pp. 114–115. Wakefield, *Heresy...*, pp. 74 & 204 n6.

BLANCHE OF MONTFERRAT, duchess of Savoy **[Monferrato]**
fl. 1480s–1490s France; Italy

Daughter of Marquis Guglielmo di Monferrato. Married Charles I of Savoy in 1485. When he died she was regent for their young son, Charles II (b.1488–d.1496). In 1495, Philippe de Commynes was present during her negotiations with the king of France and the duke of Milan.

♦ **Models. Negotiators. Politics. Regents. Widows.** ♦

Commynes, *Memoirs...*, pp. 456 & 546. *DBF,* v.8, p. 574.

BLANCHE OF NAMUR, queen of Norway and Sweden
m. 1335–1360s Belgium; Norway; Sweden

Wife of Magnus Ericsson, king of Norway and Sweden. She received several fiefs in southern Norway as her marriage portion. She and her husband gave the estate of Vadstena to (St.) †Birgitta in 1346 for the founding of her monastery.

♦ **Dowry/dower. Educated. Religious patrons.** ♦

Anderson and Zinsser, *A History of...*, p. 219. Andersson, *History...*, p. 57. Derry, *History...*, p. 67. Larsen, *History...*, pp. 194 & 203. Musset, *Les Peuples...*, p. 296.

BLANCHE OF NAVARRE
b. 1385–d. 1441 France; Italy; Spain

Daughter and heiress of †Leonor of Castile and Charles III of Navarre. Married Martin of Aragon, king of Sicily in 1404. When he died in 1409, she became regent of Sicily until she returned to Navarre in 1414. In 1419, Blanche married John II of Aragon. Mother of Carlos, prince of Viana; †Leonor (married Gaston IV de Foix); and †Blanche (first wife of Henry IV of Castile).

♦ **Estate. Queens. Regents.** ♦

Altamira, *Spain...*, pp. 257, 259, 260. Bisson, *Medieval Crown...*, pp. 129, 138, 147. Dezert, *Don Carlos...*, pp. 92–110 & 125–129. Hillgarth, *Spanish...*, pp. 228, 243, 266, 540. Leroy, *La Navarre...*, pp. 180–181. Livermore, *History...*, pp. 113, 158, 170, 179 [confuses her with daughter Blanche of Aragon]. Miron, *Queens...*, pp. 288, 309–310.

BLANCHE OF NAVARRE, countess of Champagne
c. 1180s–c. 1230 France; Spain

Daughter of Sancho VI, king of Navarre. Around 1199 married Thibaut (Theobald), count of Champagne. When he died in 1201, Blanche became regent for son Thibaut (until 1222). Fought to keep Champagne for him; won right to be direct vassal of French king; and even attended a royal parliament in 1213.

♦ **Negotiators. Popes. Regents. Soldiers. Squabbles.** ♦

Altamira, *Spain...*, p. 171. Butler, *Women...*, p. 176. Casey, "Cheshire...", p. 234. *DBF,* v. 6, p. 618. Evergates, "Chancery...," pp.

163–167. Heer, *Medieval...*, pp. 234 & 262. Robinson, *Readings...*, I, pp. 178–179. Shahar, *Fourth...*, p. 141. Valous, *Patriciat...*, p. 170.

BLANCHE OF NAVARRE, queen of France **[Blanche d'Évreux]**
b. 1335–d. 1398 France

Daughter of †Jeanne of France and Philip d'Évreux, rulers of Navarre. In 1349, Blanche married Philip VI Valois, king of France, who died a year later. She was a notable collector of art and literature. Blanche was also a peacemaker between France and Navarre.

♦ **Art patrons. Book owners. Educated. Negotiators. Widows.** ♦

Anselme, *Histoire...*, v.1, p. 283. *DBF*, v.6, p. 618. Froissart, *Chronicles...*, I, p. 90. Hughes, "Library...," p. 178. Jamison, *Life...*, I, p. 213. Leroy, *La Navarre...*, p. 129.

BLANCHE OF PONTHIEU, countess of Aumale
fl. 1340–1387 France

Wife of John V, count of Harcourt. From 1340 until 1380, Blanche owned two seigneuries, Conteville and Noyelles-sur-Mer (where she received the king of Navarre in 1357). In 1378, she purchased a third fief in Ponthieu, Buire-le-Sec, from Baudoin de Lianne.

♦ **Estate. Managers. Negotiators.** ♦

Anselme, *Histoire...*, v.3, p. 305. Belleval, *Les Fiefs...*, pp. 67–68, 90, & 246–247.

BLANCHE OF PORTUGAL **[Branca]**
b. 1259–c. 1323 Portugal

Daughter of †Beatrix de Guzman of Castile and Alfonso III of Portugal. Titular abbess of Lorvao and of Las Huelgas. Blanche supposedly fell in love with a carpenter and bore his illegitimate son. This romantic tragedy was a popular theme of several medieval literary works.

♦ **Abbesses. Adultery. Estate. Models.** ♦

Anselme, *Histoire...*, v.1, p. 582. Stephens, *Story...*, pp. 91 & 95.

BLANCHE OF SAVOY

See—BIANCA OF SAVOY.

BLOEMARDINE **[Bloemardinne of Brussels]**
d. 1336 Belgium; Flanders

Of merchant family of Brussels, Bloemardine was probably a Beguine at first. In the 1330s she was an itinerant preacher, extolling a doctrine of spiritual freedom and attracting disciples to the Brethren of the Free Spirit.

♦ **Beguines. Heretics. Mystics. Preachers.** ♦

Bynum, *Holy...*, pp. 229, 233. *Cambridge...*, VII, p. 802. Lagorio, "Continental...," p. 176. Leff, *Heresy...*, I, pp. 357 & 395–396. McDonnell, *Beguines...*, pp. 368, 490, 492–496. Russell, *Witchcraft...*, p. 224. Tuchman, *Distant...*, p. 335.

BONA [Bonne]

BONNE OF ARMAGNAC, duchess of Orleans

b. 1401–d.c. 1416 France

Daughter of †Bonne de Berry and Bernard VII, count of Armagnac. Around 1410, she became second wife of Charles of Orléans. He was captured at Agincourt in 1415 and sent to England; Bonne died soon afterward. Some of Charles' poetry was about this child-bride.

♦ **Models. Pawns.** ♦

Anselme, *Histoire...*, v.1, p. 208. Calmette, *Golden...*, p. 95. Coryn, *House...*, pp. 136, 166, 168, 206, 238, 245. Fox, *Literary...*, p. 306.

BONNE OF ARTOIS

b. 1395–d. 1425 France

Daughter of †Marie de Berry and Philip of Artois, count of Eu. In 1413, Bonne married Philip, count of Nevers (d.1415). Her second husband was Philip the Good, duke of Burgundy. She died in childbirth only a year after their marriage.

♦ **Childbirth. Models.** ♦

Anselme, *Histoire...*, v.1, pp. 241, 251. Calmette, *Golden...*, pp. 138, 170, 315, 316. Vale, *Charles...*, p. 36.

BONNE DE BERRY

m. 1376–c. 1400s France; Italy

Daughter of †Jeanne d'Armagnac and John of France, duke of Berry. Married (1) Amadeus VII of Savoy (d.1391) and (2) Bernard VII, count of Armagnac. She inherited her father's famous book, *Les Tres Riches Heures.*

See—BONNE DE BOURBON.

♦ **Book owners. Squabbles.** ♦

Anselme, *Histoire...*, v.1, pp. 107–108. Bell, "Medieval...," p. 155. Calmette, *Golden...*, p. 309. *DBF*, v.6, p. 991. Vaughan, *Philip...*, p. 53.

BONNE DE BOURBON, countess of Savoy

c. 1340s–c. 1399 Flanders; France; Italy; Switzerland

Daughter of †Isabel (de Valois) of Savoy and Pierre (I) of Bourbon. Married (1) Godfrey of Brabant and, in 1355, (2) Amadeus VI of Savoy (d.1383). Her son Amadeus VII died in 1391 and left the governance of Savoy to his mother. His widow, †Bonne de Berry, was incensed by her exclusion from power. The Berry family accused the dowager countess of murder, thus starting a bloody two year feud in the area. Finally vindicated, Bonne de Bourbon ruled Savoy until 1399.

♦ **Murder. Regents. Squabbles. Widows.** ♦

Anselme, *Histoire...*, v.1, p. 300. *DBF*, v.6, p. 991. Vaughan, *Philip...*, pp. 53, 88.

BONA OF LUXEMBOURG **[Bonne]**

b. 1316–d. 1349 Bohemia; France; Luxembourg

Daughter of John the Blind of Bohemia. In 1332, Bona married John II the Good, later king of France; mother of Charles V of France. A patron of the arts and a book collector. Supposedly her husband suspected Bona of infidelity.

♦ **Adultery. Art patrons. Book owners. Patrons of literature. Plague.** ♦

Calmette, *Golden...*, p. 25. Denieul-Cormier, *Wise...*, pp. 25, 53–4, 55, 59–60, 74, 79. Hughes, "Library...," pp. 145 & 174. Jourdain, "Memoire...," p. 503. Tuchman, *Distant...*, pp. 103 & 324.

BONA OF SAVOY, duchess of Milan **[Bonne of Savoy]**

c. 1450–c. 1505 France; Italy

Daughter of †Anne de Lusignana and Louis, duke of Savoy. Married Galeazzo Maria Sforza, duke of Milan, in 1468; children: Giangaleazzo (1469–1494, duke of Milan), †Bianca Maria (1472–1510, married Emperor Maximilian), and †Anna (1473–1497, married Alfonso d'Este). Galeazzo Maria was murdered in 1476, and Bona became regent for her young son. She also had to deal with the pope in order to obtain a posthumous absolution for her sinful husband. When she took a lower-class lover, Antonio Tassino, she lost backing for her regency, and was pushed out by Ludovic Sforza in 1480. She retired to the French court, but later returned to Italy and intrigued for Ludovic's downfall and her own reinstatement.

♦ **Banking. Builders. Politics. Popes. Regents. Widows. Women of easy virtue.** ♦

Breisach, *Caterina...*, pp. 9, 10, 27, & 41–42. Cartwright, *Beatrice...*, pp. 8, 18, 25, 70, 160, 170, 208, 216, 232, 237, & 251. Chamberlin, *World...*, pp. 259–261 & 263. Cleugh, *Chant...*, pp. 247, 249–250, & 253. Cleugh, *Medici...*, pp. 116–117, 120, 127, 144, 154, 198. Clive, *Sun...*, pp. 98–9, 105–6, 109, 120, 241. Collison-Morley, *Sforzas...*, pp. 89, 90, 99, & 119. Commynes, *Memoirs...*, I, p. 304 & II, 442, 443, & 445. Hook, *Lorenzo...*, pp. 65–6, 88, 108. Prescott, *Princes...*, pp. 107, 111–4, 128–9. Simon, *Tapestry...*, pp. 47, 52. Sizeranne, *Beatrice...*, pp. 123, 124, 135, 192, 198, & 258.

BORTE

c. 1165–1200s China; Russia

Daughter of Mongolian chief, Borte married Temuchin (who later became famous as Chingis-Khan) around 1185. Not long afterward Borte was captured and forced to become a slave concubine. Temuchin and his overlord, Togrul-Khan quickly freed Borte.

♦ **Abduction. Dowry/dower. Rape.** ♦

Spuler, *History...*, pp. 18, 19–20. Vernadsky, *Mongols...*, pp. 21–23, 24, & 45.

BOURGOT DE NOIR

fl. 1300s France

An artist, probably taught by her father, the painter Jean de Noir. Bourgot and her father, working as a team, undertook numerous commissions for royal and high-ranking patrons. King Charles V even gave the two artists a house, as partial payment for illuminating some of his books.

♦ Artists. Land/property. Merchants. ♦

Carr, "Women...," p. 9. Greer, *Obstacle...*, p. 160. Labarge, *Small Sound...*, p. 231.

(St.) BRIDGET OF SWEDEN **[St. Birgitta]**

b. 1302–d. 1373 Italy; Sweden

Daughter of Birger Persson. Married knight, Ulf Gudmarsson of Narke, when she was thirteen. They had eight children; he died around 1343. Birgitta then began her primary holy work: she started a new order and founded the first Birgittine house at Vadstena in 1346; she took a pilgrimage to Jerusalem; she wrote letters to rulers admonishing them to behave in a more Christian fashion (although she was not politically astute); she had visions (for instance, she often saw Jesus's bloody, crucified body) and performed miracles (as when she smelled sulphur in the presence of great sinners); and she helped pester Pope Urban V into returning from Avignon to Rome.

♦ Medicine. Mystics. Pilgrims. Politics. Popes. Religious patrons. Saints. Widows. Writers–Letters and theology. ♦

Andersson, *History...*, pp. 53–62. Boulding, *Underside...*, pp. 461, 464, & 465. Bynum, *Holy...*, pp. 23, 27, 213, 214, 315 n43, 377 n135. Colledge, "Alphonse...," pp. 22, 28, & 35. Harksen, *Women...*, pp. 34–35. Lagorio, "Continental...," pp. 178, 181–4. Obrist, "Swedish...," pp. 227–251. Tuchman, *Distant...*, pp. 29, 265, 343, 345.

BRITES OF PORTUGAL

See—BEATRICE OF PORTUGAL.

BRUNETTA

1475 Germany

Jewish doctor; charged with complicity in the death of a child.

♦ Childcare. Doctors/empirics. Jews. Miscreants. ♦

Friedenwald, "Jewish...," p. 220

BUCHAN, countess of

See—ISABELLA, countess of BUCHAN.

CARLOTTA D'ARAGONA **[Charlotte of Aragon]**

fl. 1490s–1500s France; Italy

Daughter of Frederick, king of Naples (r.1496). Lady-in-waiting at court of Anne of Brittany, queen of France. Carlotta was originally intended as a bride for Cesare Borgia, but she refused to marry him. She was supposedly in love with, and later married, a French nobleman named Nicholas de Laval.

♦ **Genealogy. Servants–ladies.** ♦

Chamberlin, *Fall...*, pp. 158–161, 163, 173–176, 218, 243. Cloulas, *Borgias...*, pp. 143, 150, 152, 160. Fusero, *Borgias...*, pp. 207, 209–210, & 212. Johnson, *Borgias...*, pp. 130, 132, 134, 136, 139. Prescott, *Princes...*, p. 87.

CASOTTE CRISTAL

fl. 1460s–1480s Flanders; France

A Flemish woman; wife of Thomassin. Casotte ran a well-patronized and highly profitable bathhouse/prostitution business on the rue de la Poissonnerie in Lyons during the 1470s and 1480s. An unsuccessful attempt to close her establishment was based on supposed espionage activities by Casotte and her customers.

♦ **Bathhouse. Prostitutes–procurers. Spies.** ♦

Rossiaud, *Medieval Prostitution...*, pp. 44, 45, 188–191.

CASSANDRA FEDELE

1465–1558 Italy

Educated at home in Venice by father and tutors in Latin and Greek rhetoric, history, and philosophy. Considered a prodigy and an asset to Venice. When Queen †Isabella of Castile invited Cassandra to the Spanish court, the city-state refused to allow her to leave. She wrote a book on the natural sciences and the treatment of diseases. In 1497, she married Gianmaria Mappelli, a physician. Cassandra returned to her studies after his death (c.1514), but her early promise had been dissipated by age and marriage.

♦ **Scholars. Writers–medicine.** ♦

Ennen, *Medieval...*, p. 223. Fedele, *Cassandrae....* King, "Thwarted...," pp. 295–299, & 304. King and Rabil, *Her Immaculate...*, pp. 13, 21, 23,

25, 27, 28, 48–50, 69–77, 83, 87, 126, 127, 128, 132, 142, 150, 152, & 153. Kristeller, "Learned...," p. 97.

CASTELLOZA OF PROVENCE

1212 France

Probably from Auvergne; married Turc de Mairona. She composed songs for her courtly lover, N'Arman de Breon. Four of her poems are extant.

♦ **Poets/troubadours.** ♦

Bogin, *Women...*, pp. 118–129. Boutière and Schutz, *Biographies des...*, pp. 333–334. *DBF*, v.7, pp. 1354–1355. Dronke, "Provençal...," pp. 131–152. Egan, *Vidas...*, p. 26. Moulin, *La poésie...*, pp. 79–81.

CATELINE (of Paris)

1292 France

Listed as a silkworker on la rue St. Martin; Cateline was taxed 5s in 1292 Paris.

♦ **Silkwork.** ♦

Géraud, *Paris sous...*, p. 54.

CATHERINE/KATHERINE [Caterina; Catharina; Catharine; Katharine; Katerine]

CATERINA ADORNA

See—CATHERINE OF GENOA.

KATHARINE OF ARAGON **[Catalina]**

b. 1486–d. 1536 England; Spain

Daughter of †Isabella of Castile and Ferdinand of Aragon; married Arthur, prince of Wales. After he died, Katharine was married to Arthur's younger brother, the heir apparent Henry VIII of England. Eighteen years later, Henry divorced Katharine.

♦ **Educated. Divorce. Pawns.** ♦

Altamira, *Spain...*, p. 291. Brown, *History...*, I, p. 305. Lipinska, *Histoire...*, p. 158. Miller, *Castles...*, pp. 62, 126, 157, 283, 296, 350. [There are a plethora of more substantial and definitive works about Henry VIII and Katharine which deal with her life after the year 1500.]

CATHERINE D'ARTOIS, countess of Aumale

c. 1310s–1350s France

Daughter of †Jeanne de Valois and Robert d'Artois, count of Beaumont. Wife of John II of Ponthieu, count of Aumale. Catherine confirmed their commune charter to the people of Ponthoiles in 1347.

♦ **Legal activity. Managers.** ♦

Anselme, *Histoire...*, v.1, p. 388; v.3, p. 305. Belleval, *Les fiefs...*, pp. 261–262. *DBF*, v.3, p. 1202 (this source claims that she was the daughter of Charles of Artois, count of Longueville, in which case she would be the granddaughter of Jeanne and Robert).

KATERINE (l'attachière)

1292 France

In 1292 Paris, Katerine was taxed 12d for her job making nails for buckles.

♦ **Less-affluent. Merchants.** ♦

Géraud, *Paris sous...*, p. 94.

CATHERINE OF AUSTRIA

m. 1338–d. 1349 Austria; France

Daughter of Leopold I, duke of Austria. In 1338, Catherine married Enguerrand de Coucy. Catherine made sure that her son Enguerrand VII received a good education. When her husband died in 1346, she married Conrad de Magdebourg. Both died of the plague.

♦ **Pawns. Plague. Teachers.** ♦

DBF, v.9, p. 871. Tuchman, *Distant...*, pp. 47, 63, 102.

CATHERINE OF AUSTRIA **[Catherine of Hapsburg]**

m.c. 1313–d. 1323 Austria; Italy

Daughter of Albert I of Hapsburg, duke of Austria and Holy Roman Emperor. As a widow in 1316, Catherine became the first wife of Charles, duke of Calabria (son of Robert of Anjou, king of Naples). She claimed title to the defunct Latin Empire. Catherine died childless in 1323. (Charles then married †Marie of Valois—daughter of Charles of Valois, and the mother of his two daughters, †Joanna I of Naples and Maria, wife of Charles of Durazzo.)

♦ **Estate. Pawns.** ♦

Anselme, *Histoire...*, v.1, p. 409. *Cambridge...*, VII, p. 41. Headlam, *Story...*, p. 272. Partner, *Lands...*, p. 306.

KATHERINE L'AVISE

1400s–1440s France

Wife of Pierre Esvers of Paris. Katherine had the use of a shop (numbers 5 and 6) on rue Petit Pont for life. She was a mercer, and apparently worked at her craft as a *femme sole*.

♦ **Clothworkers. Land/property.** ♦

Comptes du..., pp. 199, 236, 257, 286, 307, 336, 354, 378, 393, 416, 434, 464, 481, 513, 545, 567, 608, 650, 708, 768. Favier, *Les Contribuables...*, p. 255.

CATHERINE BENINCASA

See—(St.) CATHERINE OF SIENA.

(St.) CATHERINE OF BOLOGNA **[Caterina dei Vigri]**

1413–1463 Italy

Artist-saint; abbess of Poor Clares of Bologna. Very few paintings can be identified as Catherine's—she probably worked mostly as a miniaturist. She also composed songs for her nuns, and is often pictured playing the viola. She taught others, had visions, and wrote *Le sette armi Spirituali.*

♦ **Abbesses. Artists. Medicine. Models. Music. Relics. Saints.** ♦

A.S., Mar v.2, pp. 35–89. Clement, *Women...,* pp. 350–351. Fine, *Women...,* pp. 6–7. Greer, *Obstacle...,* pp. 175–176. McLaughlin, "Creating...," pp. 262, 263, 274–5, 278–9, 279–285, 286. Ragg, *Women...,* pp. 11–163. Sparrow, "Women...," pp. 23 & 33.

KATHERINE BOTELER

c. 1301–1332 England

An alewife in Broughton village, she also held some land. In 1327, Katherine paid tax of 12d and in 1332, she was taxed 20d.

♦ **Alewives. Land/property. Manors.** ♦

Britton, *Community...,* pp. 72, 197, 251.

CATHERINE DE BRUYÈRES

1385–1465 France

Married around 1399 to Girard Bruyères, a Parisian notary (d.1444); daughter Isabelle. Through inheritance and her own business acumen, Catherine garnered much property in Paris, including three houses on the rue des Singes. Her own large house was on the rue du Martelet Saint Jean. François Villon wrote about Parisian student riots which began with the removal of a stone from Catherine's yard. He also mocked her in his poetry about the loose women of Paris.

♦ **Land/property. Merchants. Models. Religious patrons. Widows.** ♦

Bonner, *Complete...,* p. 211. Champion, *François...,* I, pp. 54–55, 276–281, 292, 294, 301; II, pp. 162–163, 184 & 341. Lewis, *François...,* pp.92, 93 & 305.

CATHERINE OF BURGUNDY

c. 1400–d.c. 1415 France

Daughter of John the Fearless of Burgundy. (Niece of †Catherine of Burgundy, duchess of Austria—see below.) Often-betrothed, Catherine died before she could be married.

♦ **Genealogy. Pawns. Unmarried.** ♦

Denieul-Cormier, *Wise...,* p. 237. Jacob, *Fifteenth...,* p. 139. Vaughan, *Philip...,* pp. 82, 90 & n.

CATHERINE OF BURGUNDY, duchess of Austria

b. 1378–d.c. 1425 Austria; France

Daughter of †Margaret (de Male) of Flanders and Philip the Bold of Burgundy. In 1393, Catherine married Leopold III of Austria. After she became a widow (in 1410), Philip the Good of Burgundy forced her to bequeath her lands to him.

♦ **Bequests. Book owners. Edcated. Estate. Games–chess. Pawns. Widows.** ♦

Anselme, *Histoire...*, v.1, p. 238. Calmette, *Golden...*, pp. 54–55, 138, 185, 300. Hughes, "Library...," p. 31. Vaughan, *Philip...*, pp. 81, 82, 84–85.

CATERINA CALDIERA

m. 1451–d. 1463 Italy

Daughter of Venetian humanist/doctor, Giovanni Caldiera. Married Andrea Contarini in 1451. Her father wrote a commentary for Caterina and tutored her in Latin and philosophy. Caterina herself wrote the treatise *De Laudibus sanctorum*. Her education and abilities were praised by other humanists.

♦ **Scholars. Writers.** ♦

King and Rabil, *Her Immaculate...*, pp. 17, 18–19, & 132. Labalme, *Beyond...*, p. 2.

CATERINA CORNARO, queen of Cyprus

b. 1454–d. 1510 Cyprus; Italy

In 1468, Caterina married King James II of Cyprus (d.c.1473). A coup to restore Queen †Charlotte of Lusignan (after James died) failed because Venice, Caterina's city-state, stepped in to save her throne. However, she then became merely a Venetian puppet. Because her baby James III had died, Venice later forced Caterina to abdicate and the city-state itself absorbed Cyprus. From 1489 until 1510, Caterina lived on her fief of Asolo where she maintained a highly sophisticated and artistic court.

♦ **Art patrons. Models. Music. Patrons of literature. Pawns. Rulers. Widows.** ♦

Brion, *Catherine....* *Cambridge...*, IV, pp. 466, 471, 477; VII, p. 767. Cronin, *Flowering...*, pp. 103 & 210. Hill, *History...*, v.3, pp. 631–640 passim, 757–764 passim. Kristeller, "Learned...," p. 93. Norwich, *History...*, pp. 364–367 & 472.

CATHERINE DE COURTENEY

fl. 1280s–1310s France; Israel; Italy

Daughter of Beatrice of Anjou and Philip of Courteney. Titular heiress of the Eastern Latin Empire. Around 1300, Catherine became the second wife of Charles of Valois; their daughters were †Catherine and †Jeanne (de Valois).

♦ **Childcare. Estate. Popes.** ♦

Cambridge..., VII, pp. 6, 310. Denieul-Cormier, *Wise...*, p. 19. Holmes, *Florence...*, p. 167. Partner, *Lands...*, pp. 287, 292. Runciman, *Sicilian...*, pp. 270–271, 274.

CATHERINE DE COURTENEY

See—CATHERINE OF VALOIS.

CATHERINE DELORT

d. 1335 France

At court in Toulouse, this middle-aged woman admitted she had had an affair with a shepherd who took her to "witch orgies." She also "confessed" to making devilish potions and eating children. She was burned at the stake after being tortured to reveal the names of other witches.

♦ **Ecclesiastical courts–Inquisition. Punishments. Witchcraft.** ♦

Cohn, *Europe's...*, pp. 129–130, 132, 137–138. Lea, *Materials...*, p. 231. Russell, *Witchcraft...*, pp. 184–185. Summers, *Geography...*, pp. 378–379.

KATHERINE DERTFORD

fl. 1415 England

As a Lollard, Katherine was tried in Lincolnshire court for holding heretical views on the Eucharist.

♦ **Ecclesiastical courts. Lollards.** ♦

Cross, "Great...," p. 362.

KATHERINE DORE

fl. 1415 England

See—JOAN WOULBAROWE.

♦ **Apprentices–mistresses. Silkwork.** ♦

CATERINA OF FLORENCE

1400s Italy

Caterina was a *medica* at Florentine hospital, Sancta Maria Nuova, where she signed extant prescriptions.

♦ **Doctors/empirics. Medicine–hospitals.** ♦

Hughes, *Women...*, p. 142. Hurd-Mead, *History...*, p. 278. Lipinska, *Histoire...*, p. 149.

CATHERINE OF FRANCE **[Catherine Valois]**

b. 1428–d. 1446 France

Oldest daughter of †Marie of Anjou and Charles VII of France. First wife of Charles, count of Charolais (later duke of Burgundy). They married in 1439; she died childless in 1446.

♦ **Genealogy. Pawns.** ♦

Calmette, *Golden...*, pp. 156 & 161. Cleugh, *Chant...*, pp. 69, 100, & 126. Commynes, *Memoirs...*, p. 135. *DBF*, v.7, pp. 1416–1417. Vale, *Charles...*, pp. 84–5.

CATHERINE OF FRANCE, queen of England [Katherine Valois]

b. 1401–d. 1437 England; France

Daughter of †Isabeau of Bavaria and Charles VI of France. Around 1420 Catherine married Henry V of England, fulfilling a provision of the Treaty of Troyes. Her son, Henry VI, was an infant when his father died (1422). Catherine retired from court and soon found solace in the arms of a Welshman, Owen Tudor. Catherine bore Owen several children, including Edmund, earl of Richmond (father of King Henry VII). She died at Bermondsey Abbey.

♦ **Art patrons. Educated. Models. Negotiators. Pawns. Religieuses. Widows. Women of easy virtue.** ♦

Calmette, *Golden...*, pp. 115, 132, 133. Clive, *Sun...*, pp. xxxviii, 36, 187, 305. Coryn, *House...*, pp. 162, 169, 208, 209, 211, 212, 214. Griffiths, "Queen...". Griffiths and Thomas, *Making...*, pp. 1–4, 25–33, 37, 47, 53, 182–183, 187, 190–191, 198. Hutchison, *King...*, pp. 92, 93, 176, 178–179, 184, 186, 188–189, 190, 192, 194, 197–199, 208, 211, 215–217, 222–223. Jacob, *Fifteenth...*, pp. 138–142, 178, 180, 182–184, 192–195, 200–201, 214, 226. Jarman, *Crispin's...*, pp. 38, 46, 198, 199, 202, 208, 210, 212.

(St.) CATHERINE OF GENOA

[Caterina Adorna; Catherine Fieschi Adorni]

1447–1510 Italy

Noblewoman of Fieschi; forced to marry Julio Adorno. She became very pious: wore hairshirt, had visions, etc. Her major religious work included caring for the sick (even during plague outbreak), writing the *Theology of Love*, and founding a hospital in Genoa (1477). Catherine also attracted many disciples.

♦ **Medicine–hospitals. Mystics. Plague. Saints. Writers–theology.** ♦

Bonzi da Genova, *S. Caterina....* Bynum, *Holy...*, pp. 140, 142, 144, 180–6, 194, 203–206, 214, 215, 221, 223, 226, 227, 234, 250, 264, 275, 277, 279, 289, 290, 297. Catherine, *Treatise on Purgatory....* Farmer, *Oxford...*, p. 70. Hugel, *Mystical....* *Life and Sayings....* Kristeller, "Learned...," p. 94.

KATHARINE GRANDISON, countess of Salisbury

d.c. 1350 England

Daughter of William de Grandison; married William de Montacute (Montague), earl of Salisbury. Katharine held their castle for several months against Scottish troops. She was guardian of †Joan "Fair Maid of Kent." The story of her "rape" by Edward III in 1341/2 is extremely dubious.

♦ **Childcare. Models. Rape. Soldiers. Tournaments.** ♦

Bourchier, *Chronicle...*, VI, p. 191. *DNB,* v.13, pp. 660–661. Gransden, "Alleged Rape..." Hardy, *Philippa...*, pp. 129–131, 145, 194, 206. Jamison, *Life...*, I, pp. 32–35, 36, 37. Tuchman, *Distant...*, pp. 68–69.

KATHERINE HUSENBOLTZ

fl. 1450 Germany

Between 1445 and 1453, Katherine was licensed as a cooper in Strasbourg.

♦ **Merchants–coopers.** ♦

O'Faolain, *Not in...*, p. 154.

CATHERINE DE L'ISLE BOUCHARD, countess of Tonnerre

1420s France

Supposedly known for her licentious behavior, in 1423 she was godmother to the future Louis XI. Catherine frequently looked after him while he was young; in 1429, she was his governess.

♦ **Childcare. Women of easy virtue.** ♦

Champion, *Louis...*, pp. 44 & 45. Denieul-Cormier, *Wise...*, pp. 302, 303. Kendall, *Louis XI,* p. 34.

CATHERINE OF LANCASTER, queen of Castile

[Katherine; Catalina]

b. 1372–d. 1418 England; Spain

Daughter of John of Gaunt by his second wife †Constance of Castile. As granddaughter of Pedro I of Castile, she was forced to bring about peace in that country by marrying the Infante Enrique (Henry III of Castile) in 1386. After his death in 1406, Catherine was regent for their young son, John II.

♦ **Jews–treatment of. Regents. Widows. Writers–letters.** ♦

Altamira, *Spain...*, p. 238. Froissart, *Chronicles...*, I, pp. 354, 367, 368, 386, 387; II, pp. 17, 19–20, 30, 31, 77, 78, 110, 139. Green, *Letters...*, pp. 85–87. Roche, *Dona...*, pp. 12, 15, 21, 37, 39, 44, 45, 50, 51, 60, 62, 79, 80. Smith, *Spain...*, pp. 94–95.

CATHERINE MERCEYRA

1338 France

Had her own badge-selling business in Le Puy.

♦ **Badge dealers.** ♦

Cohen, "Pilgrim...," p. 202.

CATHERINE OF NAVARRE [Catherine de Foix, queen of Navarre]

b. 1468–d. 1517 France; Spain

Daughter of †Madeleine Valois (Magdalena of France) and Gaston de Foix, prince of Viana. Inherited throne of Navarre in 1483. Catherine married Jean d'Albret in 1484. They fought to keep Navarre, but with only moderate success. Son: Henry d'Albret, king of Navarre.

♦ **Estate. Negotiators. Rulers.** ♦

Anselme, *Histoire...*, v.3, p. 376. *DBF,* v.7, p. 1416. Smith, *Spain...*, p. 115.

KATHERINE NEVILLE, duchess of Norfolk

b. 1398–d. 1484 England

Daughter of †Joan Beaufort and Ralph Neville, earl of Westmoreland. Married (1) John Mowbray, duke of Norfolk (d.1432); (2) Thomas Strangways; (3) John, viscount Beaumont. In 1465, this elderly widow was married to her fourth husband, twenty-year-old John Woodville. He was the brother of the new queen, †Elizabeth Woodville, who was busily providing all her relatives with rich, socially-elevated mates. The chroniclers were appalled by the marriage of John and Katherine.

♦ **Dowry/dower. Estate. Models. Pawns. Widows.** ♦

Clive, *Sun...*, p. 114. *Coronation...*, p. 66. Jacob, *Fifteenth...*, pp. 321, 464. McFarlane, *Nobility...*, pp. 11, 153, 180. Ross, *Wars...*, p. 68. Scofield, *Life...*, I, pp. 6 & 376. St. Aubyn, *Year...*, p. 53.

CATHERINE OF PALLANZA **[Blessed Caterina]**

b. 1437–d. 1478 Italy

A hermit in the mountains near Milan, Catherine attracted a following—other women who wished to live with her under the Augustinian Rule.

♦ **Anchoresses.** ♦

Attwater, *Dictionary...*, p. 60. Effinger, *Women...*, pp. 59–60.

CATHERINE PERCY, countess of Kent

b. 1423–d. 1489 England

Daughter of †Eleanor Neville and Henry Percy, earl of Northumberland; married Edmund Grey, lord of Ruthin, who later became earl of Kent.

♦ **Genealogy.** ♦

Coronation..., p. 57. *DNB,* v.8, p. 624; v.15, p. 852.

KATHERINE DE LA POLE **[Catherine]**

c. 1410s–1470s England

Daughter of Elizabeth Mowbray and Michael de la Pole, earl of Suffolk (d.1415). Katherine was abbess of Barking from 1433 until 1473. Edmund and Jasper Tudor were in her care from 1437 through 1442.

♦ **Abbesses. Childcare.** ♦

DNB, v.16, p. 34. Griffiths and Thomas, *Making...*, p. 32. *Letters of Queen...*, p. 103. Power, *Nunneries...*, pp. 42, 263, 270, 571.

CATHARINE PYKRING

1451 England

Catharine and Isabella Hunter were whipped with a handful of flax for washing their linen on a holy day.

♦ **Ecclesiastical courts. Miscreants. Punishments.** ♦

Hair, *Bawdy...*, p. 177 (#445).

KATHERINE REBESTOECKYN

fl. 1450 Germany

During the years 1445–1453, she was licensed as a goldsmith in Strasbourg.

♦ **Goldsmiths.** ♦

O'Faolain, *Not in...*, p. 154.

KATHERINE RICHE **[Kathryn Ryche Betson]**

b. 1463–d. 1510 England

Daughter of †Elizabeth Croke (Stonor) by her first husband Thomas Ryche. In 1478, Katherine married a London wool merchant, Thomas Betson. After he died in 1486, Katherine married a London haberdasher, William Welbeck.

♦ **Educated. Land/property. Models.** ♦

Kendall, *Yorkist...*, pp. 366–368. *Stonor...*, pp. xxvii–xxviii, xxix, 2–4, 6–8, 10, 15, 22, 28, 47, 55–57, 64.

CATHERINE DE LA ROCHELLE

fl. 1400s–1420s France

A false visionary; Catherine claimed to be guided by voices of saints. When †Joan of Arc met Catherine, the future saint advised her to return to her family.

♦ **Mystics. Superstitions.** ♦

Barstow, *Joan...*, pp. 29, 65–67, 105. Pernoud, *Joan...*, p. 142. Pernoud, *Retrial...*, p. 6.

CATHERINE ROYER **[le Royer]**

c. 1401–1456 France

She and husband Henri were †Joan of Arc's hosts at Vaucouleur. Catherine testified to Joan's virtue and sincerity during the retrial in 1455.

♦ **Ecclesiastical courts–Inquisition. Land/property. Legal activity.** ♦

Anderson and Zinsser, *A History of...*, p. 152. Pernoud, *Retrial...*, pp. 75–76.

CATHERINE OF SEBASTOPOL

fl. 1380s Italy

Tuscan slave trader.

♦ **Shipping–slave traders. Slaves–trading.** ♦

Gies, *Women...*, p. 196.

CATHERINE SFORZA, countess of Forli **[Caterina]**
1463–1509 Italy

Illegitimate daughter of Galeazzo Maria Sforza, duke of Milan. In 1477, she married Pope Sixtus IV's nephew, Girolamo Riario. When the pope died, Girolamo and Catherine tried to sway the papal election. Catherine took and held the Castle Sant'Angelo. Afterwards, the couple went to live in Forli and Imola, the cities Pope Sixtus had given them. After Girolamo was assassinated (1488), Catherine had to fight to retain possession of her towns; she won this battle and was appointed regent for her son Ottaviano. In 1489 she became young Giacomo Feo's mistress and then his wife. After he was murdered, she had an affair with Giovanni de'Medici. When she became pregnant, the couple were secretly married (1497). He died in 1498, but Catherine continued to fight against Cesare Borgia; either she or one of her supporters sent Pope Alexander VI a container of poisoned messages in an attempt to destroy the power behind Cesare. Catherine was finally captured in 1500 and imprisoned for eighteen months; although she was eventually released, she had lost all her power.

♦ **Illegitimacy. Legal activity. Medicine. Murder. Popes. Prisons. Regents. Rulers. Soldiers. Women of easy virtue.** ♦

Breisach, *Caterina....* Cartwright, *Beatrice...*, pp. 20, 23, 41, 253, 330, 341 & 365. Chamberlin, *Fall...*, pp. 31, 44–45, 185, 187–197, 199, 206, 237, 239–240. Chamberlin, *World...*, pp. 101 & 199. Cleugh, *Medici...*, pp. 128, 161–162, 222–223, 225, 239, 270. Cloulas, *Borgias...*, pp. 48, 170, 173, 175. Commynes, *Memoirs...*, p. 462. Fusero, *Borgias...*, pp. 67, 133, 146, 176, 219–222. Johnson, *Borgias...*, pp. 150–154, 157, 164, 187. Prescott, *Princes...*, pp. 41, 90, 114–127, 297. Sizeranne, *Beatrice...*, pp. 195, 197 & 258.

(St.) CATHERINE OF SIENA **[Catherine Benincasa]**
1347–1380 Italy

Dedicated her life to Christ; refused marriage so that she could live in a cell at her home for three years. She had visions, cared for poor and sick, and collected disciples. Catherine worked diligently to push the papal court out of Avignon and back to Rome. She also bombarded a wide variety of political and military leaders with advice and admonitions to follow Christian teachings. Catherine perhaps starved herself to death since she preferred the Eucharist to more earthly food. Her visions included a mystical marriage with Christ; God's revelations to her were recorded in *Divine Dialogue*.

♦ **Anchoresses. Medicine. Mystics. Politics. Popes. Saints. Unmarried. Virginity. Writers.** ♦

Berrigan, "Tuscan...," pp. 252–268. Bynum, *Holy...*, pp. 7, 23, 28 ... 279, 316, 377. Colledge, "Alphonse...," pp. 20, 34 & 49. *Dialogue....* Farmer, *Oxford...*, pp. 70–71. Fawtier, *Les Oeuvres....* Fawtier,

Sainte.... Fusero, *Borgias...*, pp. 29, 30, & 34. Lagorio, "Continental...," pp. 184–191. McLaughlin, "Women...," pp. 115–124. *St. Catherine...Letters....* Volpato, "Between Prophetesses...," pp. 149–161.

KATHERINE OF SUTTON

fl. 1363–1376 England

Abbess of Barking; wrote and produced three liturgical dramas for Easter services.

♦ **Abbesses. Clothworkers. Drama. Writers–plays.** ♦

Cotton, *Playwrights...*, pp. 27–28, 213 n. Craig, *English...*, p. 36. Young, *Drama...*, I, pp. 166, 167, 177, 381; II, pp. 410–411.

(St.) CATHERINE OF SWEDEN

c. 1330–d. 1381 Sweden

Fourth child of St. †Bridget of Sweden. Catherine's husband died while she was accompanying her mother to Italy. She was associated with Bridget in many projects: advocating return of papacy to Rome; pilgrimage to Jerusalem; and working with the Birgittine Order. After Bridget died, Catherine went to the abbey of Vadstena where her reputation for piety and miracles flourished. She was the only woman summoned as a witness in the canonization process for her mother.

♦ **Models. Nuns. Pilgrims. Popes. Saints.** ♦

Attwater, *Dictionary...*, p. 61. Bynum, *Holy...*, pp. 3, 214–215. Colledge, "Alphonse...," pp. 22, 28 & 35. Lagorio, "Continental...," pp. 182–183, 185.

KATHERINE SWYNFORD, duchess of Lancaster [Katherine Roet]

b. 1350–d. 1404 England

Daughter of Flemish knight, Sir Paon Roet. Around 1368, Katherine married Sir Hugh Swynford. He died in 1372, by which time Katherine was already the mistress of John of Gaunt. This relationship lasted for some twenty-five years. Katherine bore Gaunt four children, and also served as governess to his legitimate daughters. In 1396, the couple finally married.

♦ **Adultery. Childcare. Hunting. Mistresses. Models. Servants–governesses. Teachers. Widows.** ♦

Armitage-Smith, *John...*, pp. 227, 390–393. Braddy, "Chaucer and...," p. 225. Froissart, *Chronicles...*, II, pp. 139, 140, 148, 154, 155, 158. Gardner, *Life...*, pp. 109, 113, 117, 136, 153–157, 159–162, 213, 297, 307. Given-Wilson, *English...*, pp. 50 & 130. Holmes, *Later...*, pp. 189–190. Hutchison, *King...*, pp. 17, 69, 75. Jacob, *Fifteenth...*, pp. 103, 271, 464, 473. Roche, *Dona...*, pp. 2, 7, 9–17, 19, 21–24, 28, 37, 57, 71–73, 92. Rosenthal, *Nobles...*, p. 174.

CATHERINE DE THOUARS, dame de Tiffauges

c. 1404–1450s France

Daughter/heiress of Béatrice de Montjean and Milet de Thouars. In 1420, Catherine was abducted and presumably raped by her fiancé,

Gilles de Rais. Since that effectively ruined her chances with other suitors, Catherine's parents quickly got the couple officially married. As soon as she did her duty by producing an heir, their daughter Marie, Catherine retired to a separate estate. After Gilles was executed (as a homosexual child molester/murderer), she promptly married a more congenial spouse.

♦ **Abduction. Estate. Legal activity. Pawns. Rape.** ♦

Hyatte, *Laughter...*, pp. 17, 27, 78, & 133. Robbins, *Encyclopedia...*, p. 403. Wolf, *Bluebeard...*, pp. 26–30 & 79–80.

CATHERINE DE VALOIS **[Catherine de Courteney]**

b. 1301–d.c. 1345 Byzantium, France, Greece, Italy

Daughter of †Catherine de Courteney and Charles of Valois. Married in 1313 to Philip of Taranto. As a widow, and as titular empress of Constantinople, Catherine held the last possessions of the Latin Empire in the Morea for her minor son, Robert of Taranto, prince of Achaia.

♦ **Queens. Regents. Teachers. Widows.** ♦

Cambridge..., vol. IV, pp. 452, 453, 454, 474, 476, 534, 535. Cheetham, *Greece...*, pp. 144 & 158. *DBF,* v.7, pp. 1415–6.

CATHERINE DE VAUSSELLES **[Katherine]**

fl. 1450s France

François Villon wrote of her as the "love of his life." He portrayed her as a very coquettish and fickle woman. She listened to him, charmed him, and then left him for another man.

♦ **Models. Women of easy virtue.** ♦

Champion, *François...*, I, pp. 89, 104 & 105; II, pp. 2, 6, 141, 164, 200, 302–303. Lewis, *François...*, pp. 127–129, 131, 132, 278 & 366–367.

KATHARINE VAUX

fl. 1450s–1480s England; France

A Provençal noblewoman; wife of Sir William Vaux (d.c.1474). She was a favorite lady-in-waiting to †Margaret of Anjou, queen of England. Katharine not only stayed with Margaret while the deposed queen was imprisoned in England, but she also accompanied Margaret to Anjou and witnessed her will in 1482.

♦ **Legal activity. Prisons. Servants–ladies.** ♦

Clive, *Sun...*, pp. 181, 187, 229. Scofield, *Life...*, I, p. 585; II, pp. 23 & 159.

CATERINA DEI VIGRI

See—(St.) CATHERINE OF BOLOGNA.

CATERINA VISCONTI

m. 1380–1410s Italy

Daughter of †Regina della Scala and Bernabo Visconti; married Giangaleazzo Visconti in 1380. Caterina helped her husband to acquire

Vicenza. When Giangaleazzo died in 1402, she became regent of Milan for her sons Giovanni Maria and Filippo Maria. She did a good job, but later fell in love with Francesco Barbaro. By allowing him too much influence, Caterina lost much of her own power.

♦ **Estate. Negotiators. Regents. Widows. Women of easy virtue.** ♦

Chamberlin, *Count...*, pp. 70, 98, 102, 115, 116, 173 & 220. Trevelyan, *Short...*, pp. 156 & 158.

CATHERINE OF VRABA **[Lady Catherine Vraba]**

1402 Bohemia

Widow of Conrad Kapler of Sulevice. She made large donations to Hussite sect. Particularly interested in sermons, she insisted that these be in the vernacular so that the uneducated could better understand them.

♦ **Hussites. Preachers. Religious patrons.** ♦

Klassen, *Nobility...*, p. 87.

KATHERINE WOODVILLE **[Catherine Wydeville]**

b. 1442–d. 1497 England

Daughter of †Jacquetta of Luxembourg and Richard Woodville; younger sister of Queen †Elizabeth Woodville. In 1466, Katherine married Henry Stafford, duke of Buckingham. After he was executed in 1483, Katherine married Jasper Tudor, uncle of Henry VII. Her husband later became duke of Bedford and earl of Pembroke. After he died, Katherine married Sir Richard Wingfield.

♦ **Genealogy. Pawns.** ♦

Clive, *Sun...*, pp. xxxviii, 114, 204, 291, 304. *Coronation...*, pp. 54–55. *DNB*, v.8, p. 858. Griffiths and Thomas, *Making...*, pp. 30, 99–100, 179. McFarlane, *Nobility...*, pp. 206–207. Rawcliffe, *Staffords...*, pp. 23, 28, 35, 36, 63, 80, 92, 126–8. Scofield, *Life...*, II, pp. 253, 329 n3. Strickland, *Lives...*, p. 232.

KATHARINE OF YORK, countess of Devon

b. 1479–d. 1527 England

Daughter of Elizabeth Woodville and Edward IV of England. Katharine was a useful pawn in marital negotiations until her father died. In 1495, she married William Courtenay, who later became earl of Devon.

♦ **Genealogy. Pawns.** ♦

Clive, *Sun...*, pp. 241 & 306. *DNB*, v.6, p. 616. Scofield, *Life...*, II, pp. 253 & 329 n3. Strickland, *Lives...*, p. 232.

"CAVOLAJA" OF FLORENCE

fl. 1380s Italy

Poor woman with farm on outskirts of Florence. She made a fortune by going every day into the city to sell her cabbages (the origin of her nickname "cabbageseller"). By the time she died, "Cavolaja" was so well-known and respected that bells were rung for her passing and she was accorded a pompous burial ceremony before being interred in a fine tomb.

♦ **Land/property. Merchants. Provisioning–cabbage sellers.** ♦

Boulding, *Underside...*, p. 491. Staley, *Guilds...*, p. 458.

CECILIA [Caecelia; Cecile; Cecily]

CECILE DE BÉZIERS, countess of Foix

c. 1150 — France

See—ESCLARMONDE DE FOIX and ZABELIA.

♦ **Genealogy** ♦

CECILY BONVILLE

m.c. 1475 — England

Daughter and heiress of William Bonville, lord Harington; second wife of Thomas Grey, marquis of Dorset.

♦ **Genealogy. Servants–ladies.** ♦

Clive, *Sun...*, p. 99. *DNB,* v.8, p. 645. *Stonor...*, v.2, p. 140.

CECILIA LE BOTELER

1323 — England

Accused Sir William Bradshaw of murdering of her husband. However, when the case was about to be tried, Sir William and sixty armed men "persuaded" the jury to acquit him.

♦ **Legal activity. Manors. Murder. Widows.** ♦

Bellamy, *Crime...*, p. 20. Hanawalt, "Fur Collar...," p. 7.

CECILY CHAUMPAIGNE

c. 1360s–1390s — England

Daughter of William and Agnes Chaumpaigne. Brought suit against Geoffrey Chaucer for rape (c.1380); the case may have actually involved payment of a debt. It was settled out-of-court.

♦ **Legal activity. Rape.** ♦

Braddy, "Chaucer, Alice...," p. 907. *Calendar of Plea...*, II, p. 268. Gardner, *Life...*, pp. 251–252.

CECILY FITZJOHN, countess of Hereford — **[Cecile fitzJohn]**

fl.c. 1180s — England

Daughter of †Sybil de Lacy and Payn FitzJohn. Part of Cecily's dowry included some of the extensive Lacy lands. Her first husband was Roger, earl of Hereford. She later married Walter de Mayenne.

♦ **Dowry/dower. Genealogy.** ♦

DNB, v.7, p. 1318. Wrightman, *Lacy...*, pp. 141, 148 & 175.

CECILIA OF FLANDERS

c. 1060s–d. 1127 France

Daughter of †Matilda of Flanders and William of Normandy, king of England (William the Conqueror). Cecilia received an excellent convent education in preparation for becoming a nun. She was known for writing poetry. Baudri de Bourgueil dedicated poems to Cecilia—praising her beauty and purity. Cecilia became abbess at her mother's foundation of La Trinité at Caen.

♦ **Abbesses. Models. Patrons of literature. Scholars. Unmarried. Writers.** ♦

Brown, *Normans...*, pp. 34 & 146. Gardiner, *English...*, pp. 54–55. Heinrich, *Canonesses...*, p. 196. Jourdain, "Memoire...," p. 483. Thompson, *Literacy...*, pp. 167–168. Verdon, "Les Sources...," p.233. Vitalis, *Ecclesiastical...*, II, p. 130 n1.

CECILIA OF FRANCE

b. 1098–d. 1138 France; Lebanon; Turkey

Daughter of †Bertrade de Montfort and Philip I of France; around 1108, she married Tancred of Antioch (d.1112). Cecilia later married Pons St. Gilles of Tripoli. Cecilia inherited land in Tripoli and Antioch. She aided war against Moslems.

♦ **Crusades. Estate. Soldiers.** ♦

Comnena, *Alexiad*, p. 369. Decaux, *Histoire...*, pp. 218–221. Douglas, *Norman...*, pp. 185, 189, & Table 3. Payne, *Dream...*, p. 139.

CECILIA GALLERANI

c. 1470s–1500s Italy

Mistress for over ten years to Ludovic Sforza, regent of Milan. He presumably had Leonardo da Vinci paint her portrait. Well-educated, often compared with other scholarly women. Ludovic gave her a palace when she later married Lodovico Bergamini.

♦ **Estate. Mistresses. Models. Music. Scholars. Writers.** ♦

Ady, *History...*, pp. 140, 163, 282, 310. Bellonci, "Beatrice...," pp. 288–291. Cartwright, *Beatrice...*, pp. 52–54, 89, 150, 263, 292, & 321. Simon, *Tapestry...*, pp. 96, 130, 140. Sizeranne, *Beatrice...*, pp. 38–40.

CECILIA GONZAGA

1425–d. 1451 Italy

Daughter of Gianfrancesco Gonzaga, marquis of Mantua. Corresponded with other famous humanists of her day; excelled in Greek and Latin studies. She resisted marriage in favor of piety and learning. After her father died in 1444, both Cecilia and her mother took the veil.

♦ **Nuns. Scholars. Unmarried. Virginity. Writers.** ♦

Brinton, *Ganzaga...*, pp. 68, 70–72, 98. King and Rabil, *Her Immaculate...*, pp. 17, 19–20, 44, 53–54, 91–94, 97–100, 105, 117, & 132. Kristeller, "Learned...," p. 94. Prescott, *Princes...*, pp. 152–3. Simon, *Tapestry...*, pp. 6, 33, 36–37, 39, 49, 140.

CECILY NEVILLE, duchess of Warwick

c. 1420s–d.c. 1451 England

Daughter of Richard Neville and †Alice Montagu, countess of Salisbury. Married (1) Henry Beauchamp of Warwick and (2) (c.1448) John Tiptoft, earl of Worcester.

♦ **Dowry/dower. Squabbles.** ♦

Abram, *English...*, p. 38. *DNB,* vol. 14, p. 282. Jacob, *Fifteenth...*, p. 563. Johnson, *Duke...*, pp. 59, 93n. McFarlane, *Nobility...*, pp. 87 & 201.

CECILY NEVILLE, duchess of York

b. 1415–d. 1495 England; Ireland

Daughter of †Joan Beaufort and Ralph Neville, earl of Westmoreland. Wife of Richard, duke of York; two of their sons became kings of England: Edward IV and Richard III. Cecily accompanied her husband to govern Ireland in 1449. After he and their sons were charged with treason in 1459, she successfully pleaded with Henry VI for her family and for some of her husband's confiscated fortune. She helped her sons escape to safe havens when the fight for the throne went against them. She had much influence with Edward IV, although not enough to save the life of another son, George, duke of Clarence (1478). In fact, Cecily outlived all of her sons. Cecily perhaps found consolation in her collection of religious literature, including books by several female saints. In addition to being very pious, she was spirited and a sharp-witted business woman. Through an attorney, Cecily conducted numerous profitable merchant/shipping ventures.

♦ **Book owners. Negotiators. Politics. Rebellions. Religious patrons. Shipping. Widows.** ♦

Clive, *Sun...*, pp. 3, 5, 25, 41, 101, 106, 117, 138, 142, 158, 165, 168, 236, 245, 248, 288, 291. Curtis, *Ireland...*, pp. 138 & 139. Green, *Letters...*, pp. 105–107. Halligan (ed.), *Booke...*, pp. 41n & 51. Johnson, *Duke...*, pp. 2, 10, 13, 14, 26, 47, 72, 192, 196, 211. Kendall, *Yorkist...*, pp. 423–426. McFarlane, *Nobility...*, p. 66. *Oxford...Prose*, p. 94. Rosenthal, *Nobles...*, p. 181. Scofield, *Life...*, I, pp. 1, 5, 39, 102, 147 & 170; II, pp. 207 & 408. St. Aubyn, *Year...*, pp. 42, 50, 53, 142–144, 146–148, 160–161, 204, 218, 238.

CECILIA RYGEWAY

1359 England

Convicted of murdering her husband John in 1359, she was sentenced to *peine forte et dure*—in her case, imprisonment without any food or water. Cecilia survived this treatment for forty days. King Edward III was convinced that this was a miracle, so he pardoned Cecilia.

♦ **Murder. Prisons. Punishments.** ♦

Bellamy, *Crime...*, p. 142. McCall, *Medieval...*, p. 68.

CECILE DE TURENNE

[Cecile de Comminges, countess of Turenne]

fl. 1330s–1340s Italy

Niece and "hostess" of Pope Clement VI. There was some rumor and speculation concerning just what her duties with Clement included. Apparently, however, their relationship was just that of niece and uncle.

♦ **Models. Popes. Women of easy virtue.** ♦

Cheetham, *Keepers...*, p. 157. Trevelyan, *Short...*, p. 152.

CECILY OF YORK

b. 1469–d. 1507 England

Younger daughter of †Elizabeth Woodville and Edward IV of England. Around 1487, she married John, lord Welles (d.1499). Cecily presumably later married Thomas Kymbe.

♦ **Genealogy. Pawns.** ♦

Brown, *History...*, I, pp. 267, 272, 276 & 279. Clive, *Sun...*, pp. 208, 210, 215, 240, 258, 267–8. *DNB*, v.3, pp. 1321–1322. Griffiths and Thomas, *Making...*, pp. 30, 93 & 126. Jacob, *Fifteenth...*, pp. 574–5, 586. Scofield, *Life...*, I, pp. 482–483; II, pp. 101–103 & 353.

CHARLOTTE D'ALBRET, duchess of Valence

b. 1482–d. 1514 France

Daughter of Alain d'Albret of Nérac, duke of Guyenne; married 1499 to Cesare Borgia to seal treaty between King Louis XII and Pope Alexander VI. After Cesare returned to Rome, Charlotte was detained in France by Louis XII as his insurance that Cesare would comply with the terms of their alliance. Daughter Luisa Borgia was born in 1500, but Charlotte never saw Cesare again.

♦ **Pawns. Popes. Religieuses.** ♦

Breisach, *Caterina...*, p. 197. Chamberlin, *Fall...*, pp. 179–182, 320–322, 331. Cloulas, *Borgias...*, pp. 160–162. Fusero, *Borgias...*, pp. 210–212, 215–216, 224, 295–298. Garner, *Caesar...*, pp. 71, 131, 132, 137, 310. Johnson, *Borgias...*, pp. 90–91, 139–140, 141. Norwich, *History...*, p. 381. Simon, *Tapestry...*, pp. 119 & 132. Trevelyan, *Short...*, p. 199.

CHARLOTTE OF LUSIGNAN, queen of Cyprus

c. 1440s–1487 Cyprus; Greece; Italy

Daughter and heiress of Helene Paleologa and Jean III of Cyprus. Married John of Portugal. After he was poisoned, Charlotte married Louis of Savoy. In 1460, Charlotte and her husband were deposed by her illegitimate half-brother James II Lusignan of Cyprus. Charlotte fled to the castle of Kyrenia and then escaped to Rome. Moving to Rhodes, she continued to intrigue to overthrow James and later plotted against his widow, †Caterina Cornaro. The end result of Charlotte's conspiracies was that Venice deposed her rival Caterina.

♦ **Politics. Rulers. Soldiers. Squabbles.** ♦

Cambridge..., IV, pp. 466, 471, 477. *DBF*, v.8, p. 595. Hill, *History...*, v.3, pp. 548–620 passim. Norwich, *History...*, pp. 364–365.

CHARLOTTE OF SAVOY, queen of France

b. 1439–d. 1483 France; Italy

Daughter of †Anne of Lusignan and Louis, duke of Savoy. Married Dauphin Louis (XI) of France, against his father's wishes. She was sweet, simple, pious, and fond of Louis. Charlotte was a patron of art, music, and literature. Philippe Commynes thought the king's faithfulness to Charlotte was particularly admirable because she was a good woman but not very exciting intellectually or sexually.

♦ **Art patrons. Book owners. Models. Music. Patrons of literature.** ♦

Anselme, *Histoire...*, p. 122. Champion, *Louis...*, pp. 124, 131, 249, 250–251. Cleugh, *Chant...*, pp. 109, 112, 116–117, 130, 151, 165, 211, 242, 247, 287. Commynes, *Memoirs...*, pp. 259, 377, 425 & 426. José, *La Maison...*, v.2, p. 429. Jourdain, "Memoire...," p. 503. Lewis, *King...*, pp. 90, 219 & 222. Vale, *Charles...*, pp. 164–5.

CHARLOTTE (de Valois) **[Charlotte de Brézé]**

m. 1462–d. 1476 France

Daughter of Charles VII and his mistress †Agnes Sorel. In 1462, Charlotte married Jacques de Brézé. Charlotte was killed by her husband when he returned early from a hunt and discovered her in bed with one of his knights.

♦ **Adultery. Illegitimacy. Murder.** ♦

DBF, v.7, p. 262; v.8, p. 530. Philippe, *Agnes...*, pp. 57 & 63. Vallet, *Histoire...*, v.3, pp. 13–15, 22.

Countess of CHÂTELLERAULT

fl.c. 1100 France

The wife of Aimery I, viscount of Châtellerault; her name (or nickname) was presumably Dangerosa. One of William IX of Aquitaine's many mistresses; presumably grandmother (or perhaps aunt) of †Eleanor of Aquitaine.

♦ **Abduction. Estate. Mistresses.** ♦

Cambridge..., III, p. 130 (says her name was Maubergeon). *DBF*, v.17 (fasc. 97), p. 145. Kelly, *Eleanor...*, pp. 6, 8, 109, 157, 385. Pernoud, *Eleanor...*, p. 25. Pernoud, *La femme...*, p. 145.

CHIARA GONZAGA **[Claire]**

b. 1465–d. 1503 France; Italy

Daughter of †Margaret of Bavaria and Federigo Gonzaga, marquis of Mantua. Wife of Gilbert de Bourbon, count of Montpensier (d.1496). After her sons died in Italian wars, she lived the rest of her life in poverty and seclusion at Mantua.

♦ **Dowry/dower. Pawns. Writers–letters.** ♦

Anselme, *Histoire...*, v.1, p. 315. Cartwright, *Beatrice...*, pp. 251, 305, 314 & 329. Chamberlin, *World...*, p. 168. Commynes, *Memoirs...*, II, p. 569. Prescott, *Princes...*, p. 183. Simon, *Tapestry...*, pp. 65, 67–68, 72, 117, 120, 128, 131, 165, 172.

CHILDLOVE (DE WORTH)

fl. 1250s England

An anchoress in Berkshire; her brother Lucas supported her by buying a corrody for her maintenance.

♦ **Anchoresses. Charity.** ♦

Warren, *Anchorites...*, pp. 46, 257–258, 266.

CHRISTINE [Cristina; Christina; Cristine; Crystene]

CRISTINA BLAKE

1355 England

Wife of Roger Blake. Cristina was sent to prison by London court for regrating beer (buying ale and then selling it at a higher price).

♦ **Alewives. Miscreants. Prisons.** ♦

Calendar of Plea..., I, p. 253.

CHRISTINA (of Gandersheim)

860s–900s Germany

Daughter of Oda and Liudolf of East Saxony. A nun at Gandersheim. See—ODA and HATHUMADA OF GANDERSHEIM.

♦ **Nuns.** ♦

CRYSTENE HOUGHTON **[alias Stone]**

1490 England

Convicted as a strumpet and "common bawde," Crystene was ousted from London. In 1490, when she was again found in the city, Crystene was arrested, put in the pillory, and then imprisoned for a year and one day.

♦ **Prisons. Prostitutes. Punishments.** ♦

Calendar of Letter..., L, p. 276.

CHRISTINA (of Hungary)

fl. 1060s–1090s England; Hungary; Scotland

Presumably the daughter of exiled prince Edward of England and †Agatha (of Hungary). Christina took the veil in 1086; later became abbess of Romsey. Her sister (St.) †Margaret, queen of Scotland, entrusted daughters †Matilda and †Mary to Christina. She gave them an excellent education, evidently by beating them into submission.

♦ **Abbesses. Childcare. Scholars. Teachers.** ♦

Barlow, *Edward...*, pp. 163 & 218. Duncan, *Scotland...*, pp. 118–119. Glover, *Story...*, pp. 48 & 52. Nagy, *St. Margaret...*, pp. 13 & 15. Thompson, *Literacy...*, pp. 170–171.

CHRISTINA OF MARKYATE

c. 1096–c. 1155 England

According to hagiographical tradition, this young girl—originally named Theodora—was forced to flee her home because her parents were attempting to "persuade" her to marry. Helped by various pious friends, she became a recluse. After many vicissitudes of fate and fortune (and a change of name to Christina), she became prioress of Markyate. Christina then gained a reputation for sanctity and for performing miracles. She was also an excellent embroiderer; she made a mitre and sandals for the pope.

♦ **Abbesses. Anchoresses. Artistic clothwork. Models. Mystics. Popes. Unmarried. Virginity. Writers–theology.** ♦

Bynum, *Holy...*, pp. 27, 222, 247, 281. Clark and Williams, "Impact...," pp. 161–162. Coulton, *Life...*, I, pp. 170–173. Elkins, *Holy...*, pp. 27–38, 39, 40–2, 73, 78. Farmer, *Oxford...*, pp. 77–8. Fox, *Literary...*, pp. 31, 32, 56. Holdsworth, "Christina...," pp. 185–204. McLaughlin, "Women...," pp. 108–115. Petroff, *Medieval...*, pp. 144–150. Talbot, *Christina....* Warren, *Anchorites...*, pp. 33, 34, 37, 41, 93–94, 127, 287. Zarnecki, "Contributions...," pp. 75 & 79.

CHRISTINA OF NORWAY

fl. 1130s–1160s Norway

Daughter of Sigurd I the Crusader of Norway; married powerful thane and royal adviser, Erling Skakke. She reputedly spied on King Haakon Broad-shoulders' councillors and sent word to her husband not to trust Haakon. In 1162, son Magnus (V) Erlingsson was elected king (age five) due to Erling's prestige and her royal blood.

♦ **Politics. Spies.** ♦

Boyesen, *Story...*, pp. 318, 322, 332. Larsen, *History...*, pp. 130 & 136.

CHRISTINE DE PISAN **[Pizan]**

b. 1364–d. 1429 France; Italy

Daughter of Thomas of Pisano, Christine was born in Italy, but the next year her father was called to the Parisian court of Charles V of France. From her father, a court astrologer and physician, she received an excellent education. Around 1380, Christine married Étienne de Castel. Nine years later, as a widow with three young children to support, Christine began her career as a successful writer. Among her patrons were the dukes of Burgundy and Orléans. She condemned anti-feminist literature. Many of her books extolled the value of honorable women who nurse their relatives, instill familial virtues in their young, live piously, and play an active role in the prosperity of their families and their nations. She lauded †Joan of Arc, but she wrote to †Isabeau of

Bavaria warning the queen to look after her duties as wife and mother. Among Christine's works were: *Cent Ballades, Le Livre des faits et bonnes moeurs du sage Roi Charles Quint, Le Livre des trois vertus, Le Livre de la cité des dames*, and *Le Livre des fait d'armes et de chevalerie.* She later retired to the convent of Poissy (c.1418).

♦ **Bookmaking. Politics. Religieuses. Scholars. Teachers. Widows. Writers.** ♦

Blumenfeld-Kosinski, "Christine...," pp. 279–292. Bornstein, "Military...," pp. 475–477. Brewer, *Chaucer...*, p. 66. Cartellieri, *Court...*, pp. 99–100, 113–114. Champion, *François...*, I, pp. 139, 198, 278–279; II, pp. 126 & 199. Fox, *Literary...*, pp. 271–274, 276, 277, 296, 302–303, 325, 326, 338. Gies, *Women...*, pp. 10–12, 90–91, 162, 198. Hughes, "Library...," pp. 146, 165, 171, 184. Huizinga, *Waning...*, pp. 38, 63, 102, 114, 121, 145, 250, 274, 292, 301. Legge (ed), *Anglo-Norman...*, pp. 144–150 [#99]. Matthews, "Wife...," pp. 417, 418 & 433. *Oxford...Prose*, pp. 48, 429–430. Petroff, *Medieval...*, pp. 335–346. Pisan, *City....* Sherman, "Ordo ad...," pp. 289–290. Solente, *Christine....* Tuchman, *Distant...*, pp. 221, 229–231, 250, 283, 506, 536. Willard, "Christine...", pp. 90–120. Willard, "Franco-Italian...," pp. 333–363.

CRISTINA ROKINGEHAM

1275 England

See—AGNES ROKINGEHAM.

♦ **Taverners.** ♦

(St.) CHRISTINA OF ST. TROND

[Christina Mirabilis; the Astonishing]

1150–1224 Belgium; Flanders

Lay religious woman of Liège; noted for extreme self-abuse in attempt to imitate Christ. In 1182, Christina fell into a trance and was pronounced dead. During her funeral she awoke and then levitated to the church rafters. Her *Vita* was written by Thomas de Cantimpré in 1232.

♦ **Models. Mystics. Religieuses. Saints.** ♦

Attwater, *Dictionary...*, p. 64. Bolton, "Vitae Matrum...," pp. 257, 260, & 263. Bynum, *Holy...*, pp. 24, 115, 117, 120, 120–123, 193, 203, 211, 223, 234, 273, 274. Herlihy, *Opera...*, pp. 118–119. Joly, *Le Cantique....* Lagorio, "Continental...," p. 175. McDonnell, *Beguines...*, pp. 33n, 47, 200n, 328, 380–381, 395. Petroff, *Medieval...*, pp. 184–188.

CHRISTINA OF STOMMELN **[Blessed Christina]**

1242–1312 Germany

At age ten, she professed to having a mystic marriage with Christ. From age fifteen until age forty-six, Christina was tortured by diabolical temptations and physical pain (stigmata, gushing blood, etc.).

♦ **Models. Mystics. Unmarried. Saints–popular.** ♦

Attwater, *Dictionary...*, p. 64. Bynum, *Holy...*, p. 213. Coulton, *Life...*, I, pp. 132–149. Lagorio, "Continental...," p. 175. McDonnell, *Beguines...*, pp. 87, 200, & 345. Power, *Women...*, p. 90. Power, *Nunneries...*, p. 501.

CHRISTINE SWATH

d.c. 1261 — England

Wife of William de Swath of London. Christine bit Luke le Girdeler on his finger which caused his whole body to swell until he died. She was arrested for causing Luke's death, and Christine soon died in Newgate prison.

♦ **Medicine. Miscreants. Murder. Prisons.** ♦

London Eyre...1276, p. 32 [#113].

CHRISTINA OF SWEDEN

fl. 1090–1120 — Russia; Sweden

Daughter of King Inge of Sweden; married Mstislav, prince of Novgorod (later Mstislav I of Kiev); their son was Vsevolod of Novgorod.

♦ **Genealogy.** ♦

Vernadsky, *Kievan...*, pp. 97 & 336.

CLARE [Clair; Clara]

CLARA D'ANDUZA **[Clair d'Anduze]**

c. 1210s — France

A Provençal noblewoman and troubadour. Clara was probably the wife of Bernard d'Anduze, and possibly the lover of Uc de Saint Circ.

♦ **Poets/troubadours. Women of easy virtue.** ♦

Bogin, *Women...*, pp. 130–131. Boutière and Schutz, *Biographies des...*, pp. 247 & 249. Miron, *Queens...*, p. 33. Moulin, *La poésie...*, pp. 82–83 & 176.

CLARE OF ASSISI **[Blessed Clair; St. Clare; Chiara Schiffi]**

1193–1253 — Italy

Daughter of Favorino Seisso; friend of (St.) Francis of Assisi. Founded new order—Poor Clares—associated with Franciscans. She wrote the Rule for her order, insisting on poverty, modesty, etc. Venerated as a saint.

♦ **Artistic clothwork. Nuns. Politics. Religious patrons. Saints. Virginity.** ♦

Bolton, "Vitae Matrum...," p. 262. Bolton, "Mulieres Sanctae...", pp. 150–152. Brooke and Brooke, "St. Clare...," pp. 275–287. Bynum, *Holy...*, pp. 15, 24, 74, 85, 99–102, 146, 193, 215. Claire, *Écrits*. De Robeck, *St. Clare....* Harksen, *Women...*, pp. 33–34. *Legend and Writings.... Life...Clare.* Petroff, *Medieval...*, pp. 242–244. *Rule....*

CLARA GATTERSTEDT

fl. 1300s — Germany

Nun and artist at convent of St. James at Kreuzberg. She painted a series of portraits of the abbots of Fulda.

♦ **Artists. Nuns.** ♦

Zarnecki, "Contributions...," p. 79.

CLARA HATZERLIN

c. 1430–1476 Germany

Professional book-copier (and possibly illuminator) of Augsburg. She is most famous for making a collection of folk-songs—the *Volkslieder.*

♦ **Artists. Bookmaking. Educated. Music.** ♦

Greer, *Obstacle...*, pp. 162–164. Harksen, *Women...*, p. 46. Schoenfeld, *Women...*, pp. 196 & 198–200.

(St.) CLARE OF MONTEFALCO

1268–1308 Italy

Entered monastery at age six; later became abbess of Montefalco. After her death, Clare's body did not decompose and her blood remained liquid.

♦ **Abbesses. Mystics. Saints. Unmarried.** ♦

Attwater, *Dictionary...*, p. 66. Bynum, *Holy...*, pp. 211, 213, 257, 362. Goodich, "Contours...," p. 28. Holmes, *Florence...*, pp. 53, 62–63, 65, 67.

CLARICIA [Clarice; Clarissa]

CLARICIA OF AUGSBURG

fl. 1210s–1220s Germany

Sent to convent for education and training in bookmaking. Claricia was an illuminator in the convent scriptorium; painted a self-portrait in tail of a "Q" in psalter.

♦ **Artists. Bookmaking. Educated. Religieuses.** ♦

Carr, "Women...," p. 6. Greer, *Obstacle...*, p. 158.

CLARISSA ORSINI **[Clarice]**

m. 1469–d. 1488 Italy

Of powerful Roman family; daughter of Jacopo and Maddelena Orsini; married Lorenzo de'Medici in 1469. Clarissa was strong and proud; had some influence with her husband, Lorenzo the Magnificent. She attempted to quell her son Pietro's debauchery by personally selecting his bride, †Alfonsina Orsini. Her sons' tutor called her boring, but that may have been because she did not appreciate him. Ill-health may also have made her short-tempered. Clarissa was educated and intelligent—she made sure her children received a good education.

♦ **Book owners. Educated. Negotiators. Teachers. Writers–letters.** ♦

Anderson and Zinsser, *A History of...*, pp. 384, 399–400, 440. Brion, *Medici,* pp. 55 & 128. Cleugh, *Medici...*, pp. 106–108, 160–161, 171,

196. Hook, *Lorenzo...*, pp. 23–24, 26–27, 35–36, 45, 76, 106, 111, 129, 161, 171, 176–177. Maguire, *Women...*, pp. 95, 129, 132, 138, 146–148, 150, 152–154, 161, 166–169, 171, 256.

CLARICE OF ROTOMAGO **[Clarice of Rouen]**

1312 France

Wife of Pierre Faverel. Arrested and excommunicated for practicing medicine.

♦ **Doctors/empirics. Ecclesiastical courts. Punishments–excommunicated.** ♦

Herlihy, *Opera...*, p. 113. Hughes, *Women...*, p. 144. Hurd-Mead, *History...*, p. 271. Lipinska, *Histoire...*, p. 9. Wickersheimer, *Dictionnaire...*, p. 100.

CLAUDE DES ARMOISES

1436 France

Claude was probably the most successful of the fake "†Joan of Arcs." She was given financial backing because many people believed her claims; she was later denounced in Paris. Dressed as a man, Claude fought in Rome for the pope, and then was a soldier in the Parisian garrison.

♦ **Miscreants. Popes. Soldiers. Unmarried.** ♦

Barstow, *Joan...*, pp. 66–67. Champion, *François...*, p. 249. Coulton, *Life...*, I, p. 211. Wolf, *Bluebeard...*, pp. 166 & 167.

CLEMENCE OF BARKING

c. 1160s–1190s England

Nun at Barking. She translated the *Life of Saint Catherine* from Latin into Norman French.

♦ **Bookmaking. Educated. Nuns. Writers.** ♦

Clark and Williams, "Impact...," p. 166. Elkins, *Holy...*, pp. 149, 212 (n. 17 & 18). Gardiner, *English...*, p. 60. Lejeune, "La Femme...," p. 202. McDonnell, *Beguines...*, p. 373. Power, *Nunneries...*, p. 239.

CLEMENCE OF HUNGARY, queen of France **[Clémenza d'Hongrie]**

c. 1294–d. 1328 France; Hungary

Daughter of Clemence of Hapsburg and Charles I of Hungary. In 1315, she became the second wife of Louis X of France. He died in 1316; she bore his posthumous son John, but the baby only lived a few days. Clemence then retired to a Dominican convent where she was notable for her piety.

♦ **Book owners. Queens. Religieuses. Widows.** ♦

Bell, "Medieval...," p. 185 n69. *Cambridge...*, VII, p. 334. *DBF*, vol. 8, p. 1419. Fawtier, *Capetian...*, pp. 41n, 129. Sherman, "Ordo Ad...," p. 268.

CLÉMENCE SILLONE
c. 1423–1450s Belgium; Flanders

Townswoman of Bruges, chosen as wetnurse for baby Louis (XI) of France. After he became king, Louis gave her a pension.

♦ **Childcare. Nurses–wetnurses. Servants.** ♦

Champion, *Louis...*, pp. 45 & 238. Lewis, *King...*, p. 153.

CLEMENTIA, countess of FLANDERS [Clémence de Bourgogne]
fl. 1090s–1100s Flanders

Wife of Robert II, count of Flanders. After Clementia had three sons in three years, she used "feminine arts" to prevent more pregnancies. The fact that all three of her sons died young was considered God's punishment for her use of birth control.

♦ **Childbirth–prevention. Estate. Medicine. Models. Punishments.** ♦

Bishop, *Middle...*, p. 237. Vercauteren, "Les Médecins...," pp. 72–74. Verdon, "Les Sources...," p. 223.

CLEMENTIA OF ZÄHRINGEN
m.c. 1150 Germany

Daughter of Conrad, duke of Zähringen. A great heiress, Clementia married Henry the Lion, duke of Saxony and Bavaria. They were later separated, and he remarried.

♦ **Divorce. Estate. Pawns.** ♦

Cambridge..., V, p. 357. Fuhrmann, *Germany...*, p. 163. Haverkamp, *Medieval...*, pp. 146 & 180.

(St.) COLETTE OF CORBIE [Nicolette]
1381–1447 Belgium; Flanders; France

Originally a Beguine, Colette later became an anchoress. Her visions finally led her to become the superior of Poor Clare order. She traveled to most houses of the order implementing her reformist ideas. Colette was particularly influential at Burgundian court; she acted as a negotiator and advisor to Philip the Good. She was against the efforts of (St.) †Bridget of Sweden and (St.) †Catherine of Siena to move the papacy from Avignon. Colette was especially involved with the Passion, to the extent of physically and emotionally reliving it. During such times, she suffered a great deal and could only endure a small amount of candlelight around her. She abhorred the very idea of sexual intimacy, and vigorously opposed canonization of any non-virginal woman.

♦ **Anchoresses. Beguines. Managers. Mystics. Negotiators. Orphans. Politics. Popes. Religious patrons. Saints. Virginity.** ♦

Attwater, *Dictionary...*, p. 68. Bynum, *Holy...*, pp. 15, 16, 67, 82, 88, 92, 138–9, 196, 197, 199, 204, 229, 234, 273. *Cambridge...*, VII, pp. 304, 811. *DBF*, v.9, pp. 216–217. Delaney, *Dictionary...*, p. 153. Huizinga,

Waning..., pp. 164, 170, 173, 176 & 238. Sainte-Marie Perrin, *La Belle Vie.... Vita....*

COLETTE LA MOYNESSE

1420s France

Herb seller of Paris. The Provost of Paris paid Colette for providing green herbs or vegetables, 1424–1428.

♦ **Apothecaries. Merchants. Provisioning.** ♦

Comptes du..., pp. 53 & 176.

COLETTE (of Paris)

fl. 1400s France

Parisian draper patronized by Philip, duke of Burgundy. He bought silk, etc., for covering books, and later commissioned Colette to ornament a cloth cover for a Book of Hours.

♦ **Artistic clothwork. Bookmaking. Clothworkers.** ♦

Favier, *Les Contribuables...*, p. 254 (This is evidently the same woman, although Favier believes her name may have been Marguerite Compans). Hughes, "Library of...," p. 167.

CONSTANCE [Constantia; Costanza]

CONSTANCE OF ANTIOCH

b. 1128–1160s Byzantium; Turkey

Daughter/heiress of †Alice of Jerusalem and Bohemund II of Antioch. Constance married Raymond of Poitiers (d.1149); son Bohemund III and daughter †Mary of Antioch. As a widow, Constance married Renaud of Châtillon; they had daughter †Anne. For some years Constance served as regent of Antioch.

♦ **Regents. Soldiers.** ♦

Bridge, *Crusades...*, pp. 11, 145, 147, 167, 192. *Cambridge...*, IV, pp. 359, 373, 381; V, pp. 302, 308. Douglas, *Norman...*, pp. 190 & Table 3. Hamilton, "Women...," pp. 154–155. Kelly, *Eleanor...*, p. 31. Norwich, *Kingdom...*, pp. 113 & 125. Payne, *Dream...*, pp. 134, 135, 140, 162, 168. Pernoud, *Eleanor...*, p. 68.

CONSTANCE OF ARAGON, queen of Hungary, Holy Roman Empress **[Costanza of Barcelona]**

b. 1184–d. 1222 Germany; Hungary; Italy; Spain

Sister of Pedro II of Aragon; her first husband was King Emeric (Imre I) of Hungary (d.1204); their son was King Laszlo III. In 1209, Constance married Emperor Frederick II. Despite the difference in their ages (she was ten years older than he), this union worked well. Frederick particularly respected her political wisdom. Constance was an active participant in his government; in 1212, Frederick named her vice-regent.

When Constance died, Frederick supposedly buried his crown with her as a symbol of his esteem.

♦ **Genealogy. Rulers.** ♦

Cambridge..., VI, pp. 14, 66 n1, 76, 84, 135, 138, 144. Ennen, *Medieval...*, p. 146. Leuschner, *Germany...*, p. 34. Runciman, *Sicilian...*, pp. 14, 26. Shneidman, *Rise...*, pp. 295, 319. Van Cleve, *Emperor...*, pp. 65–67, 79, 80, 107, 126.

COSTANZA OF ARAGON, queen of Sicily **[Constanca]**

m.c. 1360 Italy; Spain

Daughter of Pedro IV of Aragon and his first wife †Marie of Navarre; married King Fadrique (Frederick III) of Sicily. Her father tried to have her declared heiress of Aragon, but the *Cortes* would not recognize her as his successor. Costanza's daughter †Maria was eventually declared heiress of Sicily.

♦ **Estate. Genealogy. Queens.** ♦

Bisson, *Medieval Crown...*, pp. 107, 110. *Cambridge...*, VII, p. 591. Hillgarth, *Pere...*, pp. 6, 50, 99, 214, 380, 392–395, 398, 418, 529, 585, 586. Miron, *Queens...*, pp. 181, 189–191, 241. Shneidman, *Rise...*, pp. 83, 486–488, 492, 499.

CONSTANCE, queen of ARAGON **[Constance of Sicily; of Swabia]**

c. 1250s–d. 1302 Italy; Spain

Daughter of Manfred, king of Sicily (illegitimate son of Holy Roman Emperor, Frederick II). Around 1262, Constance married Pedro (III) of Aragon. They were the parents of (St.) †Elizabeth of Portugal, Alfonso III, Jaime, and Fadrique. She served for some time as the regent of Sicily. As a widow she retired to her duchy of Gandia. Constance died as a Poor Clare of Barcelona.

♦ **Estate. Popes. Regents. Religieuses. Widows.** ♦

Altamira, *Spain...*, p. 242. *Cambridge...*, VI, pp. 184, 198, 199; VII, pp. 6, 308, 582, 583. Desclot, *Chronicle...*, Part I, xxii, 152. Diehl, *Byzantine...*, p. 274. Fusero, *Borgias*, pp. 23 & 139. Miron, *Queens...*, pp. 111–116, 118–125. Powicke, *Thirteenth...*, pp. 252 & 253. Shneidman, *Rise...*, pp. 24–28, 46, 166, 227, 235, 246, 318, 319, 324–326, 330, 332, 337, 340, 344, 363, 381, 479. Smith, *Spain...*, pp. 66–67. Trevelyan, *Short...*, p. 116.

CONSTANCE OF ARLES, queen of France

[Constance of Toulouse]

b. 986–d. 1032 France

Daughter of †Adelaide of Anjou and William of Arles, count of Toulouse. Constance became the third wife of Robert II of France around 1003. There is much dissension over whether Hugh of Beauvais maliciously caused trouble between Constance and Robert, and whether she was implicated in Hugh's death. Constance was undoubtedly hot-tempered, energetic, and haughty. She participated in many aspects of government—advising her husband, sharing judicial proceedings, and sitting in at the Council of Orléans (1022) which was convened to deal with heretics among French clerics. She caused son Henry (I) to relinquish control of Burgundy by insisting that he give that duchy to her favorite son, Robert.

♦ **Heretics–activity against. Legal activity. Models. Murder. Politics. Squabbles.** ♦

Butler, *Women...*, pp. 38–44. *Cambridge...*, III, pp. 104, 107, 116n. *DBF*, v.9, p. 491. Decaux, *Histoire...*, pp. 188–190. Douglas, *William...*, p. 29. Ennen, *Medieval...*, p. 74. Facinger, "Study...," pp. 5, 25, 33 & 41. Guizot, *History...*, pp. 299, 301, 305. Lewis, *Development...*, pp. 338, 345, 391. Robinson, *Readings...*, I, p. 198. Stafford, *Queens...*, pp. 22–25, 30, 42, 58, 72, 77–78, 84, 97, 101, 106–108, 111, 134, 157, 159, 164, 167–168, 209. Summers, *Geography...*, pp. 359–60.

CONSTANCE OF BRITTANY

b. 1161–d. 1201 England; France

Daughter and heiress of Conan IV of Brittany. In 1182, Constance married Geoffrey of England (son of Henry II and †Eleanor of Aquitaine). After he died in 1186, Constance was regent for son Arthur. Forced to marry Raoul of Chester by Henry II, the Bretons chased him away and Constance again ruled Brittany until 1196. After she had the marriage to Raoul annulled, Constance married Guy de Thouars. She urged her son Arthur and daughter †Eleanor of Brittany (by her first husband) to rebel against King John. Constance supposedly died of leprosy.

♦ **Divorce. Leprosy. Pawns. Prisons. Rebellions. Religious patrons. Rulers.** ♦

Appleby, *John...*, pp. 12, 79, 84, 86, 94. Baldwin, *Government...*, pp. 95, 198. Barlow, *Feudal...*, pp. 332, 341, 346. Barrow, *Feudal...*, pp. 169 & 419. *DBF*, v.9, p. 492. Kelly, *Eleanor...*, pp. 136, 159, 184, 187, 349–351, 365, 366, 368, 376, 385. Le Patourel, *Feudal...*, pp. IX, 11, 12; X, 101–104, 105, 106, 108, 110, 115; XV, 163. Lloyd, *Maligned...*, pp. 9, 80, 92–3, 111, 129, 232. Pernoud, *Eleanor...*, pp. 144, 194, 235, 257, 261. Shahar, *Fourth...*, p. 146.

CONSTANCE OF BURGUNDY, queen of Castile

See—CONSTANCE OF FRANCE.

COSTANZA CALENDA **[Laurea Constantia Calenda]**

fl. 1415–1423 Italy

Daughter of Salvator Calenda, dean of medicine at University of Salerno. Wife of Baldassare de Sancto Magno. Costanza lectured at University of Naples in 1423. Unlike most female doctors, Costanza had attended some university classes and had passed an examination.

♦ **Doctors/empirics. Educated. Teachers. University.** ♦

Anderson and Zinsser, *A History of...*, pp. 416–7. Hughes, *Women...*, pp. 62 & 142. Hurd-Mead, *History...*, p. 308. Kristeller, "Learned...," p. 102. Lipinska, *Histoire...*, pp. 99–100.

CONSTANCE OF CASTILE, queen of France

c. 1140s–d. 1160 France; Spain

Daughter of Berengeria of Barcelona and Alfonso VII of Castile. Second wife of Louis VII of France; they had two daughters, †Margaret and †Alys. Constance died giving birth to Alys.

♦ **Childbirth. Pilgrims. Queens.** ♦

DBF, v.9, 492–493. Facinger, "Study...," pp. 8 & 17. Kelly, *Eleanor...*, pp. 90, 106, 108, 110, 111. Marks, *Pilgrims...*, p. 176. Pernoud, *Eleanor...*, pp. 120 & 133. Warren, *Henry...*, pp. 72, 82n, 88, 117. Winston, *Thomas...*, pp. 71 & 94–95.

CONSTANCE OF CASTILE, duchess of Lancaster [Costanza]

b. 1354–d. 1394 England; Spain

Second daughter of Pedro I the Cruel of Castile and his mistress †Maria de Padilla. Constance fled Castile with her father in 1366. In 1371 she became the second wife of John of Gaunt. From first to last hers was a political alliance, and the relationship was probably not improved by Gaunt's on-going affair with †Katherine Swynford.

♦ **Estate. Illegitimacy. Music. Pawns. Politics. Rebellions. Tournaments.** ♦

Armitage-Smith, *John...*, pp. 92, 93, 101, 119, 226, 227, 247, 249, & 357. Froissart, *Chronicles...*, I, pp. 138–139, 210, 267, 338, 339, 354–356, 364–369, 384–387, 390, 423–425; II, pp. 16, 30, 31, 78, 139. Gardner, *Life...*, pp. 110, 135, 155, 170, 172, 297. Hardy, *Philippa...*, pp. 285, 287, 303, 309. Jamison, *Life...*, I, p. 285; II, pp. 159–160 & 264. Roche, *Dona...*, pp. 11, 20, 22, 23, 24, 26, 37–9, 41, 44, 45, 50, 51, 60, 61. Stephens, *Story...*, pp. 103–104 & 113.

CONSTANCE LA DESPENSER

See—CONSTANCE OF YORK, countess of Gloucester.

CONSTANCE (FitzGilbert)

fl. 1100s England

Wife of Ralph fitzGilbert. Interested in French vernacular literature. Patroness of troubadours like David the Trouvère and Geoffrey Gaimar. Constance helped the latter gather sources for his *Lestorie des Engles* and translated some of his Latin sources.

♦ **Educated. Patrons of literature. Writers.** ♦

Jourdain, "Memoire...," p. 476. Lejeune, "La Femme...," p. 205. Thompson, *Literacy...*, pp. 180–181. Vitalis, *Ecclesiastical...*, v.4, p. xxiv.

CONSTANCE OF FRANCE

c. 1090s–1120s France; Turkey

Daughter of Philip I of France; married (1) Hugh, count of Champagne. After his death, Constance married Bohemund I of Antioch in 1106. When he died in 1111, she became regent of Taranto for her son Bohemund II. The throne was usurped and Constance imprisoned around 1118. She was freed c.1120.

♦ **Popes. Prisons. Regents. Widows.** ♦

Comnena, *Alexiad*, p. 369. Douglas, *Norman...*, pp. 39–41. Norwich, *Normans...*, pp. 285, 304–5. Ritchie, "Bohemund...," pp. 301–2. Vitalis, *Ecclesiastical...*, v.3, p. 182.

CONSTANCE OF FRANCE, queen of Castile

[Constance of Burgundy]

m.c. 1079–1110s France; Spain

Second wife of Alfonso VI of Castile. Very pious, Constance disapproved of toleration toward Islamic citizens. She was instrumental in persuading the Spanish clergy to accept and conform to the leadership of the Roman pontiff.

♦ **Politics. Popes. Religious patrons.** ♦

Altamira, *Spain...*, pp. 147–148. Effinger, *Women...*, pp. 267–272. Fletcher, *Quest...*, pp. 72, 83, 150, 153, 160–1. Livermore, *History...*, pp. 106 & 109. Miron, *Queens...*, pp. 44–46 & 57. O'Callaghan, *History...*, pp. 206 & 213. *Oxford...Europe*, pp. 197, 206.

CONSTANCE OF FRANCE, countess of Toulouse

c. 1130s–1160s England; France

Daughter of †Adelaide of Maurienne and Louis VI of France. Married Eustace, son of King Stephen of England. After Eustace died, Constance married Raymond V of Toulouse in 1154. In 1165, Constance left him, complaining to her brother, King Louis VII, that Raymond ignored her.

♦ **Abduction. Divorce. Dowry/dower. Managers.** ♦

Barlow, *Feudal...*, pp. 216, 289. Bedos Rezak, "Women...," pp. 70, 73, 75. Dunbabin, *France...*, pp. 301–302 & 377. Gesta, *Stephani...*, p. 107n. Lambert, *Medieval...*, p. 64. Pernoud, *Eleanor...*, pp. 125 & 158. Warren, *Henry...*, p. 107.

CONSTANCE OF HOHENSTAUFEN [Empress Anna of Byzantium]

b. 1232–d. 1313 Byzantium; Germany; Greece; Italy; Spain; Turkey

Illegitimate daughter of Holy Roman Emperor Frederick II; married John Vatatzes, king of Nicaea, in 1244 to produce union of two anti-papacy forces. John was totally uninterested in her; he was engaged in a scandalous affair with her lady-in-waiting. John died in 1254 and Emperor Theodore II Lascaris (John's son by his first wife, †Irene Lascaris) kept

Constance exiled from court. In 1261, Michael Paleologus usurped and Anna returned from Nicaea to Constantinople. She refused to be Michael's mistress, so he eventually returned her to Manfred of Germany, king of Sicily. In 1269, Constance retired to a convent in Spain where she died in 1313, leaving her Byzantine property to her nephew, Jaime II of Aragon.

♦ **Bequests. Dowry/dower. Illegitimacy. Models. Pawns. Queens. Religieuses. Widows.** ♦

Boulding, *Underside...*, pp. 442–443. *Cambridge...*, vol. IV, pp. 323, 429, 495, 496. Diehl, *Byzantine...*, pp. 259–275. Miron, *Queens...*, pp. 146–147.

CONSTANCE OF HUNGARY

See—KUNIGUNDA OF HUNGARY [Cunigunde].

CONSTANCE (of Hungary)

c. 1200 Bohemia; Hungary

See explanation after KUNIGUNDA (Cunigunde) OF HUNGARY.

Also see—AGNES OF BOHEMIA and ANNE OF BOHEMIA.

♦ **Genealogy.** ♦

CONSTANCE OF NORMANDY

b. 1066–d. 1090 England; France

Daughter of †Matilda of Flanders and William of Normandy, king of England (the Conqueror). In 1086, Constance married Alan IV, count of Brittany.

♦ **Genealogy.** ♦

DNB, v.13, p. 51. Warren, *Henry...*, pp. 74 & 75. Williamson, *Kings...*, p. 43.

CONSTANCE OF SICILY, Holy Roman Empress

b. 1154–d.c. 1198 Germany; Italy

Posthumous daughter/heiress of Roger II, king of Sicily, by his third wife †Beatrice of Rethel (who died giving birth to Constance). Constance married Henry VI of Germany around 1186. In 1194, she gave birth to Frederick II, Henry's son and heir. In 1197, Henry died and she kept Frederick with her to maintain her position in the regency government. She left her son in the care of the pope when she died in 1198.

♦ **Childbirth. Estate. Orphans. Pawns. Popes. Prisons. Regents.** ♦

Barraclough, *Origins...*, pp. 185, 204–5. *Cambridge...*, V, pp. 191, 198, 200, 202, 408, 453, 456, 457, 461, 464, 465, 471, 472; VI, pp. 9, 12, 13, 131, 132, 133, 162, 163. Cheetham, *Keepers...*, pp. 122, 123, 125–127. Fuhrmann, *Germany...*, pp. 164, 174, 181, 182, 186. Haverkamp, *Medieval...*, pp. 233, 235, 239, 241, 265. Kelly, *Eleanor...*, pp. 259, 265, 305, 313, 314, 336. Kennan, "Innocent III...," pp. 233–4. Norwich, *Kingdom...*, pp. 161, 288, 324–5, 331, 345–7, 354–7, 361–3, 367, 375–80,

388–90. Partner, *Lands...*, pp. 217–218, 224, 231. Pernoud, *Eleanor...*, pp. 214, 216, 228. Stephenson, *Mediaeval...*, pp. 388, 402–4. Trevelyan, *Short...*, pp. 98 & 99.

CONSTANCE OF SICILY
CONSTANCE OF SWABIA

See—CONSTANCE, queen of ARAGON.

COSTANZA VARANO

b. 1428–d.c. 1450 Italy

Daughter of Elizabetta and Pier Gentile Varano of Pesaro. Costanza was brought up and educated by her grandmother †Battista da Montefeltro, a humanist scholar herself. An accomplished Latin scholar, Costanza wrote poems, orations, and letters (like one to †Bianca Maria Visconti in 1444 and another to †Cecilia Gonzaga). In 1442, Alessandro Sforza fell in love with Costanza and they married in 1444. They established a peaceful rule and a learned court in Pesaro. Costanza had two children, †Battista and Costanzo. She died of the after-effects of the second birth.

♦ **Childbirth. Patrons of literature. Rulers. Scholars. Writers.** ♦

Collison-Morley, *Sforzas...*, p. 55. Gardiner, *English...*, pp. 149–150. Jones, *Malatesta...*, p. 191. King, "Book-lined...," p. 83. King and Rabil, *Her Immaculate...*, pp. 13, 16–18, 21, 39–44, 53–56, 132 & 134. Kristeller, "Learned...," pp. 96 & 112.

CONSTANCE OF YORK, countess of Gloucester
[Constance la Despenser]

c. 1390s–d. 1416 England

Daughter of †Isabel of Castile and Edmund of Langley, earl of Cambridge and later duke of York. When her mother died in 1392, she left Constance two small primers. Wife of Thomas le Despenser, earl of Gloucester (beheaded 1400). Constance supposedly committed adultery with Edmund, earl of Kent (their daughter later claimed that the couple had secretly married).

♦ **Adultery. Bequests. Book owners. Politics.** ♦

Bourchier, *Chronicle...*, VI, p. 191. *DNB*, v.5, p. 867; v.11, p. 552. Jacob, *Fifteenth...*, pp. 26, 56. Johnson, *Duke...*, p. 12. McFarlane, *Nobility...*, p. 236 n5.

CONTESSINA DE'BARDI

m.c. 1415–d. 1473 Italy

Heiress of wealthy Florentine family. When she married Cosimo de'Medici around 1415, he thus became manager of their bank. Her dowry also included their home, the Palazzo Bardi. Contessina had two sons, Piero and Giovanni.

♦ **Banking. Dowry/dower. Estate. Managers. Religious patrons. Writers.** ♦

Anderson and Zinsser, *A History of...*, pp. 377, 381–2, 401. Brion, *Medici...*, pp. 33 & 48. Cleugh, *Medici...*, pp. 40, 47, 70, 87, 94. Hook, *Lorenzo...*, pp. 10, 18. Maguire, *Women...*, pp. 5, 19, 20, 21, 25, 33, 41, 49, 52, 56, 58, 59, 250.

CORBA DE PÉREILLE **[Perella]**

d. 1244 France

Wife of Raimon de Péreille, lord of Montségur. Corba became a Cathar "perfect." She was captured at the Cathar fortress of Montségur and was burned for her heretical beliefs.

♦ **Cathars. Punishments. Soldiers.** ♦

Decaux, *Histoire...*, pp. 294–295. Gies, *Women...*, p. 96. Marks, *Pilgrims...*, pp. 290, 291, 294.

CORNELIE VAN WULFSKERKE

c. 1480s–1510 Switzerland

Nun at Carmelite convent of Notre Dame de Sion. Learned bookmaking and illuminating crafts from †Marguerite Scheppers. After Marguerite's death (1505), Cornelie finished the *De Tempore* gradual the two women had been working on, and then she illuminated the companion volume, *De Sancto*.

♦ **Artists. Bookmaking. Nuns.** ♦

Greer, *Obstacle...*, p. 165.

Lady de COUCY

c. 1366–d.c. 1405 England; France

Served as governess in the train of young †Isabella of France when the girl came to England as the second wife of King Richard II. The sources agree that this lady viewed her post as an opportunity to indulge herself by living in great luxury. Her extravagance finally led to her dismissal. She was sent back to France, and a more economical, English governess was appointed for Isabella. We believe this lady de Coucy was Marie de Coucy (daughter of Enguerrand VII de Coucy and †Isabella of England, countess of Bedford) who married Henri de Bar in 1384. Marie was heiress of the Coucy estates in France and possibly inherited her extravagant tendencies from her mother.

♦ **Childcare. Estate. Legal activity. Servants–childcare. Teachers.** ♦

Froissart, *Chronicles...*, II, p. 214. Gardiner, *English...*, p. 99. Hardy, *Philippa...*, pp. 283, 298, 308. Somerset, *Ladies...*, pp. 7–8. Tuchman, *Distant...*, pp. 232, 298, 314, 327, 328, 367, 423, 479, 606, 609–610, 628.

COUSTANCE (la parcheminière)

1292 France

In the 1292 Paris tax rolls, Coustance was taxed 12d for her parchment making business on the rue aus Laviendières.

♦ **Bookmaking. Less-affluent.** ♦

Géraud, *Paris sous...*, p. 29.

CRISTINA

See—CHRISTINE.

CRISTIANA LA FLAONERS

d. 1291 England

Widow of William le Fannere (or Vannere). She made light cakes called flans or flauns (like pancakes).

♦ **Less-affluent. Provisioning–pastry. Widows.** ♦

Calendar of Wills..., I, p. 105.

CUNIGUNDE/KUNIGUNDE
[Cunegonde; Cunigund; Cunigunda; Kunigunda]

KUNIGUNDE OF DENMARK, queen of Germany

See—GUNHILD OF DENMARK, queen of Germany.

KUNIGUNDE OF GOSS **[Cunegunde of Gross]**

c. 1239–1269 Austria

Abbess of Goss; presumably she and her nuns embroidered a number of altar pieces and liturgical garments.

♦ **Abbesses. Artistic clothwork.** ♦

Harksen, *Women...*, p. 97. Zarnecki, "Contributions...," p. 79.

KUNIGUNDA OF HUNGARY **[Constance; Cunigonde of Swabia]**

c. 1250s–d. 1287 Bohemia; Hungary

Married Ottokar II of Bohemia around 1261. Kunigunda was extremely strong-willed and supposedly tried to avenge her husband's death (1278). In 1283, Kunigunda fell in love with and then married Zavis of Falkenstein. Her son, Wenceslaus, had to curtail her authority to prevent power from falling to her incompetent and disreputable husband.

♦ **Politics. Women of easy virtue.** ♦

Cambridge..., VI, pp. 440, 469. Maurice, *Bohemia...*, pp. 86, 87, 100, 108, 109, 112. Runciman, *Sicilian...*, Table IV. Shneidman, *Rise...*, p. 327.

These sources all appear somewhat confused over Kunigunda. The confusion results from several family members who had the same names. We believe the following is correct: Ottokar I married a woman named †Constance (or Constantina) who was presumably of Hungarian descent. They had a son who is sometimes called Wenceslaus III but is more often known as King Wenceslaus I. This king married (as his second wife) †Cunigunda of Swabia (daughter of Philip, duke of

Swabia, and †Irene Angela—see below). King Wenceslaus I and Cunigunda of Swabia had two sons: Vladislav (who predeceased his father) and Ottokar II. Ottokar II married (as his second wife) Kunigunda—who is sometimes also known as Constance—of Hungary. She may have been the daughter of Béla IV of Hungary, but was probably his granddaughter. Ottokar II and Kunigunda had a son who became King Wenceslaus II. (His son, Wenceslaus III, is also known as Ladislas, king of Hungary.)

(St.) CUNIGUND OF LUXEMBOURG, Holy Roman Empress

c. 980s–d. 1039 Germany; Luxembourg

Daughter of Sigfrid, count of Luxembourg; wife of Holy Roman Emperor Henry II. Cunigund was Henry's partner in supervising Saxony's defense and issuing decrees on church reformation. In 1002, Cunigund became the first known woman in Germany to use her own seal. When Henry died in 1024, Cunigund settled the succession issue by handing over the royal insignia to Henry's cousin, Conrad II. She then left the political field to become a nun. Henry was named a saint in 1152 and Cunigund also became a saint shortly thereafter. The *Vita S. Cunegundis* was written around 1199. Although mostly interested in her piety, the author also particularly extolled her love of reading.

♦ Book owners. Educated. Models. Negotiators. Ordeals. Politics. Popes. Regents. Religious patrons. Religieuses. Saints. Soldiers. Widows. ♦

Attwater, *Dictionary...*, p. 74. Barlow, *Edward...*, pp. 82, 257, 284–285. Barraclough, *Origins...*, p. 74. Bedos Rezak, "Women...," p. 63. Bryce, *Holy...*, pp. 491–492. *Cambridge...*, III, pp. 218, 241, 248, 252, 254, 279. Herlihy, *Opera...*, pp. 116–117. Leyser, *Rule...*, pp. 50 & 52. Stafford, *Queens...*, pp. 76, 105, 118, 124, & 171. Stubbs, *Germany...*, pp. 123–124, 127. Thompson, *Feudal...*, I, p. 50; II, p. 427. Thompson, *Literacy...*, p. 85.

KUNIGUNDA OF NUREMBERG

c. 1400–1440 Germany

Nun at St. Catherine in Nuremberg; Kunigunda worked as both a scribe and an illuminator in the convent scriptorium.

♦ Artists. Bookmaking. Nuns. ♦

Greer, *Obstacle...*, pp. 161–162.

CUNIGUNDA OF SWABIA, queen of Bohemia

fl. 1210s–1230s Bohemia; Germany

Daughter of †Irene Angela and Philip II, duke of Swabia. Cunigunda claimed part of the Hohenstaufen estates in Swabia. She married Wenceslaus III of Bohemia (King Wenceslaus I). One of their sons was Ottokar II, king of Bohemia. As a widow, in 1232 Cunigunda founded cloister at Tišnov.

♦ **Estate. Queens. Religieuses. Religious patrons. Widows.** ♦

Cambridge..., VI, p. 100. Leuschner, *Germany...*, p. 83. Runciman, *Sicilian...*, tables IV & VI. Shneidman, *Rise...*, p. 327 (in the index this source confuses Cunigunda with †Kunigunda of Hungary, the wife of Ottokar II, but does not do so in the text). Thompson, *Feudal...*, II, p. 637.

CUNEGONDE OF SWABIA, queen of Germany

fl. 890s–910s Germany

Sister of Erchanger and Berchtold of Swabia. Cunegonde married Liutpold, margrave of Bavaria. She later married Conrad I, king of Germany (d.918), to seal an alliance. Her heir was son Arnulf of Bavaria.

♦ **Genealogy. Pawns. Queens.** ♦

Fisher, *Medieval Empire...*, I, pp. 71–72. Riché, *Les Carolingiens...*, p. 223.

CWENTHRYTH OF MERCIA **[Quendreda]**

fl. 820s England

Daughter of Aelfthryth and Cenwulf, king of Mercia. She was abbess of two rich, family establishments. In 825, the ownership of some of her extensive monastery property was disputed. Her quarrels with high-ranking churchmen over property perhaps help to explain the vindictiveness of later monastic chroniclers toward Cwenthryth. Nearly three hundred years after her death, William of Malmesbury embellished the legend of her half-brother, (St.) Kenelm of Mercia by reporting that Cwenthryth's lover murdered Kenelm. William also accused Cwenthryth of practicing magic, and stated that God punished her by making her eyes fall out. Cwenthryth is often confused with †Cyenthryth, queen of Mercia (see below), who was also the victim of "bad press."

♦ **Abbesses. Managers. Models. Murder. Witchcraft. Women of easy virtue.** ♦

Attwater, *Dictionary...*, p. 179. Butler, *Lives...*, p. 128. *Cambridge...*, III, p. 344. Campbell, *Anglo-Saxons*, pp. 106, 127, & 138. Farmer, *Oxford...*, p. 231. Wright, *Cultivation...*, p. 104.

CYENTHRYTH, queen of MERCIA **[Kynethryth]**

c. 770s–800s England

Wife of Offa, king of Mercia (d.796). Although Alcuin referred to her as pious, Cyenthryth has gone down in history as a notoriously evil queen. More notable during her own time was her role in Offa's government. He even had coins struck with her image. As a widow, she took the veil and became an assertive abbess.

♦ **Abbesses. Banking. Mistresses. Models. Murder. Rulers. Squabbles. Widows.** ♦

DNB, v.14, p. 899. Fell, *Women...*, pp. 90–91, 123. Stafford, *Queens...*, pp. 16–17, 128, 132, 182–183, 201. Wood, *Search...*, pp. 81, 85, 93, 98. Wright, *Cultivation...*, pp. 93, 97, 99, 100–103.

DANGEROSSA

See—Countess of CHÂTELLERAULT.

DELPHINE OF LANGUEDOC **[Blessed Delphina de Glandevès]**

b. 1282–d.c. 1358 France; Italy

Around 1298, Delphine married (St.) Elzéar de Sabran. She accompanied her husband to the court of Naples and became an attendant to †Sancia of Majorca, queen of Naples. For at least part of their marriage, Elzéar and Delphine followed a mutual vow of chastity. Delphine was a widow for many years. A Franciscan tertiary, she lived in self-imposed poverty in Provence. Delphine mediated local quarrels and set up an interest-free system of loans for the rural populace.

♦ **Banking. Negotiators. Religieuses. Servants. Virginity. Widows.** ♦

Attwater, *Dictionary...*, pp. 78 & 92. *DBF,* v.10, pp. 912–913. Duhamelet, *S. Elzéar et....* Goodich, "Contours...," p. 25.

DENISE [Denyse]

DENISE

fl. 1200–1215 England

Denise accused Nicholas Kam of murdering her husband Anthony. The judge in Launceston ruled that, since she did not actually witness the crime, her case was unproved. Nevertheless, Nicholas eventually had to undergo a trial by ordeal to prove his innocence since all the jurors and neighbors believed him guilty.

♦ **Legal activity. Manors. Murder. Ordeals.** ♦

Select Pleas..., I, p. 1. *Translations...*, I, p. 30.

DENISE (la barbière)

1292 France

Listed as a barber of the parish of Saint-Germain-l'Auxerrois in 1292 Paris. Denise must have had a large clientele since she paid a relatively high tax of 30s.

♦ **Barbers. Land/property.** ♦

Géraud, *Paris sous...*, p. 31. Hughes, *Women...*, p. 140.
Wickersheimer, *Dictionnaire...*, p. 117.

DENYSE LA NORMANDE
1292 France
Listed in 1292 Paris survey as an innkeeper (hostelière)—taxed 6s.
♦ Innkeepers. ♦
Géraud, *Paris sous...*, p. 24.

DENISE DE PARTENAY
1467 France
An "old wife" (*sage femme*) who was arrested because the University of Paris medical faculty accused her of illegally treating patients.
♦ Doctors/empirics. Miscreants. University. ♦
Hughes, *Women...*, p. 146. Wickersheimer, *Dictionnaire...*, p. 117.

DENISE (la sainturière)
1456/7 France
Widow of belt-maker Germain Bon Ouvrier. Denise evidently took over his business on Saint Marcel lez Paris.
♦ Apparel–accessories. Land/property. Merchants. Widows. ♦
Comptes du..., p. 893.

DENISE LA VILEYN
fl. 1270s England
Around 1270, Denise gave her land and houses in Distaf Lane, London, to Henry de Greneford on agreement that he was to care for her until she died. Henry did not carry out his part in that arrangement, so Denise took him to court and won the case.
♦ Land/property. Legal activity. ♦
London Eyre...1276, p. 111.

DENISELLE GRENIÈRES
1459 France
Supposed heretic; arrested in 1459 and tortured to reveal names of other heretics. This was beginning of persecution known as *Vauderie of Arras.*
♦ Ecclesiastical courts–Inquisition. Heretics. Punishments. ♦
Cartellieri, *Court...*, pp. 191–193. McCall, *Medieval...*, pp. 253–254.
Robbins, *Encyclopedia...*, p. 30. Summers, *Geography...*, p. 385.

DENISETTE DE NÉREL
1380 France
Recorded as a licensed schoolteacher in 1380 Paris.
♦ Teachers. ♦
Decaux, *Histoire...*, p. 355.

DENISETTE DE PERIERS
1442/3 France
A fripperer—old clothes and rags dealer—in fifteenth century Paris at number ten, rue Petit Pont.
♦ **Less-affluent. Merchants–rags.** ♦
Comptes du..., pp. 308 & 393.

DEVORGUILLA OF GALLOWAY **[Dervorgilla Balliol]**
c. 1220–d.c. 1291 Scotland
Daughter and co-heiress of Margaret of Huntingdon and Alan, lord of Galloway (d.1234). Married John Balliol; son John Balliol, king of Scotland (1292–1296). Devorguilla founded Sweetheart Abbey in husband's memory and helped endow his foundation of Balliol College at Oxford.
♦ **Estate. Religious patrons. University. Widows.** ♦
Barrow, *Feudal...*, pp. 241n, 391 & n, 420. Bryant, *Age...*, pp. 133 & 370. *DNB*, vol. 16, p. 558. Duncan, *Scotland...*, pp. 402, 413, 586. Glover, *Story...*, p. 75. Mackie, *History...*, pp. 48 & 73. Mackie, *Short...*, pp. 45 & 83. Powicke, *Thirteenth...*, pp. 581n, 602 & n, 606n, 610n, 693n.

DERVORGILLA (O'RUAIRC) **[Derbforgaill O'Rourke, of Ireland]**
b. 1109–d. 1193 Ireland
Daughter of Murchadh O'Maeleachlainn. Wife of Tiernan O'Ruairc, prince of Brefni. In 1152, Dervorgilla was abducted (possibly at her own request) by Dermot MacMurrough; he returned her to her husband the next year. The resulting feud was part of the reason that Dermot invited Norman/English soldiers into Ireland. Devorgilla eventually entered a monastery at Mellifont.
♦ **Abduction. Rape. Religieuses. Religious patrons. Squabbles. Women of easy virtue.** ♦
Appleby, *John...*, pp. 28–9. Curtis, *Ireland...*, pp. 43 & 46. *DNB*, v.14, pp. 1160–1161. Lloyd, *Maligned...*, pp. 21 & 22. Orpen, *Ireland...*, I, pp. 55–58. Otway-Ruthven, *History...*, pp. 41 & 43. Richter, *Medieval...*, p. 131.

DHUODA **[Dodane]**
m. 824–850s France
Wife of Bernard, count of Septimania. Between 841 and 843, she wrote the *Manual of Dhuoda* for their son William (later duke of Aquitaine). This guidebook to manners and morals stressed loyalty to kings and reverence to God. It was also Dhuoda who, despite her husband's excesses, managed to control their estates and retain William's patrimony.
♦ **Childcare. Educated. Managers. Pawns. Teachers. Writers.** ♦
Cabaniss, *Judith...*, pp. 13, 15, 20, 22, 51–64, 180. Decaux, *Histoire...*, pp. 184–187. Dhuoda, *Manuel pour....* Dhuoda, *Le Manuel....* Dronke, *Women...*, pp. x, 5, 29, 35–55, 91, 109, 139, 290–293. Ennen, *Medieval...*, pp. 35–36. Marchand, "Frankish...," pp. 1–29. Pernoud,

La femme..., pp. 54–65. Riché, *Les Carolingiens...*, pp. 164 & 322. Thièbaux, *The Writings...*, pp. 65–80. Wemple, *Women...*, pp. 98–99 & 188.

DIEMUD [Diemuod; Diemudis]

Note: There may have been as few as two of these Diemud nun/bookmakers, or as many as five.

DIEMUOD OF NONNBERG

d. 1135 Austria

Abbess of Nonnberg; wrote and collected sermons using nuns as copyists.

♦ **Abbesses. Bookmaking. Writers–theology.** ♦

Carr, "Women...," pp. 6–7. Greer, *Obstacle...*, pp. 157, 158, 159.

DIEMUDIS OF WESSOBRUN [Diemueth]

c. 1057–1130 Germany

Nun at Bavarian establishment of Wessobrun. Copyist and illuminator of some forty-five manuscripts. She also translated works of church fathers.

♦ **Artists. Bookmaking. Educated. Models. Nuns. Writers–translators.** ♦

Anderson and Zinsser, *A History of...*, p. 201. Carr, "Women...," pp. 6–7. Greer, *Obstacle...*, pp. 157–159. Jourdain, "Memoire...," pp. 482–483.

DIEMUD OF WESSOBRUN

fl. c. 1110s Germany

Scribe at convent of Wessobrun. Signed her initials in missal she produced.

♦ **Bookmaking. Nuns.** ♦

Carr, "Women...," pp. 6–7. Greer, *Obstacle...*, pp. 157–159. Heinrich, *Canonesses...*, pp. 191–192.

DIONYSIA [Dionisia; Dyonisia]

DIONYSIA BALDEWYNE

1302 England

She was ostracized from her community in Exeter (1302) for having friends who were commonly believed to be witches.

♦ **Punishments. Witchcraft.** ♦

Ewen, *Witchcraft...*, p. 29.

DIONISIA BOTTELE

1369 England

A *femme sole* silkworker of London. She continued her craft after she married John Bottele, a London mercer. Dionisia then became a *femme couverte.*

♦ **Silkwork. Unmarried.** ♦

Calendar of Plea..., II, p. 111.

DIONYSIA DE MOUNTCHESNY **[Munchensy]**

c. 1260s–1290s England

An heiress herself, eventually much of her lands went to her cousin Aymer de Valence, earl of Pembroke. She commissioned Walter of Bibbesworth to write a textbook with which she could teach her daughter, Dionysia. This manual covered French, feminine household tasks, courtesy, etc. Lady Dionysia was also very pious; she founded a house of minoresses at Waterbeach in 1293.

♦ **Childcare. Estate. Patrons of literature. Religious patrons. Teachers.** ♦

Clark and Williams, "Impact...," p. 166. Jenkinson, "Mary...," pp. 404, 421, 422. Jourdain, "Memoire...," p. 490. Orme, *English...*, p. 72. Power, *Women...*, p. 83.

DIONISIA DE WODEMERSTHAM

1281 England

Servant of Henry Pistor of Clerkenwell. He left land and houses to her in recognition of her good services.

♦ **Bequests. Land/property. Servants.** ♦

Calendar of Wills..., I, p. 55.

DOBRAVKA

See—DUBRAVKA.

DODA

fl. 840s Germany

Slave/servant/concubine of Lothar I, king of Germany and Holy Roman Emperor. Doda was emancipated after she bore the king an illegitimate son. (Slave women were frequently freed if they bore sons for their masters.)

♦ **Mistresses. Servants. Slaves–freed.** ♦

Stafford, *Queens...*, p. 69.

DONELLA OF BOLOGNA

1271 Italy

Professional illuminator in 1271 Bologna.

♦ **Artists. Bookmaking.** ♦

Greer, *Obstacle...*, p. 160. Munsterberg, *History...*, p. 12.

DOROTHY [Dorotea; Dorothea]

DOROTEA BOCCHI [Dorotea Bucca]

c. 1390–c. 1450 Italy

Daughter of Professor Jean Bucca, Dorotea taught medicine and moral philosophy at University of Bologna. During her long tenure, her classes were very popular with the students, and her fame as a scholar spread rapidly.

♦ **Medicine. Scholars. Teachers. University.** ♦

Anderson and Zinsser, *A History of...*, p. 416. Greer, *Obstacle...*, pp. 209, 277, & 308. Ide, *Women...*, p. 148. Lipinska, *Histoire...*, pp. 151–152.

DOROTEA CARACCIOLO [da Crema]

1490s–1503 Italy

Daughter of Roberto Malatesta. She was wife of a Neapolitan *condottiere* when she was captured in 1500 by Cesare Borgia. Dorotea supposedly refused to leave Cesare; she returned to her husband some three years later.

♦ **Abduction. Women of easy virtue.** ♦

Cloulas, *Borgias...*, pp. 190–191. Fusero, *Borgias...*, pp. 230–231. Johnson, *Borgias...*, pp. 163–164.

DOROTEA GONZAGA

b. 1449–d. 1467 Italy

Daughter of †Barbara von Brandenburg and Ludovico II Gonzaga. Dorotea's sister Susanna was to be Galeazzo Maria Sforza's wife, but she developed back trouble. Dorotea was substituted as a proposed bride. After Galeazzo Maria broke the engagement, Dorotea died, reputedly of disappointment.

♦ **Divorce–betrothal. Educated. Handicapped–curved spine. Models. Pawns. Unmarried.** ♦

Breisach, *Caterina...*, pp. 5, 8, 9. Cartwright, *Beatrice...*, p. 18. Chamberlin, *World...*, pp. 190–191. Prescott, *Princes...*, p. 107.

DOROTHEA HINDREMSTEIN

1450s Switzerland

Wife of Burgis von Hindremstein; an "old wife" of Lucerne. She was convicted (c.1454) of practicing witchcraft, and sentenced in absentia (to death at the stake). Dorothea was supposedly an expert at cursing people and animals.

♦ **Doctors/empirics. Witchcraft.** ♦

Cohn, *Europe's...*, p. 242. Kieckhefer, *European...*, p. 131. Lea, *Materials...*, p. 253.

DOROTHY OF MONTAU **[St. Dorothea]**

1347–d. 1394 Germany

Married a swordsmith named Albert; all but one of their nine children died young. Her mystical trances irritated her husband, but she finally reformed him. After Albert died, Dorothy became a recluse at Marienwerder. Her canonization process was never completed, but she still has a cult in central Europe.

♦ **Anchoresses. Models. Mystics. Pilgrims. Saints–popular.** ♦

Attwater, *Dictionary...*, p. 83. Bynum, *Holy...*, pp. 55, 88, 112, 136–137, 203–205, 210, 221, 253, 256, 257, 275, 295. Ennen, *Medieval...*, pp. 155–156. Lagorio, "Continental...," pp. 173–174. Newman, *Sister...*, p. 256.

DOROTHY OF STRYGL

fl. 1390s Bohemia; Czechoslovakia

Borrowed money from wealthier townswoman, †Anna Harbatova. When bad economy made it impossible for Dorothy to repay her creditor, Anna forced her to become a prostitute in Prague to discharge the debt.

♦ **Banking–debtors. Prostitutes.** ♦

Klassen, *Nobility...*, p. 20.

DOUCE (I) OF PROVENCE, countess of Barcelona

[Dulce; Dolza; Dolca]

m. 1112 France

Daughter of Gerberga of Provence and Gilbert, count of Gévaudan. By her marriage in 1112 to Ramon Berenguer III, count of Barcelona (as his second wife), the county of Provence became a possession of the house of Barcelona.

♦ **Estate. Legal activity.** ♦

Bisson, *Medieval Crown...*, pp. 25, 26, 37. Chaytor, *History...*, I, p. 57. *Cambridge...*, VI, p. 406. *DBF*, v.2, p. 649 (mistakenly says that she married Ramon Berenguer I of Barcelona). Farreras et al., *Histoire...*, p. 264. Shahar, *Fourth...*, p. 131. Shneidman, *Rise...*, v.1, p. 190; v.2, pp. 294, 296.

DOUCE (II) OF BARCELONA, queen of Portugal **[Dulce]**

m. 1174–d. 1198 Portugal; Spain

Daughter of †Petronilla of Aragon and Ramon Berenguer IV, count of Barcelona (so she was the granddaughter of †Douce (I) of Provence). Douce married Sancho I of Portugal in 1174. Their son and heir was Alfonso II of Portugal; they also had daughter (St.) †Theresa of Portugal.

♦ **Genealogy. Queens.** ♦

Anselme, *Histoire...*, v.1, p. 575. Shneidman, *Rise...*, v.1, pp. 13 & 179. Stephens, *Story...*, pp. 57, 63, 70.

DOUCE (III) OF PROVENCE

m.c. 1175 France ; Spain

Granddaughter of †Douce (I) by Berenguer Ramon, count of Provence. Douce (III) should have inherited Provence, but her cousin Alfonso II of Aragon (originally Ramon Berenguer V of Barcelona) took these lands from her. She was engaged to Raymond VI, count of Toulouse, but there is some doubt that an actual marriage ever took place.

♦ **Divorce. Estate. Pawns. Poets/troubadours. Squabbles.** ♦

Bogin, *Women...*, p. 171. Chaytor, *History...*, p. 68. *DBF,* v.11, p. 649. Deminska, "Polish...," pp. 289, 290. Shneidman, *Rise...*, v.2, p. 297.

Note: We have numbered the above three women because all have similar names, all were related, and they are often confused with one another. The relationships of these women is further complicated by several name changes among their male relatives. Douce (I) and her husband Ramon Berenguer III had two sons: apparently Berenguer Ramon inherited Provence while Ramon Berenguer IV became count of Barcelona. These sons then each had a daughter named Douce. Furthermore, Ramon Berenguer IV had two sons, Ramon Berenguer V and Pedro. Ramon Berenguer V inherited Aragon from his mother †Petronilla of Aragon; he changed his name in 1164 to Alfonso II of Aragon. His brother then inherited Barcelona and changed his name to Ramon Berenguer.

(St.) DOUCELINE

b. 1214–d. 1274 France

Rich townswoman of Provence. At Marseilles in 1240, she founded a house of Beguines associated with the Franciscans. She was a fanatic about self-mortification and about men—she insisted that none of her Beguines ever speak to a male (except a confessor). Douceline herself corresponded with at least one man—Charles I of Anjou, king of Sicily.

♦ **Beguines. Educated. Mystics. Religious patrons. Saints. Unmarried. Virginity. Writers–letters.** ♦

Albanes, *La Vie de....* Bynum, *Holy...*, pp. 77, 133–34, 174, 204, 213, 250, 261, 269. Coulton, *Life...*, III, pp. 54–56. *DBF,* v. 11, pp. 649–650. Gout, *La Vie de....* McDonnell, *Beguines...*, pp. 375 & 400. Power, *Nunneries...*, p. 501. Power, *Women...*, p. 90.

DRAHOMIRA

fl. 900s Bohemia

Wife of Vratislav, duke of Bohemia. During time of religious transition (from pagan to Christian practices) she was an adamant believer in the old gods. Of her two sons, (St.) Wenceslas was raised by his grandmother, but Boleslav was taught in the pagan ways by Drahomira. She was presumably the guiding force behind the murders of both Wenceslas and his grandmother †Ludmila. Pious chroniclers wrote that Drahomira later disappeared into the ground during an earthquake.

♦ **Childcare. Heretics. Models. Murder. Teachers.** ♦

Cambridge..., III, p. 184. Daniel-Rops, *Church...*, p. 555. Maurice, *Bohemia...*, pp. 24, 25–26, 27. Riché, *Les Carolingiens...*, p. 257.

DRUSIANA (Sforza)

b. 1437–1460s Italy

Illegitimate daughter of Francesco Sforza, duke of Milan, and his favorite mistress, Colombina of Acquapendente. He had Drusiana legitimized by the pope and then married her to Jacopo Piccinino. Her husband was murdered around 1465.

♦ **Illegitimacy. Pawns.** ♦

Collison-Morley, *Sforzas...*, p. 85. Commynes, *Memoirs...*, II, p. 476. Prescott, *Princes...*, pp. 174–5.

DUBRAVKA OF BOHEMIA **[Saint Dombrowska; Dobravka]**

fl. 960s–980s Bohemia; Poland

Daughter of Boleslav I of Bohemia. In effort to secure alliance and Christianize his country, Mieszko I of Poland married Dubravka around 965. Their son Boleslas I succeeded Mieszko in 992. She helped her husband turn Poland into an ally of Germany, and she advised him to become a papal vassal.

♦ **Pawns. Popes. Religious patrons.** ♦

Cambridge..., III, p. 202. Daniel-Rops, *Church...*, p. 556. Davies, *God's...*, pp. 4, 85. Duckett, *Death...*, p. 96. Halecki, *History...*, pp. 10 & 15. Thompson, *Feudal...*, II, p. 641.

DULCIA DE BOSQUETO

fl.c. 1200s France

Catholic nun; left her abbey to become a *perfecta* with her Cathar son.

♦ **Cathars. Nuns.** ♦

Abels, "Participation...," p. 230.

DULCIA TRYE

1261/2 England

London prostitute; resident of whorehouse in parish of All Hallows Colemanescherche (the house belonged to Alice la Blunde).

♦ **Prostitutes.** ♦

London Eyre...1276, p. 34.

EADBURG OF MERCIA **[Eadburh of Wessex]**
m. 789–c. 810 England; France; Germany; Italy

Daughter of †Cynethryth and King Offa of Mercia; in 789 Eadburg married King Beorthric of Wessex. She has been stereotyped as a wicked queen; variously accused of poisoning husband, poisoning councillors, stealing the king's treasury, etc. When Beorthric died, Eadburg fled to Charlemagne's court, where she was given refuge and a nunnery. She was supposedly ousted for conducting illicit affairs at this convent. Eadburg may have wandered for some time before she became a recluse. It is sometimes said that Eadburg died while on a pilgrimage to Rome—a journey she supposedly undertook in order to atone for having accidentally poisoned her husband in the year 802.

♦ **Adultery. Anchoresses. Models. Murder. Pilgrims. Queens. Religieuses. Widows.** ♦

Boyesen, *Story...,* p. 41. *DNB,* v.6, p. 306. Farmer, *Oxford...,* p. 225. Stafford, *Queens...,* pp. 17–18, 31, 96, 104–105, 134, & 177.

(St.) EADBURGA OF WINCHESTER **[Eadburh; Edburga]**
b. 921–d. 960 England

Daughter of Edward the Elder, king of Wessex and England, and his third wife, †Eadgifu of Kent. Eadburga was a nun at Winchester abbey.

♦ **Educated. Nuns. Saints.** ♦

Attwater, *Dictionary...,* p. 87. Braswell, "St. Edburga...," pp. 292–333. *DNB,* v.6, p. 423. Farmer, *Oxford...,* p. 118. Lucas, *Women...,* p. 46. Wright, *Cultivation...,* p. 50.

EADGIFU OF ENGLAND, queen of France **[Edwige; Hedwig; Ogive]**
m.c. 917–950s England; France

Daughter of Aelflaed and King Edward the Elder of Wessex/England; second wife of Carolingian king, Charles III the Simple. Eadgifu's dower lands included Tusey on Maas. After Charles died, Eadgifu enlisted the aid of her half-brother, King Athelstan, to gain the throne for her son Louis IV d'Outremer (r.936–954). She obtained loyalty oaths from French lords, insisted on hostages, retrieved possession of Nantes, and defended Laon. Once Louis married †Gerberga of Saxony, however, Eadgifu retired from political activity and moved to the convent of

Laon. In 951, she left her nunnery and was escorted to Vermandois where she married Louis' enemy, Herbert III of Vermandois, count of Meaux. She may have simply been abducted, but Louis's angry reaction to his mother's remarriage indicates that Eadgifu herself chose to wed Herbert.

♦ **Abduction. Dowry/dower. Negotiators. Politics. Religieuses. Soldiers. Squabbles. Widows.** ♦

Anselme, *Histoire...,* v.1, pp. 36 & 49. *DNB,* v.6, p. 423. Decaux, *Histoire...,* p. 175. Duckett, *Death...,* p. 46. McKitterick, *Frankish...,* pp. 313, 315, 318, 338 n29, & Tables 7 & 9. Riché, *Les Carolingiens...,* p. 241. Sismondi, *French...,* pp. 423, 424, 439. Stafford, *Queens...,* pp. 102, 110, 115, 164, 168–169, 180, & 190. Vitalis, *Ecclesiastical...,* v.3, p. 80.

EADGIFU OF KENT, queen of England

c. 910s–d.c. 968 England

Daughter of Sighelm of Kent. Last (third) wife of Edward the Elder of Wessex/England. Patroness of English monastic reform movement; close ally of Dunstan, archbishop of Canterbury. Her son Edmund ruled (940–946), then his young sons Eadwig (Edwy) and Edgar were passed over so that Eadgifu's other son, Eadred became king (946–955). Eadgifu was a powerful force at the courts of both sons. She lost this power when her grandson, Eadwig, became king, so she and Dunstan vigorously opposed his rule.

♦ **Politics. Religious patrons. Widows.** ♦

DNB, v.6, p. 423. Lucas, *Women...,* p. 44. Stafford, *Queens...,* pp. 74, 103, 111, 121, 124–126, 143–149, 151, 157–159, 161, & 208. Stafford, "Sons...," pp. 92–93.

EADGIFU OF LOMINSTER **[Aelfgyva]**

fl. 1040s England

Abbess of Lominster in Herefordshire. In 1048, Earl Swegen abducted Eadgifu and kept her as his wife for a year.

♦ **Abbesses. Abduction.** ♦

Barlow, *Edward...,* pp. 91, 103, 303, 340. Cutler, "Edith...," pp. 226–227. Eckenstein, *Woman...,* p. 202. Schulenburg, "Women's...," p. 232.

EADGYFU OF ENGLAND, queen of Burgundy and Provence
[Edgine; Ogine; Egida; Adelaide of Wessex]

fl. 920s–940s England; France

Daughter of Edward the Elder, presumably by his third wife, †Eadgifu of Kent. Eadgyfu married Louis the Blind of Lower Burgundy, king of Burgundy and Provence (d.c.932).

♦ **Genealogy. Pawns. Widows.** ♦

Anselme, *Histoire...,* v.1, pp. 60–61. Cope, *Phoenix...,* p. 64. *DNB,* v.6, p. 423. Page, *Life in...,* p. 23.

(St.) EADGYTH (of England) **[St. Edith of Wilton]**

b. 962–d. 984 England

Daughter of nun, †Wulfthryth, and King Edgar of England. Entered Wilton as a baby. When upbraided by Bishop Aethelwold for indulging in extravagant luxuries and fine clothes, Eadgyth made a rude comment regarding his clothing and his morals. She was well educated in literary and artistic skills. Eadgyth refused all positions of temporal power, preferring to remain a regular nun. She was later venerated because her relics performed miraculous cures in the next century; the monk Goscelin wrote her Vita.

♦ **Charity. Educated. Illegitimacy. Models. Nuns. Relics. Saints.** ♦

Attwater, *Dictionary...*, p. 87. Barlow, *Edward...*, pp. 28n, 69, 233, 257, 264, 271n. *DNB*, v.6, pp. 368–369 & 387. Elkins, *Holy...*, pp. 6–9, 21, 24. Farmer, *Oxford...*, p. 120. Lucas, *Women...*, p. 46. Schulenburg, "Female...," pp. 113–114. Stafford, "Sons...," pp. 79 & 97.

EADGYTH Also see—EDITH.

EADHILD OF WESSEX

d. 937 England; France

Daughter of King Edward the Elder of Wessex/England and his second wife †Aelflaed. First wife of Hugh the Great, count of Paris and duke of the Franks; mother of Hugh Capet, king of France.

♦ **Genealogy.** ♦

Cambridge..., III, pp. 82, 366. *DNB*, v.6, p. 423. McKitterick, *Frankish...*, pp. 251, 314, Table 6. Page, *Life in...*, p. 23. Riché, *Les Carolingiens...*, p. 252.

EALDGYTH (of MERCIA), queen of Wales, queen of England **[Aldgyth]**

c. 1040s–1080s England; Wales

Daughter of Aelfgifu and Aelfgar, earl of Mercia (son of Leofric and †Godgyfu—Lady Godiva). Married (1) Gruffyd ap Llewelyn, king of North Wales (d.1063), and (2) Harold II, the last Saxon king of England. After Harold died at the battle of Hastings, Ealdgyth retired to her lands in Chester.

♦ **Dowry/dower. Queens. Widows.** ♦

Barlow, *Edward...*, pp. 207, 210, 243. Barlow, *Feudal...*, pp. 71, 79. Brown, *Normans...*, pp. 137, 141, 192. *Cambridge...*, III, p. 397; V, p. 497. *DNB*, v.8, pp. 1305 & 1309. Stenton, *Anglo-Saxon...*, p. 573. Williamson, *Kings...*, p. 41.

EBBA **[Ebba "the Younger"]**

fl. 850s–880s England

Daughter of Ethelred I, king of Northumbria. As abbess of Coldingham during brutal Viking raids, Ebba protected the chastity of her nuns by horribly disfiguring their faces. She was martyred with her nuns when the Vikings returned and burned her monastery.

♦ **Abbesses. Models. Murder. Virginity–protection.** ♦

Farmer, *Oxford...*, p. 117. McNamara and Wemple, "Sanctity...," pp. 102–3. Schulenburg, "Heroics...," pp. 47–48. Wright, *Cultivation...*, p. 50.

ECGWYNA

fl. 880s–900s England

Noblewoman of Wessex; concubine (and presumably later the first wife) of Edward the Elder. In 924 their son Athelstan succeeded to crown of Wessex and Mercia.

♦ **Genealogy. Mistresses.** ♦

DNB, v.6, p. 423. Stafford, *Queens...*, pp. 65 & 70. Stafford, "Sons...," p. 88. Williamson, *Kings...*, pp. 24 & 219.

EDELINE (la barbière)

1292 France

In 1292 Paris, Edeline paid 2s tax on her barber shop on the rue au Fuerre.

♦ **Barbers. Less-affluent.** ♦

Géraud, *Paris sous...*, p. 47. Hughes, *Women...*, p. 140.

EDELINE (la paonnière)

1292 France

Edeline was taxed 2s on her business—making and ornamenting hats with peacock feathers.

♦ **Apparel–hatmakers. Less-affluent.** ♦

Géraud, *Paris sous...*, p. 78.

EDELOT (la fourmagière)

1292 France

A cheesemonger, she was taxed 12d on her business at La Ferronnerie in the 1292 Paris survey.

♦ **Less-affluent. Provisioning–dairy.** ♦

Géraud, *Paris sous...*, p. 7.

EDITH Also see: EADGYTH

EDITH OF ENGLAND, queen of Germany **[Eadgyth]**
m. 929–d. 946 England; Germany

Daughter of Edward the Elder; her brother, King Athelstan of Wessex, married her to Otto of Saxony (later Otto I the Great, Holy Roman Emperor). Edith intervened in political decisions, especially when religious foundations were involved. †Hroswitha of Gandersheim wrote that Edith was a praiseworthy queen. Two children: Liudolf, duke of Swabia, and †Liutgard of Germany.

♦ **Models. Politics. Religious patrons.** ♦

Bryce, *Holy...*, pp. 84 & 142. Bullough and Storey, *Study...*, p. 23. *DNB*, v.6, p. 423. Duckett, *Death...*, pp. 58, 61, 71, & 94. Leyser, *Rule...*, pp. 2, 19, 42, 53 & 75. Robinson, *Readings...*, I, p. 247. Stafford, *Queens...*, pp. 6, 34–35, 56, 91, 104, 110, 124, & 189. Stubbs, *Germany...*, p. 93.

EDITH PAUMER
1305 England

Widow of Robert le Paumer of London. Her will, probated in 1305, gives an indication of possessions found in average "middle-class" urban home. The items detailed by Edith included: a girdle of green silk; gold buckles; brewing utensils; ewer and basin; brass pots and pans; cauldrons; tables with trestles; cups with silver stands; gold rings; many silver spoons; bed and silk mattress; and a chest in which to keep many of these goods.

♦ **Alewives. Bequests–personal items.** ♦

Calendar of Wills..., I, pp. 175–176.

EDITH OF SCOTLAND, queen of England
See—MATILDA OF SCOTLAND, queen of England.

EDITH SWAN-NECK
fl. 1050s–1060s England

Mistress of King Harold II of England; presumably the mother of his five children. Legend states that after the Battle of Hastings, Edith was the only person who could identify Harold's body. She supposedly searched the field for his corpse, and then had him properly buried.

♦ **Genealogy. Mistresses. Models.** ♦

Barlow, *Feudal...*, pp. 79, 90. Brown, *Normans...*, pp. 137, 141, 174. *DNB*, v.8, p. 1309. Williamson, *Kings...*, p. 41.

EDITH OF WESSEX, queen of England **[Eadgytha]**
b. 1025–d. 1075 England

Oldest daughter of †Gytha of Denmark and Earl Godwine of Wessex; married King Edward the Confessor in 1045. Well-educated at nunnery of Wilton; also adept at embroidery. Implicated in murder of Earl

Gospatric. She secured appointments and favors for her brother Tostig. In 1051, Edith was sent to a nunnery during trouble between husband and father, but she reappeared at court in 1052. She was instrumental in getting *Life of King Edward* written, a history as much about Edith and her family as it is about her husband.

♦ **Artistic clothwork. Educated. Estate. Models. Murder. Negotiators. Patrons of literature. Politics. Religieuses. Religious patrons. Squabbles. Widows.** ♦

Barlow, *Edward...*, pp. 25, 65, 71, 74, 80–85, 90...284–285, 291–300, 335, 340, 343. Barlow, *Feudal...*, pp. 56, 61, 64, 66, 68, 73, 77–78, 87. Blair, *Anglo-Saxon...*, pp. 102, 106–107, 108. Brown, *Normans...*, pp. 81, 82, 106 n217, 124–125, 135–136, 244. Campbell, *Anglo-Saxons,* pp. 221, 222, 224, 233. Cutler, "Edith...," pp. 222–231. Stafford, *Queens...*, pp. 4–6, 23, 25, 28–29, 39, 41, 54–55, 82, 97–98, 101–114, 129, 162, 171, 179, 189. Stenton, *Anglo-Saxon...*, pp. 419, 495, 557, 560, 570, 588. Stephenson, *Mediaeval...*, p. 215.

EILIKA OF SAXONY **[Elicke; Elike]**

fl.c. 1100 Germany

Daughter and co-heiress of Magnus Billung, duke of Saxony (d.1106). Eilika married Otto, count of Ballenstedt and Ascania. She built a castle for the support of a monastery at Goseck.

♦ **Estate. Religious patrons.** ♦

Cambridge..., V, pp. 152, 153. Fuhrmann, *Germany...*, p. 99. Leyser, *Medieval...*, p. 187. Stubbs, *Germany...*, p. 179.

ELA, countess of SALISBURY **[Eila]**

c. 1185–c. 1240s England

Daughter and heiress of William, earl of Salisbury. In 1198, King Richard I married Ela to his illegitimate half-brother, William Longsword. After William died in 1226, Ela devoted herself to the pious life. She built an Austin convent in Wiltshire in 1232, and became abbess in 1239.

♦ **Abbesses. Estate. Pawns. Religious patrons. Widows.** ♦

Appleby, *John...*, p. 193. *DNB,* v.12, pp. 115 & 117. Lloyd, *Maligned...*, p. 364. Paris, *Chronicles...*, pp. 185, 244, 259. Shahar, *Fourth...*, p. 97. Tyerman, *England...*, pp. 211, 403 n90.

ELEANOR/LEONOR

[Alianore; Aliénor; Eleanora; Leonora; Leonore]

LEONOR OF ALBUQUERQUE, queen of Aragon

b. 1374–d. 1435 Spain

Daughter of Beatrice of Portugal and Sancho, count of Albuquerque. Originally named Urraca, she became Leonor when she married Ferdinand I of Aragon in 1395. They had several children (including

Alfonso V of Aragon, b.c.1396), and she also took in others—like the orphaned Fadrique of Aragon, count of Luna. Widowed in 1416, Leonor continued to be an active quasi-political force, arranging marriages for her children, etc.

♦ **Childcare. Negotiators. Orphans. Prisons. Religieuses. Widows.** ♦

Bisson, *Medieval Crown...*, Table VI. Miron, *Queens...*, pp. 265–285. Ryder, *Kingdom...*, p. 27.

ELEANOR OF AQUITAINE, queen of France, queen of England

c. 1122–d. 1203 England; France

Daughter of †Aénor of Châtellerault and William X, count of Poitou. Eleanor was heiress of her troubadour grandfather, William IX, duke of Aquitaine. In 1137, she married Louis VII of France. When he joined the Second Crusade, Eleanor went along at the head of a group of women. Suspected of impropriety with her uncle, Raymond of Poitiers (at Antioch); Eleanor appeared eager for a divorce. Louis agreed because they had no sons. The marriage was annulled in 1152 and Eleanor quickly married Henry of Anjou (Henry II of England). Fond of power and an excellent politician, she often personally ruled Aquitaine for some sixty-five years. She also frequently served as regent for Henry II during the years 1155 through 1170. Unfortunately for Eleanor, she then proceeded to incite his sons to rebel. (Eleanor has also been accused of hiring a sorcerer to drain the blood from Henry II's mistress †Rosamund Clifford.) Her angry husband placed Eleanor under close constraint (or "house arrest") from around 1174 until 1189 when he died. (She was not so closely confined toward the end of this period.) Once released, from 1189 until 1199 Eleanor was the real ruler of England since she was regent for her son, Richard I, who was out of the country for nearly his entire reign. Eleanor released prisoners; set up a special treasury to obtain the thirty-five tons of silver needed to ransom Richard; advised him to do homage to the Holy Roman Emperor; negotiated a marriage for the dauphin Louis VIII with her granddaughter, †Blanche of Castile; arranged Richard's marriage with †Berengaria of Navarre, and even accompanied the young bride to Sicily to join Richard. Although Eleanor retired to Fontevrault, she later reappeared to support her youngest son, King John, against her grandson, Arthur of Brittany. "Power politics" was probably her first love, but Eleanor also supported the arts—particularly as a patroness of poets like Bernard de Ventadour, Bertran de Born, and †Marie de France. Eleanor was equally interested in medicine, establishing a hospital for the sick and wounded, and sometimes helping with their care.

♦ **Art patrons. Banking. Crusades. Divorce. Educated. Legal activity. Medicine. Models. Negotiators. Patrons of literature. Politics. Popes. Prisons. Rebellions. Regents. Religieuses. Religious patrons. Rulers. Soldiers. Squabbles. Widows. Witchcraft. Women of easy virtue.** ♦

Appleby, *John...*, pp. 3, 4, 8, 9, ... 99, 108, 115, 123. Baldwin, *Government...*, pp. 10, 12, 14, 78, 94, 191, 367. Barlow, *Feudal...*, pp. 201, 232, 284, 288, 304, 326–327, 331–332, 340, 342, 357, 369, 372, 373, 376, 380. Bingham, *Crowned...*, pp. 71, 77, 102, 124, 151. Bonner (ed.), *Songs...*, pp. 5, 6, 8, 19, 32, 82, 258–260, 278. Brown, "Eleanor...," pp. 9–39. *Chronicles...*, pp. 116, 117, 132, 140–143. Ennen, *Medieval...*, pp. 124, 139–142. Ewen, *Witchcraft...*, p. 73. Fox, *Literary...*, pp. 115, 121, 134, 275, 279, 358. Hallam (ed.), *Plantagenet...*, pp. 79, 80, 81, 82, 91...261, 262, 275, 276, 278. Haskins, *Normans...*, pp. 89, 118, 120, 123, 184. Kelly, *Eleanor....* Kibler (ed.), *Eleanor....* Lloyd, *Maligned...*, pp. 5–7, 8, 13...108, 115–6, 148, 306. Markale, *Aliénore....* Meade, *Eleanor....* Norwich, *Kingdom...*, pp. 121, 122, 125, 135, 139–141, 150, 364, 372–373. Pernoud, *Eleanor....* Richardson, "Letters and Charters...," pp. 193–213. Stephenson, *Mediaeval...*, pp. 233, 319–320, 322, 326, 376, 378–400. Warren, *Henry...*, pp. 42–45, 64, 65, 78 & n, 99 n2, 101, 103, 118–121, 138, 216, 260, 308, 328, 583, 598, 600–602. Winston, *Thomas...*, pp. 31–32, 51, 64, 70, 75, 83, 93–94, 225, 234–235, 302–303, 326.

LEONOR OF ARAGON, queen of Castile

c. 1360–d. 1382 Spain

Daughter of †Leonor of Sicily and Pedro IV of Aragon; married John I of Castile; mother of Henry III of Castile (b.c.1379).

♦ **Genealogy. Pawns. Queens.** ♦

Bisson, *Medieval Crown...*, p. 134. *Cambridge...*, VII, pp. 579, 590. Hillgarth, *Pere...*, pp. 23, 35, 56, 495, 518, 578–579, 581–583, 589, 591–592. Miron, *Queens...*, p. 195. Smith, *Spain...*, pp. 93–94. Stephens, *Story...*, p. 101.

LEONORA OF ARAGON, duchess of Ferrara

1460s–d. 1493 Italy

Daughter of Ferrante I of Aragon, king of Naples, and his first wife Isabella of Taranto. In 1473, Leonora married Ercole I d'Este, duke of Ferrara; their children included †Isabella and †Beatrice d'Este. Leonora often functioned as Ercole's regent in Ferrara. She was also noted for her piety and her interest in the moral aspects of humanism. Leonora was patroness of the famed printer and teacher, Aldo Manuzio.

♦ **Art patrons. Charity. Educated. Patrons of literature. Regents. Soldiers. Writers–letters.** ♦

Cartwright, *Beatrice...*, pp. 3, 4, 6, 28, 30, 34, 38, 50, 64, 73, 107, 166, 168, 172, 177, 181, 186, 190, 195, 198, 206–207. Chamberlin, *World...*, pp. 181, 182, 184, 194, 269. Chiappini, *Eleanora....* Gundersheimer, "Women...," pp. 43–65. Hughes, "Earrings...," p. 167. Johnson, *Borgias...*, pp. 74–75. Kristeller, "Learned...," p. 93. Prescott, *Princes...*, pp. 67, 72, 74, 167, 205, 208, 210–211, 216. Trevelyan, *Short...*, p. 183.

LEONOR OF ARAGON, queen of Navarre

c. 1430s–d.c. 1480 France; Spain

Daughter of †Blanche of Navarre and John II of Aragon. Married Gaston IV de Foix. Leonor inherited the kingdom of Navarre; she is presumed to have murdered her sister †Blanche of Aragon in order to insure this inheritance.

♦ **Estate. Murder. Queens.** ♦

Dezert, *Don Carlos...*, p. 110. Hillgarth, *Spanish...*, p. 540. Leroy, *La Navarre...*, p. 181.

LEONOR OF ARAGON, queen of Portugal

m. 1427–1440s Portugal; Spain

Daughter of †Leonor of Albuquerque and King Ferdinand I of Aragon; married Edward, king of Portugal. Their son Alfonso V succeeded in 1438 at age six. Leonor opposed the regency of Pedro (Alfonso's uncle), but her opposition achieved little. She finally retired to Castile.

♦ **Politics. Regents. Soldiers. Squabbles.** ♦

Dos Passos, *Portugal...*, pp. 101, 102, 104, 110, 113–114, 122. Miron, *Queens...*, p. 284. Nowell, *History...*, pp. 33–36. O'Callaghan, *History...*, pp. 560 & 566. Stephens, *Story...*, pp. 124, 130–132.

LEONOR OF ARAGON, countess of Toulouse

[Eleanor of Provence]

m.c. 1200 France; Spain

Sister of Pedro II of Aragon; around the year 1200, she became the fifth wife of Raymond, count of Toulouse. Leonor was a patroness of troubadours and also supported the Cathar heresy. She supposedly conducted a secret Cathar ceremony while the pope celebrated Mass in the same castle.

♦ **Cathars. Models. Patrons of literature. Popes.** ♦

Boutière and Schutz, *Biographies des...*, pp. 404–407. Heer, *Medieval...*, p. 168. Lejeune, "La Femme...," p. 207. Marks, *Pilgrims...*, p. 245. O'Callaghan, *History...*, p. 249.

ELEANORA DI ARBOREA **[Eleanor di Alborea]**

c. 1360s–d.c. 1404 Italy

Daughter of Mariano IV of Sardinia; married Brancaleone de Oria. When the Sardinians rebelled and killed her brother, Ugono, Eleanora quelled the revolt and defeated the Aragonese on the battlefield. She then ruled Sardinia for over twenty years, providing peace, financial prosperity, and an outstanding legal code (which remained in force until nearly 1900).

♦ **Legal activity. Rebellions. Rulers. Soldiers.** ♦

Bisson, *Medieval Crown...*, p. 124. Boulding, *Underside...*, p. 443. Brundage, *Law, Sex...*, p. 519 Day, "Status...," p. 307. Smith, *Spain...*, pp. 71–72.

ELEANOR BEAUCHAMP, duchess of Somerset **[Alianore]**

c. 1430s–1460s England

Daughter and co-heiress of †Elizabeth Berkeley and Richard Beauchamp, earl of Warwick; married Edmund Beaufort, duke of Somerset.

♦ **Estate. Legal activity. Politics.** ♦

Clive, *Sun...*, p. xxxvi. *DNB,* v.2, p. 31. Johnson, *Duke...*, pp. 93, 103, 120, 175, 184, 193. *Letters of Queen...*, pp. 117–119. Scofield, *Life...*, I, p. 274.

ELEANOR DE BOHUN, duchess of Gloucester **[Alianor]**

c. 1360s–d. 1399 England

Daughter and co-heiress of Humphrey de Bohun, earl of Hereford and Essex. In 1374, Eleanor married Thomas of Woodstock, duke of Gloucester. In her will (1399), Eleanor bequeathed a variety of books to her son Humphrey and daughters Isabel and †Anne (of Woodstock).

♦ **Bequests. Book-owners. Estate. Models.** ♦

Froissart, *Chronicles...*, II, pp. 171, 172, 183, 185, 187, 189. Given-Wilson, *English...*, p. 44. Hardy, *Philippa...*, p. 310. McFarlane, *Nobility...*, pp. 152, 207, & 236. Rawcliffe, *Staffords...*, pp. 12, 13, 14, 15, 16, 17, 95. Robertson, *Chaucer's...*, p. 208. Tuck, *Richard...*, pp. 8–9, 191. Tyerman, *England...*, p. 261.

ELEANOR OF BRITTANY **[Eleanora, Fair Maid of Bretagne]**

fl.c. 1190s–d. 1241 England; France

Daughter of †Constance of Brittany and Geoffrey (of England). After her brother Arthur was killed by her uncle, King John, Eleanor believed she was next heir to English throne. To prevent her from becoming the focal point of rebellions, she was captured and imprisoned in 1214. Although Eleanor was well-treated (furnished with servants, elegant dresses, and plenty of food and drink), she remained a prisoner until her death.

♦ **Pawns. Prisons. Squabbles. Unmarried. Writers–letters.** ♦

DBF, v.2, pp. 6–7. Green, *Letters...*, pp. 24–27. Guilloreau, "Aliénor de...". Kelly, *Eleanor...*, pp. 278, 305, 340, 372–3. Lloyd, *Maligned...*, pp. 31, 65, 128, 146, 232, 236–7. Weiss, "Castellan...," p. 249.

ELEANOR BUTLER

See—ELEANOR TALBOT.

LEONOR OF CASTILE, queen of Aragon

c. 1200s–d.c. 1250 Spain

Daughter of †Eleanor of England and Alfonso VIII of Castile; married Jaime I of Aragon in 1221. Although he repudiated Leonor, their son Alfonso was the heir of Aragon. Leonor retired to a convent, possibly her mother's foundation of Las Huelgas.

♦ **Divorce. Religieuses.** ♦

Bisson, *Medieval Crown...*, pp. 61, 62, 65. Hillgarth, *Spanish...*, p. 169. Miron, *Queens...*, pp. 93–100. O'Callaghan, *History...*, p. 346. Shneidman, *Rise...*, pp. 8, 12, 13, 15, 23, 129, 220, 309.

LEONOR OF CASTILE, queen of Aragon

c. 1310s–d.c. 1358 Spain

Daughter of Constance and Ferdinand IV of Castile. Leonor married Jaime of Aragon, but he repudiated her in order to embrace the religious life. Leonor then married Jaime's brother, Alfonso IV of Aragon, in 1329. She influenced Alfonso to favor their son Ferdinand over his son by previous wife, Pedro (IV). Her interference caused a rebellion among the nobles. After Alfonso died in 1336, Leonor fled to a nunnery to escape Pedro's wrath. She was finally murdered because of her continued plots on behalf of her son.

♦ **Divorce. Murder. Pawns. Politics. Rebellions. Religieuses. Squabbles. Widows.** ♦

Bisson, *Medieval Crown...*, pp. 96, 97, 101, 104, 105, 112, 113. Hillgarth, *Pere...*, pp. 4, 6–8, 12, 16, 49, 138–141 ... 424, 431, 450, 494, 499, 502, 541. Miron, *Queens...*, pp. 168–176. Shneidman, *Rise...*, pp. 78, 80–91, 97, 100, 342, 343, 353, 488, 492, 498 (this source mistakenly claims that her father was Sancho IV). Smith, *Spain...*, p. 70. Sturcken, "Unconsummated...," pp. 185–201.

ELEANOR OF CASTILE, queen of England

b. 1244–d. 1290 England; Spain

Daughter of Ferdinand III of Castile and his second wife, †Jeanne de Dammartin of Ponthieu; married Edward (I) of England in 1254. Although politically motivated, theirs was an exceptionally happy royal marriage. Before he succeeded to his father's throne, Eleanor accompanied Edward to Acre on Crusade and helped nurse him when he was wounded there. Eleanor appreciated style and comfort; she insisted that her floors be carpeted in the Spanish manner. Eleanor wove tapestries and hired people to copy and make books. Her high-handed and severe methods of extracting money made her very unpopular on her dower lands. But Eleanor could also be pious and charitable; at Easter she washed the feet of the poor, while Edward gave them money.

♦ **Artistic clothwork. Bookmaking. Charity. Crusades. Dowry/dower. Games–chess. Hunting. Managers. Models. Nurses. Patrons of literature.** ♦

Altamira, *Spain...*, pp. 230–231. Aubert, "Decorative...," p. 141. Belleval, *Les fiefs...*, p. 314. Bryant, *Age...*, pp. 27, 68, 93, 95, 111–112, 127–128, 185 & 248. *Calendar of Letter...*, A, p. 224. Green, *Letters...*, pp. 46–47. Hallam (ed.), *Four...*, pp. 80, 82, 114, 119, 126, 127, 132, 133. Labarge, *Simon...*, pp. 142 & 238. Parsons, *Court....* Pernoud, *La femme...*, pp. 248–257. Prestwich, *Edward...*, pp. 9–11, 15, 17, 66, 72, 78–9, 82, 91, 104, 112, 114, 117–120, 122, 123–5, 132, 150, 217, 226, 312, 316–7, 346, 355, 363, 567. *Select...Edward I*, I, pp. cxiii, clxviii, 104–105. Somerset, *Ladies...*, p. 4. Tyerman, *England...*, pp. 5, 117, 130, 232, 235, 237–8, 429 n99.

LEONOR OF CASTILE, queen of Navarre **[Eleanor de Trastamar]**
c. 1360–1380s Spain

Daughter of †Juana Manuel and Henry II of Castile. A war was caused by Leonor's broken engagement to Fernando I of Portugal (c.1372). She eventually married Charles III of Navarre.

♦ Divorce. Pawns. Queens. ♦

Hillgarth, *Spanish...*, p. 392. Leroy, *La Navarre...*, pp. 141 & 144. Stephens, *Story...*, pp. 101–103.

ELEANOR DE CLARE **[Alianore le Despenser]**
c. 1290s–1320s England

Daughter of †Joan of England (of Acre) and Gilbert de Clare, earl of Gloucester. Around 1306 Eleanor married Hugh le Despenser the younger. As lady-in-waiting to †Isabella of France, the young queen of England, Eleanor had her own retinue and chamberlain (possibly because she was the favorite niece of her uncle King Edward II).

♦ Estate. Servants–ladies. Writers–letters. ♦

Cambridge..., VII, pp. 421, 422, 520. *DNB,* v.4, p. 383. Fryde, *Tyranny...*, pp. 28, 30, 31, 41, 62, 241. Given–Wilson, *English...*, pp. 40–41. *Household...Isabella,* p. xiv. *Stonor...*, I, p. 3.

ELEANOR COBHAM
m.c. 1429–d.c. 1456 England

Lady-in-waiting to †Jacqueline of Hainault, duchess of Gloucester. Jacqueline's husband, Humphrey of Gloucester, fell in love with Eleanor, so he divorced Jacqueline and married Eleanor. In 1441, she was charged with practicing sorcery in order to magically kill the king. Eleanor was convicted, forced to do public penance, and then imprisoned for the rest of her life. Her trial was largely a political ploy designed to bring about the downfall of her powerful husband.

♦ Divorce. Models. Prisons. Punishments. Servants. Witchcraft. Women of easy virtue. ♦

Bellamy, *Crime...*, p. 61. Butt, *History...*, pp. 511, 527–528, 530, 533. Ewen, *Witchcraft...*, pp. 37–38. Griffiths, "Trial...". Holmes, *Later...*, p. 213. Jacob, *Fifteenth...*, pp. 226, 482, 485, 486. Kieckhefer, *European...*, p. 126. Kittredge, *Witchcraft...*, pp. 81–84. Lea, *History...*, III, pp. 467, 468. Myers, "Captivity...," pp. 272–277. Robbins, *Encyclopedia...*, pp. 98–9, 162.

ELEANOR LE DESPENSER

See—ELEANOR DE CLARE.

ELEANOR OF ENGLAND, countess of Bar
b. 1265–d. 1298 England; France

Daughter of †Eleanor of Castile and Edward I of England. In 1293 Eleanor married Henry III, count of Bar.

♦ **Estate. Genealogy. Pawns.** ♦

Cambridge..., VII, p. 323. *DNB*, v.6, p. 456. Powicke, *Thirteenth...*, pp. 118n, 257–258, 263–264, 668n, 672n. Prestwich, *Edward...*, pp. 125–128, 315, 320, 325, 389. Williamson, *Kings...*, p. 72.

ELEANOR OF ENGLAND, queen of Castile **[Leonor]**

b. 1162–d. 1214 England; Spain

Daughter of †Eleanor of Aquitaine and Henry II of England. Married around 1177 to Alfonso VIII of Castile; dowry included duchy of Gascony. Her daughters included †Berenguela of Castile and Leon, †Blanche of Castile, queen of France, †Urraca of Castile, queen of Portugal, and †Leonor of Castile, queen of Aragon. Eleanor founded the abbey of Las Huelgas de Burgos. She was also interested in literature and music; she persuaded her husband to make his court a cultural center.

♦ **Dowry/dower. Models. Music. Patrons of literature. Religious patrons.** ♦

Bingham, *Crowned...*, pp. 71–72, 150 & 151. Fuhrmann, *Germany...*, pp. 159 & 168. Kelly, *Eleanor...*, pp. 103, 159, 289, 328, 340, 355, 358, 385. Livermore, *History...*, pp. 113–114 & 137. Marks, *Pilgrims...*, pp. 176 & 210. Pernoud, *Eleanor...*, pp. 102, 194, 253, 255, 258–9. Winston, *Thomas...*, pp. 110 & 225.

ELEANOR OF ENGLAND, countess of Guelders

b. 1318–d. 1355 England; Netherlands

Daughter of †Isabella of France and Edward II of England. Married around 1332 to Reginald II, count of Guelders. After his death, Eleanor was regent of Guelders.

♦ **Leprosy–suspected. Pawns. Regents. Widows.** ♦

DNB, v.6, p. 466. Haines, *Church...*, pp. 32–33. Hardy, *Philippa...*, pp. 20, 35, 54, 61, 72, 77–8, 104, 142–3. Jusserand, *Wayfaring...*, p. 99. Williamson, *Kings...*, p. 76.

ELEANOR OF ENGLAND, countess of Leicester

See—ELEANOR DE MONTFORT, countess of Leicester.

LEONOR DE GUZMAN

c. 1320s–d.c. 1352 Spain

Although married to †Maria of Portugal, Alfonso XI of Castile was much more attached to Leonor—his mistress and the mother of ten of his children. After Alfonso died, his wife supposedly imprisoned and then executed Leonor. Enrique (Henry), count of Trastamara, who usurped the throne from Alfonso's legitimate son and heir, Pedro I the Cruel, was one of Leonor's sons by Alfonso.

♦ **Mistresses. Murder. Prisons.** ♦

Armitage-Smith, *John...*, p. 36. *Cambridge...*, VII, pp. 574, 575. Hardy, *Philippa...*, pp. 165, 190, 199. Jamison, *Life...*, I, pp. 246–247, 250–253. Livermore, *History...*, pp. 143, 144. Smith, *Spain...*, p. 72.

ELEANOR OF LANCASTER

fl. 1330s–1350s England

Daughter of †Maud Chaworth and Henry, earl of Lancaster. Married (1) John Beaumont and (2) (c.1345) the recently divorced Richard, earl of Arundel.

♦ **Genealogy.** ♦

DNB, vol. 9, p. 552. Hardy, *Philippa...,* pp. 110–111. Rosenthal, *Nobles...,* pp. 177–178.

LEONOR OF LANCASTRE, queen of Portugal

1458–1525 Portugal

Daughter of Beatrix of Portugal and Ferdinand, duke of Viseu. Married John II of Portugal in 1471; their son and heir, Alfonso, died young. After John's death, Leonor influenced the line of succession, managing to obtain the throne for her brother Manuel. She was patroness of poet Gil Vicente.

♦ **Patrons of literature. Politics. Regents. Widows.** ♦

Anselme, *Histoire...,* v.1, p. 599. Dos Passos, *Story...,* pp. 161, 263. Nowell, *History...,* pp. 51, 62–63.

LEONOR LOPEZ **[Leonor Lopez Carrillo]**

c. 1350s–1400s Spain

Noblewoman of Cordoba; Leonor dictated a history/biography of her family called the *Memorias.* She and her relatives had been imprisoned by Henry II Trastamara of Castile because they had fought on the side of Pedro I the Cruel. Her father (Martin Lopez) and most of her family died in prison of plague. Leonor and her husband, Juan Ferrandez de Henestrosa, were eventually released. For a short time, Leonor was lady-in-waiting to †Catherine of Lancaster, queen of Castile. After a dispute with the queen, Leonor retired to a convent.

♦ **Plague. Politics. Prisons. Religieuses. Servants–ladies. Writers.** ♦

Ayerbe-Chaux, "Las Memorias...," pp. 11–33. Petroff, *Medieval...,* pp. 329–334. Snow, "Spanish...," p. 321.

ELEANOR DE MONTFORT, countess of Leicester
[Eleanor of England]

b. 1215–d.c. 1274 England; France

Daughter of †Isabelle of Angoulême and King John of England. Eleanor was the second wife of William Marshal, earl of Pembroke. After his death (1231), Eleanor took a vow of perpetual chastity, yet she soon married Simon de Montfort (c.1238). The marriage was annulled because of her previous vow. Simon had to go to Rome to obtain papal dispensation to regularize their marriage. When Simon died at Evesham heading up the baronial revolt, Eleanor smuggled her remaining children and a fortune in gold into France. She retired to convent of Montargis.

♦ **Crusades. Educated. Managers. Models. Rebellions. Religieuses. Virginity–vows. Widows. Writers–letters.** ♦

C.P., v.10, pp. 365–368. Gies, *Women...,* p. 120–142, 162, 188, 216, & 231. Labarge, *Baronial...,* pp. 49, 50, 51, ... Labarge, *Simon...,* pp. 69–70, 86, 100, ... Lloyd, *Maligned...,* pp. 353, 395. *Manners and Expenses...,* pp. vi, xii, xiii, xv, & xvii. Mertes, *English...,* pp. 14, 68, 82, 85. Paris, *Chronicles...,* p. 129. Prestwich, *Edward...,* pp. 29, 31, 34, 55, 64.

ELEANORA DE MONTFORT, princess of Wales

b. 1252–d. 1282 England; France; Wales

Daughter of Simon de Montfort and †Eleanor of England, countess of Leicester (Eleanor de Montfort, see above). Escaped to France with her mother after her father died at Evesham. Lived at convent of Montargis until she sailed to Wales for her wedding to Llewellyn ap Gruffydd, prince of Wales. Edward I captured her and her brother Amauric. For about two years, Eleanora was held captive to force Llewellyn to swear fealty to the English king. The couple finally married in 1278, and Eleanora exerted all her influence to keep peace between Edward I and Llewellyn. She died in 1282 giving birth to a daughter, †Gwenllian.

♦ **Abduction. Childbirth. Educated. Negotiators. Pawns. Prisons. Religieuses. Writers–letters.** ♦

Barrow, *Feudal...,* pp. 351, 352, 419. Bryant, *Age...,* pp. 61 & 66. *DNB,* v.12, p. 19. Green, *Letters...,* pp. 51–57. Gies, *Women...,* pp. 135, 140–142. Labarge, *Simon...,* pp. 100, etc.... Prestwich, *Edward...,* pp. 105, 175–176, 204.

ELEANOR NEVILLE, lady Lumley

fl. 1380s–1400s England

Daughter of John, lord Neville of Raby; sister of Ralph Neville, first earl of Westmoreland; wife of Sir Ralph Lumley (d.1400); mother of Sir John Lumley; aunt of †Eleanor Neville, countess of Northumberland.

♦ **Genealogy.** ♦

C.P., v.8, p. 270. *DNB,* v.12, p. 274. Jacob, *Fifteenth...,* p. 328.

ELEANOR NEVILLE, countess of Northumberland

fl. 1400s–1430s England

Daughter of †Joan Beaufort and Ralph Neville, earl of Westmoreland. Married (1) Richard le Despenser and (2) Henry Percy II, earl of Northumberland. She had some twelve children by her second husband.

♦ **Genealogy. Managers.** ♦

DNB, v.15, pp. 850 & 851. Jacob, *Fifteenth...,* pp. 321, 464. Johnson, *Duke...,* p. 10. Scofield, *Life...,* I, p. 6.

ELEANOR NEVILLE, lady Stanley

fl. 1450s–1470s England

Daughter of †Alice Montagu and Richard Neville, earl of Salisbury; wife of Thomas, lord Stanley.

♦ **Genealogy.** ♦

Bennett, "Good...," p. 14. *DNB,* v.14, p. 282; v.18, p. 965.

ALIÉNOR DE POITIERS

fl.c. 1440s France

Daughter of a Portuguese countess, Aliénor was brought up at the court of Burgundy. She later wrote *Les honneurs de la Cour,* an etiquette book about the manners and observances of the highest nobility. She was particularly outraged by encroachments of the lower classes upon the prerogatives of royalty.

♦ **Servants. Writers–etiquette.** ♦

Cartellieri, *Court...,* pp. 70–72. Huizinga, *Waning...,* pp. 36, 43, 106, 206. Willard, "Christine...," pp. 104, 108.

LEONOR OF PORTUGAL, queen of Aragon [Elinor]

d. 1348 Portugal; Spain

Daughter of †Beatrice of Castile and Alfonso IV of Portugal. Around 1347, Leonor became the second wife of Pedro IV of Aragon (after his first wife †Marie of Navarre died). Leonor died of the pestilence about a year later.

♦ **Plague. Queens.** ♦

Hillgarth, *Pere...,* pp. 5, 50–51, 104, 396, 420–422, 424, 427, 429, 439, 446. Shneidman, *Rise...,* pp. 488, 493, 498.

ELEANOR OF PROVENCE, queen of England

b. 1221–d. 1291 England; France

Daughter of †Beatrice of Savoy and Raymond Berengar, count of Provence. In 1236, Eleanor married Henry III of England; mother of Edward I. Eleanor's numerous relatives and Provençal retainers made her unpopular with many of her English subjects. Nevertheless, she and Henry had a happy marriage. They were well-suited since both were more interested in artistic endeavors than in governmental responsibilities. She encouraged French vernacular literature and ideals of courtly manners and love at the English court. In fact, Eleanor was a poet herself; when young she had written a courtly romance. After Henry died, she retired to Amesbury convent.

♦ **Art patrons. Patrons of literature. Religieuses. Widows. Writers–letters and poetry.** ♦

Armitage-Smith, *John...,* p. 89. Biles, "Indomitable...," pp. 113–131. Bréquigny, *Lettres de rois...,* pp. 245, 264–265, 306–307. Bryant, *Age...,* pp. 25, 112, 113, 123, 129 & 131. *Calendar of Letter...,* A, p. 90. Gardiner, *English...,* p. 61. Green, *Letters...,* pp. 34–35. Hallam (ed.),

Four..., pp. 56, 58, 59, 78, 96. *London Eyre...1276,* pp. 99, 103, 114. Prestwich, *Edward...*, pp. 4, 6–10, 20–21, 34–35, 37, 39–40, 45, 54–56, 83, 89, 122–123, 127, 132, 346, 355. Previte-Orton, *Outlines...*, p. 333. *Select...Edward I,* I, pp. xxxvii, cx, 7–9, 114–115, 139–140. Somerset, *Ladies...*, p. 4. Thompson, *Literacy...*, p. 180.

LEONOR OF SICILY, queen of Aragon

m.c. 1348–d. 1375 — Italy; Spain

Sister of King Frederick IV of Sicily; third wife of Pedro IV of Aragon (after his second wife †Leonor of Portugal died). Leonor of Sicily had much influence with her husband, and she occasionally served as his regent.

♦ **Estate. Politics. Prisons. Regents.** ♦

Bisson, *Medieval Crown...*, pp. 109, 110, 116, 120, 126. Hillgarth, *Pere...*, pp. 5–6, 22–23, 51, 113, 440, 449, 451, 484, 485, 488, 518, 544, 556, 583, 587, 589–591, 595. Hillgarth, *Spanish...*, p. 350. Miron, *Queens...*, pp. 187–196 & 201. Shneidman, *Rise...*, pp. 488, 493, 498.

ELEANOR STUART, duchess of Austria
[Eleanor of Scotland; Eleonore von Österreich]

1433–1480 — Austria; France; Scotland

Daughter of †Joan Beaufort and James I of Scotland; married Duke Sigismund of Austria in 1449. Eleanor translated a French novel, *Pontus and Sidonia,* into German.

♦ **Educated. Regents. Writers.** ♦

DNB, v.10, p. 573. Frederiksen, *Women...*, p. 65. Harksen, *Women...*, p. 54. Schoenfeld, *Women...*, p. 202.

ELEANOR TALBOT **[Lady Eleanor Butler]**

b. 1435–d. 1468 — England

Daughter of †Margaret Beauchamp and John Talbot, earl of Shrewsbury; around 1448 she married Sir Thomas Boteler. Possibly betrothed to Edward IV before he secretly married †Elizabeth Woodville. Richard III used the story to make Edward's sons seem illegitimate, and thus ineligible for the throne of England.

♦ **Divorce–betrothals. Models.** ♦

Butt, *History...*, pp. 618, 619, 626. Clive, *Sun...*, pp. 96 & 287–289. *DNB,* vol. 19, p. 323. Jacob, *Fifteenth...*, pp. 618 & 619. Scofield, *Life...*, II, p. 161. St. Aubyn, *Year...*, pp. 155–156, 158.

LEONOR TELES, queen of Portugal **[Leonor Telles de Meneses]**

c. 1350s–d. 1386 — Portugal

Wife of John Lorenzo da Cunha. Fernando I of Portugal fell in love with Leonor. The king drove her husband into exile, helped her get a divorce, and then made her his wife. After Fernando died in 1383, their daughter †Beatrix was to inherit, but she was underage and was married to John I, the king of Castile. Leonor therefore held the regency for Beatrix. Leonor's lover, John Ferandes Andeiro, count of Ourem, soon infuriated the Portuguese nobles to such an extent that many supported a coup by John of Avis—who became King John I of Portugal.

♦ **Adultery. Divorce. Regents. Rebellions. Soldiers. Widows.** ♦

Armitage-Smith, *John...*, pp. 101, 262. Froissart, *Chronicles...*, I, pp. 338, 340–344. Nowell, *History...*, pp. 17–18. Roche, *Dona...*, pp. 30–32, 34, 36, 53, 58. Stephens, *Story...*, pp. 101, 103–105, 107, 109, 110.

ELEANORA OF VERMANDOIS **[Aliénor]**

c. 1160s–d.c. 1213 Flanders; France; Netherlands

Daughter of Raoul I, count of Vermandois and his second wife †Petronilla of Aquitaine. Eleanora married (1) Geoffrey of Hainault, count of Ostrevant; (2) William IV, count of Nevers; (3) Mathew of Alsace, count of Flanders and Boulogne; and (4) Matthew III, count of Beaumont sur Oise (d.1208). Eleanora claimed Vermandois when her sister, †Isabella of Vermandois, died in 1182. She finally received Valois and St. Quentin in return for giving up her claims to Vermandois.

♦ **Charity. Estate. Squabbles.** ♦

Anselme, *Histoire...*, v.2, p. 722. Baldwin, *Government...*, pp. 15, 24, 25, 187, 200, 255, 278. *Cambridge...*, VI, p. 293. Fawtier, *Capetian...*, pp. 112, 113, 114.

ELEANOR DE WENDALE

1329 England

In 1329 Broughton village court, Eleanor was fined for regrating bread.

♦ **Manors. Miscreants. Provisioning–bakers.** ♦

Britton, *Community...*, pp. 90–91, 220, 268 n45.

ELEANOR WEST **[Lady Alianore Clifton]**

fl. 1370s–1400 England

Daughter of Sir Thomas and Lady Alice West of Hinton Marcel in Hampshire. Eloped with less wealthy Nicholas Clifton. This caused her father to petition for a change in statutes to allow male relatives to prosecute rape cases—even when the woman involved had consented to intimacy. Clifton had to buy a pardon to avoid being executed. Thereafter, women had virtually no protection under English law against rapists. Although Sir Thomas disowned her, her mother left Eleanor money and personal property in her will.

♦ **Bequests–personal items. Estate. Rape.** ♦

Fifty Earliest..., pp. 4–10. Post, "King's...," p. 160.

ELENA BAROUN

fl. 1292–1313 England

In village of Wistow she was constantly in trouble; cited for adultery, brewing, butchering infractions, forestalling, etc. She was finally prohibited the vill for her incorrigible behavior. In 1313, Ivo by Hirst was fined in Warboys village court for receiving Elena.

♦ **Adultery. Alewives. Manors. Miscreants. Provisioning–butchers. Punishments.** ♦

Hogan, "Medieval Villainy...," pp. 190–191.

ELENA OF MOSCOW, grand duchess of Lithuania, queen of Poland **[Helen]**

m. 1495 Lithuania; Poland; Russia

Daughter of Ivan III of Moscow; in 1495 she married Grand Duke Aleksandr of Lithuania as part of a peace treaty. Elena caused problems by her absolute refusal to convert to, or even tolerate, Roman Catholicism. Aleksandr and Elena became king and queen of Poland around the year 1500.

♦ **Pawns. Politics. Religieuses.** ♦

Davies, *God's...*, pp. 139, 141. Pares, *History...*, p. 98 Vernadsky, *Russia...*, pp. 14, 86–89, 93 & 94.

ELENA TAILLOUR

1292 England

Daughter of Sabine and Philip le Taillour of London. She and her sisters, Margery and Johanna, were nuns at Clerkenwell.

♦ **Bequests. Nuns.** ♦

Calendar of Wills..., I, p. 107.

ELICKE

See—EILIKA OF SAXONY.

ELISENDA DE MONCADA, queen of Aragon **[Elisen]**

m. 1322–d. 1364 Spain

Daughter of Elisenda de Pinos and Pedro de Moncada; married Jaime II of Aragon in 1322 for alliance purposes (his third wife). She had problems with Jaime's son by an earlier wife.

♦ **Pawns. Religious patrons. Squabbles.** ♦

Bisson, *Medieval Crown...*, pp. 96, 100, 125. Hillgarth, *Pere III...*, pp. 144, 173, 219, 372. Miron, *Queens...*, pp. 155–156. Shneidman, *Rise...*, pp. 66, 73, 101.

ELISIA HUNDESDICH

1307 England

Wife of William de Hundesdich of London. In his will (1307), William left his craft implements to Elisia so that she could continue their businesses of brewing and tanning.

♦ **Alewives. Bequests. Tanners. Widows.** ♦

Calendar of Wills..., I, pp. 186–187.

ELIZABETH [Elisabeth; Elizabetta] Also see: ISABELLE

ELIZABETH, lady ABERGAVENNY **[Bergavenny]**
c. 1450s–d.c. 1500 England

Her first three husbands—Robert Bassett, Richard Naylor, and John Stokker—were all wealthy merchants of London, and she received legacies from all. After John Stokker, a London draper and alderman, died in 1485, Elizabeth married yet again, but this time she married a member of the nobility—George Neville, lord Abergavenny.

♦ **Bequests. Dowry/dower. Land/property. Merchants. Widows.** ♦

C.P., v.1, p. 31. Hindley, *England...*, pp. 153–154 (she is mistakenly called Joan here). Thrupp, *Merchant...*, pp. 266 & 367.

ELIZABETH OF AUSTRIA, queen of Poland **[Hapsburg]**
m. 1454–1490s Austria; Germany; Poland

Daughter of †Elizabeth of Luxembourg and Albert Hapsburg of Austria; married Casimir Jagiello, king of Poland. A political influence on her husband, Elizabeth also believed her sons should inherit the Empire from her father. Later, used her troops to secure succession in Poland for her son Jan Olbracht (King John I).

♦ **Politics. Queens. Soldiers.** ♦

Davies, *God's...*, p. 256. Halecki, *Poland...*, pp. 95 & 96. Reddaway et al, *Cambridge...*, pp. 243, 249, 250, 257, 258.

ELIZABETH BADLESMERE
fl. 1310s–1330s England

Daughter and co-heiress of Giles, lord Badlesmere. Elizabeth married (1) Edmund Mortimer, and (2) in 1335, William de Bohun (later earl of Northampton).

♦ **Estate.** ♦

DNB, v.2, p. 772. Given-Wilson, *English...*, p. 380.

ELIZABETH BERKELEY, countess of Warwick
c. 1400–d. 1422 England

Daughter of Thomas, lord Berkeley; married Richard Beauchamp, fifth earl of Warwick.

♦ **Childbirth. Estate. Genealogy.** ♦

DNB, vol. 2, p. 31. Given-Wilson, *English...*, pp. 143–144. Jacob, *Fifteenth...*, pp. 329 & 343. McFarlane, *Nobility...*, pp. 110 n2 & 193. Ross, "Household...," pp. 81–105. Warren, *Anchorites...*, p. 203.

ELIZABETH OF BOHEMIA
c. 1300–d. 1330 Bohemia; Germany; Luxembourg

Daughter of King Wenceslaus II of Bohemia; married John of Luxembourg around 1309; son Wenceslaus became King Charles of Bohemia and then Holy Roman Emperor. In 1311, Elizabeth and John were crowned king and queen of Bohemia. Henry of Lipa fomented trouble between the couple, and Elizabeth finally fled to Bavaria. The people of Prague secured her return in 1325. Elizabeth helped victims of plague, endowed monasteries, protected the church, and was much more popular with the people of Bohemia (and with her son) than was John, who viewed Bohemia as a mere tax base.

♦ **Plague–help during. Prisons. Religious patrons. Rulers. Squabbles.** ♦

Cambridge..., VII, pp. 94, 95, 109, 117, 156, 157, 160. Harrsen, *Cursus...*, p. 56. Leuschner, *Germany...*, p. 104. Lutzow, *Bohemia...*, pp. 58–60. Maurice, *Bohemia...*, pp. 119, 123, 125–127.

ELIZABETH OF BOSNIA, queen of Hungary and Poland **[Elizabeth Kotromanić]**

c. 1339–d. 1385 Hungary; Poland

Wife of Louis of Anjou, king of Hungary and Poland. When he died in 1382, she negotiated a treaty securing the crown of Poland for their younger daughter, †Jadwiga. She also helped her older daughter †Maria rule Hungary. During civil war, Elizabeth was captured and then murdered. Some chroniclers saw this as an appropriate fate because she supposedly had Charles of Durazzo murdered to prevent him from taking the throne away from her daughter.

♦ **Negotiators. Murder. Prison. Regents. Widows.** ♦

Davies, *God's...*, p. 65. Fügedi, *Castle...*, p. 123. Halecki, *Poland...*, p. 66. Pamlényi, *History...*, pp. 78 & 620. Reddaway et al, *Cambridge...*, p. 195. Stubbs, *Later...*, pp. 143 & 165.

ELIZABETH BOURCHIER

c. 1400–d. 1433 England

Daughter and sole heiress of Idoine Lovey and Bartholomew, lord Bourchier (d.1409). Married (1) Hugh Stafford (d.1420) and (2) Sir Lewis Robessart (d.1431). After his death, she was petitioned by some of her tenants to redress wrongs committed by her high-handed husband.

♦ **Estate. Managers. Widows.** ♦

C.P., v.2, pp. 247–248. McFarlane, *Nobility...*, pp. 49 & 221.

ELIZABETH BRYENE

c. 1390 England

See—ALICE DE BRYENE and MAUD LOVELL, lady Arundel.

♦ **Genealogy.** ♦

ELIZABETH DE BURGH, countess of Ulster

c. 1332–d. 1363 England; Ireland

Daughter and sole heiress of †Matilda of Lancaster and William de Burgh, earl of Ulster. In 1342, Elizabeth married Lionel, duke of Clarence; daughter †Philippa of Clarence (married Edmund Mortimer, earl of March). Geoffrey Chaucer was a page in Elizabeth's household in the later 1350s. Elizabeth was heiress of her grandmother, †Elizabeth de Clare (see below), another great heiress. (She is often confused with this grandmother.)

♦ Estate. Genealogy. Managers. ♦

Armitage-Smith, *John...*, pp. 10, 24 & 25. Brewer, *Chaucer...*, pp. 107 & 145. Bryant, *Age...*, pp. 324–325. *Calendar of Plea...*, I, p. 153 n2. Curtis, *Ireland...*, pp. 105, 111, 113 & 122. *DNB,* v.3, pp. 331. Gardner, *Life...*, pp. 23, 90–93, 95–97, 105, 108, 109, 116, 118, 135, 271. Given-Wilson, *English...*, pp. 41–42. Hardy, *Philippa...*, pp. 133–5, 183, 250–1, 269, 271, 273, 293, 301. McFarlane, *Nobility...*, p. 213. Richter, *Medieval...*, pp. 163 & 174.

ELIZABETH DE BURGO, queen of Scotland **[Elizabeth de Burgh]**
m.c. 1304–1327 Ireland; Scotland

Daughter of Richard the Red de Burgo (de Burgh), earl of Ulster. Second wife of King Robert (I) de Bruce; son David (II). During fighting between England and Scotland, Elizabeth was captured and confined. She was well-treated, and later released.

♦ Genealogy. Prisons. Queens. ♦

Allan, "Historical...," p. 313. *DNB,* v.3, p. 128. Powicke, *Thirteenth...*, p. 716 & n. Richter, *Medieval...*, p. 153. Williamson, *Kings...*, p. 229 & Table 18.

ELIZABETH DE CLARE **[Elizabeth de Burgh, lady of Clare]**
b. 1293–d. 1360 England; Ireland

Daughter of †Joan of England (of Acre) and Gilbert de Clare; co-heiress of her brother Gilbert de Clare. Married (1) John de Burgh; (2) Theobald de Verdon (who may have abducted her); and (3) Roger Damery (d'Amory; d.1322). Among her many charitable donations, Elizabeth founded Clare College at Cambridge. (She is often called Elizabeth de Burgh and is thus confused with her granddaughter—see above.)

♦ Abduction. Charity. Estate. Legal activity. Managers. Prisons. Religious patrons. University. Widows. ♦

DNB, v. 3, p. 331; v.4, pp. 376–377. Fryde, *Tyranny...*, pp. 34, 41, 106, 110–112, 117, 230, 254. Given-Wilson, *English...*, pp. 40–42. Jenkinson, "Mary...," pp. 408, 422, 424, 428, 429. Jusserand, *Wayfaring...*, pp. 98–99. Mertes, *English...*, pp. 23, 24, 44, 45, 130, 175. Rosenthal, *Purchase...*, pp. 79–80. Shahar, *Fourth...*, p. 158.

ELIZABETH CROKE **[Elizabeth Ryche; Elizabeth Stonor]**
c. 1440s–d. 1479 England

Wealthy daughter of Margaret Gregory and John Croke, alderman of London. Married (1) Thomas Ryche of London and (2) William Stonor. Although accused of extravagance, Elizabeth was also instrumental in the expansion of William's business. In later 1470s, Elizabeth obtained a position in Queen †Elizabeth Woodville's court.

♦ **Merchants. Negotiators. Servants–ladies. Writers–letters.** ♦
Kendall, *Yorkist...*, pp. 228, 241, 377, 402. Mertes, *English...*, p. 43. *Stonor...*, v.1, pp. 148–149, 156–157, 165; v.2, pp. 2, 3, 6–27, 41–48, 53–56, 60–69, 72–77, 86–91, 98, 100, 102, 168–176, 180, 204, 208, 226, 229, 233, 237.

ELIZABETH, princess of ENGLAND
b. 1282–d. 1316 England; Netherlands; Wales

Daughter of †Eleanor of Castile and Edward I of England. Married in 1296 to John, count of Holland (d.1299). In 1302, Elizabeth married Humphrey de Bohun (later earl of Hereford). She negotiated peace between the king and disgruntled nobles.

♦ **Genealogy. Negotiators.** ♦
Barrow, *Feudal...*, pp. 293, 419. Bryant, *Age...*, p. 177. *DNB*, v.6, p. 456. McFarlane, *Nobility...*, pp. 263–264. Powicke, *Thirteenth...*, pp. 665, 680n. Prestwich, *Edward...*, pp. 111, 126–129, 132, 388, 538.

ELIZABETH OF FLANDERS, queen of France
See—ISABELLA OF HAINAULT, queen of France.

ELIZABETH OF GOERLITZ **[Gorlitz; Elisabeth of Luxembourg]**
c. 1380s–1420s Belgium; Bohemia; France; Germany; Luxembourg; Netherlands

Daughter of Richarde of Mekelbourg and John of Luxembourg. Around the turn of the fifteenth century, Elizabeth became the second wife of Anthony, count of Rethel, duke of Brabant. After his death at Agincourt, she married John of Bavaria. A great landholder, Elizabeth was nevertheless constantly in debt due to her extravagant tastes.

♦ **Banking. Estate. Squabbles.** ♦
Anselme, *Histoire...*, v.1, p. 248. Blok, *History...*, v.1, p. 299; v.2, pp. 21, 22, 27. Calmette, *Golden...*, pp. 112, 125–126, 154, 155, 156, 310. Dumont, *Histoire...*, pp. 121, 540, 542. Pirenne, *Histoire...*, v.2, pp. 228, 229, 232, 234, 235, 236, 254, 286. Vaughan, *Philip...*, p. 90.

ELISABETTA GONZAGA, duchess of Urbino
b. 1471–d. 1526 Italy

Daughter of †Margaret of Bavaria and Federigo Gonzaga, marquis of Mantua; married Guidobaldo da Montefeltre, duke of Urbino. Elisabetta collected art work, antiques, and rare books. She had been taught dancing and music, along with her more serious studies, so her court was a center of cultural and intellectual pursuits. Many of the poets and musicians of the late 1400s gathered at Urbino under her patronage.

♦ **Art patrons. Book owners. Dance. Educated. Hunting. Managers. Models. Music. Patrons of literature. Popes. Virginity.** ♦
Cartwright, *Beatrice...*, pp. 50, 57, 144, 147, 151, 187, 227. Chamberlin, *World...*, pp. 154, 161–163, 168, 195, 198–199 & 290. Cloulas, *Borgias...*, pp. 173, 196, 204, 205, 206. Cronin, *Flowering...*, pp. 96 & 98. Kelly-Gadol, "Did Women...," pp. 150–151. King and Rabil, *Her Immaculate...*,

pp. 21 & 133. Prescott, *Princes...*, pp. 165, 168, 170, 260–1, 264, 266, 269–74, 276, 277. Simon, *Tapestry...*, pp. 24, 72–74, 126, 130–132, 138, 140, 165, 169, 176, 177.

ELIZABETH HIGGINS **[Higgens; Hygouns]**

fl. 1450s–1470s England

She and her daughter owned and ran the *Black Swan* tavern (probably in London). She was a very "close friend" to Sir John (II) Paston.

♦ **Models. Taverners. Women of easy virtue.** ♦

Barron, "Lords of...," p. 110. Clive, *Sun...*, p. 188. *Paston...*, v.1, pp. 443 & 634.

ELIZABETH HOLLAND

m. 1394–d.c. 1423 England

Daughter of Thomas Holland, earl of Kent, and Alice FitzAlan (daughter of Richard FitzAlan, earl of Arundel). Elizabeth married John Neville (oldest son of Ralph Neville, first earl of Westmoreland) who died in 1420. Their son was Ralph Neville.

♦ **Dowry/dower.** ♦

C.P., v.12, pt.2, pp. 548–549. Jacob, *Fifteenth...*, pp. 8 & 320.

ELIZABETH HOWARD, countess of OXFORD

c. 1406–c. 1480 England

Daughter of Sir John Howard; heiress of Plaitz. In 1426 she secretly wed John de Vere, earl of Oxford.

♦ **Estate. Genealogy. Writers–letters.** ♦

DNB, v.20, p. 240. Green, *Letters...*, pp. 94–95. *Paston...*, I, p. 492; II, pp. 38, 43, 98–99, 277–278, 326, 591–592.

(St.) ELIZABETH OF HUNGARY **[Elizabeth of Thuringia]**

b. 1207–d. 1231 Germany; Hungary

Daughter of †Gertrud of Meran and Andrew II of Hungary; at age fourteen Elizabeth married Louis of Thuringia (1221). Elizabeth was especially interested in helping poor, sick, and orphans; cared for patients at hospital in Marburg. Elizabeth's spiritual adviser and confessor was the sadistic persecutor of heretics, Conrad von Marburg. He whipped her and encouraged her fasting and self-mortification until she died (age 24) from this abuse. Reports of Elizabeth's piety (and miracles attributed to her) caused a frenzy among worshippers at her funeral lying-in-state—the crowd tore strips from her clothing and pulled off her hair, nails, and nipples in the effort to possess holy relics of the future saint. Her body was enshrined, and miracles were quickly associated with her remains. Elizabeth was canonized only four years after her death.

♦ **Charity. Childcare. Models. Nurses. Relics. Religieuses. Religious patrons. Saints. Widows.** ♦

Bynum, *Holy...*, pp. 7, 88, 102, 135, 136, 193, 203, 204, 215, 224, 226, 233, 273, 274, 275, 282. Farmer, *Oxford...*, p. 129. Fox, *Literary...*, pp. 53–

54. Harksen, *Women...*, pp. 35–36. Haverkamp, *Medieval...*, pp. 317, 318–319. Henderson, *Short...*, pp. 109–110. Hughes, *Women...*, pp. 133–134 & 137. Montalemberg, *L'Histoire....* Uminski, *Royal....* Vauchez, "Charité...," pp. 163–173.

ELIZABETH, queen of HUNGARY

See—ELIZABETH OF LUXEMBOURG, queen of Hungary.

See—ELIZABETH OF POLAND, queen of Hungary.

ELIZABETH JUDELA

1489 England

Called a "common bawde," Elizabeth was convicted by London court for prostitution. She was led from prison to pillory at Cornhill (with minstrels advertising her sentence). She was then ousted from London.

♦ **Prostitutes. Punishments.** ♦

Calendar of Letter..., L, p. 269. Kendall, *Yorkist...*, p. 62.

ELIZABETH OF KIEV, queen of Norway, queen of Denmark [Ellisif of Novgorod]

fl. 1030s–1060s Denmark; England; Norway; Russia

Daughter of †Ingegarde of Sweden and Yaroslav I of Kiev. According to sagas, Harold Sigurdsson (later King Harold III Hardrada of Norway) joined elite Byzantine guard in order to make himself worthy of her. Upon his return, he took his new riches to Kiev where he married Elizabeth (c.1043). Elizabeth accompanied Harold to Norway, and later to England where he died in 1066. In 1068, she married King Sweyn II of Denmark to seal a peace treaty between Norway and Denmark.

♦ **Models. Pawns. Politics. Widows.** ♦

Barlow, *Edward...*, pp. 19 & 22. Boyesen, *Story...*, pp. 242, 255, 272 & 274. Jones, *Vikings...*, p. 263. Lloyd, *Maligned...*, p. xiii. Pares, *History...*, p. 35. Pernoud, *La femme...*, p. 229. Vernadsky, *Kievan...*, pp. 336 & 346.

ELIZABETH KIRKEBY

fl. 1460s–1480s England

As the widow of John Kyrkeby, a goldsmith of London (d.1482), she continued his business and carried on her own trade as a merchant, draper, and shipper. Though she allowed two suitors to help with her overseas business affairs, she never remarried. When Elizabeth died, she was very wealthy.

♦ **Clothworkers. Goldsmiths. Legal activity. Merchants. Shipping. Widows.** ♦

Abram, "Women...," p. 280. Hindley, *England...*, p. 154. Lacey, "Women...," p. 54. Thrupp, *Merchant...*, pp. 106 & n11, 107.

ELIZABETH OF LANCASTER, duchess of Exeter

b. 1363–d. 1426 England

Daughter of †Blanche of Lancaster and John of Gaunt. Elizabeth was betrothed as a child to John Hastings, earl of Pembroke. This contract was later cancelled and Elizabeth hastily wed John Holland, earl of Huntingdon (later duke of Exeter). Presumably, she and Holland had jumped the gun and Elizabeth was already pregnant. After his death (1400), she married John Cornwall, baron Fanhope.

♦ **Adultery. Divorce–betrothal. Hunting.** ♦

Armitage-Smith, *John...*, pp. 310 & 460. *DNB*, v.9, p. 1042; v.10, p. 864. Jacob, *Fifteenth...*, p. 223. Roche, *Dona...*, pp. 6, 9, 14, 20, 22, 23, 38, 44, 45. Tuck, *Richard...*, pp. 114–115.

ELIZABETH LUCY

fl. 1450s–1470s England

Mistress of Edward IV in 1460s. Mother of Arthur "Plantagenet" and Elizabeth (who married Sir Thomas Lumley). [Some historians believe Arthur's mother was named Elizabeth Wayte.]

♦ **Mistresses.** ♦

Clive, *Sun...*, pp. 96 & 289. Scofield, *Life...*, II, pp. 56 & 161. St. Aubyn, *Year...*, pp. 152 & 155.

ELIZABETH OF LUXEMBOURG, queen of Hungary

b. 1409–d.c. 1442 Austria; Bohemia; Hungary; Luxembourg; Poland

Daughter of †Barbara of Cilly and Sigismund of Luxembourg (king of Hungary and Poland, Holy Roman Emperor). Married Albert Hapsburg of Austria (who succeeded to Sigismund's titles in 1437). When her husband died in 1439, Ladislas III of Poland was chosen king of Hungary. When Elizabeth bore Albert's posthumous son, many Hungarians changed sides and supported the baby as rightful heir to the throne. Elizabeth struggled to secure the crown for her son—as detailed in memoirs/history supposedly written by †Helene Kotanner. Eventually Elizabeth's son became King Laszlo V of Hungary (r.1452–1457).

♦ **Estate. Models. Politics. Squabbles. Widows.** ♦

Fügedi, *Castle...*, p. 130. Halecki, *Poland...*, pp. 88 & 95. Harksen, *Women...*, p. 54. Maurice, *Bohemia...*, p. 314. Pamlényi, *History...*, pp. 95 & 96. Reddaway et al, *Cambridge...*, pp. 236–239.

ELIZABETH MORING

1385 England

Wife of important London citizen, Henry Moring. In city court 1385, her servant †Johanna testified that Elizabeth's embroidery business was a front for a whorehouse/"call girl" operation. Elizabeth's apprentices were actually hired out to provide intimate services to her all-male clientele. The court judged Elizabeth a harlot and a procuress.

♦ **Apprentices–mistresses. Clothworkers. Employers. Prostitutes. Punishments.** ♦

Bellamy, *Crime...*, p. 60. Labarge, *Small Sound...*, pp. 203–204. Lacey, "Women...," pp. 50–51. Riley, *Memorials...*, pp. 484–486. Robertson, *Chaucer's...*, p. 103.

ELIZABETH, countess of OXFORD

See—ELIZABETH HOWARD, countess of Oxford.

ELIZABETH PASTON

c. 1430–1470s England

Daughter of †Agnes (Berry) Paston and Judge William Paston. Her unhappy relationship with her mother is detailed in extant Paston letters. Elizabeth married Robert Poynings in 1459.

♦ **Genealogy. Writers–letters.** ♦

Barron, "Lords of...," pp. 112–113. Coulton, *Life...*, III, pp. 130–132. Haskell, "Paston...," pp. 466–467 & 470. Kendall, *Yorkist...*, pp. 378–379. *Paston...*, I, pp. 22–24, 27, 30, 42, 155–6, 198, 205–8, 445, 528, 627; II, pp. 31–2, 89, 217, 233, 247–8, 254.

ELIZABETH PERCY, countess of Westmoreland

c. 1400s–1430s England

Daughter of Elizabeth Mortimer and Henry Percy. Married (1) John, lord Clifford (d.1422) and (2) Ralph Neville, earl of Westmoreland.

♦ **Genealogy.** ♦

DNB, v.15, p, 844. Jacob, *Fifteenth...*, pp. 59 & 146.

ELIZABETH OF POLAND, queen of Hungary **[Elizabeth Lokietek]**

c. 1310s–1386 Hungary; Poland

Daughter of Ladislaus I of Poland; married Charles I of Hungary (Charles Robert of Anjou) to cement a Polish/Hungarian alliance; mother of Louis of Anjou, king of Hungary and Poland (b. 1326). Elizabeth urged Pope Clement VI to put Louis on the Neapolitan throne instead of †Joanna I. Failing at that, Elizabeth later traveled to Naples to arrange a marriage between her younger son, Andrew, and Joanna I. Elizabeth was involved in pious works—she commissioned the completion of Cathedral at Kassa; and she was interested in medicine—she invented "water of the queen of Hungary," a treatment for rheumatism made from distilled water and rosemary.

♦ **Art patrons. Medicine. Negotiators. Politics. Popes. Religious patrons. Widows.** ♦

Davies, *God's...*, p. 109. Halecki, *Poland...*, p. 49. Hurd-Mead, *History...*, p. 273. Lipinska, *Histoire...*, pp. 125–126. Pamlényi, *History...*, pp. 75, 611, 620. Reddaway et al, *Cambridge...*, pp. 120, 167, 182, 191, 197, 198, 201. Vambéry, *Hungary...*, pp. 162–163.

ELIZABETH OF POMERANIA, queen of Bohemia, Holy Roman Empress **[Elizabeth Slupsk]**

fl. 1360s–1380s Bohemia; Germany; Luxembourg; Poland

Daughter of Bogislaus V, duke of Pomerania; granddaughter of Casimir the Great of Poland. Around 1364, Elizabeth became the fourth wife of Charles IV, king of Bohemia and Holy Roman Emperor (Wenceslaus of Luxembourg). They had children Sigismund of Bohemia (later Holy Roman Emperor) and †Anne of Bohemia. Since Charles had died in 1378, Elizabeth helped arrange Anne's marriage to Richard II of England.

♦ Negotiators. Queens. Widows. ♦

Cambridge..., VII, p. 174. Davies, *God's...*, p. 98. Leuschner, *Germany...*, pp. 151–152. Lutzow, *Bohemia...*, pp. 63 & 85. Stubbs, *Later...*, p. 138.

(St.) ELIZABETH OF PORTUGAL **[Isabel of Aragon, queen of Portugal]**

1271–c. 1336 Portugal; Spain

Daughter of †Constance of Sicily, queen of Aragon, and Pedro III of Aragon. Around 1280, married Diniz of Portugal; mother of Alfonso IV and Constance, queen of Castile. Elizabeth quickly became known as "the peacemaker," especially among the members of her own (and her husband's) contentious family. Her unhappy marriage caused Elizabeth to devote more and more of her energies to pious activities. She was a fanatic about fasting, started an orphanage at Coimbra, contributed to hospitals and universities, and founded an agricultural college to prepare girls for marriage to farmers—even giving land to the graduates. Diniz died in 1325, and Elizabeth donned the habit of the Poor Clares (although she did not take vows). On a pilgrimage she miraculously restored a blind child's sight. Although many miracles were associated with her shrine at the Convent of Santa Clare in Coimbra, Elizabeth was not canonized until 1625.

♦ Charity. Childcare. Medicine. Negotiators. Pilgrims. Politics. Popes. Relics–miracles. Religieuses. Religious patrons. Saints. University. Widows. ♦

Dos Passos, *Portugal...*, pp. 42–43, 46–67. Farmer, *Oxford...*, pp. 129–130. Livermore, *History...*, pp. 156, 157, 158. Livermore, *New...*, pp. 84, 88, 89. McNabb, *St. Elizabeth....* (an uncritical biography). *Short Relation....* Stephens, *Story...*, pp. 86, 91, 92, 98.

ELIZABETH RYCHE

See—ELIZABETH CROKE.

ELIZABETH QUINTIN

1338 France

Pilgrim badge maker and seller at Le Puy. In 1338, she petitioned the court for her hereditary rights to this business.

♦ **Badge dealers. Legal activity–business.** ♦

Cohen, "Pilgrim...," p. 202.

ELIZABETH SAY

c. 1420s–d.c. 1464 England

Married in 1430s to Sir John Montgomery; in the 1440s, she lived at her manor of Cheshunt, Herefordshire. Godmother of Edward (IV), and a fervent Yorkist. Edward showed his appreciation with grants and protection for her property.

♦ **Estate. Politics. Rebellions. Widows.** ♦

Clive, *Sun...*, p. 76. *Letters of Queen...*, pp. 105–106. Scofield, *Life...*, I, pp. 1 & 2.

ELIZABETH, lady SCALES

c. 1440s–1470s England

Daughter of Thomas, lord Scales; heiress of Sandringham (and a number of other estates). Her first husband was Sir Henry Bourchier. In 1460, she married Anthony Woodville, later earl Rivers. As a principal lady-in-waiting to his sister, Queen †Elizabeth Woodville, Lady Scales received a yearly stipend of £40.

♦ **Estate. Games–cards. Servants–ladies.** ♦

Clive, *Sun...*, pp. 41, 75, 115, 204. *DNB*, v.2, p. 918. Scofield, *Life...*, I, p. 377. St. Aubyn, *Year...*, p. 52.

ELISABETH SCEPENS **[Betkin]**

fl. 1460s–c. 1490 Belgium

Student/apprentice of bookmaker William Vrelandt in Bruges. After he died (c.1476), she ran his business with William's widow. Although much of her work would then have been administrative, she must also have worked as an illuminator on some manuscripts, because Elisabeth was a member of the artists' guild from 1476 until 1489.

♦ **Apprentices. Artists. Bookmaking. Merchants. Unmarried.** ♦

Greer, *Obstacle...*, pp. 164–165. Uitz, *Legend...*, p. 100.

(St.) ELIZABETH OF SCHÖNAU

b. 1129–d. 1164 Germany

As a child, Elizabeth entered Benedictine double monastery at Schönau near Trier. Although Elizabeth's main work was among the poor, she is primarily recognized as a mystic. She was also a proponent of clerical reform.

♦ **Charity. Models. Mystics. Saints. Unmarried. Writers.** ♦

Bynum, *Holy...*, pp. 185, 264. Dean, "Elisabeth..." Dean, "Manuscripts..." Didier, "Elisabeth...," pp. 221–224. Ferrante, "Education...," p. 26. Frederiksen, *Women...*, pp. 66–67. Halligan (ed.), *Booke...*, pp. 10n, 35, 51. Lagorio, "Continental...," pp. 163, 166–167. McDonnell, *Beguines...*, pp. 281, 296 & 344. Newman, *Sister...*, pp. xvi, 36–38, 39–41, 83, 172, 182, 195, 225, 248, 255. Petroff, *Medieval...*, pp. 159–170. Power, *Nunneries...*, p. 239 Thièbaux, *The Writings...*, pp. 134–163.

ELIZABETH SCOLEMAYSTRES

1441 England

Teacher, or tutor, in 1441 London Cripplesgate area.

♦ **Teachers.** ♦

Hollaender and Kellaway, "Aliens...," p. 269. Orme, *English...*, p. 55.

ELIZABETH, lady SCROPE

1470 England

When Henry VI was re-established on the English throne, Edward IV's wife, †Elizabeth Woodville, took sanctuary. The earl of Warwick sent Elizabeth Scrope to be the deposed queen's midwife. Lady Scrope was paid £10 for helping at the birth of Edward (V) prince of Wales, and she also served as godmother to the baby at his christening.

♦ **Midwives. Servants.** ♦

Clive, *Sun...*, p. 158. Scofield, *Life...*, I, p. 546. Strickland, *Lives...*, p. 220.

ELIZABETH STAPILTON

d.c. 1450 England

Daughter of Agnes and Sir Bryan de Stapilton. At age twelve, Elizabeth married twelve-year-old William Plumpton; they had nine children.

♦ **Childcare. Genealogy.** ♦

DNB, v.15, p. 1321. *Plumpton...*, pp. xliii, xliv.

ELIZABETH STOKTON

c. 1460s–1480s England

An embroiderer and silkworker, she finished cloths which were then shipped to Italy to be sold. After her husband John Stokton, a mercer and alderman died around 1472, Elizabeth married Gerard Caniziani, another London mercer.

♦ **Artistic clothwork. Shipping. Silkwork. Widows.** ♦

Kendall, *Yorkist...*, p. 405. Thrupp, *Merchant...*, pp. 170 & 368.

ELIZABETH STONOR

See—ELIZABETH CROKE.

ELIZABETH TALBOT, duchess of Norfolk

fl. 1440s–1480s England

Daughter of †Margaret Beauchamp and John Talbot, earl of Shrewsbury; in 1460s married John Mowbray III, duke of Norfolk. She was a friend of John (II) and John (III) Paston. King Edward IV paid Elizabeth £200 to accompany his sister, †Margaret of York, to her wedding in Flanders; there Elizabeth attended banquets and tournament—*l'Arbre d'Or.* Elizabeth was also very pious; she went on barefoot pilgrimage to Walsingham. In addition, she proved to be an able negotiator; she drove a hard (and profitable) bargain with Edward IV for the marriage of her daughter †Anne Mowbray to his son Richard.

♦ **Negotiators. Pilgrims. Servants–attendants. Tournaments.** ♦

Barron, "Lords of...," p. 110. Clive, *Sun...*, pp. 129, 172, 211, 243. *DNB,* vol. 19, p. 323. Kendall, *Yorkist...*, pp. 216, 220–223, 245, 451–452. *Paston...*, I, pp. 308–9, 366, 440–492, 525–536, 553–597, 600–1, 618, 639, 655–656; II, pp. 388, 400, 432, 469–70, 475–6. Scofield, *Life...*, I, pp. 455–456, 481; II, pp. 203–204.

ELIZABETH LE VEEL **[Elizabeth Calfe]**

m. 1390 Ireland

Heiress of barony of Norragh in Kildare. In 1390, she married king of Leinster, Art Oge MacMurrough Kavanagh (d.1417). When he was refused possession of Elizabeth's estates, he ravaged English lands in several counties. He eventually claimed his bride and some of her lands.

♦ **Estate. Squabbles.** ♦

C.P., v.7, p. 158. Curtis, *Ireland...*, pp. 116 & 124. *DNB,* v.12, p. 680.

ELIZABETH OF VERMANDOIS

See—ISABELLA OF VERMANDOIS.

ELIZABETH WOODVILLE, queen of England **[Wydeville]**

b. 1437–d. 1492 England

Daughter of †Jacquetta of Luxembourg, dowager duchess of Bedford, and Richard Woodville, later earl Rivers. She was a widow (of John Grey, lord Ferrers) with two young sons when she waylaid Edward IV to beg pardons for her father and brother. In 1464, Elizabeth and Edward were secretly married. Her relatives were all quickly elevated and Elizabeth found socially and financially profitable marriage partners for most. This caused hard feelings at court, and the earl of Warwick became so angry that he switched sides, bringing Henry VI and †Margaret of Anjou back to power. Although Edward and Elizabeth regained the crown, after Edward IV died, his brother Richard III usurped the throne by claiming that Edward and Elizabeth's clandestine marriage was invalid. That made their sons illegitimate, and thus took them out of line for the English crown. These young princes presumably died in the Tower of London. Elizabeth's actions after her sons went to the Tower have been closely examined as a possible clue to what happened to the boys—and when it happened. Whatever her motives, Elizabeth and her daughters did return to court during Richard III's reign.

♦ **Educated. Games–bowling. Negotiators. Politics. Religious patrons. Servants. Widows.** ♦

Butt, *History...*, pp. 592–593, 596, 599, 600, 603, 614, 616, 617, 618, 625, 627, 628. Clive, *Sun...*, pp. 2, 40, 75, 90, ... 293, 297, 305–6.

Commynes, *Memoirs...*, pp. 219, 366, 375, 377, 378, 411. *Coronation....* Goodman, *Wars...*, pp. 67, 68, 86, 187, 210. Green, *Letters...*, pp. 110–111. Griffiths and Thomas, *Making...*, pp. 86, 90–98, 102, 107, 109, 115, 124, 126, 145, 175, 177, 180. Holmes, *Later...*, pp. 222, 224–225. Jacob, *Fifteenth...*, pp. 324, 535, 536, 546, 553, 555, 605, 617–618, 672. Kendall, *Yorkist...*, pp. 167–170, 179, 193. Myers, "Household...Woodville". Scofield, *Life...*, I, pp. 178, 332, 354...; II, pp. 439... St. Aubyn, *Year...*, pp. 48–50, 53, 54, 56, 57, 75–77... *Stonor...*, v.1, pp. xxxii, xlii, 123; v.2, pp. 14, 127–128, 146, 150–151, 159, 160.

ELIZABETH OF YORK, queen of England

b. 1466–d. 1503 England

Daughter of †Elizabeth Woodville and Edward IV of England. Married Henry VII in 1486 to fulfill arrangement which helped put Henry on the throne of England. This brought together the houses of York and Lancaster, ending the Wars of the Roses. Their children were Margaret (b.1489), Henry VIII (b.1491), and Mary (b.1496). Elizabeth also proved to be adept at negotiating marriage contracts, and was interested in literature. In fact, she translated Marguerite of Angoulême's *Mirroir de l'âme.* The *Most Pleasant Song of the Lady Bessy* is a fictionalized version of the struggle to put Henry Tudor on the throne—depicting Elizabeth as an active participant in this venture (which was probably not true).

♦ **Childbirth. Models. Negotiators. Pawns. Writers.** ♦

Butt, *History...*, pp. 621, 622, 628, 633. Cleugh, *Chant...*, pp. 220, 257–258, 275. Clive, *Sun...*, pp. 117, 146, 203–4, 208, 215, 220, 232, 240, 245, 273, 289, 297–8, 304–6. Commynes, *Memoirs...*, pp. 271–272, 366, 377, 378, 414. Griffiths and Thomas, *Making...*, pp. 4, 30, 83, 85, 88, 91, 93–96, 104–5, 115, 126, 182–3, 187, 189, 193, 196. Harvey, *Elizabeth....* Kelly, "Canonical...". McFarlane, *Nobility...*, p. 81. Mertes, *English...*, pp. 94 & 158. Scofield, *Life...*, I, p. 506; II, p. 142. St. Aubyn, *Year...*, pp. 60–61, 156, 157, 176, 189, 190, 196, 200, 202.

ELIZABETH OF YORK, duchess of Suffolk

b. 1444–d. 1503 England

Daughter of †Cecily Neville and Richard, duke of York. Around 1458, Elizabeth married John de la Pole, duke of Suffolk. Her brother Edward IV placed the deposed queen, †Margaret of Anjou, in Elizabeth's care (1471) at Ewelme in Oxfordshire. Elizabeth was paid eight marks weekly for performing this service.

♦ **Estate. Politics. Prisons–jailers. Servants–ladies.** ♦

Clive, *Sun...*, pp. 65, 243, 290. *Coronation...*, p. 40. *DNB*, vol. 16, p. 1070. Green, *Letters...*, pp. 109–110. Johnson, *Duke...*, pp. 18 & 47. Kendall, *Yorkist...*, pp. 213, 216 & 426. *Paston...*, I, pp. 169, 310, 337, 357, 366, 442, 611; II, pp. 210, 442. Scofield, *Life...*, I, p. 2; II, p. 23. *Stonor...*, v.1, pp. xliv, 117; v.2, pp. 13 & 14.

ELLEN [Elen]

ELLEN DALOK **[Elena]**

1493 England

In 1493 court, Ellen was condemned for owning a "magic book," which explained such subjects as how to tell fortunes and how to make rain. She also claimed to be able to put fatal curses on people.

♦ **Book owners. Ecclesiastical courts. Superstitions. Witchcraft.** ♦

Cohn, *Europe's...*, p. 153. Ewen, *Witchcraft...*, p. 82. Hindley, *England...*, p. 147.

ELLEN SAGE

1376 England

The widowed Ellen took over her husband John's haberdashery business as a *femme sole.*

♦ **Apparel. Merchants. Widows.** ♦

Calendar of Plea..., II, p. 213.

ELEN SKOLEMASTRE

1494 England

Teacher in Taunton; received 3s 3d from a student.

♦ **Bequests. Teachers.** ♦

Gardiner, *English...*, p. 86.

ELSE OF MEERSBURG

1450 Switzerland

In 1450 at Lucerne, Else was charged with practicing witchcraft, including accusations that she rode to witch meetings on dogs or other animals.

♦ **Witchcraft.** ♦

Kieckhefer, *European...*, p. 129. Lea, *Materials...*, p. 251.

ELSE VON ORTEMBERG

fl. 1445–1453 Germany

Between the years 1445 and 1453, Else was licensed to work as a tailor in Strasbourg.

♦ **Apparel–tailors.** ♦

O'Faolain, *Not in...*, p. 154.

ELVIRA OF CASTILE **[Gesloire]**

fl. 1090s Byzantium; France; Spain

Illegitimate daughter of Alfonso VI of Castile. In 1090, she married Raymond, count of Toulouse. In 1096, Elvira and her infant son accompanied Raymond on Crusade. The baby died on the way to the Holy Land. Raymond died in 1105.

♦ **Childcare. Crusades. Illegitimacy. Soldiers.** ♦

Anselme, *Histoire...*, v.2, p. 686. Marks, *Pilgrims...*, pp. 58 & 83. Miron, *Queens...*, pp. 58–59.

Note: We have chosen not to make two separate Elvira of Castile entries since we have been unable to determine whether the following woman is the same Elvira as the one above.

Elvira of Castile, queen of Sicily

m. 1117–d. 1135 Italy; Spain

Daughter of Alfonso VI of Castile; first wife of Roger II, king of Sicily; their seven children included William I of Sicily.

♦ **Genealogy. Queens.** ♦

Cambridge..., V, p. 191. Douglas, *Norman...*, Table 2. Norwich, *Kingdom...*, pp. 17, 35, 89n, 110n, 148. Norwich, *Normans...*, p. 297.

ELVIRA OF LEON

fl. 950s–970s Spain

Daughter of Ramiro II of Leon. When her nephew Ramiro III was left fatherless at age five (966), Elvira ran the government of Leon for him—but was not especially successful at that task.

♦ **Nuns. Regents.** ♦

Cambridge..., V, p. 191. Livermore, *History...*, pp. 96–97. O'Callaghan, *History...*, p. 125.

EMELINE (la poréeresse)

1292 France

Listed in 1292 Paris tax records as a kitchen/garden herbmonger on the rue aus Oubloiers; taxed 3s.

♦ **Apothecaries. Less-affluent.** ♦

Géraud, *Paris sous...*, p. 148.

EMELINE (la ventrière)

1292 Paris In 1292 Paris she was a midwife on the rue des Escoufles; paid 2s tax.

♦ **Less-affluent. Midwives.** ♦

Géraud, *Paris sous...*, p. 114. Hughes, *Women...*, p. 146.

EMILIA PIA

fl. 1480s–1500s Italy

Wife of Antonio da Montefeltro; she was †Elisabetta Gonzaga's best friend. Emilia directed the salon of courtiers, poets, and musicians at Elisabetta's rooms in Urbino.

♦ **Educated. Models. Patrons of literature.** ♦

Cartwright, *Beatrice...*, pp. 108, 147, 151. Cronin, *Flowering...*, p. 98. Kelly-Gadol, "Did Women...," p. 151. Prescott, *Princes...*, p. 273. Simon, *Tapestry...*, p. 176.

EMMA (of Apulia)

fl. 1080s–1100s Italy

Daughter of †Sichelgaita and Robert Guiscard. Her son Tancred succeeded her half-brother, Bohemund, as ruler of Antioch in 1111.

♦ **Genealogy.** ♦

Ritchie, "Bohemund...," p. 296. Stephenson, *Mediaeval...*, p. 388.

EMMA FITZOSBERN, countess of Norfolk

[Emma Guader; of Hereford; of Norfolk]

m. 1075–1100 Byzantium; England; France; Turkey

Daughter of Adeliza of Tosny and William FitzOsbern. In 1075, Emma's brother, Roger, earl of Hereford, married her to Ralph Guader, earl of Norfolk, to seal an alliance against William the Conqueror. Ralph left her to defend Norwich castle; she kept it for three months before surrendering (after obtaining safe passage out of the country). Ralph and Emma lived on their estates in Brittany until 1096 when they went on Crusade with Robert Curthose of Normandy. Ralph, Emma, and son Alan took part in siege of Nicaea. [Their other son was Ralph, lord of Gael and Montfort. His daughter †Amicia married Robert II de Beaumont, earl of Leicester (c.1122).]

♦ **Crusades. Estate. Genealogy. Rebellions. Soldiers.** ♦

Clark and Williams, "Impact...," p. 170. *C.P.*, v.7, p. 530. *DNB*, v.8, p. 757. Douglas, *William...*, pp. 90, 145, Table 8. Le Patourel, *Feudal...*, VI, pp. 6, 9.

EMMA OF FRANCE

[Emma of Burgundy; Emma Capet; Emma of Neustria]

fl. 910s–934 France

Daughter of Robert I of France and his first wife Beatrice. Emma took part in the negotiations which put her husband, Raoul of Burgundy, on the throne of France in 923. She also helped Raoul by defending Laon, capturing Avalon, and successfully besieging an enemy castle in 935. Emma often interceded with her husband for land grants and other privileges for the church.

♦ **Negotiators. Religious patrons. Rulers. Soldiers.** ♦

Anselme, *Histoire...*, v.1, pp. 36 & 68. Lehmann, *Rôle de la...*, pp. 145–147. McKitterick, *Frankish...*, p. 310 & Table 4. Riché, *Les Carolingiens...*, p. 242. Sismondi, *French...*, p. 418. Stafford, *Queens...*, pp. 77, 117, 119, 132, 190. Stephenson, *Mediaeval...*, p. 211, Table III. Verdon, "Les Sources...," pp. 226 & 227.

EMMA, queen of GERMANY

m.c. 827–d. 876 Germany

Wife of Louis the German, who ruled the East Frankia, or German, part of his grandfather Charlemagne's empire. Emma apparently had a role in her husband's government; in particular, her name often appeared in charters granting land, privileges, and protection to religious foundations for women. Chroniclers especially extolled her piety and wisdom.

♦ **Models. Politics. Queens. Religious patrons.** ♦

Cabaniss, *Judith...*, pp. 13 & 25. *Cambridge...*, III, p. 19. McKitterick, *Frankish...*, Table 3. Riché, *Les Carolingiens...*, p. 153. Stafford, *Queens...*, pp. 143 & 179. Wemple, *Women...*, p. 90.

EMMA HATFIELD

c. 1350s–1380s — England

As a widow, Emma took over her husband's business as a chandler. Her apprentice, Roger Gosse, was reluctant to learn from a woman. Emma eventually petitioned London court to punish the recalcitrant Roger, who was sent to Newgate prison until he was willing to be more obedient.

♦ **Apprentices–mistresses. Candlemakers. Legal activity. Widows.** ♦

Calendar of Plea..., II, p. 128.

EMMA OF ITALY, queen of France

m.c. 966–c. 990s — France; Italy

Daughter of †Adelheid of Burgundy, by her first husband, Lothar, king of Italy. Emma married King Lothar of France. She played a part in his government, going with Lothar on military campaigns and defending Verdun while he was in Laon. After Lothar died, she became regent for son Louis V. Her brother-in-law, Charles of Lorraine, accused Emma of adultery with Bishop Adalbero in order to make Louis's claim to the throne questionable—through the taint of illegitimacy. When Louis died in 987, Emma lost all governmental power.

♦ **Adultery. Regents. Soldiers. Squabbles. Widows.** ♦

Decaux, *Histoire...*, p. 175. Duckett, *Death...*, pp. 93 & 101. McKitterick, *Frankish...*, pp. 325, 327, 330, Tables 5 & 9. Riché, *Les Carolingiens...*, pp. 264 & 266. Sismondi, *French...*, p. 448. Stafford, *Queens...*, pp. 56, 77, 82, 94–5, 110, 115–7, 141, 151, 167, 175–7, 206. Verdon, "Les sources...," p. 240.

EMMA OF NORMANDY, queen of England

m. 1002–d. 1052 — Belgium; England; France

Daughter of †Gunnor (of Denmark) and Richard I, duke of Normandy; in 1002 she married Aethelred (II) of England; they had three children, including the future King Edward the Confessor. When Canute of Denmark became king of England, he married the widowed Emma. After Canute died (1035), Emma promptly seized the royal treasury in an attempt to dictate the succession. When Harold Harefoot (the son of her rival †Aelfgifu of Northampton) was officially recognized, Emma retired to Bruges. Emma's son by Canute, Harthacanute, reigned from 1040 until 1042, and allowed her to hold a position of some power in his government. Since Emma was a very ambitious woman, this may explain why she preferred her son by Canute to her son by Ethelred. As soon as Edward the Confessor became king, he stripped her of both her power and her wealth. Thereafter, until her death in 1052, she lived in retirement at Winchester. The *Encomium of Queen Emma* which she commissioned (probably in 1041) is a unique biography of an early laywoman.

♦ **Banking. Models. Ordeals. Patrons of literature. Politics. Religious patrons. Widows.** ♦

A.S., Jan. v.1, pp. 291, 292, 293, 294, 390. Barlow, *Edward...*, pp. 7, 9, 25–38, 42–53 ... 291, 298, 329, 339–341. Blair, *Anglo-Saxon...*, pp. 99–100, 103–5. Brown, *Normans...*, pp. 67 n24, 77 n76, 78, 79, 106, 110–111, 113, 139 n155. Bullough and Storey, *Study...*, p. 22. Campbell, *Anglo-Saxons,* pp. 170, 194, 199, 208, 214–16, 221, 225, 230. Campbell, "Queen...," pp. 66–79. Cutler, "Edith...," pp. 224, 230–1. Jones, *Vikings...*, pp. 358, 398–399, 403. McKitterick, *Frankish...*, p. 238. Stafford, "King's...," pp. 3–27. Stafford, *Queens...*, pp. 3–5, 40, 45, 48, 49, 58, 72, 78, 91, 102–5, 110, 139–44, 151, 157–8, 161–6, 169, 170, 177, 189, 210. Stephenson, *Mediaeval...*, p. 215. Summers, *Geography...*, p. 456. *Translations...*, IV, pp. 13–14. Vitalis, *Ecclesiastical...*, v.2, pp. 42, 134, 226.

EMMA TURK

1325 England

When her husband Paulin Turk, fishmonger of London, died in 1325, he gave her the rest of his apprentice's term of service. Thus Emma could continue to run their business.

♦ **Apprentices–mistresses. Bequests. Provisioning–fishmongers. Widows.** ♦

Calendar of Wills..., I, p. 317.

ENDE

fl. 970s Spain

Manuscript illuminator; ornamented and signed beautifully illustrated *Beatus Apocalypse.*

♦ **Artists. Bookmaking. Religieuses.** ♦

Carr, "Women...," p. 6. Greer, *Obstacle...*, p. 152. Munsterberg, *History...*, pp. 12 & 14. Petersen and Wilson, *Women...*, pp. 13–14.

ENGELBURGA

See—ANGELBERGA.

ENGELTRUDE

See—INGELTRUDE.

EREMBOURC DE BRAIÈRES

1292 France

Paid 24s in 1292 tax collection on her business as a goldsmith in Paris.

♦ **Goldsmiths. Merchants.** ♦

Géraud, *Paris sous...*, p. 26.

EREMBOURC (la florière)

1292 France

Flower seller in 1292 Paris; taxed 2s.

♦ **Less-affluent. Merchants–florists.** ♦

Géraud, *Paris sous...*, p. 122.

EREMBOURC (la potière)

1292 France

Listed as a potter at the door of St-Honoré in the parish of St. Germain L'Aucerrais. She paid 2s tax in 1292 Paris.

♦ **Less-affluent. Potters.** ♦

Géraud, *Paris sous...*, p. 9.

ERMENGARDE, Holy Roman Empress [Hermengarde; Irmengardis]

c. 780s–d. 818 France; Germany

Daughter of Count Ingram. First wife of Louis I the Pious; mother of Lothar I (b. 795) and Louis the German. Ermengarde's piety and political wisdom made her an able partner and adviser to her husband. Her death plunged Louis into deep, if temporary, depression.

♦ **Genealogy. Queens.** ♦

Carolingian..., pp. 130, 200, 208. Decaux, *Histoire...*, p. 179. Duckett, *Carolingian...*, pp. 28 & 285. Lehmann, *Rôle de la...*, p. 126. McKitterick, *Frankish...*, p. 106, & Table 3. McNamara and Wemple, "Marriage...," pp. 106–107. Riché, *Les Carolingiens...*, p. 143. Stafford, *Queens...*, pp. 91, 130, 143, 162, 187 & 190. Wemple, *Women...*, pp. 79–80, 90, 98.

ERMENGARDE OF ANJOU, duchess of Brittany

m. 1088–d. 1147 France

Daughter of Foulques IV le Rechin of Anjou and his first wife Audéarde de Beaugency. In 1088, Ermengarde married William IX, count of Poitiers, duke of Aquitaine. After they divorced in 1091, she became the second wife of Alan IV, count of Brittany. She was regent of Brittany while Alan was crusading in the East (1096–1101), and again from 1112 until his death in 1119. She then retired for a short time to Fontevrault, but soon returned to her duties as regent for her young son. Ermengarde petitioned Pope Calixtus II to reinstate her as duchess of Aquitaine, but the request was denied. Ermengarde was more successful at improving the Breton legal codes, and she also banned the exploitation of shipwrecks. That she was well-educated is indicated by a poem addressed to her from Bishop Marbodus of Rennes. In 1131, Ermengarde went on pilgrimage to the Holy Lands. After her return, her political activities gave way to pious considerations;

Ermengarde founded a monastery and supported several Cistercian establishments.

♦ **Divorce. Educated. Insanity–supposed. Legal activity. Models. Pilgrims. Popes. Regents. Religieuses. Religious patrons. Squabbles. Widows.** ♦

Casey, "Cheshire...," p. 234. Heer, *Medieval...*, p. 234. Jourdain, "Memoire...," p. 476. Lehmann, *Rôle de la...*, pp. 276–277. Marks, *Pilgrims...*, pp. 47–48, 63, 86. Pernoud, *La femme...*, pp. 143–149. Smith, "Robert...," p. 183. Thompson, *Literacy...*, p. 129. Warren, *Henry...*, pp. 74 & 75.

ERMENGARDE DE BEAUMONT, queen of Scotland

m. 1186–d. 1233 England; France; Scotland

Daughter of Richard, viscount of Beaumont (in Maine). In 1186, Ermengarde married William I the Lion, king of Scotland (d.1214), as part of a peace treaty. She was the mother of King Alexander II of Scotland.

♦ **Dowry/dower. Negotiators. Pawns. Queens. Religious patrons.** ♦

Barrow, *Feudal...*, pp. 175n, 420. *DNB*, v.21, p. 334. Duncan, *Scotland...*, pp. 209, 231–232, 251, 253 n72, 277, 413, 534. Mackie, *History...*, p. 47. Warren, *Henry...*, pp. 186, 603–604.

ERMENGARDE (of Burgundy)

c. 990s–d. 1057 France

The widowed Ermengarde married Rudolf III of Burgundy in 1011. After Rudolf died (c.1032), she became politically important as transmitter of his duchy; she opposed Eudes II of Blois.

♦ **Dowry/dower. Politics. Religious patrons. Widows.** ♦

Cambridge..., III, p. 142. *DBF*, v.12, p. 1384; v.13, p. 248. Lewis, *Development...*, pp. 301–302. Stafford, *Queens...*, pp. 102, 124, 171.

ERMENGARD (of Italy), Holy Roman Empress [Ermingart]

m.c. 821–d. 858 France; Germany; Italy

Daughter of Hugh de Tours of Alsace. Wife of Holy Roman Emperor Lothar I. Founded, supported, and owned several abbeys and nunneries. Ermengard was also an excellent embroiderer; she made a tapestry of the life of St. Peter.

♦ **Artistic clothwork. Estate. Religious patrons.** ♦

Carolingian..., pp. 109, 200. Duckett, *Carolingian...*, p. 29. McKitterick, *Frankish...*, p. 91, & Table 3. Riché, *Les Carolingiens...*, p. 152. Stafford, *Queens...*, pp. 20, 26, 27, 39, 101, 107, 139, 143, & 179. Wemple, "S. Salvatore...," p. 90. Wemple, *Women...*, pp. 90 & 92.

ERMENGARDE (of Ivrea) [Ermengarde of Tuscany]

d.c. 932 Italy

Daughter of Adelbert II and †Bertha of Tuscany. Married Adelbert of Ivrea. She ruled as regent after Adelbert died. Wealthy and beautiful, the widowed Ermengarde had numerous suitors. According to chronicler Liutprand of Cremona, Ermengarde used this situation, and her considerable "sex appeal," as tools to gain and keep power in Ivrea.

♦ **Models. Politics. Regents. Widows. Women of easy virtue.** ♦

Cambridge..., III, pp. 153, 157. Ernouf, *Histoire...*, pp. 122, 187, 220, 243–247. McNamara and Wemple, "Sanctity...," p. 109. Stafford, *Queens...*, pp. 20–21 & 138. Wright, *Works...*, pp. 96, 113–114, 148, 178.

ERMENGARD, duchess of LOMBARDY, queen of Provence [Irmengard]

m.c. 876–d.c. 896 Germany; Italy; France

Daughter of †Angelberga and Emperor Louis II; married Boso of Vienne, duke of Lombardy around 876; son Louis III the Blind born around 880. Boso took Provence from Louis II of France and made it a kingdom, largely because Ermengard pushed him to do so. She personally appealed to Emperor Charles III the Fat and, with his help, set her son Louis on the throne of Provence, while she ruled for him as regent.

♦ **Negotiators. Politics. Popes. Regents. Soldiers. Widows.** ♦

Cambridge..., III, pp. 49, 53, 56, 57, 58, 62, 137, 138. Decaux, *Histoire...*, pp. 174–175. Ernouf, *Histoire...*, pp. 50–51, 95, 122. Lehmann, *Rôle de la...*, pp. 138, 141–142. McKitterick, *Frankish...*, p. 260, Tables 3 & 4. Riché, *Les Carolingiens...*, p. 206. Stafford, *Queens...*, pp. 41, 47, 54, 118–120, 162–163, 176, & 206. Wemple, *Women...*, p. 91.

ERMENGARDE, viscountess of NARBONNE

c. 1120s–d.c. 1194 France

She inherited Narbonne from her father Aymeri II at a young age. Alphonse I, count of Toulouse, (and later his son Raymond), tried to take the vicomté under the pretext of "protecting" Ermengarde and her lands during her minority. However, Ermengarde defeated the count and quelled the rebellious nobles of Narbonne. Although she married, possibly three times, her husbands had little role in governing her lands. She was a strong supporter of King Louis VII and led military expeditions against anti-royalist forces in southern France. Ermengarde was renowned as a judge in difficult feudal legal cases. She received letters of confirmation from Louis VII, and the support of the papacy, for her rights to dispense high and low justice on her estates. Ermengarde also became recognized as a patroness of troubadours, and of various religious foundations.

♦ **Legal activity–judges. Models. Patrons of literature. Poets/troubadours. Popes. Religious patrons. Rulers. Soldiers.** ♦

Bonner (ed.), *Songs...*, pp. 8, 16, 239, 248. *DBF*, v.12, pp. 1386–1387. Decaux, *Histoire...*, pp. 213–214. Gies, *Knight...*, p. 61. Heer, *Medieval...*, p. 262. Lehmann, *Rôle de la...*, pp. 216, 285–289. Marks, *Pilgrims...*, pp. 169, 180–181. Pernoud, *Eleanor...*, pp. 125 & 152.

ERMENGARDE (of St. Adrian)

fl.c. 1180s–1210s Germany

Nun at convent of St. Adrian; illuminated *Augustini sermones* manuscript.

♦ **Artists. Bookmaking. Nuns.** ♦

Greer, *Obstacle...*, pp. 158–159.

ERMENGARD (of S. Salvatore)

c. 1106 Italy

Abbess of S. Salvatore/S. Guilia in 1106. Pope Paschal II enhanced her powers by issuing a decretal placing male priests, etc., under her authority on S. Salvatore lands.

♦ **Abbesses. Managers. Popes.** ♦

Wemple, "S. Salvatore...," p. 97.

ERMENTRUDE OF JOUARRE

fl. 850s France

Abbess of Jouarre. Used her well-connected and important family to garner lands and relics for the abbey. Ermentrude secured market and coinage rights from Charles I the Bald, king of France. She also turned her establishment into a profitable pilgrimage site.

♦ **Abbesses. Banking. Managers. Pilgrims. Politics. Relics. Religious patrons.** ♦

Guerout, "Le monastere...," pp. 75–78. Wemple, *Women...*, p. 172.

ERMENTRUDE OF ORLÉANS, queen of France
[Hirmentrude;Irmintrud]

m. 842–d. 869 France

Daughter of Engeltrude and Odo, count of Orléans; first wife of Charles I the Bald, king of France. She was a gifted embroiderer and was interested in religious foundations; Charles gave Ermentrude the nunnery of Chelles.

♦ **Artistic clothwork. Estate. Models. Religious patrons.** ♦

Carolingian..., pp. 26, 173, 211. *DBF*, v.12, p. 1388. Duckett, *Carolingian...*, p. 209. Jourdain, "Memoire...," p. 473. Lehmann, *Rôle de la...*, p. 138. McKitterick, *Frankish...*, pp. 181, 184, 195, Table 3. Riché, *Les Carolingiens...*, p. 166. Stafford, *Queens...*, pp. 39, 43, 87, 89, 91, 102, 107, 131, 179, 189, 190. Wemple, *Women...*, pp. 91, 172, 254.

ERMESSEND OF CARCASSONNE, countess of Barcelona
[Ermessenda of Béziers-Agda]

c. 980s–1050s France; Spain

Daughter of Roger the Old and Adelaise, count and countess of Carcassonne. Wife of Ramon Borell, count of Barcelona. After he died in 1018, Ermessend was regent for their son Berenguer Ramon I, and later for her grandson Ramon Berenguer I. An able and vigorous regent, she led successful military operations and revitalized Barcelona's system of justice.

♦ **Legal activity. Regents. Soldiers. Squabbles. Widows.** ♦

Daniel-Rops, *Church...*, p. 558. Farreras et al, *Histoire...*, pp. 255, 256, 264. Lewis, *Development...*, pp. 123, 275, 322, 341, 379, 380 & n, 391–392. McLaughlin, "Woman...," p. 203. Shneidman, *Rise...*, pp. 189, 190, 292, 294, 295–296.

ESCLARMONDE DE FOIX

c. 1170s–d.c. 1215 France

Possibly because of the religious/political turmoil in this region, genealogical records do not exist for many Cathar nobles—especially members of the Foix family. The best available evidence suggests that Esclarmonde was the daughter of †Cecile de Béziers and Roger Bernard, count of Foix. She was presumably married to an orthodox Catholic, Jordan de l'Isle Jordan. He apparently supported Esclarmonde, who became a leading Cathar. In 1207, she debated religious issues with orthodox theologians at Pamiers. She also helped to build Cathar fortress of Montségur and founded hospitals and schools for others of her belief.

♦ **Builders. Cathars. Managers. Medicine. Preachers. Religious patrons. Teachers.** ♦

Abels, "Participation...," pp. 227–229. Castillon, *Histoire...*, p. 230. *DBF*, v.14, p. 187. Decaux, *Histoire...*, pp. 288 & 290. Ennen, *Medieval...*, p. 130. Marks, *Pilgrims...*, pp. 252, 253, 285, 290. Sumption, *Albigensian...*, p. 60. Wakefield, *Heresy...*, p. 74.

ESCLARMUNDA DE FOIX, queen of Majorca [Sclaramonda of Foix]

m. 1275 France; Spain

Daughter of Roger Bernard III, count of Foix. Wife of James of Majorca. Supporter of the Franciscans; believed to have been the founder of a convent at Perpignan. Her daughter was †Sancia of Majorca.

♦ **Queens. Religious patrons.** ♦

Hillgarth, *Pere...*, p. 231. Musto, "Queen Sancia...," pp. 182–183. Otis, "Prostitution...," pp. 149 & 156. Shneidman, *Rise...*, pp. 29, 320.

ESTIENNE (la gravelière)

1292 France

Of the rue En Darne-Estat in 1292 Paris, Dame Estienne paid 12s on her unusual profession—as a sand and gravel collector.

♦ **Merchants. Mining.** ♦

Géraud, *Paris sous...*, p. 51.

ESTRITH OF DENMARK [Estrid]

c. 1010s–1040s Denmark

Daughter of Sweyn I Fork-beard, king of Denmark; sister of Canute of Denmark and England; married Earl Ulf of Denmark. Her son Sweyn II

Estrithsson became king of Denmark around 1048. After Estrith became a widow, Canute tried to use her to achieve an alliance with Normandy. He married her to Robert I of Normandy around the year 1030; Robert later repudiated Estrith.

♦ **Divorce. Pawns. Widows.** ♦

Barlow, *Feudal...*, pp. 2, 57, 92. Blair, *Anglo-Saxon...*, p. 105. Boyesen, *Story...*, p. 236. Brown, *Normans...*, pp. 112 n15, 138. *Cambridge...*, III, pp. 387, 389; V, p. 490. Stenton, *Anglo-Saxon...*, pp. 377, 402–403.

EUDELINE (la barbière)

1292 France

Paid 18s tax on her business on the rue Saint-Christofle in 1292 Paris.

♦ **Barbers. Land/property.** ♦

Géraud, *Paris sous...*, p. 147. Hughes, *Women...*, p. 140.

EUDELINE (la baudréere)

1292 France

In 1292 Paris, Eudeline was taxed 12d for her occupation—making parts (like soles and straps) for shoes.

♦ **Apparel–shoemakers. Less-affluent.** ♦

Géraud, *Paris sous...*, p. 147.

EUDOCIA [Eudoxia]

EUDOCIA BAIANE, empress of Byzantium

d. 901 Byzantium

In effort to gain an heir for his throne, in 899, Byzantine Emperor Leo VI married his third wife, Eudocia Baiane. In 901, she died in labor, giving birth to a son who died shortly thereafter.

♦ **Childbirth. Pawns. Queens.** ♦

Cambridge..., IV, pp. 57, 256. Jenkins, *Byzantium...*, p. 215.

EUDOXIA COMNENA **[Eudocia of Constantinople]**

fl. 1170s–1190s Byzantium; France

Daughter of Emperor Manuel I Comnenus. Jilted by her first fiance, Alfonso II of Aragon, she married William VIII of Montpellier. He repudiated Eudoxia around 1187, so she entered a monastery. Eudoxia was a patroness of troubadours and she is mentioned in some poetry

♦ **Divorce. Models. Patrons of literature. Poets/troubadours. Religieuses.** ♦

Bonner (ed.), *Songs...*, pp. 151, 280, 295. Boutière and Schutz, *Biographies des...*, p. 477. Lejeune, "La Femme...," p. 208. Shneidman, *Rise...*, pp. 38, 319, 320.

EUDOCIA OF DECAPOLIS, empress of Byzantium

m. 855 — Byzantium

She was married to Emperor Michael III in 855 by his mother Empress †Theodora of Paphlagonia. This forced union so infuriated Michael that he conspired with his uncle Bardas to rebel against Theodora.

♦ **Pawns. Queens. Rebellions.** ♦

Diehl, *Byzantine...*, p. 109. Jenkins, *Byzantium...*, p. 160.

EUDOCIA INGERINA, empress of Byzantium

c. 850s–882 — Byzantium

Daughter of Scandinavian minister at Byzantine court. In 855, fifteen-year-old Emperor Michael III fell in love with her. In a panic, his mother, Empress/Regent †Theodora of Paphlagonia, quickly married Michael to †Eudocia of Decapolis. Once Michael III seized power, he married Eudocia Ingerina to his favorite, Basil the Macedonian. Basil was forced to divorce his wife Maria in 865 and marry Eudocia. She had three sons: Leo (b.866), Stephen (b.867), and Alexander (b.870). The first of these boys, Leo, was presumed to be Michael's son and he eventually became Basileus Leo VI. As emperor, however, Basil I the Macedonian showed his preference for his first wife Maria and her son by making the boy, Constantine, co-emperor in 869.

♦ **Models. Pawns. Queens. Women of easy virtue.** ♦

Cambridge..., IV, pp. 43, 47, 50, 51, 53, 55. Diehl, *Byzantine...*, p. 109. Jenkins, *Byzantium...*, pp. 159–160, 195, & 302.

EUDOCIA MACREMBOLITISSA, empress of Byzantium

fl. 1060s–1070s — Byzantium

Wife of Byzantine Emperor Constantine X Ducas. When he died in 1067, Eudocia assumed the imperial power for her son Michael VII Ducas. In an attempt to retain the throne for her son, she then married Romanus Diogenes who became her co-regent, as Romanus IV. He was killed by the Turks in the disastrous battle of Manzikert. With the Empire in ruins, she ruled with her son, until his death in 1078.

♦ **Models. Pawns. Regents. Soldiers. Widows.** ♦

Cambridge..., IV, pp. 325, 326, 757. *Chronicles...*, pp. 41 & 42. Comnena, *Alexiad...*, pp. 107–108, 280–281. Norwich, *Normans...*, pp. 165 & 170.

EUPHEMIA [Eufemia; Eufimia; Evfimia]

EUPHEMIA OF ARNSTEIN, queen of Norway

m.c. 1295–1310s — Germany; Norway

Around 1295, Euphemia married Haakon of Norway (later King Haakon V Long-legs). This marriage improved trade, but caused trouble by bringing much Hanseatic influence into Norway. Euphemia was a patroness of writers; she was particularly fond of chivalric romances and encouraged their translation.

♦ **Educated. Models. Patrons of literature.** ♦

Boyesen, *Story...*, pp. 457 & 459. Bukdahl, *Scandinavia...*, v.1, p. 310. Larsen, *History...*, pp. 162, 174 & 189.

EVFIMIA OF KIEV, queen of Hungary

c. 1100–d. 1139 Hungary; Russia

Daughter of Vladimir II Monomach, prince of Kiev. Became second wife of King Coloman of Hungary in 1112. She soon returned home to Russia to give birth to her baby Boris. In later years, when Boris put forward his claim to the throne of Hungary, the supporters of his rival, Béla II of Hungary, claimed that Evfimia had fled Hungary because Coloman had discovered that she was committing adultery and had banished her. In that case, Boris' father was a matter of some doubt. Evfimia denied this version of the story. Boris' party claimed that Evfimia had voluntarily returned home because she was shocked by the dissolute and intrigue-ridden Hungarian court.

♦ **Adultery. Queens. Squabbles.** ♦

Cambridge..., IV, p. 356. Vernadsky, *Kievan...*, pp. 330–331.

EUFEMIA (of MECKLENBURG) **[Euphemia of Sweden]**

c. 1315–1340s Germany; Sweden

Daughter of †Ingebjorg of Norway and Duke Erik of Sweden; granddaughter of †Euphemia of Arnstein and Haakon V of Norway. Eufemia married Albert of Mecklenburg. Thanks to her royal bloodlines, her son, Albert of Mecklenburg, was offered the Swedish throne in the 1360s.

♦ **Estate. Genealogy.** ♦

Musset, *Les Peuples...*, p. 295. Scott, *Sweden...*, pp. 72 & 75.

EUPHEMIA OF WHERWELL

fl. 1226–1257 England

Abbess of Wherwell (in Hampshire). Medically knowledgeable; lauded by contemporaries for building water and sewer system under the monastery infirmary. Euphemia was also widely known as a mystic. In addition, she designed and supervised construction of new, and better, convent buildings.

♦ **Abbesses. Builders. Medicine. Models. Mystics.** ♦

Gasquet, *English...*, pp. 155–158. Gies, *Women...*, p. 68. Hughes, *Women...*, p. 118. Hurd-Mead, *History...*, pp. 164 & 223. Power, *Nunneries...*, pp. 29, 89, 90, 94, 169, 243, 501.

EUPHROSYNE OF BYZANTIUM

c. 790–830s Byzantium

Daughter of Constantine VI and his first wife, Mary of Amnia. When her father divorced her mother, Euphrosyne retired to a convent. Around 820, Emperor Michael II caused a scandal by falling in love with

Euphrosyne, removing her from the convent, and marrying her. After he died in 829, Euphrosyne quickly found a wife for her stepson Theophilus, and then retired (reputedly with relief) back to her convent.

♦ **Adultery. Negotiators. Religieuses.** ♦

Diehl, *Byzantine...,* pp. 83, 94, 97–8. Jenkins, *Byzantium...,* pp. 91 & 141.

EUPRAXIA OF KIEV, Holy Roman Empress

[Adelheid of Kiev; Praxedis]

b. 1071–d. 1109 Germany; Italy; Russia

Daughter of Vsevolod I of Kiev. Married (1) Henry the Long, marquis of Nordmark (d.1087). She then wished to become a nun at Quedlinburg, but was instead forced to become the second wife of Holy Roman Emperor Henry IV. (Her name was then changed to Empress Adelheid.) She was very unhappy at Henry's court, and later received absolution from Pope Urban II for what she claimed was her forced participation in Henry's orgies. In 1093, Adelheid fled from Germany and took refuge with †Matilda of Tuscany at Canossa. In 1099, she returned to Kiev and took back her name of Eupraxia. When Henry IV died (1106), Eupraxia took the veil at St. Andrew where her sister, †Ianka, was abbess. Her story is told in *byliny* (epic folklore of Russia) in a very romanticized version. Few western historians credit her stories; beliefs range from the idea that she was insane to the view that she was very wicked. Eupraxia was perhaps simply a useful tool in the papacy's fight against Henry IV. It is possible, however, that the relatively luxurious court of Germany did shock this prudish woman who was used to a much more ascetic way of life—a woman, moreover, who desperately wished to be free to live a celibate and strict life as a nun.

♦ **Adultery. Models. Nuns. Pawns. Popes. Widows.** ♦

Cambridge..., V, pp. 94, 145, 146. Cheetham, *Keepers...,* p. 102. Ennen, *Medieval...,* p. 73. Fuhrmann, *Germany...,* pp. 68, 69. Hampe, *Germany...,* pp. 97–98. Haverkamp, *Medieval...,* p. 121. Vernadsky, *Kievan...,* pp. 340–342.

EVFOSINIA OF POLOTSK **[Euphrosynia]**

b. 1001–d.c. 1073 Russia

Russian princess; chose to become a nun rather than marry. She was a renowned scholar and a great beauty. Evfosinia reputedly established classes for girls at her monastery.

♦ **Nuns. Scholars. Teachers. Unmarried.** ♦

Vernadsky, *Kievan...,* p. 278.

EVA OF BROUNESTOWN

fl. 1300s–1320s Ireland

See—ALICE KYTELER.

♦ **Witchcraft.** ♦

EVA MACMURROUGH **[Aoife]**

fl. 1160s–1170s Ireland

Daughter of Mor O'Toole and Dermot MacMurrough. In 1166, she accompanied her father to Bristol. He offered her hand in marriage to "Strongbow" (Richard FitzGilbert de Clare, earl of Striguil) in exchange for troops which would come to Ireland and help crush Tiernan O'Ruairc. Strongbow did travel to Ireland, and he and Eva were married in 1170. Their only child, †Isabella de Clare, was just a baby when Strongbow died in 1176.

♦ **Dowry/dower. Estate. Pawns. Widows.** ♦

Appleby, *John...*, pp. 28–9 & 89. Curtis, *Ireland...*, pp. 46, 50, 59, & 80. Curtis, *Medieval...*, pp. 49 & 131. *DNB*, v.4, pp. 391, 392. FitzGibbon, *Irish...*, pp. 107 & 108. Lloyd, *Maligned...*, pp. 22 & 23. Orpen, *Ireland...*, I, pp. 74, 197–202. Richter, *Medieval...*, pp. 132, 144. Scherman, *Flowering...*, p. 234.

EVA OF SAINT-MARTIN

fl. 1230s–d. 1265 Belgium

Beguine and famed recluse. She promoted the elevation of the Feast of the Eucharist to an official Holy Day—as initiated by her friend †Juliana of Cornillon. Eva was also a close friend of Pope Urban IV; he wrote to her in 1264 at Liège.

♦ **Anchoresses. Beguines. Educated. Popes.** ♦

Attwater, *Dictionary...*, p. 175. Bynum, *Holy...*, p. 55. Lagorio, "Continental...," p. 175. McDonnell, *Beguines...*, pp. 300, 304, 306, 308–309, 332. Weisheipl, *Friar...*, pp. 178–180.

— F —

FABRISSE RIVES

fl. 1280s–1310s France

Married a Cathar; their daughter †Grazida (Lizier) was born around 1298. Her husband soon forced Fabrisse to leave his home because she refused to convert to Catharism. To support herself, Fabrisse then became a rather incompetent wine merchant in the town of Montaillou.

♦ **Alewives. Heretics.** ♦

Dronke, *Women...*, p. 203. Ladurie, *Montaillou...*, pp. 6, 34, 65, 158, 378.

FAYDIDE OF MILLAU, countess of Toulouse [Faydide of Toulouse]

fl. 1140s France

Daughter of Gerberge, countess of Provence, and Gilbert, viscount of Millau; wife of Alphonse I, count of Toulouse. Faydide accompanied †Eleanor of Aquitaine on the Second Crusade.

♦ **Crusades. Servants–ladies.** ♦

Anselme, *Histoire...*, v.2, p. 687. Kelly, *Eleanor...*, p. 34. Pernoud, *Eleanor...*, p. 50.

FELISE (la pastéere)

1292 France

Pastry-seller of 1292 Paris; paid 2s taxes.

♦ **Less-affluent. Provisioning–pastry.** ♦

Géraud, *Paris sous...*, p. 162.

FELISE REYNARD

fl.c. 1440s–1450s France

Widow of Jean Pic, lord of Beaumont-en-Trèves. Mistress of Louis (XI) while he was in Dauphiné. They had two daughters. Louis gave both girls dowries and saw to it that they married well: Jeanne married Louis de Bourbon, Admiral of France; the other daughter married Aimar de Poitiers, lord of Saint-Vallier.

♦ **Mistresses. Widows.** ♦

Champion, *Louis...*, p. 119. Cleugh, *Chant...*, p. 106. Lewis, *King...*, p. 218.

FIAMMETTA

d. 1337 Italy

Her real name was presumably Maria d'Aquino. She was an educated beauty of Naples; married to Count Tomaso d'Aquino. Giovanni Boccaccio made her famous as *Fiammetta*—presumably his mistress and inspiration. Some scholars believe that she was the illegitimate daughter of Robert the Wise, king of Naples.

♦ **Adultery. Educated. Models. Plague.** ♦

Bernardo, "Petrarch's...," p. 66. Branca, *Boccaccio...,* pp. 17–18, 29, 42, 45, 58, 60–63, 67–69. Musto, "Queen Sancia...," pp. 186 n55. Tuchman, *Distant...,* pp. 103, 220, 221.

FIAMETTA ADIMARI

1469 Italy

Tuscan townswoman. She wrote to her husband requesting that he buy a young slave to care for their baby son once he was weaned.

♦ **Childcare. Slaves–owners. Writers–letters.** ♦

Maguire, *Women...,* pp. 142 & 224. Origo, "Domestic...," pp. 324 & 333.

FLORENCIA PINAR

fl.c. 1480s–1490s Spain

Well-educated noblewoman. Wrote erotic love poetry; three extant works.

♦ **Educated. Poets/troubadours.** ♦

Defiant...Hispanic, pp. 17–19. Snow, "Spanish...," pp. 320–332.

FORIA (of Vermandois)

1247/8 France

Jewish usurer recorded in the *Contra judaeas* (Against Jews) documents from Picardy (specifically the royal province of Vermandois) in 1247/48. Probably Foria handled small domestic loans; most of her clients were likely to have been Christian females.

♦ **Banking. Jews.** ♦

Jordan, "Jews...," p. 53.

(St.) FRANCES OF ROME **[Francesca Bussa dei Ponziani]**

1384–1440 Italy

A very wealthy woman, she married Lorenzo Ponziano in 1397. She reputedly vomited whenever her husband insisted on sexual intimacy. She and her sister-in-law were devoted to caring for the Roman poor, especially in hospitals. Frances established a group of women to help with this charitable work. Her visions included the ability to constantly see her guardian angel.

♦ **Charity. Medicine–hospitals. Mystics. Religieuses. Religious patrons. Saints. Virginity.** ♦

A.S., Mar v.2, pp. 89–219. Attwater, *Dictionary...,* pp. 110–111. Bynum, *Holy...,* pp. 215, 222, 226, 317 n52. Farmer, *Oxford...,* pp. 156–157.

FRANCESCA BENTIVOGLIO

b. 1465–1500 Italy

Daughter of Giovanni Bentivoglio of Bologna. In 1482, forty-two-year-old Galeotto Manfredi of Faenza married seventeen-year-old Francesca in order to ally himself with her powerful family. Their many marital problems soon resulted in a separation. An attempted reconciliation in 1487 was a dismal failure. In 1488, she lured Galeotto into her room and stabbed him (or had him stabbed) in the back. Francesca then tried to assume the regency for their son Astorre, but was defeated by Florentine troops. She was forced to retire to Bologna.

♦ **Murder. Pawns. Regents.** ♦

Ady, *Bentivoglio...,* pp. 66, 83–84, 87, 142–143, 148, 167. Breisach, *Caterina...,* pp. 89–90 & 125–127. Fusero, *Borgias,* pp. 146 & 230. Hook, *Lorenzo...,* pp. 175–176.

FRANCESCA DA RIMINI

d. 1285 Italy

Daughter of Giovanni da Polenta of Ravenna. Wife of Giovanni Malatesta the lame. When he discovered Francesca in bed with his brother Paolo Malatesta the handsome, Giovanni murdered the two lovers. Francesca and Paolo are among the occupants of Dante's *Hell,* in the *Divine Comedy.*

♦ **Adultery. Models. Murder–victims.** ♦

Cartwright, *Beatrice...,* p. 373. Chubb, *Dante...,* pp. 76, 179–183, 213, 425, 284, 546, 718, 724. Effinger, *Women...,* pp. 108–111. Holmes, *Florence...,* pp. 112–113, 237, 242–243. Phillips, *Dante's...,* pp. 46–47. Prescott, *Princes...,* p. 279.

FRANCESCA DE ROMANA

fl. 1321 Italy

Wife of Matteo de Romana. In 1321 she received a license from Charles, duke of Calabria, and a certificate from the University of Salerno giving her the right to practice surgery.

♦ **Educated. Surgeons. University.** ♦

Harksen, *Women...,* p. 27. Hughes, *Women...,* p. 144. Hurd-Mead, *History...,* p. 277. Lipinska, *Histoire...,* p. 99. Mozans, *Woman...,* p. 286. Uitz, *Legend...,* p. 67.

FREDERUN OF LORRAINE, queen of France **[Frérone]**

m. 907–d.c. 917 France

Became first wife of King Charles III the Simple around 907. Charles gave her the lands of Corbeny and Ponthieu for dower estates. Frederun later gave Ponthieu to the abbey of St. Corneille at Compiègne.

♦ **Dowry/dower. Queens. Religious patrons.** ♦

Riché, *Les Carolingiens...,* p. 239. Stafford, *Queens...,* pp. 37, 102, 132. Verdon, "Les Sources...," p. 242.

FRESSENDA (de Hauteville)

c. 1000s–1040s France; Italy

Second wife of Tancred de Hauteville. Her first son (b.1016) was Robert Guiscard, duke of Apulia (d.1085). Among her other six sons and three daughters was Roger I, great count of Sicily (d.1101).

♦ **Genealogy.** ♦

Cambridge..., V, p. 170. Norwich, *Kingdom...*, p. 395. Norwich, *Normans...*, pp. 39–40. Osborne, *Greatest...*, p. 40.

FREYDIS OF NORWAY

c. 980s–1010s Iceland; Norway

Daughter of Erik the Red; half-sister of Leif Ericsson. She accompanied the second Icelandic expedition to "Vinland" (North America) around A.D. 1000.

♦ **Models. Shipping–explorers & pioneers.** ♦

Boyesen, *Story...*, p. 181. Jones, *Vikings...*, p. 303. Larsen, *History...*, p. 62.

FRIDERUN (of Germany)

c. 960 Germany

Daughter of Count Wichmann the younger. She and her sister †Imma founded and ran monastery of Kemnade. Otto I helped them take possession of a vast amount of land for their convent.

♦ **Abbesses. Estate. Managers. Religious patrons.** ♦

Leyser, *Rule...*, pp. 56, 65, & 68.

FYGEN VAN BERCHEM

c. 1440s–1502 Germany

A silkworker; admitted to guild in 1455.

For more details see her sister—SEWIS VAN BERCHEM.

♦ **Apprentices. Shipping. Silkwork.** ♦

Wensky, "Women's Guilds...," p. 647.

— G —

GABRINA ALBETTI

1375 Italy

Gabrina was an old woman in 1375 when she was tried for witchcraft by secular court at Reggio. She was branded and mutilated for practicing love magic and for teaching other women to worship the Devil.

♦ **Punishments. Witchcraft.** ♦

Kieckhefer, *European...*, p. 115. Russell, *Witchcraft...*, pp. 209-210.

GALIENA (of Norfolk)

1209 England

Accused in 1209 Norfolk by †Agnes, wife of Odo, of being a witch. Galiena was cleared of this charge by successfully undergoing the hot iron ordeal.

♦ **Ordeals. Witchcraft.** ♦

Ewen, *Witchcraft...*, pp. 27-28. Robbins, *Encyclopedia...*, p. 161. Summers, *Geography...*, p. 80.

GARSENDA DE FORCALQUIER, countess of Provence

c. 1180–d.c. 1257 France

Facts about Garsenda are somewhat difficult to isolate since she is usually known by the same name as her mother, and she also had a daughter named Garsenda. Moreover, there is some dispute over whether her father's name was Bernard, Guillem IV, or Rainon of Sabran, lord of Caylar. It is known, however, that Garsenda was an heiress who married Alfonso II, count of Provence, around 1193. When he died (c.1209), she ruled Provence for their young son, Raymond Berengar IV. In 1225, Garsenda relinquished control of the region to her son, and she retired to a monastery. She is best known today as one of the female Provençal trobaritz.

♦ **Estate. Models. Patrons of literature. Poets/troubadours. Regents. Religieuses. Widows.** ♦

Bogin, *Women...*, pp. 108-109 & 170-173. Boutière and Schutz, *Biographies des...*, pp. 215, 216, 505-507. Cox, *Eagles...*, pp. 21, 118. *DBF*, v.14, p. 426. Powicke, *Thirteenth...*, p. 112 n.

GENEVIÈVE (la paonnière)

1313 France

In 1313 Paris, Genevieve was a *plummassière*—a hatmaker who used peacock feathers for making and ornamenting her hats. Evidently, Geneviève was quite successful; she was taxed £12, while two men in her line of work paid much lower taxes—75s and 18d. She used some of her money to endow a chantry.

♦ **Apparel–hatmakers. Land/property. Merchants. Religious patrons.** ♦

Lehmann, *Rôle de la...*, p. 447.

GERBERGA OF BAVARIA

b. 940–d.c. 1002 Germany

Daughter of †Judith and Henry I of Bavaria. Became abbess of Gandersheim and Regensburg. Mentor of †Hroswitha of Gandersheim who later wrote about Gerberga. She used her family connections to acquire vast lands, wealth, and privileges for Gandersheim and her foundation of St. Mary's.

♦ **Abbesses. Managers. Models. Religious patrons. Teachers.** ♦

Dictionary..., v.6, p. 313. Dronke, *Women...*, pp. 56-57, 65-66, 75-76, 79, 83, 147. Duckett, *Death...*, pp. 109, 183, & 255. Ennen, *Medieval...*, pp. 82 & 83. Leyser, *Rule...*, pp. 18, 26, 54, & 66.

GERBERGA OF SAXONY, queen of France

b. 910s–d.c. 969 France; Germany

Daughter of †Matilda (of Saxony) and Henry the Fowler, king of Germany. In 929, Gerberga married Giselbert, duke of Lotharingia. After he died (c.931), she married Louis IV d'Outremer, king of France. Despite frequent pregnancies, Gerberga negotiated alliances, headed peace treaty delegations, and defended Laon for her husband. After Louis died (954), she was equally helpful to her son, Lothar I of France, serving as his regent, accompanying him on military campaigns, assisting at the siege of Dijon, and enlisting her brother Otto I's help for Lothar. After Lothar married, Gerberga tactfully retired to her dower lands in Lotharingia.

♦ **Book owners. Dowry/dower. Negotiators. Regents. Soldiers. Widows.** ♦

Decaux, *Histoire...*, p. 175. Duckett, *Death...*, pp. 46, 59, 68-69, 79, 93, & 315. Lehmann, *Rôle de la...*, pp. 147-154. Leyser, *Rule...*, pp. 53 & 54. McKitterick, *Frankish...*, pp. 313, 316, 318, Tables 9 & 10. Robinson, *Readings...*, I, p. 247. Stafford, *Queens...*, pp. 35, 40, 50, 56, 77, 83, 89-91, 110, 115, 117-119, 123, 132, 145, 151, 160-161, 166, 176, 185, & 189. Verdon, "Les Sources...," pp. 226, 227, 240.

GERBERGA (of TOULOUSE) **[Gariberga]**

d. 834 France

Daughter of William I, count of Toulouse; sister of Bernard of Septimania. She entered convent at Chalon-sur-Sâone. When Emperor

Lothar I took the area (plundering the region and killing many inhabitants), he had Gerberga drowned, claiming that she practiced the arts of witchcraft.

♦ **Murder. Nuns. Witchcraft.** ♦

Anselme, *Histoire...*, v.2, p. 680. *Carolingian...*, pp. 135, 203. Duckett, *Carolingian...*, p. 51. Wemple, *Women...*, p. 95.

GERTRUDE OF BABENBERG

c. 1230s-1268 Austria; Bohemia; Germany; Russia

Inherited the duchy of Austria through her uncle. Married (1) Vladislav, the presumed heir of his father Wenceslaus of Bohemia. After Vladislav died, Gertrude married Herman of Baden (d.c.1250). Her third husband was Romanus, prince of Russia (Roman, prince of Galicia).

♦ **Estate. Pawns. Politics.** ♦

Cambridge..., V, p. 352; VI, pp. 437, 438. Stubbs, *Later...*, p. 71. Vernadsky, *Mongols...*, p. 145.

GERTRUDE OF BAVARIA

fl. 1150s–1180s Denmark; Germany

Daughter of Henry the Lion of Bavaria and Saxony. Around 1166, Gertrude married Frederick of Rothenburg. After his death, she married Canute VI of Denmark.

♦ **Genealogy. Queens.** ♦

Cambridge..., V, p. 387. Haverkamp, *Medieval...*, p. 231.

GERTRUDE OF FLANDERS, duchess of Lorraine

c. 1080s–1120s Belgium; Flanders; France

Daughter of Robert I the Frisian, count of Flanders, and †Gertrude of Saxony (daughter of Bernard, duke of Saxony, and widow of Florent I, count of Holland). Gertrude of Flanders married (1) Henry of Louvain, count of Brussels (d.1095), and (2) Thierry of Alsace, duke of Lorraine. Their son, Thierry of Alsace, claimed Flanders through her line. In the 1120s, she engaged in an unsuccessful feud with Emperor Henry V.

♦ **Estate. Politics. Squabbles. Widows.** ♦

Anselme, *Histoire...*, v.2, pp. 718-719. *Cambridge...*, V, pp. 164, 599. Pirenne, *Histoire...*, v.1, p. 197 & n.

GERTRUDE OF HACKEBORN

1232–1291 Germany

Daughter of Baron von Hackeborn; sister of †Mechtild of Hackeborn. Abbess of Helfta from 1251 until 1291. Gertrude served as teacher/mentor to †Gertrude the Great (see below). Her long rule saw Helfta established as a center of scholarship and mysticism.

♦ **Abbesses. Childcare. Mystics. Teachers.** ♦

Boulding, *Underside...*, pp. 454, 460-461. Bynum, *Jesus...*, pp. 175, 176, 178, 209, 210, 223, 249, 256. Halligan (ed.), *Booke...*, pp. 33, 34, 35, 37. Lagorio, "Continental...," p. 167. Leff, *Heresy...*, v.1, p. 31.

(St.) GERTRUDE VON HELFTA **[Gertrude the Great]**
b. 1256–d. 1301 Germany

Sent to convent of Helfta at age five. A mystic and writer of a collection of prayers, the *Exercitia Spirituala,* among other works.

♦ **Mystics. Nuns. Saints. Scholars. Writers–theology.** ♦

Bynum, *Holy...,* pp. 28, 58, 62, 64, 65, 84, 85, 86, 133, 151, 172, 185, 200, 211, 212, 231-2, 234, 236, 242, 261, 263, 292. *Exercises....* Farmer, *Oxford...,* pp. 169-170. Halligan (ed.), *Booke...,* pp. 34-37, 39, 44, 45. Lagorio, "Continental...," pp. 163, 167, 170-172. McDonnell, *Beguines...,* p. 374. Power, *Women...,* p. 90. Petroff, *Medieval...,* pp. 222-230.

GERTRUDE OF MEISSEN **[Gertrude of Brunswick]**
c. 1080s–d. 1117 Germany

Sister and heiress of Ekbert II of Meissen (murdered in 1090). Married (1) Dietrich, count of Katlenburg; (2) Henry the Fat, count of Nordheim (murdered 1101)—their daughters were Empress †Richenza and Gertrude, countess of Holland; and (3) Henry of Eilenburg, margrave of Meissen (d.1103). Their son Henry was born after his father's death.

♦ **Estate. Murder. Politics.** ♦

Cambridge..., V, pp. 145, 146, 152 & n, 153. Leyser, *Medieval...,* p. 187.

GERTRUD OF MERAN, queen of Hungary **[Gertrude of Merano]**
b. 1185-d.c. 1213 Austria; Germany; Hungary

Daughter of †Agnes of Dedo and Berthold IV, count of Meran and Andrechs; sister of St. †Hedwig of Silesia; mother of St. †Elizabeth of Hungary (b.1207). Wife of King Andrew II of Hungary.

♦ **Genealogy. Murder. Queens.** ♦

Butler, *Lives...,* vol. 4, p. 124. Harrsen, *Cursus...,* p. 21. Hughes, *Women...,* pp. 133-134. Hurd-Mead, *History...,* p. 181. Pamlényi, *History...,* p. 56.

GERTRUDE VAN ÖOSTEN **[Blessed Gertrude of Delft]**
d.c. 1358 Netherlands

Dutch Beguine and famed mystic of Delft. Gertrude's life story, detailing her passage from servant to saint, was useful propaganda—"proof" that Beguines were not heretics. She suffered stigmata for eighteen years. Gertrude was also a psychic with a large following.

♦ **Beguines. Mystics. Models. Servants. Superstitions.** ♦

A.S., Jan v.1, pp. 348-353. Attwater, *Dictionary...,* p. 124. Bynum, *Holy...,* pp. 28, 117, 123, 211. Goodich, "Ancilla Dei...," pp. 127-128. Lagorio, "Continental...," p. 175. McDonnell, *Beguines...,* p. 397, 399, 552.

GERTRUDE OF SAXONY, duchess of Bavaria
m.c. 1127–d. 1143 Germany

Daughter of †Richenza of Nordheim and Emperor Lothar II (Lothar of Supplinburg); married Henry the Proud, duke of Bavaria. She passed the duchy of Saxony to her son Henry the Lion. After Henry the Proud died, around 1142 Gertrude married Henry II Jasomirgott. She died in childbirth, ruining several alliance plans.

♦ **Childbirth. Estate. Models. Regents.** ♦

Cambridge..., V, pp. 153, 154, 337, 348, 349, 350. Fuhrmann, *Germany...*, pp. 118, 125, 140, 150. Hallam, *History...*, pp. 8-10. Hampe, *Germany...*, pp. 123 & 140. Haverkamp, *Medieval...*, pp. 137, 138, 139, 142, 143, 266. Stephenson, *Mediaeval...*, p. 403.

GERTRUDE OF SAXONY, countess of Holland, countess of Flanders

c. 1050s–d. 1113 Flanders; Germany; Netherlands

See her daughter—GERTRUDE OF FLANDERS, countess of Lorraine.

♦ **Estate. Widows.** ♦

GESLOIRE OF CASTILE

See—ELVIRA OF CASTILE.

GILE (la barbière)

1297 France

A Parisian barber; in 1297 she paid 2s 6d tax.

♦ **Barbers. Less-affluent.** ♦

Jacquart, *Le Milieu...*, p. 443. Michaëlsson, *Le Livre...*, p. 397.

GILE (la maçonne)

1292 France

Paid 12s on her occupation as a mason at la Pissote St. Martin in 1292 Paris.

♦ **Builders–masons. Land/property.** ♦

Géraud, *Paris sous...*, p. 59.

GILETTE OF NARBONNE

fl.c. 1300 France

Daughter of physician, Gérard of Narbonne. After his death, Gilette took over his practice, treating his patients and supposedly even curing the French king of fistula. Boccacio referred to her as *Donna Medica.*

♦ **Doctors/empirics. Models.** ♦

Hurd-Mead, *History...*, p. 272. Lipinska, *Histoire...*, p. 152.

GINEVRA (Datini)

1398–c. 1420s Italy

Slave girl; daughter of Francesco Datini by his slave/mistress. He later adopted and legitimized Ginevra. Francesco hired a tutor to coach her in reading. He also gave Ginevra a sizeable dowry and found her a husband—a respectable, young wool merchant from Prato.

♦ **Dowry/dower. Educated. Illegitimacy. Models. Slaves.** ♦

Gies, *Women...*, pp. 201-202, 206. Origo, "Domestic...," pp. 344-345.

GINEVRA D'ESTE **[Genevieve]**

c. 1418–d. 1440 Italy

Daughter of Niccolo d'Este of Ferrara. Became first wife of Sigismund Malatesta of Rimini around 1434. It was rumored that she was murdered, perhaps by her husband, in 1440.

♦ **Genealogy. Murder–suspected.** ♦

Jones, *Malatesta...*, pp. 176 & 186. Prescott, *Princes...*, pp. 285-7. Yriarte, *Rimini: Etudes...*, pp. 88-89 & 123 (an old, chatty source).

GINEVRA NOGOROLA

1417–c. 1465 Italy

Humanist scholar, well-educated in Greek and Latin. In 1438, Ginevra married Brunoro Gambara, a Brescian nobleman, and was forced to give up scholarly activities in order to raise her numerous children. She was also known for her community service work in Brescia.

♦ **Charity. Scholars. Writers.** ♦

King and Rabil, *Her Immaculate...*, pp. 11, 16-17, 18 & 131. Kristeller, "Learned...," pp. 96-97. Mozans, *Woman...*, p. 58. Robathan, "Bluestocking...," pp. 106, 107, 109.

GIOVANNA **[Giovanni; Giovannia]**

See—JEAN/JOAN.

GIRALDA DE LAURAC, lady of Lavaur

[Giraude; Geralda of Montreal]

d. 1211 France

Noted for her charity to Cathars, and for her support of poets and scholars. Giralda and her brother Aimery de Montréal defended castle of Lavaur for two months against Simon de Montfort. When the fortress fell (1211), Aimery was hanged, several hundred Cathars were burned, and Giralda was stoned to death.

♦ **Cathars. Charity. Murder–victims. Patrons of literature. Soldiers.** ♦

Decaux, *Histoire...*, p. 291. Marks, *Pilgrims...*, p. 263. Wakefield, *Heresy...*, pp. 200 & 204.

GISELA [Gisel; Gisèle; Gisla; Gisle]

GISELA

b. 781–810s France; Germany

Daughter of †Hildegard and Charlemagne. Well-educated; student of Alcuin. An avid astronomer. Alcuin and other writers extolled her love of learning. She entered convent in 814.

♦ **Astronomy. Educated. Estate. Models. Nuns.** ♦

Carolingian..., pp. 59, 186, 200. Decaux, *Histoire...,* pp. 161-162. Duckett, *Carolingian...,* p. 14. Ennen, *Medieval...,* p. 53. Jourdain, "Memoire...," p. 471. Lehmann, *Rôle de la...,* pp. 192-193.

GISELA OF BAVARIA, queen of Hungary **[Giselle]**
b. 985-d.c. 1065 Germany; Hungary

Daughter of Gisèle of Burgundy and Henry the Quarrelsome of Bavaria. Around 996, Gisela married (St.) Stephen of Hungary. Her cousin, Otto III, made the couple king and queen of Hungary. She exerted a strong Germanic influence on the court and on her husband. Gisela was very pious; she gave much of her wealth to the church.

♦ **Art patrons. Models. Politics. Religious patrons.** ♦

Bryce, *Holy...,* pp. 151 & 491. *DBF,* v.1, p. 528. Karacsonyi, *Life...,* p. 118. Kelleher, *Holy...,* pp. 21, 22, 27, 79, 80-84, 93, 94, 96. Kosztolnyik, *Five...,* pp. 12, 43, 57. Nagy, *St. Margaret...,* pp. 16-17. Pamlényi, *History...,* pp. 34 & 626.

GISELA (of France)
c. 830s–860s France; Italy

Daughter of †Judith of Bavaria and Louis I the Pious; married Eberhard de Frioul (Everard, marquis of Friuli—d.864). Her husband bequeathed his entire library to Gisela.

♦ **Book owners. Genealogy.** ♦

Bell, "Medieval...," p. 155. Cabaniss, *Judith...,* p. 36. *Cambridge...,* III, p. 47. McKitterick, *Frankish...,* p. 184. Riché, *Les Carolingiens...,* p. 300.

GISELA OF KERZENBROECK **[Gisele von Kerssenbroek]**
d.c. 1300 Germany

Nun at Rulle near Osnabrück. Worked in convent scriptorium. She copied and illustrated the *Codex Gisele.* This was illuminated with fifty-two miniatures including one of her convent community. She also signed one picture on the edge of Virgin Mary's coverlet.

♦ **Artists. Bookmaking. Nuns. Writers–copyists.** ♦

Carr, "Women...," p. 8. Greer, *Obstacle...,* pp. 158-159.

GISLA OF LORRAINE **[Gisle of Normandy]**
fl. 860s–880s France

Daughter of †Waldrada and Lothar II of Lotharingia. Married Godfried of Normandy. After he was killed, Gisla made ineffective efforts to bring peace to the area. Failing at that task, she found peace for herself by retiring to a monastery; she became abbess of Nivelles.

♦ **Abbesses. Estate. Illegitimacy. Politics. Religieuses. Widows.** ♦

Cambridge..., III, p. 60. Ernouf, *Histoire...,* pp. 69, 80, 125, 306. Wemple, *Women...,* p. xiv.

GISELA OF SWABIA, queen of Germany, Holy Roman Empress [Gisele of Germany]

c. 1000s–1043 Germany

Daughter of Gerberga of Burgundy and Herman, duke of Swabia. Gisela was a widow when she married Conrad II of Germany, later Holy Roman Emperor. She was a political asset to Conrad. In the *Deeds of Conrad II,* a contemporary described her as a peacemaker and a negotiator of "manly" wisdom. Gisela was represented in contemporary illuminations as a bringer of peace.

♦ **Book owners. Dowry/dower. Educated. Models. Negotiators. Patrons of literature. Politics. Popes. Regents. Religious patrons. Teachers.** ♦

Cambridge..., III, pp. 143n, 249, 254, 256, 264, 271, 273, 276, 280, 294; V, pp. 17, 18, 24. Ennen, *Medieval...,* pp. 67-69. Hampe, *Germany...,* pp. 34 & 37. Leyser, *Rule...,* p. 111. Stafford, *Queens...,* pp. 30 & 45. Stubbs, *Germany...,* pp. 142 & 171. Verdon, "Les Sources...," p. 247.

GIULIA

See—GUILIA.

GODA LA GABLERE

1244 England

A usurer in thirteenth-century London. Goda repented of that sin, and retired to St. Mary's convent where she atoned and became a nun.

♦ **Banking–usury. Charity. Land/property. Nuns.** ♦

London Eyre...1244, pp. 126-127.

GODEVERE OF TOËNI [Godchilde; Godehilde of Tosni]

d. 1097 England; France

An English noblewoman who married Baldwin I of Lorraine, count of Edessa. She accompanied him on the First Crusade and died en route, in Asia Minor.

♦ **Crusades.** ♦

Hamilton, "Women...," p. 145. Lehmann, *Rôle de la...,* p. 373. Payne, *Dream...,* pp. 51, 119. Tyerman, *England...,* pp. 16, 429 n99. Vitalis, *Ecclesiastical...,* v.3, pp. 128 & 129.

GODGIFU (of England) [Goda]

b. 1006–d.c. 1050 England; France

Daughter of †Emma of Normandy and King Ethelred II of England. Godgifu married Drogo of Mantes, count of the Vexin (d.1035); their son Ralf later became earl of Hereford. Godgifu's second husband was Eustace II, count of Boulogne.

♦ **Estate. Genealogy.** ♦

Barlow, *Edward...,* pp. 27, 30, 39, 41, 45, 50, 109, 219, 307-308, 340. Barlow, *Feudal...,* pp. 57, 58, 141. Brown, *Normans...,* pp. 78, 82, 103,

111, 112, 115, 123. *Cambridge...*, III, pp. 392, 393. *DNB*, v.6, p. 897. Douglas, *William...*, p. 171 & Tables 3 & 7. Wood, *Search...*, p. 210.

GODGIFU, lady of MERCIA **[Godgyfu; Lady Godiva]**
b. 1003–d.c. 1070 England

Sister of Thorold of Bucknall, sheriff of Lincolnshire. Married Leofric, ealdorman of Mercia, in later 1020s (she was probably a widow at the time). The story of Godgifu's naked ride through Coventry is extremely dubious, but she was renowned in her own time as a patroness of the church. She commissioned art works for churches, founded monasteries, endowed abbeys, and was benefactress of other pious projects. Presumably around 1060 (after Leofric's death), she retired to convent at Evesham. Godgifu was mother of at least one son, Aelfgar, earl of Mercia.

♦ **Art patrons. Models. Religieuses. Religious patrons. Widows.** ♦
Barlow, *Feudal...*, p. 56. Burbidge, *Old...*, pp. 16-40 (this is an older work, but it has much information about Godgifu). Campbell, *Anglo-Saxons*, p. 209. Schulenburg, "Women's...," pp. 235, 236. Wright, *Cultivation...*, p. 241.

GODILA (of Walbeck)
c. 986–d.c. 1030 Germany

Otto II, Holy Roman Emperor, married her to Liuthar of Walbeck around 988. When Liuthar died at Cologne in 1003, Godila quickly secured his estate for their young son, Werner.

♦ **Pawns. Regents. Widows.** ♦
Leyser, *Rule...*, pp. 41, 43, 52, 55, 72, & 120.

GORMFLATH (of Ireland) **[Gormlaith of Leinster; Kormlod]**
c. 980s–c. 1015 Ireland

Sister of Maelmora, king of Leinster. There is some confusion over Gormflath's marital/political career, but it appears that she married at least three times. Her first husband was Olaf Cuaran, ruler of Dublin who was defeated by Malachy of Meath. Their son Sitric Silkbeard later ruled Dublin. Gormflath soon married the conqueror, Malachy. He tired of her and repudiated her around 990. Nothing daunted, Gormflath proceeded to wed the great Irish leader, Brian Boru. Around 1000 he also repudiated Gormflath; she then fomented a rebellion by her brother and son. Gormflath even offered to marry Sigurd the Stout, earl of Orkney, if he would come to Ireland and help defeat Brian Boru and Malachy of Meath. The deal was agreed upon, but Brian, Sigurd, and Maelmora all died in the battle.

♦ **Divorce. Negotiators. Politics. Women of easy virtue.** ♦
Cambridge..., III, p. 324; VII, p. 532. Curtis, *Ireland...*, pp. 27-28, 29, & 30. *DNB*, v.12, p. 753; v.14, p. 978. Jones, *Vikings...*, p. 397. Scherman, *Flowering...*, pp. 221 & 222.

GRAZIDA LIZIER

b. 1298–c. 1320s France

A Cathar of Montaillou. When young, she was seduced by Cathar preacher Pierre Clergue. Grazida later married Pierre Lizier, but continued the affair with Clergue. She testified before the Inquisition about her very individual beliefs and her lack of guilt over sexual "wrongdoing."

♦ **Adultery. Cathars. Ecclesiastical courts–Inquisition. Rape.** ♦

Decaux, *Histoire...*, pp. 246-247. Dronke, *Women...*, pp. 204-210. Duvernoy, *Inquisition à Pamiers...*, pp. 302-306. Ladurie, *Montaillou...*, pp. 29, 151, 158, 159, 172-4, 370-1.

GRUOCH, queen of SCOTLAND

fl.c. 1010s–1050s Scotland

Possibly the daughter of Kenneth III of Scotland (d.1005). Gruoch was a widow with a son from a previous marriage when she married Macbeth. Duncan was killed and Macbeth succeeded to the throne of Scotland in 1040. He and Gruoch reigned until Malcolm (III) Canmore killed Macbeth in 1057. Gruoch's son Lulach then took the throne until he too was killed several months later. Unlike Shakespeare's portrayal, Macbeth and his lady seem to have been fairly good, peaceful rulers.

♦ **Models. Queens. Religious patrons.** ♦

Barlow, *Edward...*, p. 202. Brown, *History...*, I, pp. 53 & 54. *Cambridge...*, VII, pp. 553, 554 n2. Duncan, *Scotland...*, p. 99. Mackie, *History...*, p. 43.

GUALDRADA OF TUSCANY

See—WALDRADA (of Arles).

GUDA (of Germany)

fl. 1100s Germany

Nun of Westphalia; worked in bookmaking as an illuminator. She signed one of her works with a self-portrait; this *Homeliary of St. Bartholomew* is now at Frankfurt-am-Main.

♦ **Artists. Bookmaking. Nuns.** ♦

Greer, *Obstacle...*, p. 158. Harksen, *Women...*, p. 46. Munsterberg, *History...*, p. 12.

GUDRID (of Greenland) **[Thorbjornsdottir]**

fl. 990s–1000s Greenland; Iceland; Norway

As a widow, she lived in Greenland with her father-in-law, Eric the Red. While wintering in Greenland around 998, Thorfinn Karlsefni (a wealthy Icelandic merchant) met and married Gudrid. Thorfinn and Gudrid then equipped a ship and set off with some 100 passengers and a variety of livestock, to establish a colony in "Vinland" (North America). During the three years they attempted this settlement, Gudrid supposedly gave birth to the first North American white child, her son Snorri Thorfinsson. After the *Skraellings* (Native Americans) drove the colonists off, Thorfinn and Gudrid settled in Iceland.

♦ **Models. Shipping–explorers & pioneers. Widows.** ♦

Boyesen, *Story...,* p. 181. Jones, *Vikings...,* p. 300. Scherman, *Daughter...,* pp. 197-8, 220, 224.

GUGLIELMA (of Milan)

d.c. 1282 Italy

In Milan around 1271, this prophetess started a new antinomian religious movement. Guglielma's sect was led by women, and she herself claimed to be the Holy Spirit.

♦ **Antinomian. Heretics. Mystics.** ♦

Bynum, *Holy...,* p. 233. Lambert, *Medieval...,* p. 193. Newman, *Sister...,* pp. 247, 253. Russell, *Witchcraft...,* pp. 141 & 181. Wessley, "Guglielmites...," pp. 289-303.

GUIGONE DE SALINS

fl. 1440s–1460s France

Wife of Nicolas Rolin, chancellor of Burgundy (1460s). In 1443, she and her husband built a hospital in Beaune.

♦ **Medicine. Models. Religious patrons.** ♦

Calmette, *Golden...,* pp. 218 & 248. Cartellieri, *Court...,* p. 145. Hurd-Mead, *History...,* p. 320.

GUILIA FARNESE **[Giulia; Julia]**

b. 1475–1500s Italy

Daughter of Giovannia de'Caetani and Pier Luigi Farnese. In 1489, Guilia married Orso Orsini of Rome. Possibly she was already involved in passionate affair with Rodrigo Borgia. She also became a close friend and companion of Rodrigo's daughter †Lucrezia (by a previous mistress). After Rodrigo became Pope Alexander VI, the Romans reputedly called Guilia "The Bride of Christ."

♦ **Educated. Mistresses. Popes. Writers–letters.** ♦

Chamberlin, *Fall...,* pp. viii, 39-42, 80, 90, 91, 98-100, 103-105, 129, 132-136, 217, 219, 327. Cheetham, *Keepers...,* p. 190. Cloulas, *Borgias...,* pp. 53, 60, 75, 76, 89, 95-6, 97, 98, 99-100. Fusero, *Borgias,* pp. 148-149, 155, 161, 162, 170-171, 172, 173-176...etc. Johnson, *Borgias...,* pp. 82, 93, 94, 99-100, 102-103, 105. Prescott, *Princes...,* p. 18. Simon, *Tapestry...,* p. 252.

GUILLELMA DE ROSERS

fl. 1240s–1260s France

Southern French noblewoman of Rougiers. A *trobaritz,* she exchanged tensons with Lanfrancs Cigala, a lawyer and troubadour from Genoa, who was also presumably her lover.

♦ **Poets/troubadours. Women of easy virtue.** ♦

Bogin, *Women...*, pp. 134-135. Boutière and Schutz, *Biographies des...*, pp. 372 & 374.

GUILLEMETTE BENET

fl. 1320s France

Heretic arrested in Montaillou. She refused questioning by Inquisition, so was sentenced to perpetual imprisonment (c.1322).

♦ **Ecclesiastical courts-Inquisition. Heretics. Prisons. Punishments.** ♦

Dronke, *Writers...*, p. 213. Duvernoy, *Inquisition à Pamiers...*, pp. 260-267. Ladurie, *Montaillou...*, pp. 42, 45, 56, 366.

GUILLEMETTE DU LUYS

1479 France

Surgeon in the service of Louis XI, king of France. Guillemette operated the medicinal baths used by the French court. Guillemette received over £19 for her medical services to Louis (c.1479).

♦ **Bathhouse. Surgeons.** ♦

Hughes, *Women...*, pp. 89 & 144. Labarge, *Women...*, p. 178. Wickersheimer, *Dictionnaire...*, I, p. 267.

GUILLEMETTE (la tapicière)

fl. 1450s France

Rug and tapestry maker of Paris; Guillemette was one of six women mentioned by François Villon in the poem of advice given to certain ladies of Paris by the *Belle Heaulmière.* Villon termed Guillemette a "daughter of joy," who used her tapestry business as a cover for another occupation—that of a semi-professional prostitute. She was possibly the wife (or mistress) of Estienne Sergent, a seal engraver of Paris.

♦ **Artistic clothwork. Clothworkers. Models. Women of easy virtue.** ♦

Bonner, *Complete...*, p. 51. Champion, *François...*, p. 94. Lewis, *François...*, p. 277.

GUIOTE SERRE

1421–1438 France

Glover of Paris who sometimes made gloves for the French king.

♦ **Apparel–accessories.** ♦

Favier, *Les Contribuables...*, p. 137.

GUNDRADA

c. 790s–c. 820s France

Favorite cousin of Charlemagne. Her friend Alcuin wrote many letters to her. Gundrada joined her brothers, Count Wala and Abbot Adelhard of Corbie, in attempting to curtail the power of Louis I the Pious. Louis finally forced Gundrada to retire from court, and she was enclosed in the convent of St. Radegund at Poitiers.

♦ **Educated. Politics. Rebellions. Religieuses.** ♦

Cambridge..., III, p. 2. Duckett, *Carolingian...*, pp. 15 & 23. McKitterick, *Frankish...*, p. 134. Riché, *Les Carolingiens...*, p. 150.

GUNDREDA (of Warenne)

c. 1050s–d. 1085 England; Flanders

Sister of a Flemish noble who became the earl of Chester in England. Gundreda married William I of Warenne (d.1088); mother of William II of Warenne (d.1138). She was known as a generous supporter of the church.

♦ **Childbirth. Models. Religious patrons.** ♦

C.P., v.12, pt.1, p. 494. Douglas, *William...*, pp. 76, 267, 392. Le Patourel, *Feudal...*, VI, pp. 10, 11.

GUNHILD OF DENMARK, queen of Norway **[Gunnhild]**

c. 920s–c. 970 Denmark; England; Norway; Scotland

Daughter of Gorm the Old, king of Denmark; married around 930 to Erik I Blood-axe, king of Norway. She was haughty and was believed to be an expert sorceress. Later historians often credited her with many of the murders and other cruel acts committed by her husband. When Erik was forced to abdicate, the couple moved to England where they took over the region of York. After Eric died in 954, Gunhild had a eulogy/ poem composed in his honor. She then took her sons to Denmark where her brother, King Harold Blue-tooth, gave them refuge. He also gave her aid to retrieve the Norwegian throne for her son Harold Gray-pelt. Governing with Harold, Gunhild proved to be a fairly wise ruler. She probably died in Scotland.

♦ **Models. Murder. Patrons of literature. Politics. Rulers. Widows. Witchcraft.** ♦

Boyesen, *Story...*, pp. 74-86, 94-95, 99-102, 104-114, 130 & 134. Fell, *Women...*, pp. 144-145. Jones, *Vikings...*, pp. 113, 121-122, 123, 125, 131, 136 n2. Larsen, *History...*, pp. 88 & 91-92. Wood, *Search...*, pp. 155, 165.

GUNNHILD OF DENMARK, queen of Germany

[Kunigunde of England]

c. 1020s–d. 1038 Denmark; England; Germany; Italy

Daughter of †Emma of Normandy and Canute of Denmark and England. Around 1036, Gunnhild married Henry (III) of Germany. She died in Italy from heat and possibly plague.

♦ **Genealogy. Models. Plague.** ♦

Barlow, *Edward...*, pp. 27, 39, Table A. *Cambridge...*, III, pp. 263, 269, 274, 294. Fuhrmann, *Germany...*, p. 40. Norwich, *Normans...*, p. 74. Stafford, *Queens...*, pp. 186 & 188. Stubbs, *Germany...*, pp. 145, 148, 149, 222. Vitalis, *Ecclesiastical...*, v.3, p. 86.

GUNNOR (of Denmark) **[Albereda; Gunnvor]**
c. 960s–c. 1030 Denmark; France

Mistress and then wife of Richard I of Normandy, count of Rouen. Among their children were: Richard II of Normandy; Robert, archbishop of Rouen; and †Emma, queen of England (wife of both Ethelred and Canute). Gunnor was a patroness of Coutances Cathedral, and an influence in her son's government.

♦ **Mistresses. Politics. Religious patrons. Widows.** ♦

Bates, *Normandy...*, pp. 108, 112, 118, 150-151, 213. Douglas, *William...*, pp. 34, 89, 145. Jones, *Vikings...*, p. 229 n1. Le Patourel, *Feudal...*, VI, pp. 4-6, 9-10, 12-13, 17-18. McKitterick, *Frankish...*, p. 238.

GUNNORA DE STRATFORD
d. 1305 England

Well-off merchant of London. She left houses, tenements, and her part of a ship to two of her servants, William Edmund and Nicholas.

♦ **Bequests. Employers. Land/property. Merchants. Shipping–owners.** ♦

Calendar of Wills..., I, p. 169.

GUYETTE DURAND **[Guyette of Grenoble]**
fl. 1440s–1460s France

Around 1450, she was a mistress of Dauphin Louis (XI). Louis later found a husband for her, his secretary Charles de Seillons. After Charles died, Louis married Guyette to his equerry, Grace d'Archelles.

♦ **Mistresses.** ♦

Champion, *Louis...*, p. 119. Cleugh, *Chant...*, p. 106. Lewis, *King...*, p. 218.

GWENLLIAN (of Wales)
fl. 1190s-d. 1236 Wales

Daughter of Lord Rhys, a leading Welsh prince (d.1197). Ednyfed Fychan married Gwenllian to enhance his prestige; they had a son, Goronwy (d.1268). Gwenllian and Ednyfed Fychan were ancestors of the Tudor monarchs of England.

♦ **Genealogy. Pawns.** ♦

Griffiths and Thomas, *Making...*, p. 7. Rees, *Son...*, pp. 38, 39, 40, 41, 111. Williamson, *Kings...*, p. 226 & Table 16.

GWENLLIAN (of Wales)
b. 1282–d. 1337 England; Wales

Daughter of †Eleanora de Montfort and Llewellyn ap Gruffydd, prince of Wales. Her mother died giving birth to Gwenllian; and her father was killed by Edward I of England a couple of years later. Gwenllian was probably cared for and educated at the convent of Sempringham, where she later became a nun. (The theory that she may have left the convent to marry William Gorm is unlikely.)

♦ **Educated. Nuns. Orphans.** ♦

Curtis, *Medieval...*, pp. 128 & 135. *DNB*, v.12, pp. 19-20. Green, *Letters...*, p. 51-57. Lloyd, *History...*, v.2, p. 763. Power, *Nunneries...*, p. 30.

GYDA OF ENGLAND, princess of Kiev **[Gytha]**

fl. 1050s–1090s Denmark; England; Russia

Daughter of Harold II of England and (presumably) his mistress †Edith Swan-neck. After her father's defeat and death at battle of Hastings in 1066, Gyda was among the prominent Anglo-Saxons who fled to the safe haven of Denmark. The Danish king later arranged a marriage for her; Gyda became the first wife of Vladimir Monomach, prince of Kiev. Their son, Mstislav I, succeeded his father in 1125.

♦ **Genealogy. Illegitimacy. Queens.** ♦

Campbell, *Anglo-Saxons*, p. 240. *DNB*, v.8, p. 1309. Vernadsky, *Kievan...*, pp. 96 & 336.

GYTHA OF DENMARK **[Githa]**

m. 1019–1040s Denmark; England; France

Danish wife of Godwine, an important Anglo-Saxon earl; sister of Earl Ulf of Denmark. Among her children were †Edith, wife of King Edward the Confessor, and Harold, king of England in 1066. When William of Normandy conquered England, Gytha fled to France, taking along some of the English treasury to ease the hardships of relocation.

♦ **Banking. Miscreants. Religious patrons. Soldiers. Widows.** ♦

Barlow, *Edward...*, pp. 43, 52, 80, 91, 114, 126, 163, 195, 241, 302-303. Barlow, *Feudal...*, pp. 56, 63, 68, 78, 90-91. Brown, *Normans...*, p. 137. *Cambridge...*, III, p. 389; V, p. 503. Cutler, "Edith...," p. 222. Fell, *Women...*, pp. 136 & 147. Larsen, *History...*, p. 114. Schulenburg, "Women's...," p. 231. Vitalis, *Ecclesiastical...*, v.2, pp. 170-173, 178-181; v.3, pp. 224-225.

HADEWIJCH

fl. 1200s — Belgium; Flanders

Flemish Beguine; author of a number of lyrics, and of her *Visions*. Hadewijch was intensely devoted to the Eucharist.

♦ **Beguines. Music. Mystics. Writers–theology.** ♦

Bynum, *Holy...*, pp. 3–4, 27, 31, 67, 105–6, 153–161, 171, 183, 186, 205, 209, 235, 241–3, 250, 258, 263, 269, 279, 290, 292, 296, 299. Colledge, *Netherlands...*, pp. 9–12, 33–87. Ennen, *Medieval...*, pp. 132 & 135. Halligan (ed.), *Booke...*, p. 36. Lagorio, "Continental...," pp. 175, & 176–7. McDonnell, *Beguines...*, pp. 365 & 392. Vanderauwera, "Brabant...," pp. 186–203. Zum Brunn and Epiney-Burgard, *Women...*, pp. 97–139.

For so-called Hadewijch II, see Zum Brunn and Epiney-Burgard, *Women...*, pp. xxiii, xxxii, xxxiii, 109, 129–39, 176.

HAOYS (la meresse)

1292 — France

Healer in 1292 Paris at la Vile de St. Lorenz (Sorentez); Haoys paid a 7s tax.

♦ **Doctors/empirics. Land/property.** ♦

Géraud, *Paris sous...*, p. 61. Hughes, *Women...*, p. 141. Hurd-Mead, *History...*, p. 215. Lipinska, *Histoire...*, p. 118.

HAOUYS (la poulaillière)

1292 — France

In 1292 Paris tax survey Haouys paid 18s on her poultry-selling business.

♦ **Merchants. Provisioning–poultry.** ♦

Géraud, *Paris sous...*, p. 96.

HATHEBURG

fl.c. 890s–910s — Germany

Daughter of Erwin (of Merseburg); she brought much of her father's estate as dowry. Although she had taken a vow of chastity, Hatheburg became the first wife of Henry I the Fowler of Germany. He repudiated her in 909, presumably with the blessing of the church (which considered their marriage illegitimate because of her former religious vows).

Their son later rebelled against Henry because the king had retained Hatheburg's dowry.

♦ **Adultery. Divorce. Dowry/dower. Religieuses. Virginity–vows.** ♦ *Cambridge...*, III, p. 186. Duckett, *Death...*, pp. 59 & 64. Leyser, *Rule...*, pp. 12 & 60.

HATHUI (of Germany) **[Hadwig; Hedwig]**
fl.c. 920s–960s France; Germany

Daughter of Henry I the Fowler and his second wife, †Matilda, queen of Germany (Matilda of Saxony). In 938 Hathui became the second wife of Hugh the Great, count of Paris and duke of the Franks (d.956).

♦ **Genealogy. Pawns.** ♦

Duckett, *Death...*, pp. 59 & 79. Leyser, *Rule...*, p. 53. McKitterick, *Frankish...*, pp. 317, 323, Table 6. Riché, *Les Carolingiens...*, p. 252.

HATHUMODA OF GANDERSHEIM
c. 840–d. 874 Germany

After her parents (†Oda and Liudolf of East Saxony) founded Gandersheim (c.858), Hathumoda and her sisters (Gerberga and †Christina) became nuns there. As abbess, Hathumoda chose to make Gandersheim an ascetic Benedictine house and established a tradition of intellectual activity for her nuns. Her *Vita* and an elegiac poem were written by her brother, a monk named Agius.

♦ **Abbesses. Educated. Models. Religious patrons. Saints. Teachers. Unmarried.** ♦

Cambridge..., III, pp. 529 & 530. *Dictionary...*, v.6, p. 313. Wemple, *Women...*, pp. 153, 174, 280, & 297.

HAUVIETTE OF DOMREMY
c. 1410–1450s France

A childhood friend of †Joan of Arc. Married another resident of Domremy, Gérard de Syonne. In 1455, at Joan's retrial, Hauviette testified that, as a young girl, Joan was normal but very devout.

♦ **Ecclesiastical courts–Inquisition. Legal activity. Manors.** ♦

Pernoud, *Retrial...*, pp. 62–63. Stolpe, *Maid...*, pp. 28, 43, 66.

HAVISE D'ÉVREUX

See—HELVISE OF NEVERS, countess of ÉVREUX.

HAWISE OF GLOUCESTER **[Avice; Hawide; Isabelle]**
fl. 1170s–d.c. 1218 England

Daughter and co-heiress of William, earl of Gloucester. Around 1189, Hawise married Prince John of England. In 1199, John repudiated Hawise, using consanguinity as his excuse. Hawise later married Geoffrey de Mandeville (1214), and in 1217 she became the third wife of Hubert de Burgh.

♦ **Divorce. Estate.** ♦

Appleby, *John...*, pp. 19, 43, 63, 99–100, 230. Barlow, *Feudal...*, pp. 354, 371, 395, 408. Barrow, *Feudal...*, pp. 179, 187, 216, 419. Bingham, *Crowned...*, pp. 88, 100 & 149. *DNB*, vol. 10, pp. 839–840, & 844. Kelly, *Eleanor...*, pp. 191–2, 302, 361. Lloyd, *Maligned...*, pp. 15, 40, 99–100, 229, 263. Pernoud, *Eleanor...*, pp. 197, 199, 224, &258. Richardson, "Marriage...," pp. 289–290.

HAWISE MONE **[Moone; Moon]**

fl. 1430 England

Wife of Thomas Mone, a fairly wealthy merchant—presumably a shoemaker in Norfolk. Like her husband, Hawise was an avid Lollard. The couple ran a school at their home for like-minded believers.

♦ **Ecclesiastical courts. Educated. Lollards. Merchants. Teachers.** ♦

Aston, "Lollard...," pp. 443, 452. Tanner, *Norwich...*, pp. 24–26, 28, 47, 75, 86, 138–144.

---

la belle HEAULMIÈRE **[beautiful helmet seller; Jeanne]**

c. 1380–d.c. 1456 France

In 1400, she was said to be among the most beautiful women in Paris and had an important and wealthy cleric as her lover. Many years later, François Villon made the elderly Heaulmière the subject of two poems. In one, this character gives young demi-mondaines of Paris advice—to take advantage of their assets while young. In Villon's poignant *Lament* the old woman regrets her lost youth and beauty, contrasting her former loveliness with her present aged body. She was probably the "Jeanne la Heaumière" mentioned as a poor old woman in the Parisian tax records of the mid-1400s.

♦ **Less-affluent. Merchants. Models. Prostitutes.** ♦

Bonner, *Complete...*, p. 196. Cartellieri, *Court...*, pp. 117–118. Champion, *François...*, I, pp. 93–100, 198; II, pp. 140, 183, 192–194 & 196. *Comptes du...*, pp. 438 & 571. Lewis, *François...*, pp. 42, 273–274 & 276–277. Matthews, "Wife...," p. 433. Nichols, "Lyric...," p. 141.

HEDWIG OF BAVARIA, duchess of Swabia

fl. 940s–d. 994 Germany

Daughter of †Judith and Henry I of Bavaria; married Duke Burchard of Swabia. Hedwig had a reputation as a virago. She and her brother, Duke Henry the Quarrelsome, conspired to fill the bishopric of Augsburg. After Burchard died, however, the emperor paid the Bavarians back by bestowing Swabia on Otto. Hedwig and Henry rebelled, starting a war (c.975/980).

♦ **Models. Politics. Rebellions. Widows.** ♦

Cambridge..., III, pp. 204, 205n. Duckett, *Death...*, pp. 98–99. Ennen, *Medieval...*, pp. 83–84. Jenkins, *Byzantium...*, pp. 263, 269–270, & 284. Leyser, *Rule...*, pp. 53 & 54.

HEDWIG OF GERMANY

See—HATHUI (of Germany).

(St.) HEDWIG OF SILESIA

1174–1243 Austria; Germany; Poland

Daughter of †Agnes of Dedo and Berthold IV, count of Meran and Andrechs; she was educated at the convent of Franken. At age thirteen, Hedwig married Duke Henry of Silesia, whom she later converted. Although she lost her first two babies, Hedwig eventually had several children. Many of her offspring aided her at the hospitals and convents she founded and served. In particular, Hedwig was interested in caring for lepers. By 1200, her reputation for charity and piety was supplemented by reports of her miracles. For instance, Hedwig supposedly brought a hanged man back to life. After her death in 1243, Hedwig was quickly canonized (1267).

♦ **Educated. Leprosy. Medicine. Mystics. Nurses. Religious patrons. Saints.** ♦

Butler, *Lives...*, IV, p. 124. Bynum, *Holy...*, pp. 77, 211, 391 n77, 392 n85. Farmer, *Oxford...*, pp. 187–188. Harrsen, *Cursus...*, pp. 3, 4, 7, 17–22, 50, 53. Hughes, *Women...*, pp. 131–132. Hurd-Mead, *History...*, pp. 176 & 180–181.

HELEN [Helena; Helene]

HELENE DE CHAMBES

m. 1473–d.c. 1532 France

Rich heiress of Jeanne Chabot and Jean, seigneur de Montsoreau; married by Louis XI to Philippe de Commynes in 1473. Their daughter Jehanne became countess of Penthièvre in 1504.

♦ **Estate. Pawns.** ♦

Commynes, *Memoirs...*, pp. 10, 76, & 151. *DBF,* v.9, pp. 386–387. Lewis, *King...*, pp. 336 & 346.

HELEN GALRUSSYN

fl.c. 1300s–1320s Ireland

See—ALICE KYTELER.

♦ **Witchcraft.** ♦

HELENA (Guiscard)

fl. 1070s–c. 1110s Byzantium; Italy

Daughter of Robert Guiscard. She was sent to Constantinople to marry Constantine, son of Emperor Michael VII, but the marriage was called off. Alexius Comnenus finally sent Helena home after she had spent so many years in Byzantium that she was no longer useful as a marriage pawn. Roger I of Sicily gave her a home at his court where she proved to be very helpful as an expert in Greek language and customs.

♦ **Models. Pawns. Teachers. Unmarried.** ♦

Comnena, *Alexiad...*, pp. 53, 58–59, 67, 144. Norwich, *Normans...*, pp. 223–227 & 251. Osborne, *Greatest...*, pp. 342–343 & 346.

HELEN LACAPENA, empress of Byzantium

fl. 920s–930s — Byzantium

Daughter of Theodora and Romanus I Lacapenus. Married Constantine VII around 920. Their son Romanus II was born around 937. When Helen's brothers plotted to usurp the throne, she had them exiled. Nevertheless, her reputation as an intriguer who controlled her husband is probably inaccurate.

♦ **Politics. Rebellions. Regents. Women of easy virtue.** ♦

Cambridge..., IV, pp. 61, 64, 67, 98n. Jenkins, *Byzantium...*, pp. 236, 252, 254 & 262. Wright, *Works...*, pp. 124 & 190.

HELENE KOTANNER **[Kottanerin]**

fl. 1420s–1440s — Austria; Hungary

Widow of a high-ranking burgher of Ödenburg. Around 1438, she remarried and became a lady-in-waiting to †Elizabeth of Luxembourg, consort of Albert of Hapsburg, king of Hungary. Helene claimed that, after Albert's death, she stole the royal insignia at Elizabeth's order. Helene wrote her *Memoirs* about the politics of her time, and about her own exalted position in the late queen's court.

♦ **Politics. Servants Squabbles Writers** ♦

Frederiksen, *Women...*, p. 131. Harksen, *Women...*, p. 54. Uitz, *Legend...*, pp. 145–146.

HÉLISSENT (la ferpière)

1292 — France

Hélissent, of the rue Osteriche, paid 12d tax on her linen brokerage business.

♦ **Clothworkers. Less-affluent.** ♦

Géraud, *Paris sous...*, p. 5.

HELOISE (of Argenteuil) **[Héloise]**

b. 1101–d. 1164 — France

Her uncle/guardian hired the famous teacher Peter Abelard to tutor young Heloise. Their professional relationship soon blossomed into a love affair. Heloise gave birth to a son, and the couple were secretly wed (the marriage remained a secret in order to preserve Abelard's reputation as a theologian and cleric). Heloise entered a convent. Unaware of the marriage, her uncle avenged family honor by castrating Abelard. Much later, Heloise and Abelard presumably exchanged several letters. His missals show little evidence of warmth, but hers indicate that she was very intelligent, passionate, and loyal. Heloise became abbess of Argenteuil and she started the Paraclete order which soon had sister houses throughout France. (Some scholars believe that Abelard, or someone else, wrote the letters attributed to Heloise.)

♦ **Abbesses. Adultery. Educated. Models. Religious patrons. Writers–letters.** ♦

Charrier, *Heloise dans....* Dronke, *Women...,* pp. vii, ix, 21, 32, 89–90, 93, 97, 102, 107–143, 152–153, 214, 218, 302–306. Gilson, *Heloise....* Kelly, *Eleanor...,* pp. 14, 74, 87. *Letters...Heloise,* pp. 112–127. Muckle, "Personal Letters...," pp. 47–94. Pernoud, *Heloise....* Radice, "French...," pp. 90–108. Stephenson, *Mediaeval...,* pp. 297–299 & 319.

HELOYS (la miergesse)

1292 France

Dame Heloys was a healer on the rue des Jardins in 1292 Paris; taxed 5s.

♦ **Doctors/empirics.** ♦

Géraud, *Paris sous...,* p. 134. Hughes, *Women...,* p. 141. Hurd-Mead, *History...,* p. 215. Lipinska, *Histoire...,* p. 118. Wickersheimer, *Dictionnaire...,* p. 273.

HELOYS (l'uilière)

1292 France

Listed in 1292 Paris survey working at the end of the rue du Four. Heloys was taxed 12d on her oil-mongering business.

♦ **Less-affluent. Merchants–oil.** ♦

Géraud, *Paris sous...,* p. 8.

HELOYSON (la nourrice)

1292 France

Nurse on the rue des Arsis; paid 4s tax in 1292 Paris.

♦ **Less-affluent. Nurses.** ♦

Géraud, *Paris sous...,* p. 93. Hughes, *Women...,* p. 147.

HELVIDIS **[Heluidis]**

1136 France

A lay healer near Lille, she was also a noted benefactor of the church. Referred to as a *medica* in a charter from Count Thierry of Alsace.

♦ **Doctors/empirics. Religious patrons.** ♦

Vercauteren, "Les Medicins...," p. 73. Wickersheimer, *Dictionnaire...,* p. 273.

HELWISE OF NEVERS, countess of ÉVREUX

[Helvis; Helvise; Helvire; Havise]

fl.c. 1070s–1110s France

Intelligent and beautiful daughter of Adélaide of France and William, count of Nevers. Helwise also had a reputation for greed and cruelty.

She dominated her husband, William, count of Évreux (d.1118). A feud of some three years duration was begun by Helwise, who took exception to some remarks made by her sister-in-law, †Isabel de Montfort (de Conches). Helwise raised †Bertrade de Montfort.

♦ **Childcare. Models. Rulers. Squabbles.** ♦

Anselme, *Histoire...*, II, p. 479. Barthélemy, "Kinship...," pp. 138–139. Lehmann, *Rôle de la...*, p. 217. Pernoud, *La femme...*, pp. 138–9. Verdon, "Les Sources...," p. 229. Vitalis, *Ecclesiastical...*, v.4, pp. 184, 185, 212, 213.

HENRIETTE DE CRAUS

1434 France

In 1434 at Chamars, this lay healer went to the stake as a witch/heretic. It was said that her healing was accomplished with the aid of incantations and by invoking the Devil.

♦ **Doctors/empirics. Heretics. Punishments. Witchcraft.** ♦

Hughes, *Women...*, p. 145. Wickersheimer, *Dictionnaire...*, I, p. 291.

HENRIETTE LA PATRIARCHE

fl. 1440s France

Purse maker of Paris; worked at number four Notre Dame bridge.

♦ **Apparel–accessories.** ♦

Comptes du..., pp. 206, 491, 577, 610, 656, 722, 778, 850.

HERLEVA (of NORMANDY)

See—ARLETTE (of NORMANDY).

HERRAD VON LANDSBERG **[Herrade, abbess of Hohenburg]**

fl. 1150s–d. 1195 Austria; Germany

Well-educated, imaginative abbess and writer. Herrad compiled and wrote possibly the most innovative compendium or pictorial encyclopedia of the Middle Ages—the *Hortus Deliciarum.* This manuscript covered the history of the world by biblical tradition, as well as philosophy and current events. The illustrations were not only incorporated into the text, but the words were of secondary importance in many cases. This enabled even the illiterate to benefit from the *Hortus*. Herrad supplied ideas, text, and drawings for this compendium, but probably did not paint the illustrations herself. The end of the manuscript contained a picture of Herrad, her mentor †Relindis, and her canonesses at Hohenburg.

♦ **Abbesses. Artists. Bookmaking. Educated. Models. Music. Writers.** ♦

Cames, *Allégories et symboles....* Carr, "Women...," pp. 7–8. Drinker, *Music...*, pp. 198–199. Ferrante, *Women...*, pp. 4–5, ftn.6. Greer, *Obstacle...*, pp. 156–158. Heinrich, *Canonesses...*, pp. 186, 192–193. Henshaw, "Church...," pp. 12–13. Herrade, *Hortus....* Lipinska, *Histoire...*, p. 132. Munsterberg, *History...*, p. 12. Pinnow, *History...*, p. 99. Saxl, "Illustrated...," pp. 252–254.

HERSENDE (of Fontevrault) **[Hersend of Champagne]**
fl. 1090–1120s France

When Robert of Arbrissel returned to his missionary duties in 1099, he appointed Hersende as the first superior of the foundation of Fontevrault. She proved to be such an excellent administrator that, thereafter, the abbey remained in the charge of female superiors. Hersende was especially interested in medicine; she taught nuns to be healers and nurses, and she often attended patients herself.

♦ **Abbesses. Managers. Medicine. Teachers.** ♦

Eckenstein, *Woman...*, p. 194. Gold, *Lady...*, p. 95. Hurd-Mead, *History...*, pp. 167, 178 & 217. Pernoud, *La femme...*, p. 134. Smith, "Robert...," pp. 181 & 182.

HERSENDE (of France) **[Hersend of Champagne]**
fl. 1249–1259 France

A healer, called *maitresse fiscienne*. She accompanied (St.) Louis IX on Crusade in 1249. In addition to attending her royal patient, Hersende was in charge of the female camp followers. She received a life pension for her services. Probably settled in Paris around 1250 and married Jacques, the royal apothecary.

♦ **Crusades. Doctors/empirics.** ♦

Hughes, *Women...*, pp. 88–89. Hurd-Mead, *History...*, pp. 167 & 217. Labarge, *Small Sound...*, p. 174. Pernoud, *La femme...*, p. 203. Wickersheimer, *Dictionnaire...*, pp. 294–295.

HILDEGARD
c. 770 France; Germany

See—BERTHA; GISELA; and ROTRUDE.

♦ **Genealogy.** ♦

(St.) HILDEGARDE OF BINGEN
b. 1098–d. 1179 Germany

Entered Disibodenberg as a child; became abbess of that Benedictine establishment in 1137. In 1147, Hildegarde founded convent of Rupertsberg at Bingen. She was intelligent, educated, politically active (although not politically sophisticated), and a very innovative mystic and writer. Hildegarde joined (St.) Bernard of Clairvaux in calling for the Second Crusade. A prolific writer; she dictated many letters to religious leaders, and to secular rulers like Frederick Barbarossa and †Eleanor of Aquitaine. Hildegarde also wrote poems set to music, an encyclopedia containing the scientific lore of her day, a medical treatise, and the *Scivias*—a collection and interpretation of her visions—complete with illustrations probably designed by the author. Her *Ordo Virtutum,* a liturgical drama, is the earliest known "morality play." Hildegarde had a unique perception of women, the medical uses of gems, and the entire universe. Although never canonized, Hildegarde of Bingen has been venerated by many as a saint.

♦ **Abbesses. Crusades. Drama. Gems/jewelry. Medicine. Music. Mystics. Politics. Religious patrons. Saints. Scholars. Superstitions. Writers.** ♦

Bullough, "Medieval Medical...," p. 493. Bynum, *Holy...*, pp. 62, 111, 185, 236, 252, 260, 263–5, 279, 291, 292. Crombie, *Science...*, pp. 18 & 223. Drinker, *Music...*, p. 200. Dronke, *Women...*, pp. 9, 109, 144–203, 306–316, 319. Ennen, *Medieval...*, pp. 128–9, 132, 133. Farmer, *Oxford...*, pp. 193–4. Ferrante, "Education...," p. 26. Frederiksen, *Women...*, pp. 101–103. Gies, *Women...*, pp. 63–65, 68, 76–85, 87, 231. Greer, *Obstacle...*, pp. 157–158. Haverkamp, *Medieval...*, pp. 191, 198, 199, 314, 315. Hildegard, *Scivias....* Kraft, "German...," pp. 109–130. Lagorio, "Continental...," pp. 163–166, 167, 170. McDonnell, *Beguines...*, pp. 281–297. Newman, *Sister....* Pernoud, *La femme...*, pp. 49–52. Petroff, *Medieval...*, pp. 151–158. Thièbaux, *The Writings...*, pp. 105–134. Zum Brunn and Epiney-Burgard, *Women...*, pp. 1–36....

HILDEGARDE (of France)

fl.c. 810s–840s — France

Daughter of Louis I the Pious and his first wife †Ermengarde; married Gérard, count of Auvergne. In 841, Hildegarde assisted her brother Charles I the Bald, king of France, in his fight for the throne. She later became abbess at Laon.

♦ **Abbesses. Politics. Soldiers. Widows.** ♦

Cabaniss, *Judith...*, pp. 10, 36 & 39. *Carolingian...*, pp. 160, 208. Decaux, *Histoire...*, p. 175. Nelson, *Politics...*, p. 214. Riché, *Les Carolingiens...*, p. 191.

HIPPOLITA SFORZA, duchess of Calabria, queen of Naples

See—IPPOLITA SFORZA.

HIRMENTRUDE

See—ERMENTRUDE OF ORLEANS.

HODIERNA OF JERUSALEM

c. 1120s–1150s — Israel; Lebanon

See—MÉLISENDE, queen of JERUSALEM.

Also see—MORPHIA OF MELITENE.

♦ **Regents.** ♦

HODIERNE (la cerencerresse)

1292 — France

Hodierne of la Tounèlierie was taxed 2s in the 1292 Paris survey on her occupation as a comber of wool and other raw materials.

♦ **Clothworkers. Less-affluent.** ♦

Géraud, *Paris sous...*, p. 37.

HROSWITHA OF GANDERSHEIM **[Hrotsvit]**

b. 935–c. 999 Germany

Relative of †Gerberga of Bavaria and of Otto I the Great, Holy Roman Emperor. Hroswitha was well-educated in Greek and Latin. She became a canoness at Benedictine abbey of Gandersheim. Hroswitha is the first recognized medieval dramatist. She wrote saints' legends, at least six comedies, and the *Gesta Ottonis,* a history of Otto the Great. According to Hroswitha, Empress †Adelheid of Burgundy tunneled out of prison in order to appeal to Otto for help. Hroswitha was also knowledgeable about the medical beliefs of her time; she taught herbal/medical lore and treated some patients herself.

♦ **Drama. Educated. Medicine. Nuns. Writers.** ♦

Bonfante (ed.), *The Plays....* Dronke, *Women...,* pp. 55–83. Duckett, *Death...,* pp. 254–270. Ennen, *Medieval...,* pp. 82 & 83. Frederiksen, *Women...,* p. 105. Fox, *Literary...,* pp. 241 & 258. Haight, *Hrotswitha....* Hurd-Mead, *History...,* pp. 111–112. Leyser, *Rule...,* pp. 16, 17, 19, 20, 38, 47, 84 & 96. Petroff, *Medieval...,* pp. 114–135. Stafford, *Queens...,* pp. 66, 67, & 68. Thièbaux, *The Writings...,* pp. 81–90. Wilson, "Saxon...," pp. 30–63.

HRUODTRUDE

See—ROTRUDE.

HUGUETTE BALARIN

fl. 1470s France

Wife of Jacques Caille, a rich merchant and city councillor of Lyons. Louis XI stayed with them in 1475 while he was in that city. Around that same year, Jacques and Huguette endowed a hospital in Lyons to care for victims of plague and other contagions.

♦ **Charity. Medicine. Plague–hospitals. Politics.** ♦

Valous, *Patriciat...,* pp. 325 & 328.

HUGUETTE DU HAMEL

fl. 1430s–1460s France

Illegitimate daughter of Hugh Cuillerel, the abbot of Saint-Riquier. Huguette entered convent around 1439, and became abbess of Port-Royal (Pourras) near Paris around 1455. Huguette turned over financial work, etc., of the establishment to her lover, Baudes le Maistre. This love affair was not the extent of her infamy—Huguette liked to stay out all night partying with "gallants," she encouraged nuns to provide sexual services to men, and she stole some £400 of the abbey's wealth. Huguette is mentioned, as *the abbess of Pouras,* in a poem by François Villon.

♦ **Abbesses. Adultery. Illegitimacy. Miscreants. Models. Prostitutes.** ♦

Bonner, *Complete...*, p. 206. Champion, *François...*, I, p. 324; II, pp. 13–15 & 152. Lewis, *François...*, p. 117.

HUITACE (la lanière)

1292 France

Dame Huitace had a shop on the rue aus Prouvoires in 1292 Paris. She must have had a booming business as a dyer and seller of wool since she was taxed 50s on her occupation.

♦ **Clothworkers. Land/property. Merchants.** ♦

Géraud, *Paris sous...*, p. 39.

(St.) HUMILITAS

See—(St.) UMILITA OF FAENZA.

— I —

IANKA OF KIEV

fl. 1070s–1110s — Russia

Originally betrothed to Constantine Ducas of Byzantium, Ianka instead entered convent of St. Andrew at Kiev which she and her father, Vsevolod I, founded in 1086. As abbess, Ianka started a school at this convent. The girls were taught music, needlework, reading, and writing.

♦ **Abbesses. Educated. Music. Religious patrons. Teachers. Unmarried.** ♦

Boulding, *Underside...*, p. 384. Vernadsky, *Kievan...*, pp. 154, 278–279, 341, & 351.

IDA OF BOULOGNE — **[Ida of Flanders]**

c. 1160s–1200s — Flanders; France; Germany; Netherlands

Daughter and heiress of Matthew, count of Boulogne. Married (1) Gerard II, count of Gueldres (d.1180); (2) in 1183, Berthold V, duke of Zähringen; and (3) Renaud (Reginald), count of Dammartin (he supposedly abducted her). Their daughter and heiress was †Matilda of Boulogne (also known as Maude or Mahaut).

♦ **Abduction. Estate. Widows.** ♦

Anselme, *Histoire...*, v.1, p. 80; v.2, p. 722. Appleby, *John...*, p. 176. Baldwin, *Government...*, pp. 15 & 201. Tyerman, *England...*, p. 48.

IDA, countess of BOULOGNE

See—YDAIN OF LORRAINE, countess of Boulogne.

IDA OF NIVELLES

d. 1231 — Belgium

Originally a Beguine; later became abbess of the Cistercian house of La Ramée. Under Ida's leadership, this house became known as a bookmaking center—her nuns were adept at both calligraphy and painting miniatures. Ida was noted for her devotion to the Eucharist.

♦ **Abbesses. Beguines. Bookmaking. Educated.** ♦

Bynum, *Holy...*, pp. 77, 115. Bynum, *Jesus...*, pp. 180 n, 257. Lagorio, "Continental...," p. 175. McDonnell, *Beguines...*, p. 374. Weisheipl, *Friar...*, p. 178. Zum Brunn and Epiney-Burgard, *Women...*, pp. 73 & 74.

IDA DE PORTUNHALE

1298 England

Sold her infant son. Involved in baby-selling "scam" with Ella de Sor.

♦ **Childcare. Ecclesiastical courts. Miscreants.** ♦

Hair, *Bawdy...*, p. 155 (#380).

IDA OF SWABIA **[Ita]**

m. 940s–d. 986 Germany

Daughter and heiress of Hermann I, duke of Swabia. Between 940 and 947, Ida married Liudolf, son of †Edith of England and Holy Roman Emperor Otto I. Their children were Otto of Swabia and Bavaria, and †Matilda, abbess of Essen. †Hroswitha of Gandersheim wrote about the exalted position Ida and Liudolf occupied for a time, as Otto I paraded them about the Empire the couple were to inherit. (These plans came to naught when Liudolf predeceased his father.)

♦ **Estate. Models. Pawns.** ♦

Cambridge..., III, p. 191. Duckett, *Death...*, p. 72. Leyser, *Rule...*, pp. 19, 20 & 53. Riché, *Les Carolingiens...*, p. 249. Wright, *Works...*, p. 177.

IDONEA

fl. 1150s– 1160s England

Thomas Becket sent letters to this nun during his dispute with King Henry II. She was directed to transcribe, copy, and deliver papal letters to archbishop of York and witnesses. This important mission was dangerous because Idonea risked torture and death to carry it out.

♦ **Educated. Nuns. Politics.** ♦

Barlow, *Thomas...*, p. 206. Eckenstein, *Woman...*, pp. 212– 213. Ferrante, "Education...," p. 17. Knowles, *Thomas...*, p. 129. Winston, *Thomas...*, pp. 300–301.

IDONEA LE HUKESTERE

1344 England

Brought suit in London court against William Simond for taking and butchering her pregnant pig. William was found guilty; the jury awarded Idonea 7s for the loss of her sow.

♦ **Land/property. Legal activity. Merchants.** ♦

Calendar of Plea..., I, p. 158.

ILLUMINATO BEMBO **[Illuminata]**

c. 1420s–1470 Italy

Member of the great Venetian Bembo family; took vows in 1433. Companion and biographer of (St.) †Catherine of Bologna. Most interested in Catherine's piety, Sister Illuminato dismissed the saint's artistic endeavors in one sentence. Her *Specchio d'Illuminatione sulla Vita di Caterina da Bologna* was completed in 1469.

♦ **Abbesses. Writers–biography.** ♦

Fine, *Women...*, p. 7. McLaughlin, "Creating...," pp. 279, 279–280 n.46. Ragg, *Women...*, pp. 14, 18, 64, 67, 71, 111–112, 119, 132, 141, 144, 148, 151, 156, 158.

IMMA OF SAXONY

fl. 970s — Germany

See—FRIDERUN (of Germany).

♦ **Estate. Religious patrons.** ♦

INES DE CASTRO — **[Inez]**

fl. 1330s–d. 1355 — Portugal; Spain

Daughter of Pedro Fernandez de Castro of Castile and Alonça Soares de Villa Dares of Portugal; lady-in-waiting to Constance Manuel, wife of Pedro, the heir of Portugal. Pedro fell in love with Ines, and he married her after Constance died. Pedro's father, Alfonso IV, had Ines murdered in January of 1355. Pedro declared war against his father in revenge; his mother †Beatrice eventually made peace between the two. Shortly after Alfonso died, however, Pedro had Ines's body moved, crowned, and then reburied with much pomp.

♦ **Mistresses. Models. Murder. Queens.** ♦

Jamison, *Life...*, I, p. 273. Nowell, *History...*, pp. 14–15. Roche, *Dona...*, pp. 27–29, 34, 64, 67. Stephens, *Story...*, pp. 95–98, 99, 101, 103, 111.

INGEBORG [Ingebjorg; Ingibiorg]

INGEBORG OF DENMARK, queen of France

b. 1176–d. 1237 — Denmark; France

Daughter of †Gertrude of Bavaria and King Canute VI of Denmark; to seal an alliance, Ingeborg became the second wife of Philip II Augustus of France in 1193. Philip proceeded to repudiate his bride the next day. He later took a third wife, †Agnes of Meran. Ingeborg continued to fight for her rights. She enlisted Pope Innocent III's help in 1198, and with his support she continued to resist all Philip's ploys. For his part, Philip tried to legitimize his annulment and remarriage, attempted to return Ingeborg to Denmark, locked her away in various convents, and consistently mistreated her. Some twenty years after their marriage, however, Philip finally gave up and established Ingeborg as rightful queen of France.

♦ **Bequests. Divorce. Dowry/dower. Politics. Popes. Prisons. Religieuses.** ♦

Appleby, *John...*, pp. 9, 101–2, 190. Baldwin, *Government...*, pp. 80–86, 117, 118, 171, 177, 210, 270, 353, 357, 379, 380. Barlow, *Feudal...*, pp. 363, 371, 416, 419. Butler, *Women...*, pp. 137–143. Facinger, "Study...," pp. 9–10, 38–39, & 44. Geraud, "Ingeburge de...," pp. 3–27,

93–118. Hallam, *History...*, pp. 127–128. Kelly, *Eleanor...*, pp. 314, 337, 338, 366–8. Summers, *Geography...*, p. 361.

INGEBORG OF DENMARK, queen of Norway

c. 1250s–d. 1287 Denmark; Norway

Daughter of Erik Plow-penny, king of Denmark; to establish peace, she was married to Magnus VI Law-mender, king of Norway, in 1265. When he died in 1280, their son and heir, Erik II Magnusson (Priest-hater), was only twelve, so Ingeborg served as principal regent with a baronial council. Her haughty manner did not endear her to nobles or commoners. Ingeborg caused additional problems by urging one of her favorites to play pirate along the shores of Denmark (because she had never received the Danish estates to which she was entitled).

♦ **Estate. Regents. Shipping–pirates. Widows. Women of easy virtue.** ♦

Boyesen, *Story...*, pp. 451–454. Larsen, *History...*, pp. 159, 172, 173.

INGEBJORG OF NORWAY

c. 1300–1330s Norway; Sweden

Daughter of Haakon V of Norway; married in 1312 to Duke Erik of Sweden. Their son Magnus VII Eriksson was born in 1316. Around the same time, her husband was killed by his brother King Birger Magnusson of Sweden. In 1319, Ingebjorg's young son became king of Norway; soon afterwards, he also became king of Sweden. She had great power in her son's regency. She then started an affair with Knut Porse of Halland, a Danish nobleman whom she later married. Since Ingebjorg used her wealth and power to enrich her lover, the irate regency councils of both Sweden and Norway curtailed her governmental influence.

♦ **Regents. Widows. Women of easy virtue.** ♦

Andersson, *History...*, pp. 48–49. Boyesen, *Story...*, pp. 458–459, 461–462. Derry, *History...*, pp. 60 & 69. Larsen, *History...*, pp. 161, 175, 192, 193, & 198. Musset, *Les Peuples...*, pp. 209, 235, 294, 295, 296. Scott, *Sweden...*, pp. 70–71.

INGEBORG OF NORWAY

m. 1312 Norway; Sweden

Daughter of †Isabella Bruce and Erik II Magnusson (Priest-hater), king of Norway. In 1312, Ingeborg married Duke Valdemar of Sweden. (This was a double ceremony in Oslo; the other couple was †Ingebjorg of Norway—see above—and Valdemar's brother, Duke Erik of Sweden.) Ingeborg and Valdemar had a son named Erik who was born in 1316. Like Ingebjorg's husband, Valdemar was killed by his brother King Birger Magnusson of Sweden.

♦ **Murder. Pawns.** ♦

Boyesen, *Story...*, pp. 458 & 459. Scott, *Sweden...*, pp. 70–71.

INGELBERG

See—ANGELBERGA.

INGIBIORG, queen of SCOTLAND **[Ingeborg of Norway]**

m.c. 1065 Norway; Scotland

Possibly the daughter of Thorfinn, earl of Orkney (though she may have even been his widow). Around 1065 she married Malcolm III of Scotland. She had two sons by Malcolm, but the rest of her story is obscure. Malcolm may have repudiated Ingibiorg, or she may have died by 1069.

♦ **Divorce. Queens.** ♦

Barlow, *Edward...*, p. 203. Barrow, *Feudal...*, pp. 129 & 420. Brown, *History...*, I, pp. 57, 59, 65. *Cambridge...*, VII, pp. 554, 559, 560 n1. Duncan, *Scotland...*, pp. 100, 118. Glover, *Story...*, pp. 48 & 50. Mackie, *History...*, p. 39. Mackie, *Short...*, p. 28.

INGEGARDE OF SWEDEN

c. 1020 Russia; Sweden

See—ANASTASIA OF KIEV; ANNE OF KIEV; and ELIZABETH OF KIEV.

♦ **Genealogy.** ♦

INGELTRUDE

fl. 840s–860s Germany; Italy

Daughter of Count Motfried; first wife of Count Boson (of Northern Italy). In 856, Ingeltrude ran off with one of Boson's vassals. Boson enlisted papal support to retrieve his run-away wife; Ingeltrude was excommunicated in 860. At Cologne, she gained the help of Bishop Gunthar who believed, as she did, that Boson would kill her if she returned to him. She finally made a deal with Pope Nicholas I to do penance in Rome—but she died before Nicholas could reconcile Boson with her. Some of the German nobles who received lands from Ingeltrude later ran into trouble with the church because she had made these gifts without her husband's consent.

♦ **Adultery. Divorce. Estate. Politics. Popes.** ♦

Bishop, "Bishops as...," pp. 60–61, 72–74, 76. Decaux, *Histoire...*, pp. 175–177. Duckett, *Carolingian...*, p. 235. Ernouf, *Histoire...*, pp. 10, 11, 49. McNamara and Wemple, "Marriage...," p. 111. Wemple, *Women...*, pp. 86–87 & 249.

INGERID OF SWEDEN, queen of Norway

fl. 1130s–1140s Norway; Sweden

Wife of Harold Gilchrist (Gille), king of Norway. After he was killed (c.1136), she convened a council and used all her power to get her young son Inge crowned. In 1142, she caused a scandal by marrying an unimportant nobleman; he was soon assassinated.

♦ **Murder. Politics. Queens. Widows.** ♦

Boyesen, *Story...*, pp. 311, 314, 386. Larsen, *History...*, pp. 129 & 130.

INGUNN (of Iceland)

fl.c. 1110 Iceland

Mentioned in saga as a teacher at Cathedral School of Holar.

♦ **Models. Servants. Teachers.** ♦

Frank, "Iceland...," p. 484.

IPPOLITA SFORZA, duchess of Calabria, queen of Naples [Hippolita Maria]

b. 1442–1480s Italy

Daughter of †Bianca Maria Visconti and Francesco Sforza, duke of Milan. Around 1465, Ippolita married Alfonso of Aragon, duke of Calabria, and later king of Naples. Two children: Ferrante II, king of Naples, and †Isabella of Aragon, duchess of Milan. Ippolita was well-educated, especially in Greek and Latin. Her tutor dedicated several manuscripts to her. Ippolita enjoyed learning and art; she often discussed books and poetry with her friend, Lorenzo de'Medici.

♦ **Book owners. Dance. Educated. Managers. Models. Popes. Politics.** ♦

Chamberlin, *World...*, p. 269. Cleugh, *Medici...*, pp. 100, 101, 102, 105. Hook, *Lorenzo...*, pp. 19, 20, 114. King, "Book-lined...," pp. 82–83. King and Rabil, *Her Immaculate...*, pp. 20–21, 44–48, 132, 135. Kristeller, "Learned...," p. 96. Prescott, *Princes...*, pp. 67, 71, 75, 78, 251. Sizeranne, *Beatrice...*, pp. 122, 257, 260.

IRENE, empress of BYZANTIUM [Irene the Athenian]

m. 769–d. 803 Byzantium; Greece

Married future Byzantine Emperor Leo IV around the year 769. When he died in 780, Irene became regent for their ten year-old son, Constantine VI. She prevented him from assuming any role in the government, so he rebelled and began his own rule (c.790). In 797, however, Irene deposed her son and had him blinded so that he could not take the reins of government from her again. Irene was a relatively good ruler, but her main characteristics were ambition and religious fanaticism. Certainly one of her motives for keeping Constantine off the Byzantine throne was that he was an iconoclast. Not only was Irene fervent in her orthodoxy, but she also realized that iconoclasm was detrimental to Byzantine stability. Irene ruled alone from 797 until a palace coup sent her to a monastery in 802.

♦ **Legal activity. Models. Popes. Rebellions. Regents. Religieuses. Religious patrons. Rulers. Soldiers. Widows.** ♦

Cambridge..., IV, pp. 19–25, 31, 34, 35, 36, 124–126, 246, 710, 757. *Carolingian...*, pp. 73, 76, 82–83, 190–192. Diehl, *Byzantine...*, pp. 65–93. Ganshof, *Carolingians...*, pp. 34, 41, 170. Jenkins, *Byzantium...*, pp.

90–104 & 110–111. McKitterick, *Frankish...*, p. 70. Riché, *Les Carolingiens...*, pp. 107 & 124. Runciman, "Empress...," pp. 101–118.

IRENE ANGELA, Holy Roman Empress **[Irene Angia]**

m.c. 1193–d.c. 1209 Byzantium; Germany; Italy

Daughter of Byzantine Emperor Isaac II Angelus; married (1) c.1193 to Roger, duke of Apulia; and (2) c.1196 to Philip of Swabia, later Holy Roman Emperor. She influenced Philip to help retrieve the Byzantine throne for Alexius IV in 1203.

♦ **Crusades. Politics.** ♦

Bridge, *Crusades...*, p. 232. *Cambridge...*, IV, p. 417; V, pp. 202, 471, 473, 479; VI, pp. 52, 67, 72. *Chronicles...*, p. 200. Diehl, *Byzantine...*, pp. 251–252. Fuhrmann, *Germany...*, p. 184. Hampe, *Germany...*, pp. 229 & 238. Haverkamp, *Medieval...*, pp. 14 & 265. Norwich, *Kingdom...*, pp. 381, 387–388.

IRENE DUCAS, empress of Byzantium

m. 1077–d. 1123 Byzantium

In 1077, Irene married future emperor of Byzantium, Alexius Comnenus (despite his mother's protests). Irene was modest, pious, and a literary patron. At first, Alexius tended to neglect Irene since he had only married her for political reasons. After his mother, †Anna Dalassena, retired from court in the 1100s, Irene became an influential adviser to Alexius. In the struggle over his successor, however, she supported her daughter †Anna against her son John. The failure of her plots, and her husband's death in 1118, caused Irene to retire to a convent she had established.

♦ **Charity. Divorce. Educated. Models. Patrons of literature. Politics. Rebellions. Religieuses. Religious patrons. Soldiers. Widows.** ♦

Cambridge..., IV, pp. 326, 328, 342–347. *Chronicles...*, p. 66. Comnena, *Alexiad...*, pp. 12, 17, 91, 105, 109, 110, 196, 374–378, 384, 396–397, 404, 448, 452, 453, 457, 460, 473–476, 507–510, 514. Diehl, *Byzantine...*, pp. 199–225.

IRENE LASCARIS, empress of Byzantium

d. 1241 Byzantium; Greece; Turkey

First wife of John III Ducas Vatatzes, Greek emperor of Nicaea. Her son, Theodore II Lascaris ruled in Byzantium from 1254 until 1261. Irene was especially active in establishing and supporting churches, hospitals, and orphanages.

♦ **Charity. Medicine. Models. Orphans. Patrons of literature. Religious patrons. Scholars.** ♦

Cambridge..., IV, pp. 495, 498, 499. Diehl, *Byzantine...*, p. 260.

IRENE OF MONTFERRAT

See—YOLANDE OF MONTFERRAT, empress of Byzantium.

IRMENGAUDE

See—ERMENGARDE.

ISABELLE [Isabeau; Isabel; Isabella; Isabiau; Isobel]

Also see: ELIZABETH and YSABEL

ISABELLE OF ACHAIA

[Isabelle de Villehardouin, princess of Achaia]

1254–1311 Greece; Netherlands

Daughter and heiress of Anne of Comnene and William of Achaia. Married (1) in 1269, Philip of Sicily (d.1277). When Isabelle's father died, Achaia went to Philip's father, Charles I of Naples (house of Anjou). In 1289 Isabelle remarried and, until 1296, she and her new husband, Florent d'Avesnes of Hainault, ruled Achaia in peace. Their young daughter †Matilda of Hainault was betrothed to Guy II, duke of Athens. In 1300, despite a previous agreement not to remarry, Isabelle wed Philip of Savoy in an attempt to hold onto her lands. The newlyweds were ousted by Charles II of Anjou. In 1311, Isabelle died in exile in Holland.

♦ **Estate. Pawns. Rulers. Widows.** ♦

Anselme, *Histoire...*, v.1, pp. 397 & 416. *Cambridge...*, IV, pp. 444–449, 452, 474. Cheetham, *Greece...*, pp. 98, 99, 112–114, 122, 123–124, 144, 234. Diehl, *Byzantine...*, p. 280. Runciman, *Sicilian...*, pp. 138–139, 147, 196.

ISABELLE OF ANGOULEÊME, queen of England

b. 1186–d. 1246 England; France

Daughter of Alice de Courteney and Aymer, count of Angoulême. In 1200, she married King John of England; they had five children: Henry (III); Richard, earl of Cornwall; †Joan (later queen of Scotland); †Isabella (later Holy Roman Empress); and †Eleanor de Montfort (countess of Pembroke and Leicester). John died in 1216, and the queen returned to Angoulême. She quickly broke off her daughter's engagement to Hugh X de Lusignan, and married him herself. Her remarriage caused problems in both England and France; Isabelle was ambitious and she tended to push Hugh into political activity. Late in her life, she retired to Fontevrault.

♦ **Divorce. Politics. Religieuses. Widows. Writers–letters.** ♦

Appleby, *John...*, pp. 100–1, 107–8, 112, 118–9, 125, 138, 144, 185–6, 210, & 223. Bréquigny, *Lettres de rois...*, pp. 27–28. Cazel and Painter, "Marriage of...". Green, *Letters...*, pp. 28–31. Kelly, *Eleanor...*, pp. 362–6, 369, 375, 383, 387. Lloyd, *Maligned...*, pp. 102–4, 106–8, 110, ... 367, 373, 393, 394. *Manners and Expenses...*, intro. Paris, *Chronicles...*, pp. 109, 264, 267. Richardson, "Marriage...". Robinson, *Readings...*, I, p. 210. Stephens, "Early Life...," pp. 304–305. Weiss, "Castellan...," p. 249.

ISABEAU (apotiqueresse)

1320 France

Parisian records of 1320 noted that Isabeau sold bath salts and other herbal wares.

♦ **Apothecaries.** ♦

Decaux, *Histoire...*, p. 336. Lehmann, *Rôle de la...*, p. 475.

ISABEL OF ARAGON, princess of France

fl. 1250s–d. 1271 France; Spain

Daughter of †Yolande of Hungary and Jaime I of Aragon. Married Philip (III) of France around 1262. She accompanied her husband and father-in-law (Louis IX) on the Eighth Crusade. In 1271, Isabel was thrown from her horse, which caused her to give birth prematurely—she and the baby both died.

♦ **Childbirth. Crusades.** ♦

Butler, *Women...*, p. 253. *Cambridge...*, VI, p. 359. Fawtier, *Capetian...*, pp. 128 & 165. Jordan, *Louis...*, p. 216 & n. Lehmann, *Rôle de la...*, p. 388. Miron, *Queens...*, p. 104. Powicke, *Thirteenth...*, pp. 239–240 & n. Shneidman, *Rise...*, p. 330.

ISABELLA OF ARAGON, duchess of Milan

c. 1472–d. 1524 Italy

Daughter of †Ippolita Sforza and Alfonso of Aragon, king of Naples; in 1489, Isabella married Giangaleazzo Sforza, titular duke of Milan; mother of Francesco, Ippolita, and Bona. Only Bona survived past childhood (she married Sigismund I, king of Poland). When Isabella moved to Milan as a new bride, she discovered that her husband was so weak-willed and hedonistic that his uncle Ludovic Sforza was actually running the duchy. Isabella was strong and courageous; she attempted to interest Giangaleazzo in governing Milan, but to no avail. When Giangaleazzo died in 1494, Ludovic took over Milan and became duke in his own name. He gave Bari to Isabella for her retirement.

♦ **Educated. Estate. Models. Pawns. Politics. Squabbles. Writers.** ♦

Cartwright, *Beatrice...*, pp. 49, 69, 80, 99, 118, 124, 160, 167, 169, 176, 230, 237, 250, 265, 269, 328, 353. Chamberlin, *Fall...*, pp. 112, 119, 122–124, 131. Chamberlin, *World...*, pp. 182, 266, 269–270. Cleugh, *Medici...*, pp. 198 & 201. Collison-Morley, *Sforzas...*, pp. 149–158. Commynes, *Memoirs...*, pp. 444, 446, 461, 602. Fusero, *Borgias...*, pp. 159, 288, 290–291. Prescott, *Princes...*, pp. 8, 13–14, 79–80, 83, 134. Sizeranne, *Beatrice...*, pp. 122–124, 126, 130–132, 135, 137–138, 142, 147, 151, 153, 155, 183, 259, 260. Trevelyan, *Short...*, pp. 188–189, 191.

ISABELLA OF ARAGON, queen of Portugal

b. 1470–d. 1498 Portugal; Spain

First child of †Isabella, queen of Castile and Aragon, and Ferdinand of Aragon. In 1490, she married Prince Alfonso of Portugal; after his death

(1491), she married Manuel I, king of Portugal (in 1497). Isabella died giving birth to their only child, Miguel. (He was sworn heir to the three kingdoms—Aragon, Castile, and Portugal—in 1498, but he died at age two.) Like her parents, Isabella was very pious and intensely orthodox. Before she would consent to wed Manuel I, Isabella forced him to expel the Jews from Portugal.

♦ **Childbirth. Jews–treatment of. Religious patrons.** ♦

Altamira, *Spain...*, p. 291. Miller, *Castles...*, pp. 73, 78, 104, 106, 126, 128, 144, 157–159, 161, 165, 166, 172–173, 175–176, 197, 202. Nowell, *History...*, pp. 57–58 & 68–69. Smith, *Spain...*, p. 115. Stephens, *Story...*, pp. 163, 170, 171, 173, 174.

ISABEAU OF BAVARIA, queen of France

[Elizabeth; Isabelle; Isabella]

1370–1435 France; Germany

Daughter of †Taddea Visconti and Stephen III of Bavaria. Married Charles VI the Mad of France in 1385; they had twelve children. Isabeau has gone down in history as a nymphomaniac and as the woman who signed away France—by agreeing to the Treaty of Troyes. This document dispossessed her son (the dauphin Charles VII), betrothed her daughter †Catherine to Henry V of England, and made the English king future heir to the French throne. Isabeau evidently had few abilities as a ruler. It was widely believed that she was the mistress of Louis, duke of Orléans. She was especially unpopular with Parisians who considered her frivolous and a spendthrift. Her bad reputation may have been largely caused by her foreign ways and the unfortunate bouts of insanity suffered by her husband. She certainly compromised her reputation (but not necessarily her virtue) with the duke of Orléans. Furthermore, due to pressure by the duke of Burgundy, Isabeau may have had no option but to agree to the Treaty of Troyes.

♦ **Adultery. Art patrons. Book owners. Models. Music. Negotiators. Patrons of literature. Pilgrims. Politics. Regents. Religious patrons. Tournaments** ♦

Bell, "Medieval...," pp. 157–8, 161, 163, 165. Calmette, *Golden...*, pp. 58, 74, 75, 79, 92, 119, 122, 306, 307. Cartellieri, *Court...*, pp. 36–37, 42, 47, 51, 110–111. Chamberlin, *Count...*, pp. 40, 67, 176, 177–179. Champion, *François...*, I, pp. 6, 144, 198, 216; II, pp. 299, 304, 315. Cleugh, *Chant...*, pp. 13–14, 43, 140. Coryn, *House...*, pp. 12, 17, 24, 31, 40...201, 203, 206, 211, 212. Decaux, *Histoire...*, pp. 375–392, 394–404, 434–435. Froissart, *Chronicles...*, I, pp. 285–286; II, pp. 53, 54, 56, 58, 75, 90, 92, 100–101, 106, 108, 113, 129, & 130. Huizinga, *Waning...*, pp. 51, 97, 145, 214, 225, 236. Hutchison, *King...*, pp. 56, 156–157, 177–179, 185–186, 192, 211. Jarman, *Crispin's...*, pp. 24, 199, 202, 206. Legge (ed.), *Anglo-Norman...*, p. 252 (#170). Pisan, *City...*, p. 212. Tuchman, *Distant...*, pp. xvii, 436–440, 478–481, 517, 529–531, 540, 542–543, 547, 556, 581, 609, 618. Vale, *Charles...*, pp. 21, 23, 30–1, 48–9, 94.

ISABEL BEAUMONT

c. 1340 England

See—BLANCHE OF LANCASTER and MATILDA OF LANCASTER, duchess of Zealand.

♦ **Genealogy.** ♦

ISABEL, lady BERKELEY

See—ISABEL MOWBRAY, lady Berkeley.

ISABEL DE BORGIA **[Isabel da Borja]**

c. 1410–d. 1468 Spain

Daughter of Francisca Marti and Domingo de Borja. Married Jofré de Borja y Doms (d.c.1439). Mother of: Beatrice, Damiata, Juana, Tecla, Pedro Luis, and Rodrigo (later Pope Alexander VI). Favorite sister of Alonso Borja (later Pope Calixtus III), he sent money home for Isabel, found marriage partners for her daughters, and helped her sons start their careers. Isabel was also a religious benefactress; she personally established at least one chapel.

♦ **Popes. Religious patrons. Widows.** ♦

Chamberlin, *Fall...*, p. xxiv. Cloulas, *Borgias...*, pp. 4 & 11. Fusero, *Borgias...*, pp. 23 & 60. Johnson, *Borgias...*, pp. 8, 9, 17, 35, 36.

ISABELLE OF BOURBON, countess of Charolais

fl. 1430s–d. 1465 Flanders; France

Daughter of †Agnes of Burgundy and Charles, duke of Bourbon. Became second wife of Charles the Bold (later duke of Burgundy), around 1450; mother of his heiress, †Marie of Burgundy—born in 1457.

♦ **Models. Politics.** ♦

Anselme, *Histoire...*, v.1, p. 308. Calmette, *Golden...*, pp. 164 & 176. Cartellieri, *Court...*, pp. 63, 71, 215. Cleugh, *Chant...*, pp. 126–130, 151, 193. *DBF*, v.6, p. 1391 & v.8, p. 554. Denieul-Cormier, *Wise...*, p. 331. Huizinga, *Waning...*, pp. 41 & 43. Willard, "Christine...," p. 108.

ISABEL, lady BOURCHIER, countess of Essex

[Isabella Plantagenet; of York]

fl. 1440s–1470s England

Daughter of †Anne Mortimer and Richard, earl of Cambridge (later duke of York). Aunt of Edward IV and Richard III, kings of England. Wife of Henry Bourchier, earl of Essex (d.1483); their son was Sir Henry Bourchier. Isabel was a literary patron on a small scale.

♦ **Book owners. Patrons of literature.** ♦

Coronation..., p. 66. *DNB*, v.2, p. 918. Johnson, *Duke...*, pp. 26 & 229. Kendall, *Yorkist...*, p. 318.

ISABELLA OF BRIENNE

See—YOLANDE (of Jerusalem).

ISABELLA BRUCE, queen of Norway **[Isabella de Brus]**
b. 1280–d.c. 1359 Norway; Scotland

Daughter of Robert Bruce and †Marjorie, countess of Carrick; sister of Robert I (Bruce), king of Scotland. She became second wife of Erik Magnusson, king of Norway, in the 1290s to cement Scottish/Norwegian alliance. Mother of †Ingeborg of Norway (married Valdemar of Sweden). Isabella lived in retirement for some sixty years after Eric's death in 1299.

♦ **Pawns. Queens. Widows.** ♦

Boyesen, *Story...*, pp. 456 & 459. Larsen, *History...*, pp. 172–173. Mackie, *History...*, p. 54. Powicke, *Thirteenth...*, pp. 611n., 613.

ISABELLA, countess of BUCHAN **[Isabel of Fife]**
fl.c. 1300–1310s Scotland

Daughter of Duncan, earl of Fife; wife of John Comyn, earl of Buchan. Unlike her husband, Isabella was a staunch nationalist. Deputizing for her brother (another Duncan, earl of Fife) who was an English prisoner, in 1306 she crowned Robert I (Bruce), king of Scotland. Isabella was later captured by the English forces while defending Berwick. She was imprisoned for some time in an iron cage.

♦ **Politics. Prisons. Soldiers.** ♦

Barrow, *Feudal...*, p. 406. Bryant, *Age...*, pp. 180, 181, 187. *C.P.*, v.2, p. 375. Hallam (ed.), *Four...*, p. 158. Mackie, *History...*, pp. 78 & 79. Mackie, *Short...*, p. 65. Power, *Women...*, p. 45. Powicke, *Thirteenth...*, pp. 714 & 716. Prestwich, *Edward...*, pp. 109, 508–509.

ISABELLA, queen of CASTILE and Aragon **[Isabella the Catholic]**
b. 1451–d. 1504 Spain

Daughter of John II of Castile and his second wife, Isabel of Portugal. Married Ferdinand of Aragon around 1469. In 1474, she became queen of Castile when her brother Henry IV the Impotent died. However, her claim was disputed by †Juana of Castile (*la Beltraneja*), daughter of Henry's wife †Juana of Portugal, but not, most people suspected, Henry's daughter. Some five years later, Isabella became undisputed ruler of Castile and her husband became king of Aragon. He wished to also govern Castile, but his claims were rejected and the couple ruled together. They restructured the bureaucracy of Castile and enhanced its worldwide prestige. Renowned today as the patroness of Columbus, Isabella was also interested in religious and intellectual pursuits. She even hired a female tutor to improve her Latin. Isabella built wartime tent hospitals, and erected permanent foundations during more peaceful years. Extremely pious, Isabella and Ferdinand revamped the Inquisition and she persecuted the Spanish Jews. However, Isabella refused to allow captured Native Americans to be sold as slaves, insisting that they should be converted to Christianity.

♦ **Ecclesiastical courts–Inquisition. Educated. Jews. Legal activity. Medicine. Popes. Religious patrons. Rulers. Shipping–explorers. Soldiers. Squabbles. Teachers.** ♦

Altamira, *Spain...*, pp. 225, 261–263, 269, 273, 277, 282, 285, 291, 293, 308. Chamberlin, *Fall...*, pp. 18–21, 93, 108–109, 137, 144–146, 164, 176, 178, 243–244, 310–312, 315–316. Cleugh, *Chant...*, pp. 169, 252, 255. Commmynes, *Memoirs...*, I, pp. 321, 322, 368; II, pp. 415, 425, 450, 498, 500, 578–582, 584, 586, 591n. Ennen, *Medieval...*, pp. 251–253. Fusero, *Borgias...*, pp. 128–130. Gardiner, *English...*, pp. 151–153. Johnson, *Borgias...*, pp. 73–74, 83, 116. King and Rabil, *Her Immaculate...*, p. 21. Lipinska, *Histoire...*, p. 158. Miller, *Castles...*, pp. 33–37, 44–46, 51–64, ... 261, 331. Norwich, *History...*, pp. 369, 371, 379, 392. Oliviera, *Iberian...*, pp. 171, 180, 209, 210, 211, 220, 245. *Oxford...Europe,* pp. 279–283. Previte-Orton, *Outlines...*, pp. 530–537. Smith, *Spain...*, pp. 92, 100–101, 103–104, 111, 116, 123, 125, 129, 135, 138, 156–157. Stephens, *Story...*, pp. 134, 135, 163, 171.

ISABEL OF CASTILE, countess of Cambridge, duchess of York

b. 1356–d. 1392 England; Spain

Youngest daughter of †Maria de Padilla and Pedro I of Castile; she fled Castile with her father in 1366. Around 1372, Isabel married Edmund of Langley, earl of Cambridge, and later duke of York (a younger son of Edward III of England). Unlike her sedate elder sister (†Constance of Castile, duchess of Lancaster), Isabel was very worldly and ambitious.

♦ **Illegitimacy. Pawns. Politics.** ♦

Armitage-Smith, *John...*, pp. 92, 93, & 357. *Cambridge...*, VII, pp. 447 & 579. Froissart, *Chronicles...*, I, pp. 138, 139, 210. Hardy, *Philippa...*, pp. 285, 287, 309–10. Jamison, *Life...*, I, p. 285; II, pp. 159–160. Roche, *Dona...*, pp. 11 & 32.

ISABELLA DE CLARE, countess of Pembroke

b. 1170s–1190s England; Ireland

Only daughter and heiress of †Eva MacMurrough and Richard de Clare (Strongbow). One of the richest heiresses in England, she married William Marshall in 1189. He became earl of Pembroke and lord of Leinster in her right. Mother of William Marshall, earl of Pembroke and †Isabella Marshall (who married (1) in 1217, Gilbert de Clare and (2) in 1231, Richard, earl of Cornwall).

♦ **Estate. Pawns.** ♦

Appleby, *John...*, pp. 89, 173, 228. Bingham, *Crowned...*, p. 98. *C.P.*, v.10, p. 358. Curtis, *Ireland...*, pp. 59, 66, 69. Curtis, *Medieval...*, p. 93. Orpen, *Ireland...*, II, pp. 5, 133, 201–202, 211. Richter, *Medieval...*, p. 145.

ISABEL DE CONCHES

See—ISABEL DE MONTFORT.

ISABELLA DE DESPENSER, countess of Arundel

divorced 1344 England

Daughter of †Eleanor de Clare and Hugh le Despenser the younger; married Richard, earl of Arundel. They obtained a divorce in 1344, claiming both had been forced to wed as children.

♦ **Divorce. Ecclesiastical courts.** ♦

DNB, v.9, p. 552. Rosenthal, *Nobles...,* pp. 177–178.

ISABEL DESPENSER, countess of Warwick

c. 1405–d.c. 1440 England

Daughter of †Constance of York and Thomas le Despenser, earl of Gloucester. Married (1) Richard Beauchamp, lord Abergavenny (d.1422) and (2) Richard Beauchamp, earl of Warwick in 1423 (Isabel was his second wife).

♦ **Art patrons. Bequests. Estate. Models.** ♦

DNB, v.2, p. 31. *Fifty Earliest...,* pp. 116–119. Jacob, *Fifteenth...,* p. 329. Johnson, *Duke...,* pp. 3, 13, 26. McFarlane, *Nobility...,* pp. 188 & 193.

ISABELLA OF ENGLAND, countess of Bedford

b. 1332–d.c. 1379 England; France

Oldest daughter of †Philippa of Hainault and Edward III of England. Isabella was said to be her father's favorite daughter, even though she was extremely stubborn and extravagant. Around 1365, she married Enguerrand VII de Coucy; they had two daughters: †Marie (b.1366; see lady de Coucy) and †Philippa (b.1367).

♦ **Divorce. Educated. Estate. Tournaments.** ♦

Froissart, *Chronicles...,* I, pp. 34 & 49. Hardy, *Philippa...,* pp. 78, 81, 83–4, 301, 306, 308–9. Riley, *Memorials...,* p. 431. Tuchman, *Distant...,* pp. 80, 90–91, 205, 207, 220–221, 239, 246, 247, 261, 281–282, 284, 297, 301, 303–304, 349, 351. Wentersdorf, "Clandestine...," p. 219.

ISABELLA OF ENGLAND, Holy Roman Empress

b. 1214–d. 1241 England; Germany; Italy

Daughter of †Isabelle of Angoulême and King John of England. Around 1235, Isabella married Holy Roman Emperor Frederick II. Their daughter †Margaret was born in 1237 and son Henry was born in 1238. Isabella died of a fever caused by childbirth.

♦ **Childbirth. Pawns. Queens.** ♦

Appleby, *John...,* p. 223. *Cambridge...,* VI, pp. 88, 97–99, 105, 117, 152, 251, 267. *DNB,* v.10, pp. 499–500. Hallam (ed.), *Four...,* pp. 43, 54, 56. Haverkamp, *Medieval...,* p. 251. Labarge, *Simon...,* pp. 39, 57, 58, 155. Lloyd, *Maligned...,* pp. 353 & 395. *Manners and Expenses...,* Intro. Paris, *Chronicles...,* pp. 98 & 181. Payne, *Dream...,* p. 328. Powicke, *Thirteenth...,* pp. 59, 72, 593n. Stubbs, *Later...,* pp. 28–29.

ISABELLA D'ESTE, marquessa of Mantua

1474–1539 Italy

Older daughter of †Leonora of Aragon and Ercole I d'Este, duke of Ferrara; married Francesco Gonzaga, marquis of Mantua in 1490. Well-educated, Isabella particularly enjoyed collecting Greek and Roman art. She also established a literary court where musicians and poets, like Niccolo da Coreggio, gathered. The famous teacher/printer, Aldo Manuzio, printed and bound a volume of Petrarch and Virgil for Isabella. She bullied Leonardo da Vinci into doing a sketch of her in 1499. Although her marriage was a fairly happy one, Isabella did not fit either the medieval or Renaissance ideal of an obedient wife. When her husband was captured, she ruled well in his place, but took her time about securing his release. She later refused to sell any more of her jewels for Francesco.

♦ **Art patrons. Banking. Book owners. Dance. Drama. Educated. Gems/jewelry. Hunting. Models. Managers. Music. Patrons of literature. Popes. Rulers. Writers–letters.** ♦

Bellonci, "Beatrice...," pp. 284–289, 291, 294–300. Cartwright, *Beatrice...*, pp. 4, 30, 33, 36, 40, 50, 52, 53...304, 308, 312, 321, 326, 344, 353, 356. Cartwright, *Isabella....* Chamberlin, *Fall...*, pp. 112, 252–253, 257–263, 275, 276. Chamberlin, *World...*, pp. 154, 168, 171, 172–175, 182, 199, 269. Cloulas, *Borgias...*, pp. 196, 205–8, 216–7, 224, 271, 275, 277, 288. Collison-Morley, *Sforzas...*, pp. 149–158. Cronin, *Flowering...*, pp. 97, 103, 216. Johnson, *Borgias...*, pp. 196, 202, 203, 205. King and Rabil, *Her Immaculate...*, pp. 21 & 133. Kristeller, "Learned...," p. 93. Marek, *Bed....* Meyer, *First....* Prescott, *Princes...*, pp. 114, 133, 136, 143, 163–185, 205, 215, 276. Simon, *Tapestry...*, pp. 8, 20, 67–69, 71–72, 74–78...197, 202, 214–216, 221, 249, 268. Sizeranne, *Beatrice...*, pp. 28, 84, 260. Verheyen, *Paintings....*

ISABELLE DE FERIÈVES

1317 France

Helped †Mahaut, countess of Artois, make a love philter to reunite Mahaut's daughter, †Jeanne of Burgundy, and son-in-law, the future Philip V of France. Isabelle stated that this concoction included blood, vervain, daisy, and liver-wort.

♦ **Apothecaries. Superstitions. Witchcraft.** ♦

Butler, *Women...*, pp. 267–268. Thorndike, *History...*, p. 21.

ISABELLA DE FORTIBUS, countess of Devon and Aumale [de Redvers; de Forz]

1237–1293 England; Wales

Daughter of †Amice de Clare and Baldwin de Redvers. A widow by age twenty-three, Isabella controlled her own estates and was probably the richest single woman in England. Her extensive lands supported thousands of sheep. She had banking interests, numerous manors, and a salt mining/processing operation. Isabella was also an occasional political force; she was a strong supporter of the baronial rebellion led by Simon de Montfort in the 1260s.

♦ **Banking. Legal activity. Managers. Merchants. Politics. Rebellions. Squabbles. Widows.** ♦

Bryant, *Age...*, pp. 39 & 118. *DNB,* v.16, p. 829. Denholm-Young, "Yorkshire...," pp. 389–420. Holmes, *Later...*, pp. 21 & 23. Labarge, *Baronial...*, pp. 10, 49, & 98. Labarge, *Simon...*, pp. 86, 100, 248. Mate, "Profit...," pp. 326–334. McFarlane, *Nobility...*, pp. 13, 256–259, 264. Powicke, *Thirteenth...*, pp. 364–365, 518. Prestwich, *Edward...*, pp. 62, 103, 268, 292, 294, 341, 352–353. Salzman, *Life...*, pp. 23 & 29. *Select... Edward I.,* I, pp. lxx, 120–128.

ISABELLE OF FRANCE **[Blessed Isabella]**

1225–1270 France

Daughter of †Blanche of Castile and Louis VIII of France. Well-educated, especially in Latin. Co-founder of the Franciscan abbey of Longchamp in the late 1250s. †Agnes d'Harcourt wrote her biography.

♦ **Crusades. Educated. Estate. Models. Religieuses. Religious patrons. Unmarried. Virginity.** ♦

Goodich, "Contours...," p. 24. Jordan, *Louis...*, pp. 9 & n, 10–12, 68 & n, 189n. Jourdain, "Memoire...," p. 484. McDonnell, *Beguines...*, p. 401. Thompson, *Literacy...*, p. 146.

ISABELLA OF FRANCE, queen of England

1292–1358 England; France

Daughter of †Jeanne de Navarre and Philip IV the Fair of France. In 1308, Isabella married Edward II of England. Although her husband neglected her and took her property, he sent Isabella to France in 1325 to negotiate a treaty. Edward then sent his young son and heir to France. After Isabella became Roger Mortimer's lover, the couple plotted to overthrow her husband. In 1326, Isabella, Mortimer, and Edward (III) landed in England and attracted many rebels to the young prince's standard. Edward II was captured and presumably killed, while Edward III was crowned. Isabella and Mortimer were the most powerful forces in the regency government, but they became extremely unpopular by their extravagance and misuse of power. In 1330, Isabella lost her power and position when Edward III began to rule by himself. She also lost her lover since Edward III had Mortimer executed.

♦ **Adultery. Banking. Crusades. Dowry/dower. Hunting. Negotiators. Pilgrims. Rebellions. Regents. Religieuses. Widows. Writers–letters.** ♦

Bryant, *Age...*, pp. 188, 197–199, 214, 224–237, 242, 262, 292, 309. Butt, *History...*, pp. 174, 179, 211, 213, 223–230, 232, 238, 239, 245, 271. *Calendar of Plea...*, I, pp. 18, 21, 29, 41–43, 59, 62, 65, 66, 87. Froissart, *Chronicles...*, I, pp. 2–5. Fryde, *Tyranny...*, pp. 1, 5, 16, 18, 50, 61, 76, 77...177–197, 202, 207–211, 216. Gardner, *Life...*, pp. 5, 27, 36, 42, 43,

46–48, 95, 113, 122, 261. Hallam (ed.), *Four...*, pp. 137, 162, 170, 172...224, 230, 231, 232, 234. Hardy, *Philippa...*, pp. 17–30, 33–41, ... 203, 218, 253–4. *Household... Isabella.* Le Patourel, *Feudal...*, XI, pp. 35, 45; XII, p. 175. Prestwich, *Edward...*, pp. 395, 398, 452, 549–550, 553. Riley, *Memorials...*, pp. 72, 73, 99, 105, 107, 199. Somerset, *Ladies...*, p. 5. Tuchman, *Distant...*, pp. 45, 75, 76. Tyerman, *England...*, pp. 238, 240, 242, 246. Wood, "Queens...," pp. 385, 387, 391, 398.

ISABELLA OF FRANCE, queen of England

1387–1409 England; France

Daughter of †Isabeau of Bavaria and Charles VI of France. Became second wife of Richard II of England in 1396. After Richard was deposed and Henry IV was crowned, Isabella eventually returned to France. In 1405, she married Charles of Angoulême, later duke of Orléans. Isabella died giving birth.

♦ **Childbirth. Dowry/dower. Educated. Models. Pawns. Queens.** ♦

Armitage-Smith, *John...*, p. 396. Calmette, *Golden...*, pp. 60, 95, 306. Coryn, *House...*, pp. 50, 52, 53, 81, 82, 84, 108, 133. Froissart, *Chronicles...*, II, pp. 85, 120, 128–130, 138–140, 145, 155, 157, 158, 167, 169, 171, 193, 203, 206, 210, 214, 215. Holmes, *Later...*, pp. 199–200. Huizinga, *Waning...*, p. 225. Hutchison, *King...*, pp. 56, 91, 179. Jacob, *Fifteenth...*, pp. 67, 108, 109, 484. Jones, *Ducal...*, pp. 134 & 137. Mirot, *Isabelle....* Somerset, *Ladies...*, pp. 7–8.

ISABELLE OF FRANCE, duchess of Milan **[Isabelle de Valois]**

b. 1348–d.c. 1372 France; Italy

Daughter of †Bona of Luxembourg and John II of France. To obtain part of the ransom he needed, her father married the eleven-year-old Isabelle to Giangaleazzo Visconti of Milan in 1360. Mother of †Valentine Visconti (later duchess of Orléans). Well-educated book collector. Isabelle died having her fourth baby at age twenty-four.

♦ **Book owners. Childbirth. Dowry/dower. Educated. Pawns.** ♦

Cartellieri, *Court...*, p. 89. Chamberlin, *Count...*, pp. 40 & 67. Coryn, *House...*, pp. 15 & 17. Seward, *Hundred...*, p. 100. Tuchman, *Distant...*, pp. 201, 269–270.

ISABELLA OF FRANCE, queen of Navarre **[Isabelle de Valois]**

1241–1271 France; Spain

Daughter of †Marguerite of Provence and (St.) Louis IX of France. Her father prepared an instruction manual for Isabella; the theme was obedience to parents and husbands. Isabella married Thibaut II, king of Navarre.

♦ **Book owners. Educated. Queens.** ♦

Anselme, *Histoire...*, v.1, p. 86. Guizot, *History...*, p. 457. Hurd-Mead, *History...*, p. 209. Leroy, *La Navarre...*, p. 44.

ISABELLA OF GLOUCESTER

See—HAWISE OF GLOUCESTER.

ISABEL GOBBE

1364 England

A stockfishmonger of London. She taught this trade to male apprentices.

♦ **Apprentices–mistresses. Provisioning–fishmongers.** ♦

Calendar of Plea..., I, p. 275.

ISABELLA OF HAINAULT, queen of France **[Elizabeth]**

c. 1170–d. 1190 Flanders; France

Daughter of †Margaret of Alsace and Baldwin VIII, count of Flanders (Baldwin V of Hainault). Around 1180, Isabella married Philip II Augustus of France. Their son, the future Louis VIII, was born in 1187. Isabella died giving birth to twins when she was only twenty years old.

♦ **Childbirth. Divorce. Dowry/dower. Models. Queens.** ♦

Appleby, *John...*, p. 96. Baldwin, *Government...*, pp. 15, 18, 25, 26, 81, 82, 357, 370–371, 375. Bingham, *Crowned...*, p. 150. *Cambridge...*, VI, pp. 287, 291, 292, 304, 324, 331. Decaux, *Histoire...*, pp. 268–271. Facinger, "Study...," p. 38. Fawtier, *Capetian...*, pp. 51–52, 56, 111, 112, 113. Pernoud, *Eleanor...*, pp. 193 & 210. Wolff, "Baldwin...," p. 282.

ISABELLA HODERE

1283 England

Widow of London merchant, Peter le Hodere. Isabella received brewhouse and shops from his will. In 1283, Isabella and her new husband, Richard Horn, challenged Peter's will because she had been joint property owner.

♦ **Alewives. Bequests. Land/property. Legal activity. Merchants. Widows.** ♦

Calendar of Wills..., I, p. 64.

ISABELLA OF JERUSALEM

1160s–1200s Israel; Lebanon

Daughter of †Maria Comnena and Amalric of Jerusalem. Married Onfroy (Humphrey) de Toron. When her half-sister †Sibylla died in 1190, Isabella inherited rights to kingdom of Jerusalem. In order to keep her throne, however, Isabella was forced to get a divorce and then marry Conrad of Montferrat, lord of Tyre. In 1192, Conrad was murdered, and Isabella married Henry II, count of Champagne (d.1197). Her fourth husband was Amaury of Lusignan (d.1205). Isabella passed the title of "Queen of Jerusalem" on to Mary, her daughter by Conrad.

♦ **Divorce. Estate. Murder. Pawns. Queens.** ♦

Barlow, *Feudal...*, pp. 358–359. Bingham, *Crowned...*, pp. 105 & 111. Bridge, *Crusades...*, pp. 195, 222, 248. *Cambridge...*, V, pp. 309, 311,

314. *Chronicles...*, pp. 152, 153, 247. Decaux, *Histoire...*, pp. 222–223. Hamilton, "Women...," pp. 163, 165, 167–169, 171–173. Kelly, *Eleanor...*, pp. 269, 270, 280, 281. Payne, *Dream...*, pp. 193, 195, 236, 252, 254.

ISABELLA OF JERUSALEM, Holy Roman Empress

See—YOLANDE (of Jerusalem).

ISABEL OF LEICESTER

See—ISABEL OF VERMANDOIS, countess of Leicester.

ISABEL OF LORRAINE, queen of Naples

1420s–1440s France; Italy

Daughter/heiress of †Margaret of Bavaria and Charles, duke of Lorraine; married René I, duke of Anjou. Isabel helped René acquire territories, fought for him in Sicily, and served as his regent.

♦ **Dance. Models. Negotiators. Regents. Soldiers.** ♦

Cleugh, *Chant...*, pp. 70, 77, 175. Cloulas, *Borgias...*, p. 11. Commynes, *Memoirs...*, II, p. 600. *DBF*, v.2, p. 1297. Denieul-Cormier, *Wise...*, p. 291. Lewis, *King...*, p. 180. Marks, *Pilgrims...*, p. 304. Vale, *Charles...*, pp. 49 & 92.

ISABELLA MARSHALL, countess of Cornwall

b. 1200–d. 1240 England

See—ISABELLA DE CLARE, countess of Pembroke.

♦ **Estate. Genealogy.** ♦

ISABELLE DE MELUN, countess of Dreux and Eu

fl. 1320s–1350s France

See—JEANNE D'ARTOIS, countess of Dreux.

♦ **Estate.** ♦

ISABIAU (la mergesse) **[Ysabiau]**

1292 France

Popular lay healer of 1292 Paris in parish of Ste. Opportune; paid 6s tax.

♦ **Doctors/empirics.** ♦

Géraud, *Paris sous...*, p. 57. Hurd-Mead, *History...*, p. 215. Lipinska, *Histoire...*, p. 118.

ISABEL DE MONTFORT **[Isabel de Conches; Conches-Toëni]**

fl. 1070s–1100s France

Daughter of Simon de Montfort; married Ralph of Conches. A three year feud was started because she insulted her sister-in-law, †Helwise of Nevers, countess of Évreux. Isabel was generous and gay; she dominated her husband, but was loved by most of her people. Strong-willed, she was particularly noted for donning armor and riding with her troops. Isabel retired to a convent after Ralph died.

♦ Models. Religieuses. Soldiers. Squabbles. ♦

Barthélemy, "Kinship...," p. 138. Hollister, *Medieval Europe...,* p. 161. McLaughlin, "Woman...," pp. 203–204. Verdon, "Les Sources...," p. 229. Vitalis, *Ecclesiastical...,* III, pp. 126–129; IV, pp. 212–218.

ISABEL MOWBRAY, lady Berkeley **[Isabella; Isobel]**

c. 1410s–1460s England

Younger daughter of Thomas Mowbray, duke of Norfolk. Married (1) Sir Henry Ferrers of Groby and (2) James, lord Berkeley. Isabel was spirited and courageous. In her second husband's fight to claim the barony of Berkeley, she was an able supporter, especially in the legal arena. Isabel was even imprisoned by her opponent, †Margaret Beauchamp, countess of Shrewsbury.

♦ Estate. Legal activity. Managers. Prisons. Squabbles. Writers. ♦

Abram, *English...,* p. 35. *DNB,* v. 19, p. 323. Gies, *Women...,* p. 213. Kendall, *Yorkist...,* pp. 412–413, 414. McFarlane, *Nobility...,* p. 155.

ISABEL NEVILLE, duchess of Clarence **[Isobel]**

b. 1451–d. 1476 England

Daughter of Richard Neville and †Anne Beauchamp, countess of Warwick. Married George, duke of Clarence in 1469. It is extremely unlikely that Isabel was murdered, as her husband claimed—even though he had †Ankarette Twynyho executed for the crime.

♦ Childbirth. Estate. Murder–suspected. ♦

Butt, *History...,* pp. 601, 608. Cleugh, *Chant...,* pp. 199 & 208. Clive, *Sun...,* pp. 98, 123, 142, 146, 151–4, 198, 200, 234–5, 237–8. Commynes, *Memoirs...,* pp. 212 & 215. Jacob, *Fifteenth...,* pp. 555, 579. Ross, *Wars...,* pp. 33, 68, 77. Scofield, *Life...,* I, pp. 494–5, 533; II, pp. 184, 210–11. St. Aubyn, *Year...,* pp. 54–55, 58–60.

ISABEL NORMAN

c. 1400 England

London trader and silkworker. Isabel cut out the middle-man in her silkwork operations by buying her materials through Genoese merchants who shipped the silk from Cyprus. Isabel must have been very prosperous to be able to finance such expeditions.

♦ Merchants. Shipping. Silkwork. ♦

Dale, "London...," p. 329.

ISABEL PLUMPTON

m.c. 1424 England

Daughter of William and Alice Plumpton. Married Sir Stephen de Thorp of Gowsell. Isabel owned the manor of Sacomburs.

♦ Managers. Writers–letters. ♦

Plumpton..., pp. xxxix, xl–xli, 218–220, 241–242.

ISABELLA OF PORTUGAL, duchess of Burgundy

b. 1397–d. 1471 Flanders; France; Portugal

Daughter of †Philippa of Lancaster and John I of Portugal. In 1430, Isabella became the third wife of Philip the Good, duke of Burgundy. Their son, Charles the Bold was born in 1433. Isabella was imperious, charming, serious-minded, and very intelligent. She was an excellent politician and diplomat; her husband often sent Isabella to negotiate his treaties. She was also a religious patron, and a benefactress to educators and writers.

♦ **Educated. Models. Negotiators. Patrons of literature. Regents. Religieuses. Religious patrons. Teachers.** ♦

Calmette, *Golden...*, pp. 138, 147, 150, 152–154, 167, 170, 171, 187, 199, 201, 204, 209, 233, 238, 315, 328. Cartellieri, *Court...*, pp. 55, 56, 61, 67, 170, 215. Champion, *Louis...*, pp. 78–79, 102, 103, 127, 135, 136. Cleugh, *Chant...*, pp. 49, 62, 78, 79, 85, 90, 124, 126, 128, 131–132, 163. Clive, *Sun...*, pp. 58, 93, 129, 130. Commynes, *Memoirs...*, pp. 96 & 210. Latten, "Isabelle de..." Roche, *Dona...*, pp. 72, 87, 88, 92, 93, 98, 99. Stephens, *Story...*, pp. 125 & 134. Willard, "Isabel of...," pp. 961–969.

ISABEL DE REDVERS

See—ISABELLA DE FORTIBUS.

ISABEL ROMÉE **[Isabel of Vouthon]**

c. 1400s–d. 1458 France

Mother of †Joan of Arc; Isabel encouraged her daughter's piety and taught her the *Creed, Hail Mary,* etc. During Joan's retrial on heresy charges, Isabel was the petitioner of record.

♦ **Childcare. Ecclesiastical courts–Inquisition. Legal activity. Manors. Teachers.** ♦

Barstow, *Joan...*, pp. xiii, 70, 74. Lowell, *Joan...*, pp. 19–21, 49, 72, 345, 351. Pernoud, *Retrial...*, pp. 30, 31, 33, 216. Stephenson, *Mediaeval...*, pp. 499–500.

ISABEL OF SAVOY **[Valois]**

c. 1330 France

See—BLANCHE OF BOURBON; BONNE DE BOURBON; and JEANNE DE BOURBON, queen of France.

♦ **Genealogy.** ♦

ISABELLA DE TOPPESHAM

1350 England

Called a *hostelere* in London court records of 1350. She was found guilty of stealing money one of her boarders had entrusted to her. Isabella was sent to prison until she repaid this money, plus a further sum in fines.

♦ **Banking. Innkeepers. Miscreants. Prisons.** ♦

Calendar of Plea..., I, p. 233.

ISABELLE DE VALOIS

See—ISABELLE OF FRANCE.

See—ISABEL OF SAVOY.

ISABELLA OF VERMANDOIS, countess of Flanders [Elizabeth]

c. 1140s–d. 1183 Flanders; France

Daughter and heiress of †Petronilla of Aquitaine and Raoul, count of Vermandois. In 1156, Isabella married Philip of Alsace, count of Flanders. She was known as a patroness of troubadours. Isabella supposedly had to relinquish Vermandois to her husband as the price of his forgiveness for her infidelity. She died childless in 1183.

♦ **Estate. Patrons of literature. Women of easy virtue.** ♦

Anselme, *Histoire...*, v.1, p. 534. Baldwin, *Government...*, pp. 8, 15, 17, 24. *Cambridge...*, VI, pp. 292, 293. Fawtier, *Capetian...*, pp. 111, 112, 113. Kelly, *Eleanor...*, pp. 164, 183, 385. Pernoud, *Eleanor...*, p. 152.

ISABEL OF VERMANDOIS, countess of Leicester, Meulan, and Surrey [Elizabeth of Leicester; Isabel de Warenne]

c. 1080s–1130s England; France

Daughter of Hugh de Crépy le Grand, count of Vermandois. Around 1098, Isabel married Robert I de Beaumont, earl of Meulan, who became earl of Leicester in her right. Their twin sons—Waleran and Robert II de Beaumont—were born in 1101. Not long after her husband died in 1118, Isabel married William II de Warenne, earl of Surrey (who had supposedly abducted her).

♦ **Abduction. Childbirth. Estate. Widows.** ♦

Barlow, *Feudal...*, p. 182. C.P., v.7, p. 526. *DNB*, v.9, p. 546. Le Patourel, *Feudal...*, VI, pp. 11, 13–15.

ISABELLE DE VESCY [Isabella de Beaumont]

c. 1270s–d.c. 1335 England; France

Daughter of Louis de Brienne; sister of Henry de Beaumont; married John de Vescy (d.1289). Influential lady-in-waiting to †Isabelle of France, queen of England.

♦ **Estate. Legal activity. Rebellions. Servants–ladies.** ♦

DNB, v.20, p. 287. Fryde, *Tyranny...*, p. 48, 225. *Household...Isabella*, XIV. Prestwich, *Edward...*, pp. 372, 550. Prestwich, "Isabella...," pp. 148–152.

ISABELLETTE OF EPINAL

c. 1405–1455 France

Peasant of Domremy; wife of Géraudin of Épinal. She testified at †Joan of Arc's retrial. Isabellette claimed that Joan was more pious than most of her peers. She never danced, and sometimes she would let a poor person have her bed while she slept on the floor.

♦ **Ecclesiastical courts–Inquisition. Legal activity. Manors.** ♦

Pernoud, *Joan...*, p. 18. Pernoud, *Retrial...*, pp. 65–66.

ISEUT DE CAPIO

b. 1140 France

Provençal troubadour; exchanged verses with †Almucs de Castelnau.

♦ **Poets/troubadours.** ♦

Bogin, *Women...*, pp. 92–93 & 165–166. Boutière and Schutz, *Biographies des...*, pp. 422–424. Egan, *Vidas...*, pp. 6–7.

ISOTTA DEGLI ATTI

b. 1431–d.c. 1470 Italy

Mistress and then third wife of Sigismund Malatesta, lord of Rimini. She was intelligent, educated, and influential. Sigismond found her especially useful as a diplomatic envoy. After Sigismond died, Isotta and their son, Sallustro, tried to rule Rimini—until popular revolts forced her to ask for help from Venice. Eventually Isotta's government was overthrown and it was rumored that she was poisoned.

♦ **Educated. Mistresses. Models. Murder. Negotiators. Regents. Soldiers. Widows.** ♦

Collison-Morley, *Sforzas...*, pp. 49–51. Jones, *Malatesta...*, pp. 204, 213, 241, 243, 245–247, 295n, 300n, 324–325, 332. Prescott, *Princes...*, pp. 287–9, 295, 296.

ISOTTA NOGAROLA

1418–1466 Italy

Daughter of Bianca Borromeo Nogarola of Verona; tutored by humanist Martino Rizzoni. A Latin and Greek scholar, Isotta translated and wrote poetry. She also corresponded with other humanists, and †Costanza Varano extolled Isotta's abilities. Isotta chose not to marry; instead, she continued her scholarly activities from 1441 until 1466, concentrating on sacred authors and subjects.

♦ **Book owners. Models. Religieuses. Scholars. Unmarried. Writers.** ♦

Gardiner, *English...*, pp. 149–150. King and Rabil, *Her Immaculate...*, pp. 13, 16–18, 22, 27–29, 55–69, 78, 83, 111–114, 116, 117, 121, 132, 135, 136, 141, 142, 148–150. King, "Religious...," pp. 807–22. Kristeller, "Learned...," p. 96. Nogarola, *Isotae....* Robathan, "Bluestocking...," pp. 106–111.

ITA

See—IDA.

IVETTA OF HUY **[Yvette]**

1157–1228 Belgium; Flanders

Married at thirteen, at age eighteen Ivetta was a widow with three sons. She left her children with her father and opened a charitable hospice for pilgrims. Later Ivetta, her father, and two of her sons joined the Cistercians, where Ivetta attracted numerous followers, especially women.

♦ **Models. Pilgrims–hospices. Religieuses. Widows.** ♦

Bolton, "Vitae Matrum...," pp. 258, 260, 261, 263. Bynum, *Holy...,* pp. 215, 249 n2. Herlihy, *Opera...,* p. 120. Lagorio, "Continental...," p. 175. McDonnell, *Beguines...,* pp. 151–152.

— J —

JACOBA FELICIE **[Jacqueline Felicia de Almania]**

c. 1290–1322 France

Arrested in Paris for practicing medicine without license. At her trial, witnesses swore she had cured them when licensed male physicians had failed. She was found guilty and ordered to close her practice. Evidently Jacoba was too much competition for university doctors.

♦ **Doctors/empirics. Miscreants. Punishments.** ♦

Herlihy, *Opera...*, pp. 113–114. Hughes, *Women...*, pp. 91 & 96. Hurd-Mead, *History...*, p. 271. Lipinska, *Histoire...*, pp. 119–120. Pernoud, *La femme...*, p. 203. Power, Women, pp. 87–88. Tuchman, *Distant...*, p. 228. Wickersheimer, *Dictionnaire...*, p. 317.

JACOBA (of Passau)

1474 Austria; Italy

Licensed to practice as a doctor during plague outbreak in 1474 Florence.

♦ **Doctors/empirics. Plague.** ♦

Hughes, *Women...*, p. 142. Hurd-Mead, *History...*, p. 312. Lipinska, *Histoire...*, p. 149.

JACOBINA (medica)

1304 Italy

Daughter of a doctor, Bartholomew; he probably gave Jacobina her medical training. She practiced medicine in Bologna; a male contemporary called her a great surgeon.

♦ **Doctors/empirics. Surgeons.** ♦

Hughes, *Women...*, p. 142. Hurd-Mead, *History...*, p. 224. Lipinska, *Histoire...*, p. 150.

JACQUELINE OF HAINAULT

[Jacoba van Beijeren, countess of Hainault and Holland]

1401–1436 England; Flanders; France; Netherlands

Daughter/heiress of Margaret of Burgundy and William VI, count of Hainault and Holland. Around 1416, she married John of France, duke of Touraine. He died in 1416 and her cousin, the duke of Burgundy, arranged for Jacqueline to wed their relative, Duke John IV of Brabant.

Bored to distraction by her new husband, Jacqueline divorced John and then married Humphrey, duke of Gloucester, in 1422. Her precipitate actions forced Jacqueline and Humphrey into a fight for her inheritance. The pope dissolved their marriage in 1428, and Philip the Good of Burgundy defeated Humphrey's forces. Jacqueline continued to fight. Captured and imprisoned in Ghent, Jacqueline disguised herself as a page, escaped, and resumed the fight in Holland. Eventually she was forced to sign the Treaty of Delft, giving the duke of Burgundy final inheritance of her lands and control over her own right to remarry. Despite this treaty, Jacqueline soon wed Franz von Borselen and continued to fight for her lands. After the duke of Burgundy captured Franz, he gave Jacqueline a choice between her husband's life and her lands; she then signed away all rights to her inheritance.

♦ **Adultery. Estate. Divorce. Popes. Soldiers. Squabbles.** ♦

Butt, *History...*, pp. 503, 504, 506, 510, 511, 527. Calmette, *Golden...*, pp. 54, 112, 125–126, 138, 139–142, 154, 306. Cartellieri, *Court...*, pp. 112–113. Coryn, *House...*, pp. 108, 157, 223–225. Holmes, *Later...*, pp. 204–205. Hutchison, *King...*, pp. 132, 206, 215. Jacob, *Fifteenth...*, pp. 164, 225, 226, 229, 245. Motley, *Rise...*, p. 35. Seward, *Hundred...*, pp. 202, 207. Vaughan, *Philip...*, pp. 82, 91 & n, 92.

JACQUELINE MACHECOUE **[Mother Machecou]**

c. 1420s–d.c. 1460 France

Wife of Arnoulet Machecou, a poultry caterer of Paris. As a widow (c.1438-1460), she continued his business, which made her quite wealthy and well-known. Jacqueline owned a house with gardens in the St-Martin quarter of Paris. She also owned and operated a poultry/cook shop, the *Golden Lion* in the Saunerie. She was probably the Jaquelot la Macherre who was listed as a poulterer in 1451-1453 Parisian tax records.

♦ **Land/property. Merchants. Models. Provisioning–poultry. Widows.** ♦

Champion, *François...*, I, pp. 99n., 267, 294; II, pp. 148, 321, 325–326. *Comptes du...*, p. 773. Lewis, *François...*, pp. 180 & 304.

JACQUELINE (la saacière)

1292 France

Paid 12d tax in 1292 Paris on her occupation—making purses.

♦ **Apparel–pursemakers. Less-affluent.** ♦

Géraud, *Paris sous...*, p. 40.

JACQUETTA OF LUXEMBOURG, duchess of Bedford

[Jacquette de St. Pol]

b. 1416-d.c. 1472 England; France; Luxembourg

Daughter of Pierre of St. Pol; around 1433, Jacquetta became the second wife of the English regent of France, John, duke of Bedford. Soon after he died, Jacquetta secretly married a less socially-elevated nobleman, Richard Woodville, later earl Rivers. They were the parents of Queen †Elizabeth Woodville. Accused of image magic, Jacquetta countered with a defamation of character suit, which she won. She was thereby acquitted of all charges. Jacquetta served as an envoy from the city of London in negotiations with Queen †Margaret of Anjou.

♦ **Legal activity. Negotiators. Witchcraft.** ♦

Bellamy, *Crime...*, p. 61. Clive, *Sun...*, pp. 13–15, 40–1, 99, 101, 103, 105, 112, 117–8, 133, 137, 145, 155, 288. *Coronation...*, pp. 41–54. *DNB*, v.10, p. 870. Ewen, *Witchcraft...*, p. 38. Kendall, *Yorkist...*, pp. 167, 168, 171. Kieckhefer, *European...*, p. 136. *Paston...*, I, pp. 140, 315, 339, 564; II, pp. 389 & 540. Robbins, *Encyclopedia...*, p. 162. Scofield, *Life...*, I, pp. 51, 145, 372, 498–499. St. Aubyn, *Year...*, pp. 48 & 50.

JADWIGA OF HUNGARY, queen of Poland
[Jadzwiga; Jodwiga; Hedwig]
b. 1372–d. 1399 Hungary; Poland

Younger daughter of †Elizabeth of Bosnia and Louis I the Great of Hungary and Poland. When her father died, Jadwiga's sister †Maria became queen of Hungary, but the Poles chose Jadwiga as their queen (1384). They also insisted that she marry Jagiello, grand duke of Lithuania (1386). Jagiello agreed to convert to Roman Catholicism for this marriage. Their union worked out relatively well, and they often ruled together. Jadwiga was especially effective in negotiations and making treaties. In 1399 she died giving birth to a baby who also soon died.

♦ **Childbirth. Negotiators. Rulers. Religious patrons. University.** ♦

Benes and Pounds, *Poland*, p. 40. Davies, *God's...*, pp. 112, 113, 116, 117, 118, 135, 211. Fügedi, *Castle...*, p. 123. Gardner, *Queen Jadwiga....* Halecki, *History...*, pp. 65–74, 76, 80. Pamlényi, *History...*, p. 78 Pares, *History...*, pp. 64–65, 69, 76. Pinnow, *History...*, p. 150.

JANE HAROLD **[Jone]**
1414 England

Admitted to the guild of brewers in 1414 London; she was entitled to wear the brewers' livery.

♦ **Alewives. Merchants. Miscreants.** ♦

Lacey, "Women...," p. 51.

JANE SHORE **[Elizabeth Lambert]**
c. 1450–1500s England

Daughter of Amy Marshall and John Lambert, a London mercer. Jane married William Shore, another London merchant. She was the mistress of King Edward IV from approximately 1465 until 1472. She was extolled as witty, literate, beautiful, and kind to others. Although Edward IV gave Jane at least one house and other financial assets, she reputedly refused to follow the lead of some royal mistresses by selling favors or influence. After Edward's death, she was poor and neglected. Accused of practicing witchcraft in 1483, no proof was found and she was acquitted. Jane was later imprisoned at Lud Gate, probably for poverty. Sir Thomas More (writing for Henry VII) accused Richard III of a variety of harassments directed at Jane. Her story has been a perennial favorite with authors and playwrights.

♦ **Educated. Mistresses. Models. Prisons. Witchcraft.** ♦

Butt, *History...*, p. 617. Bellamy, Crime..., p. 61. Clive, *Sun...*, pp. 96–7, 241–2, 274, 286–7. Ewen, *Witchcraft...*, p. 38. Kendall, *Yorkist...*, pp. 168, 417–420. Kieckhefer, *European...*, p. 141. Lewis, *King...*, p. 276. More, *History...*, p. 48. *Oxford...Prose*, pp. 408, 410–412, 492. Robbins, *Encyclopedia...*, p. 162. Scofield, *Life...*, II, pp. 161–162. St. Aubyn, *Year...*, pp. 122–124, 127, 130, 151.

JANE STONOR **[Joan]**

fl.c. 1450s England; France

Presumably the illegitimate daughter of William de la Pole, duke of Suffolk. Married Thomas (II) Stonor. During 1480s Jane and their son, William, quarrelled over distribution of Thomas's estate. She willed much of her extensive property to various religious foundations.

♦ **Bequests. Educated. Illegitimacy. Legal activity. Managers. Religious patrons. Squabbles. Widows. Writers–letters.** ♦

Kendall, *Yorkist...*, p. 406. *Stonor...*, v.1, pp. xxiii, xxv-xxvi, xxxii, xxxv, xlii, xlvi-xlvii, 62–63, 97, 101, 109–110, 122, 146–147, 157, 162–165; v.2, pp. 16, 135, 151, 168, 176, 186.

JEAN/JOAN [Giovanna; Jeanne; Jehanne; Joanna; Johanna; Juana]

JOAN OF ACRE, countess of Gloucester

See—JOAN OF ENGLAND, countess of Gloucester.

JOANNA OF ARAGON, queen of Naples

m. 1477–d. 1517 Italy; Spain

Daughter of John II of Aragon. Became second wife of Ferrante I of Naples. After his death in 1494, Joanna served as regent in Sicily.

♦ **Regents. Widows.** ♦

Cartwright, *Beatrice...*, p. 6. Cloulas, *Borgias...*, p. 53. Commynes, *Memoirs...*, II, pp. 479, 572, 602, 603. Prescott, *Princes...*, p. 67.

JUANA OF ARAGON, queen of Castile **[Juana *la Loca*]**

b. 1479–d.c. 1555 Spain

Daughter of †Isabella of Castile and Ferdinand II of Aragon. Married Philip the Fair of Austria and Burgundy. Their son, Charles (V,) was born around 1501. Already unstable, Juana apparently suffered from insanity after her husband died in 1506. Although she inherited Castile from her mother, she was not allowed to rule it. Juana's father thus kept control of both Castile and Aragon while she was essentially imprisoned for some forty-five years.

♦ **Educated. Insanity. Prisons. Queens. Widows. Writers–letters.** ♦

Altamira, *Spain*, pp. 292–294. Chamberlin, *Fall...*, pp. 178, 315–317, 318–320. Cloulas, *Borgias...*, pp. 223, 262, 304, 317–8. Henderson, *Short...*, p. 229. Miller, *Castles...*, pp. 15, 68, 85, 107, 157, 160–170, 181–199, 201–227, ..., 315–330, 348–353 (an opinionated and somewhat romanticized version of Juana's life). Motley, *Rise...*, p. 49. Pinnow, *History...*, p. 172. Smith, *Spain,* pp. 116–117 & 119.

(St.) JOAN OF ARC **[Jeanne d'Arc]**

b. 1412–d. 1431 France

At the age of seventeen, Joan was guided by her "voices of angels" to leave her village of Domremy and seek out the uncrowned king of France, Charles VII, to offer him her services. Riding with the French army, Joan assisted the raising of the siege of Orléans, and then won victories at Jargeau, Meung, Beaugency, Patay, Troyes, and Reims (where she had Charles crowned). Joan was finally captured at Compiègne in May of 1430, just over a year after her arrival at Charles's court. Both sides viewed her with awe, and the English believed they could only win if Joan were dead. However, they feared making her a martyr. Thus the English/Burgundian forces coerced Inquisitors to try Joan as a heretic and a witch. She was found guilty of various heresies—such as claiming to be in a state of grace, and pretending to have visions. She was executed as a relapsed heretic in 1431. A number of miracles and prophecies were associated with Joan and her death. Once the French gained control of their country, Charles VII had Joan's case reopened by the Inquisition in 1455. During the next year evidence was examined, witnesses heard, and points argued by numerous legal experts. Several irregularities in Joan's original trial made it possible to rehabilitate her in July of 1456 and to canonize her in the twentieth century. Her importance has continued to be a matter for debate during the past five hundred years. Regardless of her military role, however, it seems clear that she lowered English morale and raised French hopes at a very opportune time—thereby aiding the French cause in a substantial manner.

♦ **Ecclesiastical courts–Inquisition. Heretics. Manors. Models. Mystics. Prisons. Punishments. Saints. Soldiers. Superstitions. Unmarried. Virginity–importance. Witchcraft.** ♦

Barstow, *Joan....* Belleval, *Les fiefs...*, pp. 116–117. Bourassin, *Jeanne....* Calmette, *Golden...*, pp. 100, 133–134, 145, 147, 227, 317. Champion, *François...*, I, pp. 144–146, 169; II, pp. 118, 128n, 187, 202, 240, 260, 381. Champion, *Louis...*, pp. 6n, 46, 48, 61, 133, 256. Champion, *Procés....* Cleugh, *Chant...*, pp. 16–18, 25, 33, 42–44, 54, 57, 68, 70, 92, 97, 295. Ennen, *Medieval...*, pp. 248–251. Farmer, *Oxford...*, pp. 211–213. Fox, *Literary...*, pp. 7, 14, 69–70, 275–288, 319, 360. Grandeau,

Jeanne.... Grayeff, *Joan....* Haskins, *Normans...*, pp. 10, 19, 143–144. Jacob, *Fifteenth...*, pp. 246–248, 249, 250–252. Lowell, *Joan....* Lyonne, *Jeanne....* Margolis, *Joan....* Pernoud, *Joan....* Pernoud, *Retrial....* Scott, *Jeanne....* Sermoise, *Jeanne....* Stolpe, *Maid....* Tierney, *Western...*, pp. 568–571 & 592. Vale, *Charles...*, pp. 25, 45–68 passim, 151–4, 158, 196, 209. Wolf, *Bluebeard...*, pp. 110–113, 166–167.

JEANNE D'ARMAGNAC

c. 1365 France

See—BONNE DE BERRY and MARIE DE BERRY

♦ **Genealogy.** ♦

JEANNE D'ARTOIS, countess of Dreux

c. 1360s–1410s France

Daughter of †Isabelle de Melun and her second husband Jean d'Artois, count of Eu. Married Simon de Thouars to unite the branches of family with rights to two important seigneuries in Vimeu. Her betrothal contract stated if their marriage remained childless, the estates would pass to Jeanne's relatives. Both estates eventually did pass to Jeanne's nephew, Charles d'Artois, count of Eu.

♦ **Dowry/dower. Estate. Pawns.** ♦

Belleval, *Les fiefs...*, pp. 84, 304–305. *DBF*, v.3, pp. 1202–1203.

JOAN OF ARUNDEL, countess of Hereford and Essex

See—JOAN FITZALAN, countess of Hereford and Essex.

JEANNE D'AUXERRE

d. 1366 France

Practiced as a surgeon at Chalon-sur-Saône.

♦ **Surgeons.** ♦

Hughes, *Women...*, p. 144. Wickersheimer, *Dictionnaire...*, v.2, p. 505.

JOAN DE BAR, countess of Surrey

m.c. 1306–1361 England; France

Daughter of †Eleanor of England and Henry III, count of Bar. Wife of John de Warenne, earl of Surrey (d.1347).

♦ **Dowry/dower.** ♦

DNB, v.20, pp. 825 & 828. Given-Wilson, *English...*, p. 136. Powicke, *Thirteenth...*, pp. 138n, 517.

JOAN, lady BEAUCHAMP

fl. 1460s England

Wife of John, lord Beauchamp. Joan supposedly tried to use image magic to dispose of her husband.

♦ **Miscreants. Witchcraft. Women of easy virtue.** ♦

Emden, *Biographical...*, p. 1749. Hindley, *England...*, p. 146. Scofield, *Life...*, II, pp. 188–190.

JOHANNA BEAUFLOUR

d.c. 1327 England

Widow of Thomas Beauflour. She was a brewer and property owner in London.

♦ **Alewives. Bequests. Charity. Land/property. Widows.** ♦

Calendar of Wills..., I, p. 321.

JOAN BEAUFORT, queen of Scotland **[Johanna]**

fl. 1410s–1450s England; Scotland

Daughter of †Margaret Holland and John Beaufort, earl of Somerset. In 1424, Joan married James I of Scotland (who presumably wrote poetry to/about her). Mother of Isabel, †Margaret, and James II of Scotland. After her husband died (c.1438), Joan married Sir James Stewart of Inverneath as a protector for her son. This ploy failed, and Joan's power was nullified, although she was allowed to keep Stirling Castle.

♦ **Estate. Models. Pawns. Politics. Prisons. Regents. Widows.** ♦

Brown, *History...*, I, pp. 210, 223–224. Cleugh, *Chant...*, p. 21. Glover, *Story...*, p. 99. Mackie, *History...*, p. 97. Mackie, *Short...*, pp. 86 & 89. *Oxford...Prose*, pp. 71, 72–79. Power, "Position...," p. 429.

JOAN BEAUFORT, countess of Westmoreland **[Joanna Neville]**

b. 1379–d. 1440 England

Daughter of John of Gaunt and his mistress †Katherine Swynford. Joan was legitimized when her parents finally married. When Joan's first husband, Sir Robert Ferrers, died, she became the second wife of Ralph Neville, first earl of Westmoreland (d.1425). Their children included: †Cecily Neville, duchess of York; †Anne Neville, duchess of Buckingham; and Richard Neville, earl of Salisbury. Joan was strong-willed and had some influence with her half-brother who became King Henry IV of England.

♦ **Book owners. Charity. Illegitimacy. Politics. Religieuses. Widows. Writers–letters.** ♦

Armitage-Smith, *John...*, p. 391. Green, *Letters...*, pp. 82–83. Jacob, *Fifteenth...*, pp. 320–323, 335, 464, 666. Johnson, *Duke...*, pp. 1, 2, 10, 33, 135. McFarlane, *Nobility...*, p. 67. Orme, *English...*, p. 25. Power, *Nunneries...*, p. 418. Rosenthal, *Nobles...*, pp. 136–137. Ross, *Wars...*, p. 31. Scofield, *Life...*, I, p. 5. Tyerman, *England...*, pp. 303, 305. Warren, *Anchorites...*, pp. 206 & 207.

JEANNE DE BELLEVILLE **[Jeanne de Clisson]**

fl. 1340s England; France

Wife of Olivier III de Clisson; mother of the more famous Olivier IV de Clisson. After Philip VI of France summarily executed her husband in 1343, Jeanne became the king's implacable enemy. From Brittany, she conducted a variety of armed skirmishes against the French. At sea, Jeanne harassed French ships. In 1344, she and her troops entered a

French-occupied castle and wiped out the entire garrison. She later escaped to the English court and married Gautier de Bentley.

♦ **Models. Politics. Popes. Soldiers. Widows.** ♦

Borderie, *Histoire...*, v.3, pp. 483, 492, 595. Butler, *Women...*, p. 302. *DBF*, v.9, pp. 14–15. Decaux, *Histoire...*, pp. 374–375. Hallam (ed.), *Four...*, p. 201. Jamison, *Life...*, I, p. 56. Lehmann, *Rôle de la...*, p. 484.

JOAN DE BOHUN, countess of Hereford and Essex

See—JOAN FITZALAN, countess of Hereford and Essex.

JEHANNE (la bouchière)

1292 France

A butcher in 1292 Paris, Jehanne paid a tax of 6s.

♦ **Merchants. Provisioning–butchers.** ♦

Géraud, *Paris sous...*, p. 59.

JEANNE DE BOULOGNE, duchess of Berry

b. 1375–1410s France

Daughter of Aliénor de Comminges and Jean II, count of Auvergne and Boulogne. As a young ward of Gaston Phoebus, count of Foix, Jeanne married (c.1389) the elderly Jean, duke of Berry. She then joined the ranks of †Isabeau of Bavaria's attendants. In 1392 at the *bal des ardents,* this young girl was the only person quick-witted enough to save her nephew-in-law, King Charles VI of France, from the flames engulfing the "savage" dancers. She threw her robe over the king and smothered the flames. Jeanne later married George, lord of La Tremoille.

♦ **Dance. Models. Orphans. Servants–ladies.** ♦

Anselme, *Histoire...*, v.1, p. 105. Coryn, *House...*, pp. 21, 22, 38, 40, 42, 44, 45. Froissart, *Chronicles...*, I, pp. 50–51, 53, 54, 108. Jamison, *Life...*, II, pp. 36–37. Tuchman, *Distant...*, pp. 477 & 531.

JEANNE DE BOULOGNE, queen of France

c. 1330s–1360s France

Daughter of William XII of Auvergne; married (1) Philip of Burgundy; their son was Philip of Rouvres. After her husband died (c.1346), she became the second wife of John II the Good, king of France. She predeceased her second husband.

♦ **Art patrons. Estate. Models. Queens.** ♦

Calmette, *Golden...*, pp. 15, 23, 25, 293. Champion, *François...*, p. 204. Deniuel-Cormier, *Wise...*, pp. 55, 60–61, 76. Froissart, *Chronicles...*, I, pp. 50, 71, 90. Sherman, "Ordo ad...," p. 68.

JEANNE DE BOURBON **[Jeanne de Clermont]**

b. 1310–c. 1360s France

Daughter of Marie de Hainault and Louis of Clermont, duke of Bourbon. (Jeanne was the sister of Pierre I and the aunt of †Jeanne de Bourbon, queen of France.) Married Guy VII de Forez, lord of Ussel; mother of Louis, Jean, and Jeanne de Forez. Very pious, Jeanne de Bourbon was noted for giving alms to poor, and for various other generous religious donations.

♦ **Bequests. Charity. Estate. Religious patrons.** ♦

Anselme, *Histoire...*, v.1, p. 298. Mure, *Histoire...*, I, pp. 399, 403, 409, 411, 461–463. Valous, *Patriciat...*, pp. 369 & 433.

JEANNE DE BOURBON, queen of France

b. 1338–d. 1378 France

Daughter of †Isabelle (de Valois) of Savoy and Pierre I of Bourbon. Married Charles V of France in 1350; mother of Charles VI, who supposedly inherited his mental instability from her. She joined her husband in founding a Celestine monastery. Jeanne also commissioned a golden statue of the Virgin for this establishment. She died of childbirth fever at the age of forty.

♦ **Art patrons. Book owners. Childbirth. Insanity. Models. Religious patrons.** ♦

Champion, *François...*, pp. 15, 17, 18. Denieul-Cormier, *Wise...*, pp. 75, 76, 123, 132–134, 153, 154, 156, 377. Froissart, *Chronicles...*, I, pp. 83, 119, 155. Hughes, "Library...," p. 178. Sherman, "Ordo ad...," pp. 256–292. Tuchman, *Distant...*, pp. 314, 326, 332, 359, 439.

JEANNE DE BOURGOGNE, queen of France

See—JEANNE OF BURGUNDY, queen of France.

JEHANNE (la boutonnière)

1292 France

In 1292 Paris, Jehanne operated a button-making shop on the rue de Merderel. She must have had a relatively successful business since she was taxed 16s.

♦ **Apparel–accessories. Land/property.** ♦

Géraud, *Paris sous...*, p. 43.

JEHANNE DE BRETAGNE

c. 1440s France

Prostitute of Paris; in François Villon's *Testament,* with tongue in cheek, the poet left her a license to run a school of love.

♦ **Bequests. Models. Prostitutes.** ♦

Cartellieri, *Court...*, p. 117. Champion, *François...*, I, pp. 94, 111, 112; II, p. 164. Lewis, *François...*, p. 303.

JEHANNE DE BRIGUE **[la Cordière]**

1356–1391 France

Charged with sorcery: wax image and love magic. She also admitted summoning up a demon named Haussibut. Jehanne was convicted but was not executed for several months because it was thought she was pregnant. She was finally burned in 1391.

♦ **Punishments. Witchcraft.** ♦

Cohn, *Europe's...*, p. 197. Robbins, *Encyclopedia...*, pp. 379–381. Russell, *Witchcraft...*, pp. 214–215.

JOAN BUCKLAND

d.c. 1450 England

Managed her own small estate in Northamptonshire as a widow. Had a number of servants and tenants. Among her furniture was a trestle table, two carved chairs, and a blue bed. She left plate and vestments to the local church.

♦ **Bequests. Employers. Managers. Religious patrons. Widows.** ♦

Kendall, *Yorkist...*, pp. 337, 342, 345. Power, *Women...*, pp. 49–50.

JEANNE OF BURGUNDY, queen of France [Artois; Bourgogne]

b. 1293–d. 1329 France

Daughter of †Mahaut of Artois and Othon IV, count of Burgundy. In 1307 Jeanne married Philip of Poitiers (later Philip V of France). Jeanne was involved in two witchcraft cases with her mother. In 1314, Jeanne was accused of adultery in a famous case involving all of King Philip IV's daughters-in-law. She was found innocent; evidently Jeanne had merely covered up the indiscretions of †Blanche and †Margaret of Burgundy. Although Philip believed in her innocence, many chroniclers were not so forgiving. Historians also accuse her of having had a number of Flemish women killed during a rebellion in 1302. Jeanne left some of her estate to found the college of Bourgogne.

♦ **Adultery. Educated. Models. Murder. Politics. Prisons. Religious patrons. University. Witchcraft.** ♦

Butler, *Women...*, pp. 260–265. Champion, *François...*, pp. 217 & 218. *DBF,* v.3, p. 1207. Decaux, *Histoire...*, pp. 362–365. Fawtier, *Capetian...*, pp. 53 & 162. Sherman, "Ordo ad...," p. 268.

JEANNE OF BURGUNDY, queen of France

1311–1348 France

Daughter of †Agnes of France and Robert II of Burgundy. Married Philip of Valois (later Philip VI, king of France) in 1328; mother of John the Good of France. Well-educated; a patron of arts and scholars; very pious. She was heartily disliked and considered cruel. Died of plague 1348/1349.

♦ **Art patrons. Book owners. Educated. Patrons of literature. Plague. Politics. Regents.** ♦

Calmette, *Golden...*, pp. 15, 23, 25, 293. Denieul-Cormier, *Wise...*, pp. 9, 19, 21, 23, 37, 41, 44, 46–47, 53–55, 58, 146–147, 377. Fowler, *Age...*, p. 184. Hughes, "Library...," p. 145. Sherman, "Ordo ad...," p. 268. Tuchman, *Distant...*, 45, 103, & 134.

JUANA OF CASTILE **[Joanna la Beltraneja]**

b. 1462–d. 1530 Spain

Possibly the daughter and heiress of Henry IV of Castile and his second wife, †Juana of Portugal. However, it was popularly believed that Henry was impotent and that Juana was the illegitimate daughter of her mother's presumed lover, Beltran de le Cueva. At different times, Henry named both his daughter, Juana, and his sister, †Isabella of Castile, as successors. When he died in 1474, both women spent the next five years fighting for undisputed possession of Castile. In 1475, Juana married her uncle Alfonso V of Portugal, and he aided her in the battle for Castile. Nevertheless, in 1479, Isabella won the fight. Juana then retired to a convent.

♦ **Divorce. Illegitimacy. Models. Religieuses. Rulers. Squabbles.** ♦

Altamira, *Spain...*, pp. 239, 261–262. Commynes, *Memoirs...*, pp. 321–322, 368. Fusero, *Borgias*, p. 128. Miller, *Castles...*, pp. 29–30, 36, 40, 41, 44, 51–55, 72–74, 76, 78–80, 86–88, 95, 100, 105, 106, 244n, 350. Nowell, *History...*, pp. 44–45. Smith, *Spain...*, pp. 101–103. Stephens, *Story...*, pp. 134, 135.

JEANNE CLARISSE

1322 France

See—AGNES AVESOT.

♦ **Doctors/empirics. Employers.** ♦

Wickersheimer, *Dictionnaire...*, v.2, p. 505.

JEANNE "CONVERSA"

fl. 1320s France

Wife of Jean Liblous. On the advice of the medical faculty of Paris, Jeanne was arrested and convicted of illegally practicing medicine (c.1325).

♦ **Doctors/empirics. Miscreants. University.** ♦

Hughes, *Women...*, p. 145. Hurd-Mead, *History...*, pp. 271–272. Lipinska, *Histoire...*, p. 119. Power, *Women...*, p. 88. Wickersheimer, *Dictionnaire...*, v.2, p. 505.

JEANNE DE CRESPI

d. 1349 France

Jeanne was a barber until she became a nun at Longchamp.

♦ **Barbers. Nuns.** ♦

Hughes, *Women...*, p. 140. Wickersheimer, *Dictionnaire...*, v.2, p. 505.

JEHANNE (la cristalière)

1292 France

Sold crystal in 1292 Paris; she paid a 2s tax.

♦ **Less-affluent. Merchants.** ♦

Géraud, *Paris sous...*, p. 127.

JEANNE DE CUSEY

1438 France

At Dijon, Jeanne and her husband, Girart de Cusey, practiced as barbers. They were implicated in several poisonings and accused of practicing surgery and medicine without license.

♦ **Barbers. Doctors/empirics. Miscreants. Surgeons.** ♦

Hughes, *Women...*, pp. 141 & 145. Wickersheimer, *Dictionnaire...*, v.2, pp. 505–506.

JEANNE DABENTON

d.c. 1372 France

Leader of heretic sect—*Turlupins,* or *Society of the Poor.* Jeanne and several of her companions were burned along with their writings.

♦ **Antinomian. Punishments. Writers.** ♦

Barstow, *Joan...*, pp. 39–40. Cohn, *Pursuit...*, p. 169. McDonnell, *Beguines...*, pp. 500–502. Tuchman, *Distant...*, p. 335.

JEANNE DE DAMMARTIN, queen of Castile

m. 1237–d. 1279 France; Spain

Daughter of †Marie, countess of Ponthieu and Aumale, and Simon de Dammartin, count of Aumale. Second wife of Ferdinand III of Castile (d.c.1252); mother of †Eleanor of Castile, queen of England. An heiress, Jeanne patronized the arts and various religious establishments. Joan of Acre (Princess †Joan of England) lived in Ponthieu with her grandmother Jeanne for much of her early life. Around 1260, she married Jean de Nesle, lord of Falvy.

♦ **Art patrons. Childcare. Estate. Religious patrons. Widows.** ♦

Anselme, *Histoire...*, v. 2, p. 507; v. 3, p. 304. Powicke, *Thirteenth...*, pp. 73 & n, 235. Prestwich, *Edward...*, pp. 123, 126, 316.

JEANNE DE DIVION

c. 1320s–1330s Flanders; France

When Jeanne's cleric-lover died, †Mahaut of Artois forced her to leave Arras. Jeanne then joined †Jeanne de Valois, wife of Robert d'Artois, in a plot to take Artois from Mahaut. At Jeanne's trial in Paris, she confessed to forging documents and was executed.

♦ **Mistresses. Punishments. Squabbles.** ♦

Butler, *Women...*, pp. 278–279. Castries, *Lives...*, p. 104. Jamison, *Life...*, I, p. 39.

JEANNE DUPRÉ

1447/9 France

Tallow chandler of fifteenth century Paris on the rue de la Harpe.

♦ **Candle makers–tallow. Land/property.** ♦

Comptes du..., p. 554.

JOAN OF ENGLAND **[Joan of Woodstock]**
b. 1335–d. 1348 England

Daughter of †Philippa of Hainault and Edward III of England. Joan died of plague while on her way to Castile to marry Pedro I the Cruel.

♦ **Pawns. Plague. Tournaments.** ♦

Bryant, *Age...*, p. 382. Gardner, *Life...*, p. 114. Hardy, *Philippa...*, pp. 83–4, 93, 102–5, 107, 110, 119–24, 132–3, 139, 164–5, 182–3, 190–3, 198–200, 284, 287, 301, 304. Hohler, "Court...," pp. 172–174. Tuchman, *Distant...*, pp. 103, 216, 310n.

JOAN OF ENGLAND, countess of Gloucester **[Joan of Acre]**
1272–1307 England

Daughter of †Eleanor of Castile and Edward I of England; married (1) Gilbert de Clare, earl of Gloucester, in 1290. He died in 1295, and (c.1298) Joan married Ralph de Monthermer.

♦ **Crusades. Dowry/dower. Genealogy. Managers.** ♦

Barrow, *Feudal...*, pp. 293, 419. Bryant, *Age...*, pp. 123, 124, 163. *Calendar of Plea...*, I, p. 63 n2. McFarlane, *Nobility...*, pp. 260, 261, 263, 267. Powicke, *Thirteenth...*, pp. 268, 329, 512. Prestwich, *Edward...*, pp. 79, 126–129, 312, 317, 343, 348–351, 439, 538. Riley, *Memorials...*, pp. 45–46. Tyerman, *England...*, p. 236.

JOAN (OF ENGLAND), princess of Gwynedd **[princess of Wales]**
m. 1204-d. 1237 England; Wales

Illegitimate daughter of John, king of England. In 1204, Joan's father married her to Llewelyn the Great, prince of Gwynedd.

♦ **Illegitimacy. Negotiators. Pawns. Writers–letters.** ♦

Appleby, *John...*, pp. 36, 175, 180. Barlow, *Feudal...*, pp. 411, 414. Barrow, *Feudal...*, pp. 217, 219, 421. Bingham, *Crowned...*, p. 168. Brooke, *From Alfred...*, p. 197. *Cambridge...*, VI, p. 251; VII, pp. 514, 515. *DNB*, v.10, p. 825. Griffiths and Thomas, *Making...*, pp. 5, 6, & 9. Lloyd, *Maligned...*, pp. 199 & 210. Powicke, *Thirteenth...*, pp. 45, 391, 393, 395.

JOAN OF ENGLAND, queen of Scotland **[Joan Make-peace]**
b.c. 1210–d.c. 1237 England; France; Scotland

Daughter of †Isabella of Angoulême and King John of England. Spent much of her youth in France since she was betrothed to Hugh X de Lusignan. When her father died and her mother married her fiancé, Joan was returned to England. In 1221, she married Alexander II of Scotland.

♦ **Divorce. Pawns. Queens.** ♦

Appleby, *John...*, pp. 36, 174, 211. Barrow, *Feudal...*, pp. 249, 263–264, 419, 420. Bingham, *Crowned...*, pp. 71 & 168. Brown, *History...*, I, p. 113. *DNB*, v.10, pp. 825–826. Duncan, *Scotland...*, pp. 250, 252, 526, 534. Lloyd, *Maligned...*, pp. 234, 235, 237, 353, 395. Mackie, *History...*, p. 47. *Manners and Expenses...*, intro. Stephens, "Early Life...".

JOAN OF ENGLAND, queen of Scotland

[Joanna Make-peace; Plantagenet; of the Tower]

b. 1321–d. 1362 England; France; Scotland

Daughter of †Isabelle of France and Edward II of England. At age seven, Joan married David de Brus (later David II of Scotland) to seal a peace treaty. Much of his reign was spent in exile; Joan finally stopped accompanying him in 1359.

♦ **Divorce–separation. Pawns. Queens.** ♦

Allan, "Historical...," pp. 344–345. Brown, *History...*, I, pp. 167 & 179. Bryant, *Age...*, p. 233. Butt, *History...*, pp. 236, 242. Glover, *Story...*, p. 85. Hardy, *Philippa...*, pp. 20, 35, 48, 53–4, 80, 131, 135, 204, 234, 246–7, 254, 272–3, 301. Mackie, *History...*, pp. 86 & 88. Mackie, *Short...*, p. 72. Wentersdorf, "Clandestine...," p. 219.

JOANNA OF ENGLAND, queen of Sicily, countess of Toulouse

b. 1165–d. 1199 Byzantium; England; France; Italy

Daughter of †Eleanor of Aquitaine and Henry II of England; married 1177 to William II of Sicily (d.1189). As a widow she accompanied her new sister-in-law, †Berengaria of Navarre, on part of the Second Crusade. In 1196, Joanna became the fourth wife of Raymond VI, count of Toulouse. As she was dying of the after-effects of childbirth in 1199, Joanna became a last-minute nun of Fontevrault.

♦ **Childbirth. Crusades. Nuns. Queens. Soldiers. Widows.** ♦

Anderson and Zinsser, *A History of...*, p. 275. Barlow, *Feudal...*, pp. 339, 356–357, 360, 364, 371. Barrow, *Feudal...*, pp. 182, 183, 419. Bingham, *Crowned...*, pp. 71, 102, 103, 109, 132, 134. Bridge, *Crusades...*, pp. 210–212. Kelly, *Eleanor...*, pp. 103, 132, 159, ... 354–5, 385, 387. Lloyd, *Maligned...*, pp. 6, 61, 65, 93. Marks, *Pilgrims...*, pp. 176, 245, 269, 292. Norwich, *Kingdom...*, pp. 303–304, 309–311, 320, 324, 355, 367–368, 370, 372–373, 380. Pernoud, *Eleanor...*, pp. 102, 158, 172–3, ... 214–5, 219, 237, 241, 252–3.

JUANA ENRIQUEZ, queen of Aragon

fl. 1440s–1460s Spain

Second wife of John II of Aragon; mother of Ferdinand II, king of Aragon and Castile. An active political force, Juana was bright and very ambitious. In fact, it was rumored that she was guilty of poisoning her stepson Carlos in order to clear a path for her own son to take the throne.

♦ **Models. Murder. Politics.** ♦

Bisson, *Medieval Crown...*, pp. 148–152. Cleugh, *Chant...*, pp. 166 & 167. Commynes, *Memoirs...*, I, pp. 173, 174, & 175. Fusero, *Borgias*, p. 128. Miller, *Castles...*, pp. 56 & 161. Miron, *Queens...*, pp. 298–299, 307–325.

JOAN EVERARD

1288–1301 England

Cited numerous times in Broughton village court for brewing fees. In 1297, she ran the village equivalent of a tavern in a room she rented at John Crane's house.

♦ **Alewives. Manors. Taverners.** ♦
Britton, *Community...*, pp. 26, 203, 251 n42.

JEANNE D'ÉVREUX, queen of France
m. 1326–d. 1370 France

Daughter of Margaret of Artois and Louis of France, count of Évreux. Third wife of Charles IV of France. Jeanne commissioned several art works which she gave to various religious establishments. One of these was a particularly fine silver statue of the Virgin which held relics.

♦ **Art patrons. Book owners. Models. Negotiators. Relics. Religious patrons.** ♦
Anselme, *Histoire...*, v.1, p. 97. Bell, "Medieval...," pp. 181–183 n28, n39. Champion, *François...*, I, p. 205. *DBF*, v.8, p. 518. Froissart, *Chronicles...*, I, p. 90. *Hours of Jeanne....* Jamison, *Life...*, I, p. 213. Kidson, *Medieval...*, p. 121. Paris, "Livres...". Pisan, *City...*, p. 34. Sherman, "Ordo ad...," p. 269 & 282.

JOAN FAUCONBERG
b. 1406–d. 1490 England

Daughter of Sir Thomas Fauconberg (d.1407). Joan was supposedly retarded or insane (a condition she was believed to have inherited from her father). Despite this handicap, her inherited wealth and estates led her guardian, Ralph Neville, to marry Joan to his sixth son by †Joan Beaufort—William Neville. All three of their daughters predeceased her. In the 1430s, William was summoned to Parliament (as Lord Fauconberg in her right), and in 1461 he became earl of Kent. After he died (c.1462), despite Joan's age and mental condition, she was quickly married to John Berwyk of Kendal.

♦ **Estate. Handicapped. Insanity. Orphans. Pawns. Widows.** ♦
Clive, *Sun...*, p. 6. *C.P.*, v.5, pp. 281 & 285. *DNB*, v.14, pp. 304 & 305. Jacob, *Fifteenth...*, p. 324.

JEANNE FILLEUL
1424–1498 France

Lady-in-waiting to Margaret (Stuart) of Scotland, the dauphine of France. She shared Margaret's love of poetry and of writing verses. One of Jeanne's *rondeaux* (relating the pain of losing a lover) is extant.

♦ **Poets/troubadours. Servants–ladies-in-waiting.** ♦
Champion, *Louis...*, p. 107. Lewis, *King...*, p. 178. Moulin, *La poésie...*, pp. 101–102.

JOAN FITZALAN, lady Bergavenny
[Joan Beauchamp, lady Abergavenny]
b. 1375–d. 1435 England

Daughter of Elizabeth de Bohun and Richard III FitzAlan, earl of Arundel (d.1397). Around 1390, Joan married William Beauchamp, lord Bergavenny (d.1411).

♦ **Dowry/dower. Managers. Squabbles.** ♦

Butt, *History...*, p. 522. *C.P.*, v.1, pp. 26 & 28. *DNB*, v.7, p. 100. Given-Wilson, *English...*, p. 147. Jacob, *Fifteenth...*, p. 329. Johnson, *Duke...*, p. 8.

JOAN FITZALAN, countess of Hereford and Essex
[Joan de Bohun; Joan of Arundel]

c. 1370s–d. 1419 England

Daughter of †Eleanor of Lancaster and Richard II FitzAlan, earl of Arundel (d.1376). Wife of Humphrey de Bohun, earl of Hereford and Essex; mother of †Eleanor, duchess of Gloucester and †Mary (wife of Henry Bolingbroke—later King Henry IV). During Cheshire uprising in 1400, Joan intervened to save the earl of Huntingdon. She protected him at her castle until popular pressure forced her to release him to be executed.

♦ **Legal activity. Managers. Politics. Rebellions. Widows. Writers.** ♦

DNB, v.7, p. 97. Jacob, *Fifteenth...*, pp. 26 & 63. Legge (ed), *Anglo-Norman...*, pp. 81, 84–85, 388, 399–400, 416–417, 422. McNiven, "Cheshire...," pp. 385–386. *Nuisance...*, pp. 170–171 (#'s 633 & 644). Wylie, *History...*, v.1, pp. 103–104.

JEANNE OF FLANDERS, duchess of Brittany

See JEANNE DE MONTFORT.

JEANNE OF FLANDERS

b. 1200–d. 1244 Flanders

Daughter and heiress of †Marie (II) of Champagne and Baldwin IX of Flanders. Her parents died (or were lost) on Crusade, so Jeanne inherited at age five. Until she was twelve, Jeanne and her sister †Margaret were in the care of Philip II of France. Jeanne then married Ferdinand, prince of Portugal. When he was imprisoned, Jeanne ran Flanders essentially alone until her death. A religious patron, she was especially helpful to the Beguines. Her second husband (m.c.1237) was Thomas, count of Maurienne.

♦ **Beguines. Orphans. Religious patrons. Rulers.** ♦

Baldwin, *Government...*, pp. 203–204, 247, 271. Casey, "Cheshire...," p. 234. Gies, *Merchants...*, p. 84. Heer, *Medieval...*, p. 262. Herlihy, *Opera...*, pp. 60 & 68. Le Patourel, *Feudal...*, XV, pp. 169 & 171. McDonnell, *Beguines...*, pp. 111–112, 201, 205, 208–209, 213. Stephens, *Story...*, p. 70. Wolff, "Baldwin...," pp. 286–299.

JEHANNE (la fouacière)

1292 France

A very successful Parisian merchant. Jehanne paid a high tax of six livres on her business as a baker of a special type of white bread.

♦ **Land/property. Merchants. Provisioning–bakers.** ♦

Géraud, *Paris sous...*, p. 28.

JEANNE OF FRANCE, duchess of Brittany
m. 1397–1420s France

Daughter of †Isabeau of Bavaria and Charles VI of France; married in 1397 to John VI of Brittany (see †Jeanne de Montfort). In long-running feud between two branches of family for control of Brittany, Jeanne was an able assistant to her husband. When he was captured and imprisoned by †Marguerite de Clisson, Jeanne called an assembly at which she delivered an emotional appeal for help. Displaying her young sons as the rightful heirs of Brittany, Jeanne raised an army and besieged Châteauceaux. Thanks largely to Jeanne's efforts, Jean VI was finally released and confirmed as duke of Brittany.

♦ **Educated. Politics. Soldiers. Squabbles.** ♦

Bell, "Medieval...," pp. 163, 165. Denieul-Cormier, *Wise...*, pp. 233, 234, 252. Durtelle, *Bretagne...*, pp. 272–273 & 284. Jones, *Ducal...*, p. 134. Wolf, *Bluebeard...*, p. 23.

(St.) JEANNE OF FRANCE, duchess of Orléans [St. Joan of Valois]
1464–1505 France

Daughter of †Charlotte of Savoy and Louis XI, king of France. Around 1475 she married Louis of Orléans. When he became king (Louis XII), he divorced Jeanne (1498) to marry Charles VIII's widow, †Anne of Brittany. Jeanne then retired to convent she had founded. She was canonized in 1950.

♦ **Divorce. Handicapped. Religious patrons. Saints.** ♦

Borderie, *Histoire...*, v.4, pp. 484, 504, 589–592. Calmette, *Golden...*, pp. 85, 275, 341. Cloulas, *Borgias...*, pp. 153, 154, 155. Coryn, *House...*, pp. 270, 271, 273–275, 279–282, 287, 289, 311, 344. Denieul-Cormier, *Wise...*, pp. 346 & 351. Destefanis, *Louis....* Forster, *Good....* Fusero, *Borgias*, pp. 209–210. Johnson, *Borgias...*, pp. 135–136. Trevelyan, *Short...*, pp. 198 & 199.

JEANNE OF FRANCE, queen of Navarre
b. 1308–c. 1349 France; Spain

Daughter of †Margaret of Burgundy and Louis X of France. She should have inherited the kingdom of France when Louis died, but was denied the crown due to her gender. Her uncle, Philip V of France, also displaced her as heiress of Champagne. Jeanne married Philip d'Évreux around 1317. Around 1338, they inherited Navarre. Her daughter Joanna of Navarre was engaged to Pedro IV of Aragon. She refused to wed, however, and entered a convent. Another daughter, †Marie, then married Pedro IV. Jeanne and Philip were also the parents of Charles II the Bad of Navarre; †Agnes of Navarre, countess of Foix; and †Blanche of Navarre, queen of France.

♦ **Estate. Orphans. Pawns. Queens. Squabbles.** ♦

Anselme, *Histoire...*, v.1, p. 92. Calmette, *Golden...*, pp. 12–13 & 25. *Cambridge...*, VII, pp. 334, 335, 341, 350. Decaux, *Histoire...*, pp. 366–368. Evergates, "Chancery...," p. 173. Le Patourel, *Feudal...*, XII, p. 174. Shneidman, *Rise...*, pp. 99, 353, 354, 366.

JEHANNE GAULTIÈRE

1445/6 France

Listed as a tapestry/rug maker at Number One on the rue Petit Pont near le Petit Chastelet in 1440s Paris, Jehanne paid a 24s tax.

♦ **Artistic clothwork. Clothworkers. Land/property.** ♦

Comptes du..., pp. 435 & 567.

JOAN DE GENVILLE **[Joan de Joinville]**

b. 1286–d. 1356 England; Ireland

Daughter of Matilda de Lacy and Geoffrey de Genville. Heiress of Lacy earldom of Meath. Married Roger de Mortimer of Wigmore (c.1306).

♦ **Estate. Prisons. Squabbles.** ♦

Curtis, *Ireland...*, p. 93. *DNB*, v.13, pp. 1034 & 1038. Fryde, *Tyranny...*, pp. 40 & 63. Powicke, *Thirteenth...*, p. 517 & n. Waugh, "Marriage...," p. 194.

JOAN GRENE

1364 England

Wife of William atte Grene. Joan had to promise London court of 1364 that she would discontinue running a brothel in her house.

♦ **Land/property. Miscreants. Prostitutes.** ♦

Calendar of Plea..., II, p. 7. Lacey, "Women...," p. 50.

JOHANNA HADHAM

1308 England

Daughter of William de Hadham, a London tanner. From his will, she received a house, tanning equipment, and personal items, including: brasier and utensils (wood, silver, and iron), skins, wool and linen cloths, other linens, and a feather bed. Her father appointed Richard le Ussher to be her guardian until she came of age.

♦ **Bequests–personal items. Orphans.** ♦

Calendar of Wills..., I, p. 199.

JOAN HART

1480 France

Mistress of Robert Cely in Calais. When Joan got pregnant, she demanded, and may have sued for, financial support from Robert.

♦ **Legal activity. Models. Mistresses.** ♦

Cely..., p. 28. Gies, *Merchants...*, p. 260. Kendall, *Yorkist...*, p. 291.

JOAN HOLLAND, duchess of Brittany

[Joan, countess of Richmond]

m.c. 1365–d. 1384 England; France

Daughter of †Joan of Kent and Thomas Holland; second wife of John V de Montfort, duke of Brittany (see †Jeanne de Montfort, duchess of Brittany).

♦ **Dowry/dower. Estate. Squabbles.** ♦

Anselme, *Histoire...,* v.1, p. 453. Jamison, *Life...,* II, p. 205. Jones, *Creation...,* pp. 176–177, 267. Jones, *Ducal...,* pp. 40, 41, 45, 96, 97, 99, 172, 173n, 183n, 184n, 185n, 186, 189–192.

JOAN HUNT

fl. 1360s England

Owner of bathhouse of ill repute outside London. Had a problem with her servant, Thomas Bunny. London court eventually released him from his contract because Joan had instructed her lover to beat Thomas.

♦ **Bathhouse. Employers. Land/property. Legal activity. Prostitutes.** ♦

Abram, "Women...," p. 281. *Calendar of Plea...,* II, p. 54. Lacey, "Women...," p. 50.

JOAN OF KENT, princess of Wales

[Joan Plantagenet; Fair Maid of Kent]

1328–1385 England

Daughter of †Margaret Wake and Edmund, earl of Kent. At age twelve, Joan secretly married Thomas Holland. While he was fighting in Prussia, her guardians married Joan to William de Montacute (Montague), earl of Salisbury. Holland finally retrieved his wife, by pleading his case at the papal court, in 1349. He died in 1360, and in 1361 Joan secretly married the Black Prince, Edward, prince of Wales (d.1377); their son was Richard II of England. Especially in her later years, Joan became known as a peacemaker—most often between her powerful brother-in-law, John of Gaunt, and angry Londoners. Joan was an early patron and protector of John Wycliffe.

♦ **Adultery. Divorce. Lollards. Managers. Models. Negotiators. Orphans. Popes. Rebellions. Religious patrons. Widows. Writers–letters.** ♦

Armitage-Smith, *John...,* pp. 25, 59, 149, 155, 291, 294. Brewer, *Chaucer...,* pp. 31–33. Bryant, *Age...,* pp. 318, 323–324, 416, 426–427, 456, 477, 525, 532, 533, 539. *C.P.,* v.7, pp. 150–154. *DNB,* v.10, pp. 829–830. Froissart, *Chronicles...,* I, pp. 102, 110, 121, 136, 148–149, 214, 216, 221, 222, 227–228, 230. Gardner, *Life...,* pp. 114–115, 173, 183, 230, 245, 260–262, 271. Hardy, *Philippa...,* pp. 57, 130–1, 139, ... 301, 308, 310. Holmes, *Later...,* pp. 170 & 185. Jamison, *Life...,* II, pp. 11–12, 24, 78–79, 83. Riley, *Memorials...,* pp. 325, 362, 449. Tuchman, *Distant...,* pp. 219, 243, 288, 317. Tuck, *Richard...,* pp. 32, 37, 65, 73, 79, & 95. Wentersdorf, "Clandestine...," pp. 203–231.

JEANNE LAISNE **[Jehanne Hachette]**

b. 1454–1480s France

When Charles of Burgundy besieged Beauvais in 1472, women fought beside men and held the town for Louis XI of France. Jeanne was singled out for praise since she had captured the Burgundian standard by herself. She was rewarded with a number of royal favors, including a good marriage with dowry to Colin Pilon, and tax exemptions. Jeanne was probably the model for the legendary, axe-wielding Jehanne Hachette.

♦ **Clothworkers. Dowry/dower. Models. Soldiers.** ♦

Barstow, *Joan...*, p. 124. Butler, *Women...*, pp. 425–430. Calmette, *Golden...*, p. 188. Champion, *Louis XI*, p. 208. Cleugh, *Chant...*, p. 215. Decaux, *Histoire...*, pp. 449–450. Lewis, *King...*, p. 256.

JEANNE DE LATILLY

1319 France

Charged with using sorcery to harm Charles of Valois; she was acquitted at her trial.

♦ **Legal activity. Miscreants. Witchcraft.** ♦

Kieckhefer, *European...*, p. 110. Lehugeur, *Histoire...*, p. 416.

JEANNE DE LAVAL

c. 1440s–d. 1498 France; Italy

Daughter of Isabel de Bretagne and Guy XIII, count of Laval. Jeanne became the second wife of René I of Anjou around 1450. He gave a tournament at Saumur for Jeanne and also wrote poetry for her.

♦ **Models. Queens. Tournaments.** ♦

Anselme, *Histoire...*, v.1, p. 232. Champion, *François...*, I, pp. 180 & 181; II, p. 55. Cleugh, *Chant...*, p. 175. Marks, *Pilgrims...*, pp. 306 & 311–313. Pernoud, *La femme...*, p. 102.

JOAN DE LA LEE

1342 England

Owner of a *corrody* with Bynedone Abbey; in 1342 she sold it to William de Mussendene.

♦ **Religious patrons–corrodies.** ♦

Calendar of Plea..., I, p. 204.

JEHANNE LECOINTE

1447/9 France

Successful mercer of Paris near the place aux Veaulx, Jehanne paid a 48s tax.

♦ **Clothworkers. Land/property. Merchants.** ♦

Comptes du..., p. 580.

JOAN LENELONDE **[Joan Shench]**

fl. 1290s–c. 1340 England

Daughter and heiress of Stephen de Lenelonde, through whom she became hereditary keeper of Fleet Prison and part of Westminster Palace. Her husband John Shench received these posts in right of his wife. Joan was in charge of Fleet, while John lived at the palace. In 1303 a robbery of the king's wardrobe took place in which John may have been involved. Their son, John, inherited the posts from his mother around 1340.

♦ **Estate. Prisons–jailers.** ♦

Calendar of Plea..., I, p. 186. Tout, "Burglary...," pp. 348–353.

JEHANNE (la loirrière)

1292 France

In 1292 Paris Jehanne was a belt and strap-maker on rue de Cul-de-Sac; she paid a tax of 3s.

♦ **Apparel–accessories. Less-affluent.** ♦

Géraud, *Paris sous...*, p. 79.

JOHANNA (of London)

1385 England

Servant who confessed to London court that she had been forced by †Elizabeth Moring to be a prostitute.

See—ELIZABETH MORING.

♦ **Legal activity. Prostitutes. Servants.** ♦

JUANA MANUEL, queen of Castile **[Juana de Villena]**

b. 1339–d. 1381 France; Spain

Daughter of Blanche de la Cerda and Juan Manuel. Married usurper of Castilian throne, Henry II (Enrique de Trastamara), who defeated Pedro I the Cruel in 1369. Henry died in 1379 and was succeeded by their son Juan I. They also had a daughter, †Leonor of Castile, queen of Navarre. The family was pictured in *Virgin of Tobed*.

♦ **Models. Queens. Rebellions. Widows.** ♦

Altamira, *Spain*, pp. 235 & 238. Hillgarth, *Pere...*, pp. 579 & 580. Jamison, *Life...*, I, pp. 280–281, 283, 286; II, pp. 65 & 67.

JEANNE DE MILIÈRES

fl. 1450s France

Mistress of Parisian, Robert Vallée. Mentioned in the *Legacy* of François Villon. Since she "wore the pants" in her relationship with Robert, Villon bequeathed his trousers to Jeanne.

♦ **Bequests. Mistresses. Models.** ♦

Bonner, *Complete...*, p. 186. Champion, *François...*, II, p. 22. Lewis, *François...*, p. 245.

JEANNE DE MONTFORT, duchess of Brittany **[Joan of Flanders]**

m. 1329–1370s England; Flanders; France

Daughter of Louis de Nevers, count of Flanders. Married John (IV) de Montfort, duke of Brittany. In fight over control of her husband's duchy, Jeanne took over military operations when John was imprisoned. Her military strategies were excellent, and she maintained her forces and castles until help arrived from England. In later years, while in exile in England, Jeanne suffered a mental breakdown, which was probably brought on by the stress and hardships of previous years.

♦ **Insanity. Models. Politics. Soldiers. Squabbles.** ♦

Butler, *Women...*, pp. 285–307. *Calendar of Plea...*, I, p. 154. Decaux, *Histoire...*, pp. 372–373. Dupouy, *Histoire...*, pp. 115, 117–118, 120, 122, 126. Froissart, *Chronicles...*, I, pp. 28, 29, 30, 32. Jamison, *Life...*, I, pp. 18, 27, 30, 36, 37, 43–46, 63, 64. Jenkinson, "Mary...," p. 411. Jones, *Creation...*, pp. 197, 200, 202, 204–205, 207n, 210, 212–213, 265. Jones, *Ducal...*, pp. 1 & 16. Tuchman, *Distant...*, pp. 76–80.

Note: There is some confusion among historians over the assignment of numbers to the many Johns who inherited Brittany. Arthur II (d.1312) had two sons by his first wife (Marie of Limoges): John III (d.1341 without legitimate issue) and Guy of Brittany. Arthur II remarried, but he was related to his second wife, †Yolande de Dreux (apparently they did not first obtain a papal dispensation). The presumed illegitimacy of Arthur's second marriage allowed Guy of Brittany's daughter, †Jeanne de Penthièvre, to claim that she was the only legitimate heir. Therefore, Jeanne de Montfort's husband (Arthur and Yolande's son, John) is sometimes not numbered among the legitimate dukes of Brittany. However, we have chosen the other option—which is equally popular—and have continued to number him John IV of Brittany (and his son is thus John V, etc.)

JOAN DE MUNCHENSI, countess of Pembroke
[Munchesney; Mountchesney]

m.c. 1247–d. 1307 England

Daughter and heiress of Warin de Munchensi; married William de Valence. Notable for distributing alms and feeding the poor. Daughter Isabel married John de Hastings, so Joan's lands eventually went to that family.

♦ **Charity. Estate. Legal activity. Widows.** ♦

Cambridge..., VI, pp. 266–267. *DNB*, v.21, p. 376. Jenkinson, "Mary...," p. 404. Johnstone, "Poor Relief...," pp. 165–166. Mertes, *English...*, pp. 82, 213. Paris, *Chronicles...*, pp. 109–110. *Select...Edward I*, I, pp. 23–25. Waugh, "Marriage...," pp. 201–202.

JOANNA I, queen of NAPLES
[Joanna, countess of Provence; Joanna of Sicily; Giovanna I]

b. 1326–d.c. 1382 Italy

Daughter of Charles of Calabria and †Marie of Valois. Inherited kingdom of Naples from her grandfather, Robert the Wise of Anjou, in 1343. Married Andrew of Hungary; suspected of murdering him in 1345. His brother, Louis the Great of Hungary, tried to annex Naples and thereby caused more turmoil for the city-state. The rest of Joanna's reign was no calmer. She also married Louis of Taranto, Jayme of Majorca, and Otto of Brunswick, but had no children. Joanna was a supporter of Pope Clement VII against Pope Urban VI. Urban excommunicated and deposed Joanna for naming Louis, duke of Anjou, as her heir. Her replacement, Charles III of Durazzo, murdered Joanna since she refused to acknowledge him.

♦ **Educated. Models. Murder. Pawns. Popes. Rulers.** ♦

Anselme, *Histoire...,* v.1, pp. 409–411. Berrigan, "Tuscan...," pp. 265–268. De Feo, *Giovanna....* Froissart, *Chronicles...,* I, pp. 90, 138, 165, 166, 238. Fusero, *Borgias*, pp. 32, 33, 51. Jamison, *Life...,* II, pp. 84–85. McCall, *Medieval...,* p. 195. Musto, "Queen Sancia...," pp. 187–188. *St. Catherine...Letters,* p. 286. Trevelyan, *Short...,* p. 145. Tuchman, *Distant...,* pp. 212, 349, 351, 353, 356, 397, 418, 429.

JOANNA II, queen of NAPLES **[Giovanna II]**

b. 1374–d. 1435 Italy

Daughter of Charles III of Durazzo; in 1414, Joanna succeeded her brother Ladislaus as ruler of Naples. The chaos that began during the reign of Joanna I continued under Joanna II. She had several husbands and lovers, but remained childless. Thus Joanna swung back and forth over who was to inherit—Alfonso V of Aragon or René of Anjou.

♦ **Rulers. Widows. Women of easy virtue.** ♦

Altamira, *Spain*, p. 257. Bisson, *Medieval Crown...,* pp. 138, 139, 142, 144. Cleugh, *Medici...,* pp. 38 & 60. Cloulas, *Borgias...,* pp. 9 & 11. Collison-Morley, *Sforzas*, pp. 16–17, 18, 23, 25–26, 29. Fusero, *Borgias*, p. 51. Johnson, *Borgias...,* pp. 18 & 22. Partner, *Lands...,* pp. 392–393, 397, 399, 405–406, 408, 412. Prescott, *Princes...,* pp. 53–55. Smith, *Spain*, p. 98. Trevelyan, *Short...,* pp. 162 & 167.

JOAN OF NAVARRE, queen of England **[Jeanne; Joanna]**

1370–1437 England; France; Spain

Daughter of Charles II the Bad of Navarre. In 1386, Joan became the third wife of John V, duke of Brittany (see †Jeanne de Montfort). Widowed in 1399, Joan became regent of Brittany for a short time. She then married Henry IV of England in 1403. After Henry died, her stepson Henry V imprisoned Joan on witchcraft charges. She was so well-treated during the three years she was under house arrest, that it seems clear Henry V was using the sorcery accusations as a pretext to "borrow" Joan's financial resources.

♦ **Dowry/dower. Pawns. Prisons. Regents. Widows. Witchcraft.** ♦

DNB, v.10, pp. 830–832. Hutchison, *King...,* pp. 74–75, 102, 126, 127, 200–201, 214. Jacob, *Fifteenth...,* pp. 63, 72, 477, 478, 480, 482. Jarman, *Crispin's...,* pp. 52, 80, 81, 185, 194. Jones, *Creation...,* pp. 123 n53, 136, 142 n129, 175, 177–180, 183, 185–187, 189–196, 246, 250, 258–260. Jones, *Ducal...,* pp. 120, 136, 213–214. Kittredge, *Witchcraft...,* pp. 79–80. Legge (ed), *Anglo-Norman...,* p. 430 (#367). Myers, "Captivity...," pp. 263–284.

JEANNE OF NAVARRE, queen of France

b. 1273–d. 1305 France

Daughter and heiress of †Blanche of Artois and Henry III, count of Champagne and king of Navarre. In 1284, Jeanne married the future king of France, Philip IV. She was pious and interested in education and literature. Jeanne commissioned Joinville to write memoirs of (St.) Louis IX. When she died in 1305, her will stipulated that much of her fortune was to be used founding the College of Navarre at the University of Paris.

♦ **Bequests. Estate. Patrons of literature. Religious patrons. University.** ♦

Benton, "Philip...," pp. 283–285. Champion, *François...*, pp. 36–37 & 41. Evergates, "Chancery...," pp. 172–173. Fawtier, *Capetian...*, pp. 4, 36, 81, 126n, 127–129, 166, 203. Heer, *Medieval...*, p. 204. Leroy, *La Navarre...*, pp. 44–46. Lewis, *François...*, p. 15. Robbins, *Encyclopedia...*, p. 162. Shneidman, *Rise...*, pp. 311, 365, 366. Stephenson, *Mediaeval...*, pp. 445, 464 & 466. Summers, *Geography...*, p. 376. Thompson, *Literacy...*, p. 132.

JEANNE PAYNEL

b. 1404–d.c. 1456 France

Daughter and heiress of Foulques Paynel, lord of Hambuie and Bricquebec. Orphaned at age four, her guardians contracted a marriage for Jeanne with Gilles de Rais. The threat of scandal caused the Parlement of Paris to void this betrothal and change her guardians. Jeanne later married Louis d'Estouteville. Henry V of England blocked the couple into their fortress in Normandy where she aided her husband in defense of their lands.

♦ **Orphans. Pawns. Prisons. Religious patrons. Soldiers.** ♦

Decaux, *Histoire...*, p. 375. Lehmann, *Rôle de la...*, p. 490. Wolf, *Bluebeard...*, p. 22.

JOAN PELHAM

1399 England

Wife of Sir John Pelham. Defended castle Pevensey for Henry IV in 1399.

♦ **Soldiers.** ♦

Salzman, *Life...*, p. 265. Wylie, *History...*, v.2, p. 112.

JEANNE DE PENTHIÈVRE **[Joan de Blois]**

c. 1320s–d. 1384 France

Daughter of Jeanne of Avaugour (d.1327) and Guy of Brittany (younger son of Arthur II of Brittany). In 1337, Jeanne married Charles de Blois. She had some claim to the duchy of Brittany (see †Jeanne de Montfort, duchess of Brittany), so she tenaciously opposed John IV de Montfort's rule and allied herself with Philip VI of France. She fought for her rights, captured and killed one of John IV's top supporters, called a citizen assembly, and negotiated a treaty. In 1363 Joan's stubborness made it impossible to conclude peace negotiations. Her husband's death in 1364 forced her to sign the Treaty of Guérande in 1365. Although she lost the duchy, she gained several estates and financial aid. Furthermore, if the male de Montfort line failed, the duchy was to revert to her heirs.

♦ **Models. Negotiators. Politics. Rulers. Soldiers. Squabbles. Widows.** ♦

Anselme, *Histoire...*, v.1, pp. 450–451. Dupouy, *Histoire...*, pp. 115, 117–118, 120, 122, 126. Durtelle, *Bretagne...*, p. 333. Froissart, *Chronicles...*, I, pp. 21, 85–89, 135. Gies, *Knight...*, pp. 145, 148, 158, 164. Jamison, *Life...*, I, pp. 23, 65, 198, 211–213; II, pp. 134, 157, 159, 296, 297, 303. Jones, *Creation...*, pp. 113, 123 n51, 135, 176, 197, 204, 209–211, 253, 265–266, 268–269, 293, 298, 341. Jones, *Ducal...*, pp. 1, 16, 99. Tuchman, *Distant...*, pp. 76–77, 365.

JUANA OF PORTUGAL, queen of Castile

fl. 1450s–1470s — Portugal; Spain

Daughter of †Leonor of Aragon and Edward of Portugal. In 1455, Juana became the second wife of Henry IV of Castile. They had no children until a daughter was born in 1462. It was popularly supposed that Henry was impotent and that Juana of Portugal had a lover (Beltran de le Cueva) who was the father of her daughter, †Juana of Castile, called *la Beltraneja* after her presumed father.

♦ **Models. Queens. Women of easy virtue.** ♦

Altamira, *Spain*, p. 239. Commynes, *Memoirs...*, pp. 321, 368. Fusero, *Borgias*, p. 128. Miller, *Castles...*, pp. 28–30, 37, 44, 48, 49, 52–54, 72–74. Nowell, *History...*, p. 44. Smith, *Spain*, p. 101. Stephens, *Story...*, p. 134.

JEANNE POTIER

1491 — France

Started "group possession" at her convent in Cambrai in 1491. It was believed that Jeanne was an hysterical nymphomaniac and a witch.

♦ **Insanity. Nuns. Virginity–stress of. Witchcraft.** ♦

Robbins, *Encyclopedia...*, p. 393. Summers, *Geography...*, p. 386.

JEHANNE POUFILLE

fl. 1440s–1450s — France

Jehanne plied her trade—making silk hats and/or kerchiefs—near the Notre Dame bridge in mid-fifteenth-century Paris.

♦ **Apparel–hats. Silkwork.** ♦

Comptes du..., pp. 209, 446, 494, 581, 658, 725, 782.

JEANNE POUPONNE

fl. 1420s — Belgium

Townswoman of Bruges; wetnurse to future Louis XI of France.

♦ **Childcare. Nurses–wetnurses. Servants.** ♦

Champion, *Louis...*, p. 45. Denieul-Cormier, *Wise...*, p. 303. Lewis, *King...*, p. 153.

JOANNA ROWLEY

1479 — England

As a widow, Joanna became a wealthy long-distance trader. In 1479 she imported sugar from Portugal, and in 1480 she not only received shipments of oil and wax from Lisbon, but she also shipped in woad and wine from Spain.

♦ **Merchants. Shipping. Widows.** ♦

Abram, "Women...," p.176–180. Carus-Wilson, "Overseas...," p. 242.

JEANNE SAIGNANT

fl. 1440s–1460s France

A bathhouse owner/manager in Dijon for at least twenty years. With the backing of her husband and many highly-placed friends, the intelligent and charming Jeanne ran a very profitable prostitution business at her bathhouse.

♦ **Bathhouse. Land/property. Prostitutes.** ♦

Rossiaud, *Medieval Prostitution...,* pp. 31, 39, 41, 45, 109, 111, 132, 187 & 191.

JEHANNE (la tapicière)

1292 France

Dame Jehanne owned a large and profitable carpet/tapestry making business in 1292 Paris—taxed 6 livres.

♦ **Artistic clothwork. Clothworkers. Land/property.** ♦

Géraud, *Paris sous...,* p. 51.

JEANNE OF TOULOUSE

b. 1220–d. 1271 France

Daughter and heiress of Sanchia of Aragon and Raymond VII of Toulouse; around 1236, Jeanne married Alphonse of Poitiers (Alphonse of France, count of Poitou). She accompanied Alphonse on both the Seventh and Eighth Crusades. She and her husband both died on the way home from the eighth venture.

♦ **Bequests. Crusades. Estate.** ♦

Anselme, *Histoire...,* v.1, p. 83. *DBF,* v. 2, pp. 309–311. Fawtier, *Capetian...,* pp. 122–125, 152, 203. Jordan, *Louis...,* pp. 17, 216 & n. Lehmann, *Rôle de la...,* p. 388. Marks, *Pilgrims...,* pp. 292–293, 299. Strayer, *Albigensian...,* pp. 137 & 142. Wakefield, *Heresy...,* pp. 127, 156, 165, 166.

JOHANNA TRAVERS

d.c. 1295 England

Well-to-do merchant; owned property and wharf in London. Some of her shops and houses were left to her maid, Matilda, and to her clerk, John.

♦ **Bequests. Employers. Land/property. Merchants. Shipping.** ♦

Calendar of Wills..., I, p. 122.

JEANNE DE VALOIS

c. 1310s–d. 1363 France

Daughter of Charles of Valois by his second wife, †Catherine de Courteney. Jeanne married (1) Charles of Taranto and (2) Robert d'Artois. In the fight over the lands of †Mahaut of Artois, Jeanne even used fraud as a weapon to help Robert acquire the estates she felt should be theirs.

♦ **Managers. Miscreants. Politics. Prisons. Squabbles.** ♦

Butler, *Women...*, p. 278. *DBF,* v.8, pp. 553–554. Hardy, *Philippa...*, p. 91.

JEANNE DE VALOIS, countess of Hainault

c. 1290s–d.c. 1352 Flanders; France; Netherlands

Daughter of Charles of Valois and his first wife, Marguerite d'Anjou (daughter of Charles II of Anjou, king of Sicily). Sister of Philip VI of France. In 1305 Jeanne married William III the Good, count of Holland and Hainault (d.1337). After he died, Jeanne entered convent and became abbess. She negotiated daughter †Philippa's marriage to Edward III of England, and peace between Philip VI and Edward III (c.1341).

♦ **Abbesses. Negotiators. Patrons of literature. Politics. Widows.** ♦

Armitage-Smith, *John...*, p. 4. Bryant, *Age...*, pp. 289–290. *DBF,* v.1, p. 1426. *DNB,* v.15, p. 1050. Froissart, *Chronicles...*, I, p. 19. Hardy, *Philippa...*, pp. 27–8, 30, 32, 75, 77, 100, 121–2, 136, & 301. Jamison, *Life...*, I, pp. 16, 38, 43. Jourdain, "Memoire...," p. 503.

JEHANNE (la verrière)

1292 France

Taxed 2s on her glass-making occupation in 1292 Paris.

♦ **Less-affluent. Merchants–glass.** ♦

Géraud, *Paris sous...*, p. 99.

JEANNE VILLAIN

1487 France

Wife of Henri Villain of Fontvannes. In 1487 Troyes, this empiric was accused of using diabolic means to cure her patients.

♦ **Doctors/empirics. Witchcraft.** ♦

Hughes, *Women...*, p. 146. Wickersheimer, *Dictionnaire...*, v.2, p. 506.

JOAN WARING **[Johanna]**

c. 1370s–1410s England

Nurse of baby Henry (V) of England.

♦ **Nurses–wetnurses. Servants–childcare.** ♦

Hutchison, *King...*, pp. 15 & 77. Jarman, *Crispin's...*, p. 81.

JOAN LA WHYCCHERE

1349 England

See—AGNES WOMBE.

♦ **Servants.** ♦

JOHANNA WOLSY

1382 England

A London water carrier named Alan hired a magician, Robert Berewold, to determine who had stolen a mazer from Matilda of Eye. Using bread, a wooden peg, and four knives, Robert magically "discovered" that Johanna was the thief. She took Alan to court for defamation of character. Johanna was acquitted; Alan was sentenced to the pillory.

♦ **Legal activity. Superstitions. Witchcraft.** ♦

Bellamy, *Crime...*, p. 63.

JOAN WOULBAROWE

c. 1400 England

Apprenticed to †Katherine Dore to learn silk-working trade. Joan and Katherine had numerous disagreements which flared up in London courts even after Joan had served her apprenticeship and was a silkwoman in her own right.

♦ **Apprentices. Legal activity. Silkwork. Squabbles.** ♦

Dale, "London...," pp. 326–327.

JEANNETTE [Jehannette]

JEANNETTE CAMUS

1443/1448 France

Empiric of Dijon; arrested for practicing medicine illegally. Jeannette was eventually banished from the town.

♦ **Doctors/empirics. Miscreants. Punishments.** ♦

Hughes, *Women...*, p. 145. Wickersheimer, *Dictionnaire...*, v.2, p. 506.

JEANNETTE CHARLES

1401 Switzerland

Daughter of Richard Charles of Geneva. Accused of sorcery and diabolism.

♦ **Ecclesiastical courts–Inquisition. Unmarried. Witchcraft.** ♦

Lea, *Materials...*, p. 247.

JEANNETTE DU FOSSÉ

1421 France

Parisian barber; taxed 2s.

♦ **Barbers. Less-affluent.** ♦

Favier, *Les Contribuables...*, p. 103. Hughes, *Women...*, p. 140. Wickersheimer, *Dictionnaire...*, v.2, p. 506.

JEANNETTE LA PETITE

1427 — France

Parisian lady of pleasure, arrested for not dressing as a prostitute. Jeannette was publicly chastised: her furs were confiscated, and her ornate silver belt was donated to charity.

♦ **Prostitutes. Punishments.** ♦

Champion, *François...*, p. 92. Decaux, *Histoire...*, p. 360. Harksen, *Women...*, p. 26.

JOLETTA DE DREUX, queen of Scotland

See—YOLANDE DE DREUX, queen of Scotland.

JOURDENETTE (nourrice)

1292 — France

Nurse for Guillaume Bourcel on the rue des Arsis; Jourdenette paid a 4s tax in 1292 Paris.

♦ **Less-affluent. Nurses.** ♦

Géraud, *Paris sous...*, p. 93. Hughes, *Women...*, p. 147.

JUDITH, duchess of BAVARIA

c. 920s–970s — Germany

Daughter of Arnulf the Bad of Bavaria; married Henry I, who became duke of Bavaria (c.938). When he died in 955, Judith was regent for son Henry the Quarrelsome. One of her daughters, †Hedwig, married Burchard of Swabia. Judith was quite pious; she even took a pilgrimage to Jerusalem. A political conspiracy in which she was involved in the 970s failed, and she retired to a convent.

♦ **Pilgrims. Politics. Regents. Religieuses. Squabbles. Widows.** ♦

Cambridge..., III, pp. 191, 204, 205 & n. Duckett, *Death...*, p. 77. Ennen, *Medieval...*, p. 62. Leyser, *Rule...*, pp. 29, 53, 72, 161.

JUDITH OF BAVARIA, Holy Roman Empress

b. 802–d. 843 — France; Germany

Daughter of Welf of Bavaria; in 819 became second wife of Louis I the Pious; mother of †Gisela and Charles the Bald. Judith had a bad reputation with chroniclers because she was so ambitious and strong-willed. She used all her charms on Louis to persuade him to set aside his three adult sons and make her son Charles his heir. Judith supervised Charles's education, was a skilled harpist, and did excellent needlework. However, Judith is best remembered for the charges of adultery, incest, and witchcraft leveled at her by her enemies. Twice she was banished from court, but each time she managed to win back her pious husband's affections and regain her position of power.

♦ **Artistic clothwork. Adultery. Educated. Models. Music. Patrons of literature. Politics. Religieuses. Religious patrons. Squabbles. Superstitions. Teachers. Witchcraft.** ♦

Cabaniss, *Judith...*, pp. 7–50, 54, 62, 100, 107–108, 177. *Carolingian...*, pp. 24–26, 105, 130–131, 134–135, 144, 150, 200–203, 210. Duckett, *Carolingian...*, pp. 29, 33–34, 37–39, 40–43, 45–46, 50, 52–53, 74, 80, 85, 132–133, 171. Jourdain, "Memoire...," p. 473. Lehmann, *Rôle de la...*, pp. 125–135. McKitterick, *Frankish...*, pp. 5, 136, 165, 169, 170, 174, 176, 181, Table 3. McNamara and Wemple, "Marriage...," p. 106. Riché, *Les Carolingiens...*, pp. 152, 163, 167, 290. Stafford, *Queens...*, pp. 18–20, 24–25, 29, 40, 56–57, 69, 82, 83, 90, 93–94, 100, 107, 112, 130, 145, 156, 164, 166, 179, 180. Wemple, "S. Salvatore...," p. 90. Wemple, *Women...*, pp. 80–81, 90, 92, 95, 171, 195, 243, 254, 296.

JUDITH OF BAVARIA, duchess of Swabia

m. 1121–d.c. 1131 Germany

Daughter of †Wulfhild of Saxony and Henry the Black, duke of Bavaria. Judith married Frederick II the One-eyed, duke of Swabia, and was the mother of Emperor Frederick I Barbarossa.

♦ **Dowry/dower. Relics.** ♦

Cambridge..., V, pp. 153, 381. Fuhrmann, *Germany...*, pp. 138, 152. Haverkamp, *Medieval...*, pp. 133, 138, 158–159. Stubbs, *Germany...*, p. 198.

JUDITH, queen of ENGLAND

b. 843–870s England; Flanders; France

Daughter of †Ermentrude of Orléans and Charles the Bald, king of the Franks. In 856, Judith married the elderly king Aethelwulf of Wessex. Two years later, he died and she married his oldest son, Aethelbald (d.860). The church made him divorce Judith because she was his stepmother. Her father then forced her to retire to a convent at Senlis. Shortly thereafter, Judith escaped and secretly married Baldwin I of Flanders (d.879). Although her father tried to annul this marriage, the pope ruled that it was legitimate.

♦ **Adultery. Divorce. Educated. Popes. Religieuses. Widows.** ♦

Campbell, *Anglo-Saxons*, p. 142. Duckett, *Carolingian...*, pp. 219–223. Dunbabin, *France*, pp. 69, 72, 102. Ennen, *Medieval...*, pp. 57–61. Ernouf, *Histoire...*, pp. 10 & 11. Hodgkin, *History...*, II, pp. 512, 514, 516, 624, 632, 634. James, *Origins...*, pp. 81, 176, 180–181. McKitterick, *Frankish...*, pp. 194–195, 249, Table 3. McNamara and Wemple, "Marriage...," p. 112. Riché, *Les Carolingiens...*, p. 189. Stafford, "King's...," pp. 3–27. Stafford, *Queens...*, pp. 37, 46–47, 48, 55, 84, 129, 130–131, 145, 168, 170, 202. Wemple, *Women...*, pp. 84, 171, 245–246.

JUDITH OF ÉVREUX

b. 1047–d.c. 1089 Italy

Daughter of William, count of Évreux; first wife of Roger I of Sicily (m.c.1062). Judith helped Roger in his fight to conquer Sicily; she commanded the defense of Troina.

♦ **Soldiers.** ♦

Crawford, *Rulers...*, pp. 250 & 391. Curtis, *Roger...*, pp. 474–475. Hurd-Mead, *History...*, pp. 116, 118–119. Norwich, *Normans...*, pp. 146–147, 151–154, 156, 176, 192, 278. Osborne, *Greatest...*, pp. 153, 158, 223, 224–227, 228, 241–243, 246, 253, 329, 415, 433, 460. Smith, *Sicily...*, p. 24.

JUDITH OF FLANDERS

b. 1032–d. 1094 England; Flanders; Germany

Daughter of †Adela of France and Baldwin V, count of Flanders. Around 1050, Judith married Tostig Godwineson. She was the owner of famous *Gospel Book* which was covered in gold and jewels. Judith accompanied Tostig on pilgrimage to Rome in 1061. After he died in 1066, Judith married Welf, duke of Bavaria. She later retired, as a widow, to Weingarten Abbey in Bavaria.

♦ **Book owners. Pilgrims. Religieuses. Widows.** ♦

Bell, "Medieval...," p. 175. Barlow, *Edward...*, pp. 108, 114, 120, 195–196, 200, 210, 341. Barlow, *Feudal...*, pp. 63–64, 68, 79. Brown, *Normans...*, p. 142. Campbell, *Anglo-Saxons*, pp. 170, 192, 225. *DNB*, v.19, pp. 998 & 1001. Douglas, *William...*, p. 78. Stubbs, *Germany...*, pp. 179 & 198. Vitalis, *Ecclesiastical...*, II, pp. 140–141 & 281.

JUDITH (OF GERMANY) **[Judith Maria; Sophie]**

b. 1047–c. 1110 Germany; Hungary; Poland

Daughter of †Agnes of Poitou and Holy Roman Emperor Henry III. Married (1) (c.1059) Solomon of Hungary and (2) (c.1088) Vladislaw of Poland. An educated woman, Judith attempted to Germanize Polish literature and later tried to influence the succession in Poland.

♦ **Educated. Miscreants. Patrons of literature. Politics. Widows.** ♦

Cambridge..., V, pp. 113, 133. *DBF*, v.1, p. 755. Kosztolnyik, *Five...*, pp. 75 & 76. Reddaway et al, *Cambridge...*, pp. 43 & 71. Thompson, *Feudal...*, II, pp. 426, 600, 602. Thompson, *Literacy...*, p. 93.

JUDITH OF SCHWEINFURT

m.c. 1030 Bohemia; Germany

Daughter of an important noble family. She was educated at a convent until young Bratislav I (Vratislav), duke of Bohemia, abducted and married her.

♦ **Abduction. Educated. Religieuses.** ♦

Cambridge..., III, pp. 299, 300. Thompson, *Feudal...*, II, p. 629.

JULIANA BERNERS

c. 1380–1420s England

Although some scholars believe she was not the author, Dame Juliana is generally credited with having written the *Book of Saint Albans*—a treatise about hunting, hawking, fishing, and heraldry. She showed wide knowledge of contemporary veterinary practice, as well as a good, common sense approach.

♦ Hunting. Writers. ♦

Abram, *English...*, p. 44. Berners, *Book of St.....* Bishop, *Middle...*, p. 99. Hurd-Mead, *History...*, p. 255. Jacob, "Book...," pp. 99–118. Jacob, *Fifteenth...*, p. 665. *Oxford... Prose,* pp. 144 & 450. Power, *Nunneries...*, pp. 240 & 308.

JULIANA (BONAVENTURE)

1275 England

Illegitimate daughter of Richard Bonaventure, merchant of London. He remembered Juliana in his will as if she were one of his three legitimate children.

♦ Bequests. Illegitimacy. ♦

Calendar of Wills..., I, p. 21.

JULIANA (CORDWANER)

d. 1263 England

Wife of Richard le Cordwaner of London. An argument while playing chess ended with her death when her opponent, David de Bristoll, accidentally stabbed Juliana.

♦ Games–chess. Murder. ♦

London Eyre...1276, p. 42 (#151).

JULIANA OF CORNILLON [Blessed Julienne de Mont-Cornillon]

1193–1258 Belgium

Prioress of Mont-Cornillon near Liège. Juliana was reputedly well-versed in Latin and French; she was also a mystic and a writer. Her work on the Eucharist was finished by her best friend, the recluse †Eva of St. Martin.

♦ Abbesses. Educated. Mystics. Relics. Writers–theology. ♦

Bynum, *Holy...*, pp. 24, 55, 77, 88, 115, 116, 119–122, 124, 203, 204, 225, 232, 235–7, 249, 253. Goodich, "Countours...," pp. 25, 30, 31. Jourdain, "Memoire...," p. 484. McDonnell, *Beguines...*, pp. 4, 98, 297, 299–309, 312, 332–335, 374, 394–397, & 446.

(St.) JULIANA FALCONIERI [Giuliana]

c. 1270–1341 Italy

Florentine tertiary; before 1300 she started a religious community especially for females devoted to Virgin Mary. This Third Order of the Servite order was patronized by the Dominicans.

♦ Medicine. Religieuses. Religious patrons. Saints. ♦

Attwater, *Dictionary...*, p. 175. Bynum, *Holy...*, p. 257. Effinger, *Women...*, p. 51. Farmer, *Oxford...*, p. 227. Goodich, "Contours...," p. 21. Holmes, *Florence...*, p. 119.

JULIANA DE LEYBOURNE, countess of Huntingdon

b. 1303–c. 1368 England

Daughter of Alice de Tony and Thomas de Leybourne; granddaughter and heiress of William Leybourne. Around 1320, Juliana married John de Hastings, lord Hastings. In 1325, she married Sir Thomas le Blount, and in 1328 she wed William de Clinton (d.1354), who was created earl of Huntingdon in 1337. She was very pious; around 1361, she gave one of her manors to an Augustinian abbey. Her will left everything to charity.

♦ **Bequests. Charity. Estate. Managers. Religious patrons.** ♦

C.P., v.7, pp. 638–639. Given-Wilson, *English...*, p. 37. Tuck, *Richard...*, p. 75.

JULIANA HAUTEYN

c. 1290 England

See—ALICE ROMAYN and ROESIA DE BORFORD.

♦ **Bequests. Land/Property.** ♦

JULIAN OF NORWICH

c. 1343–1420s England

Well-educated gentlewoman of Norfolk. After an illness she had several visions. Julian became a recluse, writing about and interpreting her mystical experiences in *Revelations of Divine Love.*

♦ **Anchoresses. Educated. Mystics. Writers.** ♦

Bradley, "Julian...," pp. 195–216. Bynum, *Holy...*, pp. 185, 200, 235, 256, 264, 266–7, 269, 289–90, 292. Farmer, *Oxford...*, p. 423. Jones, "English...," pp. 269–296. Julian, *Showings....* Molinari, *Julian....* Provost, "English...," pp. 299, 312–313. Rosenthal, *Nobles...*, p. 96. Thièbaux, *The Writings...*, pp. 221–234. Warren, *Anchorites...*, pp. 13, 41, 181, 203, 214, 252, 286. Windeatt, "Julian...," pp. 1–17.

JULIANE (la potière)

1292 France

Potter in 1292 Paris; also made metal implements. Taxed 2s.

♦ **Less-affluent. Potters.** ♦

Géraud, *Paris sous...*, p. 52.

JULIANA ROOS

1332 England

Juliana and her husband John le Roos were weavers of London. Their guild accused the couple of making a cloth which did not fit industry standards. Juliana and John cut it off the loom before the cloth could be seized. In court, they declared it had been made for their own use. The court found the facts were correct, so no judgement was made.

♦ **Clothworkers. Legal activity. Miscreants.** ♦

Calendar of Plea..., I, p. 99.

JUTTA OF SPONHEIM **[Blessed Jutta of Disibodenberg]**

d. 1136 Germany

A noblewoman, the sister of Count Meginhard of Sponheim. Jutta was an outstanding mystic and recluse. The sickly child, †Hildegarde of

Bingen, was placed in Jutta's care. By the time Hildegarde was grown, Jutta had attracted a community of nuns. When she died in 1136, Hildegard became prioress of this group in Disibodenberg.

♦ **Abbesses. Anchoresses. Childcare. Educated. Models. Mystics. Teachers.** ♦

Delaney, *Dictionary...*, pp. 286 & 336. Ennen, *Medieval...*, p. 128. Gies, *Women...*, pp. 63, 64, 68, 76. Kraft, "German...," p. 110. Newman, *Sister...*, pp. 5, 8. O'Faolain, *Not in...*, p. 139. Pernoud, *La femme...*, p. 48.

KASIA (of Byzantium)

fl. 820s–840s — Byzantium

Young noblewoman of Byzantium. In a line-up to pick emperor's wife, Kasia was supposedly the most beautiful woman but Emperor Theophilus was afraid of her because she was too witty and intelligent. Instead of becoming empress, Kasia founded a convent where she retired; she amused herself by composing religious poetry and witty secular poems, some of which are extant.

♦ **Educated. Models. Religieuses. Religious patrons. Unmarried. Writers.** ♦

Bridge, *Crusade...*, pp. 36–37 (tells her story but does not name her).
Diehl, *Byzantine...*, pp. 95–96.

KATELINE DE COSTER — **[Catherine of Courtrai]**

fl. 1330s–1360 — England; Flanders

Second wife of Jacob van Artevelde of Ghent (who temporarily united Flemish towns to preserve neutrality for the wool/cloth business). In 1340s, Kateline undertook three missions to England for Jacob. After he was killed in 1345, Kateline escaped to England where she lived until 1359, when it was safe for her to return to Flanders.

♦ **Clothworkers. Merchants. Negotiators. Widows.** ♦

Gies, *Merchants...*, pp. 180–182. Hardy, *Philippa...*, pp. 115–6.

KATHERINE — **[Katharine; Katerine]**

See—CATHERINE.

KRISTIN (of Iceland)

c. 1450 — Iceland

Managed her home and staff in Iceland; her extant letters deal with details of administering a large estate.

♦ **Managers. Writers–letters.** ♦

Frank, "Iceland...," p. 484.

KUNIGUNDE — **[Kunegunde; Kunigunda]**

See—CUNEGUNDE.

KYNETHRYTH

See—CYENTHRYTH, queen of MERCIA.

— L —

LAURA **[Laura de Noves; de Sade]**

c. 1308–d. 1348 France

Married Hugh de Sade in 1325. Around 1327 at Avignon, Laura met Petrarch, who was presumably inspired to write lyric poetry about her. She died in 1348 of the plague.

♦ **Models. Plague.** ♦

Bernardo, "Petrarch's...," p. 53. Bishop, "Petrarch...," pp. 153, 167–168. Chamberlin, *World...,* p. 53. Effinger, *Women...,* pp. 91–95. Marks, *Pilgrims...,* pp. 297–299.

LAURA CERETA **[Laura Serina]**

1469–1499 Italy

Laura was educated, mostly by her father Silvestro, in math, astrology, Latin, and Greek. At age fifteen, she married Pietro Serina, a businessman of Brescia. Laura corresponded with other humanists, defended education for women, and in 1488 published a volume of letters. She may have also taught philosophy at Padua.

♦ **Astrology. Scholars. Teachers. Writers.** ♦

Cereta, *Laurae....* King and Rabil, *Her Immaculate...,* pp. 21, 23, 27, 29, 77–86, 122, 123, 124, 132, 140–142, 150, 151. Kristeller, "Learned...," p. 97. LaBalme, *Beyond...,* p. 2. Lipinska, *Histoire...,* p. 152. Rabil, *Laura....*

LAURETTE DE SAINT-VALÉRY

fl.c. 1200 France

Wife of Aléaume de Fontaines. In Amiens, Laurette was known for her charity and for nursing the poor.

♦ **Charity. Medicine. Nurses.** ♦

DBF, v.1, p. 1373. Hughes, *Women...,* p. 144. Wickersheimer, *Dictionnaire...,* v.2, p. 522.

LEONETTA (medica)

fl. 1300s Italy

Wife of Giovanni di Gorzano; Leonetta practiced as a doctor in Padua and Turin.

♦ **Doctors/empirics.** ♦

Hughes, *Women...,* p. 142. Hurd-Mead, *History...,* p. 278. Lipinska, *Histoire...,* p. 148.

LEONOR **[Leonora]**

See—ELEANOR.

LESCELINE, countess of EU **[Lescelina]**

c. 1030s–1060 France

Wife of William I, count of Eu. Mother of Robert, count of Eu, and of Hugh, bishop of Lisieux. Lesceline was widely known as a religious patroness, the founder of churches, abbeys, and other pious establishments. As a widow she chose to embrace the religious life.

♦ **Estate. Managers. Models. Religieuses. Religious patrons. Widows.** ♦

Brown, *Normans...*, p. 27. *Cambridge...*, V, p. 493. Douglas, *William...*, pp. 97, 112, 115, 124, 150, 209. Farmer, "Persuasive...," p. 522. Forester (trans.), *Ordericus...*, v.1, p. 382; v.2, p. 106.

LISA STROZZI

fl.c. 1400 Italy

Wife of Filippo Strozzi; she was a Tuscan slave owner.

♦ **Educated. Slaves–owners.** ♦

Origo, "Domestic...," p. 343.

(St.) LIUTBERGA **[Liutbirg of Saxony]**

d.c. 880 Germany

Liutberga was removed from her convent so that she could serve as assistant estate manager to Countess Gisla of Saxony. (Liutberga later ran the estate herself.) When she got older she returned to the cloister and possibly became a nun at Wendhausen. While there, she attracted visitors who wanted her advice on estate management or who wished for her to teach their daughters. Liutberga was eventually allowed to become a recluse. Her prophecies and sermons increased her fame.

♦ **Anchoresses. Artistic clothwork. Educated. Managers. Models. Music. Mystics. Preachers. Religieuses. Saints. Servants. Teachers. Unmarried.** ♦

Herlihy, *Opera...*, pp. 88–90. Leyser, *Rule...*, p. 59. McNamara and Wemple, "Sanctity...," p. 105. Schulenburg, "Female...," pp. 117 & n.65. Wemple, *Women...*, pp. 99–100, 145, 171, 173–174, 296–297.

LIUTGARD [Liudgard; Liutgarde; Lutgard]

(St.) LUTGARD OF AYWIÈRES

[Liutgard of Tongern; Lutgard of St. Trond]

b. 1182–d.c. 1246 Belgium; Flanders

Entered Benedictine convent of St. Trond around 1194. She became prioress shortly before moving to Cistercian convent at Aywières in

1206. Lutgard went blind around 1235. She was a mystic and an individualistic *muliere sanctae*. Thomas de Cantimpré wrote her *Vita*.

♦ **Abbesses. Handicapped. Models. Mystics. Relics. Saints. Writers.** ♦

Bolton, "Vitae Matrum...," pp. 259–261, 263, 265, 267, 269. Bynum, *Holy...*, pp. 64, 77, 86, 115–123 passim, 148, 171, 174, 211, 212, 213, 222, 230, 234, 247, 250, 273, 274. Halligan (ed.), *Booke...*, pp. 31, 36, 39, 43n, 44. Lagorio, "Continental...," pp. 171, 175. McDonnell, *Beguines...*, pp. 17, 20, 24, 47, 91, 97, 108, 200, 315, 316, 318, 329, 374, 393, 395, 416, 446. Power, *Nunneries...*, pp. 500 & 52.

LIUTGARD OF GERMANY **[Liutgarde of Franconia]**

m. 947–d. 953 France; Germany

Daughter of †Edith of England and Emperor Otto I. In 947, Liutgard married Conrad the Red, duke of Lorraine. They were ancestors of Emperor Conrad II.

♦ **Genealogy.** ♦

Barraclough, *Origins...*, p. 74. *Cambridge...*, III, pp. 191, 105n, 215, 249, 253. Duckett, *Death...*, pp. 61 & 67. Leyser, *Rule...*, p. 53. Stephenson, *Mediaeval...*, pp. 244, 246, Table 4. Stubbs, *Germany...*, pp. 91, 141.

LIUTGARD OF VERMANDOIS **[Leutgarde]**

c. 920–d.c. 979 France

Daughter of †Adela of France and Herbert (II), count of Vermandois; heiress of several important estates, such as Melun. Liutgard married (1) William I of Normandy and (2) Thibaut I, count of Blois and Chartres—Eudes I of Blois was their son.

♦ **Estate. Genealogy.** ♦

Anselme, *Histoire...*, v.1, p. 49. *DBF*, v.17, fasc. 97, p.152. McKitterick, *Frankish...*, pp. 323–324, & Table 7.

LOBA DE PUEINAUTIER

c. 1200s–1220s France

Wife of Jourdain de Cabaret. Supposedly had numerous lovers. She was extolled by troubadour Peire Vidal, who was presumably one of her paramours.

♦ **Adultery. Models. Patrons of literature.** ♦

Boutière and Schutz, *Biographies des...*, pp. 369–373, 384–386, 389–391. Decaux, *Histoire...*, pp. 246, 248–249.

LOMBARDA

c. 1190–c. 1230s France

Noblewoman of Toulouse; she wrote poetry in *trobar clus* style of best Provençal troubadours. She was probably also a noted Cathar.

♦ **Cathars. Poets/troubadours.** ♦

Bogin, *Women...*, pp. 114–117 & 174–175. Boutière and Schutz, *Biographies des...*, pp. 416–419. Egan, *Vidas...*, pp. 64–66. Wakefield, *Heresy...*, pp. 235 & 237.

LORETTA DE BRAOSE, countess of Leicester **[de Briouze]**
m.c. 1196–d.c. 1270 England

Daughter of †Maud (of St. Valery) and William de Braose; married Robert Beaumont, earl of Leicester. As a childless widow, Loretta spent nearly sixty years as a recluse in Kent. She aided development of first English Franciscan community. In 1265, Simon de Montfort, earl of Leicester, consulted Loretta about the political/administrative duties involved in the stewardship of England.

♦ **Anchoresses. Politics. Religious patrons. Widows.** ♦

Clark and Williams, "Impact...," pp. 162–163. Labarge, *Women...,* pp. 126–128. Powicke, "Loretta...," pp. 147–168. Shahar, *Fourth...,* p. 97. Warren, *Anchorites...,* pp. 25, 110, 121–122, 165–167, 185, 286.

LOUISE OF SAVOY, duchess of Angoulême
b. 1476–d.c. 1531 France

Daughter of †Marguerite de Bourbon and Philip II of Savoy, count of Bresse. In 1491, Louise married Charles, count of Angoulême; daughter †Marguerite was later queen of Navarre, and son François eventually became King Francis I of France. Louise was ambitious, lively, and intelligent. She made an excellent regent after Charles died in 1496. She was also well-educated. Her physician dedicated a book on *Excellent Women* to her.

♦ **Book owners. Childcare. Educated. Models. Politics. Regents. Widows.** ♦

Commynes, *Memoirs...,* pp. 310 & 312. Decaux, *Histoire...,* pp. 477–485. Fusero, *Borgias,* p. 299. Hurd-Mead, *History...,* p. 325. Mayer, *Great Regent....* Putnam, *Marguerite...,* pp. 1, 2, 3, 4, 5, 7, 8...etc. (A readable but less scholarly biography of her daughter).

LUCIA BROCADELLI **[Blessed Lucia Brocolelli; Lucy Narni]**
1476–1544 Italy

Married around 1490 to Pietro, a Milanese count, after three years Lucia was supposedly still a virgin. In 1494, she joined a third order of St. Dominic. In 1496, she was blessed with stigmata. While a nun at Viterbo, she brought fame to the area through various holy manifestations. Lucia supposedly danced with angels and was taught to read and write by St. †Catherine of Siena—who evidently took a temporary leave of absence from heaven for that purpose. Lucia also talked frequently with Christ. Ercole d'Este, duke of Ferrara, offered her a more important position (and a wider audience), so Lucia helped him kidnap her. In 1499, she became the first abbess of the convent of St. Catherine at Ferrara. Her arrogance made many of her nuns leave the convent. After Ercole's death, she was deposed because she was a very incompetent superior.

♦ **Abbesses. Abduction. Educated. Mystics. Virginity.** ♦

Attwater, *Dictionary...,* pp. 191–2. Cloulas, *Borgias...,* p. 59. Holweck, *Biographical...,* p. 624. Prescott, *Princes...,* pp. 213–4.

LUCIA MARLIANI

fl. 1470s Italy

Countess of Melzo; mistress of Galeazzo Maria Sforza. He gave her estates, titles, jewels, and many other presents. Beautiful and intelligent, Lucia was also an influential political adviser to her lover.

♦ **Estate. Gems/jewelry. Mistresses. Politics.** ♦

Ady, *History...*, pp. 109, 110, 113. Cartwright, *Beatrice...*, p. 18 (some confusion in this source). Collison-Morley, *Sforzas...*, p. 111.

LUCIA TASSEBURGH

d. 1326 England

Wife of Thomas Tasseburgh of Norwich. Lucia murdered him, so she was burned at the stake for committing petty treason—killing one's master.

♦ **Murder. Punishments.** ♦

Hanawalt, "Female...," p. 265.

LUCIENNE OF ROCHEFORT

m.c. 1105 France

Daughter of Guy, count of Rochefort. Married the future King Louis VI of France but the marriage was annulled in 1107 due to consanguinity.

♦ **Divorce. Pawns.** ♦

Anselme, *Histoire...*, p. 74. Castries, *Lives...*, p. 60. Duby, *Private...*, p. 128.

LUCREZIA D'ALAGNO

c. 1440s–1450s Italy

Mistress of Alfonso of Aragon, king of Naples. Lucrezia even visited Pope Calixtus III in an effort to obtain dispensation to marry Alfonso and have his union with †Maria of Castile annulled. Lucrezia had no success with this ploy.

♦ **Divorce. Mistresses. Models. Popes.** ♦

Cloulas, *Borgias...*, p. 31. Fusero, *Borgias*, pp. 54, 99–100. Johnson, *Borgias...*, pp. 22 & 48. Miron, *Queens...*, pp. 292, 294, 304–305. Prescott, *Princes...*, pp. 62–3. Ryder, *Kingdom...*, pp. 55 n.5.

LUCREZIA BORGIA

b. 1480–d. 1519 Italy

Daughter of Rodrigo Borgia (later Pope Alexander VI) and his mistress †Vanozza Catanei. Lucrezia was well-educated—in Greek, Latin, French, Spanish, and Italian—by her cousin †Adriana del Mila. Lucrezia also loved to dance and to write poetry. In 1493, Lucrezia married Giovanni Sforza, lord of Pesaro. In 1497, her father made her get this union annulled, and then married her to Alfonso of Aragon, later duke of Bisceglia. He was murdered in 1500, possibly by Lucrezia's brother Cesare. In 1501, Lucrezia married Alfonso d'Este, duke of

Ferrara. As duchess, she was praised for her virtue and intelligence. She had five children by Alfonso, dying in childbirth in 1519.

♦ **Art patrons. Book owners. Charity. Childbirth. Childcare. Dance. Divorce. Dowry/dower. Educated. Illegitimacy. Models. Murder. Music. Patrons of literature. Pawns. Popes. Regents. Religieuses. Writers.** ♦

Brion, *Medici*, p. 137. Cartwright, *Beatrice...*, pp. 149, 165, 184, 338. Chamberlin, *Fall...*, pp. 33, 35, 37–40,...etc..., 322, 327–331. Chamberlin, *World...*, pp. 105–107, 182–183. Cloulas, *Borgias...*, pp. 52, 59–60, 74–77...282–5, 287–8, 299–300. Cronin, *Flowering...*, pp. 30, 50, 96, 97, 98, 102, 103, 210, 216. Ennen, *Medieval...*, pp. 224–248. Fusero, *Borgias*, pp. 135, 142, 148, 150, 159, 161, 162, 170, 171, 172, 173–176, 199–203, 205–206, 217, 218, 225–227, 240, 285, 286, 289, 291–293. Johnson, *Borgias...*, pp. 36–37, 65, 79, 80, 90–91, 93, 94, 97–103, 116, 119, 123, 129, 131, 132, 140–141, 150, 156, 158–162, 165, 166, 185, 190–207. Prescott, *Princes...*, pp. 41, 215–19, 223–9, 232, 237–8, 264, 341. Simon, *Tapestry...*, pp. 96, 115, 116, 126, 130–131, 140, 146, 150–152. Trevelyan, *Short...*, pp. 196, 202, 203–204.

LUCREZIA CRIVELLI

fl. 1490s Italy

Maid of honor to †Beatrice d'Este, duchess of Milan. In 1496, she became the mistress of Ludovic Sforza, duke of Milan. Their son Gianpaolo was born in 1497. Leonardo da Vinci presumably painted Lucrezia's portrait for Ludovic. After Beatrice died, Ludovic ended his relationship with Lucrezia, but gave her several estates to make up for his desertion.

♦ **Land/property. Mistresses. Models. Servants–ladies.** ♦

Bellonci, "Beatrice...," p. 295. Cartwright, *Beatrice...*, pp. 302, 321, 379. Prescott, *Princes...*, pp. 137 & 138. Simon, *Tapestry...*, pp. 96, 130, 140. Sizeranne, *Beatrice...*, pp. 80 & 82.

LUCREZIA DONATI

b.c. 1455–1470s Italy

Young wife of Niccolo Ardinghelli. In 1469, Lorenzo de'Medici gave a tournament in her honor (also to celebrate his engagement to †Clarissa Orsini). He and Lucrezia had a long and affectionate affair/friendship.

♦ **Adultery. Models. Tournaments.** ♦

Cleugh, *Medici...*, pp. 106, 126, 186. Hook, *Lorenzo...*, pp. 16–17, 51, 77. Maguire, *Women...*, pp. 133 & 136.

LUCREZIA D'ESTE

m. 1487 Italy

Illegitimate daughter of Ercole I d'Este of Ferrara; 1487 married Annibale Bentivoglio of Bologna.

♦ **Educated. Illegitimacy. Models.** ♦

Breisach, *Catherine...*, p. 89. Cartwright, *Beatrice...*, pp. 33, 36, & 37. Prescott, *Princes...*, p. 205.

LUCREZIA DE'MEDICI
See—NANNINA DE'MEDICI.

LUCREZIA DE'MEDICI
b. 1470–d.c. 1540s Italy

Daughter of †Clarissa Orsini and Lorenzo de'Medici. In 1488, Lucrezia married Jacopo Salviati. When the Medici were in exile, she worked on their behalf to get the family reinstated. Lucrezia was guardian of †Catherine Sforza's son, Giovanni de'Medici. She was also a religious patron and a papal supporter.

♦ **Art patrons. Childcare. Educated. Politics. Popes. Religious patrons. Writers.** ♦

Cleugh, *Medici...*, pp. 160, 175, 239. Hook, *Lorenzo...*, pp. 36, 58, 83, 151, 185. Maguire, *Women...*, pp. 146, 174, & 176.

LUCREZIA TORNABUONI
b. 1425–d. 1482 Italy

Around 1444, Lucrezia married Piero de'Medici. She was very involved in the education and care of her sons, even to the extent of picking Lorenzo's wife. Lucrezia was intelligent, a good businesswoman, and a wise political aid to her husband and son. She also had a civilizing influence—as art patron and supporter of writers. Very pious, Lucrezia was a noted writer of religious hymns.

♦ **Art patrons. Bathhouse. Charity. Managers. Models. Music. Negotiators. Patrons of literature. Politics. Scholars. Teachers. Writers–hymns.** ♦

Anderson and Zinsser, *A History of...*, pp. 374, 399–400, 428. Brion, *Medici*, pp. 104 & 205. Chamberlin, *World...*, p. 191. Cleugh, *Medici...*, pp. 87, 101, 107, 114, 119, 155–157, 188, 190, 240–241. Hook, *Lorenzo...*, pp. 6, 8–9, 11, 13, 16, 23, 26, 76, 83, 106, 157–158. Kristeller, "Learned...," p. 92. Maguire, *Women...*, pp. 54, 61, 62, 64–69, 78, 80, 86, 93, 101, 116, 120, 129, 251.

LUCY ATTE LEE
1301 England

Wife of Reginald atte Lee on the manor of Cashio in Hertfordshire. Reginald wished to divorce Lucy; he offered her all their property to not oppose the divorce, and to stay away from him.

♦ **Divorce. Land/property. Manors.** ♦

Homans, *English...*, p. 174.

LUDMILA (of Bohemia) **[Saint Ludmila]**
c. 870s–d.c. 920 Bohemia; Czechoslovakia

Wife of Borivoj of Bohemia; influenced her son Vratislav to make duchy of Bohemia Christian. She was opposed by her daughter-in-law †Drahomira who led the pagan believers. Ludmila had the care and education of one of her grandsons, (St.) Wenceslaus. She was later murdered, probably by order of Drahomira, and is counted a martyr for the faith.

♦ **Childcare. Models. Murder. Politics. Religious patrons. Saints. Teachers. Widows.** ♦

Cambridge..., III, p. 184; VI, p. 432. Daniel-Rops, *Church...*, p. 555. Farmer, *Oxford...*, p. 400. Maurice, *Bohemia...*, pp. 22–24. Thompson, *Feudal...*, II, p. 622. Tierney, *Western...*, p. 216.

LYDWINE OF SCHIEDAM **[Blessed Lydwine; Lidwina]**

1380–1433 Netherlands

In 1395, Lydwine became bedridden with ulcerated sores. Her story is largely concerned with medical details of this trial sent by God, and with the punishments God inflicted on those who were not nice enough to Lydwine. God even sent Lydwine a mystical vision of one priest being tortured in Hell after his death for having mistreated her. She asked God to have rats eat all the chickens belonging to another unkind cleric from the neighboring monastery. Apparently there was an on-going feud between Lydwine and her family and the neighboring monks and priests who were suspicious of the validity of her visionary/holy powers.

♦ **Medicine. Models. Mystics. Squabbles.** ♦

Attwater, *Dictionary...*, p. 193. Brugman, *Iohannis Brugman....* Bynum, *Holy...*, pp. 25, 124–130, 196, 198, 200, 204, 205, 211, 222, 223, 228, 233, 234, 273, 274, 280, 297. Coulton, *Life...*, IV, pp. 302-306. Herlihy, *Opera...*, pp. 171–172. Huysman, *St. Lydwine....* Power, *Nunneries...*, p. 501.

— M —

MABEL [Mabil; Mabille; Mabile; Mabella]

MABEL OF BELLÊME

[Mabille Talvas; de Montgomery; de Mont Gomerii]

m.c. 1050–d.c. 1078 France

Daughter and heiress of William Talvas; she owned estates in Normandy and Maine. Around 1050, Mabel married Roger of Montgomery; they had several sons. The couple founded the abbey of St. Martin. Much more ambitious and grasping than her husband, Mabel ran their estates, led military campaigns, and forcibly acquired lands at the expense of others. Carrying on her father's feud with the founders of a nearby monastery, Mabel occupied the establishment while she and her troops literally ate the monks out of house and home. During another feud, she supposedly poisoned her rival. Mabel was murdered around 1078 by Hugh Bunel (or de Ialgeio) because she had stolen his inheritance. The medieval legend of her death stated that Mabel was beheaded in her own room after her bath.

♦ **Managers. Models. Murder. Religious patrons. Soldiers.** ♦

Bates, *Normandy...*, pp. 79, 80, 81, 104, 161 & 243. Brown, *Normans...*, pp. 36, 48, 53. *DBF*, v.5, p. 1342. Decaux, *Histoire...*, pp. 212–213. Duby, *Private...*, pp. 102 & 148. Lehmann, *Rôle de la...*, p. 227. Le Patourel, *Feudal...*, VI, pp. 17, 18, 19. Verdon, "Les Sources...," p. 228. Vitalis, *Ecclesiastical...*, v.II, pp. 46–48, 54–56, 66–68, 90, 122, 362–365; v.III, pp. xxiv, xix, 134–138, 140, 160; v.IV, pp. xxiv-xxv, 132 n4, 152 & 158.

MABEL OF BURY ST. EDMUNDS

fl. 1230s–1240s England

Lay woman, professional embroiderer. Commissioned by Henry III of England to make liturgical garments and altar pieces. Mabel was allowed to design the work and was paid £10 for one piece. Henry later gave her some rabbit fur for a robe to show his appreciation of a job well done.

♦ **Artistic clothwork. Artists. Merchants.** ♦

Carr, "Women...," pp. 8–9. Lancaster, "Artists...," pp. 82–85, 87, & 91. Parker and Pollack, *Old...*, p. 60.

MABILE (la regratière)

1292 France

Mabile eked out a living by hawking bread at the door of the Louvre in Paris; she paid small 12d tax.

♦ **Less-affluent. Provisioning–bakers.** ♦

Géraud, *Paris sous...*, p. 5.

MABEL RICH

fl. 1200s England

Wife of Edward Rich; mother of (St.) Edmund, archbishop of Canterbury. Encouraged religious training and fasting in her children. For the good of her own soul, Mabel wore sackcloth pressed to her skin with two iron plates.

♦ **Charity. Childcare. Models. Religieuses.** ♦

Boulding, *Underside...*, p. 470. *DNB,* v.6, p. 406. Hurd-Mead, *History...*, p. 223.

MACETE DE RUILLY

d. 1391 France

A Parisian court condemned her for hiring a witch, making wax images, etc. The witch she had hired, †Jehanne de Brigue, vowed that Macete wished to get rid of her husband who beat her. Macete would thus be free to continue an affair with a local curate. Both women were burned at the stake.

♦ **Punishments. Witchcraft. Women of easy virtue.** ♦

Robbins, *Encyclopedia...*, pp. 379–381. Russell, *Witchcraft...*, pp. 214–215.

MADELEINE [Maddalena; Magdelena]

MADDALENA BONSIGNORI

fl.c. 1300s Italy

Scholar/lecturer on philosophy, law, and medicine at the University of Bologna. Maddalena also wrote a treatise—*De Legibus connubialis*—on the law's treatment of women.

♦ **Legal activity. Medicine. Scholars. Teachers. University. Writers.** ♦

Effinger, *Women...*, p. 104. Greer, *Obstacle...*, p. 209. Hurd-Mead, *History...*, p. 278. Lipinska, *Histoire...*, p. 151.

MADDALENA DE'MEDICI

b. 1473–d. 1519 Italy

Daughter of †Clarissa Orsini and Lorenzo de'Medici of Florence. Sacrificed at marriage altar to achieve alliance and economic advantages for her father. Around 1488, he forced Maddalena to marry an older man with a very unsavory reputation—Pope Innocent VIII's son, Franceschetto Cibo.

♦ **Educated. Pawns. Popes. Writers–letters.** ♦

Breisach, *Caterina...*, p. 106. Cleugh, *Medici...*, pp. 160, 161, 196. Fusero, *Borgias*, p. 146. Hook, *Lorenzo...*, pp. 36, 83, 129, 171, 174, 177. Maguire, *Women...*, pp. 146 & 181. Trevelyan, *Short...*, p. 186.

MADDALENA SCROVEGNI

1356–1429 Italy

Well-educated member of a noble family of Padua. In 1376, Maddalena married a nobleman of Reggio; she soon returned to Padua as a widow. In 1390, Maddalena and her family fled to Venice. From there, she corresponded with other humanists. Antonio Loschi wrote panegyric verse about Maddalena's education, intelligence, and purity.

♦ **Models. Scholars. Widows. Writers.** ♦

King, "Goddess...," pp. 103–108. King and Rabil, *Her Immaculate...*, pp. 11–13, 16, 26, 33–35, 131. Kristeller, "Learned...," pp. 93 & 96.

MADELEINE VALOIS **[Magdalena of France]**

b. 1444–1480s France

Daughter of †Marie of Anjou and Charles VII of France; married Gaston de Foix, prince of Viana.

♦ **Genealogy. Regents.** ♦

Commynes, *Memoirs...*, II, p. 430. *DBF*, v.7, p. 1416; v.8, p. 530; v.14, p. 206. Leroy, *La Navarre...*, pp. 181–182, 191. Scofield, *Life...*, I, pp. 10–11. Smith, *Spain*, pp. 114–115. Vale, *Charles...*, pp. 173 & 224.

MAHAUT [Maheut]

MAHAUT OF ARTOIS

c. 1270s–d.c. 1328 France

Daughter and heiress of Amicia de Courtenay and Robert II of Artois. Around 1285, she married Othon IV, count of Burgundy. Both of their daughters, †Blanche and †Jeanne of Burgundy, married men who became kings of France, but only Jeanne survived to become queen. Mahaut was an effective ruler of her vast estates and was in sole charge for some twenty years after her husband died. She promoted the cloth industry, arts, music, and literature; Mahaut collected a large library for herself and had several chess sets made for her favorite game. Mahaut also made liberal donations to the church, and was particularly concerned with hospitals and with medical care for her subjects. She was also involved in several witchcraft cases.

♦ **Art patrons. Book owners. Clothworkers. Estate. Games–chess. Legal activity. Medicine. Music. Politics. Religious patrons. Rulers. Soldiers. Widows. Witchcraft.** ♦

Aubert, "Decorative...," p. 137. Butler, *Women...*, pp. 256–281. Casey, "Cheshire...," p. 235. *DBF*, v.3, pp. 1206–1209. Hurd-Mead, *History...*, pp. 270–271. Jamison, *Life...*, I, pp. 37–39. Kieckhefer, *European...*, p. 110. Lehmann, *Rôle de la...*, pp. 216–217. Richard, "Les Livres...". Richard, *Mahaut....* Russell, *Witchcraft...*, p. 172.

MAHAUT DE BRABANT **[Mahaud]**
m. 1237–d. 1288 France

Daughter of Henry II, duke of Brabant and Marie of Swabia (daughter of †Irene Angela and Philip of Swabia); married Robert of France (second son of Louis VIII and †Blanche of Castile) who then became count of Artois. In 1255, Mahaut married Guy II de Châtillon.

♦ **Genealogy. Popes. Widows.** ♦

Anselme, *Histoire...*, v.2, p. 792. Butler, *Women...*, p. 200. *DBF*, v.3, p. 1202. Stephenson, *Mediaeval...*, p. 445 Table X.

MAHEUT (la chapelière)
1292 France

In 1292 Paris, Maheut made hats at la Ferronnerie; she paid small 12d tax.

♦ **Apparel–hatmakers. Less-affluent.** ♦

Géraud, *Paris sous...*, p. 7.

MAHAUT DE CHÂTILLON **[St. Pol]**
c. 1310 France

See—BLANCHE OF BOURBON and BLANCHE OF FRANCE.

♦ **Genealogy.** ♦

MAHAUT DE DAMMARTIN

See—MATILDA OF BOULOGNE, queen of Portugal.

MAHEUT (la feutrière)
1292 France

Maheut evidently had a booming business making and selling felt in 1292 Paris, since she paid a large tax of 4 livres and 12 sous.

♦ **Clothworkers. Land/property. Merchants.** ♦

Géraud, *Paris sous...*, p. 88.

MAHAUT OF HAINAULT

See—MATILDA OF HAINAULT.

MAHEUT (la pescheresse)
1292 France

Fishwife of 1292 Paris; paid 3s tax on her business.

♦ **Less-affluent. Provisioning–fishmongers.** ♦

Géraud, *Paris sous...*, p. 133.

MALFRID OF KIEV, queen of Norway, queen of Denmark

c. 1100s–1130s Denmark; Norway; Russia

Daughter of †Christina of Sweden and Mstislav I of Kiev, prince of Novgorod; married Sigurd I, king of Norway. Around 1125 he repudiated her and married another woman. After Sigurd died in 1130, Malfrid married King Erik of Denmark.

♦ **Divorce. Pawns.** ♦

Boyesen, *Story...*, pp. 302 & 304. Larsen, *History...*, p. 112. Vernadsky, *Kievan...*, p. 336.

MANFREDA

See—MAYFREDA.

MARGARET [Margaretha; Margarida; Margarita; Margherita; Marguerite]

MARGHERITA

1391 Italy

Slave and mistress of Gregorio Dati of Florence; mother of his illegitimate son—born in 1391.

♦ **Mistresses. Slaves.** ♦

O'Faolain, *Not in...*, p. 170.

MARGARET ALDOBRANDESCHI

c. 1260s–1300 Italy

Wealthy Tuscan heiress; around 1270 she married Guy de Montfort. Her second husband, Orsello Orsini, died in 1295, and she soon married Roffred Gaetani. At that time, Margaret already had a Sienese lover who was rumored to have murdered his wife in order to have Margaret. In 1298, she obtained a divorce from Roffred. Her many marriages, her "loose behavior," and her fight with the papacy caused her to lose some of her vast estates.

♦ **Adultery. Divorce. Estate. Murder. Popes. Soldiers.** ♦

Cambridge..., VII, pp. 8, 12, 17. Collison-Morley, *Sforzas...*, p. 20. Holmes, *Florence...*, pp. 22 & 168. Partner, *Lands...*, pp. 279, 287–288, 295.

MARGARET OF ALSACE

m. 1169–d. 1194 Flanders; Netherlands

Daughter of †Sybille of Anjou and Thierry of Alsace, count of Flanders. In 1169, Margaret married Baldwin V of Hainault (Baldwin VIII, count of Flanders); their daughter was †Isabella of Hainault.

♦ **Estate. Genealogy.** ♦

Anselme, *Histoire...*, v.2, pp. 723–724. Decaux, *Histoire...*, p. 268. Wolff, "Baldwin...," p. 281.

MARGARET OF ANJOU, queen of England

b. 1430–d. 1482 England; France

Daughter of René I of Anjou and his first wife, †Isabel of Lorraine. In 1445, Margaret married Henry VI of England. They were a happy couple and Margaret was a loving mother, but she had a disastrous effect on the English political scene. Henry's bouts of insanity prompted Margaret to take a particularly active governmental role. She promoted the divisions among the nobility which led to the Wars of the Roses. Although a good military leader, Margaret was an ineffective diplomat and negotiator. In 1471, Margaret and Henry were captured and their son killed. Margaret was returned to Anjou where she died in 1482.

♦ **Book owners. Hunting. Models. Negotiators. Prisons. Religious patrons. Rulers. Squabbles. Soldiers. Writers.** ♦

Butt, *History...*, pp. 529, 531–533, 544, 554, 555, 557–559, 562–566, 571, 588–589, 591, 596, 598–600, 607. Champion, *Louis...*, pp. 89–90, 101, 158, 159, 203, 211, 223. Cleugh, *Chant...*, pp. 69–70, 76–81, 95, 135–139, 147, 159, 162–164, 171, 199, 200, 207, 223, 280, 300. Clive, *Sun...*, pp. 3, 5, 11, 12, ... 228, 229, 246, 306. Commynes, *Memoirs...*, pp. 225, 428–429. Erlanger, *Margaret....* (a rather opinionated biography). Goodman, *Wars...*, pp. 1, 25–27, 41–42, 44–46, 52, 56–58, 66–67, 78, 80–82, 204, 215, 220. Green, *Letters...*, pp. 94–99. Griffiths and Thomas, *Making...*, pp. 33–34, 39, 41, 49, 51–52, 55, 57, 61–62, 65–67, 69, 72–73, 75. Hindley, *England...*, pp. 63–65, 67, 70, 71. Holmes, *Later...*, pp. 207, 216, 218–223. Huizinga, *Waning...*, pp. 11, 73, 300. Jacob, *Fifteenth...*, pp. 397, 441, 465, 475–578 ... 564, 567–569, 579, 670, 671. Johnson, *Duke...*, pp. 46, 49, 58, 66, 72, 74, 97, 122 ... 208, 214, 219, 220, 222. Kendall, *Yorkist...*, pp. 162, 175, 414, 420–423, 466, 474, 497. Lee, "Reflections...," pp. 183–217 passim. *Letters of Queen.....* Myers, *Household...Margaret.* *Oxford...Prose*, pp. xiv, 38–41, 417, 427. Ross, *Wars...*, pp. 24, 25, 32, 35–37, 47, 50–53, 59–60, 62, 65, 85–86, 90, 93, 116, 122, 124–126, 128, 138, 143, 147–148. Scofield, *Life...*, I, pp. 116–117, 134, 176–177, 247–248, 558, 583, 589; II, pp. 23, 27, 159. St. Aubyn, *Year...*, pp. 38, 39, 43–46, 48, 55, 57, 58. Vale, *Charles...*, pp. 66, 90, 104, 161, 182, 188.

MARGARET OF ARTOIS, countess of Flanders

See—MARGARET OF FRANCE, countess of Flanders.

MARGARET DE AUDLEY, lady Stafford **[Audele]**

m. 1336 England

Daughter of †Margaret de Clare, countess of Gloucester, and Hugh de Audley. Margaret married Ralph, lord Stafford; their children were Ralph and Hugh de Stafford.

♦ **Estate. Genealogy.** ♦

C.P., v.5, p. 719. *DNB*, v.18, p. 866. Given-Wilson, *English...*, pp. 40–42. Rawcliffe, *Staffords...*, pp. 8, 9, 10.

MARGARET OF AUSTRIA

b. 1480–d. 1530 Austria; Flanders; France; Netherlands; Spain

Daughter of †Marie of Burgundy and Maximilian of Austria. Well-educated at French court in arts, medicine, and science. In 1497, Margaret married Juan, prince of Aragon and Castile. He died in the same year, and Margaret gave birth to a stillborn baby. In 1501, she married Philibert of Savoy (d.1505). In 1504, she became regent of the Netherlands. Margaret was an excellent ruler. She was an art patron, raised her nephew Charles I of Spain (Holy Roman Emperor Charles V), and served as a mediator.

♦ **Art patrons. Childbirth. Childcare. Educated. Medicine. Negotiators. Pawns. Regents. Rulers. Widows.** ♦

Altamira, *Spain*, p. 291. Cleugh, *Chant...*, pp. 255–256, 275, 287–290. Clive, *Sun...*, pp. 233, 265, 274, 292–3. Commynes, *Memoirs...*, pp. 366, 384, 399, 404, 410, 411, 413, 415, 421, 449, 450, 585. Iongh, *Margaret...* (a popular biography). Miller, *Castles...*, pp. 166–168, 170–175, 182, 188, 198, 203, 207, 217, 245, 249, 291, 297, 350. Smith, *Spain*, pp. 116, 138, 149.

MARGARET OF AUSTRIA

See—MARGARET OF BABENBURG.

MARGUERITE (l'avenière)

1292 France

Sold oats and corn in 1292 Paris; taxed 14s.

♦ **Merchants. Provisioning–grains.** ♦

Géraud, *Paris sous...*, p. 13.

MARGARET OF BABENBERG **[Margaret of Austria]**

b. 1210s–1260s Austria; Bohemia; Germany

Daughter of Leopold of Austria; married (1) Henry (son of Emperor Frederick II) in 1225. After Henry died, she took vow of chastity and entered Dominican convent at Trier. However, Ottakar II of Bohemia forced her to marry him in hopes of collecting the Austrian crown for himself. (She was one of two claimants for throne of Austria.) He soon repudiated her in order to marry †Kunigunda of Hungary. Margaret presumably returned to the convent.

♦ **Adultery. Divorce. Estate. Pawns. Queens. Religieuses. Virginity–vows. Widows.** ♦

Cambridge..., VI, pp. 88, 89, 91, 93, 437, 438. Harrsen, *Cursus...*, p. 52. Haverkamp, *Medieval...*, p. 262. Maurice, *Bohemia...*, pp. 85 & 86. Runciman, *Sicilian...*, p. 26. Stubbs, *Later...*, p. 72. Van Cleve, *Emperor...*, pp. 355 & 360.

MARGUERITE (la barbière)

1310 France

A barber of Pas-de-Calais; in 1310, †Mahaut of Artois paid Margaret 6s for healing a child's wound.

♦ **Barbers.** ♦

Hughes, *Women...*, p. 140. Labarge, *Women...*, p. 177. Wickersheimer, *Dictionnaire...*, v.2, p. 537.

MARGARET OF BAVARIA

c. 1410s–1420s Austria; France; Germany

See—ALISON DUMAY and ISABEL OF LORRAINE, queen of Naples.

♦ **Divorce. Genealogy.** ♦

MARGARET OF BAVARIA

c. 1470 Austria; Germany; Italy

See—CHIARA GONZAGA and ELISABETTA GONZAGA, duchess of Urbino.

♦ **Genealogy.** ♦

MARGARET BEAUCHAMP, countess of Shrewsbury

m.c. 1433–d. 1467 England

Oldest daughter of †Elizabeth Berkeley and Richard Beauchamp, earl of Warwick. Around 1433, Margaret married John Talbot, first earl of Shrewsbury; their children: John, Humphrey, Lewis, †Eleanor, and †Elizabeth Talbot. Margaret was strong-willed and ambitious. She continued her mother's fight for the Berkeley estates for some thirty years.

♦ **Managers. Politics. Squabbles.** ♦

Champion, *Louis...*, p. 101. *DNB,* v.19, p. 323. Johnson, *Duke...*, p. 103. Kendall, *Yorkist...*, pp. 413–414.

MARGARET BEAUFORT, countess of Richmond and Derby

1443–1509 England

Daughter of John Beaufort, duke of Somerset, and Margaret Beauchamp (daughter of Sir John Beauchamp of Bletsoe). Married: (1) John de la Pole (heir of Suffolk)—annulled 1453; (2) in 1455, Edmund Tudor, earl of Richmond (d.1456)—their son Henry, later became Henry VII of England; (3) Henry Stafford (d.1482), the second son of Humphrey, first duke of Buckingham; and (4) Thomas, lord Stanley, later earl of Derby (d.1504). Margaret was well-educated, cultured, and pious. She commissioned, translated, and/or published several religious books. She was an art patron, started many schools, and endowed hospitals. Due to the political climate, Margaret rarely saw her son Henry during his early years. Nevertheless, she worked tirelessly to help him return to England, and to set him on the throne. Once Henry became king, Margaret served him well as an occasional political advisor.

♦ **Art patrons. Divorce. Educated. Estate. Patrons of literature. Politics. Religious patrons. Teachers. Widows. Writers.** ♦

Bennett, "Good...," p. 15. Butt, *History...*, pp. 533, 537, 541, 547, 621, 622. Clive, *Sun...*, pp. 72–3, 107, 157, 192, 245, 253, 291, 295, 304–5. *DNB,* v. XVIII, pp. 859, 964, 965. Gardiner, *English...*, pp. 103–106. Goodman, *Wars...*, pp. 86–87, 90, 134, 210. Griffiths and Thomas, *Making...*, pp. 30, 35–37, 42, 47–48, 60, 68–69, 71, 82–83, 85, 88, 91–103, 108–115, 124, 127, 146, 156, 175, 178, 183–190. Jacob, *Fifteenth...*, pp. 476, 492, 621, 627, 632. Kendall, *Yorkist...*, pp. 426–428. McFarlane, *Nobility...*, pp. 206 & 207. Mertes, *English...*, pp. 43, 54, 85, 144, 145, 210. Orme, *Education...*, p. 18. *Oxford...Prose,* pp. 438–439, 442. Power, *Women...*, p. 48. Ross, *Wars...*, pp. 92, 93, 97–99. Scofield, *Life...*, I, pp. 8 & 202–203. St. Aubyn, *Year...*, pp. 126, 168–169, 189, 190, 193, 198.

MARGARET DE BOHUN, countess of Devon [Margaret Courteney]

b. 1315–d. 1391 England

Daughter of †Elizabeth of England and Humphrey de Bohun, earl of Hereford. Married Hugh Courteney, earl of Devon (d.1377).

♦ **Book owners. Educated. Managers. Widows. Writers–letters.** ♦

C.P., v.6, p. 469. *DNB,* v.4, p. 1267. McFarlane, *Nobility...*, p. 236. *Stonor...*, v.1, pp. 27–28.

MARGUERITE LA BONNE ESTRANEE

fl. 1440s–1450s France

At Number Nine Petit Pont in Paris, Marguerite made and sold linen cloth.

♦ **Clothworkers–linen. Land/property.** ♦

Comptes du..., pp. 650 & 708.

MARGARET DE BOTREAUX, lady Hungerford

c. 1420s–d. 1477 England

Daughter of Elizabeth Beaumont and William de Botreaux; married Robert, lord Hungerford (d.1459). Interested in piety and education, Margaret founded a least one school. In the 1450s, she used much of their wealth to ransom their son, Robert, lord Moleyns. When she wrote her will in 1476, she bemoaned the fact that she had been obliged to deplete the family fortune by paying ransoms.

♦ **Banking. Bequests. Charity. Legal activity. Managers. Religious patrons. Teachers. Widows. Writers.** ♦

C.P., v.6, pp. 617–618. Hindley, *England...*, pp. 154, 185. McFarlane, *Nobility...*, pp. 29, 126, 127. Orme, *Education...*, pp. 18, 143–146.

MARGUERITE DE BOURBON

fl. 1460–d. 1483 France

Daughter of †Agnes of Burgundy and Charles I, duke of Bourbon. In 1472 Marguerite married Philip II of Savoy, count of Bresse; mother of †Louise of Savoy.

♦ **Dowry/dower. Genealogy.** ♦

Anselme, *Histoire...*, v.1, p. 308. Commynes, *Memoirs...*, p. 98.

MARGUERITE DE BOURBON, queen of Navarre

fl. 1230s–d. 1257 France; Spain

Daughter of Béatrix de Montlucon and Archambaud VIII of Bourbon. Third wife of Thibaut of Champagne, king of Navarre (d.1253). She was regent for their minor son, Thibaut (d.1270).

♦ **Regents. Widows. Writers–letters.** ♦

Anselme, *Histoire...*, v.2, p. 843. Bréquigny, *Lettres de rois...*, p. 92. Fawtier, *Capetian...*, p. 127. Leroy, *La Navarre...*, p. 44. Shneidman, *Rise...*, p. 311.

MARGARET OF BRABANT, countess of Flanders

fl. 1350s–d. 1368 Belgium; Flanders

Daughter of John III of Brabant; married Louis III de Male, count of Flanders; mother of †Margaret (de Male) of Flanders, duchess of Burgundy.

♦ **Book owners. Murder. Prisons.** ♦

Hardy, *Philippa...*, pp. 102, 139, 165, 170, 172. Hughes, "Library...," pp. 31 & 34. Tuchman, *Distant...*, p. 93. Vaughan, *Philip...*, p. 95.

MARGARET OF BRABANT, Holy Roman Empress

fl. 1290s–d.c. 1311 Belgium; Germany; Italy; Luxembourg

Daughter of John I of Brabant; married Henry VII of Luxembourg; crowned empress around 1308. Margaret was pious, charitable, and very sensible, so she was quite popular and was a good advisor to her husband.

♦ **Charity. Negotiators. Plague.** ♦

Blok, *History...*, Gen. Table. Braunstein, "Toward...," p. 557. *Cambridge...*, VII, pp. 32, 33, 34, 94, 99. Chubb, *Dante...*, pp. 609–610, 622–623, 642–643.

MARGARET DE BRAOSE **[de Briouze]**

fl.c. 1190s–1220s England; France

Daughter of †Maud (of St. Valery) and William de Braose. When her mother and brother were captured in 1210, Margaret and her husband, Walter de Lacy, escaped King John's wrath by fleeing to France. King John later granted Margaret some land on which to found a nunnery to benefit the souls of her father, mother, and brother.

♦ **Estate. Politics. Religious patrons.** ♦

DNB, v.11, p. 391. Powicke, "Loretta...," pp. 149, 158, 160, 165.

MARGARET OF BURGUNDY **[Marguerite de Bourgogne]**

m. 1305–d. 1314 France

Daughter of †Agnes of France and Robert II, duke of Burgundy; married the future Louis X of France. She was imprisoned for her part in adultery scandal involving three daughters-in-law of Philip IV of France.

Margaret supposedly dallied with her lovers, Philippe and Gautier d'Aulnay at the Tour de Nesle. Marguerite died—or was killed—in prison. Her daughter was †Jeanne of France, queen of Navarre.

♦ **Adultery. Models. Prisons.** ♦

Butler, *Women...*, pp. 260–262. Calmette, *Golden...*, pp. 15 & 23. Champion, *François...*, pp. 217 & 218. Champion, *Louis...*, p. 299. *DBF*, v.4, p. 644. Decaux, *Histoire...*, pp. 362–365. Denieul-Cormier, *Wise...*, p. 61. Fawtier, *Capetian...*, pp. 53 & 129.

MARGARET OF BURGUNDY

b. 1393–d. 1442 France

Daughter of †Margaret of Hainault (of Bavaria) and Duke John the Fearless of Burgundy. Married (1) Louis of Guyenne (d. 1415) and (2) Arthur, count of Richemont. †Christine de Pisan wrote *Livre de Trois Vertus* for Margaret.

♦ **Book owners. Dowry/dower. Educated. Widows.** ♦

Calmette, *Golden...*, pp. 144 & 316. Coryn, *House...*, p. 127. Vale, *Charles...*, pp. 35–6. Vaughan, *Philip...*, pp. 82, 91 & n. Willard, "Christine...," pp. 97 & 98.

MARGARETHA CARTHEUSERIN **[Karthauserin]**

fl. 1452–1470 Germany

Nun at St. Catherine's in Nuremberg; scribe and illuminator. Probably Margaretha did most of the script while her fellow nuns produced most of the miniatures.

♦ **Bookmaking. Educated. Nuns. Writers–copyists/scribes.** ♦

Carr, "Women...," p. 8. Greer, *Obstacle...*, pp. 161–162. Harksen, *Women...*, p. 46.

MARGUERITE (la chanevacière)

1292 France

Marguerite was a well-to-do cloth merchant; for making and selling hemp cloth, she paid extremely high £7 15s in the 1292 Paris tax collection.

♦ **Clothworkers–hemp. Land/property. Merchants.** ♦

Géraud, *Paris sous...*, p. 21.

MARGARET OF CITTA DI CASTELLO

[Blessed Margaret of Meteola]

c. 1287–1320 Italy

Blind and deformed from birth, the orphaned Margaret became a Dominican tertiary as well as a servant. She was particularly known for caring for children. To benefit working parents, she even established what might be called a "day care center" in modern terms.

♦ **Childcare. Handicapped. Orphans. Religieuses. Servants.** ♦

Attwater, *Dictionary...*, p. 200. Bynum, *Holy...*, pp. 145, 273, 308 n6, 360 n174. Goodich, "Ancilla Dei...," pp. 130–131. Goodich, "Contours...," p. 24.

MARGARET DE CLARE, countess of Gloucester

c. 1290s–1330s England

Daughter of †Joan of England (of Acre) and Gilbert de Clare, earl of Gloucester. Married (1) Piers Gaveston and (2) (in 1317) Hugh de Audele (Audley). Owned property in London as well as eventually inheriting the honour of Gloucester. The Despensers took some of her estate.

♦ **Estate. Negotiators. Rebellions.** ♦

Calendar of Plea..., I, pp. 63 & 87–88. Fryde, *Tyranny...*, pp. 34, 35, 62. Gardner, *Life...*, p. 42. Given-Wilson, *English...*, pp. 40–41. Hallam (ed.), *Four...*, p. 170. Rawcliffe, *Staffords...*, p. 8.

MARGUERITE DE CLISSON, countess of Penthièvre

[Margaret de Blois]

fl. 1380s–1420s France

Daughter of Olivier de Clisson; married Jean de Penthièvre (d.1404). Marguerite vigorously carried on her husband's fight for the duchy of Brittany. She allied herself with the dauphin Louis, and then imprisoned Duke John VI of Brittany (see †Jeanne de Montfort). Marguerite eventually lost the war and was forced to flee the country.

♦ **Managers. Negotiators. Prisons. Soldiers. Squabbles. Widows.** ♦

Durtelle, *Bretagne*, pp. 271, 282–283, 285. Froissart, *Chronicles...*, I, pp. 381–382, 396, 398–401. Jones, *Creation...*, pp. 52, 269, 272, 274–275, 277, 282, 343. Jones, *Ducal...*, p. 99. Wolf, *Bluebeard...*, pp. 22–26.

MARGARET COBBE

fl. 1469–1476 England

Midwife to †Elizabeth Woodville, queen of England. Among other gifts, she received £10 gold annually.

♦ **Midwives. Nurses. Servants.** ♦

Hurd-Mead, *History...*, p. 313. Strickland, *Lives...*, pp. 220, 222 n1. Talbot and Hammond, *Medical...*, pp. 209–210.

MARGUERITE (la cordière)

1292 France

Dame Marguerite was a successful rope-maker in Paris; she paid tax of 40s in 1292.

♦ **Land/property. Merchants–rope.** ♦

Géraud, *Paris sous...*, p. 138.

(St.) MARGARET OF CORTONA **[Blessed Marguerite]**

b. 1247–d. 1297 Italy

Known as a penitential saint. Margaret was a young nobleman's mistress for several years and bore his illegitimate child. After her lover was killed, Margaret repented her loose ways and became a Franciscan tertiary. She had visions, cared for the sick, and worked to convert other sinners.

♦ **Medicine. Mistresses. Mystics. Negotiators. Preachers. Saints. Unmarried.** ♦

A.S., Feb. v.3, pp. 302–363. Attwater, *Dictionary...*, p. 200. Bynum, *Holy...*, pp. 2, 24, 58, 86, 140, 141, 145–147, 171, 172, 177, 204, 214, 221, 229, 233, 253, 256. Cuthbert, *Tuscan Penitent....* Farmer, *Oxford...*, p. 261. Goodich, "Contours...," p. 29. Holmes, *Florence...*, pp. 53, 55, 62–65, 67, 119. Mauriac, *St. Margaret....* Robbins, *Encyclopedia...*, p. 257.

MARGARET COURTENEY, countess of Devon

See—MARGARET DE BOHUN, countess of Devon.

MARGHERITA DATINI **[Margherita di Domenico Bandini]**

b. 1360–d. 1423 Italy

In 1376 married wealthy merchant, Francesco Datini of Prato (d.1410). Margherita ran large household, assisted by several slaves. Possibly because one of these was her husband's mistress, Margherita was uncomfortable and mistrustful of her slaves.

♦ **Childcare. Educated. Managers. Slaves–owners. Widows. Writers–letters.** ♦

Anderson and Zinsser, *A History of...*, pp. 139, 374–6, 379, 385, 440, 442, 443. Gies, *Merchants...*, pp. 191–193. Gies, *Women...*, pp. 184–207, 212, 228–232. Origo, "Domestic...," pp. 341–345.

MARGARET OF DENMARK, queen of Norway

b. 1353–d. 1412 Denmark; Norway; Sweden

Daughter of Waldemar IV of Denmark (d.1375); married Haakon VI of Norway; son Olaf V. After Haakon died in 1380, Margaret became regent of Denmark and Norway for five-year-old Olaf who died in 1387. By 1389, Margaret defeated Albert of Mecklenburg and became Sweden's acknowledged ruler. She negotiated the *Union of Kalmar* to protect Scandinavia from absorption by German Hanseatic League. Although she was regent for her nephew Eric of Pomerania (whom she personally educated), Margaret was the real ruler of Scandinavia even after he came of age in 1401. She was a particularly effective leader, securing peace, protecting peasant farmers, and stabilizing the Scandinavian economy. Margaret reportedly died of plague on board her ship in 1412.

♦ **Childcare. Educated. Negotiators. Plague. Regents. Religious patrons. Rulers. Shipping. Soldiers. Teachers. Widows.** ♦

Andersson, *History...*, pp. 51, 62, 72–73, 75–77. Derry, *History...*, pp. 69–75. Larsen, *History...*, pp. 196–199, 203–204, 208, 212. Musset, *Les Peuples...*, pp. 298–303. Oakley, *History...*, pp. 78 & 81. Previte-Orton, *Outlines...*, pp. 425–430. Previte-Orton, *Shorter...*, pp. 913–914. Scott, *Sweden...*, pp. 77–86, 87, 113, 167.

MARGARET EBNER
1291–1351 Germany

Nun in convent of St. Mary at Medingen. As her health declined, her visions increased. Heinrich von Nördlingen believed she had psychic gifts. Her *Revelations* detail her visions.

♦ **Mystics. Nuns. Writers.** ♦

Braunstein, "Toward...," pp. 614, 625, 626, 627. Goodich, "Contours...," p. 31. Harksen, *Women...*, p. 34. Howell et al, "Documented...," p. 119. Lagorio, "Continental...," pp. 172–173. McDonnell, *Beguines...*, p. 404.

MARGARET ELYOTT
1496 England

In London court of 1496, Margaret charged that her husband Nicolas was in violation of ecclesiastical marital rules since he no longer rendered the conjugal debt (was no longer making love to her). Nicolas was admonished to return home and fulfill his marital obligations.

♦ **Ecclesiastical courts. Legal activity–conjugal debt.** ♦

Hair, *Bawdy...*, p. 117 (#270).

(St.) MARGARET OF ENGLAND [Marguerite of Sauve Benité]
d. 1192 England; France

Presumably an English nun before she moved to France. She was evidently fond of traveling since she made pilgrimages to the Holy Land and a variety of other sites. She eventually settled as a Cistercian nun at Sauve Benité. Her shrine there later became a holy site due to the many miracles which were attributed to her relics.

♦ **Nuns. Pilgrims. Relics. Saints.** ♦

Attwater, *Dictionary...*, pp. 200–201. Farmer, *Oxford...*, p. 261. Mongour, *Sainte Marguerite....*

MARGARET OF ENGLAND, duchess of Brabant
b. 1275–d. 1318 Belgium; England

Daughter of †Eleanor of Castile and Edward I of England. Married John II, duke of Brabant in 1290.

♦ **Genealogy.** ♦

Bryant, *Age...*, pp. 123–124. *DNB*, v.6, p. 456. Pirenne, *Histoire...*, I, p. 339; II, p. 10. Powicke, *Thirteenth...*, pp. 268, 511, 512, 513, 664, 680. Prestwich, *Edward...*, pp. 111, 126–127, 129, 317, 387. Williamson, *Kings...*, p. 72.

MARGARET OF ENGLAND, countess of Pembroke
b. 1346–d.c. 1362 England

Daughter of †Philippa of Hainault and Edward III of England. First wife of John de Hastings, earl of Pembroke.

♦ **Genealogy.** ♦

DNB, v.9, p. 132. Hardy, *Philippa...,* pp. 152, 168, 178, 184, 206, 230–1, 252, 255–6, 258, 262, 266, 269, 273, 298, 301, 304, 311. Rosenthal, *Nobles...,* p. 174.

MARGARET OF ENGLAND, queen of Scotland

b. 1240–d.c. 1274 England; Scotland

Daughter of †Eleanor of Provence and Henry III of England. In 1251 at York, Margaret married Alexander III of Scotland; daughter †Margaret was born in 1261. Queen Margaret felt that she was mistreated in her new home, and she made sure that her family in England was aware of her unhappiness. This caused problems between England and Scotland.

♦ **Dowry/dower. Queens. Squabbles. Writers–letters.** ♦

Brown, *History...,* p. 120. *DNB,* v.1, pp. 264–266. Duncan, *Scotland...,* pp. 536, 560, 561, 563–566, 569, 571, 573, 576, 577, 589, 590. Glover, *Story...,* pp. 71 & 72. Lancaster, "Artists...," p. 88. Mackie, *History...,* p. 47. Mackie, *Short...,* p. 47. Powicke, *Thirteenth...,* pp. 571, 582, 585, 588, 589–591, 593. Prestwich, *Edward...,* pp. 57 & 356.

MARGARETHA VAN EYCK

fl.c. 1400–d.c. 1430 Belgium; Flanders

Believed to have been the sister of famed artist Jan van Eyck. She was presumably an illuminator in Bruges. Margaretha may also have worked on some of her brother's larger paintings.

♦ **Artists. Bookmaking.** ♦

Clement, *Women...,* pp. xvi & 119–120. Crowe, *Early...,* pp. 129–132. Greer, *Obstacle...,* pp. 29 & 164. Jany, "Women...," p. 253. Munsterberg, *History...,* p. 18.

MARGARET, countess of FLANDERS

b. 1202–d.c. 1280 Flanders

Daughter of †Marie (II) of Champagne and Baldwin IX of Flanders. Margaret's parents died on Crusade around 1205. In 1212, she married Bourchard d'Avesnes of Hainault—a marriage which was called illegitimate. Margaret later married William of Dampierre. She fought to have only her sons by William inherit. After Margaret's sister †Jeanne died in 1244, Margaret ruled Flanders, encouraged economic growth, accompanied Louis IX on Crusade, and aided the Beguines.

♦ **Beguines. Crusades. Divorce. Orphans. Popes. Religious patrons. Rulers. Squabbles.** ♦

Bryant, *Age...,* p. 114. *Cambridge...,* VI, pp. 109, 111, 127, 128, 130, 359. Heer, *Medieval...,* p. 262. Herlihy, *Opera...,* pp. 60 & 68. Jordan, *Louis...,* pp. 44 & 45. Lehmann, *Rôle de la...,* p. 388. Le Patourel, *Feudal...,* XV, pp. 169 & 171. McDonnell, *Beguines...,* pp. 111–112, 201, 209, 213. Werveke, "Industrial...," pp. 240–241. Wolff, "Baldwin...," pp. 286–299.

MARGARET OF FLANDERS, duchess of Burgundy

[Margaret de Male]

b. 1349–d. 1405 Flanders; France

Daughter and heiress of †Margaret of Brabant and Louis III de Male, count of Flanders (d.1384). Married (1) Philip of Rouvres (d.1361). In 1369, Margaret married Philip the Bold, duke of Burgundy; mother of John the Fearless.

♦ **Art patrons. Book owners. Builders. Educated. Estate. Games. Music. Negotiators. Patrons of literature. Regents. Teachers.** ♦

Armitage-Smith, *John...*, pp. 28–31. Bryant, *Age...*, pp. 426 & 440. Calmette, *Golden...*, pp. 21, 33–36, 54, 55, 61, 75, 185, 231, 301, 306. Cartellieri, *Court...*, pp. 1–2 & 29. Commynes, *Memoirs...*, pp. 294 & 330. Froissart, *Chronicles...*, I, pp. 173, 277, 299; II, pp. 101, 106, 108, 134–137, 140, 162, 165, 173, 174, 177, 178, 181. Hughes, "Library...," pp. 145–188 passim. Palmer, "England,...," pp. 343, 352, 358. Tuchman, *Distant...*, pp. 257–258, 492, 520, 523, 576, 606. Vaughan, *Philip...*, pp. 4–6, 16, 18, 32, 38, 52 ... 191–193, 204, 212, 219n, 234, 239.

MARGARET OF FRANCE, queen of England

b. 1282–d. 1318 England; France

Daughter of Philip III of France and his second wife, †Marie de Brabant. In 1299, Margaret became the second wife of elderly King Edward I of England (d.1307). Their children were Thomas of Brotherton and Edmund of Woodstock. Margaret was a patroness of the church and of artists and architects during her ten years of widowhood.

♦ **Art patrons. Charity. Music. Queens. Religious patrons. Widows.** ♦

Bryant, *Age...*, pp. 169, 170, 172, 175, 177, 179, 183. *Calendar of Wills...*, I, pp. 337–338. Hardy, *Philippa...*, p. 19. McFarlane, *Nobility...*, p. 264. Prestwich, *Edward...*, pp. 115, 129–131, 164, 379, 395–396, 483, 501, 510, 520–521, 533, 550, 557. Riley, *Memorials...*, p. 55.

MARGARET OF FRANCE, countess of Flanders

[Margaret of Artois]

b. 1310–d. 1382 Flanders; France

Daughter of †Jeanne of Burgundy and Philip V of France. Margaret married Louis of Nevers, count of Flanders (d.1346); their son was Louis III de Male, count of Flanders (d.1384).

♦ **Managers. Negotiators. Politics.** ♦

Anselme, *Histoire...*, v.2, p. 738. Armitage-Smith, *John...*, p. 29. Palmer, "England...," p. 347. Vaughan, *Philip...*, pp. 3, 5, 13, 16–18, 21, 113, 129, 153–154, 165, 210.

MARGARET OF FRANCE, queen of Hungary

b. 1158–d.c. 1197 England; France; Hungary

Daughter of Louis VII of France and his second wife, †Constance of Castile. Married Henry "the young king," prince of England (son of

Henry II and †Eleanor of Aquitaine). After he died in 1183, Margaret became the second wife of King Béla III of Hungary.

♦ **Dowry/dower. Legal activity. Models. Queens.** ♦

Baldwin, *Government...*, pp. 19–20, 28, 35, 269, 363. Barlow, *Feudal...*, pp. 288, 301, 350. Barlow, *Thomas...*, pp. 55, 57, 58, 60–61, 67, 204, 206, 208, 210, 269. Bingham, *Crowned...*, pp. 71, 74, 89 & 121. *Cambridge...*, V, pp. 611, 612; VI, pp. 294, 301, 467. *DNB,* v.9, pp. 546 & 547. Hallam (ed.), *Plantagenet...*, pp. 104, 108, 124, 130, 164, 176, 178. Kelleher, *Holy...*, p. 108, Table 1. Kelly, *Eleanor...*, pp. 106, 108, 111, 117 ... 229, 285, 289, 331. Pamlényi, *History...*, p. 60. Pernoud, *Eleanor...*, pp. 120, 122, 123, 133, 148, 157, 185. Warren, *Henry...*, pp. 72, 77, 88, 90, 111, 145, 506, 582, 598, 609, 611.

MARGARET OF HAINAULT, duchess of Burgundy
[Marguerite of Bavaria]

fl. 1370s–1410s — Flanders; France; Germany

Daughter of Margaret of Brieg and Albert of Bavaria. Married (c.1385) John of Nevers (later John the Fearless, duke of Burgundy); their son Philip the Good of Burgundy was born in 1396. Margaret was well-educated and pious. she was also known as a very austere woman.

♦ **Dowry/dower. Educated. Models.** ♦

Coryn, *House...*, p. 107. Denieul-Cormier, *Wise...*, pp. 170 & 172. Froissart, *Chronicles...*, I, p. 299; II, p. 162. Vaughan, *Philip...*, pp. 86–88, 93, 109.

MARGARET OF HAINAULT, Holy Roman Empress

c. 1310s–d. 1356 — Flanders; Germany; Netherlands

Daughter of †Jeanne de Valois and William the Good, count of Hainault and Holland. Married Louis of Bavaria, later Holy Roman Emperor. Margaret was a supporter of Beguine communities; she also introduced the *florin* in Hainault.

♦ **Banking. Beguines. Estate. Religious patrons. Squabbles. Widows.** ♦

Cambridge..., VII, pp. 129, 134, 146, 449. *DNB,* v.15, p. 1050. Gardner, *Life...*, p. 117. Hardy, *Philippa...*, pp. 30, 32, 42, 65, 105, 107, 149, 166, 225. Hazlitt, *Coinage...*, p. 394. McDonnell, *Beguines...*, p. 212. Stubbs, *Later...*, pp. 105 & 115.

MARGARET HOLLAND, duchess of Clarence

c. 1390s–d.c. 1437 — England

Daughter of Alice FitzAlan and Thomas Holland, earl of Kent. She married (1) John Beaufort of Somerset (d.1410). Around 1412, Margaret married Thomas of Lancaster, duke of Clarence (d.1421).

♦ **Managers.** ♦

Given-Wilson, *English...*, pp. 51–52. Griffiths and Thomas, *Making...*, pp. 30 & 35. Kelly, "Canonical...," pp. 286–289. McFarlane, *Nobility...*, p. 112. Williamson, *Kings...*, p. 86.

MARGARET, lady HUNGERFORD

See—MARGARET DE BOTREAUX, lady Hungerford.

MARGARET OF HUNGARY **[Blessed Margaret]**

1242–1271 Hungary

Daughter of Béla IV, king of Hungary. Margaret was a nun; noted for extreme piety and self-abuse. She has been identified with the Dominicans, and even with a group of Hungarian Beguines. Popularly claimed as a national saint; she reputedly prevented the Danube from overflowing.

♦ **Beguines. Nuns. Saints–popular. Servants. Virginity.** ♦

Attwater, *Dictionary...*, p. 201. Bynum, *Holy...*, pp. 135, 136, 146, 203, 204, 222, 275. Fügedi, *Castle...*, p. 87. Goodich, "Ancilla Dei...," p. 134. Goodich, "Contours...," pp. 20, 23, 29. Pamlényi, *History...*, p. 609.

MARGUERITE JOLI

fl. 1450s–c. 1479 France

Wife of Robert (or Robin) Turgis, a Parisian wine merchant. He owned the celebrated tavern (written about by François Villon) *Pomme de Pin* on the rue de la Juiverie. Marguerite was a member of a confraternity with a Parisian church, where she had Robert's anniversary service (c.1473). She was authorized to take over Robert's business, which she ran until around 1478. Among her other charitable donations, Marguerite contributed a £4 rent from one of her houses to the abbesses of Longchamp.

♦ **Alewives. Bequests. Charity. Land/property. Models. Religious patrons. Taverners. Widows.** ♦

Champion, *François...*, I, p. 135; II, pp. 370–371. Lewis, *François...*, pp. 43 & 129.

MARGARET LACY, countess of Lincoln **[Margaret de Quincy]**

c. 1220s–d. 1266 England

Daughter and heiress of Ranulf, earl of Lincoln and Chester; second wife of John de Lacy, and mother of his heir, Edmund Lacy, earl of Lincoln. After her husband died, Margaret commissioned Robert Grosseteste to compile a book for her about estate management.

♦ **Book owners. Managers. Patrons of literature. Widows.** ♦

Anderson and Zinsser, *A History of...*, p. 289. Barrow, *Feudal...*, pp. 332 & 333. *DNB*, v. XI, p. 380. Gardiner, *English...*, pp. 65–66. Power, *Women...*, p. 47.

MARGARET OF LEICESTER, countess of Winchester

[Margaret Beaumont]

c. 1170s–d. 1235 England

Daughter of †Petronilla of Grandmesnil and Robert III de Beaumont, earl of Leicester (d.1190); became co-heiress of the earldom (with her sister †Amicia of Leicester) when her brother Robert IV, called fitzParnel, died. Margaret married Saer de Quincy, first earl of Winchester; mother of Robert, Roger, Reginald, and Hawyse, countess of Oxford.

♦ **Estate. Genealogy.** ♦

DNB, v.16, pp. 556–557. Labarge, *Simon...,* pp. 17 & 35. Powicke, "Loretta...," p. 154. Powicke, *Thirteenth...,* p. 75n. Waugh, "Marriage...," p. 200n.

MARGARET LINDSAY

1435 England

A court in Edlingham, Northumberland, acquitted Margaret of withcraft charges in 1435. Three men had accused her of planting a magic stake which had made them impotent.

♦ **Superstitions. Witchcraft.** ♦

Ewen, *Witchcraft...,* p. 37. Hair, *Bawdy...,* p. 182 (#461).

MARGARET OF LOGY, queen of Scotland [Margaret Drummond]

b. 1323–d.c. 1375 Scotland

Daughter of Sir Malcolm de Drummond. Around 1340 she married Sir John Logie (d.c.1359). In 1363, Margaret became second wife of King David II of Scotland. She was generally considered to be an unworthy queen. In 1369, David divorced her. Although Margaret went to Rome to appeal the divorce, David died before the decision could be reversed.

♦ **Divorce. Legal activity. Models. Pilgrims. Popes.** ♦

Allan, "Historical...," pp. 334–360. Brown, *History...,* I, p. 179. Mackie, *History...,* p. 88.

MARGUERITE OF LORRAINE, duchess of Alencon [Blessed Margaret]

b. 1463–d. 1521 France

Married René of Alençon; when he died, Marguerite had to care for her three young children and rule their duchy. She was also known for her piety and her charity to the poor. In 1519, Marguerite retired to a convent of Poor Clares.

♦ **Charity. Regents. Religieuses. Widows.** ♦

Attwater, *Dictionary...,* p. 201. *DBF,* v.1, p. 1417. Putnam, *Marguerite...,* pp. 64, 79, 84, 88–89, 145, 347.

MARGARET OF MAINE

fl. 1040s–1060s France

Daughter of †Bertha of Chartres and her second husband Hugh, count of Maine. When he died around 1051, Margaret and her mother and brother (Herbert II) fled from Geoffrey Martel, count of Anjou, to asylum with William of Normandy. In the 1060s, she was betrothed to William's oldest son, Robert Curthose (sources differ over whether or not the actual marriage ever took place).

♦ **Estate. Models. Pawns. Politics.** ♦

Barlow, *Feudal...*, pp. 139–140. Bates, *Normandy...*, p. 82. *DNB*, v.16, p. 1235. Douglas, *William...*, Tables 7 & 9. Vitalis, *Ecclesiastical...*, v.2, pp. 116–117, 304–305, 310–311.

MARGARET MARSHALL, countess of Norfolk

[Margaret Brotherton; Seagrave; Plantagenet]

m. 1338–d.c. 1399 England

Daughter of Thomas Brotherton, earl of Norfolk and marshal of England (d.1338). Married John de Segrave (d.1353) who became earl of Norfolk in Margaret's right. Her second husband was Walter Mauny (Walter de Many; d.1372). Margaret inherited vast estates, was politically active, and was noted for her donations to various religious establishments. In 1397, she was created duchess in her own right.

♦ **Childcare. Estate. Managers. Politics. Religious patrons. Squabbles. Widows.** ♦

Calendar of Plea..., I, pp. 174 & 185–186. Given-Wilson, *English...*, pp. 50, 53, 102, 148. McFarlane, *Nobility...*, pp. 65–66, 100, 137–138. Riley, *Memorials...*, p. 431. Robertson, *Chaucer's...*, p. 25. Rosenthal, *Nobles...*, pp. 107–108 & 139–140. Tuck, *Richard...*, pp. 52, 95–96, 174.

MARGARET MAULTASCH

[Margaretha Maultasche, countess of Tyrol]

m.c. 1330–d.c. 1370 Austria; Bohemia; Germany

Daughter and heiress of Henry, duke of the Tyrol. Around 1330, Margaret married John Henry of Bohemia. Around 1340, Margaret fell in love with Louis of Brandenburg (Emperor Louis of Bavaria's son) and drove her husband out. To obtain a divorce, she claimed that John had been bewitched into impotency. She then married Louis of Brandenburg. John was the brother of Charles IV (who later became Holy Roman Emperor), so this situation caused political upheavals as Charles tried to help avenge John's honor.

♦ **Adultery. Divorce. Politics. Popes. Superstitions.** ♦

Cambridge..., VII, pp. 126, 128, 129, 133, 147, 160, 161. Henderson, *Short...*, pp. 143–144. Kieckhefer, *European...*, p. 113. Lutzow, *Bohemia*, pp. 61 & 65. Maurice, *Bohemia*, pp. 146 & 147. Stubbs, *Later...*, pp. 112, 133.

MARGARET OF METEOLA

See—MARGARET OF CITTA DI CASTELLO.

MARGUERITE OF NAPLES

1394–1414 Germany; Italy

Supposedly graduated from medical course at the University of Salerno. She wrote poetry in her spare time. In 1394, Marguerite was one of three licensed female eye specialists in Frankfurt-am-Main. In 1414, she was listed as a physician at the royal court.

♦ **Doctors/empirics–eye doctors. Educated. University. Writers.** ♦

Hurd-Mead, *History...*, pp. 273 & 308. Lipinska, *Histoire...*, p. 153.

MARGARET OF NAVARRE, queen of Sicily **[Margaret Ramirez]**

b. 1128–d. 1183 Italy; Spain

Daughter of Margaret Laigle and Garcia IV Ramirez, king of Navarre. Married William, later king of Sicily, in the 1140s. Although they had four sons, it was rumored that William neglected Margaret and kept a harem for his pleasure. She, in turn, supposedly had an illicit attachment to William's chief administrator, Maio of Bari. After Maio died, however, Margaret became a helpful advisor to her husband. When William died in 1166, their heir William II was just a boy, so Margaret became regent of Sicily. She probably also became the paramour of Stephen du Perche, her chancellor and cousin. This attachment caused a loss of her popularity. Stephen was soon deported, and all her power and authority in the regency were taken away. In 1170, Margaret founded the Benedictine abbey of Maniace, and in 1176 she established the Church of S. Marco d'Alunzio.

♦ **Adultery. Prisons. Regents. Relics. Religious patrons. Widows.** ♦

Barlow, *Thomas...*, pp. 199 & 259. *Cambridge...*, V, p. 197. Curtis, *Roger...*, p. 294. Norwich, *Kingdom...*, pp. 169, 216–217, 220, 223, 225, 235, 259–251, 254–261, 271, 274, 276–280, 282–285, 287–288, 290, 296–302, 320n, 321, 404. Norwich, *Normans...*, p. 54. Smith, *History...*, v.2, p. 40.

MARGARET NEVILLE

c. 1350s–d. 1372 England

Daughter of Ralph, lord Neville of Raby; married Henry, lord Percy, first earl of Northumberland. Their son was Henry Percy (Hotspur).

♦ **Genealogy.** ♦

Armitage-Smith, *John...*, pp. 256–257. *DNB,* v.15, p. 850. Jacob, *Fifteenth...*, p. 9.

MARGARET NEVILLE, countess of Oxford

fl. 1450s–1480s England

Daughter of Richard Neville and †Alice Montagu, countess of Salisbury; sister of Richard Neville, earl of Warwick (the Kingmaker). Around 1465, she married John de Vere, earl of Oxford, who was captured and attainted for plotting against Edward IV (1474). Margaret received a pardon, but her lands were never returned. It was said that she lived on charity, and by doing artistic needlework.

♦ **Artistic clothwork. Estate. Models. Rebellions.** ♦

Clive, *Sun...*, pp. 81, 142, 173, 194, 304. *DNB,* v.20, pp. 241 & 242. Kendall, *Yorkist...*, p. 220. *Paston...*, I, p. 449; II, pp. 399, 447–448, 476–477. Scofield, *Life...*, I, p. 481; II, p. 89.

MARGARET, queen of NORWAY

b. 1209–1240s Norway

Daughter of Earl Skule Baardsson; married 1225 to King Haakon IV Haakonsson of Norway (Haakon the Old) to bring peace to the country. She identified herself totally with her husband's interests and became known as an excellent wife and mother.

♦ **Pawns. Queens.** ♦

Boyesen, *Story...*, pp. 407 & 413. Larsen, *History...*, p. 149.

MARGARET, "the Maid of NORWAY"

[Margaret of Scotland and Norway]

b. 1283–d. 1290 Norway

Daughter of †Margaret of Scotland and Eric II of Norway. In 1285, she became titular queen of Scotland. Betrothed to Edward, prince of Wales, in 1290, she was on her way to get married and assume the Scottish throne when she died at Orkney.

♦ **Pawns. Queens.** ♦

Barrow, *Feudal...*, pp. 252, 387, 388, 390, 408, 420. Brown, *History...*, I, pp. 128, 134–136. Bryant, *Age...*, pp. 125–129 & 233. Glover, *Story...*, pp. 70 & 71. Larsen, *History...*, p. 172. Mackie, *History...*, pp. 46 & 54. Mackie, *Short...*, pp. 55–56. Prestwich, *Edward...*, pp. 358–360, 362, 367, 374–375.

MARGARET OF NORWAY, queen of Scotland

[Margaret of Denmark]

b. 1456–d. 1486 Denmark; Norway; Scotland

Daughter of Christian I, king of Norway, Sweden, and Denmark. In 1469, she married King James III of Scotland. Margaret was beloved by her Scottish subjects who thought her a kind and charming queen. She was the mother of James IV of Scotland.

♦ **Dowry/dower. Queens.** ♦

Boyesen, *Story...*, pp. 480–481. Brown, *History...*, I, pp. 260–261 & 266–267. Derry, *History...*, p. 79. Mackie, *History...*, p. 105.

MARGUERITE D'OINGT **[Marguerite de Duyn]**

fl. 1280s–1300s France

Prioress of Poletins (a house near Lyons). Marguerite could read and write excellent Latin as well as the vernacular. In addition to the *Life of St. Beatrice,* Marguerite also wrote *Speculum* and *Meditations* about her own visions.

♦ **Abbesses. Educated. Mystics. Writers.** ♦

Bynum, *Holy...*, pp. 130, 185, 247, 249, 254, 261, 265, 266. Duraffour et al, *Les Oeuvres....* Jourdain, "Memoire...," p. 494. Lejeune, "La Femme...," p. 202. Muir, *Literature...*, pp. 160 & 171. Petroff, *Medieval...*, pp. 290–293. Valous, *Patriciat...*, p. 140.

MARGARET PAGE

1324 England

She and her husband John were the servants of John and Alemanna de Triple, a London merchant and his wife. When John de Triple died in 1324, he left Margaret and her husband a horse, furred robes, silver cups, and other items.

♦ **Bequests–personal items. Servants.** ♦

Calendar of Wills..., I, p. 311.

MARGARET PASTON **[Margaret Mauteby]**

1423–1484 England

Daughter of Margery Berney and John Mauteby. Married John (I) Paston around 1440. Margaret raised her eight children (including John II and John III) and managed the Paston estates since John was usually away from home on business. She was not well-educated, but could read and write a little. She also held manor courts, moved her family to avoid the plague, and defended her home against armed attackers. Margaret went on pilgrimage to Walsingham to acquire benefits for her husband's health. She wrote numerous letters to John which indicate they were a very happy couple, but her children, especially her daughters, seem to have had little affection for Margaret.

♦ **Childcare. Educated. Legal activity. Managers. Pilgrims. Plague. Soldiers. Widows. Writers–letters.** ♦

Barron, "Lords...," pp. 101–117. Clive, *Sun...*, pp. 68, 76, 85, 130, 140, 145, 196, 213. Coulton, *Life...*, III, pp. 127–128. Gies, *Women...*, pp. 210–232. Haskell, "Paston...," pp. 460–471. Kendall, *Yorkist...*, pp. 35–38, 196, 206, 214, 217, 233, 242, 254–255, 315, 318, 388, 403–411, 434–435, 451, 457–361, 467. *Oxford...Prose*, pp. 39–40, 41–42, 427 & 428. *Paston....*

MARGARET PORETE **[Marguerite of Porète]**

d. 1310 Belgium

An unattached Beguine, preacher, and scholar. She translated the Bible and wrote *Mirror of Simple Souls* which proclaimed a mystical pantheism. The Inquisition tried Margaret as a heretic and then burned both the book and its author.

♦ **Beguines. Educated. Ecclesiastical courts–Inquisition. Heretics. Mystics. Punishments. Unmarried. Writers.** ♦

Barstow, *Joan...*, pp. xvi, 25, 34, 36–38, 62, 97. Bryant, "French...," pp. 204–226. Bynum, *Holy...*, pp. 22, 185–6, 277, 279, 290, 296, 384 n208. Dronke, *Women...*, pp. viii-xi, 202–203, 209, 211, 213, 215, 217–228, 275–278, 318–319. Lambert, *Medieval...*, pp. 176–179. Leff, *Heresy...*, v.1, pp. 319, 355, 368, 369–371. McDonnell, *Beguines...*, pp. 367, 490–492, 500, 523, 541. Muir, *Literature...*, pp. 7, 171–172. *Oxford...Prose*, pp. 95–96 & 436. Petroff, *Medieval...*, pp. 294–298. Porète, *Le Miroir....* Zum Brunn and Epiney-Burgard, *Women...*, pp. 143–175....

MARGARITA DE PRADES, queen of Aragon

m.c. 1409–d. 1451 Spain

She was supposed in love with a nobleman her own age when she was forced to marry elderly King Martin of Aragon. It is believed that she returned to her former lover when Martin died. In the 1420s, Margarita entered a convent; she later became abbess of Bonrepos.

♦ **Abbesses. Adultery. Pawns. Queens.** ♦

Bisson, *Medieval Crown...*, p. 130. Miron, *Queens...*, pp. 242, 247–248, 252, 261–264. O'Callaghan, *History...*, p. 542.

MARGUERITE OF PROVENCE, queen of France

b. 1220–c. 1280 France

Oldest daughter of †Beatrice of Savoy and Raymond Berengar of Provence. Married Louis IX of France in 1234. Accompanied Louis on the Seventh Crusade. They had eleven children. After Louis's mother †Blanche of Castile died (1252), Marguerite tried to exercise a similar influence over her husband and son. Because she was politically naive, however, Louis had little trust in her.

♦ **Book owners. Crusades. Estate. Patrons of literature. Politics. Soldiers. Writers–letters.** ♦

Bell, "Medieval...," pp. 162 & 166. Bréquigny, *Lettres de rois...*, pp. 42–43, 129–130, 136, 145–148, 151, 154, 186–187, 209, 212, 217–218, 251–255, 265–266, 276–283. Bridge, *Crusades...*, pp. 265–6, 272. Decaux, *Histoire...*, p. 356. Gies, *Women...*, pp. 55–56, 110–112, 116, 119. Jordan, *Louis...*, pp. 4–7, 12, 126, 129, 188 & n, 206n, 216. Lehmann, *Rôle de la...*, p. 341. Powicke, *Thirteenth...*, pp. 73, 119, 164, 178, 184, 234, 239, 244, 246, 247, 248–250, 286, 288. Sivéry, *Marguerite de....* Vercauteren, "Les Médecins...," p. 83.

MARGARET ROCLIFFE

fl. 1460s England

Granddaughter of Sir William Plumpton. Educated in French and various religious subjects.

♦ **Educated. Models.** ♦

Orme, *English...*, p. 55. *Plumpton...*, p. 8.

MARGARIDA DE ROUSSILLON **[Saurimonde de Peiralada]**

fl. 1180–1220 France

Noblewoman from Perpignan area; her second husband was Raymond de Roussillon. Troubadour Guillem de Cabestaina used her as model for tragic romance in which the heroine falls in love with a page in her husband's household. When the husband discovers the affair, he kills the page and serves the man's heart to his wife for dinner. After realizing what she has eaten, the heroine committs suicide. The story became quite popular in French romantic poetry, and Margarida is often identified with the details of Guillem's tale. Far from committing suicide, however, the real Saurimonde/Margarida outlived her husband, and later married Adhemar de Mosset.

♦ **Models. Patrons of literature. Women of easy virtue.** ♦

Boutière and Schutz, *Biographies des...*, pp. 530–555 passim. Butler, *Women...*, pp. 110–114. Decaux, *Histoire...*, p. 249.

MARGUERITE SALUZZIO

1460 Italy

Popular doctor of Piedmont; wife of Ugonino Saluzzo. Crowds sometimes followed her while she traveled the countryside as her patients lined up for treatment. Marguerite was particularly noted for her herbal/medical knowledge.

♦ **Apothecaries. Doctors/empirics. Educated.** ♦

Hurd-Mead, *History...*, p. 308. Lipinska, *Histoire...*, p. 153.

MARGUERITE (la savonnière)

1292 France

Made and/or sold soap in 1292 Paris; paid small tax—12d.

♦ **Less-affluent. Merchants–soap.** ♦

Géraud, *Paris sous...*, p. 98.

MARGUERITE SCHEPPERS **[Grietkin]**

d. 1505 Germany; Switzerland

Professional illuminator; helped start convent scriptorium at Sion. Worked with nuns on missal and on the *De Tempore* gradual.

♦ **Artists. Bookmaking. Religieuses.** ♦

Greer, *Obstacle...*, pp. 164–165.

(St.) MARGARET, queen of SCOTLAND **[Margaret of Hungary]**

b. 1046–d. 1093 England; Hungary; Scotland

Presumably the daughter of exiled prince Edward of England and †Agatha (of Hungary). After Edward died, Agatha took her children to England, and then on to Scotland where King Malcolm III (Canmore) soon married Margaret. Margaret loved the prerogatives of royalty, but this and her pro-English tendencies often made her unpopular. Along with her elegance and her jeweled books, however, Margaret was also very pious. She reformed the Scottish Church, gave to charity, and personally fed the poor and sick.

♦ **Book owners. Medicine. Music. Religious patrons. Saints.** ♦

Baker, "Nursery...," pp. 119–142. *DNB,* v.12, pp. 1017–1019. Duncan, *Scotland...*, pp. 117–125, 127, 129, 132, 134, 146, 151, 241, 453, 558, 559, 562, 611–612. Eckenstein, *Woman...*, p. 207. Farmer, *Oxford...*, p. 262. Glover, *Story...*, pp. 48, 56, 58, 63–64. Mackie, *Short...*, pp. 25–28, 35. Nagy, *St. Margaret...*. Thompson, *Literacy...*, pp. 170–171. Turgot, "Life...".

MARGARET OF SCOTLAND, queen of Norway

b. 1261–d. 1283 Norway; Scotland

Daughter of †Margaret of England and Alexander III of Scotland. Married Eric II of Norway in 1281. In 1283, she died giving birth to daughter †Margaret "the Maid of Norway."

♦ **Childbirth. Queens.** ♦

Barrow, *Feudal...*, pp. 252, 387, 420. Boyesen, *Story...*, p. 456. Brown, *History...*, I, pp. 124 & 128. Bryant, *Age...*, p. 125. Duncan, *Scotland...*, pp. 577 & 592. Glover, *Story...*, pp. 71–72. Larsen, *History...*, p. 172. Mackie, *History...*, pp. 46 & 54.

MARGARET OF SCOTLAND [Margaret Stuart, dauphine of France]

1425–1445 France; Scotland

Daughter of †Joan Beaufort and James I of Scotland; in 1436 she married the dauphin Louis (later Louis XI of France) as part of a peace/alliance treaty. She was young and gay, but of delicate health. Margaret especially liked to write poetry and hold literary salons. Her husband hated her, had her spied on, and probably indirectly contributed to her early death from tuberculosis.

♦ **Dance. Educated. Music. Patrons of literature. Pawns. Poets/troubadours. Tournaments.** ♦

Barbé, *Margaret....* Brown, *History...*, I, p. 216. Champion, *Louis...*, pp. 48, 50–52, 106–108, 112. Cleugh, *Chant...*, pp. 15, 21, 23, 29, 33, 56, 59–61, 68, 71, 79–81, 83–89, 109, 130, 300. Harksen, *Women...*, p. 54. Huizinga, *Waning...*, p. 197. Lewis, *King...*, pp. 161, 169, 171, 175–182, 193. Mackie, *History...*, p. 100. Moulin, *La Poesie...*, p. 101. Pernoud, *Retrial...*, p. 74.

MARGARET (OF SICILY)

b. 1237–1260s Germany; Italy

Daughter of †Isabel of England and Emperor Frederick II. Married Albert, margrave of Meissen; their son Frederick was born in 1257.

♦ **Genealogy.** ♦

Haverkamp, *Medieval...*, p. 262. Van Cleve, *Emperor...*, p. 495.

MARGARET STOKE

1375 England

Owned bake-shop and public oven in London.

♦ **Employers. Land/property. Legal activity. Provisioning–bakers.** ♦

Calendar of Plea..., II, p. 187.

MARGARET OF SWEDEN, queen of Norway, queen of Denmark

m.c. 1101 Denmark; Norway; Sweden

Daughter of King Inge of Sweden; married around 1101 to Magnus III Barefoot, king of Norway (d.1103). She was known as "the peacemaker." Margaret later married Nicholas Svensson, king of Denmark.

♦ **Dowry/dower. Pawns. Queens.** ♦
Boyesen, *Story...*, p. 288. Larsen, *History...*, pp. 115–116.

MARGARET OF SWEDEN, queen of Norway
m. 1184–1210s — Norway; Sweden

Daughter of King Eric the Saint of Sweden. Married King Sverre Sigurdsson of Norway (d.1202). Margaret was proud and imperious; she was unable to forgive a supposed insult by her stepson, the new king, Haakon Sverresson. It was widely believed that she poisoned Haakon at a Christmas feast—he died January 1204. Margaret refused to take part in the ordeal, but her substitute died of his burns.

♦ **Murder. Ordeals. Queens. Religious patrons. Widows.** ♦
Boyesen, *Story...*, pp. 358, 362, 381–383. Larsen, *History...*, p. 143.

MARGHERITA DI TRENTO — **[Margherita la Bella]**
d. 1307 — Italy

Lover and supporter of Dolcino, the leader of a cult following a form of militant Joachism. Captured, tortured, and then burned for her beliefs.

♦ **Adultery. Antinomian. Ecclesiastical courts–Inquisition. Preachers. Punishments.** ♦
Chubb, *Dante...*, p. 471. Leff, *Heresy...*, v.1, pp. 192 & 194. Wakefield, *Heresy...*, pp. 404 & 758 n2.

MARGUERITE DE TURENNE
fl. 1140s — France

As widow of the viscount of Limoges, Marguerite married Eble III of Ventadour. Bernard de Ventadour supposedly considered her his inspiration. Although she claimed her feelings for the poet had never resulted in a physical relationship, Eble repudiated Marguerite. There is some confusion over her dates of marriage and death. Furthermore, since Eble III also married Alais of Montpellier, Bernard's verses may have been written to/about Alais rather than Marguerite.

♦ **Divorce. Models. Patrons of literature. Women of easy virtue.** ♦
Bonner (ed.), *Songs...*, p. 257. Boutière and Schutz, *Biographies des...*, p. 24. *DBF*, v.6, p. 91. Marks, *Pilgrims...*, pp. 162–164.

MARGARET DE VALOIS

See—MARGARET OF FRANCE.
See—BLANCHE OF FRANCE.

MARGARET WAKE, countess of Kent — **[Margaret, baroness Wake]**
c. 1300s–d. 1349 — England

Sister and heiress of Thomas, lord Wake of Liddell. Margaret was the widow of John Comyn of Badenoch when she married Edmund of Woodstock, earl of Kent, in 1325. They were the parents of †Joan "Fair Maid of Kent." Margaret may have written some of her husband's treasonable correspondence.

♦ **Educated. Estate. Politics. Rebellions. Writers.** ♦

DNB, v.6, p. 412. McFarlane, *Nobility...,* p. 240. Wentersdorf, "Clandestine...," p. 204.

MARGARET WAVERE

c. 1460s–1480s England

As prioress of Catesby, she allowed buildings to go unrepaired, stole and pawned silverware, kept the nuns short of provisions, and allowed her lover to visit her. Despite these misdeeds, there was no one to replace her, so Margaret continued in her position of authority.

♦ **Abbesses. Adultery. Miscreants.** ♦

Kendall, *Yorkist...,* p. 262. Power, *Nunneries...,* pp. 81, 82, 84–86, 94, 220, 299, 388, 460, 489, 583, 584.

MARGARET WORTHHAM

d. 1460s England

Prioress of Augustinian canonesses at Cornworthy, Devonshire. Contracted to board and teach several young girls.

♦ **Abbesses. Childcare. Educated. Legal activity. Teachers.** ♦

Orme, *Education...,* p. 204.

MARGARET OF YORK, duchess of Burgundy

b. 1446–d. 1503 England; Flanders; France

Daughter of †Cecily Neville and Richard, duke of York; sister of Edward IV and Richard III, kings of England. In 1468, Margaret married Charles the Bold of Burgundy (his third wife). Margaret became a useful political advisor to, and negotiator for, Charles. She was also a patroness of the printer William Caxton. After Charles died (1477), Margaret remained an implacable enemy of Louis XI of France; she also helped arrange the marriage of her stepdaughter †Marie of Burgundy to Maximilian of Austria.

♦ **Dwarves. Educated. Estate. Models. Negotiators. Patrons of literature. Politics. Tournaments. Widows.** ♦

Calmette, *Golden...,* pp. 176–178, 185, 195, 209, 238–239, 285, 329, 343. Cartellieri, *Court...,* pp. 88, 101, 124–125, 128, 138, 157, 160–162, 169–170. Cleugh, *Chant...,* pp. 196, 199–200, 204, 234–238, 258, 270. Clive, *Sun...,* pp. 25, 66, 119, 120, 123, 127–32, 138, 165, 217–8, 229, 232–3, 251–2, 293. Commynes, *Memoirs...,* pp. 7, 117–118, 210, 346, 348, 351, 380, 381. *Coronation...,* p. 41. Hommel, Marguerite.... Huizinga, *Waning...,* pp. 123, 216, 229. Kendall, *Yorkist...,* p. 186. Ross, *Wars...,* pp. 73, 74, 104, 117. Scofield, *Life...,* I, pp. 2, 404–405, 431, 462–464; II, pp. 182–185 & 284–297. St. Aubyn, *Year...,* pp. 54, 59, 218.

MARGARET OF YPRES

1216–1237 Belgium

Presumably a merchant's daughter, she entered a convent when her father died. Although of a retiring nature, Margaret led a group of followers—

amici spirituales—directed by the Dominicans and devoted to the Eucharist. Her *Vita* was written in 1240 by Thomas de Cantimpré.

♦ **Beguines. Models. Religieuses.** ♦

Bolton, "Vitae Matrum...," pp. 258–259, 260–266. Bynum, *Holy...,* pp. 24, 115, 116, 117, 119, 120, 200, 203, 214, 247, 256, 351 n35. Lagorio, "Continental...," p. 175. McDonnell, *Beguines...,* pp. 98 & 200 n.

MARGUERITE DE YPRES

1322 Belgium; France

A Parisian surgeon; in 1322 she was prohibited from further practice because she had no license.

♦ **Miscreants. Surgeons.** ♦

Hughes, *Women...,* p. 143. Power, *Women...,* p. 88. Uitz, *Legend...,* p. 67. Wickersheimer, *Dictionnaire...,* v.2, p. 537.

MARGERY [Margerie; Marjery; Marjorie; Marjory]

MARGERY BAXTER **[Margery Backster]**

fl.c. 1400 England

Lollard of Norwich; she was especially dubious of the doctrine of transubstantiation. Margery also believed that all good and true believers were "priests."

♦ **Ecclesiastical courts. Lollards.** ♦

Aston, "Lollard...," pp. 443, 451–452. Fines, "Studies in...," p. 67 n3. Lambert, *Medieval...,* pp. 257 & 268. Tanner, *Norwich...,* pp. 13–15, 17–18, 20, 22, 26, 28, 41–51, 72. Thomson, *Later Lollards...,* p. 130.

MARGERY BREWS

See—MARGERY PASTON.

MARJORY BRUCE

b. 1294–d.c. 1318 Scotland

Daughter of Robert VIII de Bruce (Robert I, king of Scotland) by his first wife Isabella of Mar. Marjory married Walter FitzAlan, the High Steward of Scotland; their son was Robert II, first Stuart king of Scotland. Marjory was captured by the English near Tain, along with her stepmother †Elizabeth de Burgo. Robert later exchanged some high-ranking English prisoners in order to obtain the freedom of his female relatives. Marjory died in childbirth.

♦ **Childbirth. Prisons.** ♦

Brown, *History...,* I, pp. 154 & 162. Bryant, *Age...,* pp. 209 & 212. *DNB,* v.3, pp. 121 & 128. Glover, *Story...,* p. 87. Mackie, *History...,* pp. 61, 79, 82 & 84. Mackie, *Short...,* p. 79. Powicke, *Thirteenth...,* p. 685 & n. Prestwich, *Edward...,* p. 509.

MARGERY (of CALAIS)

fl. 1470s–1480s France

Mistress of English merchant, George Cely, at Calais; they had two children.

♦ **Mistresses. Models.** ♦

Cely..., p. 110. Gies, *Merchants...*, p. 260. Kendall, *Yorkist...*, p. 291.

MARJORIE, countess of CARRICK

m.c. 1266–c. 1290s Scotland

Daughter and heiress of Neil, earl of Carrick. Married (1) Adam of Kilconquhar (c.1266). He died in 1270 on Crusade at Carthage. Supposedly, Marjorie then fell in love with handsome Robert Bruce (VII) and kidnapped him in order to marry him; he became earl of Carrick in her right. Their son was Robert I (Bruce), king of Scotland.

♦ **Abduction. Estate. Models. Widows.** ♦

Brown, *History...*, I, p. 134. Bullough and Storey, *Study...*, p. 131. *DNB*, v.3, p. 117. Duncan, *Scotland...*, pp. 400 & 585. Glover, *Story...*, p. 75. Mackie, *History...*, p. 48.

MARGERY (of FROCESTOR)

1265 England

A widow who held twenty-four acres on the manor of Frocestor. As a land holder in her own right, the numerous services she owed her lord were detailed in manor court rolls.

♦ **Land/property. Manors. Widows.** ♦

Boulding, *Underside...*, pp. 482–483. O'Faolain, *Not in...*, pp. 160–161.

MARGERY OF HALES

fl.c. 1300–1310s England

An empiric on Worcestershire manor of Hales. Not very popular, she was once thrown into the river to determine if she was a witch.

♦ **Doctors/empirics. Manors. Ordeals. Witchcraft.** ♦

Labarge, *Small Sound...*, p. 175. Rubin, *Medieval...*, p. 187. Talbot and Hammond, *Medical...*, p. 209.

MARGERIE DE HAUSTEDE

fl. 1280s England

Lady-in-waiting to †Eleanor of Castile, queen of England. Margerie was in charge of caring for the queen's jewels and she also ran errands for Eleanor. Margerie's post was important enough to warrant allocating a room at Westminster Palace especially for her.

♦ **Gems/jewelry. Servants–ladies.** ♦

Somerset, *Ladies...*, p. 4.

MARGERY HAYNES

1430s–c. 1460 England

Although her husband was a villein in Wiltshire, when he died in 1435 he was worth nearly £500. Margery paid £150 for the right to keep his lands and to pick her own second husband. She also took over her late husband's three mills. By the time she died, Margery was even wealthier than William had been. She kept two servants, had built two houses, and held several tenements, shops, and other property.

♦ **Employers. Land/property. Merchants. Manors. Widows.** ♦

Anderson and Zinsser, *A History of...*, p. 426. Kendall, *Yorkist...*, p. 200.

MARGERY DE HONYLANE **[Margery of Honilane]**

fl. 1360s–1370s England

Assertive prioress of St. Helen's at Bisshopesgate, London.

♦ **Abbesses. Land/property. Legal activity. Managers.** ♦

Nuisance..., pp. 129, 136, 158.

MARJERY JOURDEMAIN **[Jurdane]**

d.c. 1444 England

Known as the "witch of Eye." She was employed by †Eleanor Cobham, duchess of Gloucester, as a sorceress. Marjery and Eleanor were both arrested and accused of practicing witchcraft. Marjery was tortured and burned.

♦ **Punishments. Witchcraft.** ♦

Butt, *History...*, p. 528. Ewen, *Witchcraft...*, pp. 37–38. Griffiths, "Trial...," pp. 387 & 391. Kittredge, *Witchcraft...*, pp. 81–83, 106, 115. Robbins, *Encyclopedia...*, pp. 162, 165, 531.

MARGERY KEMPE

b. 1373–d.c. 1438 England

Daughter of John Brunham; wife of John Kempe, a townsman of Lynn. Margery eventually abandoned her unsuccessful business enterprises and her large family in order to devote herself to a more pious lifestyle. She was a mystic and derived great satisfaction from numerous pilgrimages. Her lack of respect for some clerics led to suspicions of heresy. Her religious calling seemed to be dominated by emotionalism and a flair for dramatics; her loud wailing (or "cryings") often made her an uncomfortable person to be around. Margery dictated her memoirs, the first English autobiography, in the 1430s.

♦ **Alewives. Ecclesiastical courts. Heretics–accused. Land/property. Merchants. Mystics. Pilgrims. Religieuses. Writers–biography.** ♦

Atkinson, *Mystic....* Bynum, *Holy...*, pp. 7, 28, 88, 99, 193, 206, 215, 219, 221, 246, 247, 263, 269, 270, 280, 291. Fries, "Margery...," pp. 217–235.

Goodman, "Piety...," pp. 347–358. Goulianos, *By a Woman Writt...*, pp. 3–20. Hindley, *England...*, pp. 3, 17, 20, 120, 123, 149, 151, 155, 158, 178. Jacob, *Fifteenth...*, pp. 273, 296, 685–687. Jones, "English...," pp. 270–271. Kempe, *Book....* *Oxford...Prose*, pp. xxi, 95, 98–101, 437–438. Provost, "English...," pp. 297–319. Warren, *Anchorites...*, pp. 24, 37, 69.

MARGERY PASTON

b. 1449–d.c. 1490s England

Daughter of John (I) and †Margaret (Mauteby) Paston. At age seventeen, Margery fell in love with, and then secretly married, the Paston estate bailiff, Richard Calle. Her parents tried to get the union annulled; when they could not do so, they treated Margery as an outcast.

♦ **Miscreants. Models. Punishments.** ♦

Gies, *Women...*, pp. 223–225. Haskell, "Paston...," pp. 467–469. Hindley, *England...*, pp. 152–153. Kendall, *Yorkist...*, pp. 315, 394, 400. *Paston...*, I, pp. 157, 242, 243, 244, 287, 308, 326, 327, 328, 339, 341–343, 348, 351, 388, 409, 524, 529, 540, 541, 549; II, pp. 81 & 393.

MARGERY PASTON **[Margery Brews]**

m. 1477–d. 1495 England

Daughter of Sir Thomas and Elizabeth Brews of Norfolk. Married John (III) Paston in 1477. They were a happy, affectionate couple; wrote many letters to each other.

♦ **Dowry/dower. Land/property. Writers–letters.** ♦

Barron, "Lords...," p. 111. Coulton, *Life...*, III, pp. 132–137. Kendall, *Yorkist...*, pp. 233, 349, 385–391. *Oxford...Prose*, pp. 42–43, 428. *Paston...*, I, pp. 378, 387, 499, 500–501, 511, 600–613, 616, 621, 627, 647, 662–669; II, pp. 413, 436, 438, 441, 445, 457, 461, 469, 470.

MARGERY RUSSELL

fl. 1360s–c. 1380 England

A widow of Coventry and a successful long-distance trader. She had merchandise taken at sea by pirates, so Margery obtained *letters of marque* against the offending Spanish city. She then proceeded to seize two ships from that port in compensation for her losses.

♦ **Legal activity. Merchants. Shipping–pirates. Widows.** ♦

Abram, *English...*, p. 36. Carus-Wilson, "Overseas...," p. 243. Hindley, *England...*, p. 158. Power, *Women...*, p. 56.

MARGERY TWYNYHO

fl. 1480s–d. 1505 England

Abbess of Godstow; commissioned an inventory of abbey documents.

♦ **Abbesses. Managers. Patrons of literature.** ♦

Bullough and Storey, *Study...*, p. 146. Davis, *Medieval Cartularies...*, p. 101 (#887).

MARGOT DE LA BARRE **[Coingnet]**
d. 1390 France

Wandering prostitute believed to have magic powers. Hired by Marion la Droiturière to make her lover impotent. At Paris, both women were tortured and then burned.

♦ **Prostitutes. Punishments. Unmarried. Witchcraft.** ♦

Cohn, *Europe's...*, p. 196. Labarge, *Women...*, p. 216. Russell, *Witchcraft...*, p. 214.

MARGOT (la gantière)
1292 France

Glove-maker of 1292 Paris; paid 2s tax.

♦ **Apparel–accessories. Less-affluent.** ♦

Géraud, *Paris sous...*, p. 150.

MARGOT (la GROSSE)
1450s France

Parisian prostitute with a house near Notre Dame. This establishment was frequented by bad company and was often the site of brawls and stabbings. Margot was one of François Villon's associates. In the *Ballad of la Grosse Margot,* Villon wrote about his life with Margot—serving food and wine to her customers, fighting over money, etc.

♦ **Land/property. Models. Prostitutes.** ♦

Bonner, *Complete...*, pp. 105–107 & 211. Cartellieri, *Court...*, p. 117. Champion, *François...*, I, pp. 89 & 171; II, pp. 2, 71, 164, 184, 194–195. Lewis, *François...*, pp. 300–303.

MARGOT DE HAINAULT
1400–1430s Flanders; France

Twenty-eight-year-old woman from Hainault. She captivated Parisians in 1427 by defeating the best male tennis players. Margot's backhand was said to be particularly effective.

♦ **Models. Games–tennis.** ♦

Champion, *François...*, p. 84. Lewis, *King...*, p. 52. Shirley, *Parisian...*, p. 320.

MARGOT PIPELARDE
fl. 1310 France

A spicer and herbalist in Arras. Margot sold aromatic sachets and pomegranates, among other kitchen and medicinal herbs.

♦ **Apothecaries.** ♦

Decaux, *Histoire...*, p. 336. Lehmann, *Rôle de la...*, p. 474.

MARION LA DENTUE **[Marion l'Idole]**
fl. 1450s–1460s France

Parisian prostitute who owned a brothel on the rue des Quatre Filz Aymon, near the Temple. In the *Testament* of François Villon, he left Marion license to run a "school of love."

♦ **Bequests. Land/property. Models. Prostitutes.** ♦

Bonner, *Complete...*, pp. 108–109 & 212. Cartellieri, *Court...*, p. 117. Champion, *François...*, I, pp. 89, 102, 111; II, pp. 80 & 164–165. Lewis, *François...*, p. 303.

MARIOTTA CONVERS **[Mariota; Mary]**
1385 England

A London pawnbroker; a customer sued her for selling his jewel to a Lombard.

♦ **Banking. Gems/jewelry. Merchants–pawnbrokers. Miscreants. Prisons.** ♦

Calendar of Plea..., VI, pp. 30 & 35. Lacey, "Women...," pp. 52–53.

MAROTE (DE DOUAI)
1304 France

Widow of Jean de Douai, a goldsmith of Arras. Took over husband's business; in 1304 recorded selling gold boxes for over £50.

♦ **Goldsmiths. Widows.** ♦

Lehmann, *Rôle de la...*, p. 435. Richard, *Mahaut...*, pt. 18, p. 2.

MAROZIA OF ROME **[Marotia]**
b. 885–d.c. 938 Italy

Daughter of †Theodora and Theophylacte of Rome. Cleric/historian Liutprand of Cremona described Marozia as depraved; she was supposedly the mistress of Pope Sergius III. She married (1) Alberic, duke of Spoleto; (2) Guido of Tuscany; (3) Hugh of Provence. Her son Alberic was prince of the Romans, and she had her son John elected Pope John XI. Marozia ruled Rome as a *Senatrix*. Her third husband's plots to remove Alberic caused her son to force Hugh back to Lombardy while Marozia herself lost her power. She was compelled to retire to a convent.

♦ **Adultery. Models. Murder. Politics. Popes. Prisons. Religieuses. Rulers. Widows.** ♦

Brusher, *Popes...*, pp. 240, 244, 246, 248, 252. Bryce, *Holy...*, p. 86. *Cambridge...*, III, pp. 151, 153, 154, 241, 455. Cheetham, *Keepers...*, pp. 76 & 77. Duckett, *Death...*, pp. 55–58, 70, 163, 166. Ernouf, *Histoire...*, pp. 210–212, 221, 226. Kelly, *Oxford...*, pp. 122–3, 124. Partner, *Lands...*, pp. 79–83. Riché, *Les Carolingiens...*, p. 231. Robinson, *Readings...*, I, pp. 251–252. Stafford, *Queens...*, pp. 20, 52–53, 138. Wright, *Works...*, pp. 92–93, 117, 133.

MARTHA [Marthe; Mata; Matha]

MATHA D'ARMAGNAC, duchess of Gerona

[Mata, duchess of Girona]

m. 1373–d. 1378 France; Spain

Daughter of Béatrix de Clermont and Jean I, count of Armagnac. Married Juan of Aragon, duke of Gerona. An avid correspondent; wrote to relatives and even petitioned the king for favors for her staff.

♦ **Managers. Writers.** ♦

Bisson, *Medieval Crown...*, p. 121. Hillgarth, *Pere...*, p. 589. Javierre Mur, "Matha de...," pp. 107–247. Miron, *Queens...*, pp. 210–217, & 232.

MARTHA BORETSKY

[Marfa Boretskaia; Posadnitsa; the Mayoress]

fl. 1420s–c. 1480 Russia

Of rich Novgorod boyar family, her husband, Mayor Isaak Andreevich Boretsky, died in 1459. Martha then managed the family lands and businesses. A supporter of the Eastern Church, she gave much land to Solovki monastery. Martha also led Novgorod in alliance negotiations with Lithuania in order to protect the region from take-over attempts by Prince Ivan III of Moscow. Despite her efforts and advice, the alliance fell through and Novgorod became a Muscovy possession. Martha and several other top boyars were captured and imprisoned (c.1478).

♦ **Managers. Merchants. Models. Negotiators. Prisons. Religious patrons. Rulers. Soldiers. Widows.** ♦

Kluchevsky, *History...*, pp. 367–368. Pares, *History...*, pp. 91 & 93. Vernadsky, *Russia...*, pp. 45–46, 48, 53, 59, 65–66.

MARTHA (of PARIS)

c. 1230s–1240s France

Parchmenter of Paris; she and her husband Adam worked on the rue Saint Geneviève.

♦ **Bookmaking. Less-affluent.** ♦

Branner, "Manuscript...," p. 65. Carr, "Women...," p. 9.

MARTHE (of PARIS)

fl. 1450s France

Presumably one of François Villon's loves. He may have consoled himself for the fickleness of †Catherine de Vausselles with the charming Marthe. In a mannered ballad he used her name in acrostic with his own.

♦ **Models. Women of easy virtue.** ♦

Bonner, *Complete...*, p. 199. Champion, *François...*, I, pp. 89, 104, 185; II, pp. 7, 10, 146, 183, 200. Lewis, *François...*, pp. 130–132 & 284.

MARY [Maria; Marie]

MARIE OF ANJOU, queen of France

c. 1410s–1460s France

Daughter of †Yolande of Aragon and Sicily and Louis II of Anjou. Married Charles VII of France; son Louis XI born 1423. Marie was gentle, pious, and uninterested in politics. She bore with patience her husband's affair with †Agnes Sorel—who was given better rooms and clothes than Marie herself.

♦ **Queens. Religious patrons. Writers–letters.** ♦

Cartellieri, *Court...*, p. 114. Champion, *Louis...*, pp. 43–45, 51, 53, 102, 106, 110, 111. Cleugh, *Chant...*, pp. 11–14, 16, 19, 22, 24, 27–28, 33, 59, 68, 77, 79, 84, 86, 88, 89, 97, 144, 159, 165, 168. Denieul-Cormier, *Wise...*, pp. 237–238, 254, 281, 293, 302–304, 363. Frager, *Marie....* Lewis, *King...*, pp. 152 & 175. Vale, *Charles...*, pp. 22–3, 24, 75, 89, 91–2, 95, 190, 192.

MARY OF ANTIOCH, empress of Byzantium

c. 1150s–d.c. 1182 Byzantium

Daughter of †Constance of Antioch and Raymond of Poitiers. Second wife of Manuel Comnenus; son Alexius II. When Manuel died in 1180, she became regent for her twelve-year-old son. Her top advisor (and also her lover) the *protosebastos* Alexius Comnenus made Mary very unpopular, as did her alliance with the Latins in Constantinople. Her stepdaughter †Maria Comnena plotted to bring down Mary's government and Andronicus Comnenus eventually usurped the throne. Her son Alexius was finally forced to sign her death warrant.

♦ **Murder. Rebellions. Regents. Widows. Women of easy virtue.** ♦

Bridge, *Crusades...*, pp. 189–91. *Cambridge...*, IV, pp. 375, 379, 380–382, 757. Diehl, *Byzantine...*, pp. 247–248. Hill, *History...*, pp. 311–312. Norwich, *Kingdom...*, pp. 270, 304, 326–330.

MARIA D'AQUINO

See—FIAMMETTA.

MARIA OF ARAGON, queen of Portugal

b. 1482–d.c. 1517 Portugal; Spain

Daughter of †Isabella, queen of Castile, and Ferdinand of Aragon. Her sister †Isabella died in 1498. Isabella's husband, Emmanuel, king of Portugal, then married Maria (c.1500). She and Emmanuel had eight children and, reputedly, a happy marriage.

♦ **Pawns. Queens.** ♦

Altamira, *Spain,* p. 291. Miller, *Castles...*, pp. 119, 126, 157, 160, 166, 177, 178, 203. Stephens, *Story...*, p. 174.

MARIE D'ATAINVILLE

1292 France

A tanner (mesgeicière) in 1292 Paris; paid tax of 2s.

♦ **Less-affluent. Tanners.** ♦

Géraud, *Paris sous...*, p. 25.

MARY OF ATHOLL, countess of Boulogne

See—MARY OF SCOTLAND, countess of Boulogne.

MARIE D'AVIGNON **[Marie Robine]**

fl.c. 1390s–1410s France

Told Charles VII of France about her dream that a virgin wearing armor would deliver France from its enemies.

♦ **Mystics. Politics. Superstitions. Virginity.** ♦

Barstow, *Joan...*, pp. 63–4, 95, 97. Pernoud, *Retrial...*, pp. 5 & 88. Vale, *Charles...*, p. 50.

MARIE (la barbière)

1292 France

Barber on the rue aux Escrivains in 1292 Paris; paid 12d tax.

♦ **Barbers. Less-affluent.** ♦

Géraud, *Paris sous...*, p. 157. Hughes, *Women...*, p. 140.

MARIE DE BERRY, duchess of Bourbon

b. 1373–d. 1434 France

Daughter of †Jeanne d'Armagnac and John, duke of Berry. In 1386 she married Louis of Blois (d.1391). Marie later married Philip d'Artois, count of Eu. By age twenty-three, she was again a widow. Her third husband was John of Clermont, duke of Bourbon (d.1433). †Christine de Pisan dedicated a poem about losses at Agincourt to Marie.

♦ **Book owners. Educated. Managers. Models. Patrons of literature. Widows.** ♦

Anselme, *Histoire...*, v.1, pp. 107 & 303–304. Bell, "Medieval...," p. 155. Froissart, *Chronicles...*, II, pp. 13, 17, 109, 162, 173, 202–205. Jarman, *Crispin's...*, p. 181. Pisan, *City...*, p. 213.

MARIE DE BLANSY

1404 France

With the help of three men, Marie attempted to invoke diabolic aid to cure Charles VI of insanity. She was condemned and burned in Paris because her spells were ineffective.

♦ **Doctors/empirics. Insanity. Punishments. Witchcraft.** ♦

Hughes, *Women...*, p. 145. Wickersheimer, *Dictionnaire...*, v.1, p. 313.

MARY OF BLOIS, countess of Boulogne **[Mary of Boulogne]**
b. 1136–d. 1181 England; Flanders; France

Daughter of †Matilda of Boulogne and Stephen of Blois, king of England. Well-educated at convent. King Henry II considered her too great an heiress for her lands to go to religious establishments, so he forced her to marry Matthew of Flanders in 1160. Matthew then became earl of Boulogne in her right. After several years (and two daughters), the marriage was dissolved and Mary returned to the convent.

♦ **Abbesses. Divorce. Educated. Estate. Nuns. Pawns. Politics. Spies. Writers–letters.** ♦

Anselme, *Histoire...*, v.2, p. 722. Barlow, *Thomas...*, pp. 223, 580. *DNB*, v.13, p. 54. Eckenstein, *Woman...*, pp. 201 & 207. Elkins, *Holy...*, pp. 69, 74, 150, 189 n.25, 212 n.19. Green, *Letters...*, pp. 11–13.

MARIE OF BOHEMIA, queen of France **[Marie of Luxembourg]**
d.c. 1324 Bohemia; France; Luxembourg

Daughter of †Margaret of Brabant and Holy Roman Emperor Henry VII. Became second wife of Charles IV of France in 1322. Died of the after-effects of a premature birth.

♦ **Childbirth. Negotiators. Queens.** ♦

Butler, *Women...*, p. 262. *Cambridge...*, VII, pp. 160, 338, 339. Castries, *Lives...*, p. 97. *DBF*, v.8, p. 518. Sherman, "Ordo ad...," p. 269. Stubbs, *Later...*, pp. 104 & 105.

MARY DE BOHUN
b. 1370–d.c. 1394 England

Daughter and co-heiress of †Joan FitzAlan and Humphrey de Bohun, earl of Hereford and Essex. Around 1382, Mary married Henry of Bolingbroke (later King Henry IV)—his father John of Gaunt supposedly "rescued" her from the convent for this wedding.

♦ **Childbirth. Estate. Religieuses.** ♦

Armitage-Smith, *John...*, pp. 287 & 357. Given-Wilson, *English...*, p. 44. Hutchison, *King...*, pp. 15, 16, 74. Jarman, *Crispin's...*, pp. 32 & 201. McFarlane, *Nobility...*, pp. 152, 177, 207, 243. Rawcliffe, *Staffords...*, pp. 13, 14, 15. Robertson, *Chaucer's...*, p. 60. Tuck, *Richard...*, pp. 8–9, 160.

MARIE OF BOURBON, duchess of Calabria
b. 1426–d. 1448 France

Daughter of †Agnes of Burgundy and Charles I of Bourbon. In 1437, Marie married Jean d'Anjou, duke of Calabria. Attended tourney and danced with the dauphine, †Margaret (Stuart) of Scotland, and with †Marie of Cleves. Marie of Bourbon gave knight Jacques de Lalaing a pearl collaret and a ruby ring as tokens.

♦ **Dance. Models. Tournaments.** ♦

Anselme, *Histoire...*, v.1, p. 233. Cartellieri, *Court...*, p. 95. Champion, *Louis...*, pp. 90, 104 & 105. Commynes, *Memoirs...*, p. 600. Vale, *Charles...*, p. 74.

MARIE DE BRABANT, queen of France

m. 1275–d. 1321 — Flanders; France

Daughter of Alix of Burgundy and Henry III, duke of Brabant. Second wife of Philip III of France. She was accused of killing his children by his first wife, †Isabel of Aragon, but was found innocent. She was a literary patron; Adenet le Roi wrote *Cleomades* for Mary.

♦ **Book owners. Legal activity. Murder. Patrons of literature. Politics.** ♦

Anselme, *Histoire...*, v.1, p. 88. Bréquigny, *Lettres de rois...*, p. 267. Butler, *Women...*, p. 253. Fawtier, *Capetian...*, pp. 35, 166, 205, 217. Jourdain, "Memoire...," p. 488. Lejeune, "La Femme...," p. 207. Powicke, *Thirteenth...*, pp. 239, 240, 647. Sherman, "Ordo ad...," p. 269.

MARIE DE BRABANT, Holy Roman Empress, countess of Boulogne — **[Marie of Louvain]**

b. 1188–d. 1260 — Flanders; France; Germany

Daughter of Henry I, duke of Brabant, and his first wife Mahaut of Flanders. Marie married Otto IV of Brunswick, Holy Roman Emperor, in 1214. (His first wife, †Beatrice of Swabia—the older—died in 1212.) Otto died in 1218, and Marie later married Baldwin of Courteney. She inherited the county of Boulogne after her cousin Mahaut de Dammartin (†Matilda of Boulogne, queen of Portugal) died.

♦ **Estate. Religious patrons. Widows.** ♦

Anselme, *Histoire...*, v.2, p. 791. Blok, *History...*, Gen. Table. *Cambridge...*, VI, pp. 66 n1, 78. McDonnell, *Beguines...*, pp. 114, 221, 305. Pirenne, *Histoire...*, v.1, p. 231.

MARIE OF BRITTANY, duchess of Anjou, queen of Sicily — **[Marie de Blois]**

m. 1360–1390s — France; Italy

Daughter of †Jeanne de Penthièvre and Charles de Blois. Married Louis I of Anjou around 1374. She continued to fight for Naples on behalf of her son, Louis II of Anjou.

♦ **Politics. Prisons. Queens. Regents. Soldiers. Widows.** ♦

Anselme, *Histoire...*, v.1, p. 229. *Cambridge...*, VII, p. 297n. *DBF*, v.8, p. 559. Pernoud, *La femme...*, pp. 101–102. Tuchman, *Distant...*, pp. 423, 429, 433, 434, 454, 484, 488, 490.

MARIE OF BURGUNDY

b. 1457–d. 1482 — Austria; Flanders; France

Daughter and heiress of Charles the Bold, duke of Burgundy and his second wife, †Isabelle of Bourbon. Her father died in 1477, and Marie married Maximilian of Austria. Their son Philip was born in 1478 and daughter †Margaret was born in 1480. A great heiress, Marie was caught between the demands of Flemish merchants and those of Louis XI of France—who constantly tried to deprive her of most of her lands and power. Brought up at one of the most brilliant courts of the time,

Marie was well-educated and had even been given music lessons by Pierre Beurse. In 1482, Marie died from a fall which occurred while she was hunting. She was deeply mourned by her people and her husband.

♦ **Dwarves. Educated. Estate. Hunting. Models. Music. Rulers. Tournaments.** ♦

Boase, "Mortality...," p. 242. Bryce, *Holy...*, pp. 357 & 361. Calmette, *Golden...*, pp. 185, 188–190, 196, 232, 237, 273, 275, 282, 283, 285, 286, 320, 325. Cartellieri, *Court...*, pp. 21, 71, 157, 162. Champion, *Louis...*, pp. 228, 263, 265, 273–275, 288. Cleugh, *Chant...*, pp. 129, 206–207, 211–213, 232–239, 244–245, 251, 255, 275, 279, 287. Clive, *Sun...*, pp. 42, 119, 120, 130, 232, 233, 237, 240, 265, 266, 292–3. Commynes, *Memoirs...*, pp. 203, 209, 231, 250, 307, 325, 329, 330, 332, 334, 340–353, 373, 375, 378–385, 397, 404, 411, 416. Pinnow, *History...*, p. 169. Scofield, *Life...*, II, pp. 235–236. Stephenson, *Mediaeval...*, p. 582.

MARIA OF CASTILE, queen of Aragon

b. 1401–d. 1458 Spain

Daughter of †Catherine of Lancaster and Henry III of Castile. Married Alfonso V of Aragon in 1415. When he became ruler of Naples, she was the "governor of Aragon" for him (1434-1458). An able soldier and negotiator, Maria proved to be a wise ruler. Her policies generally supported the lower classes and the craftspeople in the cities. She also patronized arts, literature, and ecclesiastical reform.

♦ **Art patrons. Childcare. Negotiators. Patrons of literature. Popes. Religious patrons. Rulers. Soldiers.** ♦

Altamira, *Spain...*, p. 259. Cloulas, *Borgias...*, pp. 9–10. Johnson, *Borgias...*, pp. 16, 17, 48. Miron, *Queens...*, pp. 286–306. Ryder, *Kingdom...*, pp. 37, 42, 104, 111, 112, 117n, 181, 207, 229, 235, 241, 249, 254, 275, 279, 308n, 309n, 312, 354n. Smith, *Spain...*, p. 98.

MARIE I OF CHAMPAGNE

See—MARIE OF FRANCE, countess of Champagne.

MARIE OF CHAMPAGNE, countess of Flanders

[Marie II of Champagne]

b. 1174–d. 1204/5 Flanders; France

Daughter of †Marie of France and Henry I of Champagne. Around 1186, Marie married Baldwin IX of Flanders; parents of †Jeanne and †Margaret of Flanders. An enthusiastic patron of vernacular literature and troubadour poetry. When her daughters were mere toddlers, Marie left to accompany Baldwin on Crusade, where she died (he presumably died, too).

♦ **Childcare. Crusades. Patrons of literature. Plague.** ♦

Anselme, *Histoire...*, v.2, p. 726. Baldwin, *Government...*, pp. 203–204. Thompson, *Literacy...*, p. 141. Wolff, "Baldwin...," pp. 285–287.

MARY OF CLERMONT

See—MARIE, countess of PONTHIEU and Aumale.

MARIE OF CLEVES, duchess of Orléans

b. 1427–d. 1487 France

Around 1441 she became the third wife of Charles of Orléans; mother of Anne, †Marie, and Louis of Orléans (later Louis XII of France). Marie enjoyed tournaments and dancing; she once gave Jacques de Lalaing a gold and ruby rod and a large diamond as tokens. Marie wrote poetry and Charles also wrote verses to her. In a panegyric verse to her daughter, François Villon called Marie of Cleves good, gentle, and wise. After Charles died in 1465, Marie became regent for her son. She was an ally of Charles of Burgundy; wrote warning to him that the king was using forced marches to hurry his men into a surprise confrontation with Charles. Marie's second husband was Jean, lord of Rabockenges.

♦ **Book owners. Dance. Models. Politics. Regents. Spies. Tournaments. Widows. Writers.** ♦

Anselme, *Histoire...*, v.1, p. 208. Bell, "Medieval...," p. 182 n28. Calmette, *Golden...*, p. 154. Cartellieri, *Court...*, p. 95. Champion, *Louis...*, pp. 104–105. Champion, *François...*, II, pp. 20, 105–110, 312. Commynes, *Memoirs...*, I, p. 102. Lewis, *François...*, p. 159. Moulin, *La poésie...*, pp. 103–104. Vale, *Charles...*, p. 85.

MARIA COMNENA, princess of Byzantium [Mary of Byzantium]

b. 1152–d.c. 1182 Byzantium

Daughter of Emperor Manuel Comnenus by his first wife, †Bertha of Sulzbach. For some years, Maria was heir apparent. Around 1168, her father and his new wife, †Mary of Antioch, had a son Alexius (II) who thus replaced Maria as next ruler of Byzantium. Maria then married Ranier of Montferrat. When her father died in 1180, Maria hatched plot to overthrow her half brother and her stepmother/regent, Mary of Antioch. Maria planned to replace them with her husband Ranier and herself as rulers. This proposed coup not only failed, it also opened the way for her cousin Andronicus to usurp. He soon had Maria and Ranier executed.

♦ **Murder. Politics. Rebellions. Spies. Squabbles.** ♦

Cambridge..., IV, pp. 370, 371, 372, 379, 380. Diehl, *Byzantine...*, p. 248. Norwich, *Kingdom...*, pp. 270–271, 302–305, 327, 330. Payne, *Dream...*, p. 265.

MARIA COMNENA, queen of Jerusalem

m. 1167–d. 1217 Byzantium; Israel

Daughter of John of Byzantium. In 1167, she married Amalric of Jerusalem. Maria supposedly used devious arts to acquire political power. She later became regent of Jerusalem. Her second husband was Balian of Ibelin.

♦ **Negotiators. Politics. Regents.** ♦

Bridge, *Crusades...*, p. 179. Hamilton, "Women...," pp. 161, 163, 165, 166, 169. Hill, *History...*, v.2, p. 75. Ide, *Women...*, A, p. 114. Payne, *Dream...*, pp. 173, 208.

MARY CONVERS

See—MARIOTTA CONVERS.

MARIE, lady de COUCY

See—Lady de COUCY.

MARIE DE COUCY, queen of Scotland

m. 1239–c. 1260 France; Scotland

Daughter of Enguerrand de Coucy; in 1239 became second wife of Alexander II of Scotland (d.1249); mother of Alexander III (b.c.1241). As queen-mother, in 1257, she reputedly added impetus to nationalist Scottish plots. Marie's second husband was John de Brienne (John of Acre).

♦ **Politics. Queens. Widows.** ♦

Brown, *History...*, I, pp. 116 & 122. Coulton, *Life...*, III, p. 18. Duncan, *Scotland...*, pp. 534, 535, 554, 558–560, 570, 573, 587. Mackie, *History...*, p. 47.

MARY OF ENGLAND

b. 1344–d.c. 1362 England; France

Daughter of †Philippa of Hainault and Edward III of England. Married in 1361 to John V de Montfort, who became duke of Brittany around 1364 (see †Jeanne de Montfort, duchess of Brittany). Mary died a few months after their marriage.

♦ **Dowry/dower. Pawns.** ♦

Anselme, *Histoire...*, v.1, p. 453. *DNB,* v.6, p. 487. Jones, *Creation...*, pp. 176, 259n, 267. Jones, *Ducal...*, p. 17. Tuchman, *Distant...*, p. 310n. Williamson, *Kings...*, p. 79.

MARIA ENRIQUEZ, duchess of Gandia [Maria Enriquez de Luna]

b. 1476–d.c. 1536 Spain

Around 1493, Maria married Giovanni Borgia, duke of Gandia (illegitimate son of Pope Alexander VI); their children were: Isabel and Juan II, duke of Gandia. When her husband was murdered in 1497, Maria denounced her brother-in-law, Cesare Borgia, as the murderer. She even tried to interest †Isabella, queen of Castile, and Ferdinand of Aragon in obtaining justice for her. As regent, Maria ably held Gandia for her son, proving to be a strong and energetic ruler. She was also very devout—Maria gave to charity, built hospitals, took care of the poor, etc. In 1512, she took vows and became Sister Gabriella of the Poor Clares, and in the 1530s was elected abbess.

♦ **Abbesses. Art patrons. Charity. Medicine. Murder. Popes. Regents. Religious patrons. Widows.** ♦

Chamberlin, *Fall...*, pp. 108–111, 156–157, 176, 310, 315, 330. Cloulas, *Borgias...*, pp. 53, 78, 80–1, 124, 137, 301–3. Fusero, *Borgias*, pp. 140–141, 163, 166, 301, 305. Johnson, *Borgias...*, pp. 90–91, 132, 134, 218–220.

MARIE (la fanière)

1292 France

Paid 2s tax on her hay-selling business in 1292 Paris.

♦ **Less-affluent. Merchants–hay.** ♦

Géraud, *Paris sous...,* p. 14.

MARIE DE FRANCE

fl.c. 1150s–1180s England; France

Very little is known of this writer except that she was probably born in Normandy, wrote her *Lais* by 1167, and spent some time at the English court, possibly as a beneficiary of the patronage of †Eleanor of Aquitaine. We can also assume that she was of noble birth. (Some scholars identify Marie as the sister of King Henry II of England, who later became abbess of Shaftesbury.) Marie translated Aesop's *Fables* and wrote other works, but her most famous writings are her romantic, verse novelettes, called the *Lais.* In most of these works—like *Guigemar, Équitan,* and *Le Fresne*—Marie addressed different types of love, from physical to transcendental emotions. Marie dealt much more fairly and sympathetically with her female characters than did most male poets. Her works were enduringly popular during the Middle Ages, and were even translated into Norwegian—among other languages.

♦ **Abbesses. Educated. Poets/troubadours. Writers.** ♦

Bogin, *Women...,* p. 36. Clark and Williams, "Impact...," pp. 176–177. Dronke, *Women...,* pp. viii, 84, 97, 281. Ferrante, "French...," pp. 64–89. Ferrante and Hannings (eds.), *Lais....* Fox, *Literary...,* pp. 140, 145, 167–171, 172, 176, 178, 179, 200, 209, 212, 226. Freeman, "The Power...." Kelly, *Eleanor...,* pp. 165, 184, 192. Mickel, *Marie....* Mickel, "Reconsideration...," pp. 40–65. Muir, *Literature...,* pp. 64–68. Nichols, "Lyric...," pp. 149 & 152. Pernoud, *Eleanor...,* pp. 115, 152–153. Sienaert, *Les lais de....* Thièbaux, *The Writings...,* pp. 197–206.

MARIE OF FRANCE, duchess of Brabant

b. 1198–d. 1238 Flanders; France

Daughter of †Agnes of Meran and Philip II of France. Legitimized around 1202, Marie was quickly betrothed to Arthur of Brittany. He died in 1204, so she married (1211) Philip of Namur. He died a year later, and she became the second wife of Henry I, duke of Brabant, in 1213.

♦ **Dowry/dower. Illegitimacy. Pawns.** ♦

Anselme, *Histoire...,* v.1, p. 80; v.2, p. 791. Baldwin, *Government...,* pp. 86, 98, 165, 203, 209–210, 269, 275. Barlow, *Feudal...,* p. 372. *Cambridge...,* VI, pp. 289 & 317.

MARIE OF FRANCE, countess of Champagne

[Marie I of Champagne]

b. 1145–d. 1198 France

Daughter of Louis VII of France and his first wife, †Eleanor of Aquitaine. Around 1160 Marie married Henry I the Liberal of Champagne. When he died in 1181, Marie became regent until 1187, when her son Henry II reached his majority. She was again regent while he was on Crusade, and after his death in 1197 at Acre. Marie was a good ruler and was lauded as such by contemporary authors. Today she is especially known as a patroness of literature—particularly of the courtly love poetry of troubadours.

♦ Educated. Models. Patrons of literature. Poets/troubadours. Regents. Widows. ♦

Benton, "Court...," pp. 551, 553–554, 561–564, 567, 578, 580–581, 586–589. Ennen, *Medieval...*, pp. 139, 141, 142. Fox, *Literary...*, pp. 121, 126, 128, 129, 145, 149, 161, 162, 180, 195. Kelly, *Eleanor...*, pp. 28, 76, 80, 82, 106, 126, 160, 164, 173, 183, 192, 194, 226, 281, 308, 328, 358, 385. Marks, *Pilgrims...*, pp. 137, 178–182, 187, 190, 300, 303. Matthews, "Wife...," p. 423. Pernoud, *Eleanor...*, pp. 46, 96, 120, 123, 152, 153, 185, 220, 253. Pernoud, *La femme...*, pp. 116–120. Thompson, *Literacy...*, pp. 142–143. Tierney, *Western...*, pp. 292, 330, 452, 453, 454.

MARY OF GELDERS, queen of Scotland [Gueldres; Gelderland]
b. 1433–d.c. 1464 Netherlands; Scotland

Daughter of Arnold, duke of Gelders. In 1449, Mary married James II of Scotland (d.1460); they had two daughters: †Mary and Margaret; and three sons: James III, Alexander, and John. After her husband died, Mary became regent for James III. She had her own powerful party, and even interfered in English politics to the extent of aiding Queen †Margaret of Anjou. Although she probably did take lovers (such as lord Hailes), Mary was an able and dedicated ruler. She also founded a church and hospital at Trinity.

♦ Medicine. Regents. Religious patrons. Soldiers. Widows. Women of easy virtue. ♦

Brown, *History...*, I, pp. 229, 249–251, 254–256. Clive, *Sun...*, pp. 29, 53, 98. Goodman, *Wars...*, pp. 57, 59, 62. Jacob, *Fifteenth...*, pp. 523 & 527. Mackie, *History...*, pp. 98 & 104. Mackie, *Short...*, p. 105. Scofield, *Life...*, I, pp. 116–117, 134, 176–177, 247–248, 290, 310. Vale, *Charles...*, pp. 84–5.

MARY HERVEY
fl. 1390s England

Governess and teacher of the children of †Mary de Bohun and Henry Bolingbroke (later Henry IV of England).

♦ Teachers. Servants–childcare. ♦

Gardiner, *English...*, p. 99. Legge (ed), *Anglo-Norman...*, p. 400 (#334). McFarlane, *Nobility...*, p. 243.

MARIA, queen of HUNGARY
b. 1365–d.c. 1394 Germany; Hungary

Oldest daughter and heiress of †Elizabeth of Bosnia and Louis the Great (of Anjou), king of Hungary and Poland. When her father died in 1382, Maria became queen of Hungary while her sister †Jadwiga was designated ruler of Poland. Maria married Sigismund, margrave of Brandenburg, later king of Hungary, Germany, and Bohemia, and Holy Roman Emperor. Maria was captured and imprisoned until Sigismund was forced to buy her freedom with certain concessions to Hungarian nobles.

♦ **Abduction. Estate. Prisons. Rulers.** ♦

Davies, *God's...,* pp. 109–110, 112. Fügedi, *Castle...,* p. 123. Halecki, *History...,* p. 66. Pamlényi, *History...,* pp. 78, 621, 626. Pares, *History...,* p. 64. Pinnow, *History...,* p. 150. Reddaway et al, *Cambridge...,* pp. 192, 194, 195, 205. Stephenson, *Mediaeval...,* p. 511, Table XVI.

MARY OF KIEV, queen of Poland **[Marie Dobrogneva]**

fl.c. 1040s-1060s Poland; Russia

Sister of Yaroslav I of Kiev; married King Kazimir I of Poland.

♦ **Queens.** ♦

Pares, *History...,* p. 35. Pernoud, *La femme...,* p. 231.

MARIA LACAPENA, empress of Bulgaria

m. 927 Bulgaria; Byzantium

Princess of Byzantium, Emperor Romanus (I) Lacapenus married her to Peter, emperor of Bulgaria. She brought Byzantine cultural and political influence to her new home.

♦ **Pawns. Politics. Queens.** ♦

Cambridge..., IV, pp. 66 & 238. Jenkins, *Byzantium...,* pp. 244, 252, & 262.

MARIA DE LUNA, queen of Aragon

c. 1370s–1407 Spain

Daughter of Brianda d'Agouth and Count Lope of Luna. Married Martin I of Aragon in 1372. In the 1390s, Maria was regent of Aragon while Martin was in Sicily.

♦ **Childcare. Regents. Soldiers.** ♦

Chaytor, *History...,* p. 200. Farraras et al, *Histoire...,* pp. 322–323, 327, 339–340. Hillgarth, *Pere...,* p. 589. Miron, *Queens...,* pp. 33, 227, 238–255, 258–260. O'Callaghan, *History...,* p. 539.

MARIE OF LUXEMBOURG

See—MARIE OF BOHEMIA, queen of France.

MARIA DE MALLA

fl. 1260s–1290s Spain

A fairly well-to-do woman of Barcelona; wife of Pere de Malla. After his death, Maria took over his shipping ventures. From the late 1270s until the early 1290s, she expanded her commercial enterprises by sending her sons (and other employees) to trade with Majorca, North Africa, and the Byzantine Empire. She traded a variety of commodities—such as oil, wax, silk, skins, and pepper.

♦ **Employers. Land/property. Merchants. Shipping. Widows.** ♦
Abulafia, "Catalan...," pp. 220–221 & notes.

MARIE (la mareschale)
1292 France

Evidently Marie did a fairly good business as a blacksmith in 1292 Paris since she was required to pay a tax of 27s.

♦ **Blacksmiths. Land/property.** ♦
Géraud, *Paris sous...*, p. 42.

MARIA "la MEDICA"
1480 Italy

At Brescia in 1480, this popular lay healer was tried by the Inquisition as a witch. It was believed she had sex with demons, attended sabbats, and used the Devil's help to kill children. Maria was sentenced to life in prison.

♦ **Doctors/empirics. Ecclesiastical courts–Inquisition. Prisons. Punishments. Witchcraft.** ♦
Kieckhefer, *European...*, p. 139. Russell, *Witchcraft...*, pp. 260-261.

MARIE (la meresse)
1292 France

Lay healer who worked near l'Hôpital de Lourcinnes in 1292 Paris; she paid a tax of 10s.

♦ **Doctors/empirics. Land/property.** ♦
Géraud, *Paris sous...*, p. 173. Hughes, *Women...*, p. 141. Hurd-Mead, *History...*, p. 215. Lipinska, *Histoire...*, p. 118.

MARIA DE MOLINA, queen of Castile
c. 1270s–d. 1321 Spain

Married Sancho IV, king of Castile. When he died in 1295 she was regent for minor son, Ferdinand IV. She was an excellent ruler—wise, politically astute, strong, and charismatic. As king, Ferdinand did not treat her well, but around 1312 Maria was again called upon to restore order and act as regent for her grandson Alfonso XI who inherited the throne at age one.

♦ **Regents. Widows.** ♦
Altamira, *Spain*, p. 236. *Cambridge...*, VII, p. 573. Effinger, *Women...*, pp. 300–306. Livermore, *History...*, pp. 140–142. Shneidman, *Rise...*, pp. 341, 343, 345, 358, 469. Smith, *Spain*, pp. 65, 68, & 69.

MARIE OF MONTPELLIER, queen of Aragon
c. 1180–1210s France; Italy; Spain

Daughter and heiress of †Eudoxia Comnena and William VIII of Montpellier (d.1202). Married around 1192 to Barral of Marseilles, who soon died. Marie then married elderly Bernard, count of Comminges. He died in 1201 in the midst of a divorce fight. In 1204, Marie married

Pedro II of Aragon. Although she bore his son and heir, Jaime I, Pedro soon tried to divorce her. Marie fled to Rome to escape her husband's wrath, and to contest the divorce.

♦ **Divorce. Estate. Pawns. Popes. Squabbles.** ♦

Altamira, *Spain,* p. 162. Bonner (ed.), *Songs...,* p. 239. Chaytor, *History...,* pp. 68–69. Lacarra and Gonzales, "Les Testaments de...," pp. 105–120. Marks, *Pilgrims...,* p. 264. O'Callaghan, *History...,* pp. 249 & 334. Shneidman, *Rise...,* pp. 34, 38, 158, 295, 298, 304, 305.

MARIE OF NAVARRE, queen of Aragon **[Marie d'Évreux]**
m. 1338–d. 1347 France; Spain

Daughter of †Jeanne of France and Philip d'Évreux, king of Navarre. First wife of Pedro IV of Aragon. Marie was noted both for her piety and her extravagance.

♦ **Childbirth. Dowry/dower. Pawns. Religious patrons. Queens.** ♦

Hillgarth, *Pere...,* pp. 5, 38, 43, 49–50, 185, 213–215, 219, 288, 369, 380, 391–393, 395–396. Leroy, *La Navarre...,* p. 129. Miron, *Queens...,* pp. 81–92. Shneidman, *Rise...,* pp. 87, 89, 103, 354, 488.

MARY OF OIGNIES **[Blessed Mary]**
b. 1177–d. 1213 Belgium

Although she married at age fourteen, Mary was already devoted to virginity and piety. She persuaded her husband that they should not permit sexual intimacy in their relationship, and later talked him into working with her at a leper colony. A proselytizing mystic, Mary attracted numerous followers to her individualistic beliefs. She was part of the new emphasis on the humanity of Christ, and she also stressed chastity, work, poverty, converting heretics, and teaching. Although Mary herself did not preach, she aided Jacques de Vitry with his sermons. In 1207, Mary moved to the isolated convent of St. Nicholas at Oignies where she attracted more followers, and performed miraculous conversions. Jacques de Vitry wrote her *Vita,* which not only included the inspirational life story of Mary, but incorporated a propaganda effort to gain official ecclesiastical recognition for Beguines in general.

♦ **Beguines. Leprosy. Medicine. Models. Mystics. Preachers. Relics. Religieuses. Teachers. Virginity.** ♦

Bolton, "Mulieres Sanctae...," pp. 144–145. Bolton, "Vitae Matrum...," pp. 255–257, 260–263, & 268. Bynum, *Holy...,* pp. 7, 24, 59, 112, 115–124 passim, 130, 193, 199, 203, 204, 209, 213–215, 221, 227–229, 234, 250, 255, 274, 275. Coulton, *Life...,* III, p. 27. Leff, *Heresy...,* v.1, p. 18. McDonnell, *Beguines...,* pp. 51, 145, 150–151, 382, & 392. Neel, "Origins...," pp. 244–8, 250, 252, 254, 255, 256, 258, 259. Petroff, *Medieval...,* pp. 179–183. Power, *Nunneries...,* p. 525.

MARIE D'ORLÉANS
b. 1457–d. 1493 France

Daughter of Charles, duke of Orléans, and his third wife, †Marie of Cleves. François Villon wrote panegyric verses to her. Marie married Jean de Foix, count of Étampes and viscount of Narbonne.

♦ **Dance. Estate. Models.** ♦

Anselme, *Histoire...*, v.1, p. 208. Bonner, *Complete...*, p. 218. Champion, *François...*, I, pp. 44, 46, 47; II, pp. 105–110. Coryn, *House...*, pp. 257, 273, 275. Lewis, *François...*, pp. 159, 167–168.

MARIA DE PADILLA

fl. 1340s–d. 1361 Spain

Mistress of Pedro I of Castile; mother of his children. After her death, Pedro claimed they had been married so the children were legitimate.

♦ **Mistresses. Politics. Superstitions.** ♦

Armitage-Smith, *John...*, p. 37. *Cambridge...*, VII, pp. 575, 576, 579. Jamison, *Life...*, I, pp. 248, 249, 251, 284, 285. Livermore, *History...*, pp. 144, 145, 163. Smith, *Spain*, pp. 72–73.

MARIE, countess of PONTHIEU and Aumale [Mary of Clermont]

c. 1200s–d.c. 1251 France

Daughter of †Alys of France and William II, count of Ponthieu. Wife of Simon de Dammartin, count of Aumale; Marie inherited many fiefs in Ponthieu. She gave one of these—Arguel—to her third daughter †Philippa when the girl married Otho, count of Gueldres. Marie was also a noted literary patroness; Gerbert de Montreuil dedicated more than one of his works to her. In 1243, Marie married her second husband, Mathieu de Montmorency (d.1250).

♦ **Dowry/dower. Estate. Models. Patrons of literature.** ♦

Anselme, *Histoire...*, v.3, pp. 302–303. Belleval, *Les fiefs...*, pp. 15–16, 90, 246–247. Fawtier, *Capetian...*, pp. 160–161. Lejeune, "La Femme...," p. 207. Prestwich, *Edward...*, p. 316.

MARIA OF PORTUGAL, queen of Castile

c. 1310s–1350s Portugal; Spain

Daughter of †Beatrice of Castile and Alfonso IV of Portugal; married Alfonso XI of Castile in 1327; son Pedro I, the Cruel, was born around 1334. After Pedro was born, Alfonso neglected Maria and again treated his mistress †Leonor de Guzman as his consort. When Alfonso XI died in 1350, Maria supposedly had her rival Leonor executed.

♦ **Murder. Pawns. Queens. Squabbles.** ♦

Armitage-Smith, *John...*, pp. 35 & 36. *Cambridge...*, VII, pp. 574–576. Jamison, *Life...*, I, pp. 246–247 & 250–252. Smith, *Spain*, p. 72. Stephens, *Story...*, pp. 92 & 93.

MARY OF SCOTLAND

b. 1451–1488 Denmark; Scotland

Daughter of †Mary of Gelders and James II of Scotland. In 1467, Mary married Thomas Boyd, earl of Arran. When his life was threatened by plot against him, Mary warned Thomas and fled with him to Denmark (c.1469). After his death, she returned to Scotland, and in 1474, Mary wed James, lord Hamilton; their son was also named James.

♦ **Pawns. Spies. Widows.** ♦

Brown, *History...*, I, pp. 250, 259, 261, 262. *C.P.*, v.6, pp. 255–256. Mackie, *History...*, pp. 105–106.

MARY OF SCOTLAND, countess of Boulogne **[Mary of Atholl]**

b. 1085–1110s France; Scotland

Daughter of (St.) †Margaret and Malcolm III of Scotland. Educated at Romsey Abbey by her aunt †Christina of Hungary. Married Eustace III, count of Boulogne; their daughter, †Matilda of Boulogne (b.1102), was later queen of England.

♦ **Educated. Genealogy.** ♦

Barrow, *Feudal...*, pp. 115, 417, 420. Duncan, *Scotland...*, pp. 124, 126, 218. Eckenstein, *Woman...*, p. 207. Glover, *Story...*, pp. 52 & 65. Mackie, *History...*, pp. 46–47.

MARIA OF SICILY

fl.c. 1370s–d. 1401 Italy; Spain

Daughter of †Costanza of Aragon and King Frederick III of Sicily. She became the orphaned heir to the throne of Sicily when her father died around 1377. Maria was abducted by an ally of Pedro IV of Aragon who then married her to his grandson, Martin II the Younger, heir of Aragon.

♦ **Abduction. Estate. Orphans. Pawns.** ♦

Chamberlin, *Count...*, pp. 69–70. Chaytor, *History...*, pp. 190, 191, 192, 196. Hillgarth, *Pere...*, pp. 57, 586–587, 593, 594, 596–598, 600. Miron, *Queens...*, p. 241. O'Callaghan, *History...*, p. 542. Runciman, *Sicilian...*, p. 328 & Table III. Smith, *Spain*, p. 95.

MARY OF ST. POL, countess of Pembroke **[Marie de Sancto Paulo]**

b. 1304–c. 1380s England; France

Daughter of Mary of Brittany and Guy IV de Châtillon, count of St. Pol. Around 1320 she became the third wife of Aymer de Valence, earl of Pembroke. He died around 1324 and she survived him for over fifty years. As a childless widow, Mary devoted her energies and wealth to a variety of pious causes. In 1347 she founded Pembroke College at Cambridge. She also established convents, and gave generously to a number of religious institutions.

♦ **Bequests. Book owners. Charity. Dowry/dower. Estate. Legal activity. Managers. Politics. Relics. Religieuses. Religious patrons. University. Widows.** ♦

Bryant, *Age...*, pp. 213 & 362. *Calendar of Plea...*, II, p. 242. *Calendar of Wills...*, I, p. 310. *DNB*, v.1, p. 761. Jenkinson, "Mary...," pp. 401–430. Power, *Women...*, p. 48. Riley, *Memorials...*, p. 553. Robertson, *Chaucer's...*, pp. 22 & 24. Rosenthal, *Purchase...*, pp. 67–69.

MARIE OF VALOIS

m.c. 1324–d. 1331 France; Italy

See—CATHERINE OF AUSTRIA [Catherine of Hapsburg].

♦ **Genealogy.** ♦

MARIE DE VENTADOUR

b. 1165–c. 1220s France

Daughter of Helis de Castelnau and Ramon II of Turenne; she married Eble V of Ventadour around 1180. Marie wrote poetry herself, and she also was an influential patroness of troubadours.

♦ **Patrons of literature. Poets/troubadours.** ♦

Bogin, *Women...,* pp. 98–101, 168–169. Boutière and Schutz, *Biographies des...,* pp. 75–77, 170–179, 208–209, 212–214, 457, 460, 461. Egan, *Vidas...,* pp. 68–69. Marks, *Pilgrims...,* pp. 104, 195, 208, 223.

MARIA OF VIVAR, countess of Barcelona

m.c. 1095 Spain

Daughter of †Ximena and Rodrigo Diaz of Vivar—*le Cid.* Around 1095, Maria became the first wife of Ramon Berenguer III, count of Barcelona; their son was Ramon Berenguer IV.

♦ **Genealogy. Models.** ♦

Altamira, *Spain,* p. 154. *Cambridge...,* VI, pp. 401 & 402. Clissold, *In Search...,* pp. 169–191, 213, 229. Effinger, *Women...,* p. 267. Fletcher, *Quest...,* pp. 178–179, 187. Shneidman, *Rise...,* p. 294.

MASSIOTA (la Lavendere)

1365 England

Professional laundress of London; earned very little. Had to promise city aldermen that she would restrain her tongue and behave herself.

♦ **Laundresses. Less-affluent. Miscreants.** ♦

Calendar of Plea..., II, p. 26. Kendall, *Yorkist...,* p. 340. Thrupp, *Merchant...,* p. 139 n116.

MATHA

See—MARTHA.

MATHELINE FAURÉ

1335 France

See—ARMANDE ROBERT.

♦ **Witchcraft.** ♦

MATILDA / MAUD

Also see—MECHTILD.

MATILDA, countess of ALIFE

See—MATILDA OF SICILY, countess of Alife.

MATILDA OF ANJOU, princess of England, abbess of Fontevrault **[Alice; Isabella]**
c. 1110s–1160s England; France

Even though she had entered a convent as a girl, Matilda's father, Foulques V of Anjou, insisted that she marry William of England (son of King Henry I) in 1119. William drowned in the wreck of the *White Ship* the next year, so Matilda returned to Fontevrault. She became abbess in 1148.

♦ **Abbesses. Dowry/dower. Educated. Pawns. Widows.** ♦

Barlow, *Feudal...*, pp. 196–197. Chambers, *Norman...*, pp. 158 & 163. *DNB*, v.21, p. 337. Jourdain, "Memoire...," p. 475. Kelly, *Eleanor...*, pp. 342, 345, 354. Pernoud, *Eleanor...*, pp. 92, 93–94, 243. Pernoud, *La femme...*, pp. 150–153.

MATILDA OF BOULOGNE, queen of England
b. 1105–d. 1152 England; France

Daughter of †Mary (of Atholl), princess of Scotland, and Eustace III, count of Boulogne. Around 1120, Matilda married Stephen of Blois, who later became king of England. In the ongoing war for English throne between the Empress †Matilda and King Stephen, Queen Matilda was an able and courageous assistant to her husband. She negotiated alliance with King David I of Scotland. After Stephen was captured, Queen Matilda gathered his army and captured Robert of Gloucester. She obtained Stephen's release by trading him for Robert.

♦ **Negotiators. Regents. Soldiers.** ♦

Barlow, *Feudal...*, pp. 183, 201, 206–207, 210, 212, 219–221, 233–234, 250–251, 258, 267, 271. Brown, *History...*, I, p. 82. *Cambridge...*, V, pp. 543, 544, 548, 551. Chambers, *Norman...*, pp. 165, 180–181, 189, 191–192, 196. *Gesta Stephani...*, pp. 80–88 passim, 107n. Glover, *Story...*, p. 65. Green, *Letters...*, p. 13. Mackie, *History...*, p. 47.

MATILDA OF BOULOGNE, queen of Portugal
[Maude; Mahaut de Dammartin]
b. 1202–d. 1258 France; Portugal

Daughter and heiress of †Ida of Boulogne and Renaud (Reginald), count of Dammartin. In 1216, Matilda married Philip Hurepel. After he died in 1233, Matilda married Alfonso III of Portugal. He repudiated Matilda in 1249 so that he could marry †Beatrice de Guzman.

♦ **Art patrons. Divorce. Estate. Religious patrons.** ♦

Appleby, *John...*, p. 177. Baldwin, *Government...*, pp. 201–202.

MAUD DE BRAOSE **[Matilda de Briouze; of St. Valery]**
d. 1210 England; France; Ireland; Wales

Probably the daughter of Bernard of St. Valéry. Wife of William de Braose. She refused to give King John her son William as a hostage because she claimed that John had murdered his nephew Arthur. She and her son were captured and starved to death.

♦ **Estate. Murder. Politics. Prisons.** ♦

Barlow, *Feudal...*, pp. 411 & 413. Barrow, *Feudal...*, pp. 204–205. Bingham, *Crowned...*, p. 167. *Cambridge...*, VII, p. 543. Orpen, *Ireland...*, II, pp. 236, 256, 258. Powicke, "Loretta...," pp. 148, 150–151, 156–157, 158.

MAUD CHAWORTH

c. 1310 England

See—ELEANOR OF LANCASTER and MATILDA OF LANCASTER.

♦ **Genealogy.** ♦

MATILDA DE BURGHAM

1321 England

Servant of Robert and Johanna de Derby of London. When Robert died (c.1321), he bequeathed a shop to Matilda.

♦ **Bequests. Land/property. Servants.** ♦

Calendar of Wills..., I, p. 292.

MAUD CLIFFORD, countess of Cambridge

c. 1400s–1440s England

Daughter of Thomas, lord Clifford. Maud was the second wife of Richard, earl of Cambridge (his first wife was †Anne Mortimer).

♦ **Genealogy.** ♦

DNB, v.16, p. 1061. Jacob, *Fifteenth...*, p. 146. Johnson, *Duke...*, pp. 26 & 229.

MATILDA OF ENGLAND, duchess of Bavaria and Saxony

b. 1156–d.c. 1189 England; Germany

Daughter of †Eleanor of Aquitaine and Henry II of England. Around 1167 she married Henry the Lion of Bavaria and Saxony; their sons included: Otto IV, Holy Roman Emperor, and William of Brunswick. Matilda was interested in poetry—troubadour Bertran de Born found her especially inspirational.

♦ **Educated. Models. Patrons of literature. Regents.** ♦

Appleby, *John...*, pp. 9, 23, 92, 159, 260. Barlow, *Feudal...*, pp. 326, 339, 349–350. Barrow, *Feudal...*, pp. 182 & 419. Bryce, *Holy...*, p. 206. *Cambridge...*, V, pp. 402, 460, 469; VI, pp. 294, 299. Eckenstein, *Woman...*, p. 201. Ennen, *Medieval...*, pp. 142–144. Fuhrmann, *Germany...*, pp. 152, 159, 168, 179. Hallam (ed.), *Plantagenet...*, pp. 112, 113, 114, 225. Haverkamp, *Medieval...*, pp. 223 & 266. Kelly, *Eleanor...*, pp. 103, 110, 129, 134, 191, 207–11, 229, 289, 336, 346. Lloyd, *Maligned...*, pp. 6, 91, 339. Marks, *Pilgrims...*, pp. 198–199. Norwich, *Kingdom...*, p. 370. Pernoud, *Eleanor...*, pp. 102, 142, 180, 194, 240. Warren, *Feudal...*, pp. 78, 104, 221–223, 278, 600, 603.

MATILDA OF ENGLAND, Holy Roman Empress

b. 1102–d. 1164 England; France; Germany

Daughter of †Matilda of Scotland and Henry I of England. Married (1) around 1113, Henry V of Germany, Holy Roman Emperor (d.1124);

and (2) around 1128, Geoffrey of Anjou (Plantagenet; d.1150). Her son Henry, by her second husband, became Henry II, king of England. Matilda was strong-willed, shrewd, and courageous. Although officially her father's heir to the throne of England (1135), Matilda's crown was usurped by her cousin Stephen of Blois before she could reach England. For the next twenty years, the Empress conducted war for the throne—and finally succeeded in having her son named heir. Matilda gave to pious charities; she was also a literary patron and a papal supporter.

♦ Charity. Divorce. Dowry/dower. Educated. Models. Negotiators. Patrons of literature. Pawns. Politics. Popes. Religious patrons. Rulers. Soldiers. Squabbles. Widows. Writers. ♦

Barlow, *Feudal...,* pp. 174, 195, 197–203, 216–224, 251, 257, 268, 284, 286. Barlow, *Thomas...,* pp. 23, 27–28, 104, 107, 127, 135, 145, 150–151, 161. Bullough and Storey, *Study...,* p. 98. Ferguson, *Survey...,* pp. 182 & 188. Fuhrmann, *Germany...,* pp. 87, 94, 104, 117, 133. *Gesta Stephani...,* pp. 35, 58–59, 75–100 passim, 118, 136. Green, *Letters...,* p. 9–10. Hallam (ed.), *Plantagenet...,* pp. 43, 45–8, 52, 60, 62, 63, 65, 68, 69, 73–4, 102. Haverkamp, *Medieval...,* pp. 129, 135, 137, 266. Heinrich, *Canonesses...,* p. 199. Hollister, "Anglo-Norman...," pp. 19–42. Kelly, *Eleanor...,* pp. 75, 77, 84, 88, 91, 92, 113, 114, 161, 174, 192, 254, 264. Lejeune, "La Femme...," p. 205. Lloyd, *Maligned...,* pp. 20–1, 382. Mackie, *Short...,* pp. 39 & 41. Pain, *Empress....* Pernoud, *Eleanor...,* pp. 80, 88, 96, 100, 102, 106, 114, 134, 138, 142. Thompson, *Literacy...,* p. 174. Warren, *Henry...,* pp. 11, 12, 14, 16, 17–20, 23–36, 60 ... 260, 333, 363, 367, 476. Winston, *Thomas...,* pp. 64, 174, 225, 332, 338. Wrightman, *Lacy...,* pp. 79–80.

MATILDA OF ESSEN

b. 949–d.c. 1011 — Germany

Daughter of Liudolf and †Ida of Swabia; granddaughter of †Edith of England and Emperor Otto I. Abbess of Essen from 973 until 1011. Well-educated in Latin, she commissioned several religious art works.

♦ Abbesses. Art patrons. Book owners. Educated. Religious patrons. ♦

Campbell, *Anglo-Saxons,* pp. 170 & 171. Duckett, *Death...,* p. 295. Leyser, *Rule...,* p. 53. Stenton, *Anglo-Saxon...,* pp. 342 & 455.

MATILDA OF FLANDERS, queen of England

b. 1031–d. 1083 — England; Flanders; France

Daughter of †Adela of France and Baldwin V, count of Flanders. In 1053, Matilda married William of Normandy ("the Conqueror"), later king of England. Matilda was extremely well-educated, and she saw to it that their children also received a good education. She proved to be a firm, wise ruler when she governed Normandy while William was in England. One legend attributes the *Bayeux Tapestry* to Matilda, but she was probably not even involved in commissioning its manufacture. She founded the abbey of the Holy Trinity at Caen. Matilda raided numerous

English religious houses for precious items with which to enrich her own French foundations.

♦ **Artistic clothwork. Educated. Miscreants. Models. Regents. Relics–theft. Religious patrons. Teachers.** ♦

Barlow, *Feudal...*, pp. 65, 82, 91, 142, 198. Bates, *Normandy...*, pp. 76, 130, 151, 199, 250, 258. Brown, *Normans...*, pp. 142, 146, 149, 180, 189, 192, 194, 199, 202, 208, 244, 246. *DNB*, v.13, pp. 50 & 51. Decaux, *Histoire...*, pp. 209–210. Douglas, *William...*, pp. 47, 75–80, 185, 213, 236, 243, 249, 335, 369–370, 391–395. Haskins, *Normans...*, pp. 11, 61, 77, 186. Heinrich, *Canonesses...*, p. 196. Jourdain, "Memoire...," p. 474. Thompson, *Literacy...*, pp. 167–168. Vitalis, *Ecclesiastical...*, v.II, pp. 130–131.

MATILDA OF FRANCE **[Matilda of Burgundy]**
fl. 940s–970s France

Daughter of †Gerberga of Saxony and King Louis IV d'Outremer of France; offered as a matrimonial pawn by her brother King Lothar of France to Conrad the Pacific of Burgundy. Her dowry included the counties of Lyons and Vienne. She was a generous patron to the abbey of Cluny and also intervened with her husband to obtain land grants and privileges for other religious establishments. Matilda was often more energetic than her husband; in 965, she destroyed a castle that had been illegally built on her lands.

♦ **Dowry/dower. Legal activity. Managers. Pawns. Religious patrons. Soldiers.** ♦

Anselme, *Histoire...*, v.1, p. 37. Lewis, *Development...*, pp. 235, 259, 275. McKitterick, *Frankish...*, pp. 265, 322, tables 5 & 9. Riché, *Les Carolingiens...*, p. 256. Stafford, *Queens...*, pp. 88 & 124.

MAUD FRANCIS, countess of Salisbury **[Matilda Fraunceys]**
c. 1370s–1400s England

Daughter of Agnes and Adam Fraunceys, a London merchant and alderman. Maud's marriages enriched her and elevated her social status. She married (1) a rich London merchant, John Aubrey (d.1380); (2) Sir Alan Buxhall; (3) John de Montacute, earl of Salisbury. After he died (c.1400), Maud ended her marital career. She received several manors from the king for her maintenance and retired to her estates.

♦ **Dowry/dower. Estate. Merchants. Widows.** ♦

Brewer, *Chaucer...*, p. 65. *DNB*, v.13, p. 654. Thrupp, *Merchant...*, pp. 266, 322, 341.

MATILDA, queen of GERMANY **[Matilda of Saxony]**
c. 910s–d. 969 Germany

A member of a powerful clan—with extensive dowry lands in Saxony and Lotharingia—Matilda was presumably raised in a convent until she married Henry I the Fowler, king of Germany. She made political prophecies, founded Quedlinburg, and was considered saintly. Matilda favored her son Henry over her elder son, Otto I the Great. As king (936), Otto deprived Matilda of her lands and forced her from court.

After some ten years, however, she regained her position as a political and religious force. Liutprand of Cremona thought highly of Matilda.

♦ **Dowry/dower. Educated. Models. Mystics. Politics. Religieuses. Religious patrons. Widows.** ♦

Cambridge..., III, pp. 185, 186, 203. Duckett, *Death...*, pp. 59, 67, 93, 283. Leyser, *Rule...*, pp. 10, 12, 14, 16, 21, 22, 26, 28, 47, 53, 55, 62, 65, 67, 72, 75, 85, 87, & 90. Pernoud, *La femme...*, pp. 46–47. Riché, *Les Carolingiens...*, pp. 247 & 249. Stafford, *Queens...*, pp. 3, 7, 11, 12, 22, 28, 32–34, 74, 89, 90, 101, 104, 106, 108, 110, 120–121, 124, 143, 144, 156–160, 164, 166, 168, 178, 182–185, 189, & 209. Wright, *Works...*, p. 153.

MATILDA OF HAINAULT, princess of Achaia

d. 1331 — Flanders; Greece; Italy

Daughter of †Isabella of Achaia (Villehardouin) and Florent d'Avesnes of Hainault. Married (1) Guy, duke of Athens and (2) Louis of Burgundy. Twice widowed, Matilda was later imprisoned by Robert the Wise of Naples for refusing to marry John of Durazzo (of Gravino).

♦ **Estate. Pawns. Prisons. Regents. Widows.** ♦

Anselme, *Histoire...*, v.1, pp. 416 & 417. *Cambridge...*, IV, pp. 452, & 474. Cheetham, *Greece...*, pp. 122–123, 129, 130, 132, 144, 145, 232.

MATILDA OF LANCASTER **[Maud]**

fl. 1310s–1340s — England

Daughter of †Maud Chaworth and Henry, third earl of Lancaster (thus she was sister of Henry, first duke of Lancaster). Married William de Burgh, earl of Ulster; mother of †Elizabeth de Burgh. After William died in 1332, Maud married Ralph Ufford (d.1346).

♦ **Genealogy. Managers.** ♦

Calendar of Plea..., I, p. 179. *DNB,* v.3, p. 331; v.9, p. 552; v.20, p. 10.

MATILDA OF LANCASTER, duchess of Zealand **[Maud]**

fl. 1340–d. 1362 — England; Netherlands

Daughter and co-heiress of †Isabel Beaumont and Henry, first duke of Lancaster (d.1361). In 1344, she married Ralph de Stafford (d.1348). In 1352, Matilda married William of Bavaria, duke of Zealand. When she returned to England to check on her new estates, Matilda fell victim to the plague. Her estates then passed to her sister, †Blanche of Lancaster.

♦ **Estate. Plague.** ♦

Armitage-Smith, *John...*, pp. 13 & 20. *DNB,* v.9, p. 556. Froissart, *Chronicles...*, I, p. 75. Hardy, *Philippa...*, pp. 151, 225, 247–8, 256, 265, 267, 272–3, 298. McFarlane, *Nobility...*, p. 86. Roche, *Dona...*, pp. 5, 6. Wentersdorf, "Clandestine...," pp. 219 & 230.

MATILDA OF LEICESTER

1389 — England

Anchoress of Leicester. Matilda was arrested and questioned about possible Lollard beliefs. She renounced her unorthodox views, after which she was allowed to return to her religious pursuits.

♦ **Anchoresses. Bequests. Ecclesiastical courts. Lollards.** ♦

Cross, "Great...," p. 360. Lambert, *Medieval...*, p. 248. Warren, *Anchorites...*, pp. 79–81, 87, 110, 176.

MAUD LOVELL, lady Arundel

fl. 1410s–d. 1436 England; France

Daughter of †Elizabeth Bryene and Robert Lovell. Married (1) Sir Richard Stafford (d.1427). Around 1429, Maud became the second wife of John, earl of Arundel (after the death of his first wife, Constance of Fanhope). The imprisoned Charles of Orléans was enamored of Maud, and he often wrote poetry for her. She died less than a year after her second husband.

♦ **Models. Prisons. Widows.** ♦

C.P., v.1, p. 248. Jacob, *Fifteenth...*, p. 484.

MATILDA DE LUCY

c. 1360s–d. 1398 England

Daughter of Margaret de Multon and Thomas de Lucy, lord Lucy. Heiress of her brother Anthony, lord Lucy. Married (1) Gilbert de Umfraville (d.1381) and (2) second wife of Henry, lord Percy (created earl of Northumberland in 1377).

♦ **Estate. Pawns.** ♦

C.P., v.8, p. 254. Given-Wilson, *English...*, p. 134. Jacob, *Fifteenth...*, p. 54.

MAUD MAKEJOY **[Matill' Makejoye]**

c. 1306 England

Dancer and acrobat who entertained at English court in 1306.

♦ **Dance–professional. Less-affluent.** ♦

Chambers, *Stage...*, II, p. 238. Clark and Williams, "Impact...," p. 160. Prestwich, *Edward...*, p. 117.

MATILDA MARESFLETE

1404 England

Taught religion for guild of the Holy Trinity in Lincolnshire.

♦ **Preachers. Teachers.** ♦

Abram, *English...*, p. 218. Gardiner, *English...*, p. 76. Orme, *English...*, p. 55.

MATILDA OF NORTHUMBERLAND, queen of Scotland

[Maud of Huntingdon]

c. 1080s–d.c. 1130 England; France; Scotland

Daughter of Judith of Lens (niece of William the Conqueror) and Waltheof, earl of Northumberland and Huntingdon. Married (1) Simon de Senlis (Simon of St. Liz) and (2) David I, king of Scotland (r.1124-1153).

♦ **Estate. Queens.** ♦

Barlow, *Feudal...*, p. 182. Barrow, *Feudal...*, pp. 135 & 420. *Cambridge...*, VII, p. 558. *DNB*, v.5, p. 567. Duncan, *Scotland...*, pp. 134, 217, 218, 223. Mackie, *History...*, pp. 47 & 49. Warren, *Henry...*, p. 176.

MATILDA OF QUEDLINBURG **[Mathilda]**
fl. 954–d. 999 Germany

Daughter of †Adelheid of Burgundy and Otto I. Matilda was abbess of her grandmother's (†Matilda, queen of Germany) foundation of Quedlinburg. She was an expert at artistic clothwork, and she supervised her nuns in embroidering very ornate clothing and altar pieces. In the 980s, Matilda was regent for her nephew, Otto III. In that capacity, Matilda led an army in the defeat of the invading Wends in 983. She also shared her medical and historical knowledge with her cousin, †Hroswitha of Gandersheim.

♦ **Abbesses. Artistic clothwork. Medicine. Models. Patrons of literature. Regents. Soldiers.** ♦

Cambridge..., III, p. 174. Duckett, *Death...*, pp. 108, 125, 146, 181. Ennen, *Medieval...*, pp. 64, 66, 83. Heinrich, *Canonesses...*, p. 189. Hurd-Mead, *History...*, p. 112. Leyser, *Rule...*, pp. 27, 44, 49, 53, 66, 72, 87, 89. Stafford, *Queens...*, pp. 115, 121, 141, 184, 185.

MATILDA OF ROTTENBURG, countess Palantine **[Mechtild]**
fl. 1450s Germany

Patroness of literary reforms and humanist writers. Numerous authors dedicated their works, or translations, to Princess Matilda. A founder of universities—Tübingen and Freiburg.

♦ **Book owners. Models. Patrons of literature. University.** ♦

Bell, "Medieval...," p. 181 n28. Harksen, *Women...*, p. 54. Schoenfeld, *Women...*, pp. 202–203.

MATILDA OF SAVOY, queen of Portugal
m. 1146–d. 1157 Portugal

Daughter of Mahaut of Albon and Amadeus II of Savoy, count of Maurienne; married Alfonso Henriques I of Portugal. Matilda helped to arrange marriages for her daughters.

♦ **Negotiators. Queens.** ♦

Anselme, *Histoire...*, v.1, p. 574. José, *La Maison...*, p. 50. Stephens, *Story...*, pp. 41 & 54.

MATILDA OF SCOTLAND, queen of England
[Eadgyth; Edith; Maud; "Good Queen Mold"]
b. 1080–d. 1118 England; Scotland

Daughter of (St.) †Margaret and Malcolm III of Scotland. Educated at convent of Romsey by her very strict but learned aunt, †Christina of Hungary. In 1100, Matilda married King Henry I of England. She was patroness of musicians and Latin writers, particularly interested in religious works. Matilda was also very pious. She founded hospitals, encouraged charity to the poor, repaired roads and bridges, and corresponded with Pope Paschal II in order to heal the breach between Henry and Anselm, archbishop of Canterbury.

♦ **Educated. Medicine. Models. Music. Ordeals. Patrons of literature. Politics. Popes. Religieuses. Religious patrons. Writers–letters.** ♦

Davis, *First...*, p. 280. Duncan, *Scotland...*, pp. 124 & 126. Elkins, *Holy...*, pp. 2–5, 176–177 n., 183 n.5. Glover, *Story...*, pp. 50, 52, 53 & 65. Green, *Letters...*, p. 1–6. Lejeune, "La Femme...," p. 205. Mackie, *Short...*, p. 29. Pernoud, *La femme...*, pp. 150–152. Thièbaux, *The Writings...*, pp. 165–179. Thompson, *Literacy...*, pp. 170–171.

MATILDA OF SICILY, countess of Alife **[Matilda of Alife]**

fl. 1120s–1130s Italy

Daughter of Roger I of Sicily; married Rainulf of Alife (d.1139). Around 1131, Matilda fled home to Sicily with her son, imploring her half brother, Roger II, to protect her from Rainulf's cruelty. Rainulf rebelled in an attempt to retrieve Matilda (and her large dowry lands). After her husband was defeated, Matilda returned to him, but lost some of her lands to Roger. She is thought to have commissioned Alexander of Telese to write a biography of Roger II.

♦ **Dowry/dower. Patrons of literature. Politics. Squabbles.** ♦

Douglas, *Norman...*, Table 2. Norwich, *Kingdom...*, pp. 18, 32, 405. Norwich, *Normans...*, pp. 282, 309, 340. Osborne, *Greatest...*, Table.

MATILDA OF TUSCANY

b. 1046–d. 1115 Italy

Daughter and heiress of †Beatrice and Boniface II of Tuscany (murdered 1052). In 1069, Matilda married Godfrey V the Hunchback of Lorraine (murdered in 1076). This formidable countess personally extended and ruled her vast lands. Matilda was fluent in several languages, including Latin. She corresponded with learned contemporaries, studied legal codes, and collected manuscripts. A firm papal supporter, she fought Emperors Henry IV and V at the negotiating table and on the military field. She was one of the papacy's witnesses to Henry IV's penance at her castle of Canossa. In 1089, the pope persuaded forty-three-year-old Matilda to wed seventeen-year-old Welf V of Bavaria. This union was condemned by many observers; the couple separated by 1095. Although Henry IV was never able to subdue Matilda on the battlefield, his son Henry V vanquished her troops and forced Matilda to name him as her heir. Since originally her lands had been willed to the Papal See, these estates were fought over for a hundred years after Matilda's death.

♦ **Book owners. Divorce. Educated. Estate. Legal activity. Models. Negotiators. Politics. Popes. Prisons. Religious patrons. Rulers. Soldiers. Squabbles. Widows.** ♦

Barraclough, *Origins...*, pp. 92, 108, 125, 126, 129, 131, 133, 151, 157, 163, 184–186, 204, 212. Bryce, *Holy...*, pp. 160 & 168. Duff, *Matilda....* Fuhrmann, *Germany...*, pp. 65, 66, 69, 75, 84, 90. Hampe, *Germany...*, pp. 58–59, 80, 83–84, 91, 96, 97, 100, 113. Harksen, *Women...*, pp. 41–42. Haverkamp, *Medieval...*, pp. 96, 111, 114–118, 121, 122, 126, 129–132. Henderson, *Short...*, pp. 67–70. Huddy, *Matilda....* Norwich, *Normans...*, pp. 202–203, 207, 213, 235, 237, 263, 266, 305. Pernoud, *La femme...*, pp. 66, 237–239, 242–246. Pinnow, *History...*, pp. 72, 74, 76, 77, & 81. Previte-Orton, *Outlines...*, pp. 211–214. Stubbs, *Germany...*, pp. 150, 170, 171, 174, 177, 179, 185–186, 187, 200, 219. Thompson, *Literacy...*, pp. 69–70. Trevelyan, *Short...*, pp. 74, 76, 96 & 99.

MAUD DE VERE, countess of Oxford

c. 1320–d.c. 1410 England

Heiress of Giles, lord Badlesmere; around 1336, married John de Vere, earl of Oxford.

♦ **Estate. Legal activity. Managers.** ♦

Calendar of Plea..., II, p. 251. *DNB,* v.20, pp. 221 & 239. Legge (ed), *Anglo-Norman...*, pp. 64–65 (#20). Tuck, *Richard...*, p. 78.

MATILDA YONGE

1328 England

Widow of John le Yonge, merchant and brewer of London. Their sons received the brewhouse, but John left his house and shop to Matilda, along with the terms of his two apprentices.

♦ **Alewives. Apprentices–mistresses. Bequests. Land/property. Merchants. Widows.** ♦

Calendar of Wills..., I, p. 341.

MAUD

See—MATILDA.

(St.) MAURA OF TROYES

d.c. 861 France

Worked at Cathedral of Troyes; wove vestments for Bishop Prudentius, who later wrote her *Vita*.

♦ **Artistic clothwork. Models. Saints. Servants.** ♦

Attwater, *Dictionary...*, p. 209. Schulenburg, "Female...," p. 117. Wemple, *Women...*, p. 146.

MAYFREDA DE PIROVANO **[Manfreda]**

c. 1270s–d.c. 1300 Italy

Follower of †Guglielma of Milan. Mayfreda claimed she was starting a new religious age—with herself as pope, heading up a group of female cardinals. The male clergy was not amused; Mayfreda was burned at the stake as a heretic.

♦ **Antinomian. Heretics. Popes. Punishments.** ♦

Boulding, *Underside...*, p. 452. *Cambridge...*, VI, p. 708. Lambert, *Medieval...*, p. 193. Wessley, "Guglielmites...," pp. 294–296, 298–299, & 302.

MECHTILD

Also see—MATILDA.

MECHTILD VON HACKEBORN

b. 1241–d. 1299 Germany

Younger sister of abbess, †Gertrude of Hackeborn, Mechtild also entered the convent of Helta. A singer, choir director, scholar, and mystic, Mechtild's visions are compiled in the *Liber Spiritualis Gratiae.* She also instructed novices and taught at the convent school.

♦ **Models. Music. Mystics. Nuns. Scholars. Teachers. Writers.** ♦

Boulding, *Underside...*, pp. 460–461. Bynum, *Holy...*, pp. 62, 139, 185, 232, 254, 261, 356 n121, 391 n78, 404 n32. Halligan (ed.), *Booke...*, pp. 36–37, 45. Lagorio, "Continental...," pp. 163, 167–168. McDonnell, *Beguines...*, p. 374. *Oxford...Prose,* pp. 101–102 & 438. Power, *Nunneries...*, pp. 239 & 500.

MECHTHILD OF MAGDEBURG

b. 1212–d.c. 1283 Germany

A former Beguine, this mystic was a Dominican tertiary for some time. Mechthild entered the convent at Helfta around 1275. Her visions are recorded in *The Flowing Light of the Godhead.*

♦ **Beguines. Educated. Handicapped. Mystics. Nuns. Writers–theology.** ♦

Ancelet-Hustache, *Mechtilde...*, pp. 152–160. Boulding, *Underside...*, pp. 424 & 460–461. Bynum, *Holy...*, pp. 3, 27, 31, 106, 133, 186, 209, 222, 229, 235–6, 242, 250, 263, 265, 271, 279, 290, 291. Halligan (ed.), *Booke...*, pp. 34–36. Howard, "German...," pp. 153–185. Lagorio, "Continental...," pp. 163, 168–170, 171. McDonnell, *Beguines...*, p. 374. Power, *Nunneries...*, pp. 500, 525, 533. *Revelations....* Thièbaux, *The Writings...*, pp. 207–220. Zum Brunn and Epiney-Burgard, *Women...*, pp. 37–68.

MÉLISENDE, queen of JERUSALEM [Mélisinde; Mélisande]

m. 1129–d. 1161 Israel

Oldest daughter and heiress of †Morphia of Melitene and King Baldwin II of Jerusalem (d.1131). Married Foulques V of Anjou; they ruled Jerusalem from 1131 until Foulques died in 1144. Their son and heir, Baldwin III, was a minor, so Mélisende was regent for the next five years. She was a just and firm regent; she maintained peace until 1149. Baldwin then not only wished to rule alone, but he also wanted to deprive his mother of her possessions and power. She lost the small war which followed, but had enough backers, including many ecclesiastics, to retain her possessions and some influence. She and Baldwin later achieved a working relationship because his alliances with northern states depended on this—Mélisende's niece, †Constance of Antioch, was ruling in Antioch, and Mélisende's sister †Hodierna was regent of Tripoli. Mélisende was a major supporter of the church—building leper hospitals, founding convents, etc. She was also interested in the arts and commissioned the production of many illuminated manuscripts.

♦ **Adultery. Art patrons. Book owners. Crusades. Educated. Leprosy. Models. Medicine. Negotiators. Patrons of literature. Politics. Regents. Religious patrons. Rulers. Squabbles. Widows.** ♦

Bridge, *Crusades...*, pp. 11, 145, 148, 161, 167. *Chronicles...*, pp. 116, 143, 144. Decaux, *Histoire...*, pp. 221–222. Hallam (ed.), *Plantagenet...*, pp. 38, 77, 104. Hamilton, "Women...," pp. 148–157. Harksen, *Women...*, p. 44. Kelly, *Eleanor...*, pp. 65–7. Lehmann, *Rôle de la...*, pp. 382–384. Payne, *Dream...*, pp. 133–5, 138, 140, 141, 149, 151, 152, 158, 159, 161, 162, 168. Pernoud, *Eleanor...*, pp. 48, 70–1, 89. Pernoud, *La femme...*, pp. 66 & 147. Tyerman, *England...*, pp. 29, 30, 47, 48, 52.

MENGARDE BUSCALH

c. 1300s–1320s France

Had affair with Pierre Clergue, Cathar preacher of Montaillou. Probably followed his lead with regard to heretical ideas, but she was not very firm in those beliefs. In particular, Mengarde insisted on trying to save her child's life, rather than strictly following Cathar precepts that suggested death was most desirable.

♦ **Adultery. Cathars. Childcare. Ecclesiastical courts–Inquisition. Heretics.** ♦

Dronke, *Women...*, pp. 209–210. Ladurie, *Montaillou...*, p. 155.

MERCURIADE OF SALERNO

fl.c. 1200 Italy

A surgeon and teacher of medicine at Salerno. She presumably wrote four medical treatises on topics such as ointments, the treatment for fever, and how to heal wounds.

♦ **Educated. Medicine. Surgeons. Teachers. Writers–medicine.** ♦

Hughes, *Women...*, p. 147. Hurd-Mead, *History...*, pp. 225 & 276. Lipinska, *Histoire...*, p. 99. Mozans, *Woman...*, p. 286.

MICHELLE OF FRANCE **[Machaèle de Valois]**

d. 1422 France

Daughter of †Isabeau of Bavaria and Charles VI of France. First wife of Philip the Good, duke of Burgundy. Patroness of the van Eycks.

♦ **Art patrons. Dowry/dower. Educated.** ♦

Bell, "Medieval...," p. 163. Calmette, *Golden...*, pp. 110–111, 128, 132–133, 135, 138, 170. Cartellieri, *Court...*, p. 41. Crowe, *Early...*, p. 38. Denieul-Cormier, *Wise...*, pp. 233, 234, 249. Huizinga, *Waning...*, pp. 34 & 41. Jacob, *Fifteenth...*, p. 256. Vaughan, *Philip...*, pp. 82 & 91.

MICHIÈLE (la ventrière)

1292 France

A *sage-femme* and midwife of 1292 Paris on La Grant rue St. Martin, Michièle was only taxed 2s.

♦ **Less-affluent. Midwives.** ♦

Géraud, *Paris sous...*, p. 62. Hughes, *Women...*, p. 146.

MILESSENT (la cerenceresse)

1292 France

Clothworker in 1292 Paris, she paid a 2s tax on her business as a comber.

♦ **Clothworkers. Less-affluent.** ♦

Géraud, *Paris sous...*, p. 97.

MORPHIA OF MELITENE, queen of Jerusalem

d.c. 1128 Greece; Israel

Daughter of Gabriel of Melitene. Despite her adherence to her Greek Orthodox religion, Morphia and Baldwin II of Jerusalem were said to be a very happy couple. Four daughters: †Mélisende, †Hodierna, †Alice, and Yvetta. Especially while Baldwin was a Turkish captive, Morphia played an active political role, and she even negotiated his release.

♦ **Negotiators. Politics.** ♦

Bridge, *Crusades...*, pp. 139, 144. *DBF,* v.5, pp. 871–873. Hamilton, "Women...," pp. 147–148.

MYFANWY (Tudor) **[Mevanwy]**

fl.c. 1350s–1370s Wales

Wife of Goronwy ap Tudor (Gronw Fychan), famous Welsh leader; she was of a noble family of North Wales. A contemporary poet extolled Myfanwy as courageous, proud, and refined.

♦ **Models.** ♦

DNB, v.19, p. 1217. Griffiths and Thomas, *Making...*, p. 20.

— N —

NANNINA DE'MEDICI **[Lucrezia]**
b. 1447–d.c. 1482 Italy

Daughter of †Lucrezia Tornabuoni and Piero de'Medici. In 1466, she married Bernardo Rucellai; they had six children.

♦ **Dowry/dower. Educated. Pawns. Writers–letters.** ♦

Brucker, *Florence...*, p. 125. Cleugh, *Medici...*, p. 107. Hook, *Lorenzo...*, p. 6. Maguire, *Women...*, pp. 62 & 70.

NESTA **[Nest]**
c. 1080s–1120s Wales

Daughter of Rhys ap Tewdwr, prince of South Wales. Mistress of King Henry I of England and of Stephen, constable of Cardigan. In 1112 Nesta married Gerald of Windsor, constable of Pembroke. She was presumably also abducted (perhaps by her own request) by Owain ap Cadwgan. Nesta's descendants by all these liasons started a number of important Irish-Norman families.

♦ **Abduction. Genealogy. Mistresses.** ♦

Appleby, *John...*, pp. 28 & 172. Barlow, *Feudal...*, p. 334. Barrow, *Feudal...*, pp. 171 & 421. Curtis, *Ireland...*, p. 48. Curtis, *Medieval...*, pp. 10, 39, & Table. *DNB*, v.7, p. 164; v.9, p. 451. Lloyd, *Maligned...*, pp. 22–3, 25, 28, 196. Orpen, *Ireland...*, I, pp. 18, 94–97. Otway-Ruthven, *History...*, p. 43.

NICHOLE [Nicole; Nicola]

NICOLE (la boursière)
1292 France

Purse, or pouch, maker of 1292 Paris; paid 4s tax.

♦ **Apparel–accessories. Less-affluent.** ♦

Géraud, *Paris sous...*, p. 25.

NICOLE (l'erbière)
1292 France

Sold medicinal herbs and other spices on a small scale; paid 12d tax in 1292 Paris survey.

♦ **Apothecaries. Less-affluent.** ♦

Géraud, *Paris sous...*, p. 149.

NICOLE (l'esperonnière)

1292 France

Worked as a spur-maker in 1292 Paris; paid small tax of 12d.

♦ **Less-affluent. Merchants.** ♦

Géraud, *Paris sous...*, p. 94.

NICOLA DE LA HAY **[Nicholaa; Nicolaa de la Haye]**

1216 England

Wife of Gerard de Camville; she was in charge of Lincoln castle as hereditary constable. Nicola valiantly held the fortress for King John, and then for his son, young King Henry III.

♦ **Estate. Servants. Soldiers.** ♦

Appleby, *John...*, p. 47. Barrow, *Feudal...*, p. 257 & n. Bingham, *Crowned...*, p. 186. Labarge, *Baronial...*, p. 39. Lloyd, *Maligned...*, p. 366. Powicke, *Thirteenth...*, p. 11. Salzman, *Life...*, p. 265.

NICOLE (la saunière)

1292 France

Had a fairly good business in 1292 Paris selling salt on la grant rue St. Martin; paid 12s tax.

♦ **Land/property. Merchants. Provisioning–salt.** ♦

Géraud, *Paris sous...*, p. 63.

NOËL (of France)

1319 Flanders; France

In 1319, she was hired as a singer by †Mahaut, countess of Artois.

♦ **Music–professional.** ♦

Rokseth, *Les femmes...*, p. 474.

NORTHILDA

822 France

Petitioned court at Reims to grant her a divorce because she claimed her husband forced her to have "unnatural sex" with him. The synod punished her husband with heavy penances but refused to grant Northilda a divorce.

♦ **Divorce–denied. Ecclesiastical courts. Legal activity.** ♦

McNamara and Wemple, "Marriage...," p. 106. Wemple, *Women...*, p. 104.

NOTEKINA HOGGENHORE

1261/2 England

Prostitute residing in whorehouse in parish of All Hallows Colemanes-cherche in London.

♦ **Prostitutes.** ♦

London Eyre...1276, p. 34.

NOVELLA D'ANDREA

c. 1350s–1360s Italy

Daughter of law professor Giovanni d'Andrea. She supposedly studied and taught at University of Bologna. †Christine de Pisan wrote about Novella.

♦ **Models. Scholars. Teachers. University.** ♦

Greer, *Obstacle...*, p. 209. Herlihy, *Opera...*, p. 158. Labalme, *Beyond...*, p. 3. Lipinska, *Histoire...*, p. 151. Pisan, *City...*, p. 154. Tuchman, *Distant...*, p. 228.

ODA

b. 810–d. 913 Germany

Married East Saxon noble, Liudolf. They founded Brunhausen monastery in 852; transferred to Gandersheim in 858. She outlived all but one daughter, †Christina, of her very large family; Oda supposedly lived to be over one hundred years old.

♦ **Abbesses. Religious patrons.** ♦

Dictionary..., v.6, p. 313. Leyser, *Rule...*, pp. 52–55. Riché, *Les Carolingiens...*, p. 186. Wilson, *Medieval...*, p. 31.

ODELINE

fl.c. 1090s–1110s France

Daughter of Ralph, castellan of Mantes. Married Ansold of Marle; sons Peter and Ralph. She and Ansold were very pious; among their religious donations, they gave a quarry to a church near Mantes. After they had been married for some years, Ansold asked her to release him from his marriage vows because he wished to become a monk. Odeline eventually agreed to his request.

♦ **Divorce–separation. Mining. Models. Religious patrons.** ♦

Vitalis, *Ecclesiastical...*, pp. 180–181, 184–185, 186–187, 196– 198.

ODETTE DE CHAMPDIVERS

fl. 1390s–1410s France

Odette was a novice at a convent when Queen †Isabeau of Bavaria supposedly picked the girl to be a mistress/companion for King Charles VI in his spells of insanity.

♦ **Insanity–caretakers. Mistresses. Religieuses.** ♦

Castries, *Lives...*, p. 118. Coryn, *House...*, pp. 167 & 168. Tuchman, *Distant...*, p. 542.

OELUN **[Ogelun Eke]**

c. 1150s–1190s China; Russia

Oelun was presumably a member of a rival clan when Esugay-Bagatur captured and married her. The oldest of their five children was Temuchin. Esugay died in 1177, leaving Oelun in charge of a large extended family. After her son achieved prominence as the great

Chingis-Khan, he took care to see that his mother lived in luxury with many servants.

♦ **Abduction. Squabbles. Teachers. Widows.** ♦

Cambridge..., IV, p. 632. Vernadsky, *Mongols...*, pp. 20–22, 30, & 32.

OGIVE, queen of FRANCE

See—EADGIFU OF ENGLAND, queen of France.

(St.) OLGA, princess of KIEV

b. 890s–d. 969 Russia

Married at young age to Igor, prince of Kiev. Their son and heir was underage when Igor died in 945, so Olga assumed the regency. She avenged Igor's death, started tax collections, and instituted central depots for trade and for tariffs. Olga was not only a wise and energetic ruler, she also brought Christianity to her region. She travelled to Constantinople in 957. Her fictionalized story is told in the *Book of Annals*.

♦ **Banking. Estate. Merchants. Models. Regents. Religious patrons. Saints. Soldiers. Widows.** ♦

Attwater, *Dictionary...*, p. 227. Duckett, *Death...*, p. 95. Florinsky, *Russia...*, pp. 10 & 18. Jenkins, *Byzantium...*, p. 265. Kluchevsky, *History...*, pp. 16 & 59. Pares, *History...*, pp. 28, 31, & 35. Pernoud, *La femme...*, pp. 227 & 228. Riché, *Les Carolingiens...*, p. 257. Scott, *Sweden...*, pp. 23 & 31. Stephenson, *Mediaeval...*, p. 182. Vernadsky, *Kievan...*, pp. 32, 36, 38–42, 45, 46, 57, 62, 154, 190, 256, 274, 340, 352.

ONORATA RODIANA **[Rodiani]**

c. 1410s–d. 1452 Italy

Semi-legendary artist/soldier, there is much dispute over the accuracy of her life story. Born near Cremona, as a young woman Onorata gained a reputation as an artist who specialized in difficult *affresco* technique. Gabrino Fondolo commissioned her to decorate his palace in this style. While at work, Onorata stabbed a young noble in order to protect her virtue. Onorata supposedly escaped to the mountains and fought with mercenary soldiers. After she was pardoned, she returned to finish Fondolo's palace. When her city was attacked by Venice, Onorata led one group of soldiers to victory, but she was mortally wounded.

♦ **Artists. Models. Murder. Soldiers. Unmarried. Virginity.** ♦

Clement, *Women...*, pp. 293–294. Greer, *Obstacle...*, pp. 172–173. Petersen and Wilson, *Women...*, p. 22.

Madame d'OR

fl.c. 1421–1434 Flanders; France

Blonde female dwarf at the court of Philip the Good, duke of Burgundy. She was one of the entertainers at a banquet for the new duchess, †Isabella of Portugal.

♦ **Dance. Dwarves. Servants.** ♦

Calmette, *Golden...*, p. 233. Huizinga, *Waning...*, p. 17.

(St.) OSBURGA OF COVENTRY

c. 970s–d.c.1016 England

First abbess of Coventry. Many miracles were associated with her relics.

♦ **Abbesses. Relics. Saints.** ♦

Attwater, *Dictionary...*, p. 229. Farmer, *Oxford...*, p. 302.

OTA (of Norway) **[Auor]**

fl.c. 820s–840s Ireland; Norway

Wife of Viking, Thorgest (Turgesius), conqueror of the kingdoms of Ulster, Connacht, and Meath. Her husband was killed by the Irish (led by Malachy I) in 845. She was reputedly a pagan prophetess.

♦ **Models. Mystics. Superstitions.** ♦

Curtis, *Ireland...*, p. 23. *DNB,* v.19, p. 819. Jones, *Vikings...*, pp. 206, 214–215. Scherman, *Flowering...*, p. 216.

OTTA OF S. SALVATORE

fl. 1030s–1040s Italy

One of the most powerful Italian abbesses of her time. She was in charge of S. Salvatore/S. Giulia in Brescia in 1046 when she intervened with Henry III of Germany to relieve the people on her lands of taxes.

♦ **Abbesses. Managers. Politics.** ♦

Wemple, "S. Salvatore...," p. 97.

— P —

PARISINA MALATESTA, duchess of Ferrara [Parisina of Rimini]
b. 1408–d.c. 1425 Italy

At age fourteen she married Nicolo III d'Este, duke of Ferrara. Parisina soon fell in love with Ugo, Nicolo's illegitimate son. When Nicolo caught Ugo and Parisina in bed together, both were executed.

♦ **Adultery. Models. Murder. Music.** ♦

Fusero, *Borgias*, pp. 238 & 322 n23. Gardner, *Dukes...*, pp. 34–40, 49, 505. Johnson, *Borgias...*, pp. 197 & 199. Prescott, *Princes...*, pp. 187–188. Ragg, *Women...*, pp. 26–27, 130.

PAULE VIGUIER
1335 France

See—ARMANDE ROBERT.

♦ **Witchcraft.** ♦

"PEARL IN THE EGG"
1306 England

Presumably the stage name of one of the singers/minstrels who performed at Westminster in 1306.

♦ **Music–professional.** ♦

Chambers, *Stage...*, II, p. 238. Labarge, *Baronial...*, p. 180.

PENTECOUSTE (la fruitière)
1292 France

Fruitmonger in 1292 Paris; paid 2s tax.

♦ **Less-affluent. Provisioning–fruit.** ♦

Géraud, *Paris sous...*, p. 77.

PERNA
c. 1460 Italy

Jewish doctor. Around 1460, Perna applied for license to practice medicine in Fano.

♦ **Doctors/empirics. Jews. Legal activity.** ♦

Friedenwald, "Jewish...," I, p. 220.

PERONNE LOESSART

fl. 1420s–1440s France

Testified before Inquisition court at the trial of Gilles de Rais. She had allowed her ten-year-old son Robin to be taken to Gilles' castle in 1438 because she was assured that he was to become a page. However, the boy had never been seen or heard from again—leaving a strong presumption that he was one of the victims of Gilles' murderous passion.

♦ **Childcare. Ecclesiastical courts–Inquisition. Legal activity. Manors.** ♦

Hyatte, *Laughter...*, pp. 13, 129–131. Summers, *Geography...*, p. 393. Wolf, *Bluebeard...*, pp. 137–138.

PERRETTE [Peretta; Perette; Perrotte]

PERRETTE LA HANCÉ

1446/7 France

Parisian barber on la grant rue St. Jacques; paid 30s tax.

♦ **Barbers. Land/property.** ♦

Comptes du..., p. 496. Jacquart, *Le Milieu...*, p. 467.

PERRETTE LA MAUGARNIE

1399 France

Apprenticed to †Poncette Aubry to learn linen draper's craft. In 1399 Paris, Perrette brought suit against her mistress for not teaching her.

♦ **Apprentices. Clothworkers. Legal activity.** ♦

O'Faolin, *Not in...*, pp. 158–159.

PERETTA PERONNE **[Perette of Rouen]**

b. 1360–d.c. 1411 France

A *sage-femme,* midwife, and/or surgeon of Rouen. Prosecuted in Paris for witchcraft and for practicing medicine as an unlicensed physician. Imprisoned for some time, Peretta was later acquitted by order of King Charles VI.

♦ **Midwives. Miscreants. Prisons. Surgeons. Witchcraft.** ♦

Hughes, *Women...*, pp. 110 & 146. Hurd-Mead, *History...*, p. 269. Wickersheimer, *Dictionnaire...*, v.3, p. 222.

PERRETTE LA TOUTAINE

1421 France

Tavern keeper in 1421 Paris.

♦ **Taverners.** ♦

Favier, *Les Contribuables...*, p. 209.

PERRINE MARTIN **[La Meffraye]**
c. 1400–d.c. 1441 France

Arrested as accomplice of Gilles de Rais in 1440. She was burned at the stake. Perrine was said to be a very skillful procurer for Gilles; she allegedly lured numerous young boys to their deaths.

♦ **Ecclesiastical courts–Inquisition. Prostitutes–procurers. Punishments.** ♦

Hyatte, *Laughter...*, pp. 43–45, 67, 78, 142, 146. Wolf, *Bluebeard...*, pp. 153–154 & 239n.

PERRONELLE [Péronelle; Peronnelle; Perrenelle; Perronnele; Perronnelle]

PÉRONNELLE D'ARMENTIÈRES
b. 1340 France

Daughter of Gonthier d'Unchair of Champagne. Well-educated, Péronnelle taught and composed poetry. When she was about eighteen, she corresponded with, and then met, the poet/musician Guillaume de Machaut. They may have had an affair at that time. Probably she was more enamored of his fame than of the sixty-year-old man himself. He immortalized Péronnelle in *Le Livre du Voir Dit.* She proved to be fickle, however, since she soon broke off her relationship with Machaut in order to marry a more "suitable" man.

♦ **Educated. Models. Music. Teachers. Women of easy virtue. Writers.** ♦

Cartellieri, *Court...*, p. 99. *DBF,* v.1, p. 755. Fox, *Literary...*, p. 296. Huizinga, *Waning...*, pp. 109–111. Moulin, *La poésie...*, pp. 88–91.

PÉRRONNELE (l'espicière)
1292–1319 France

In 1292 Paris, Dame Pérronele was an extremely prosperous spicer—selling a variety of herbs and spices. She paid the very large tax of £7 at that time. She was probably the same Pérronnele *l'erbière* who went from Paris to Artois in 1319 to take herbal medicines and advice to Countess †Mahaut.

♦ **Apothecaries. Land/property. Medicine. Merchants.** ♦

Decaux, *Histoire...*, p. 336. Géraud, *Paris sous...*, p. 139. Hughes, *Women...*, p. 144. Hurd-Mead, *History...*, p. 271. Wickersheimer, *Dictionnaire...*, v.2, p. 597.

PÉRRONNELE (la lavendière)
1292 France

Laundress of 1292 Paris—taxed 2s.

♦ **Laundresses. Less-affluent.** ♦

Géraud, *Paris sous...*, p. 77.

PÉRRONELE (la nourrice)

1292 France

Of the rue des Arsis in 1292 Paris; she was nurse to Pierre de Fournay.

♦ **Less-affluent. Nurses.** ♦

Géraud, *Paris sous...*, p. 93. Hughes, *Women...*, p. 147.

PETRONILLA OF AQUITAINE, countess of Vermandois
[Aelith; Aeliz; Péronelle]

b. 1124–1140s France

Daughter of †Aénor of Châtellerault and William X of Aquitaine. Her older sister, †Eleanor of Aquitaine, queen of France, used her influence to help Petronilla marry Raoul of Vermandois. Raoul first had to divorce his wife Eleanor of Champagne. This caused a great deal of strife for all concerned. Petronilla and Raoul had a son, Raoul II, and daughters, †Eleanora and †Isabella (of Vermandois).

♦ **Divorce. Models. Squabbles.** ♦

Cambridge..., V, p. 606. *DBF*, v.1, pp. 658–659; v.2, p. 1. Kelly, *Eleanor...*, pp. 6, 22–23, 27, 386. Lloyd, *Maligned...*, pp. xxiv-xxv. Pernoud, *Eleanor...*, pp. 35, 36, 42, 74.

PETRONILLA, queen of ARAGON, countess of Barcelona

b. 1135–d.c. 1173 Spain

Daughter of Inez de Poitiers and Ramiro II, king of Aragon. Since her father returned to his monastery not long after her birth, Petronilla was married at a young age to Ramon Berenguer IV, count of Barcelona, who ruled Aragon for her at first (later she became co-ruler). Barcelona and Aragon were united under their heir, Alfonso II (originally named Ramon Berenguer V). Petronilla also had a daughter, †Douce (II) of Barcelona, queen of Portugal.

♦ **Estate. Pawns. Rulers.** ♦

Altamira, *Spain...*, pp. 156, 159, 263. Bisson, *Medieval Crown...*, pp. 3, 16–17, 27, 31. Bonner (ed.), *Songs...*, p. 239. *Cambridge...*, VI, pp. 405, 406, 410. Fusero, *Borgias*, p. 19. Livermore, *History...*, p. 112. Merriman, *Rise...*, v.1, p. 277. Miron, *Queens...*, p. 62. Shneidman, *Rise...*, pp. 191, 280, 285, 286, 291, 292, 294, 296, 297, 309, 487. Smith, *Spain...*, pp. 57–58. Stephens, *Story...*, p. 57.

PETRONILLE OF COMMINGES, countess of Bigorre
[Pétronelle; Pérronelle]

c. 1180s–d. 1240s France; Spain

Daughter of Bernard, count of Comminges, and Étiennette de Bigorre. Her mother's heiress, Petronille was raised at the court of Aragon. She married five times, which caused inheritance squabbles among her three daughters—†Alice de Montfort, Mathes, and Pétronille—and their heirs.

♦ **Bequests. Charity. Educated. Managers. Negotiators. Orphans. Religieuses. Religious patrons. Squabbles.** ♦

Colomez, *Histoire...*, pp. 43–73 passim. Labarge, *Simon...*, pp. 131–132.

PETRONILLE OF FONTEVRAULT **[de Cheville; de Craon]**

b. 1093–d.c. 1148 France

Robert d'Arbrissel appointed her abbess of Fontevrault in 1115. She was well-educated, an excellent leader, and determined to protect her institution's position and power. Petronille also commissioned the production of Robert's *Vita*.

♦ **Abbesses. Legal activity. Managers. Patrons of literature. Popes.** ♦

Eckenstein, *Woman...*, p. 194. Gold, *Lady...*, pp. 95 & 97. Hurd-Mead, *History...*, p. 178. Marks, *Pilgrims...*, p. 62. Martiniere, "Une Falsification de...," pp. 1–45. Pernoud, *Eleanor...*, p. 93. Pernoud, *La femme...*, pp. 131–133, 134. Smith, "Robert...," pp. 183 & 184.

PETRONILLA OF GRANDMESNIL, countess of Leicester
[Pétronille de Parnel, heiress of Grantmesnil]

c. 1145–d. 1212 England

Married in the later 1150s to Robert III de Beaumont, earl of Leicester (d.1190); mother of Robert IV, †Margaret, and †Amicia of Leicester. Petronilla actively pursued land and estate rights. She acquired the right to hold a profitable market at Ware.

♦ **Estate. Legal activity. Managers. Merchants. Widows.** ♦

C.P., v.7, pp. 532–533. *DNB,* v.2, p. 68. Powicke, "Loretta...," pp. 152, 154, 155.

PETRONILLA OF MEATH

d. 1320s Ireland

See—ALICE KYTELER.

Only one in the case who was burned at the stake.

♦ **Ecclesiastical courts. Punishments. Witchcraft.** ♦

PETRONILLA OF TEYE

1320 England

On manor of Dunmow, Essex, the widowed Petronilla gave her land to son John on condition that he give her a room, a cow, four sheep, and a pig. He was also bound to provide other necessities for her.

♦ **Land/property. Legal activity. Manors. Widows.** ♦

Homans, *English...*, p. 145.

PETRONILLA TURK

1338–d. 1349 England

In 1338, Petronilla went to court regarding dispute over protection and fortification of a wharf she had rented to William de Brikelesworth. The London court decided that William would fortify the structure, but that he could then keep the wharf for longer than the original contract had specified. In 1349 Petronilla willed this same wharf, along with her shops and brewing utensils to her son Richard.

♦ **Alewives. Bequests. Land/property. Legal activity. Merchants. Shipping.** ♦

Calendar of Plea..., I, p. 177.

PHELIPOTE (la fritière)

1292 France

Sold fried fish on la rue de Merderel in 1292 Paris—paid 2s tax.

♦ **Less-affluent. Provisioning–fish.** ♦

Géraud, *Paris sous...*, p. 43.

PHILIPPA [Phelippe; Phillippia]

PHILIPPA OF ANTIOCH

b. 1146–c. 1170s Turkey

Daughter of Bohemund II of Antioch. In 1166, Philippa had a short and scandalous affair with forty-eight-year-old Andronicus Comnenus.

♦ **Adultery. Models.** ♦

Bridge, *Crusades...*, pp. 131 & 190. *Cambridge...*, IV, pp. 375 & 381. Norwich, *Kingdom...*, p. 328.

PHILIPPA OF CHAMPAGNE

fl.c. 1200–c. 1240 France; Israel

Daughter of †Isabella of Jerusalem and Henry II of Champagne. Around 1214, Philippa married Erard I of Brienne, lord of Rameru and Venisy. Philippa and Erard challenged Thibaut and †Blanche for the rights to the county of Champagne.

♦ **Estate. Squabbles.** ♦

Anselme, *Histoire...*, v.2, p. 841. Baldwin, *Government...*, pp. 197 & 341. Fawtier, *Capetian...*, p. 127. Robinson, *Readings...*, I, pp. 178–179.

PHILIPPA OF CLARENCE, countess of March

b. 1355–d.c. 1381 England

Only daughter and heiress of Lionel, duke of Clarence, and †Elizabeth de Burgh, countess of Ulster. In 1368, Philippa married Edmund Mortimer, earl of March.

♦ **Estate. Genealogy.** ♦

Armitage-Smith, *John...*, p. 25. Bryant, *Age...*, p. 447. *C.P.*, v.3, p. 245. *DNB*, v.11, p. 1215; v. 13, p. 1018. Given-Wilson, *English...*, pp. 41–42. Hardy, *Philippa...*, pp. 273, 290, 306, & 309. McFarlane, *Nobility...*, p. 86. Rosenthal, *Nobles...*, pp. 186–187.

PHILIPPA OF COIMBRA
1450 Portugal
Daughter of Pedro, duke of Coimbra. It took Philippa a year to illustrate a *Gospel* book which she later gave to the convent of Odivellas.
♦ **Artists. Bookmaking. Book owners. Religious patrons.** ♦
Greer, *Obstacle...*, p. 167.

PHILIPPA DE COUCY, countess of Oxford
b. 1367–1390s England; France
Daughter of †Isabella of England and Enguerrand VII de Coucy. Heiress of her mother's English lands—Philippa stayed in that country while her sister Marie (see lady de †Coucy) lived in France. Around 1379, Philippa married Robert de Vere, earl of Oxford. He divorced her in order to marry †Agnes de Launcreona.
♦ **Divorce. Estate. Models.** ♦
Froissart, *Chronicles...*, I, pp. 407 & 417. Hardy, *Philippa...*, pp. 284, 298, 308–9. Tuchman, *Distant...*, pp. 233, 298, 321, 446, 466–469, 473, 518, 563, 628. Tuck, *Richard...*, p. 78.

PHILIPPA DE DAMMARTIN, countess of Gueldres
[Philippe; Philipotte]
fl.c. 1240s–1270s France; Netherlands
See—MARIE, countess of PONTHIEU and Aumale.
♦ **Dowry/dower. Managers.** ♦
Belleval, *Les fiefs...*, pp. 16 & 314.

PHILIPPA OF ENGLAND, queen of Norway, Denmark, and Sweden
b. 1394–d.c. 1430 Denmark; England; Norway; Sweden
Well-educated daughter of †Mary de Bohun and Henry IV of England. Around 1406, Philippa married young Eric of Pomerania, king of Norway, Denmark, and Sweden. They had no children, but Philippa was a wise and capable helper for Eric. She held council meetings in Sweden, was regent occasionally in Norway, was a benefactress to Birgittine monasteries, and helped improve Eric's popularity through her own kindness and charm.
♦ **Educated. Negotiators. Regents. Religious patrons.** ♦
Andersson, *History...*, p. 77. Derry, *History...*, p. 74. Hurd-Mead, *History...*, p. 280. Jacob, *Fifteenth...*, pp. 69, 196, 318. Larsen, *History...*, pp. 212 & 213. McFarlane, *Nobility...*, pp. 243 & 244. Musset, *Les Peuples...*, p. 303. Seward, *Hundred...*, p. 150.

PHILIPPA OF HAINAULT, queen of England
b. 1314–d. 1369 Belgium; England; Flanders; Netherlands
Daughter of †Jeanne de Valois and William III the Good, count of Hainault and Holland. Around 1328, Philippa married Edward III of

England. Her husband gave her much of the wool-growing region of Norwich as dower lands. Philippa proceeded to import Flemish clothmakers to teach the craft to the English. She thereby started the cloth manufacturing business and greatly improved the financial position of the residents of that area. She supposedly even sponsored a tournament for their entertainment. Patroness of Froissart and presumably of Chaucer, Philippa also founded and endowed Queen's College. Equally interested in medicine, she started hospitals and was both patroness and patient of the noted female doctor, Caecelia of Oxford. Although she supposedly intervened personally to save the lives of the burghers of Calais, Philippa could also act as a soldier. While regent of England for her husband (who was fighting in France), Philippa was said to have ridden with her soldiers against the Scottish troops and captured King David. She provided her husband's court with culture, fashion, glamor, wisdom, and a high moral tone. She also provided Edward with plenty of children. Philippa was extolled as an excellent wife, mother, and queen by her husband, children, and subjects.

♦ **Book owners. Childcare. Clothworkers. Dowry/dower. Educated. Legal activity. Medicine. Models. Negotiators. Patrons of literature. Prisons. Regents. Religious patrons. Soldiers. Tournaments. University.** ♦

Armitage-Smith, *John...*, pp. 1–5, 75, 390. Bellamy, *Crime...*, p. 86. Brewer, *Chaucer...*, pp. 22, 30, 36, & 43. Bryant, *Age...*, pp. 226, 230, 236, 239, 255, 282, 320, 442. Butt, *History...*, pp. 223, 236, 244, 289, 330. *Calendar of Plea...*, I, p. 156; II, p. 119. Davis, *First...*, pp. 273–276. Fowler, *Age...*, pp. 191–192, 195. Fox, *Literary...*, pp. 286 & 299. Froissart, *Chronicles...*, I, pp. iii, 13, 18, 19, 32, 45–47, 66, 77, 78, 95, 126–127, 143, 175, 195, 381; II, pp. 118, 139, 203. Gardner, *Life...*, pp. 47, 60, 91, 95, 99, 109, 113–115, 117, 118, 153–157, 172–173, 179, 230, 271. Hallam (ed.), *Four...*, pp. 208, 233, 240, 251, 252, 253, 280, 294, 298. Hardy, *Philippa....* Jamison, *Life...*, I, pp. 32, 42, 63; II, pp. 118–119. Power, *Women...*, p. 75. Riley, *Memorials...*, pp. 170–171, 186, 326–327. Somerset, *Ladies...*, p. 5. Tuchman, *Distant...*, pp. 51, 70, 93, 94, 215, 216, 261, 475.

PHILIPPA OF LANCASTER, queen of Portugal

b. 1360–d. 1415 England; Portugal

Daughter of †Blanche of Lancaster and John of Gaunt. In 1387, Philippa married King John I of Portugal; their sons included King Edward I of Portugal and Henry the Navigator. Philippa was well-educated, popular, and pious. Her husband respected Philippa's intelligence and advice. Evidently he was also fond of her; on their tombs John and Philippa's effigies hold hands. She died of plague some years before John.

♦ **Art patrons. Astronomy. Educated. Hunting. Models. Negotiators. Patrons of literature. Plague. Politics. Teachers. Tournaments. Writers–letters.** ♦

Armitage-Smith, *John...*, pp. 227, 310, 319–320, 335–336. Froissart, *Chronicles...*, I, pp. 354, 356, 367–368, 384–388, 390, 423; II, pp. 111 & 139. Green, *Letters...*, pp. 78–81. Legge (ed), *Anglo-Norman...*, pp. 73–74, 347–348, 360–362, 372–373. Livermore, *History...*, p. 165. Nowell, *History...*, pp. 21, 22, 27–28. Roche, *Philippa....* Stephens, *Story...*, pp. 113, 122, 125, 127.

PHELIPPE (la miergesse)

1292 France

Of the rue Gervese-Lohareuc; in 1292 Paris, Phelippe paid 3s tax on her occupation as a lay healer.

♦ **Doctors/empirics. Less-affluent.** ♦

Géraud, *Paris sous...*, p. 138. Hughes, *Women...*, p. 141. Hurd-Mead, *History...*, p. 215. Lipinska, *Histoire...*, p. 118.

PHILIPPE DE MONCADA

d.c. 1215 France

Her genealogy is unclear, but she was presumably the wife of Raymond Roger, count of Foix, and the sister-in-law of the notable Cathar, †Esclarmonde de Foix. Philippe was a Cathar deaconess who took in many fellow heretics at her castle of Dun. The poet Guiraut Riquier found Philippe quite inspirational.

♦ **Cathars. Managers. Models.** ♦

Abels, "Women...," p. 229. Anselme, *Histoire...*, v.3, p. 345. *DBF*, v.14, p. 187. Marks, *Pilgrims...*, pp. 252 & 279. Wakefield, *Heresy...*, p. 74.

PHILIPPA MORTIMER, countess of Arundel

b.c. 1375–d.c. 1400 England

Daughter of †Philippa of Clarence and Edmund, earl of March. Married (1) John Hastings, earl of Pembroke (d.1389); (2) in 1392, Richard, earl of Arundel (d.c.1397); and (3) Thomas Poynings, lord St. John.

♦ **Genealogy. Models.** ♦

Bourchier, *Chronicle...*, VI, p. 191. *DNB*, v.7, pp. 99–100; v.13, p. 1018. Froissart, *Chronicles...*, IV, p. 50. Roche, Dona..., p. 72. Tuck, *Richard...*, p. 191.

PHILLIPPIA, countess of POITOU **[Philippa of Toulouse]**

fl. 1080s–1110s France; Spain

Daughter of Guillaume de Toulousain. After her first husband, Sancho IV, king of Aragon, died in 1094, Phillippia married William, seventh count of Poitou (William IX of Aquitaine). During 1101 and 1102, she served as regent for him in Aquitaine. She retired to Fontevrault around 1116.

♦ **Queens. Regents. Religieuses.** ♦

Bogin, *Women...*, p. 35. Kelly, *Eleanor...*, pp. 6, 15, 109. Marks, *Pilgrims...*, pp. 48–49, 57–59, 62, 65–66, 83, 84, 86, 89, 92. Pernoud, *Eleanor...*, pp. 25, 26, 34, 125.

PHILIPPA ROET **[Philippa Chaucer]**

c. 1340s–d. 1387 England; Flanders

Lady-in-waiting to †Philippa of Hainault, queen of England, and to †Constance of Castile, duchess of Lancaster. Sister of †Katherine Swynford. Married the poet, Geoffrey Chaucer, around 1365.

♦ **Models. Servants–ladies.** ♦

Braddy, "Chaucer and...," pp. 224–225. Brewer, *Chaucer...*, pp. 41 & 45. Fowler, *Age...*, p. 195. Gardner, *Life...*, pp. 11, 20, 91, 117, 118, 135, 153–157, 159–167, 173, 179, 209, 250, 272, 279. Hardy, *Philippa...*, p. 303. Roche, *Dona...*, pp. 2, 6, 16, 21.

PHILIPPINE DE PORCELLET

c. 1250s–c. 1300 France

Beguine; disciple and friend of (St.) †Douceline. Presumably wrote Douceline's *Vita*.

♦ **Beguines. Nuns. Writers.** ♦

Coulton, *Life...*, III, pp. 54–56. McDonnell, *Beguines...*, p. 400.

PIERINA DE BUGATIS

1390 Italy

In 1390 Milan, Pierina "confessed" to a variety of witchcraft practices.

♦ **Superstitions. Witchcraft.** ♦

McCall, *Underworld...*, pp. 251–252. Russell, *Witchcraft...*, pp. 212–213.

PIERRILLE ROLAND

1335 France

See—ARMANDE ROBERT.

♦ **Witchcraft.** ♦

PONCETTE AUBRY

1399 France

See—PERRETTE LA MAUGARNIE.

♦ **Apprentices–mistresses. Clothworkers. Legal activity. Miscreants.** ♦

PRAXEDIS

See—EUPRAXIA OF KIEV.

PRÉGENTE OF MELUN

fl. 1440s France

Lady-in-waiting to †Margaret (Stuart) of Scotland, dauphine of France. Prégente was also a member of Margaret's literary salon. Margaret's husband, the future Louis XI of France, hated Prégente because he felt she encouraged his wife in frivolous activities.

♦ Educated. Servants–ladies. Writers. ♦

Champion, *Louis...*, p. 109. Lewis, *King...*, p. 179.

PROUS BONETTA **[Na Prous Bonetta]**

d.c. 1325 France

First affiliated with Beguines, she became an iconoclastic religious. In 1325, she confessed to heretical/feminist beliefs and was burned at the stake.

♦ Antinomian. Beguines. Ecclesiastical courts–Inquisition. Punishments. Unmarried. ♦

Barstow, *Joan...*, pp. xvi, 38, 95. Boulding, *Underside...*, p. 452. Leff, *Heresy...*, v.1, pp. 3, 213–215, 217. May, "Confessions...," pp. 11, 19–20, 27. Petroff, *Medieval...*, pp. 284–289. Wessley, "Guglielmites...," pp. 294 & 300.

QUINTINE VAN DEN ZANDE

fl. 1300s — Belgium; Flanders

After her father (Ghiselbrecht van den Zandes) died, Quintine took over his hostel business for a brief period. When she married her second husband, Simon van Vaernewijc, he ran the inn with her help.

♦ **Bequests. Innkeepers. Land/property. Widows.** ♦

Nicholas, *Domestic Life...*, p. 87.

QUENDREDA

See—CWENTHRYTH OF MERCIA.

— R —

RAGNHILD OF DENMARK, queen of Norway **[Ragnild]**
fl. 870s–890s Denmark; Norway

Daughter of King Erik the Younger of Jutland. Married Harold Fair-hair of Norway; mother of Erik I Blood-axe, king of Norway.

♦ **Genealogy. Queens.** ♦

Boyesen, *Story...*, p. 68. Jones, *Vikings...*, p. 94. Larsen, *History...*, p. 84. Wood, *Search...*, p. 154.

RAGNHILD (of Ringerike), queen of Norway **[Ragnild]**
fl. 840s–850s Norway

Daughter of the king of Ringerike. Legend says that Halfdan the Swarthy, ruler of parts of Norway, fell in love with Ragnhild when he rescued her from kidnappers. She had prophetic dreams about their famous son Harold Fair-hair (b.850).

♦ **Abduction. Models. Mystics.** ♦

Boyesen, *Story...*, pp. 47–48. Jones, *Vikings...*, pp. 85–86. Larsen, *History...*, p. 81.

RAOULINE LA MALINGRÉ
c. 1440–1445 France

Raouline of Number Ten rue Petit Pont, was a Parisian linen worker/ seller.

♦ **Clothworkers–linen. Land/property.** ♦

Comptes du..., pp. 199, 245, 291, 341.

REBECCA GUARNA
fl.c. 1200 Italy

Doctor and writer in Salerno; famed for herbal-medical knowledge. Wrote three treatises on medicine—including details about treatment of fevers and how to use urine samples in diagnoses.

♦ **Apothecaries. Doctors/empirics. Writers–medicine.** ♦

Hughes, *Women...*, p. 147. Hurd-Mead, *History...*, pp. 225, 276–277. Lipinska, *Histoire...*, p. 99. Mozans, *Woman...*, p. 286.

REGINA DELLA SCALA
c. 1340s–d. 1385 Italy

Member of ruling family of Vicenza, the city passed through Regina to her daughter Caterina. Regina was the wife of Bernabo Visconti; mother of seventeen of his children. She was supposedly the only person who could control his rages.

♦ **Estate. Managers. Models.** ♦

Chamberlin, *Count...*, pp. 23, 27, 74. Trevelyan, *Short...*, p. 156. Tuchman, *Distant...*, pp. 254 & 344.

RELINDIS OF HOHENBURG
fl. 1100s Germany

Abbess/reformer at Hohenburg. Well-educated herself, Relindis taught novices liberal arts, astronomy, and mathematics. Her most famous pupil was †Herrad von Landsberg.

♦ **Abbesses. Astronomy. Childcare. Educated. Teachers.** ♦

Carr, "Women...," p. 7. Heinrich, *Canonesses...*, p. 143. Jourdain, "Memoire...," p. 475.

RICHARDIS
fl. 850s–880s Germany

Wife of the future Holy Roman Emperor Charles III the Fat. He repudiated Richardis, declaring the marriage was never consummated. Richardis admitted that she was still a virgin. In the attempt to gain his divorce, Charles then accused her of adultery. Richardis underwent an ordeal to clear herself of that charge. She then entered nunnery of Andelau, and later became abbess.

♦ **Abbesses. Adultery–accusations. Divorce. Ordeals. Politics. Popes. Religious patrons. Virginity.** ♦

McKitterick, *Frankish...*, pp. 176, 285, Table 3. Riché, *Les Carolingiens...*, pp. 186 & 211. Stafford, *Queens...*, pp. 77, 82, 94, 96, 102, 179, 180. Wemple, *Women...*, pp. 104 & 171.

RICHARDIS VON STADE
d. 1152 Germany

A nun at Rupertsberg. Richardis was companion, friend, and scribe to †Hildegarde of Bingen. Richardis became abbess of Bassum in 1151.

♦ **Abbesses. Educated. Models. Writers.** ♦

Anderson and Zinsser, *A History of...*, p. 188. Kraft, "German...," p. 111. Lucas, *Women...*, p. 142. Newman, *Sister...*, pp. 6, 222–223, 225, 247. Zum Brunn and Epiney-Burgard, *Women...*, pp. 2, 5, 6, 7.

RICHENZA OF NORDHEIM, Holy Roman Empress **[Richsa]**
m.c. 1100–d.c. 1141 Germany; Italy

Heiress of duchy of Saxony and of Brunswick (she was presumably the daughter of †Gertrude of Meissen (or Brunswick) and Henry the Fat of Nordheim; granddaughter of Otto of Nordheim). Richenza married

Lothar II of Supplinburg, Holy Roman Emperor; she was crowned empress in 1132 in Italy. In 1136, she again accompanied Lothar and his army to Italy. Lothar died during their return journey in 1137. Richenza had sometimes acted with Lothar as a co-ruler; this experience served her well in Saxony where she became regent for her grandson Henry the Lion.

♦ **Estate. Models. Negotiators. Popes. Regents. Rulers. Soldiers. Widows.** ♦

Cambridge..., V, pp. 152, 153, 334, 340, 346–349, 364, 365. Ennen, *Medieval...*, pp. 142–143. Fuhrmann, *Germany...*, pp. 99, 120, 127. Hampe, *Germany...*, p. 125. Haverkamp, *Medieval...*, pp. 142 & 266. Leyser, *Medieval...*, p. 187. Leyser, *Rule...*, p. 119. Norwich, *Kingdom...*, pp. 8, 25–27, 42, 58. Stubbs, *Germany...*, pp. 179, 181, 188, 189.

RICHEUT (la meresse)

1292 France

In 1292 Paris, Richeut was a lay healer of the Parish of Saint-Gervais; she paid 3s tax.

♦ **Doctors/empirics. Less-affluent.** ♦

Géraud, *Paris sous...*, p. 108. Hughes, *Women...*, p. 141. Hurd-Mead, *History...*, p. 215. Lipinska, *Histoire...*, p. 118.

RICHILDE OF AUTUN

m. 870 France; Germany

Presumably the daughter of Count Beuves (or Biwin) and Richild (of Lotharingia). Richilde is thought to have been the mistress of Charles the Bald, king of France, before she became his wife in 870. Crowned Empress in 877. When Charles died, he entrusted Richilde with royal insignia and regalia. She was to settle succession issues by handing these over to Charles's son Louis the Stammerer. Although Richilde first attempted to have her brother crowned, she eventually gave the royal symbols to Louis.

♦ **Mistresses. Politics. Popes. Widows.** ♦

Anselme, *Histoire...*, v.1, p. 34. *Cambridge...*, III, pp. 45, 53, & 137. Lehmann, *Rôle de la...*, pp. 138–144. McKitterick, *Frankish...*, pp. 181, 184, 195, 259, Tables 3 & 4. Riché, *Les Carolingiens...*, pp. 196 & 321. Stafford, *Queens...*, pp. 26, 40, 41, 87, 105, 171, & 176. Wemple, *Women...*, p. 93.

RICHILDE, countess of FLANDERS

c. 1030s–d.1086 Flanders; Netherlands

Daughter of Ranier VI, count of Hainault. Around 1051, the widowed Richilde married Baldwin VI of Flanders. Widowed again, in 1070 she took over the regency and ruled Flanders and Hainault for their underage son. She was very unpopular, in part because her third husband was from Normandy. She led her troops against Robert the Frisian, and later in the Crusades.

♦ **Crusades. Legal activity. Prisons. Regents. Soldiers. Widows.** ♦

Barlow, *Feudal...*, p. 140. Decaux, *Histoire...*, p. 213. Douglas, *William...*, pp. 224 & 225. Dunbabin, *France...*, pp. 209, 211, 222. Fawtier, *Capetian...*, p. 105. Harksen, *Women...*, p. 16. Lehmann, *Rôle de la...*, p. 213. Pernoud, *La femme...*, pp. 179–180.

RICHOLDA

1271/2 England

Owned whorehouse on Bredstrete in London. One of her customers stabbed another client, so Richolda and several of her ladies were arrested and taken to Newgate. She was later acquitted and released.

♦ **Land/property. Murder. Prisons. Prostitutes.** ♦

London Eyre...1276, pp. 63–64.

ROESIA DE BORFORD **[Rose Burford]**

d. 1329 England

Daughter of †Juliana Hauteyn and Thomas Romayn, a London pepperer and alderman who died in 1312. Wife of John of Burford, a London merchant—like her father, a pepperer and alderman. Roesia received 100 marks for making a cope decorated with coral; †Isabella of France, queen of England, bought the vestment to send as a present to the pope. Executor of husband's will (1318), as a widow Roesia engaged in various business and legal transactions. Her own will, written in 1329 and proved that same year in London, indicates that Roesia was a very well-to-do merchant in her own right. She owned tenements in the city (she bequeathed some of these to pious uses) and manors in the country. Roesia also taught the wool trade to at least one apprentice. Her son James inherited her property in Surrey, Kent, and Sussex (some of which she had inherited from her mother).

♦ **Apprentices–mistresses. Artistic clothwork. Bequests. Charity. Clothworkers. Gems/jewelry. Land/property. Legal activity. Merchants. Popes. Widows.** ♦

Calendar of Plea..., II, p. 3 *Calendar of Wills...*, I, p. 303. Labarge, *Small Sound...*, p. 230. Power, *Women...*, pp. 56–57. Thrupp, *Merchant...*, pp. 171 n36 & 327. Uitz, *Legend...*, p. 40.

ROGNEDA OF POLOTSK, princess of Kiev

c. 960s–980s Russia

Daughter of Rogvolod of Polotsk. Legend reports that she turned down a proposal from Vladimir I of Kiev. He then led an army to Polotsk, killed her father, and married Rogneda by force (974). Supposedly, she later tried to murder Vladimir.

♦ **Abduction. Models. Murder.** ♦

Kluchevsky, *History...*, pp. 95 & 109. Vernadsky, *Kievan...*, pp. 39, 57, 59, 74, 182.

ROIANTKEN

b. 810–d.c. 860s France

Wife of Count Deuerhoiarn of Redon. Owned much property in Brittany— some of which she bought for herself and which she later gave to the church.

♦ **Dowry/dower. Estate. Managers. Religious patrons.** ♦

Wemple, *Women...*, p. 119.

(St.) ROSALIA OF PALERMO

d. 1160 Italy

Patron saint of Palermo and of sailors. She was supposedly a recluse who lived in caves overlooking the sea. Presumably her prayers saved her city twice from the plague.

♦ **Anchoresses. Models. Plague. Saints.** ♦

Attwater, *Dictionary...*, p. 264. Effinger, *Women...*, pp. 54–55.

ROSAMUND CLIFFORD

c. 1150s–d. c. 1176 England

Though some scholars have questioned her existence, she is usually said to have been the mistress of Henry II, king of England, during the 1160s and early 1170s. When Rosamund fell seriously ill, she retired to Godstow and took the veil before her death in 1176.

♦ **Mistresses. Models. Religieuses. Witchcraft.** ♦

Appleby, *John...*, pp. 17 & 274. Coulton, *Life...*, v.3, pp. 5–6. Ewen, *Witchcraft...*, p. 73. Heer, *Medieval...*, p. 134. Kelly, *Eleanor...*, pp. 150–1, 153, 192, 193, 239, & 384. Marks, *Pilgrims...*, p. 177. Pernoud, *Eleanor...*, pp. 134–6, 140, 170, 172. Warren, *Henry...*, pp. 119, 601 & n3. Winston, *Thomas...*, pp. 140 & 234–235.

ROSE NOSTERFELD

1364 England

Wife of London merchant, William Nosterfeld. In 1364, William and Rose were accused of selling ale by one-third short weight, and of counterfeiting the seals for this short weight of ale. They admitted to the ale charge and were fined. William and Rose denied counterfeiting seals, however, and the London jury acquitted the couple of that charge.

♦ **Alewives. Miscreants.** ♦

Calendar of Plea..., II, p. 6.

ROSE O'CONNOR, countess of Meath **[Rose of Monmouth]**

c. 1160s–1180s Ireland

Daughter of Rory O'Connor, high king of Ireland. Married (1) Baderon of Monmouth and (2) Hugh II de Lacy.

♦ Genealogy. Pawns. ♦

Barlow, *Feudal...*, p. 348. Curtis, *Ireland...*, pp. 63 & 64. Curtis, *Medieval...*, pp. 86, 128, and table. Wrightman, *Lacy...*, pp. 194 & 206.

ROSE SAVAGE

1282 England

Accused John de Clifford of raping her. John pointed out discrepancies in her petition, so Rose's case was denied and she was jailed. With the king as petitioner, the case continued, and John (although absent) was found guilty since the whole neighborhood knew of his crime.

♦ Abduction. Legal activity. Punishments. Rape. ♦

Bellamy, *Crime...*, p. 104. Prestwich, *Edward...*, p. 282. *Select...Edward I,* I, pp. 101–102.

(St.) ROSE OF VITERBO **[Rosa]**

1235–1253 Italy

She is believed to have been a Franciscan tertiary of too low social status to join local convent. She preached on the streets of Viterbo and used her saintly influence to oppose heretics and Ghibellines. Rose had quite a following, and many miracles were attributed to her. Her saintliness was "proved" by the fact that, after death, her body did not decay.

♦ Models. Preachers. Politics. Relics. Religieuses. Saints. Unmarried. ♦

Abate, *S. Rosa....* Attwater, *Dictionary...*, p. 264. Bynum, *Holy...*, pp. 145, 146, 273, 364 n213, 392 n85, 396 n13. Goodich, "Contours...," p. 28. Herlihy, *Opera...*, pp. 121–122. Huizinga, *Waning...*, p. 128.

ROTHILD OF CHELLES

c. 880s–920s France

Abbess of Chelles until her nephew, Charles III the Simple of France removed her and put a Lotharingian man in her place. Rothild's powerful family (including Robert I of France, her son Hugh, count of Maine, and her son-in-law, Hugh the Great, count of Paris and duke of the Franks) rose against Charles. He fled, but this did not stop the war between Charles and Robert I which had been touched off by the ill-treatment of Rothild.

♦ Abbesses. Politics. Squabbles. ♦

Anselme, *Histoire...*, v.1, p. 69. James, *Origins...*, p. 182. McKitterick, *Frankish...*, pp. 185 & 309.

ROTRUDE **[Hruodtrude; Rothrud; Rotrud]**

b. 775–d.c. 810 France; Germany

Charlemagne's favorite legitimate daughter (by wife †Hildegard). At an early age Rotrude was betrothed to Constantine VI, so Charlemagne hired a famous Byzantine scholar to tutor her in Greek. Although the marriage plans fell through, Rotrude continued her studies in liberal arts, theology, etc. Alcuin, and other contemporary writers, lauded her intelligence and education. Probably around the year 800, Rotrude had an affair with Count Rorigo; their children started the large and important Rorico clan. Rotrude later retired to monastery of Chelles.

♦ **Adultery. Educated. Models. Religieuses.** ♦

Carolingian..., pp. 91, 187, 194. Decaux, *Histoire...*, pp. 161–162. Duckett, *Carolingian...*, p. 14. Ganshof, *Carolingians...*, p. 170. Jenkins, *Byzantium...*, p. 97. Jourdain, "Memoire...," pp. 471–472. Lehmann, *Rôle de la...*, pp. 192–193. McKitterick, *Frankish...*, pp. 70 & 184. Riché, *Les Carolingiens...*, p. 140. Stafford, *Queens...*, p. 55. Wemple, *Women...*, pp. 79 & 179.

ROZA

fl.c. 930 France; Italy

Daughter of Gualbert de Pavie. She was said to be extremely beautiful, so she was nicknamed "Venus" after she became the mistress of Hugh of Arles. Hugh made their son Theobald archbishop of Milan at a very young age, and this act of nepotism caused a great scandal.

♦ **Mistresses. Models.** ♦

Ernouf, *Histoire...*, pp. 309–310. Stafford, *Queens...*, p. 53. Wright, *Works...*, pp. 128 & 152–153.

ROZALA OF LOMBARDY, countess of Flanders
[Susanna, princess of France]

c. 960s–d.c. 1003 Flanders; France; Italy

Daughter of †Willa of Tuscany and Berengar II, count of Ivrea and king of Italy. Married Arnulf II, count of Flanders. After he died in 988, she married Hugh Capet's heir, Robert the Pious. This arranged marriage was a dismal failure. Not only was there an age gap between the two, but they had absolutely no liking for one another. By 990, Robert had repudiated Rozala, but he then refused to return her dowry—the lands of Montreuil.

♦ **Divorce. Dowry/dower. Models. Pawns. Squabbles.** ♦

Duckett, *Death...*, p. 122. Dunbabin, *France...*, pp. 102, 136, 217. Facinger, "Study...," pp. 10, 12, 22. Fawtier, *Capetian...*, p. 50. McKitterick, *Frankish...*, pp. 252 & 323. Marks, *Pilgrims...*, p. 27. Pernoud, *La femme...*, p. 178. Riché, *Les Carolingiens...*, p. 267. Stafford, *Queens...*, pp. 42, 74, 83, 102, 176, 190.

— S —

SABINA VON STEINBACH

fl. 1225–1240 Austria; Germany

Sabina supposedly helped a master builder/sculptor make the statues at Strassburg Cathedral.

♦ **Artists. Builders.** ♦

Anderson and Zinsser, *A History of...*, p. 412. Carr, "Women...," p. 8. Petersen and Wilson, *Women...*, pp. 20–21, 22, 121.

SAINTE (la paintre)

1292 France

A painter, probably of statues and pictures; paid 3s tax in 1292 Paris.

♦ **Artists. Less-affluent.** ♦

Géraud, *Paris sous...*, p. 160.

SAIV KAVANAGH **[Sabina; Saive]**

m.c. 1463 Ireland

Daughter of Donal Reagh, king of Leinster. Saiv married James Butler; they were parents of Piers Butler, later earl of Ossory and Ormond. Because Saiv was a native of Ireland, it was not until 1467 that the marriage was officially acknowledged.

♦ **Estate. Genealogy. Legal activity. Squabbles.** ♦

Curtis, *Ireland...*, pp. 142 & 145. *DNB,* v.3, p. 524.

SANCIA [Sancha; Sanche; Sanchia]

SANCIA D'ARAGONA, princess of Squillace

b. 1479–d. 1506 Italy

Illegitimate daughter of Alfonso of Calabria (later Alfonso II of Naples). In 1494, she married Rodrigo Borgia's (Pope Alexander VI's) illegimate son, Joffré Borgia. Sancia was good-natured, fun loving, and promiscuous. Presumably her sexual conquests included Joffré's brothers, Juan and Cesare Borgia.

♦ **Adultery. Childcare. Divorce–separations. Estate. Illegitimacy. Models. Popes. Prisons.** ♦

Cartwright, *Beatrice...*, pp. 221 & 225. Chamberlin, *Fall...*, pp. viii, 111, 115–118, 124, 153–158, 184, 207, 218–224, 295, 311, 326. Cloulas, *Borgias...*, pp. 84, 87–8, 122–4, 164, 230, 249, 259, 271, 284, 298. Fusero, *Borgias...*, pp. 163, 168, 186, 191, 225–227, 259, 269–270, 291. Johnson, *Borgias...*, pp. 36–37, 90–91, 94–95, 100, 101, 119–120, 127–129, 132, 140, 158. Prescott, *Princes...*, pp. 73 & 80–81.

SANCHA OF CASTILE, queen of Aragon
b. 1154–1200s Spain

Daughter of Alfonso VII of Castile; married Alfonso II of Aragon in 1174; mother of Pedro II of Aragon. She and her husband had political, marital, and financial difficulties. In 1196, the widowed Sancha retired to a convent she had established at Sijena.

♦ **Dowry/dower. Politics. Religieuses. Religious patrons. Soldiers. Squabbles. Widows.** ♦

Deminska, "Polish...," pp. 287, 290. Miron, *Queens...*, pp. 71–80, 81. Shneidman, *Rise...*, p. 182.

SANCHA, queen of LEON AND CASTILE
fl. 1020–d. 1067 Spain

Daughter of Alfonso V of Leon and his wife—apparently Elvira Gonzalez of Galicia. Married Ferdinand (Fernando) I of Castile around 1032, which eventually united the two kingdoms.

♦ **Queens.** ♦

Altamira, Spain..., p. 110. Effinger, *Women...*, p. 290. Fletcher, *Quest...*, pp. 68, 71, 90, 115–6.

SANCIA OF MAJORCA, queen of Naples **[Sanchia of Aragon]**
b. 1286–d. 1345 Italy; Spain

Daughter of †Esclaramunda de Foix and James II of Majorca. Second wife of King Robert the Wise of Naples. Very pious, Sancia supported Franciscan establishments and wished to enter a convent herself. She disagreed with the pope over the orthodoxy of the Spiritual Franciscans. When Robert died, he left Sancia as regent for his granddaughter †Joanna I of Naples. Sancia was soon pushed aside and she retired to a convent (c.1343).

♦ **Heretics. Popes. Regents. Religieuses. Religious patrons. Widows.** ♦

Anselme, *Histoire...*, v.1, p. 408. Musto, "Queen Sancia...," pp. 179–214. Shneidman, *Rise...*, p. 93.

(St.) SANCHA OF PORTUGAL
b. 1180–d. 1229 Portugal

Daughter of †Douce (II) of Barcelona and Sancho I of Portugal. Very pious, she soon became a nun. Introduced Franciscans into Portugal. Sancha may have become abbess of Lorvao.

♦ **Abbesses. Nuns. Religious patrons. Saints.** ♦

Anselme, *Histoire...*, v.1, p. 576. Holweck, *Biographical...*, p. 883. Stephens, *Story...*, p. 74.

SANCHIA OF PROVENCE

b. 1225–d. 1261 England; France

Third daughter of †Beatrice of Savoy and Raymond Berengar, count of Provence. In 1243, Sanchia became the second wife of Richard, earl of Cornwall, later king of the Romans.

♦ **Models. Queens.** ♦

Armitage-Smith, *John...*, pp. 89–90. *Cambridge...*, VI, pp. 119, 126, 266. Labarge, *Simon...*, pp. 67–68. Paris, *Chronicles...*, pp. 199 & 201. Powicke, *Thirteenth...*, pp. 100, 104, 105, 107, 119. Runciman, *Sicilian...*, pp. 59–60, 71, 72. Shneidman, *Rise...*, p. 299. Wakefield, *Heresy...*, pp. 157–158.

SANCHE SNOTH

fl. 1360s England

A London broker, she acted as a middleman for a skinner.

♦ **Merchants–furs.** ♦

Lacey, "Women...," p. 52.

SARAH [Sara; Sarra; Sarre]

SARRA (of Broughton)

fl. 1292 England

Servant of Roger Gylbert in Broughton village; Sarra was also a brewer.

♦ **Alewives. Manors. Servants. Unmarried.** ♦

Britton, *Community...*, p. 236.

SARAH OF MEATH

fl. 1310s–1330s England; Ireland

See—ALICE KYTELER.

Sarah escaped with Alice.

♦ **Witchcraft.** ♦

SARRE (la mirgesse)

1292 France

Doctor in Paris at l'Atacherie; taught medical skills to her daughter Florian who may have practiced medicine with her mother.

♦ **Doctors/empirics. Jews. Teachers.** ♦

Géraud, *Paris sous...*, p. 179. Herlihy, *Opera...*, pp. 146–147. Hughes, *Women...*, p. 141. Hurd-Mead, *History...*, p. 215. Lipinska, *Histoire...*, p. 118. Wickersheimer, *Dictionnaire...*, v.2, p. 732.

SARA OF SAINT-GILLES

1326 France

Jewish doctor of Marseilles; widow of Abraham. She also taught medicine to other women. In 1326, Sara was licensed to train a male apprentice.

♦ **Apprentices–mistresses. Doctors/empirics. Jews. Teachers. Widows.** ♦

Friedenwald, "Jewish...," p. 217. Harksen, *Women...*, pp. 27–28. Hughes, *Women...*, p. 145. Hurd-Mead, *History...*, pp. 158, 214, 269. Jacquart, *Le Milieu...*, p. 85. Lipinska, *Histoire...*, p. 118. Wickersheimer, *Dictionnaire...*, v.2, p. 732.

SARAH STROBY

1316 England

Wife of Hugh de Strubby. In his will of 1316, Hugh left his shops and tavern to Sarah to run.

♦ **Bequests. Land/property. Merchants. Taverners. Widows.** ♦

Calendar of Wills..., I, p. 269.

SARA (of Wurzburg)

1419 Germany

Jewish doctor; granted license to practice medicine in Wurzburg on annual payment of 10 florin tax. She was so successful that she later bought a house in town.

♦ **Doctors/empirics. Jews. Land/property.** ♦

Friedenwald, "Jewish...," pp. 218–219. Hughes, *Women...*, p. 143. Hurd-Mead, *History...*, p. 312. Lipinska, *Histoire...*, p. 124.

SAURIMONDE DE PEIRALADA

See—MARGARIDA DE ROUSSILLON.

SCLERENA (of Byzantium)

c. 1010s–d.c. 1045 Byzantium

Permanent mistress of Constantine Monomachus; followed him into exile. When he became Basileus by marrying Empress †Zoe the Porphyrogenita in 1042, Sclerena took up residence at Byzantine palace where she had her own apartments. Zoe acquiesced in this arrangement, so Sclerena was accorded most of the privileges of a legitimate consort.

♦ **Mistresses. Models. Religious patrons.** ♦

Cambridge..., IV, pp. 109, 110, 115. Daniel-Rops, *Church...*, p. 525. Diehl, *Byzantine...*, pp. 162–166 & 168.

SEDILE (la fournière)
1292 France

Tended public oven in 1292 Paris; paid 12d tax.

♦ **Less-affluent. Provisioning–bakers.** ♦

Géraud, *Paris sous...*, p. 53.

SEDILLON ROSSIGNOL
1425/6 France

Taxes on her property near door of Saint Honore in Paris were remitted because she agreed to keep the gate and wall in good repair.

♦ **Builders. Land/property.** ♦

Comptes du..., pp. 72–73.

SERLIN **[Zerline]**
1428 Germany

Jewish doctor; oculist of Frankfurt-am-Main.

♦ **Doctors/empirics–eye doctors. Jews.** ♦

Friedenwald, "Jewish...," p. 219. Hughes, *Women...*, p. 143. Hurd-Mead, *History...*, p. 312. Lipinska, *Histoire...*, p. 123.

SERSIVE LA BÉRANGIÈRE
1380 France

Listed as one of twenty-one licensed female schoolteachers in 1380 Paris.

♦ **Teachers.** ♦

Decaux, *Histoire...*, p. 355.

SEWIS VAN BERCHEM
1450s–d. 1483 Germany

An unmarried clothworker, Sewis was admitted to the silkmakers guild in 1462. She and her sister †Fygen served on the guild committee, trained many apprentices, and were quite prosperous.

♦ **Apprentices. Clothworkers. Land/property. Legal activity. Merchants. Shipping. Silkwork. Unmarried.** ♦

Wensky, "Women's Guilds...," p. 647.

SIBILLINA BISCOSSI **[Blessed]**
1287–1367 Italy

Blind girl of Pavia; at age twelve became servant at Dominican convent.

♦ **Anchoresses. Handicapped. Orphans. Servants.** ♦

Attwater, *Dictionary...*, p. 273. Goodich, "Ancilla Dei...," pp. 125 & 131.

SIBYL [Sibila; Sibilia; Sibylla; Sibylle; Sybil; Sybilla; Sybille]

SIBYLLA OF ACERRA, queen of Sicily

fl. 1170s–1190s Italy; Germany

Daughter of Roger, count of Acerra; married Tancred of Lecce, king of Sicily. When he died in 1194, their underage son William III became the last Norman king of Sicily. Sibylla served as his regent—making a courageous last stand against Henry VI. After his victory Henry sent her to Germany where she and her daughters eventually escaped, or were granted their freedom.

♦ Prisons. Regents. Soldiers. Widows. ♦

Cambridge..., V, pp. 202, 203, 470, 471; VI, p. 133. Norwich, *Kingdom...,* pp. 380, 382–383, 385–386, 388.

SYBILLE OF ANJOU, countess of Flanders

c. 1110s–1170s Flanders; France

Daughter of Foulques V of Anjou. Around 1124, Sybille married (1) William Clito. This marriage was annulled about a year later. Around 1130, Sybille married Thierry of Alsace, count of Flanders; their children included : Philip of Alsace, count of Flanders, and †Margaret of Alsace, countess of Hainault. Sybille's dowry—the county of Maine—caused a variety of territorial disputes. She often served as her husband's liege-lord in the late 1140s, defending their lands against Baldwin IV, count of Hainault.

♦ Crusades. Divorce. Dowry/dower. Legal activity. Politics. Regents. Soldiers. Widows. ♦

Anselme, *Histoire...,* v.2, p. 721. Barlow, *Feudal...,* pp. 197, 199, & 234. Bedos Rezak, "Women...," p. 63. Hallam (ed.), *Plantagenet...,* p. 104. Kelly, *Eleanor...,* pp. 34 & 66. Payne, *Dream...,* p. 185. Pernoud, *Eleanor...,* p. 50. Warlop, *Flemish...,* v.1, pt. 1, pp. 83, 165, 228, 235, 303.

SYBILLE DE CHÂTEAU-PORCIEN [Sybil de Coucy]

c. 1060s–1090s France

Wife of Godefroi, count of Namur. Sybille evidently felt that her husband was away fighting too often, so when Enguerrand (I) de Coucy offered to replace her absent spouse, Sybille accepted. Godefroi later returned home to fight for his wife and property in an exceptionally bloody feud. Since he lost this war, Sybille and her lands remained with Enguerrand.

♦ Divorce. Managers. Squabbles. Women of easy virtue. ♦

Decaux, *Histoire...,* pp. 215–216. Duby, *Private...,* p. 139 (not named in this source). Tuchman, *Distant...,* pp. 5–6.

SYBIL OF CONVERSANO

c. 1080s–d.c. 1103 France; Italy

Daughter of Geoffrey of Conversano, lord of Brindisi (grandson of Tancred of Hauteville). Sybil married Robert Curthose, oldest son of William of Normandy, the Conqueror of England. Their son, William Clito, was born around 1101. Sybil's dowry financed Robert's efforts to retrieve the duchy of Normandy. Orderic Vitalis claimed that Sybil was poisoned, but William of Malmesbury opined that her death was a result of problems incurred in childbirth. Both chroniclers extolled Sybil as a virtuous wife.

♦ **Childbirth. Dowry/dower. Models.** ♦

Barlow, *Feudal...,* pp. 170, 175, 194. *DNB,* v.16, p. 1241. Douglas, *Norman...,* pp. 15 & 31. Forester (trans.), *Ordericus...,* v.3, pp. 66, 256, 272, 341, 343; v.4, p. 86.

SIBILLA (of England), queen of Scotland

c. 1100s–d. 1121 England; Scotland

Illegitimate daughter of Henry I of England; married Alexander I of Scotland. After her death, Alexander founded a church in her memory.

♦ **Illegitimacy. Queens.** ♦

Barrow, *Feudal...,* pp. 132–133, 420. Brown, *History...,* I, p. 69. Chambers, *Norman...,* p. 154. *DNB,* v.1, pp. 259 & 261. Glover, *Story...,* pp. 53–54. Mackie, *History...,* p. 47.

SIBILIA DE FORCIA, queen of Aragon

m. 1377–d. 1407 Spain

Widow of Artal de Forcia. Mistress and then wife of Pedro IV of Aragon. Her stepson John I accused Sibilia of witchcraft and theft. She had probably at least schemed against him. After being tortured and imprisoned, she was finally released to live in poverty and obscurity.

♦ **Mistresses. Politics. Prisons. Widows. Witchcraft.** ♦

Bisson, *Medieval Crown...,* pp. 116, 117, 121, 122, 126. Chaytor, *History...,* pp. 192, 194–195, 204. Hillgarth, *Pere...,* pp. 6, 93, 104, 585, 593, 600. Miron, *Queens...,* pp. 201, 202.

SIBYLLA OF JERUSALEM

m.c. 1176–d. 1190 Israel

Daughter of †Agnes of Courtenay and Amalric I of Jerusalem. Married (1) William of Montferrat (d.1177) and (2) Guy de Lusignan around 1180. She was crowned queen of Jerusalem in 1186. In 1187, she unsuccessfully defended the city against Saladin. Sibylla died in an epidemic of 1190, thus touching off another contest for Jerusalem.

♦ **Educated. Estate. Negotiators. Rulers. Soldiers.** ♦

Bridge, *Crusades...*, pp. 12, 197, 221. *Cambridge...*, V, pp. 309 & 310. *Chronicles...*, pp. 152, 160, 181, 247. Decaux, *Histoire...*, pp. 222–223. Hamilton, *Women...*, pp. 163–172. Kelly, *Eleanor...*, pp. 268 & 269. Payne, *Dream...*, pp. 185, 193, 198, 199, 236, 265. Pernoud, *Eleanor...*, p. 121. Tyerman, *England...*, pp. 51 & 68.

SYBIL DE LACY

c. 1180 England

See—AGNES FITZJOHN and CECILY FITZJOHN.

♦ **Charity. Estate.** ♦

SICHELGAITA OF SALERNO, duchess of Apulia **[Sikelgaita]**

b. 1040–d. 1090 Italy

Daughter of duke of Salerno; second wife of Robert Guiscard; mother of Roger Borsa. In contemporary writing—like that of †Anna Comnena—Sichelgaita was described as a large, fearsome woman, wearing armor, rallying troops, and fighting like a man. She succeeded in dispossessing Robert's older son Bohemund of Antioch; her own son Roger was named heir. Sichelgaita supposedly even tried to poison Bohemund with one of her medical potions.

♦ **Medicine. Models. Politics. Soldiers. Widows.** ♦

Cambridge..., V, pp. 174 & 182. *Chronicles...*, pp. 52 & 55. Comnena, *Alexiad...*, pp. 59, 66, 147, 192. Gies, *Women...*, p. 24. Hollister, *Medieval Europe...*, pp. 173, 174. Norwich, *Kingdom...*, pp. 36, 334, 386. Norwich, *Normans...*, pp. 116–118, 146, 153, 183, 195–197, 201, 210, 217, 231–232, 245–247, 249–251, 258–259. Ritchie, "Bohemund...," pp. 293–295.

SIGRID, queen of SWEDEN

c. 970s–1000 Denmark; Sweden

Wife of Erik the Victorious of Sweden; mother of his heir, King Olaf. According to sagas, as a widow, Sigrid executed several men for presuming to propose marriage to her. This was supposed to be the origin of her quarrel with Olaf Tryggvesson of Norway.

♦ **Estate. Models. Murder. Politics. Widows.** ♦

Boyesen, *Story...*, pp. 152, 154, 161, 163, 182. Jones, *Vikings...*, pp. 136 & 365.

SIMONE OF BYZANTIUM

b. 1292–1330s Byzantium; Russia

Daughter of Andronicus II of Byzantium. Married around age six to forty-year-old Kral of Serbia, Stephen Miloutin. Stephen was subject to jealous rages which terrified Simone. She attempted to enter convent to escape him, but was forced to return to Serbia. After Stephen died,

Simone retired to a convent at Constantinople. Her nephew Andronicus (III) caused a scandal by attempting to seduce Simone at her nunnery.

♦ **Models. Nuns. Pawns.** ♦

Cambridge..., IV, pp. 532 & 533. Diehl, *Byzantine...*, pp. 277, 280–282, 285.

SIMONETTA CATTANEO **[Simonetta Vespucci]**

b. 1459–d. 1476 Italy

Wife of Marco Vespucci of Florence. Friend, and possibly lover, of Lorenzo de'Medici, who held tournament for her in 1475. He also wrote poetry about her, as did Politian. Botticelli presumably painted her portrait. Simonetta died young of tuberculosis.

♦ **Educated. Models. Tournaments. Women of easy virtue.** ♦

Cleugh, *Medici...*, pp. 126–127. Hook, *Lorenzo...*, pp. 16, 50, 78. Sizeranne, *Beatrice...*, pp. 85, 161, & 172.

SLYMINA FORT

fl. 1270s–1290s England

Wife of Fictavin le Fort, a Jewish merchant of London. She owned houses in Cattestrete. Apparently Slymina was one of the Jews expelled from the kingdom by Edward I in 1290.

♦ **Jews. Land/property.** ♦

Calendar of Wills..., I, pp. 202–203.

SOPHIA, queen of BOHEMIA

fl. 1380s–1420s Bohemia; Czechoslovakia

Wife of Wenceslaus of Bohemia. Supporter and protector of John Hus. When her husband died in 1419, she was appointed regent. She had been a good influence on Wenceslaus, but as regent Sophia was allowed too little freedom of action to enable her to keep the peace.

♦ **Hussites. Regents. Religious patrons. Widows.** ♦

Klassen, *Nobility...*, pp. 78, 89, 123–124. Lambert, *Medieval...*, p. 315. Leff, *Heresy...*, v.2, p. 620, 621, 688, 693, 695, 696. Lutzow, *Hussite...*, pp. 3–4, 14, 19, 35. Maurice, *Bohemia...*, pp. 184, 192, 202, 233, 235, 236, 242, 243, 247.

SOPHIA OF GANDERSHEIM

b. 975–d. 1039 Germany

Daughter of †Theophano of Byzantium and Otto II of Germany. Abbess of Gandersheim and Essen. Sophia was proud and willful. These qualities, and her passion for acquiring property, led to a great deal of strife for her family.

♦ **Abbesses. Estate. Managers. Politics. Popes.** ♦

Anderson and Zinsser, *A History of...*, pp. 198–199. *Cambridge...*, III, p. 255. Duckett, *Death...*, pp. 182–183. Ennen, *Medieval...*, pp. 81, 82, 83. Leyser, *Rule...*, pp. 49–50, 54, 66, 89, 94, 172.

SOPHIA, princess of MOSCOW **[Zoe Paleologa]**

b. 1448–d.c. 1503 Byzantium; Italy; Russia

Niece of Constantine XI of Byzantium. Received some schooling as a papal ward. The pope married her in 1472 to Ivan III of Moscow—and her name was changed to Sophia. A visitor, †Clarissa Orsini, indicated that Sophia suffered from obesity. In her new home, she was influential in elevating the status and ceremony surrounding the prince of Moscow. Sophia also encouraged artistic production and supported the Orthodox Church. She fought for and gained the crown for her son Vasili III.

♦ Art patrons. Educated. Handicapped. Models. Orphans. Politics. Popes. Religious patrons. Squabbles. ♦

Maguire, *Women...*, pp. 148–149. Pares, *History...*, pp. 93–94, 95, 99. Vernadsky, *Russia...*, pp. 17–26 & 122–130.

SOPHIE (of GERMANY), queen of Hungary, queen of Poland

See—JUDITH (of GERMANY).

STEPHANIA (of Rome)

c. 960s–1000s Italy

Probably the sister of Pope John XIII who granted her the town of Palestrina. Widow of Roman rebel leader Crescentius, Stephania was rumored to have avenged her husband's execution by poisoning Otto III in 1002.

♦ Estate. Models. Murder. Popes. Widows. Women of easy virtue. ♦

Bryce, *Holy...*, p. 147. Partner, *Lands...*, p. 91.

Countess of STRATHEARN **[Strathern]**

fl. 1300s–1320s Scotland

She was imprisoned for life for plotting to depose King Robert I of Scotland. The *Dictionary of National Biography* indicates that her name was Maria. Other sources say that she was Agnes Comyn (daughter of Alexander Buchan; aunt of another of the conspirators, William Soulis), a suggestion that makes more sense, and seems to have more supporting evidence in its favor. Some doubt remains as to whether her husband was Malise VI or Malise VII, earl of Strathearn.

♦ Models. Politics. Prisons. Spies. ♦

Allan, "Historical...," p. 353. Barrow, *Robert...*, p. 430. *Calendar...Scotland*, v.3, p. 42. *DNB*, v.19, pp. 36–37. Nicholson,

Scotland..., p. 102. Paul, *Scots...*, VI, pp. 135–137, & VIII, pp. 241–250. *Scalacronica...*, p. 144. Scott, *Robert...*, p. 198.

SUBH OF CORDOBA **[Aurora]**
c. 950s–990s Spain

Harem wife of Hakam II, Caliph of Cordoba, and mother of his only two sons. The younger of these survived to become Hisham II in 976. Since he was a minor, the government was run by Subh and her lover, Abi Amir (al-Mansur). He eventually pushed Subh aside and made Hisham into little more than a puppet.

♦ **Mistresses. Negotiators. Pawns. Regents. Widows.** ♦

Bendiner, *Rise...*, pp. 222–226, 229, 230. *Cambridge...*, III, pp. 424, 425, 426. Jackson, *Making...*, pp. 47 & 48. Livermore, *History...*, pp. 86 & 87. O'Callaghan, *History...*, pp. 126 & 129.

SUSANE (la coiffière)
1292 France

Successful coif maker (headdress/scarf) of 1292 Paris—paid 70s tax.

♦ **Apparel–hatmakers. Land/property. Merchants.** ♦

Géraud, *Paris sous...*, p. 13.

SUSANNA OF FRANCE

See—ROZALA OF LOMBARDY.

SVANHILD OF ESSEN
c. 1060–d.c. 1090 Germany

Abbess of powerful house of Essen on the Ruhr. She had most of the privileges and powers of a bishop. Svanhild built a chapel for this establishment and was responsible for the production of the famous *Gospel Book of Essen* which was covered in gold and jewels.

♦ **Abbesses. Bookmaking. Builders. Managers. Religious patrons.** ♦

Kashnitz, "Gospel...," pp. 122–166.

SYBILLE

See—SIBYL.

SYSSOH GALRUSSYN **[Syssok]**
fl. 1300s–1320s Ireland

See—ALICE KYTELER.

♦ **Witchcraft.** ♦

— T —

TADDEA VISCONTI **[Thadee]**

fl. 1360s–1370s Germany; Italy

Daughter of Bernabo Visconti. First wife of Stephen of Bavaria; mother of †Isabeau of Bavaria, queen of France (b.1370).

♦ **Genealogy.** ♦

Coryn, *House...*, p. 17. Tuchman, *Distant...*, p. 436.

TAMARA, queen of GEORGIA **[Thamar]**

c. 1160s–d. 1213 Russia

Daughter of King George III of Georgia, she inherited his crown in 1184. Tamara was forced to marry twice in attempts to secure her throne, but she was a better ruler than either husband. She eventually banished her first husband. Tamara not only ruled well, but patronized the arts—especially literature.

♦ **Art patrons. Divorce. Educated. Models. Patrons of literature. Rulers. Soldiers.** ♦

Cambridge..., VII, p. 612. Toumanoff, "Relationship...," pp. 299–312. Uitz, *Legend...*, p. 38. Vernadsky, *Kievan...*, pp. 357, 359, 360.

TANGLOST

c. 1480–1500 England

Accused of practicing wax image magic, home-wrecking, and adultery. Supposed to have killed her lover's wife by witchcraft. Ousted from the community by the bishop of St. David's, Tanglost then hired Margaret Hackett to help make wax images to kill the cleric.

♦ **Adultery. Ecclesiastical courts. Murder. Prisons. Witchcraft.** ♦

Kieckhefer, *European...*, p. 139. Kittredge, *Witchcraft...*, pp. 85–86. Martin, "Clerical...," pp. 374–376. Thomas, *Religion...*, p. 467.

TARUB (of Cordoba)

fl. 830s–850s Spain

Favorite mistress of Abd-er Rahman II, emir of Cordoba. Tarub supposedly tried to poison him, his heir presumptive, and others in order to put her own son Abdallah on the throne. Her plots failed, but she retained her position in the harem.

♦ Mistresses. Murder–attempted. Politics. ♦

Bendiner, *Rise...*, pp. 88–89, 122–123, 132. *Cambridge...*, III, pp. 416, 417. Jackson, *Making...*, pp. 29–30.

TENXWIND OF ANDERNACH **[Tengswich]**

c. 1130s–1170s Germany

She was a well-to-do townswoman; became abbess of Augustinian nunnery. She and †Hildegarde of Bingen conducted a heated correspondence over social and religious questions. Tenxwind, who believed in emulating the poverty of Christ and His disciples, upbraided Hildegarde for excluding all but wealthy, noble women from her convent.

♦ Abbesses. Writers. ♦

Ennen, *Medieval...*, p. 128. Haverkamp, *Medieval...*, pp. 191, 199, 329. Newman, *Sister...*, pp. 35n., 85, 221–222. Zum Brunn and Epiney-Burgard, *Women...*, p. 6.

TEODORINA (Cibo) **[Teodorina Usodimare]**

c. 1450s–1490s Italy

Daughter of Pope Innocent VIII. Married Genoese merchant, Gerardo Usodimare.

♦ Illegitimacy. Models. Pawns. Popes. ♦

Bell, *Short...*, p. 285. Brusher, *Popes...*, p. 422. Cloulas, *Borgias...*, p. 54. Creighton, *History...*, IV, p. 150. Maguire, *Women...*, p. 180.

THAMAR

See—TAMARA.

THEODA OF MAINZ **[Theuda; Thiota]**

847 Germany

Prophetess of Mainz whose followers turned away from the church. She was condemned by clerics. Theoda was whipped until she returned to orthodoxy and gave up the practice of fortune-telling.

♦ Ecclesiastical courts. Heretics. Mystics. Preachers. Punishments. ♦

Lambert, *Medieval...*, pp. 9, 25, 26, 59. Russell, *Dissent...*, pp. 107–108, 111–113, 118, 238, 248, 252. Schulenburg, "Female...," p. 116. Wemple, *Women...*, p. 145.

THEODORA, empress of BYZANTIUM

fl. 1250s–1260s Byzantium; Greece

Wife of Greek ruler of Nicaea, Theodora was crowned empress at Constantinople when her husband became Michael VIII Paleologus in 1261. When he tried to divorce her, Theodora resisted and even enlisted the support of the Patriarch of Constantinople. Michael was forced to give up his divorce and remarriage plans.

♦ Divorce–opposition to. Queens. ♦
Diehl, *Byzantine...*, pp. 272–273. Norwich, *History...*, p. 159.

THEODORA COMNENA, duchess of Austria
fl. 1130s–1150s Austria; Byzantium

Well-educated; literary patroness. Niece of Manuel Comnenus, emperor of Byzantium. She became his mistress in the 1140s. In 1148, Theodora became the second wife of Henry of Austria (Henry II Jasomirgott of Babenberg).

♦ Educated. Mistresses. Models. Patrons of literature. Pawns. ♦
Bell, "Medieval...," pp. 184–5 n69. Bridge, *Crusades...*, p. 162. *Cambridge...*, v.IV, p. 363. Fuhrmann, *Germany...*, p. 150. Haverkamp, *Medieval...*, pp. 145 & 223. Norwich, *Kingdom...*, pp. 115, 137, 328. Pernoud, *Eleanor...*, p. 60.

THEODORA COMNENA, queen of Jerusalem
b. 1147–1180s Byzantium; Israel

Daughter of Isaac Comnenus; her uncle Manuel Comnenus, emperor of Byzantium, married Theodora to Baldwin III of Jerusalem around 1158. As a twenty-one-year-old widow, Theodora fell in love with a notorious womanizer, her cousin Andronicus Comnenus. They lived together in various places—and she gave birth to two sons. In 1182, Andronicus returned to Constantinople and usurped the crown. Theodora was probably then sent to a convent.

♦ Abduction. Mistresses. Queens. Religieuses. Scholars. ♦
Bridge, *Crusades...*, pp. 130, 173, 190. *Cambridge...*, IV, pp. 363, 374, 381. Hamilton, "Women...," pp. 157–159, 162, 174. Norwich, *Kingdom...*, pp. 328–330. Payne, *Dream...*, pp. 166 & 173.

THEODORA OF PAPHLAGONIA, empress of Byzantium
[St. Theodora]
b. 810s–c. 860 Byzantium

Emperor Theophilus chose Theodora as his wife. Their son Michael III was very young when Theophilus died in 842, so Theodora served as regent for the next fourteen years. Theodora restored orthodoxy—for which the Eastern Church canonized her. However, she was wise enough to make this a slow change with little fanaticism or violence. Theodora was moderate, wise, courageous, and a good military leader. On the other hand, she cruelly stamped out the Paulician sect, and she brought about her own downfall by not allowing her son any part in the government. Around 856, he and Theodora's brother Bardas usurped the throne. She then retired to a convent.

♦ Regents. Religieuses. Religious patrons. Saints. Soldiers. ♦
Cambridge..., IV, pp. 34, 40, 41, 42, 43, 46, 133, 139, 217, 246. Daniel-Rops, *Church...*, pp. 503–505. Diehl, *Byzantine...*, pp. 95–113. Jenkins, *Byzantium...*, pp. 141, 150, 151, 154–160, 166, 170–171.

THEODORA THE PORPHYROGENITA, empress of Byzantium
b. 989–d. 1056 Byzantium

Daughter of co-emperor Constantine VIII. When he died in 1028, she and her older sister †Zoe became co-rulers, but Theodora was quickly "encouraged" to retire to a convent. In 1042, rebels forced her to return to her public/governmental role. Theodora proved to have wit and courage, but was not very interested in ruling; moreover, she and Zoe were unable to work well together. After Zoe and her last husband Constantine Monomachus died, Theodora again left the convent in 1055 to assume the role of empress. She governed fairly well until her death some two years later.

♦ **Religieuses. Rulers. Unmarried.** ♦

Cambridge..., IV, pp. 84, 94, 96, 100, 107, 108, 109, 115, 116, 319, 597. Diehl, *Byzantine...*, pp. 137, 154, 158, 166, 168, 169, 172–173. Jenkins, *Byzantium...*, pp. 339, 344, 361–363, 371. Leyser, *Rule...*, p. 107. Norwich, *Normans...*, pp. 45 & 63–64.

THEODORA OF ROME
c. 870s–920s Italy

Ambitious and determined wife of Theophylacte, governor of the Roman Senate. Mother of the *Senatrix* †Marozia of Rome. Theodora may have been the mistress of Pope John X (whom her daughter Marozia reputedly murdered), but it is equally possible that her bad reputation was undeserved. Chronicler Liutprand of Cremona reviled Theodora and both her daughters, Marozia and Theodora the Younger, for their sexual exploits and loose morals.

♦ **Mistresses. Models. Politics. Popes.** ♦

Cambridge..., III, pp. 151, 455; IV, pp. 256, 259. Cheetham, *Keepers...*, p. 76. Duckett, *Death...*, pp. 55, 231. Ernouf, *Histoire...*, pp. 208, 214–216. Kelly, *Oxford...*, pp. 120, 121, & 122. Osborne, *Greatest...*, pp. 110–111. Partner, *Lands...*, p. 79. Riché, *Les Carolingiens...*, p. 231. Stafford, *Queens...*, pp. 30 & 138. Trevelyan, *Short...*, p. 64. Wright, *Works...*, pp. 92–93.

THEOPHANO, empress of BYZANTIUM **[St. Theophano]**
c. 860s–d. 897 Byzantium

Supposedly too plain and pious to please her husband, Leo VI. Theophano lived in childless seclusion, while Leo kept a mistress. After Theophano died, however, Leo erected a church in her honor.

♦ **Divorce. Pawns. Prisons. Religieuses. Queens. Saints.** ♦

Cambridge..., IV, pp. 55, 56, 59, 256. Jenkins, *Byzantium...*, pp. 199, 214.

THEOPHANO, empress of BYZANTIUM **[Anastaso]**
b. 940–c. 980 Byzantium

Theophano was reputedly a taverner's daughter and a beautiful courtesan before Emperor Romanus II fell in love with and married her in

956. When he died in 963, Theophano assumed the regency for their two sons Basil II and Constantine VIII. She was unpopular, and many believed she had murdered Romanus. Theophano married a popular general, Nicephorus Phocas, to shore up her position. She then fell in love with his nephew, John Tzimisces. In 969, Theophano helped John murder Nicephorus. After her lover was securely on the throne, he sent Theophano to a convent. When her sons became co-rulers (976), they returned Theophano to court, but she was no longer a political force.

♦ **Models. Murder. Regents. Religieuses. Widows. Women of easy virtue.** ♦

Cambridge..., IV, pp. 64–65, 67–72, 77–79, 81, 84, 145, 757. Diehl, *Byzantine...*, pp. 114–135. Duckett, *Death...*, pp. 90–91. Stephenson, *Mediaeval...*, pp. 181–182.

THEOPHANO OF BYZANTIUM, Holy Roman Empress [Theophanu]

b. 958–d. 991 — Byzantium; Germany

Daughter of †Theophano and Romanus II. In 972, Theophano married Otto II, later Holy Roman Emperor. She brought Byzantine influence in arts and letters to her new home. Theophano also saw to it that her son Otto (III) received a good education. After Otto II died in 983, Theophano shared in her son's regency government. She was an able and energetic ruler.

♦ **Art patrons. Educated. Negotiators. Patrons of literature. Pilgrims. Popes. Regents. Teachers. Widows.** ♦

Barraclough, *Origins...*, p. 62. Bryce, *Holy...*, pp. 139–140, 144, 491. *Cambridge...*, III, pp. 80, 103, 167, 169, 171, 172, 173, 203, 205n, 207, 209, 210, 211, 212; IV, pp. 68, 77, 81, 94, 147. Cheetham, *Keepers...*, pp. 80 & 82. Duckett, *Death...*, pp. 92, 98, 101, 106–107, 124, 211, 294. Ennen, *Medieval...*, pp. 61, 62–3, 64–6, 82. Jenkins, *Byzantium...*, pp. 293–295, 321. Lehmann, *Rôle de la...*, pp. 251–252. Leyser, *Medieval...*, pp. 88, 90, 107, 117–120. Leyser, *Rule...*, pp. 44, 49, 53, 55, 89–90. Nelson, *Politics...*, pp. 373–374, 399 n130. Norwich, *History...*, pp. 46 & 47. Norwich, *Normans...*, pp. 5 & 13. Partner, *Lands...*, pp. 92 & 96. Pinnow, *History...*, pp. 37–38. Riché, *Les Carolingiens...*, pp. 261, 266, 337. Stafford, *Queens...*, pp. 1, 9, 30, 48, 88–90, 102, 103, 110–111, 118, 132, 136, 139–144, 149–150, 154–155, 161, 179, 186, 190, 210. Stubbs, *Germany...*, pp. 110–111, 112–113, 119. Vernadsky, *Kievan...*, p. 63.

THERESA [Teresa]

TERESA DE CARTAGENA

fl. 1400s — Spain

Deaf nun; among other works, she wrote two volumes about spiritual growth and physical infirmities.

♦ **Handicapped. Nuns. Writers.** ♦

Deyermond, "El Convento...," pp. 19–29. Snow, "Spanish...," p. 321.

THERESA OF CASTILE, countess of Portugal
b. 1080–d.c. 1130 Portugal; Spain

Illegitimate daughter of Alfonso VI of Castile; half-sister of †Urraca of Castile. Her father married Theresa to Henry of Burgundy around 1095 with a dowry of Oporto and Coimbra. When Henry died around 1112, their son Alfonso Henriques was very young, so Theresa served as his regent. She continued Henry's policies—building an independent kingdom of Portugal. Unscrupulous and ambitious, Theresa was, nonetheless, a capable and courageous ruler. She led troops, encouraged urban growth, and instilled national feelings in the Portugese. Idolized by poets, her passionate love affair with Fernando Peres caused some decline in her popularity. Her son wrested control of Portugal from her in 1128, but it was Theresa's previous efforts which allowed Alfonso Henriques to become first king of an independent Portugal (1143).

♦ **Adultery. Illegitimacy. Models. Prisons. Regents. Soldiers. Squabbles. Widows.** ♦

Altamira, *Spain...*, pp. 169–170. Dos Passos, *Story...*, pp. 17 & 18–19. Jackson, *Making...*, pp. 71 & 76. Livermore, *History...*, pp. 108–110. Nowell, *History...*, pp. 6–7. Shneidman, *Rise...*, pp. 282 & 297. Smith, *Spain...*, p. 57. Stephens, *Story...*, pp. 18, 20, 22–32, 34–37, 43, 48, 59, 98.

TERESA DE ENTENZA **[Teresa d'Entença]**
m. 1312–d. 1327 Spain

Daughter and heiress of Constanca d'Antillo and Gombau de Entenza, count of Urgel. Married Alfonso IV of Aragon; mother of Pedro IV. In the 1320s Teresa ruled Urgel.

♦ **Childbirth. Estate. Rulers.** ♦

Bisson, *Medieval Crown...*, pp. 101 & 104. Chaytor, *History...*, pp. 161, 166. Hillgarth, *Pere...*, pp. 3–4, 133, 136–138, 148, 154, 156, 158, 159, 161, 163, 173. Miron, *Queens...*, pp. 20, 160–165. Shneidman, *Rise...*, pp. 66, 68, 156, 486.

THERESA OF PORTUGAL, countess of Flanders
m. 1183 Flanders; Portugal

Youngest daughter of Alfonso Henriques of Portugal; married Philip, count of Flanders. Both historians and troubadours reported that her departure broke the king's heart, causing him to soon die.

♦ **Models. Negotiators.** ♦

Dos Passos, *Story...*, pp. 38–39. McLaughlin, "Woman...," p. 199. Stephens, *Story...*, pp. 58 & 72.

(St.) THERESA OF PORTUGAL, queen of Leon **[Blessed Teresa]**
b. 1176–d. 1250 Portugal; Spain

Daughter of †Douce (II) of Barcelona and Sancho I of Portugal. In 1191, her father married Theresa to her cousin Alfonso IX of Leon. The pope forced Alfonso to repudiate Theresa on grounds of consanguinity, and in 1195 she returned to Portugal. She later became a nun in convent at Lorvao which she had founded. There is some dispute over her official religious status, although she was supposedly canonized in 1705.

♦ **Divorce. Nuns. Pawns. Popes. Religious patrons. Queens. Saints.** ♦

Attwater, Dictionary..., p. 285. Holweck, *Biographical...*, p. 883. Stephens, *Story...*, pp. 63, 64, 70, 71.

THEUTBERGA, queen of LOTHARINGIA **[Tetberga]**
m. 855–870s France; Germany; Switzerland

Sister of Hubert, abbot of Saint-Maurice. Forced into a political marriage with Lothar II of Lotharingia. Since they had no children, he soon wanted to divorce Theutberga so that he could marry his mistress †Waldrada—who was also the mother of his children. Lothar sent Theutberga to close confinement in convent of Avenay and he later accused her of incest with her brother Hubert. Since her substitute survived the ordeal, she was found innocent of that charge. When Lothar imprisoned Theutberga, she appealed to Pope Nicholas I, who ruled in her favor. The pope insisted the couple must live together, but their marital strife continued until Lothar died in 869.

♦ **Adultery. Divorce. Models. Ordeals. Pawns. Popes. Prisons. Religieuses.** ♦

Bishop, "Bishops as...," pp. 53–55, 58, 61–63, 65–66, 68, 70–72, 74–75, & 81. *Cambridge...*, III, pp. 38–45, 449. Duckett, *Carolingian...*, pp. 223–238 & 258. Ennen, *Medieval...*, p. 56. McNamara and Wemple, "Marriage...," pp. 110–111. Riché, *Les Carolingiens...*, pp. 177 & 184. Stafford, *Queens...*, pp. 29, 39, 75–76, 83, 130, 177, 180. Wemple, *Women...*, pp. 84–87, 90–91, 104, 171.

THOMASINE DINHAM
fl. 1470 England

Became prioress at Cornworthy, Devonshire. Because Jane Knight, the mother of two of Thomasine's students, refused to pay for her daughters' education, Thomasine had to sue Jane for the money.

♦ **Abbesses. Childcare. Legal activity. Teachers.** ♦

Orme, *Education...*, p. 204. Power, *Women...*, p. 81.

THOMASSE (la talemelière)
1292 France

Baked and sold her own bread; paid 5s tax in 1292 Paris.

♦ **Provisioning–bakers.** ♦

Géraud, *Paris sous...*, p. 109.

THORA OF NORWAY
m.c. 1049–1060s Norway

Mistress of Harold III Hardrada of Norway; she may have been the mother of his sons and successors, Magnus II and Olaf. Although Harold already had a wife, †Elizabeth of Kiev, he married Thora and she was accorded honors as his queen.

♦ **Mistresses. Queens. Soldiers.** ♦

Barlow, *Edward...*, pp. 22 & Table B. Boyesen, *Story...*, p. 255. Lloyd, *Maligned...*, p. xiii.

THYRA OF DENMARK, queen of Norway **[Thryri]**
c. 970s–d. 1000 Denmark; Norway; Sweden

Daughter of Harold Gormsson of Denmark. Married (1) Styrbjorn of Sweden. After his death, Thyra's brother, King Sweyn I Fork-beard of Denmark, forced her to marry Burislav, king of Wendland. She ran away and married Olaf Tryggvesson, king of Norway. His death in the year 1000 may have been caused in part by his efforts to recover some of her vast dowry lands.

♦ **Divorce. Dowry/dower. Models. Pawns. Widows.** ♦

Boyesen, *Story...*, pp. 154, 161, 168, 171, 214. Jones, *Vikings...*, pp. 128, 136, 137.

TIBORS D'OMELAS, countess of Angoulême **[Tibour]**
c. 1130–d.c. 1181 France

Daughter of Tibors d'Orange and Guilhem d'Omelas; sister of poet Raimbaut d'Orange. Married (1) Gaufroy de Mornas, and (2) c. 1150, Bertrand des Baux. A supporter of troubadours, Tibors also wrote some poetry herself.

♦ **Models. Patrons of literature. Poets/troubadours.** ♦

Bogin, *Women...*, pp. 80–81 & 162–163. Boutière and Schutz, *Biographies des...*, pp. 498–499. Dronke, *Women...*, pp. 99–100 & 299. Egan, *Vidas...*, pp. 105–106. Lejeune, "La Femme...," p. 207.

TIFFANIA
[Thyphainne; Tiphaine; Tyfaine; Tyfainne; Typhainne]

TYPHAINNE (la blazennière)
1292 France

Paid 4s tax in 1292 Paris on her rather unusual occupation—recovering saddles with new leather.

♦ **Less-affluent. Merchants–saddlers.** ♦

Géraud, *Paris sous...*, p. 95.

TYFAINNE (mestresse de l'école)
1292 France

Schoolmistress of the rue aux Ours; paid 2s taxes in 1292 Paris.

♦ **Less-affluent. Teachers.** ♦

Géraud, *Paris sous...*, p. 54.

TIPHAINE RAGUEL **[Epiphanie Raguenel; Ravenel]**
b. 1330–d.c. 1372 France

Daughter of Sir Robin Ravenel and Jeanne de Dinan, heiress of Bellière. Married around 1362 to Bertrand du Guesclin, later Constable of France. Rich, beautiful, and well-educated, Tiphaine used astrology to predict future events. After her marriage, Tiphaine rarely saw her husband, and she was solely responsible for managing their property—a task she performed extremely well.

♦ **Astronomy. Educated. Managers. Nodels. Superstitions.** ♦

Decaux, *Histoire...*, pp. 199–200. Gies, *Knight...*, pp. 154, 163, 164. Jamison, *Life...*, I, pp. 143, 147–149; II, pp. 80, 141–144, 160.

THYPHAINNE (la toière)
1292 France

Dame Thyphainne of the rue aus Prouvoires paid 20s tax in 1292 Paris on her unusual occupation—making pillowcases.

♦ **Clothworkers. Land/property.** ♦

Géraud, *Paris sous...*, p. 39.

TODA, queen of NAVARRE **[Theuda; Tota]**
c. 920s–960s Spain

Regent for her son, King Garcia Sanchez, Toda was a principal leader of Christian Spain for over forty years. To retrieve the throne of Leon for her grandson Sancho the Fat, she took him to Cordoba for a weight reduction course. Despite Christendom's general horror, Toda also used her Islamic allies from Cordoba to secure the throne for Sancho.

♦ **Medicine. Negotiators. Regents. Rulers. Soldiers. Widows.** ♦

Altamira, *Spain...*, pp. 115, 116, 120, 133. Bendiner, *Rise...*, pp. 201, 203–206. *Cambridge...*, III, pp. 421–423. Jackson, *Making...*, pp. 38–40 & 43. Livermore, *History...*, pp. 85, 94, 95, 98. Smith, *Spain...*, p. 54.

TROTULA OF SALERNO
c. 1040s–1090s Italy

Famed midwife/doctor of Salerno. Credited with writing two medical treatises—one was on cosmetics and the other included a wealth of detail about childbirth and its problems. However, scholars continue to debate questions such as "Who was Trotula?", "Did she really exist?", and "Where did she receive her education?".

♦ **Doctors/empirics–obstetrics. Midwives. Models. Writers–medicine.** ♦

Bullough, "Medieval Medical...," p. 495. Herlihy, *Opera...*, pp. 104–106. Hughes, *Women...*, pp. 105, 147. Hurd-Mead, *History...*, pp. 127–154. LaBalme, *Beyond...*, p. 3. Lipinska, *Histoire...*, pp.87–98. Mason-Hohl, "Trotula...". Trotula, *Diseases....*

TRYNGEN IME HOVE

c. 1450–1501 Germany

Wife of Mertyn Ime Hove; an extremely competent and prosperous silk weaver in Cologne. In 1462, Tryngen had a large number of apprentices and purchased a huge amount of silk. She also helped her husband in his import/export business with England.

♦ **Apprentices. Clothworkers. Land/property. Legal activity. Merchants. Shipping. Silkwork.** ♦

Wensky, "Women's Guilds...," pp. 645–646.

TURAKINA **[Toragana]**

fl. 1230s–1240s China; Russia

Wife of Great Khan Ugedey (Ogadai Khan). When he died in 1241, Turakina directed state business on behalf of their son Guyuk. At her instigation, Guyak was named Great Khan in 1246.

♦ **Models. Negotiators. Regents. Slaves. Soldiers. Widows.** ♦

Cambridge..., IV, p. 640. Spuler, *History...*, pp. 65, 66, 127. Vernadsky, *Mongols...*, pp. 59–60 & 124.

— U —

ULRICHA DE FOSCHUA

fl. 1351 — Germany

Noted female oculist practicing near Munich. A grateful patient bequeathed a house and garden to Ulricha.

♦ **Bequests. Doctors/empirics–eye. Land/property.** ♦

Hurd-Mead, *History...*, p. 272. Lipinska, *Histoire...*, p. 122.

(St.) UMILIANA DEI CHERCHI

c. 1220–d. 1246 — Italy

Married in 1236; her husband soon died. Umiliana then became a tertiary in her home town of Florence; known for her visions of the Baby Jesus.

♦ **Mystics. Saints. Widows.** ♦

Battelli, *La leggenda....* Bynum, *Holy...*, pp. 24 & 396 n21. Goodich, "Contours...," p. 25. Herlihy, "Children...," pp. 126–127. Holmes, *Florence...*, p. 64. Holweck, *Biographical...*, pp. 495–496.

(St.) UMILITA OF FAENZA — **[St. Humilitas; Umiltá]**

b. 1226–d. 1310 — Italy

Both Umilita and her husband were extremely pious; eventually both embraced the religious life. Umilita was a recluse before she became the head of a house of nuns near Faenza. She founded a second house at Florence. Umilita was also renowned for her preaching.

♦ **Abbesses. Anchoresses. Preachers. Religious patrons. Saints. Writers.** ♦

Attwater, *Dictionary...*, p. 143. Bynum, *Holy...*, pp. 140, 145, 215, 234, 248. Goodich, "Contours...," pp. 22 & 25. Petroff, *Medieval Women's...*, pp. 7, 20, 21, 27, 28, 55 n, 61, 231, 235–236, 241, 247–253.

URRACA, queen of CASTILE

c. 1090–d.c. 1126 — Spain

Daughter of †Constance of France and Alfonso VI of Castile and Leon. In 1109 her father died, leaving his lands to Urraca who spent the rest of her life fighting for them. Despite a love affair with Gomez of

Candespina, in 1109 Urraca married Alfonso I of Aragon in an effort to secure her lands. They were later divorced, so she and her son Alfonso VII of Castile had to fight her ex-husband for the rights to Leon and Castile.

♦ **Adultery. Divorce. Models. Rulers. Soldiers. Squabbles. Widows.** ♦

Altamira, *Spain...*, pp. 162, 169, 170. *Cambridge...*, VI, pp. 403–405. Effinger, *Women...*, pp. 278–282. Fletcher, *Quest...*, pp. 119, 153, 187–8. Fusero, *Borgias...*, p. 17. Jackson, *Making...*, pp. 71–73. Livermore, *History...*, pp. 108–111. Miron, *Queens...*, pp. 20 & 43–61. Reilly, *Kingdom....* Smith, *Spain...*, p. 57. Stephens, *Story...*, pp. 18, 21, 23, 24, 28–30. Tyerman, *England...*, p. 25.

URRACA OF CASTILE, queen of Portugal

m.c. 1200–1220s Portugal; Spain

Daughter of †Eleanor (Leonor) of England and Alfonso VIII of Castile. Married Alfonso II of Portugal; mother of Sancho II. Urraca was known for her charity and piety; she built hospitals and convents.

♦ **Medicine. Religious patrons. Queens.** ♦

Bingham, *Crowned...*, p. 151. Gies, *Women...*, pp. 97–98 & 114. Kelly, *Eleanor...*, pp. 359 & 361. Marks, *Pilgrims...*, p. 211. Pernoud, *Eleanor...*, pp. 259–260. Stephens, *Story...*, pp. 70 & 74.

URRACA GONZALEZ, queen of Leon

c. 940s–970s Spain

Daughter of Fernan Gonzalez, count of Burgos and of Castile. He forced Urraca to marry Ordono III of Leon. After Ordono's death, Fernan insisted that Urraca marry Ordono IV, and later forced her to marry Sancho, the presumed heir of Navarre.

♦ **Pawns. Queens. Widows.** ♦

Cambridge..., III, p. 422. Jackson, *Making...*, pp. 38–39. Leroy, *La Navarre...*, p. 189. Miron, *Queens...*, pp. 27–30. Smith, *Spain...*, p. 54.

URRACA OF PORTUGAL, queen of Leon

m.c. 1160–1180s Portugal; Spain

Daughter of †Matilda of Savoy and Alfonso I (Alfonso Henriques)of Portugal. Around 1160, Urraca became the first wife of Ferdinand II of Leon and Gallicia; mother of Alfonso IX. She and Ferdinand were separated because they were related within the prohibited degree of consanguinity. Urraca attempted to obtain a papal dispensation for their marriage but was unsuccessful. (Ferdinand remarried in 1179.) During their marriage, Urraca had some role in governmental and religious affairs. In 1169, Urraca signed a charter for the Order of the Templars; in 1174, she signed another act in concert with Ferdinand.

♦ **Divorce. Politics. Popes. Queens. Religious patrons.** ♦

Anselme, *Histoire...*, v.1, p. 574. Stephens, *Story...*, pp. 54 & 63.

UTA OF NIEDERMÜNSTER

c. 975–995 Germany

Abbess of Bavarian convent. She led the house to concentrate on producing manuscripts and other artistic projects.

[In the early 1000s, one of her successors was also named Uta; under this woman—Uta II—the *Uta Codex* was produced, indicating that the book-making/artistic trend remained.]

♦ **Abbesses. Art patrons. Bookmaking.** ♦

Kelleher, *Holy...*, pp. 78-80, 86, 88, 94. [Uta II: *Ibid.*, pp. 78, 89, 94.]

— V —

VALENTINE VISCONTI, queen of Cyprus

m.c. 1380 — Cyprus; Italy

One of Bernabo Visconti's many illegitimate children. Married Peter II, king of Cyprus.

♦ **Illegitimacy. Queens.** ♦

Hill, *History...*, v.2, pp. 357, 382n, 417, 423, 425, 430n. Norwich, *History...*, p. 248.

VALENTINE VISCONTI, duchess of Orléans **[Valentine of Milan]**

m.c. 1388–d. 1408 — France; Italy

Daughter of †Isabelle of France and Giangaleazzo Visconti, duke of Milan. Valentine was described by contemporaries as beautiful, cultured, kind, and well-educated. When she married Louis, duke of Orléans, she brought forks, books, and extravagant clothing to her new homeland. She and Queen †Isabeau of Bavaria were rivals at everything. Her later years were spent away from court for her own safety, since Isabeau had accused Valentine of witchcraft. After Louis of Orléans was murdered in 1407, Valentine fortified her home, and then returned to Paris to seek justice.

♦ **Book owners. Childcare. Dance. Educated. Insanity. Legal activity. Music. Religious patrons. Soldiers. Squabbles. Widows. Witchcraft.** ♦

Calmette, *Golden...*, pp. 58, 81–2, 89, 91, 92. Cartellieri, *Court...*, pp. 44, 47, 49. Chamberlin, *Count...*, pp. 67, 89–93, 109–113. Collas, *Valentine....* Commynes, *Memoirs...*, pp. 455 & 460. Coryn, *House...*, pp. 1–5, 15–18, 24–25, 40, 47, 55–60, 67, 77–78, 98, 127–128, 133, 251, 328. Denieul-Cormier, *Wise...*, pp. 183, 184, 199, 207–209, 217, 221, 242, 248. Froissart, *Chronicles...*, II, pp. 54–55, 164–165. Jourdain, "Memoire...," p. 496. Norwich, *History...*, pp. 322, 361, 370, 372. Pernoud, *Retrial...*, pp. 102–103. Pisan, *City...*, pp. 212–213. Tuchman, *Distant...*, pp. 478, 514, 529, 540–541, 556, 581. Willard, "Christine...," p. 94.

VANOZZA CATANEI

b. 1445–d. 1518 — Italy

Beautiful young woman of Mantua. During the years 1470 through 1483, Vanozza was the mistress of Rodrigo Borgia—who later became

Pope Alexander VI. She was the mother of several of his children: Cesare, Juan, †Lucrezia and Joffré. Vanozza was cultured and pious, a good mother, and an excellent business woman. Her high-ranking clerical lover enabled her to amass a fortune in hotels and other real estate.

♦ **Adultery. Banking. Educated. Innkeepers. Land/property. Merchants. Mistresses. Popes. Religious patrons. Writers–letters.** ♦

Chamberlin, *Fall...*, pp. 33–41, 96, 98, 103–104, 107, 111, 128, 136, 147–148, 153, 217, 300, 326–327, 330. Cheetham, *Keeper...*, pp. 188–190. Cloulas, *Borgias...*, pp. 45, 51–2, 107, 130, 298–299. Fusero, *Borgias...*, pp. 120, 135–138, 191, 292. Johnson, *Borgias...*, pp. 65, 78–80, 90–91, 108, 124–125, 194, 199. Simon, *Tapestry...*, pp. 146–147.

VIOLANTE OF HUNGARY, queen of Aragon

See—YOLANDE OF HUNGARY, queen of Aragon.

VIOLANTE VISCONTI

b. 1354–d.c. 1385 Italy

Daughter of †Bianca of Savoy and Galeazzo Visconti of Pavia, who paid a huge dowry for her marriage in 1368 to the widower, Lionel, duke of Clarence. After his death, Violante was soon forced to marry young Otto Paleolgo, marquis of Montferrat (who soon met with a violent end). Violante was then married to Ludovico Visconti, lord of Lodi. He was later jailed (and possibly killed) by her brother Giangaleazzo Visconti. Violante returned home where she soon died, reportedly worn out from her troubled marital career.

♦ **Dowry/dower. Models. Pawns. Widows.** ♦

Armitage-Smith, *John...*, p. 24. Chamberlin, *Count...*, pp. 41–42 & 114. *C.P.*, v.3, p. 258. *DNB*, v.11, pp. 1216–1217. Gardner, *Life...*, pp. 109 & 190. Hardy, *Philippa...*, pp. 289–293. Tuchman, *Distant...*, pp. 253–254, 256–257, & 269. Vaughan, *Philip...*, p. 4.

VIRDIMURA OF SICILY

1376 Italy

Wife of physician Pasquale of Catania. In 1376, Virdimura was granted permission by royal court to practice medicine throughout the kingdom. Not only did she pass medical tests, but many patients and doctors testified on her behalf. Virdimura then chose to practice among the poor.

♦ **Charity. Doctors/empirics. Jews. Legal activity.** ♦

Friedenwald, "Jewish...," pp. 217–218.

— W —

WALDRADA **[Waldrade]**
c. 840s–870s France; Germany

Mistress of Lothar II of Lotharingia; mother of his son Hugh. Lothar tried to divorce his barren wife †Theutberga in order to marry Waldrada; in fact, Waldrada was actually crowned in 862. Theutberga fought back, even accusing Waldrada of witchcraft and appealing to Pope Nicholas I. When Lothar died in 869, the issue was still unsettled, and Waldrada continued to be recognized only as his mistress. She later took the veil at Remiremont and was absolved by Pope Adrian II.

♦ **Divorce. Mistresses. Models. Popes. Queens. Religieuses. Witchcraft.** ♦

Bishop, "Bishops as...," pp. 55, 66, 70. *Cambridge...*, III, pp. 38, 40, 41–44. Duckett, *Carolingian...*, pp. 223–238 & 258. Ennen, *Medieval...*, p. 56. Ernouf, *Histoire...*, pp. 1–76. Jenkins, *Byzantium...*, p. 180. McKitterick, *Frankish...*, pp. 178–179. Riché, *Les Carolingiens...*, p. 177. Stafford, *Queens...*, pp. 29, 70, 75–76, 130. Wemple, *Women...*, pp. 84–86, 90, 94, 195, 249.

WALDRADA (of Arles) **[Gualdrada of Tuscany]**
fl. 970s France; Germany; Italy

Illegitimate daughter of Hubert (of Arles). Married Pietro Candiano IV, doge of Venice, although he had to send his first wife Giovana to a monastery to do so. In 976, Waldrada's husband and baby son were killed by Venetian mob. Waldrada escaped to German court, but kept up harassment and plotting against Venice for revenge.

♦ **Divorce. Dowry/dower. Illegitimacy. Politics. Rebellions. Squabbles. Widows.** ♦

Cambridge..., III, p. 170; IV, pp. 402, 403. Ernouf, *Histoire...*, pp. 357–360. Norwich, *History...*, pp. 41–42 & 44–45.

Lady WALGRAVE **[Elizabeth Fraye]**
fl. 1460s–1480s England

Friend of John (II) Paston. She was probably the widowed Dame Elizabeth Walgrave, daughter of Sir John Fraye and Dame Agnes Saye, who was named as her mother's executrix in 1478.

♦ **Bequests. Legal activity. Models. Widows.** ♦

Calendar of Plea..., VI, pp. 137–139. Kendall, *Yorkist...*, p. 343. *Paston...*, I, pp. 478, 480, 499.

WILLA

c. 920 Italy

See—BERTHA OF TUSCANY and WILLA OF TUSCANY.

♦ **Genealogy.** ♦

WILLA OF TUSCANY, queen of Italy

c. 930s–d.c. 966 Italy

Daughter of †Willa and Boson, marquis of Tuscany. Wife of Berengar II (d.966), marquis of Ivrea and king of Italy. Ambitious and courageous, Willa was a good military leader and an adviser to her husband. She also took care that their daughters received an education. Willa was given a bad reputation by chroniclers, especially Liutprand of Cremona. He claimed Willa engaged in a love affair with her daughter's tutor.

♦ **Childcare. Models. Politics. Prisons. Rulers. Soldiers. Teachers. Women of easy virtue.** ♦

Cambridge..., III, pp. 157, 159, 162, 163. Duckett, *Death...*, pp. 82, 85, 167, 209. Ernouf, *Histoire...*, pp. 333–341. Robinson, *Readings...*, I, p. 258. Sismondi, *French...*, pp. 412–413. Stafford, *Queens...*, pp. 20, 24, 25, 54, 118, 119, 136, 206. Wright, *Works...*, pp. 109, 150, 182, 199–200.

(St.) WULFHILDA OF BARKING

d.c. 980s England

King Edgar attempted to abduct Wulfhilda, but she managed to escape his amorous clutches. She founded a convent in Dorset, and later became abbess of Barking. Though Wulfhilda was eventually ousted from that position, she returned to the post shortly before her death.

♦ **Abbesses. Abduction–attempted. Mystics. Religious patrons. Saints. Virginity.** ♦

Attwater, *Dictionary...*, p. 315. Esposito, "La vie...," pp. 10–26. Elkins, *Holy...*, pp. 6, 7, 9. Farmer, *Oxford...*, pp. 411–412. Schulenburg, "Female...," p. 114.

WULFHILD OF SAXONY

fl. 1100–1120s Germany

Daughter and co-heiress of Magnus Billung, duke of Saxony (d.1106). Wulfhild married Henry the Black, later duke of Bavaria and Saxony (d.1126); mother of Henry the Proud, duke of Bavaria.

♦ **Estate. Genealogy.** ♦

Cambridge..., V, pp. 152, 153, 154, 337. Fuhrmann, *Germany...*, p. 99. Leyser, *Medieval...*, p. 187. Stubbs, *Germany...*, p. 179.

(St.) WULFTHRYTH, queen of ENGLAND

d.c. 988 England

Though there is some disagreement on their marital status, Wulfthryth was presumably the wife of Edgar of England, and definitely the mother of (St.) †Eadgyth (of Wilton). Sources are unclear about whether Wulfthryth refused to stay with Edgar, or whether he repudiated her. However, not long after Eadgyth was born in 962, Wulfthryth retired from court and was given the position of abbess of Wilton.

♦ **Abbesses. Divorce. Queens. Saints.** ♦

Attwater, *Dictionary...*, p. 310. *DNB*, v.6, pp. 368–369. Stafford, *Queens...*, pp. 32, 74, 179, 180. Stafford, "Sons...," p. 79.

WYNFLAED

d.c. 950 England

Wynflaed's will revealed that she was a wealthy woman and that she was concerned for her female family members and slaves. One of the latter, Wulfwaru, was given her freedom. Wynflaed left her weaver, Eadgifu, and seamstress, Aethelgifu, to her granddaughter. Most of Wynflaed's other possessions—including clothing, jewelry, estates, bed linens, horses, and books—went to her daughter, Aethelflaed.

♦ **Bequests–personal items. Book owners. Clothworkers. Estate. Gems/jewelry. Religious patrons. Slaves–owners. Widows.** ♦

Fell, *Women...*, pp. 41, 43–45, 49, 95–96, 102, 107. Page, *Life in...*, pp. 63–64, 68, 71, 73, 74, 139, 151, 168. Whitelock, *Anglo-Saxon...*, pp. 10–15.

XIMENA DIAZ **[Jimena]**

m.c. 1075–c. 1116 Spain

Relative of Alfonso VI of Castile; he gave her in marriage to his best soldier/leader, Rodrigo Diaz of Vivar (*le Cid*). They had two daughters before Don Rodrigo died in 1099. Ximena ruled in Valencia until 1102.

♦ **Estate. Models. Pawns. Regents. Soldiers. Widows.** ♦

Altamira, *Spain...*, pp. 152 & 154. *Cambridge...*, VI, pp. 400–401. Clissold, *In Search...*, pp. 29–31, 56, 76–78, 100–102, 145–152, 168, 171, 175, 178, 197, 204–206, 209, 211–217, 223–227, 230–232. Fletcher, *Quest...*, pp. 95, 97–8, 121–3 ... 192, 196, 199. Shneidman, *Rise...*, p. 147.

XIMENA, queen of LEON

fl. 900s Spain

Basque woman, queen of Alfonso III the Great of Leon. Ximena supposedly influenced her husband in some political decisions.

♦ **Estate. Politics. Queens.** ♦

Livermore, *History...*, pp. 92 & 94.

YDAIN OF LORRAINE, countess of Boulogne **[Yde; Ida]**
fl. 1040s–1060s France

Daughter of Godfrey IV, duke of Lorraine; Ydain was well-educated and pious. Second wife of Eustace II, count of Boulogne; mother of Godfrey, Baldwin, and Eustace. A popular cautionary tale revolved around Ydain's love for her sons, and the dangers of allowing servants to nurse noble babies. Eustace was supposedly once nursed by a servant so he was never as brilliant as his brothers.

♦ **Childcare. Educated. Models. Superstitions.** ♦

A.S., Ap. v.2, p. 892. Barlow, *Edward...*, pp. 219, 307–308. Coulton, *Life...*, III, pp. 30–31. DBF, v.16, p. 432. Payne, *Dream...*, p. 50. Thompson, *Literacy...*, p. 137. Vitalis, *Ecclesiastical...*, II, pp. 206–207.

YDETTE OF METZ
1456 Germany

In Cologne court, Ydette "confessed" she had caused bad weather by magical means. Other associates testified that she took them to witch meetings and gave them magic ointments.

♦ **Witchcraft.** ♦

Kieckhefer, *European...*, p. 131. Lea, *History...*, III, p. 457. Lea, *Materials...*, pp. 253–254.

YOLANDE OF ANJOU
b. 1428–d. 1483 France

Younger daughter of †Isabel of Lorraine and René I of Anjou; married Ferry II of Lorraine, count of Vaudemont; their son was René, duke of Lorraine. In 1481, Yolande took the title of queen of Jerusalem and Sicily, after the death of her cousin Charles IV of Anjou.

♦ **Genealogy. Queens.** ♦

Anselme, *Histoire...*, v.1, p. 232. Cleugh, *Chant...*, pp. 227 & 280. *DBF*, v.2, pp. 1297–1298.

YOLANDE OF ARAGON, duchess of Anjou, queen of the two Sicilies **[Yolande of Sicily]**
b. 1380–c. 1430s France; Italy; Spain

Daughter of Yolande de Bar and John I of Aragon. In 1400, Yolande married Louis II of Anjou, later king of Sicily (d.1422). As regent of Anjou, she ruled firmly and wisely. Yolande also negotiated treaties and marriages, found troops for †Joan of Arc, and affirmed the Maid's virginity.

♦ **Book owners. Childcare. Medicine. Negotiators. Regents. Soldiers. Virginity. Writers.** ♦

Bell, "Medieval...," p. 155. Borderie, *Histoire...*, IV, p. 225. Coryn, *House...*, pp. 160, 197, 198, 223, 237, 255. Decaux, *Histoire...*, pp. 392–404, 434. Denieul-Cormier, *Wise...*, pp. 178, 179, 237, 238, 240, 254, 255, 260, 261, 291, 297, 308, 338. Lehmann, *Rôle de la...*, pp. 505–512. Myers, "Household...," p. 11. Pernoud, *Retrial...*, pp. 82 & 140. Tierney, *Western...*, p. 567. Tuchman, *Distant...*, p. 488. Vale, *Charles...*, pp. 22, 27, 35, 39, 41, 49–51, 71–2, 91.

YOLANDE DE DREUX **[Yolande of Brittany]**
b. 1219–d. 1272 France

Daughter of †Alix of Brittany and Pierre Mauclerc, comte de Dreux. Yolande was betrothed in 1231, but †Blanche of Castile forbade her to marry because she was heiress of many estates. In 1238, Yolande finally married Hugh XI de Lusignan, count of La Marche and Angoulême (d.1260), with the county of Penthièvre as her dowry.

♦ **Estate. Orphans. Pawns.** ♦

Anselme, *Histoire...*, v.1, p. 446; v.3, pp. 79–80. Borderie, *Histoire...*, III, pp. 312, 319, 329, 382, 390, 400, 401, 407, 416, 418, 493, 615. Powicke, *Thirteenth...*, p. 93.

YOLANDE DE DREUX, queen of Scotland
[Joletta; Yolette de Montfort]
c. 1270s–1300s France; Scotland

Daughter of Robert IV, count of Dreux; in 1285, Yolande became second wife of Alexander III of Scotland—he died that same winter. She later became the second wife of Arthur II, duke of Brittany; their son, John IV de Montfort, duke of Brittany, was born around 1293 (see †Jeanne de Montfort, duchess of Brittany, for more).

♦ **Dance. Estate. Models. Queens. Superstitions. Widows.** ♦

Anselme, *Histoire...*, v.1, p. 451. Barrow, *Feudal...*, pp. 252 & 420. Brown, *History...*, I, pp. 128–129. Coulton, *Life...*, III, p. 20. *DNB*, v.1, p. 266. Mackie, *History...*, p. 47. Mackie, *Short...*, p. 55. Powicke, *Thirteenth...*, pp. 93, 597, 598 & n. Prestwich, *Edward...*, pp. 358 & 360.

YOLANDE OF HUNGARY, queen of Aragon **[Violante]**
m. 1236–1251 Hungary; Spain

Daughter of Yolande de Courtenay and Andrew II of Hungary; second wife of Jaime I of Aragon. Mother of Pedro III, and grandmother of St. †Elizabeth of Portugal. Strong-willed, Yolande had a sometimes disruptive political influence on her husband and country.

♦ **Genealogy. Politics.** ♦

Bisson, *Medieval Crown...*, pp. 65 & 67. Miron, *Queens...*, pp. 98–110. O'Callaghan, *History...*, p. 346. Shneidman, *Rise...*, pp. 19–23, 26, 98, 131, 220, 310, 319.

YOLANDE (of Jerusalem), Holy Roman Empress
[Elizabeth; Isabella von Brienne]
b. 1207–d.c. 1229 Germany; Israel; Italy

Daughter of Marie of Montferrat and John of Brienne; heiress of the kingdom of Jerusalem. Married around 1225 to Holy Roman Emperor Frederick II (after his first wife, †Constance of Aragon, died in 1222). Frederick thereby claimed Yolande's kingdom of Jerusalem. She died young, a few days after giving birth to son Conrad (IV).

♦ **Childbirth. Estate. Pawns. Queens.** ♦

Bridge, *Crusades...*, pp. 254–255. *Cambridge...*, V, pp. 314, 315, 316; VI, pp. 99, 144, 147. Cheetham, *Keepers...*, p. 134. *Chronicles...*, pp. 247, 256, 257, 258. Hampe, *Germany...*, pp. 261 & 264. Haverkamp, *Medieval...*, pp. 13, 246, 253. Leuschner, *Germany...*, p. 50. Mure, *Histoire...*, v.1, p. 511. Payne, *Dream...*, pp. 307, 308, 311. Trevelyan, *Short...*, p. 105.

YOLANDE OF MONTFERRAT, empress of Byzantium
[Empress Irene]
b. 1273–d. 1317 Byzantium; Italy

In 1284, Yolande married widower Andronicus II of Byzantium. After her four children were born, Yolande nagged Andronicus constantly to make their children his heirs. Yolande was eventually forced to move to Thessalonica, but she continued to scheme on behalf of her children.

♦ **Queens. Squabbles.** ♦

Boulding, *Underside...*, pp. 442–443. Diehl, *Byzantine...*, pp. 276–286.

YOLANDE DE VALOIS, duchess of Savoy **[Yolande of France]**
b. 1434–d. 1478 France

Daughter of †Marie of Anjou and Charles VII of France. Married in 1452 to Amadeus IX, duke of Savoy. After he died in 1472, Yolande was regent for their son Philibert. She was captured by Charles of Burgundy, but her brother King Louis XI of France obtained her release.

♦ Abduction. Book owners. Negotiators. Politics. Prisons. Regents. Widows. ♦

Anselme, *Histoire...*, v.1, p. 118. Bell, "Medieval...," p. 176. Calmette, *Golden...*, pp. 267–8, 277–8. *Cambridge...*, VII, pp. 207, 208. Cleugh, *Chant...*, pp. 26, 100, 227–228, 249–250, 252. Commynes, *Memoirs...*, pp. 303, 305, 306, 308, 310–312, 393, 402n. Kendall, *Louis XI*, pp. 243, 254, 268, 298, 303, 308, 310–311. Vale, *Charles...*, p. 73.

YOLETTE DE DREUX, queen of Scotland

See—YOLANDE DE DREUX, queen of Scotland.

YSABEL [Ysabelle; Ysabiau]

Also see: ISABEL

YSABEL (la commanderesse)

1292 France

Employment agent for servants on la rue aux Commanderesses in 1292 Paris—Ysabel paid 5s tax.

♦ Recommandresses. ♦

Géraud, *Paris sous...*, p. 115.

YSABELLE DE L'ESPINE

fl. 1445–1449 France

Paid small tax of 4s on her job as a *revenderesse de fil* in mid-fifteenth century Paris—Ysabelle was a retailer of thread.

♦ Clothworkers. Less-affluent. Merchants–thread. ♦

Comptes du..., pp. 435, 481, 567, 610.

YSABIAU (la ferpière)

1292 France

Ysabiau was presumably a *fripperer*—seller of used clothing, furniture, etc.—on the rue Renier-Bourdon. Paid 3s tax in 1292 Paris survey.

♦ Less-affluent. Merchants–second-hand items. ♦

Géraud, *Paris sous...*, p. 17.

YSABEL DE LA HEUSE

1292 France

Innkeeper of hostelry on the rue Saint-Christofle in 1292 Paris; Ysabel was taxed 8s.

♦ Innkeepers. Land/property. ♦

Géraud, *Paris sous...*, p. 147.

YSABEL (la meresse)

1292 France

Must have been a popular lay healer on the rue de Frépillon, since she paid tax of 24s in 1292 Paris.

♦ **Doctors/empirics. Land/property.** ♦

Géraud, *Paris sous...*, p. 65. Hughes, *Women...*, p. 141. Hurd-Mead, *History...*, p. 215. Wickersheimer, *Dictionnaire...*, v.1, p. 312.

YSABIAU (la nourrice)

1292 France

Ysabiau of la Ferronnerie was listed in 1292 Paris rolls as nurse to Jehan de Fossez, an ironmonger. Ysabiau paid a tax of 12s.

♦ **Land/property. Nurses.** ♦

Géraud, *Paris sous...*, p. 22. Hughes, *Women...*, p. 147.

YSABELET LA BLANCHE

1421 France

Paid small tax in 1421 Paris; she was probably a prostitute.

♦ **Less-affluent. Merchants. Prostitutes.** ♦

Favier, *Les Contribuables...*, p. 142.

YVETTE OF HUY

See IVETTA OF HUY.

— Z —

ZABELIA

fl.c. 1200 France

A rather vague or shadowy figure due to the lack of information about Foix at this period. Her existence is documented, but many historians do not attempt to give her a first name. It appears that Zabelia was the daughter of †Cecile de Béziers and Roger Bernard, count of Foix; thus she was the sister of the Cathar leader, †Esclarmonde de Foix. Zabelia married Roger II de Comminges (d.1211). She was a patroness of the Waldensian movement.

♦ **Charity. Religious patrons. Waldensians.** ♦

Anselme, *Histoire...*, v.2, p. 642. Castillon, *Histoire...*, p. 230. Decaux, *Histoire...*, p. 290. Marks, *Pilgrims...*, p. 252. Sumption, *Albigensian...*, p. 60.

ZAIDA OF SEVILLE, queen of Castile

fl.c. 1050s Spain

Daughter of Emir of Seville, Abn Abed. Mistress/wife of Alfonso VI of Castile; died giving birth to his only son, Sancho. Alfonso's desire to make Sancho his heir was resisted because Zaida was of the Islamic faith.

♦ **Childbirth. Queens.** ♦

Altamira, *Spain...*, p. 133. Jackson, *Making...*, p. 71. Miron, *Queens...*, pp. 44, 46, 48. Oliviera, *Iberian...*, p. 111. Stephens, *Story...*, p. 23.

(St.) ZITA OF LUCCA **[Sitha]**

b. 1218–d.c. 1275 Italy

Servant of Faytinelli family for nearly fifty years. Mutilated her own face so that she would not be attractive to men. Noted for liberal almsgiving, and for kindness to those on "death row."

♦ **Charity. Handicapped. Saints. Servants. Unmarried. Virginity–protection.** ♦

A.S., Ap. v.3, pp. 502–532. Attwater, *Dictionary...*, p. 319. Farmer, *Oxford...*, pp. 418–9. Goodich, "Ancilla Dei...," pp. 128–130 & 136. Goodich, "Contours...," p. 24.

ZOE CARBOUNOPSINA, empress of Byzantium
fl. 902–920 Byzantium

Mistress of Leo VI of Byzantium by 902. He had married three times (including another Zoe) but had no sons. When Zoe gave birth to his son in 905, Leo secretly married her to legitimize the boy (Constantine Porphyrogenitus). This unleashed a religious war since fourth marriages were illegal in the Eastern Church. The issue was settled to Leo's satisfaction by 907. In 914, Zoe became regent. Although very capable, her military losses in Bulgaria decreased her popularity. In 919, Zoe abdicated her governmental role to become "Sister Anna" at a nearby convent.

♦ **Divorce. Mistresses. Nuns. Regents. Soldiers. Widows.** ♦

Cambridge..., IV, pp. 57, 60, 61, 142, 256. Jenkins, *Byzantium...*, pp. 203, 215–216, 220–222, 225, 228–236.

ZOE PALAEOLOGA

See—SOPHIA OF MOSCOW.

ZOE THE PORPHYROGENITA, empress of Byzantium
b. 978–d.c. 1049 Byzantium

Daughter of Constantine VIII. She had spent her life in *Gynaeceum* and so was still a virgin when, at age fifty, her father married her to Romanus Argyrus (1028). Constantine died shortly after the wedding, leaving the Empire to the newlyweds. Finally free, but neglected by her sixty-year-old husband, Zoe soon took lovers. In 1034, she and her paramour Michael presumably murdered Romanus and then got married. As Emperor Michael IV, her former lover feared Zoe and neglected her. After his death in 1041, his nephew became Michael V. This young man arrested Zoe, causing a popular uprising which placed both Zoe and her sister †Theodora on the throne. Zoe hated Theodora, so she soon married Constantine Monomachus and returned Theodora to the convent. Elderly Zoe then settled down to piety, and to friendship with Constantine since he already had a mistress.

♦ **Adultery. Legal activity. Murder. Pawns. Prisons. Rebellions. Rulers. Virginity–forced.** ♦

Comnena, *Alexiad...*, pp. 185n & 186. Diehl, *Byzantine...*, pp. 137–171. Jenkins, *Byzantium...*, pp. 321, 324–325, 339, 341, 344, 346. Leyser, *Rule...*, p. 107. Norwich, *Normans...*, pp. 45–46 & 63–64.

DATES

Women Cross Referenced by First Date

Dates through 900:

769–803	Irene, empress of Byzantium
770–800	Cyenthryth, queen of Mercia
770 fl.	Hildegard
775–810	Rotrude
780–818	Ermengarde, Holy Roman Empress
781–820	Gisela
789–810	Eadburg of Mercia
790–830	Euphrosyne of Byzantium
800–850	Asa, queen of Agdir
800 fl.	Bertha
800 fl.	Gundrada
802–843	Judith of Bavaria, Holy Roman Empress
810–840	Hildegarde (of France)
810–913	Oda
810–860	Roiantken
810–860	Theodora of Paphlagonia
820 fl.	Cwenthryth of Mercia
821–858	Ermengard (of Italy), Holy Roman Empress
822	Northilda
824 m.	Dhuoda
827–876	Emma, queen of Germany
830–860	Adelaide of Tours
830–860	Bertha de Sens, countess of Vienne
830–860	Gisela (of France)
830 fl.	Kasia (of Byzantium)
830 fl.	Ota (of Norway)
833–861	Amalberga
834 d.	Gerberga (of Toulouse)
840–890	Angelberga
840 fl.	Bertha of Avenay
840 fl.	Doda
840–874	Hathumoda of Gandersheim
840 fl.	Ragnhild (of Ringerike)
840 fl.	Tarub (of Cordoba)
840–870	Waldrada
842–869	Ermentrude of Orléans
843–870	Judith, queen of England
847	Theoda of Mainz
850–880	Ebba
850 fl.	Ermentrude of Jouarre
850–882	Eudocia Ingerina, empress of Byzantium
850 fl.	Ingeltrude
853–888	Aethelswith of Wessex, queen of Mercia
855 m.	Eudocia of Decapolis, empress of Byzantium
855 m.	Theutberga, queen of Lotharingia
860–890	Bertha of Tuscany
860 fl.	Gisla of Lorraine
860 fl.	Richardis
860–897	Theophano, empress of Byzantium
861 d.	Maura of Troyes (St.)
870 fl.	Adelaide, queen of France
870–900	Ageltrudis (of Spoleto)
870–910	Bertilla
870–920	Ludmila (of Bohemia)
870 m.	Richilde of Autun
870–920	Theodora of Rome
872–918	Aethelflaed, lady of the Mercians
875 fl.	Ansgard
876–896	Ermengard, duchess of Lombardy, queen of Provence
880–920	Adelaide of Roumainmoutier

880–920	Aelfthryth of Wessex
880 fl.	Christina (of Gandersheim)
880 d.	Liutberga (St.)
880 fl.	Ragnhild of Denmark
880–920	Rothild of Chelles
885–938	Marozia of Rome
890 fl.	Aud "the Deep–Minded"
890–969	Olga, princess of Kiev (St.)
900 fl.	Cunegunde of Swabia
900 fl.	Drahomira
900 fl.	Ecgwyna
900 fl.	Hatheburg
900 fl.	Ximena, queen of Leon

Dates 901 through 1000:

901 m.	Aelflaed
901 d.	Eudocia Baiane, empress of Byzantium
902–920	Zoe Carbounopsina
907–917	Frederun of Lorraine, queen of France
910–940	Adela of France [Adele]
910–940	Eadgyfu of England, queen of Burgundy and Provence
910–968	Eadgifu of Kent, queen of England
910–934	Emma of France
910–969	Gerberga of Saxony, queen of France
910–969	Matilda, queen of Germany
915	Bertha of Italy
917–950	Eadgifu of England, queen of France
920–970	Gunhild of Denmark, queen of Norway
920 fl.	Helen Lacapena, empress of Byzantium
920–970	Judith, duchess of Bavaria
920–979	Liutgard of Vermandois
920–960	Toda, queen of Navarre
920 fl.	Willa
921–960	Eadburga of Winchester (St.)
927 m.	Maria Lacapena [Mary]
929–946	Edith of England, queen of Germany
930 fl.	Bertha of Swabia
930–950	Bertha of Tuscany
930 fl.	Bezole
930 fl.	Roza
930–966	Willa of Tuscany, queen of Italy
932 d.	Ermengarde (of Ivrea)
933–999	Adelheid of Burgundy, Holy Roman Empress
935–999	Hroswitha of Gandersheim
936 m.	Alda of Arles
937 d.	Eadhild of Wessex
938–1005	Beatrice (of France), duchess of Haute–Lorraine
940–970	Aelfgifu
940–1002	Gerberga of Bavaria
940 fl.	Hathui (of Germany)
940–994	Hedwig of Bavaria
940–986	Ida of Swabia
940–970	Matilda of France
940–980	Theophano, empress of Byzantium
940–970	Urraca Gonzalez
945–980	Aethelflaed of Damerham
947 m.	Liutgard of Germany
949–1020	Adelaide of Anjou
949–1011	Matilda of Essen
950–1002	Aelfthryth
950–970	Elvira of Leon
950–990	Subh of Cordoba
950 d.	Wynflaed
954–999	Matilda of Quedlinburg
958–991	Theophano of Byzantium, Holy Roman Empress
960–1000	Adelaide (Capet), queen of France
960 fl.	Astrid of Norway
960 b.	Friderun (of Germany)
960–1030	Gunnor (of Denmark)
960–990	Rogneda of Polotsk
960–1003	Rozala of Lombardy
960–1000	Stephania (of Rome)
962–984	Eadgyth (of England) (St.)
963–1011	Anne, princess of Byzantium
964–1025	Bertha of Chartres
966–990	Emma of Italy, queen of France
970–1020	Aasta Grönske
970 fl.	Bertheida
970 fl.	Dubravka of Bohemia
970 fl.	Ende
970 fl.	Imma of Saxony
970–1016	Osburga of Coventry (St.)
970–1000	Sigrid, queen of Sweden
970–1000	Thyra of Denmark
970 fl.	Waldrada (of Arles)
975–1039	Sophia of Gandersheim
975–995	Uta of Niedermünster
977–1045	Adelheid of Germany, abbess of Quedlinburg
978–1049	Zoe the Porphyrogenita
980–1050	Ermessend of Carcassonne, countess of Barcelona

980 fl.	Freydis of Norway
980–1015	Gormflath (of Ireland)
980 d.	Wulfhilda of Barking (St.)
985–1065	Gisela of Bavaria, queen of Hungary
986–1032	Constance of Arles, queen of France
986–1030	Godila (of Walbeck)
988 d.	Wulfthryth, queen of England (St.)
989–1056	Theodora the Porphyrogenita
990 fl.	Astrid (of Denmark)
990–1057	Ermengarde (of Burgundy)
990 fl.	Gudrid (of Greenland)
990–1039	Cunigund of Luxembourg, Holy Roman Empress (St.)
1000–1040	Aelfgifu of Northampton
1000 fl.	Almodis (I) of Limoges
1000 fl.	Bethoc of Scotland
1000–1043	Gisela of Swabia, queen of Germany

Dates 1001 through 1100:

1001–1073	Evfosinia of Polotsk
1002–1052	Emma of Normandy
1003–1070	Godgifu, lady of Mercia
1006–1050	Godgifu (of England)
1010–1040	Estrith of Denmark
1010–1050	Gruoch, queen of Scotland
1010–1045	Sclerena (of Byzantium)
1019–1068	Agnes of Anjou
1019 m.	Gytha of Denmark
1020 fl.	Arlette (of Normandy)
1020 fl.	Astrid of Sweden
1020 fl.	Fressenda (de Hauteville)
1020 fl.	Ingegarde of Sweden
1024–1080	Anne of Kiev
1025–1075	Edith of Wessex, queen of England
1030–1091	Adelheid of Savoy [Adelaide]
1030 fl.	Adela of France [Adele]
1030–1077	Agnes of Poitou, Holy Roman Empress
1030–1060	Anastasia of Kiev
1030–1076	Beatrice, marchioness of Tuscany
1030–1060	Elizabeth of Kiev
1030 m.	Judith of Schweinfurt
1030–1060	Lesceline, countess of Eu
1030 fl.	Otta of S. Salvatore
1030–1086	Richilde, countess of Flanders
1031–1083	Matilda of Flanders
1032–1094	Judith of Flanders
1037 fl.	Sancha, queen of Leon and Castile [Sancia]
1038 d.	Gunnhild of Denmark, queen of Germany
1040 fl.	Agatha (of Hungary)
1040–1105	Anna Dalassena [Anne]
1040 fl.	Eadgifu of Lominster
1040–1080	Ealdgyth (of Mercia)
1040–1060	Margaret of Maine
1040 fl.	Mary of Kiev
1040–1090	Sichelgaita of Salerno
1040–1090	Trotula of Salerno
1046–1093	Margaret, queen of Scotland (St.)
1046–1115	Matilda of Tuscany
1047–1089	Judith of Évreux
1047–1110	Judith (of Germany)
1049–1122	Alberada of Buonalbergo
1049 m.	Thora of Norway
1050 fl.	Aubrée d'Ivry
1050–1060	Edith Swan–neck
1050–1113	Gertrude of Saxony, countess of Holland
1050–1085	Gundreda (of Warenne)
1050–1090	Gyda of England
1050–1078	Mabel of Bellême
1050 fl.	Ydain of Lorraine
1050 fl.	Zaida of Seville
1057–1130	Diemudis of Wessobrun [Diemud]
1060–1080	Agnes d'Évreux, countess of Montfort
1060–1127	Cecilia of Flanders
1060 fl.	Eudocia Macrembolitissa, empress of Byzantium
1060–1090	Sybille de Château–Porcien [Sibyl]
1060–1090	Svanhild of Essen
1062–1138	Adele, countess of Blois and Chartres
1063–1135	Almodis (III) of Toulouse
1065 m.	Ingibiorg, queen of Scotland
1066–1087	Bertha of Susa
1066–1090	Constance of Normandy
1070–1120	Agnes of Germany
1070 fl.	Christina (of Hungary) [Christine]
1070–1110	Helena (Guiscard) [Helen]
1070–1110	Helwise of Nevers, countess of Évreux
1070–1110	Ianka of Kiev
1070–1100	Isabel de Montfort [Isabelle]
1071 d.	Almodis (II) de La Marche, countess of Barcelona

1071–1109	Eupraxia of Kiev, Holy Roman Empress
1072–1118	Adela of Flanders, queen of Denmark
1072–1094	Bertha of Holland
1075–1119	Bertrade de Montfort, queen of France
1075 m.	Emma FitzOsbern, countess of Norfolk
1077–1123	Irene Ducas, empress of Byzantium
1080–1120	Agnes, countess of Aix
1080–1130	Alice de Clare
1080–1129	Almodis (IV), countess of La Marche
1080–1110	Constance of France, queen of Castile
1080 fl.	Emma (of Apulia)
1080–1120	Gertrude of Flanders, duchess of Lorraine
1080–1130	Isabel of Vermandois, countess of Leicester
1080–1130	Matilda of Northumberland, queen of Scotland
1080–1118	Matilda of Scotland
1080–1120	Nesta
1080–1110	Phillippia, countess of Poitou [Philippa]
1080–1103	Sybil of Conversano [Sibyl]
1080–1130	Theresa of Castile
1083–1148	Anna Comnena [Anne]
1085–1110	Mary of Scotland, countess of Boulogne
1088–1147	Ermengarde of Anjou, duchess of Brittany
1089–1118	Adelaide of Savona
1090–1120	Christina of Sweden [Christine]
1090–1120	Constance of France
1090 fl.	Elvira of Castile
1090–1117	Gertrude of Meissen
1090 fl.	Hersende (of Fontevrault)
1090–1110	Odeline
1090–1126	Urraca, queen of Castile
1090 fl.	Ximena Diaz
1093–1148	Petronille of Fontevrault
1095 m.	Maria of Vivar [Mary]
1096–1155	Christina of Markyate [Christine]
1097 d.	Godevere of Töeni
1098–1138	Cecilia of France
1098–1179	Hildegarde of Bingen (St.)
1100 fl.	Châtellerault (countess of)
1100 fl.	Clementia, countess of Flanders
1100 fl.	Constance (FitzGilbert)
1100 fl.	Diemud of Wessobrun
1100 fl.	Eilika of Saxony
1100–1139	Evfimia of Kiev [Euphemia]
1100 fl.	Guda (of Germany)
1100–1130	Malfrid of Kiev, queen of Norway, queen of Denmark
1100 fl.	Relindis of Hohenburg
1100–1141	Richenza of Nordheim, Holy Roman Empress
1100–1121	Sibilla (of England) [Sibyl]
1100–1120	Wulfhild of Saxony

Dates 1101 through 1200:

1101–1164	Heloise of Argenteuil
1101 m.	Margaret of Sweden, queen of Norway
1102–1164	Matilda of England, Holy Roman Empress
1103–1151	Adelicia of Louvain, queen of England
1105 m.	Lucienne of Rochefort
1105–1152	Matilda of Boulogne, queen of England
1106	Ermengard (of S. Salvatore)
1109–1193	Dervorgilla (O'Ruairc)
1110 fl.	Beatrice de Vesci
1110 fl.	Ingunn (of Iceland)
1110–1160	Matilda of Anjou
1110–1170	Sybille of Anjou, countess of Flanders [Sibyl]
1112 m.	Douce (I) of Provence
1115–1154	Adelaide of Maurienne, queen of France
1117–1135	Elvira of Castile, queen of Sicily
1120 fl.	Aénor of Châtellerault
1120 fl.	Agnes of Saarbrücken
1120 fl.	Amicia de Gael, countess of Leicester
1120–1194	Ermengarde, viscountess of Narbonne
1120 fl.	Matilda of Sicily, countess of Alife
1121–1175	Bethlem of Greci
1121–1131	Judith of Bavaria, duchess of Swabia
1122–1203	Eleanor of Aquitaine
1124–1140	Petronilla of Aquitaine, countess of Vermandois
1126 m.	Alice of Jerusalem, princess of Antioch
1127 d.	Ava of Melk
1127–1143	Gertrude of Saxony, duchess of Bavaria

1128–1160	Constance of Antioch
1128–1183	Margaret of Navarre, queen of Sicily
1128 d.	Morphia of Melitene
1129–1164	Elizabeth of Schönau (St.)
1129–1161	Mélisende, queen of Jerusalem
1130–1178	Ada of Warenne
1130–1170	Beatrice de Dia
1130–1195	Bertha of Swabia, duchess of Lorraine
1130–1160	Christina of Norway [Christine]
1130–1160	Constance of France, countess of Toulouse
1130–1170	Tenxwind of Andernach
1130–1181	Tibors d'Omelas
1135–1185	Agnes of Courtenay
1135 d.	Diemuod of Nonnberg [Diemud]
1135–1173	Petronilla, queen of Aragon
1136	Helvidis
1136 d.	Jutta of Sponheim
1136–1181	Mary of Blois
1140–1170	Ada of Scotland, countess of Holland
1140–1170	Adelaide de Porcairques
1140–1184	Beatrice of Burgundy
1140 fl.	Faydide of Millau, countess of Toulouse
1140 fl.	Hodierna of Jerusalem
1140 fl.	Ingerid of Sweden
1140–1183	Isabella of Vermandois, countess of Flanders
1140 b.	Iseut de Capio
1140 fl.	Marguerite de Turenne [Margaret]
1140 fl.	Theodora Comnena
1145–1206	Adele of Champagne, queen of France
1145–1198	Marie of France, countess of Champagne [Mary]
1145–1212	Petronilla of Grandmesnil, countess of Leicester
1146 m.	Bertha of Sulzbach
1146–1157	Matilda of Savoy
1146–1170	Philippa of Antioch
1147 b.	Almucs de Castelnau
1147–1185	Theodora Comnena, queen of Jerusalem
1149–1190	Alix of France, countess of Blois and Chartres
1150 fl.	Cecile de Béziers [Cecilia]
1150–1224	Christina of St. Trond [Christine]
1150 m.	Clementia of Zähringen
1150 fl.	Constance of Castile, queen of France
1150–1170	Gertrude of Bavaria
1150 fl.	Idonea
1150–1182	Mary of Antioch
1150–1180	Marie de France [Mary]
1150–1190	Oelun
1150–1176	Rosamund Clifford
1152 m.	Beatrice of Rethel, queen of Sicily
1152–1182	Maria Comnena, princess of Byzantium [Mary]
1152 d.	Richardis von Stade
1153	Adelheid of Vohburg
1154–1184	Anne de Châtillon
1154–1198	Constance of Sicily, Holy Roman Empress
1155–1195	Herrad von Landsberg
1156–1189	Matilda of England, duchess of Bavaria
1157–1228	Ivetta of Huy
1158–1197	Margaret of France, queen of Hungary
1160–1200	Alys of France [Alice]
1160–1210	Amicia of Leicester
1160–1190	Clemence of Barking
1160–1213	Eleanora of Vermandois [Eleanor]
1160 fl.	Eva MacMurrough
1160–1200	Ida of Boulogne
1160 d.	Rosalia of Palermo (St.)
1160–1200	Sancha of Castile
1160–1213	Tamara, queen of Georgia
1160 m.	Urraca of Portugal
1161–1201	Constance of Brittany
1162–1214	Eleanor of England, queen of Castile
1163–1230	Berengaria of Navarre, queen of England
1165–1200	Borte
1165–1199	Joanna of England, queen of Sicily [Jean]
1165–1220	Marie de Ventadour [Mary]
1167–1217	Maria Comnena, queen of Jerusalem [Mary]
1169–1194	Margaret of Alsace
1170–1201	Azalais de Rocamartina [Adelaide]
1170 fl.	Agnes of Dedo
1170 fl.	Basilia de Clare
1170–1228	Beatrice of Viennois, countess of Albon
1170–1215	Esclarmonde de Foix
1170–1190	Eudoxia Comnena

1170–1218 Hawise of Gloucester
1170–1190 Isabella de Clare [Isabelle]
1170–1190 Isabella of Hainault, queen of France [Isabelle]
1170–1235 Margaret of Leicester
1170 fl. Rose O'Connor
1171–1199 Adelaide of Toulouse
1171–1220 Agnes of France
1174–1198 Douce (II) of Barcelona
1174–1243 Hedwig of Silesia (St.)
1174–1204 Marie of Champagne, countess of Flanders [Mary]
1175 m. Amicia of Gloucester
1175 m. Douce (III) of Provence
1176–1237 Ingeborg of Denmark, queen of France
1176–1190 Sibylla of Jerusalem [Sibyl]
1176–1250 Theresa of Portugal, queen of Leon (St.)
1177–1213 Mary of Oignies
1180–1220 Affreca of Man, countess of Ulster
1180–1201 Agnes of Meran
1180–1221 Alice de Montmorency
1180 fl. Blanche of Laurac
1180–1230 Blanche of Navarre, countess of Champagne
1180 fl. Cecily FitzJohn [Cecilia]
1180–1257 Garsenda de Forcalquier
1180 fl. Isabella of Jerusalem [Isabelle]
1180–1220 Margarida de Roussillon [Margaret]
1180–1240 Marie of Montpellier [Mary]
1180–1240 Petronille of Comminges
1180–1229 Sancha of Portugal (St.) [Sancia]
1180 fl. Sibylla of Acerra [Sibyl]
1180 fl. Sybil de Lacy [Sibyl]
1182–1246 Lutgard of Aywières (St.) [Liutgard]
1183 m. Theresa of Portugal, countess of Flanders
1184–1203 Agnes of Meissen
1184–1222 Constance of Aragon, queen of Hungary
1184–1210 Margaret of Sweden, queen of Norway
1185–1240 Ela, countess of Salisbury
1185–1240 Gertrud of Meran [Gertrude]
1186–1233 Ermengarde de Beaumont, queen of Scotland
1186–1246 Isabelle of Angoulême, queen of England
1188–1252 Blanche of Castile, queen of France
1188–1260 Marie de Brabant, Holy Roman Empress
1190–1241 Annora de Braose
1190–1241 Eleanor of Brittany
1190 fl. Ermengarde (of St. Adrian)
1190–1236 Gwenllian (of Wales)
1190–1230 Lombarda
1190–1220 Margaret de Braose
1192 d. Margaret of England (St.)
1193 m. Agnes von Staufen
1192–1253 Clare of Assisi
1193–1209 Irene Angela, Holy Roman Empress
1193–1258 Juliana of Cornillon
1195–1246 Alix of Champagne, queen of Cyprus [Alice]
1196–1270 Loretta de Braose
1197–1246 Berenguela of Castile
1198–1238 Marie of France, duchess of Brabant [Mary]
1199–1230 Alix of Brittany [Alice]
1199–1251 Alix de Vergy, duchess of Burgundy [Alice]
1200 fl. Abella of Salerno
1200 fl. Constance (of Hungary)
1200 fl. Dulcia de Bosqueto
1200 fl. Leonor of Aragon, countess of Toulouse [Eleanor]
1200–1250 Leonor of Castile, queen of Aragon [Eleanor]
1200 fl. Hadewijch
1200–1240 Isabella Marshall [Isabelle]
1200–1244 Jeanne of Flanders [Jean]
1200 fl. Laurette de Saint-Valéry
1200 fl. Mabel Rich
1200–1251 Marie, countess of Ponthieu and Aumale [Mary]
1200 fl. Mercuriade of Salerno
1200–1240 Philippa of Champagne
1200 fl. Rebecca Guarna
1200–1220 Urraca of Castile, queen of Portugal
1200 fl. Zabelia

Dates 1201 through 1300:

1202–1280 Margaret, countess of Flanders
1202–1258 Matilda of Boulogne, queen of Portugal
1204–1237 Joan of England, princess of Gwynedd [Jean]
1205–1282 Agnes of Bohemia

1207–1231	Elizabeth of Hungary (St.)
1207–1229	Yolande (of Jerusalem), Holy Roman Empress
1209	Agnes (of Norfolk)
1209	Galiena (of Norfolk)
1209–1240	Margaret, queen of Norway
1210–1250	Anne, princess of Bohemia
1210 fl.	Clara d'Anduza [Clare]
1210	Claricia of Augsburg
1210–1230	Cunigunda of Swabia, queen of Bohemia
1210–1237	Joan of England, queen of Scotland [Jean]
1210 fl.	Loba de Pueinautier
1210–1260	Margaret of Babenberg
1210 d.	Maud de Braose [Matilda]
1211 d.	Giralda de Laurac
1212 fl.	Castelloza of Provence
1212–1283	Mechtild of Magdeburg
1214 d.	Beatrice de Warenne
1214–1274	Douceline (St.)
1214–1241	Isabella of England, Holy Roman Empress [Isabelle]
1215–1274	Eleanor de Montfort, countess of Leicester
1215 d.	Philippe de Moncada
1216–1237	Margaret of Ypres
1216	Nicola de la Hay [Nichole]
1218–1275	Zita of Lucca (St.)
1219 m.	Beatrice of Swabia, queen of Castile
1219–1272	Yolande de Dreux
1220–1240	Adelasia of Torres, queen of Sardinia
1220–1260	Alix de Mâcon [Alice]
1220	Alice de Montfort
1220–1284	Amice de Clare [Amicia]
1220–1266	Beatrice of Savoy, countess of Provence
1220–1291	Devorguilla of Galloway
1220–1271	Jeanne of Toulouse [Jean]
1220–1280	Marguerite of Provence, queen of France [Margaret]
1220–1266	Margaret Lacy
1220–1246	Umiliana dei Cherchi (St.)
1221–1291	Eleanor of Provence, queen of England
1223 d.	Agnes de Condet
1224 d.	Agnes FitzJohn
1225–1270	Isabelle of France
1225–1240	Sabina von Steinbach
1225–1261	Sanchia of Provence [Sancia]
1226–1257	Euphemia of Wherwell
1226–1310	Umilita of Faenza
1230–1265	Eva of Saint-Martin
1230–1268	Gertrude of Babenberg
1230 fl.	Mabel of Bury St. Edmunds
1230–1257	Marguerite de Bourbon, queen of Navarre [Margaret]
1230 fl.	Martha (of Paris)
1230–1240	Turakina
1231 d.	Aurembaix, countess of Urgel
1231 d.	Ida of Nivelles
1232–1313	Constance of Hohenstaufen
1232–1291	Gertrude of Hackeborn
1235–1253	Rose of Viterbo (St.)
1236–1251	Yolande of Hungary, queen of Aragon
1237–1293	Isabella de Fortibus [Isabelle]
1237–1279	Jeanne de Dammartin, queen of Castile [Jean]
1237–1288	Mahaut de Brabant
1237–1260	Margaret (of Sicily)
1239–1269	Kunigunde of Goss [Cunigunde]
1239–1260	Marie de Coucy, queen of Scotland [Mary]
1240–1304	Beatrice de Guzman
1240–1274	Margaret of England, queen of Scotland
1240–1270	Philippa de Dammartin
1241 d.	Irene Lascaris, empress of Byzantium
1241–1271	Isabella of France, queen of Navarre [Isabelle]
1241–1299	Mechtild von Hackeborn
1242–1275	Beatrice of England
1242–1312	Christina of Stommeln [Christine]
1242–1271	Margaret of Hungary
1243–1288	Alix of Brittany [Alice]
1244 d.	Corba de Péreille
1244–1290	Eleanor of Castile, queen of England
1244	Goda la Gablere
1246–1267	Beatrice of Provence
1247	Foria (of Vermandois)
1247–1307	Joan de Munchensi [Jean]
1247–1297	Margaret of Cortona (St.)
1249	Hersende (of France)
1250–1290	Agnes d'Harcourt
1250 fl.	Alice Hulle
1250–1309	Angela of Foligno
1250 fl.	Childlove (de Worth)

1250–1302 Constance, queen of Aragon
1250–1287 Kunigunda of Hungary [Cunigunde]
1250 fl. Guillelma de Rosers
1250–1287 Ingeborg of Denmark, queen of Norway
1250–1300 Philippine de Porcellet
1250 fl. Theodora, empress of Byzantium
1251 Alice (of Stratford)
1252–1320 Blanche of France
1252–1282 Eleanora de Montfort [Eleanor]
1254–1311 Isabelle of Achaia
1256–1301 Gertrude von Helfta
1259–1323 Blanche of Portugal
1260–1290 Dionysia de Mountchesny
1260–1300 Margaret Aldobrandeschi
1260–1290 Maria de Malla [Mary]
1261 d. Christine Swath
1261 Dulcia Trye
1261–1283 Margaret of Scotland, queen of Norway
1261 Notekina Hoggenhore
1263 d. Juliana (Cordwaner)
1265–1295 Agnes de Monceaux
1265–1298 Eleanor of England, countess of Bar
1265 Margery (of Frocestor)
1266–1290 Beatrice Portinari
1266–1290 Marjorie, countess of Carrick [Margery]
1268–1317 Agnes da Montepulciano (St.)
1268 m. Beatrice of Falkenstein
1268 d. Beatrice of Nazareth
1268–1308 Clare of Montefalco (St.)
1269–1302 Blanche of Artois
1270 fl. Agnes of Huntingdon
1270 fl. Denise la Vileyn
1270–1341 Juliana Falconieri (St.)
1270–1328 Mahaut of Artois
1270–1321 Maria de Molina [Mary]
1270–1300 Mayfreda de Pirovano
1270–1300 Yolande de Dreux, queen of Scotland
1271 Donella of Bologne
1271–1336 Elizabeth of Portugal (St.)
1271 d. Isabel of Aragon, princess of France [Isabelle]
1271 Richolda
1272–1307 Joan of England, countess of Gloucester [Jean]
1273–1305 Jeanne of Navarre, queen of France [Jean]
1273–1317 Yolande of Montferrat
1274 d. Aveline de Forz, countess of Aumale
1275 fl. Agnes Rokingeham
1275 d. Angele de la Barthe [Angela]
1275 Cristina Rokingeham [Christine]
1275 m. Esclarmunda de Foix, queen of Majorca
1275 Juliana (Bonaventure)
1275–1318 Margaret of England, duchess of Brabant
1275–1321 Marie de Brabant, queen of France [Mary]
1279–1325 Agnes of France
1280–1351 Agnes of Hapsburg, queen of Hungary
1280–1348 Alice Lacy, countess of Lancaster
1280–1309 Alice la Wymplere
1280 Avice Gardebois
1280–1310 Catherine de Courteney
1280–1359 Isabella Bruce [Isabelle]
1280–1335 Isabelle de Vescy
1280 fl. Margerie de Haustede [Margery]
1280 fl. Slymina Fort
1281 fl. Agnes Brid
1281 Dionisia de Wodemerstham
1282 fl. Alice Bokerel
1282–1358 Delphine of Languedoc
1282–1316 Elizabeth, princess of England
1282 d. Guglielma (of Milan)
1282–1337 Gwenllian (of Wales)
1282–1318 Margaret of France, queen of England
1282 Rose Savage
1283–1310 Blanche of Anjou, queen of Aragon
1283 Isabella Hodere [Isabelle]
1283–1290 Margaret, "the Maid of Norway"
1284–1308 Agnes Molton
1285 d. Francesca da Rimini
1286–1356 Joan de Genville [Jean]
1286–1345 Sancia of Majorca
1287–1320 Margaret of Citta di Castello
1287–1367 Sibillina Biscossi [Sibyl]
1288–1330 Elizabeth of Bohemia
1288 fl. Joan Everard [Jean]
1290 Agnes Thomas
1290 d. Amice la Plomere [Amicia]
1290–1320 Eleanor de Clare

1290 fl.	Fabrisse Rives
1290–1352	Jeanne de Valois, countess of Hainault [Jean]
1290–1322	Jacoba Felicie
1290 fl.	Juliana Hauteyn
1290–1311	Margaret of Brabant, Holy Roman Empress
1290–1330	Margaret de Clare
1290 fl.	Marguerite d'Oingt [Margaret]
1291 d.	Cristiana la Flaoners
1291–1351	Margaret Ebner
1292	Adelie l'Erbière [Adele]
1292	Aalis (la barbière) [Alice]
1292	Aales (la chandelière) [Alice]
1292	Aelis (la poissonière) [Alice]
1292	Aaeles (la tapicière) [Alice]
1292	Aalis (l'ymaginière) [Alice]
1292	Alison (la nourrice)
1292	Ameline (la bouchière)
1292	Ameline (la cordoanière)
1292	Ameline (la couturière)
1292	Anès (la cervoisière) [Anne]
1292	Anès (la gueinnière) [Anne]
1292	Anès (la taupière) [Anne]
1292	Ascelinne (la deicière)
1292	Aveline (la barbière)
1292	Aveline (la chapelière)
1292	Aveline (l'estuverresse)
1292	Béatriz (la buffretière) [Beatrice]
1292	Bietrix (la metresse) [Beatrice]
1292	Berte (la tartrière)
1292	Cateline (of Paris)
1292	Katerine (l'attachière) [Catherine]
1292	Coustance (la parcheminière) [Constance]
1292	Denise (la barbière)
1292	Denyse la Normande [Denise]
1292	Edeline (la barbière)
1292	Edeline (la paonnière)
1292	Edelot (la fourmagière)
1292	Elena Taillour
1292	Emeline (la poréeresse)
1292	Emeline (la ventrière)
1292	Erembourc de Braieres
1292	Erembourc (la florière)
1292	Erembourc (la potière)
1292	Estienne (la gravelière)
1292	Eudeline (la barbière)
1292	Eudeline (la baudreere)
1292	Felise (la pasteere)
1292	Gile (la mâconne)
1292	Haouys (la poulaillière)
1292	Haoys (la meresse)
1292	Hélissent (la ferpière)
1292	Heloys (la miergesse)
1292	Heloys (l'uilière)
1292	Heloyson (la nourrice)
1292	Hodierne (la cerencerresse)
1292	Huitace (la lanière)
1292–1358	Isabella of France, queen of England [Isabelle]
1292	Isabiau (la mergesse) [Isabelle]
1292	Jacqueline (la saacière)
1292	Jehanne (la bouchière) [Jean]
1292	Jehanne (la boutonnière) [Jean]
1292	Jehanne (la cristalière) [Jean]
1292	Jehanne (la fouacière) [Jean]
1292	Jehanne (la loirrière) [Jean]
1292	Jehanne (la tapicière) [Jean]
1292	Jehanne (la verrière) [Jean]
1292	Jourdenete (nourrice)
1292	Juliane (la potière)
1292	Mabile (la regratière) [Mabel]
1292	Maheut (la chapelière) [Mahaut]
1292	Maheut (la feutrière) [Mahaut]
1292	Maheut (la pescheresse) [Mahaut]
1292	Marguerite (l'avenière) [Margaret]
1292	Marguerite (la chanevacière) [Margaret]
1292	Marguerite (la cordière) [Margaret]
1292	Marguerite (la savonnière) [Margaret]
1292	Margot (la gantière)
1292	Marie d'Atainville [Mary]
1292	Marie (la barbière) [Mary]
1292	Marie (la fanière) [Mary]
1292	Marie (la mareschale) [Mary]
1292	Marie (la meresse) [Mary]
1292	Michiele (la ventrière)
1292	Milessent (la cerenceresse)

1292	Nicole (la boursière) [Nichole]
1292	Nicole (l'erbière) [Nichole]
1292	Nicole (l'esperonnière) [Nichole]
1292	Nicole (la saunière) [Nichole]
1292	Pentecouste (la fruitière)
1292	Pérronnele (la lavendière) [Pérronelle]
1292	Pérronele (la nourrice) [Pérronelle]
1292	Phelipote (la fritière)
1292	Phelippe (la miergesse) [Philippa]
1292	Richeut (la meresse)
1292	Sainte (la paintre)
1292	Sarra (of Broughton) [Sarah]
1292	Sarre (la mirgesse) [Sarah]
1292	Sedile (la fournière)
1292–1330	Simone of Byzantium
1292	Susane (la coiffière)
1292	Thomasse (la talemelière)
1292	Typhainne (la blazennière) [Tiffania]
1292	Tyfainne (mestresse de l'école) [Tiffania]
1292	Thyphainne (la toière) [Tiffania]
1292	Ysabel (la commanderesse)
1292	Ysabiau (la ferpière) [Ysabel]
1292	Ysabel de la Heuse
1292	Ysabel (la meresse)
1292	Ysabiau (la nourrice) [Ysabel]
1293–1360	Elizabeth de Clare
1293–1329	Jeanne of Burgundy [Jean]
1294–1325	Agnes Page
1294–1328	Clemence of Hungary
1294–1318	Marjory Bruce [Margery]
1295–1326	Blanche of Burgundy
1295–1310	Euphemia of Arnstein, queen of Norway
1295 d.	Johanna Travers [Jean]
1297–1332	Agnes de Broughton
1297–1332	Agnes Kateline
1297–1306	Beatrice Brounying
1297	Gile (la barbière)
1298–1320	Grazida Lizier
1298	Ida de Portunhale
1300 fl.	Alice Kyteler
1300 fl.	Beatrice Candia
1300 fl.	Bourgot de Noir
1300 fl.	Clara Gatterstedt [Clare]
1300 fl.	Elena Baroun
1300 fl.	Eva of Brounestown
1300 fl.	Gilette of Narbonne
1300 d.	Gisela of Kerzenbroeck
1300–1330	Ingebjorg of Norway
1300 fl.	Joan Lenelonde [Jean]
1300 fl.	Leonetta (medica)
1300 fl.	Maddalena Bonsignori [Madeleine]
1300–1314	Margaret of Burgundy
1300–1349	Margaret Wake
1300 fl.	Margery of Hales
1300–1340	Matilda of Lancaster
1300 fl.	Pérronnele (l'espicière) [Pérronelle]
1300 fl.	Quintine van den Zande

Dates 1301 through 1400:

1301–1332	Katherine Boteler [Catherine]
1301–1345	Catherine de Valois
1301	Lucy atte Lee
1302–1373	Bridget of Sweden (St.)
1302	Dionysia Baldewyne
1303	Alice of Rallingbury
1303–1368	Juliana de Leybourne, countess of Huntingdon
1304–1327	Elizabeth de Burgo, queen of Scotland
1304	Jacobina (medica)
1304	Marote (de Douai)
1304–1380	Mary of St. Pol
1305 fl.	Agnes Russell
1305 d.	Alice de Wylesdone
1305	Edith Paumer
1305 d.	Gunnora de Stratford
1306–1361	Joan de Bar, countess of Surrey [Jean]
1306	Maud Makejoy [Matilda]
1306	Pearl in the Egg
1307	Elisia Hundesdich
1307 d.	Margherita di Trento [Margaret]
1308	Johanna Hadham [Jean]
1308–1348	Laura
1309	Avice la Wymplere
1310 fl.	Avis Wade
1310 fl.	Beatrice of Planisolles
1310 fl.	Beatrice Puttock
1310–1350	Catherine d'Artois
1310–1358	Leonor of Castile, queen of Aragon [Eleanor]

1310–1330 Elizabeth Badlesmere
1310–1386 Elizabeth of Poland, queen of Hungary
1310 fl. Helen Galrussyn
1310 fl. Isabella, countess of Buchan [Isabelle]
1310–1360 Jeanne de Bourbon [Jean]
1310–1349 Jeanne of France, queen of Navarre [Jean]
1310–1363 Jeanne de Valois [Jean]
1310 fl. Mahaut de Châtillon
1310 Marguerite (la barbière) [Margaret]
1310–1382 Margaret of France, countess of Flanders
1310–1356 Margaret of Hainault, Holy Roman Empress
1310 d. Margaret Porete
1310–1350 Maria of Portugal [Mary]
1310 fl. Margot Pipelarde
1310 fl. Maud Chaworth [Matilda]
1310 fl. Mengarde Buscalh
1310 fl. Strathearn (countess of)
1310 fl. Syssoh Galrussyn
1311–1348 Jeanne of Burgundy, queen of France [Jean]
1312 Anastasia Spychefat
1312 Clarice of Rotomago [Claricia]
1312 m. Ingeborg of Norway
1312–1327 Teresa de Entenza [Theresa]
1313 fl. Agnes Cook (le Keu)
1313 Alice Romayn
1313 fl. Ameline (la miresse)
1313 Basilia Maderman
1313–1323 Catherine of Austria
1313 Geneviève (la paonnière)
1314–1369 Philippa of Hainault
1315–1340 Eufemia (of Mecklenburg) [Euphemia]
1315–1391 Margaret de Bohun, countess of Devon
1316–1348 Blanche of France
1316–1349 Bona of Luxembourg
1316 Sarah Stroby
1317 Isabelle de Ferièves
1318–1355 Eleanor of England, countess of Guelders
1319 Jeanne de Latilly [Jean]
1319 Noel (of France)
1320–1360 Agnes Chaucer
1320–1353 Anne of Savoy, empress of Byzantium
1320 fl. Annota Lange
1320 Belota (the Jew)
1320–1352 Leonor de Guzman [Eleanor]
1320 fl. Guillemette Benet
1320 Isabeau (apotiqueresse) [Isabelle]
1320 fl. Jeanne "Conversa" [Jean]
1320 fl. Jeanne de Divion [Jean]
1320–1384 Jeanne de Penthièvre [Jean]
1320–1410 Maud de Vere, countess of Oxford [Matilda]
1320 d. Petronilla of Meath
1320 Petronilla of Teye
1320 fl. Sarah of Meath
1321 Agnes Francou
1321 Baddlesmere (lady)
1321 fl. Francesca de Romana
1321–1362 Joan of England, queen of Scotland [Jean]
1321 Matilda de Burgham
1322 fl. Agnes Avesot
1322–1364 Elisenda de Moncada, queen of Aragon
1322 Jeanne Clarisse [Jean]
1322 Juliana Roos
1322 Marguerite de Ypres [Margaret]
1323 Cecilia le Boteler
1323–1375 Margaret of Logy
1324 Alice Barley
1324 Margaret Page
1324 d. Marie of Bohemia [Mary]
1324–1331 Marie of Valois [Mary]
1325 Emma Turk
1325 d. Prous Bonetta
1326–1370 Jeanne d'Évreux, queen of France [Jean]
1326–1382 Joanna I, queen of Naples [Jean]
1326 d. Lucia Tasseburgh
1326 Sara of Saint-Gilles [Sarah]
1327 d. Johanna Beauflour [Jean]
1328–1385 Joan of Kent [Jean]
1328 Matilda Yonge
1329 Eleanor de Wendale
1329–1370 Jeanne de Montfort [Jean]
1329 d. Roesia de Borford
1330–1380 Agnes of Navarre
1330 Alice Staundon
1330 fl. Bayalun
1330 fl. Beatrice of Castile, queen of Portugal

1330–1381	Catherine of Sweden (St.)
1330 fl.	Cecile de Turenne [Cecilia]
1330 fl.	Isabelle de Melun
1330 fl.	Isabel of Savoy
1330–1360	Jeanne de Boulogne, queen of France [Jean]
1330–1370	Margaret Maultasch
1330–1372	Tiphaine Raguel [Tiffania]
1331 d.	Matilda of Hainault, princess of Achaia
1332–1363	Elizabeth de Burgh
1332–1379	Isabella of England, countess of Bedford [Isabelle]
1335 b.	Alice atte March
1335 d.	Anne–Marie de Georgel
1335 fl.	Armande Robert
1335–1360	Blanche of Namur
1335–1398	Blanche of Navarre, queen of France
1335 d.	Catherine Delort
1335–1348	Joan of England (of Woodstock) [Jean]
1335	Matheline Fauré
1335 fl.	Paule Viguier
1335	Pierrille Roland
1336 d.	Bloemardine
1336 m.	Margaret de Audley, lady Stafford
1337 d.	Fiametta
1338	Alice Donbely
1338 fl.	Agnes, countess of Dunbar
1338	Agnes (of Holbourne)
1338	Agnes Sigily
1338	Alice de Lincoln
1338	Alice Montacute
1338	Alice Tredewedowe
1338	Beatrice la Welsshe
1338–1361	Blanche of Bourbon
1338	Catherine Merceyra
1338	Elizabeth Quintin
1338–1378	Jeanne de Bourbon, queen of France [Jean]
1338–1399	Margaret Marshall
1338–1347	Marie of Navarre [Mary]
1339–1385	Elizabeth of Bosnia
1339–1381	Juana Manuel, queen of Castile [Jean]
1340	Alice Denecoumbe
1340–1387	Blanche of Ponthieu
1340–1399	Bonne de Bourbon, countess of Savoy
1340 fl.	Eleanor of Lancaster
1340 fl.	Isabel Beaumont
1340 fl.	Jeanne de Belleville [Jean]
1340 fl.	Kateline de Coster
1340–1361	Maria de Padilla [Mary]
1340–1385	Regina della Scalla
1341–1369	Blanche of Lancaster
1342	Joan de la Lee [Jean]
1343–1420	Julian of Norwich
1344 fl.	Agnes de Bury
1344	Idonea le Hukestere
1344 fl.	Isabella de Despenser, countess of Arundel
1344–1362	Mary of England
1346–1362	Margaret of England, countess of Pembroke
1347–1380	Catherine of Siena (St.)
1347–1394	Dorothy of Montau
1348 d.	Leonor of Portugal, queen of Aragon [Eleanor]
1348–1375	Leonor of Sicily, queen of Aragon [Eleanor]
1348–1372	Isabelle of France, duchess of Milan
1349	Agnes Wombe
1349–1400	Alice Perrers
1349 d.	Catherine of Austria
1349 d.	Jeanne de Crespi [Jean]
1349	Joan la Whycchere [Jean]
1349–1405	Margaret of Flanders, duchess of Burgundy
1349 d.	Petronilla Turk
1350	Agnes Mundene
1350–1415	Alice de Bryene
1350 fl.	Alice Cantebrugge
1350 fl.	Bianca of Savoy
1350 d.	Katharine Grandison [Catherine]
1350–1404	Katherine Swynford [Catherine]
1350–1400	Leonor Lopez [Eleanor]
1350–1386	Leonor Telles, queen of Portugal [Eleanor]
1350	Isabella de Toppesham [Isabelle]
1350–1368	Margaret of Brabant, countess of Flanders
1350 fl.	Novella d'Andrea
1350 fl.	Péronnelle d'Armentières [Pérronelle]
1351 fl.	Ulricha de Foschua
1353–1368	Beatrice of Castile
1353–1412	Margaret of Denmark
1354	Agnes atte Holte
1354–1394	Constance of Castile, duchess of Lancaster
1354–1384	Violante Visconti
1355	Alice atte Harpe

1355	Alice Stanford
1355	Cristina Blake [Christine]
1355 d.	Ines de Castro
1355–1381	Philippa of Clarence
1356–1392	Isabel of Castile, duchess of York [Isabelle]
1356–1391	Jehanne de Brigue [Jean]
1356–1429	Maddalena Scrovegni [Madeleine]
1358 d.	Gertrude van Öosten
1359	Cecilia Rygeway
1360	Antoinette de Bellegarde
1360–1390	Cecily Chaumpaigne
1360 m.	Costanza of Aragon, queen of Sicily [Constance]
1360–1382	Leonor of Aragon, queen of Castile [Eleanor]
1360–1404	Eleanora di Arborea [Eleanor]
1360–1399	Eleanor de Bohun, duchess of Gloucester
1360 b.	Leonor of Castile, queen of Navarre [Eleanor]
1360 fl.	Emma Hatfield
1360–1410	Jeanne d'Artois [Jean]
1360 fl.	Joan Hunt [Jean]
1360–1423	Margherita Datini [Margaret]
1360–1390	Marie of Brittany, duchess of Anjou [Mary]
1360–1398	Matilda de Lucy
1360 fl.	Margery de Honylane
1360 fl.	Myfanwy (Tudor)
1360–1411	Peretta Peronne [Perrette]
1360–1415	Philippa of Lancaster, queen of Portugal
1360 fl.	Sanche Snoth [Sanica]
1360 fl.	Taddea Visconti
1363–1426	Elizabeth of Lancaster
1364	Agnes Irlond
1364	Beatrice Bassett
1364–1429	Christine de Pisan
1364	Isabel Gobbe [Isabelle]
1364	Joan Grene [Jean]
1364	Rose Nosterfeld
1365–1384	Joan Holland, duchess of Brittany [Jean]
1365–1394	Maria, queen of Hungary [Mary]
1365	Massiota (la Lavendere)
1366–1394	Anne of Bohemia
1366–1405	Coucy (lady de)
1366 d.	Jeanne d'Auxerre [Jean]
1367–1390	Philippa de Coucy
1369–1390	Anne de Many, countess of Pembroke
1369	Dionysia Bottele
1370 fl.	Alexandra Crowe [Alessandra]
1370	Alice Horsford
1370–1380	Alice de Lye
1370–1401	Annabella Drummond, queen of Scotland
1370–1438	Anne of Woodstock
1370–1408	Antonia Daniello
1370–1450	Beatrice d'Estellin
1370 fl.	Katherine of Sutton [Catherine]
1370–1400	Eleanor West
1370 fl.	Elizabeth of Pomerania
1370–1435	Isabeau of Bavaria [Isabelle]
1370–1419	Joan FitzAlan [Jean]
1370–1437	Joan of Navarre, queen of England [Jean]
1370–1400	Margaret of Hainault, duchess of Burgundy
1370 fl.	Margery Russell
1370–1394	Mary de Bohun
1370–1407	Maria de Luna [Mary]
1370–1401	Maria of Sicily [Mary]
1370–1400	Maud Francis [Matilda]
1371	Agnes de Sechelles
1371–1390	Beatrix of Portugal, queen of Castile [Beatrice]
1372–1418	Catherine of Lancaster
1372–1399	Jadwiga of Hungary
1372 d.	Jeanne Dabenton [Jean]
1372 d.	Margaret Neville
1373 d.	Agnes Pickerell
1373–1438	Margery Kempe
1373–1378	Matha d'Armagnac [Martha]
1373–1434	Marie de Berry [Mary]
1374–1435	Leonor of Albuquerque [Eleanor]
1374–1435	Joanna II, queen of Naples [Jean]
1375 fl.	Alice Shether
1375	Gabrina Albetti
1375–1424	Jeanne de Boulogne, duchess of Berry [Jean]
1375–1435	Joan FitzAlan, lady Bergavenny [Jean]
1375	Margaret Stoke
1375–1400	Philippa Mortimer
1376 fl.	Agnes Cook
1376 m.	Bonne de Berry [Bona]
1376	Ellen Sage
1376 fl.	Virdimura of Sicily
1377–1407	Sibilia de Forcia [Sibyl]
1378–1425	Catherine of Burgundy, duchess of Austria

1400–1430 Margot de Hainault
1400–1440 Maud Clifford, countess of Cambridge [Matilda]
1400–1441 Perrine Martin
1400 fl. Teresa de Cartagena [Theresa]

Dates 1401 through 1505:

1401–1416 Bonne of Armagnac [Bona]
1401–1437 Catherine of France, queen of England
1401–1456 Catherine Royer
1401–1436 Jacqueline of Hainault
1401 Jeannette Charles
1401–1458 Maria of Castile [Mary]
1402–1432 Anne of Burgundy, duchess of Bedford
1402 Catherine of Vraba
1404–1450 Catherine de Thouars
1404–1456 Jeanne Paynel [Jean]
1404 d. Marie de Blansy [Mary]
1404 Matilda Maresflete
1405–1440 Barbara of Cilly, Holy Roman Empress
1405–1455 Isabellette of Epinal
1406–1480 Elizabeth Howard, countess of Oxford
1406–1490 Joan Fauconberg [Jean]
1407–1471 Alessandra Strozzi
1408–1425 Parisina Malatesta
1409–1442 Elizabeth of Luxembourg
1409–1451 Margarita de Prades [Margaret]
1410–1476 Agnes of Burgundy, duchess of Bourbon
1410–1450 Agnese del Maino [Agnes]
1410–1420 Aelips de Beauchamp [Alice]
1410–1466 Alix la Bourgolle [Alice]
1410–1468 Alice Drayton
1410 fl. Anna of Mochov [Anne]
1410–1470 Katherine de la Pole [Catherine]
1410 fl. Ginevra (Datini)
1410–1450 Hauviette (of Domremy)
1410–1468 Isabel de Borgia [Isabelle]
1410–1440 Isabel Despenser, countess of Warwick [Isabelle]
1410–1460 Isabel Mowbray, lady Berkeley [Isabelle]
1410–1460 Marie of Anjou [Mary]
1410–1436 Maud Lovell, lady Arundel [Matilda]
1410–1452 Onorata Rodiana
1412–1431 Joan of Arc (St.) [Jean]
1413 Alice (Poplar)
1413–1463 Catherine of Bologna (Caterina dei Vigri)
1414 Jane Harold
1415 fl. Alison la Jourdain
1415 fl. Katherine Dertford [Catherine]
1415 fl. Katherine Dore [Catherine]
1415–1495 Cecily Neville, duchess of York [Cecilia]
1415–1473 Contessina de'Bardi
1415 fl. Margaret of Bavaria
1416–1472 Jacquetta of Luxembourg
1417–1465 Ginevra Nogorola
1418–1440 Ginevra d'Este
1418–1466 Isotta Nogarola
1419 Sara (of Wurzburg) [Sarah]
1420–1450 Agnes Sorel
1420 fl. Alison la Métaille
1420–1460 Anne de Lusignan
1420 Catherine de l'Isle Bouchard
1420–1451 Cecily Neville [Cecilia]
1420 Colette la Moynesse
1420–1464 Elizabeth Say
1420–1440 Helene Kotanner
1420 fl. Isabel of Lorraine [Isabelle]
1420–1460 Jacqueline Machecoue
1420 fl. Jeanne Pouponne [Jean]
1420–1477 Margaret de Botreaux, lady Hungerford
1420–1480 Martha Boretsky
1421–1438 Guiote Serre
1421 Jeannette du Fosse
1421–1434 Or (Madame d')
1421 Perrette la Toutaine
1421 Ysabelet la Blanche
1422–1492 Anne Beauchamp, countess of Warwick
1422–1481 Barbara von Brandenburg
1422 d. Michelle of France
1423–1489 Catherine Percy, countess of Kent
1423–1450 Clemence Sillone
1423 fl. Costanza Calenda [Constance]
1423–1484 Margaret Paston
1424–1468 Bianca Maria Visconti
1424–1460 Blanche of Aragon
1424 m. Isabel Plumpton [Isabelle]
1424–1498 Jeanne Filleul [Jean]
1425–1451 Cecilia Gonzaga
1425–1482 Lucrezia Tornabuoni
1425–1445 Margaret of Scotland

1425	Sedillon Rossignol
1426–1448	Marie of Bourbon [Mary]
1427–1497	Beatrice di Correggio
1427 m.	Leonor of Aragon, queen of Portugal [Eleanor]
1427	Jeannette la Petite
1427–1487	Marie of Cleves [Mary]
1428–1446	Catherine of France
1428–1450	Costanza Varano [Constance]
1428	Serlin
1428–1483	Yolande of Anjou
1429–1456	Eleanor Cobham
1430–1484	Agnes Forster
1430–1460	Antigone (of Gloucester)
1430	Beatrice of Monyons
1430–1476	Clara Hätzerlin [Clare]
1430–1480	Leonor of Aragon, queen of Navarre [Eleanor]
1430–1460	Eleanor Beauchamp, duchess of Somerset
1430–1470	Elizabeth Paston
1430 fl.	Hawise Mone
1430–1470	Illuminato Bembo
1430 fl.	Joan Beaufort, queen of Scotland [Jean]
1430–1482	Margaret of Anjou
1430–1460	Margery Haynes
1430 fl.	Peronne Loessart
1431 d.	Alison Dumay
1431–1470	Isotta degli Atti
1432	Agnese Arizonelli [Agnes]
1433–1480	Eleanor Stuart, duchess of Austria
1433–1467	Margaret Beauchamp, countess of Shrewsbury
1433–1464	Mary of Gelders, queen of Scotland
1434	Henriette de Craus
1434–1478	Yolande de Valois
1435 d.	Agnes Bernauer
1435	Beatrice Sharpe
1435–1468	Eleanor Talbot
1435	Margaret Lindsay
1436	Claude des Armoises
1437–1478	Catherine of Pallanza
1437–1460	Drusiana (Sforza)
1437–1492	Elizabeth Woodville
1438–1461	Agnes Desjardins
1438	Jeanne de Cusey [Jean]
1439–1476	Anne of York, duchess of Exeter
1439–1483	Charlotte of Savoy
1440 fl.	Agnes Broumattin
1440–1487	Charlotte of Lusignan
1440 fl.	Aliénor de Poitiers [Eleanor]
1440–1479	Elizabeth Croke
1440–1470	Elizabeth, lady Scales
1440 fl.	Felise Reynard
1440–1502	Fygen van Berchem
1440 fl.	Henriette la Patriarche
1440 fl.	Huguette du Hamel
1440 fl.	Jehanne de Bretagne [Jean]
1440–1498	Jeanne de Laval [Jean]
1440 fl.	Jehanne Poufille [Jean]
1440–1460	Jeanne Saignant [Jean]
1440 fl.	Marguerite la Bonne Estranée [Margaret]
1440 fl.	Pregente of Melun
1440	Raouline la Malingré
1441	Elizabeth Scolemaystres
1442–1512	Katherine Woodville [Catherine]
1442	Denisette de Periers
1442–1480	Ippolita Sforza
1443–1509	Margaret Beaufort
1444–1503	Elizabeth of York, duchess of Suffolk
1444–1480	Madeleine Valois
1444 d.	Marjery Jourdemain [Margery]
1445 fl.	Alice Henley
1445	Jehanne Gaultière [Jean]
1445 fl.	Jeannette Camus
1445–1518	Vanozza Catanei
1445 fl.	Ysabelle de l'Espine [Ysabel]
1446–1472	Battista Sforza
1446–1503	Margaret of York
1446	Perrette la Hance
1447–1510	Catherine of Genoa
1447–1482	Nannina de'Medici
1448	Jeanne Dupré [Jean]
1448 fl.	Jehanne Lecointe [Jean]
1448–1503	Sophia, princess of Moscow
1449–1467	Dorotea Gonzaga [Dorothy]
1449–1490	Margery Paston
1450–1500	Agrippina of Moscow
1450–1485	Alice Chester
1450 fl.	Anne Shirley
1450 fl.	Antoinette de Villequier
1450–1490	Beatrice of Aragon
1450–1505	Bona of Savoy
1450 fl.	Katherine Husenboltz [Catherine]
1450 fl.	Katherine Rebestoeckyn [Catherine]
1450 fl.	Catherine de Vausselles

1450 fl. Dorothea Hindremstein [Dorothy]
1450–1470 Eleanor Neville, lady Stanley
1250–1500 Elizabeth, lady Abergavenny
1450 d. Elizabeth Stapilton
1450–1480 Elizabeth Talbot
1450 fl. Else of Meersburg
1450 fl. Else von Ortemberg
1450 fl. Guigone de Salins
1450 fl. Guillemette (la tapicière)
1450 fl. Guyette Durand
1450 fl. Isabel, lady Bourchier [Isabelle]
1450–1500 Jane Shore
1450–1494 Jane Stonor
1450 d. Joan Buckland [Jean]
1450 fl. Juana Enriquez, queen of Aragon [Jean]
1450 fl. Jeanne de Milières [Jean]
1450 Kristin (of Iceland)
1450 fl. Lucrezia d'Alagno
1450–1479 Marguerite Joli [Margaret]
1450–1480 Margaret Neville, countess of Oxford
1450 Margot (la Grosse)
1450 fl. Marion la Dentue
1450 fl. Marthe (of Paris) [Martha]
1450 fl. Matilda of Rottenburg
1450 fl. Philippa of Coimbra
1450–1483 Sewis van Berchem
1450–1490 Teodorina (Cibo)
1450–1501 Tryngen Ime Hove
1451–1463 Caterina Caldiera [Catherine]
1451 Catharine Pykring [Catherine]
1451–1504 Isabella, queen of Castile and Aragon [Isabelle]
1451–1476 Isabel Neville [Isabelle]
1451–1488 Mary of Scotland
1452–1470 Margaretha Cartheuserin [Margaret]
1454–1510 Caterina Cornaro, queen of Cyprus [Catherine]
1454–1490 Elizabeth of Austria
1454–1480 Jeanne Laisne [Jean]
1455–1470 Lucrezia Donati
1456–1485 Anne Neville, queen of England
1456–1491 Antonia Uccello
1456 Denise (la sainturière)
1456–1486 Margaret of Norway, queen of Scotland
1456 Ydette of Metz
1457–1482 Marie of Burgundy [Mary]
1457–1493 Marie d'Orléans
1458–1525 Leonor of Lancastre [Eleanor]
1459 Deniselle Grénières
1459–1476 Simonetta Cattaneo
1460–1500 Adriana del Mila
1460–1480 Agnes Butler
1460 fl. Agnes Deyntee
1460 fl. Alison (of Port–Royal)
1460–1522 Anne of Beaujeu
1460 fl. Anne Devereux
1460–1510 Anne Stafford
1460–1480 Casotte Cristal
1460 fl. Katharine Vaux [Catherine]
1460–1493 Leonora of Aragon, duchess of Ferrara [Eleanor]
1460 fl. Elizabeth Higgins
1460–1480 Elizabeth Kirkeby
1460 fl. Elizabeth Lucy
1460–1490 Elisabeth Scepens [Elizabeth]
1460 fl. Joan, lady Beauchamp [Jean]
1460 fl. Juana of Portugal [Jean]
1460–1483 Marguerite de Bourbon [Margaret]
1460 fl. Margaret Rocliffe
1460 Marguerite Saluzzio [Margaret]
1460 d. Margaret Worthham
1460 Perna
1461 Alice Knyvet
1462 m. Charlotte (de Valois)
1462–1530 Juana of Castile [Jean]
1463 Bertrande of Avignon
1463–1509 Catherine Sforza
1463–1510 Katherine Riche [Catherine]
1463–1521 Marguerite of Lorraine [Margaret]
1463 m. Saiv Kavanagh
1464–1505 Jeanne of France, duchess of Orléans [Jean]
1465–1471 Anne Holland
1465–1558 Cassandra Fedele
1465–1503 Chiara Gonzaga
1465–1500 Francesca Bentivoglio
1465 d. Isabelle of Bourbon
1466–1503 Elizabeth of York, queen of England
1467 Denise de Partenay
1468 Alson Potkyn
1468 d. Ambroise de Lore
1468 Beaugrant (Madame de)

COUNTRIES

Women Cross Referenced by Country

AUSTRIA
Agnes Bernauer
Agnes of Dedo
Agnes of Germany
Agnes of Hapsburg, queen of Hungary
Agnes of Meran
Anastasia of Kiev
Ava of Melk
Bianca Maria Sforza
Catherine of Austria
Catherine of Austria
Catherine of Burgundy, duchess of Austria
Kunigunde of Goss [Cunigunde]
Diemuod of Nonnberg [Diemud]
Eleanor Stuart, duchess of Austria
Elizabeth of Austria
Elizabeth of Luxembourg
Gertrude of Babenberg
Gertrud of Merano [Gertrude]
Hedwig of Silesia (St.)
Helene Kotanner
Herrad von Landsberg
Jacoba (of Passau)
Margaret of Austria
Margaret of Babenberg
Margaret of Bavaria
Margaret of Bavaria
Margaret Maultasch
Marie of Burgundy [Mary]
Sabina von Steinbach
Theodora Comnena

BELGIUM
Adelicia of Louvain, queen of England
Anees de Quinkere [Anne]
Beatrice of Nazareth
Blanche of Namur
Bloemardine
Christina of St. Trond [Christine]
Clemence Sillone
Elizabeth of Goerlitz
Elisabeth Scepens [Elizabeth]
Emma of Normandy
Eva of Saint-Martin
Gertrude of Flanders, duchess of Lorraine
Hadewijch
Ida of Nivelles
Ivetta of Huy
Jeanne Pouponne [Jean]
Juliana of Cornillon
Lutgard of Aywières (St.) [Liutgard]
Margaret of Brabant, countess of Flanders
Margaret of Brabant, Holy Roman Empress
Margaret of England, duchess of Brabant
Margaretha van Eyck [Margaret]
Margaret Porete
Marguerite de Ypres [Margaret]
Margaret of Ypres
Mary of Oignies
Philippa of Hainault
Quintine van den Zande

BOHEMIA
Agnes of Bohemia
Agnes de Launcreona
Anne, princess of Bohemia
Anne of Bohemia, queen of England
Anna Harbatova [Anne]
Anna of Mochov [Anne]
Barbara of Cilly, Holy Roman Empress
Blanche of France

BULGARIA

BYZANTIUM

CHINA

CYPRUS

CZECHOSLOVAKIA

DENMARK

Gytha of Denmark
Ingeborg of Denmark, queen of France
Ingeborg of Denmark, queen of Norway
Malfrid of Kiev, queen of Norway, queen of Denmark
Margaret of Denmark
Margaret of Norway, queen of Scotland
Margaret of Sweden, queen of Norway
Mary of Scotland
Philippa of England
Ragnhild of Denmark
Sigrid, queen of Sweden
Thyra of Denmark

ENGLAND

Adelicia of Louvain, queen of England
Aelfgifu
Aelfgifu of Northampton
Aelflaed
Aelfthryth of Wessex
Aethelflaed of Damerham
Aethelflaed, lady of the Mercians
Aethelswith of Wessex, queen of Mercia
Agnes Asser
Agnes Brid
Agnes de Broughton
Agnes Brundyssch
Agnes de Bury
Agnes Butler
Agnes Chaucer
Agnes de Condet
Agnes Cook
Agnes Cook (le Keu)
Agnes Deyntee
Agnes FitzJohn
Agnes Forster
Agnes (of Holbourne)
Agnes atte Holte
Agnes of Huntingdon
Agnes Irlond
Agnes Kateline
Agnes Knetchur
Agnes de Launcreona
Agnes Molton
Agnes de Monceaux
Agnes Mundene
Agnes (of Norfolk)
Agnes Page
Agnes Paston
Agnes Pickerell
Agnes Rokingeham
Agnes Russell
Agnes Sadler
Agnes Sigily
Agnes Thomas
Agnes Wombe
Alexandra Crowe [Alessandra]
Alice Barley
Alice Bokerel
Alice de Bryene
Alice Burle
Alice Cantebrugge
Alice Chaucer, duchess of Suffolk
Alice Chester
Alice de Clare
Alice Denecoumbe
Alice Dexter
Alice Donbely
Alice Drayton
Alys of France [Alice]
Alice atte Harpe
Alice Henley
Alice Horsford
Alice Hulle
Alice Knyvet
Alice Lacy, countess of Lancaster
Alice de Lincoln
Alice de Lye
Alice atte March
Alice Montacute
Alice Montagu, countess of Salisbury
Alice Perrers
Alice (Poplar)
Alice of Rallingbury
Alice Romayn
Alice Seford
Alice Shedyngton
Alice Shether
Alice Stanford
Alice Staundon
Alice (of Stratford)
Alice Tredewedowe
Alice de Wylesdone
Alice la Wymplere (le Wimpler)
Alson Potkyn
Amice de Clare [Amicia]
Amicia of Gloucester
Amicia de Gael, countess of Leicester
Amicia of Leicester
Amice la Plomere [Amicia]
Anastasia Spychefat
Ankarette Twynyho
Anne Beauchamp, countess of Warwick
Anne of Bohemia, queen of England
Anne of Caux
Anne Devereux

Anne Holland
Anne de Many, countess of Pembroke
Anne Mortimer
Anne Mowbray
Anne Neville, duchess of Buckingham
Anne Neville, queen of England
Anna Palmer [Anne]
Anne Paston
Anne Shirley
Anne Stafford
Anne of Woodstock
Anne of York
Anne of York, duchess of Exeter
Annora de Braose
Antigone (of Gloucester)
Aveline de Forz, countess of Aumale
Avice Gardebois
Avice la Wymplere
Avis Wade
Baddlesmere (lady)
Basilia de Clare
Basilia Maderman
Beatrice Bassett
Beatrice Brounying
Beatrice of England
Beatrice of Falkenstein
Beatrice of Portugal
Beatrice Puttock
Beatrice Sharpe
Beatrice de Vesci
Beatrice de Warenne
Beatrice la Welsshe
Berengaria of Navarre, queen of England
Blanche of Artois
Blanche of Lancaster
Blanche, princess of England
Katharine of Aragon [Catherine]
Katherine Boteler [Catherine]
Katherine Dertford [Catherine]
Katherine Dore [Catherine]
Catherine of France, queen of England
Katharine Grandison [Catherine]
Catherine of Lancaster
Katherine Neville [Catherine]
Catherine Percy, countess of Kent
Katherine de la Pole [Catherine]
Catharine Pykring [Catherine]
Katherine Riche [Catherine]
Katherine of Sutton [Catherine]
Katherine Swynford [Catherine]
Katharine Vaux [Catherine]
Katherine Woodville [Catherine]
Cecily Bonville [Cecilia]
Cecilia le Boteler
Cecily Chaumpaigne [Cecilia]
Cecily FitzJohn [Cecilia]
Cecily Neville [Cecilia]
Cecily Neville, duchess of York [Cecilia]
Cecilia Rygeway
Cecily of York [Cecilia]
Childlove (de Worth)
Cristina Blake [Christine]
Cristiana la Flaoners [Christine]
Crystene Houghton [Christine]
Christina (of Hungary) [Christine]
Christina of Markyate [Christine]
Cristina Rokingeham [Christine]
Christine Swath
Clemence of Barking
Constance of Brittany
Constance of Castile, duchess of Lancaster
Constance (FitzGilbert)
Constance of France, countess of Toulouse
Constance of Normandy
Constance of York, countess of Gloucester
Coucy (lady de)
Cwenthryth of Mercia
Cyenthryth, queen of Mercia
Denise la Vileyn
Dionysia Baldewyne
Dionysia Bottele
Dionysia de Mountchesny
Dionisia de Wodemerstham
Dulcia Trye
Eadburg of Mercia
Eadburga of Winchester (St.)
Eadgyfu of England, queen of Burgundy and Provence [Eadgifu]
Eadgifu of England, queen of France
Eadgifu of Kent, queen of England
Eadgifu of Lominster
Eadhild of Wessex
Ealdgyth (of Mercia)
Ebba
Ecgwyna
Edith of England, queen of Germany
Eadgyth (of England) (St.) [Edith]
Edith Paumer
Edith Swan-neck
Edith of Wessex, queen of England
Ela, countess of Salisbury
Eleanor of Aquitaine
Eleanor Beauchamp, duchess of Somerset
Eleanor de Bohun, duchess of Gloucester

Eleanor of Brittany
Eleanor of Castile, queen of England
Eleanor de Clare
Eleanor Cobham
Eleanor of England, countess of Bar
Eleanor of England, countess of Guelders
Eleanor of England, queen of Castile
Eleanor of Lancaster
Eleanor de Montfort, countess of Leicester
Eleanora de Montfort [Eleanor]
Eleanor Neville, lady Lumley
Eleanor Neville, countess of Northumberland
Eleanor Neville, lady Stanley
Eleanor of Provence, queen of England
Eleanor Talbot
Eleanor de Wendale
Eleanor West
Elena Baroun
Elena Taillour
Elisia Hundesdich
Elizabeth, lady Abergavenny
Elizabeth Badlesmere
Elizabeth Berkeley, countess of Warwick
Elizabeth Bourchier
Elizabeth Bryene
Elizabeth de Burgh
Elizabeth de Clare
Elizabeth Croke
Elizabeth, princess of England
Elizabeth Higgins
Elizabeth Holland
Elizabeth Howard, countess of Oxford
Elizabeth Judela
Elizabeth of Kiev
Elizabeth Kirkeby
Elizabeth of Lancaster
Elizabeth Lucy
Elizabeth Moring
Elizabeth Paston
Elizabeth Percy, countess of Westmoreland
Elizabeth Say
Elizabeth, lady Scales
Elizabeth Scolemaystres
Elizabeth, lady Scrope
Elizabeth Stapilton
Elizabeth Stokton
Elizabeth Talbot
Elizabeth Woodville
Elizabeth of York, queen of England
Elizabeth of York, duchess of Suffolk
Ellen Dalok
Ellen Sage
Elen Skolmastre [Ellen]
Emma FitzOsbern, countess of Norfolk
Emma Hatfield
Emma of Normandy
Emma Turk
Ermengarde de Beaumont, queen of Scotland
Euphemia of Wherwell
Galiena (of Norfolk)
Goda la Gablere
Godevere of Töeni
Godgifu (of England)
Godgifu, lady of Mercia
Gundreda (of Warenne)
Gunnhild of Denmark, queen of Germany [Gunhild]
Gunhild of Denmark, queen of Norway
Gunnora de Stratford
Gwenllian (of Wales)
Gyda of England
Gytha of Denmark
Hawise of Gloucester
Hawise Mone
Ida de Portunhale
Idonea
Idonea le Hukestere
Isabelle of Angoulême, queen of England
Isabel Beaumont
Isabel, lady Bourchier [Isabelle]
Isabel of Castile, duchess of York [Isabelle]
Isabella de Clare [Isabelle]
Isabella de Despenser, countess of Arundel [Isabelle]
Isabel Despenser, countess of Warwick [Isabelle]
Isabella of England, countess of Bedford [Isabelle]
Isabella of England, Holy Roman Empress [Isabelle]
Isabella de Fortibus [Isabelle]
Isabella of France, queen of England [Isabelle]
Isabella of France, queen of England [Isabelle]
Isabel Gobbe [Isabelle]
Isabella Hodere [Isabelle]
Isabella Marshall [Isabelle]
Isabel Mowbray, lady Berkeley [Isabelle]
Isabel Neville [Isabelle]
Isabel Norman [Isabelle]
Isabel Plumpton [Isabelle]
Isabelle de Toppesham [Isabelle]

Isabelle de Vescy
Isabel of Vermandois, countess of Leicester [Isabelle]
Jacqueline of Hainault
Jacquetta of Luxembourg
Jane Harold
Jane Shore
Jane Stonor
Joan de Bar, countess of Surrey [Jean]
Joan, lady Beauchamp [Jean]
Johanna Beauflour [Jean]
Joan Beaufort, queen of Scotland [Jean]
Joan Beaufort, countess of Westmoreland [Jean]
Jeanne de Belleville [Jean]
Joan Buckland [Jean]
Joan of England (of Woodstock) [Jean]
Joan of England, countess of Gloucester [Jean]
Joan of England, princess of Gwynedd [Jean]
Joan of England, queen of Scotland [Jean]
Joan of England, queen of Scotland [Jean]
Joanna of England, queen of Sicily [Jean]
Joan Everard [Jean]
Joan Fauconberg [Jean]
Joan FitzAlan [Jean]
Joan FitzAlan, lady Bergavenny [Jean]
Joan de Genville [Jean]
Joan Grene [Jean]
Johanna Hadham [Jean]
Joan Holland, duchess of Brittany [Jean]
Joan Hunt [Jean]
Joan of Kent [Jean]
Joan de la Lee [Jean]
Joan Lenelonde [Jean]
Johanna (of London) [Jean]
Jeanne de Montfort [Jean]
Joan de Munchensi [Jean]
Joan of Navarre, queen of England [Jean]
Joan Pelham [Jean]
Joanna Rowley [Jean]
Johanna Travers [Jean]
Joan Waring [Jean]
Joan la Whycchere [Jean]
Johanna Wolsy [Jean]
Joan Woulbarowe [Jean]
Judith, queen of England
Judith of Flanders
Juliana Berners
Juliana (Bonaventure)
Juliana (Cordwaner)
Juliana Hauteyn
Juliana de Leybourne, countess of Huntingdon
Julian of Norwich [Juliana]
Juliana Roos
Kateline de Coster
Loretta de Braose
Lucia Tasseburgh
Lucy atte Lee
Mabel of Bury St. Edmunds
Mabel Rich
Margaret of Anjou
Margaret de Audley, lady Stafford
Margaret Beauchamp, countess of Shrewsbury
Margaret Beaufort
Margaret de Bohun, countess of Devon
Margaret de Botreaux, lady Hungerford
Margaret de Braose
Margaret de Clare
Margaret Cobbe
Margaret Elyott
Margaret of England (St.)
Margaret of England, duchess of Brabant
Margaret of England, countess of Pembroke
Margaret of England, queen of Scotland
Margaret of France, queen of England
Margaret of France, queen of Hungary
Margaret Holland
Margaret Lacy
Margaret of Leicester
Margaret Lindsay
Margaret Marshall
Margaret Neville
Margaret Neville, countess of Oxford
Margaret Page
Margaret Paston
Margaret Rocliffe
Margaret, queen of Scotland (St.)
Margaret Stoke
Margaret Wake
Margaret Wavere
Margaret Worthham
Margaret of York
Margery Baxter
Margery (of Frocestor)
Margery of Hales
Margerie de Haustede [Margery]
Margery Haynes
Margery de Honylane
Marjery Jourdemain [Margery]
Margery Kempe

Margery Paston
Margery Paston
Margery Russell
Margery Twynyho
Mariota Convers
Mary of Blois
Mary de Bohun
Mary of England
Marie de France [Mary]
Mary Hervey
Mary of St. Pol
Massiota (la Lavendere)
Matilda of Anjou
Matilda of Boulogne, queen of England
Maud de Braose [Matilda]
Matilda de Burgham
Maud Chaworth
Maud Clifford, countess of Cambridge [Matilda]
Matilda of England, duchess of Bavaria
Matilda of England, Holy Roman Empress
Matilda of Flanders
Maud Francis [Matilda]
Matilda of Lancaster
Matilda of Lancaster, duchess of Zealand
Matilda of Leicester
Maud Lovell, lady Arundel [Matilda]
Matilda de Lucy
Maud Makejoy [Matilda]
Matilda Maresflete
Matilda of Northumberland, queen of Scotland
Matilda of Scotland
Maud de Vere, countess of Oxford [Matilda]
Matilda Yonge
Nicola de la Hay [Nichole]
Notekina Hoggenhore
Osburga of Coventry (St.)
Pearl in the Egg
Petronilla of Grandmesnil, countess of Leicester
Petronilla of Teye
Petronilla Turk
Philippa of Clarence
Philippa de Coucy
Philippa of England
Philippa of Hainault
Philippa of Lancaster, queen of Portugal
Philippa Mortimer
Philippa Roet
Richolda
Roesia de Borford
Rosamund Clifford
Rose Nosterfeld
Rose Savage
Sanchia of Provence [Sancia]
Sanche Snoth [Sancia]
Sarra (of Broughton) [Sarah]
Sarah of Meath
Sarah Stroby
Sibilla (of England) [Sibyl]
Sybil de Lacy [Sibyl]
Slymina Fort
Tanglost
Thomasine Dinham
Walgrave (lady)
Wulfhilda of Barking (St.)
Wulfthryth, queen of England (St.)
Wynflaed

FLANDERS

Adela of Flanders, queen of Denmark
Adela of France
Aelfthryth of Wessex
Anees de Quinkere [Anne]
Beatrice of Nazareth
Bloemardine
Bonne de Bourbon, countess of Savoy
Casotte Cristal
Christina of St. Trond [Christine]
Clementia, countess of Flanders
Clemence Sillone [Clementia]
Eleanora of Vermandois
Gertrude of Flanders, duchess of Lorraine
Gertrude of Saxony, countess of Holland
Gundreda (of Warenne)
Hadewijch
Ida of Boulogne
Isabelle of Bourbon
Isabella of Hainault, queen of France [Isabelle]
Isabella of Portugal [Isabelle]
Isabella of Vermandois, countess of Flanders [Isabelle]
Ivetta of Huy
Jacqueline of Hainault
Jeanne de Divion [Jean]
Jeanne of Flanders [Jean]
Jeanne de Montfort [Jean]
Jeanne de Valois, countess of Hainault [Jean]
Judith, queen of England
Judith of Flanders
Kateline de Coster
Lutgard of Aywières (St.) [Liutgard]

Margaret of Alsace
Margaret of Austria
Margaret of Brabant, countess of Flanders
Margaretha van Eyck [Margaret]
Margaret, countess of Flanders
Margaret of Flanders, duchess of Burgundy
Margaret of France, countess of Flanders
Margaret of Hainault, duchess of Burgundy
Margaret of Hainault, Holy Roman Empress
Margaret of York
Margot de Hainault
Mary of Blois
Marie de Brabant, queen of France [Mary]
Marie de Brabant, Holy Roman Empress [Mary]
Marie of Burgundy [Mary]
Marie of Champagne, countess of Flanders [Mary]
Marie of France, duchess of Brabant [Mary]
Matilda of Flanders
Matilda of Hainault, princess of Achaia
Noel (of France)
Or (Madame d')
Philippa of Hainault
Philippa Roet
Quintine van den Zande
Richilde, countess of Flanders
Rozala of Lombardy
Sybille of Anjou, countess of Flanders [Sibyl]
Theresa of Portugal, countess of Flanders

FRANCE

Adelaide of Anjou
Adelaide (Capet), queen of France
Adelaide, queen of France
Adelaide of Maurienne, queen of France
Adelaide de Porcairques
Azalais de Rocamartina [Adelaide]
Adelaide of Roumainmoutier
Adelheid of Savoy [Adelaide]
Adelaide of Toulouse
Adelaide of Tours
Adele, countess of Blois and Chartres
Adele of Champagne, queen of France
Adelie l'Erbière [Adele]
Adela of France [Adele]
Adela of France [Adele]
Adelicia of Louvain, queen of England
Aelips de Beauchamp
Aénor of Châtellerault
Agnes, countess of Aix
Agnes of Anjou
Agnes Avesot
Agnes Broumattin
Agnes of Burgundy, duchess of Bourbon
Agnes Desjardins
Agnes d'Évreux, countess of Montfort
Agnes of France
Agnes of France
Agnes Francou
Agnes d'Harcourt
Agnes of Meran
Agnes of Navarre
Agnes of Poitou, Holy Roman Empress
Agnes de Sechelles
Agnes Sorel
Aalis (la barbière) [Alice]
Alix la Bourgolle [Alice]
Alix of Brittany [Alice]
Alix of Brittany [Alice]
Alix of Champagne, queen of Cyprus [Alice]
Aales (la chandelière) [Alice]
Alice de Clare
Alys of France [Alice]
Alix of France, countess of Blois and Chartres [Alice]
Alice de Montfort
Alice de Montmorency
Alix de Mâcon [Alice]
Aelis (la poissonière) [Alice]
Aaeles (la tapicière) [Alice]
Alix de Vergy, duchess of Burgundy [Alice]
Aalis (l'ymaginière) [Alice]
Alison Dumay
Alison la Jourdain
Alison la Métaille
Alison (la nourrice)
Alison (of Port-Royal)
Almodis (I) of Limoges
Almodis (II) de La Marche, countess of Barcelona
Almodis (III) of Toulouse
Almodis (IV), countess of La Marche
Almucs de Castelnau
Ambroise de Lore
Ameline (la bouchière)
Ameline (la cordoanière)
Ameline (la couturière)
Ameline (la miresse)
Amicia de Gael, countess of Leicester

Anastaise of Paris [Anastasia]
Angele de la Barthe [Angela]
Angelberga
Anne of Beaujeu
Anne of Brittany, queen of France
Anne of Burgundy, duchess of Bedford
Anne of Caux
Anès (la cervoisière) [Anne]
Anne de Châtillon
Anès (la gueinnière) [Anne]
Anne of Kiev
Anne de Lusignan
Anès (la taupière) [Anne]
Anne-Marie de Georgel
Ansgard
Antigone (of Gloucester)
Antoinette de Bellegarde
Antoinette de Villequier
Arlette (of Normandy)
Armande Robert
Ascelinne (la deicière)
Aubrée d'Ivry
Aveline (la barbière)
Aveline (la chapelière)
Aveline (l'estuverresse)
Béatriz (la buffretière) [Beatrice]
Beatrice of Burgundy
Béatrice de Dia
Beatrice of England
Béatrice d'Estellin
Beatrice (of France, duchess of Haute-Lorraine
Bietrix (la metresse) [Beatrice]
Beatrice of Monyons
Beatrice of Planisolles
Beatrice of Provence
Beatrice of Savoy, countess of Provence
Beatrice of Viennois, countess of Albon
Beaugrant (madame de)
Belota (the Jew)
Berengaria of Navarre, queen of England
Berte (la tartrière)
Bertha
Bertha of Avenay
Bertha of Chartres
Bertha of Holland
Bertha de Sens, countess of Vienne
Bertha of Swabia
Bertha of Swabia, duchess of Lorraine
Bertha of Tuscany
Bertha of Tuscany
Bertrade de Montfort, queen of France
Bertrande of Avignon
Bezole
Blanche of Artois
Blanche of Bourbon
Blanche of Burgundy
Blanche of Castile, queen of France
Blanche of France
Blanche of France
Blanche of Laurac
Blanche of Montferrat, duchess of Savoy
Blanche of Navarre
Blanche of Navarre, countess of Champagne
Blanche of Navarre, queen of France
Blanche of Ponthieu
Bonne of Armagnac [Bona]
Bonne of Artois [Bona]
Bonne de Berry [Bona]
Bonne de Bourbon, countess of Savoy [Bona]
Bona of Luxembourg
Bona of Savoy
Bourgot de Noir
Carlotta d'Aragona
Casotte Cristal
Castelloza of Provence
Cateline (of Paris)
Catherine d'Artois
Katerine (l'attachière) [Catherine]
Catherine of Austria
Katherine l'Avise [Catherine]
Catherine de Bruyères
Catherine of Burgundy
Catherine of Burgundy, duchess of Austria
Catherine de Courteney
Catherine Delort
Catherine of France
Catherine of France, queen of England
Catherine de l'Isle Bouchard
Catherine Merceyra
Catherine of Navarre
Catherine de la Rochelle
Catherine Royer
Catherine de Thouars
Catherine de Valois
Catherine de Vausselles
Katharine Vaux [Catherine]
Cecile de Béziers
Cecilia of Flanders
Cecilia of France
Charlotte d'Albret
Charlotte of Savoy
Charlotte (de Valois)
Châtellerault (countess of)

Grazida Lizier
Guigone de Salins
Guillelma de Rosers
Guillemette Benet
Guillemette du Luys
Guillemette (la tapicière)
Guiote Serre
Gundrada
Gunnor (of Denmark)
Guyette Durand
Gytha of Denmark
Haoys (la meresse)
Haouys (la poulaillière)
Hauviette (of Domremy)
Heaulmière (la belle)
Helene de Chambes [Helen]
Hélissent (la ferpière)
Heloise of Argenteuil
Heloys (la miergesse)
Heloys (l'uilière)
Heloyson (la nourrice)
Helvidis
Helwise of Nevers, countess of Évreux
Henriette de Craus
Henriette la Patriarche
Hersende (of Fontevrault)
Hersende (of France)
Hildegard
Hodierne (la cerencerresse)
Huguette Balarin
Huguette du Hamel
Huitace (la lanière)
Ida of Boulogne
Ingeborg of Denmark, queen of France
Isabelle of Angoulême, queen of England
Isabeau (apotiqueresse) [Isabelle]
Isabel of Aragon, princess of France [Isabelle]
Isabeau of Bavaria [Isabelle]
Isabelle of Bourbon
Isabella of England, countess of Bedford [Isabelle]
Isabelle de Ferièves
Isabelle of France
Isabella of France, queen of England [Isabelle]
Isabella of France, queen of England [Isabelle]
Isabelle of France, duchess of Milan
Isabella of France, queen of Navarre [Isabelle]
Isabella of Hainault, queen of France [Isabelle]
Isabel of Lorraine [Isabelle]
Isabelle de Melun
Isabiau (la mergesse) [Isabelle]
Isabel de Montfort [Isabelle]
Isabella of Portugal [Isabelle]
Isabel Romée [Isabelle]
Isabel of Savoy
Isabella of Vermandois, countess of Flanders [Isabelle]
Isabel of Vermandois, countess of Leicester [Isabelle]
Isabelle de Vescy
Isabellette of Épinal
Iseut de Capio
Jacoba Felicie
Jacqueline of Hainault
Jacqueline Machecoue
Jacqueline (la saacière)
Jacquetta of Luxembourg
Jane Stonor
Joan of Arc (St.) [Jean]
Jeanne d'Armagnac
Jeanne d'Artois [Jean]
Jeanne d'Auxerre [Jean]
Joan de Bar, countess of Surrey [Jean]
Jeanne de Belleville [Jean]
Jehanne (la bouchière) [Jean]
Jeanne de Boulogne, duchess of Berry [Jean]
Jeanne de Boulogne, queen of France [Jean]
Jeanne de Bourbon [Jean]
Jeanne de Bourbon, queen of France [Jean]
Jehanne (la boutonnière) [Jean]
Jehanne de Bretagne [Jean]
Jehanne de Brigue [Jean]
Jeanne of Burgundy, queen of France [Jean]
Jeanne of Burgundy, queen of France [Jean]
Jeanne Clarisse [Jean]
Jeanne "Conversa" [Jean]
Jeanne de Crespi [Jean]
Jehanne (la cristalière) [Jean]
Jeanne de Cusey [Jean]
Jeanne Dabenton [Jean]
Jeanne de Dammartin, queen of Castile [Jean]
Jeanne de Divion [Jean]
Jeanne Dupré [Jean]
Joan of England, queen of Scotland [Jean]
Joan of England, queen of Scotland [Jean]

Joanna of England, queen of Sicily [Jean]
Jeanne d'Évreux, queen of France [Jean]
Jeanne Filleul [Jean]
Jehanne (la fouacière) [Jean]
Jeanne of France, duchess of Brittany [Jean]
Jeanne of France, queen of Navarre [Jean]
Jeanne of France, duchess of Orléans [Jean]
Jehanne Gaultière [Jean]
Joan Hart [Jean]
Joan Holland, duchess of Brittany [Jean]
Jeanne Laisne [Jean]
Jeanne de Latilly [Jean]
Jeanne de Laval [Jean]
Jehanne Lecointe [Jean]
Jehanne (la loirrière) [Jean]
Juana Manuel, queen of Castile [Jean]
Jeanne de Milières [Jean]
Jeanne de Montfort [Jean]
Joan of Navarre, queen of England [Jean]
Jeanne of Navarre, queen of France [Jean]
Jeanne Paynel [Jean]
Jeanne de Penthièvre [Jean]
Jeanne Potier [Jean]
Jehanne Poufille [Jean]
Jeanne Saignant [Jean]
Jehanne (la tapicière) [Jean]
Jeanne of Toulouse [Jean]
Jeanne de Valois [Jean]
Jeanne de Valois, countess of Hainault [Jean]
Jehanne (la verrière) [Jean]
Jeanne Villain [Jean]
Jeannette Camus
Jeannette du Fossé
Jeannette la Petite
Jourdenete (la nourrice)
Judith of Bavaria, Holy Roman Empress
Judith, queen of England
Juliane (la potière) [Juliana]
Laura
Laurette de Saint-Valéry
Lesceline, countess of Eu
Liutgard of Germany
Liutgard of Vermandois
Loba de Pueinautier
Lombarda
Louise of Savoy
Lucienne of Rochefort
Mabel of Bellême
Mabile (la regratière)
Macete de Ruilly
Madeleine Valois
Mahaut of Artois
Mahaut de Brabant
Maheut (la chapelière) [Mahaut]
Maheut (la feutrière) [Mahaut]
Mahaut de Châtillon
Maheut (la pescheresse) [Mahaut]
Margaret of Anjou
Margaret of Austria
Marguerite (l'avenière) [Margaret]
Marguerite (la barbière) [Margaret]
Margaret of Bavaria
Marguerite la Bonne Estranée [Margaret]
Marguerite de Bourbon [Margaret]
Marguerite de Bourbon, queen of Navarre [Margaret]
Margaret de Braose
Margaret of Burgundy
Margaret of Burgundy
Marguerite (la chanevacière) [Margaret]
Marguerite de Clisson [Margaret]
Marguerite (la cordière) [Margaret]
Margaret of England (St.)
Margaret of Flanders, duchess of Burgundy
Margaret of France, queen of England
Margaret of France, countess of Flanders
Margaret of France, queen of Hungary
Margaret of Hainault, duchess of Burgundy
Marguerite Joli [Margaret]
Marguerite of Lorraine [Margaret]
Margaret of Maine
Marguerite d'Oingt [Margaret]
Marguerite of Provence, queen of France [Margaret]
Margarida de Roussillon [Margaret]
Marguerite (la savonnière) [Margaret]
Margaret of Scotland
Marguerite de Turenne [Margaret]
Margaret of York
Marguerite de Ypres [Margaret]
Margery (of Calais)
Margot de la Barre
Margot (la gantière)
Margot (la Grosse)
Margot de Hainault
Margot Pipelarde
Marion la Dentue
Marote (de Douai)
Matha d'Armagnac [Martha]
Martha (of Paris)
Martha (of Paris)
Marie of Anjou [Mary]

Marie d'Atainville [Mary]
Marie d'Avignon [Mary]
Marie (la barbière) [Mary]
Marie de Berry [Mary]
Barie de Blansy [Mary]
Mary of Blois
Marie of Bohemia [Mary]
Marie of Bourbon [Mary]
Marie de Brabant, queen of France [Mary]
Marie de Brabant, Holy Roman Empress [Mary]
Marie of Brittany, duchess of Anjou [Mary]
Marie of Burgundy [Mary]
Marie of Champagne, countess of Flanders [Mary]
Marie of Cleves [Mary]
Marie de Coucy, queen of Scotland [Mary]
Mary of England
Marie (la fanière) [Mary]
Marie de France [Mary]
Marie of France, duchess of Brabant [Mary]
Marie of France, countess of Champagne [Mary]
Marie (la mareschale) [Mary]
Marie (la meresse) [Mary]
Marie of Montpellier [Mary]
Marie d'Orléans [Mary]
Marie, countess of Ponthieu and Aumale [Mary]
Mary of St. Pol
Mary of Scotland, countess of Boulogne
Marie of Valois [Mary]
Marie de Ventadour [Mary]
Matheline Fauré
Matilda of Anjou
Matilda of Boulogne, queen of England
Matilda of Boulogne, queen of Portugal
Maud de Braose [Matilda]
Matilda of England, Holy Roman Empress
Matilda of Flanders
Matilda of France
Maud Lovell, lady Arundel [Matilda]
Matilda of Northumberland, queen of Scotland
Maura of Troyes (St.)
Mengarde Buscalh
Michelle of France
Michiele (la ventrière)
Milessent (la cerenceresse)
Nicole (la boursière) [Nichole]
Nicole (l'erbière) [Nichole]
Nicole (l'esperonnière) [Nichole]
Nicole (la saunière) [Nichole]
Noel (of France)
Northilda
Odeline
Odette de Champdivers
Or (madame d')
Paule Viguier
Pentecouste (la fruitière)
Peronne Loessart
Perrette la Hance
Perrette la Maugarnie
Peretta Peronne [Perrette]
Perrette la Toutaine
Perrine Martin
Péronnelle d'Armentières [Pérronelle]
Pérronnele (l'espicière) [Pérronelle]
Pérronnele (la lavendière) [Pérronelle]
Pérronele (la nourrice [Pérronelle]
Petronilla of Aquitaine, countess of Vermandois
Petronille of Comminges
Petronille of Fontevrault
Phelipote (la fritière)
Philippa of Champagne
Philippa de Coucy
Philippa de Dammartin
Phelippe (la miergesse) [Philippa]
Philippe de Moncada [Philippa]
Phillippia, countess of Poitou [Philippa]
Philippine de Porcellet
Pierrille Roland
Poncette Aubry
Pregente of Melun
Prous Bonetta
Raouline la Malingré
Richeut (la meresse)
Richilde of Autun
Roiantken
Rothild of Chelles
Rotrude
Roza
Rozala of Lombardy
Sainte (la paintre)
Sanchia of Provence [Sancia]
Sarre (la mirgesse) [Sarah]
Sara of Saint-Gilles [Sarah]
Sedile (la fournière)
Sedillon Rossignol
Sersive la Berangière
Sybille of Anjou, countess of Flanders [Sibyl]
Sybille de Château-Porcien [Sibyl]
Sybil of Conversano [Sibyl]

Susane (la coiffière)
Theutberga, queen of Lotharingia
Thomasse (la talemelière)
Tibors d'Omelas
Typhainne (la blazennière) [Tiffania]
Tyfainne (mestresse de l'école) [Tiffania]
Tiphaine Raguel [Tiffania]
Thyphainne (la toière) [Tiffania]
Valentine Visconti, duchess of Orléans
Waldrada
Waldrada (of Arles)
Ydain of Lorraine
Yolande of Anjou
Yolande of Aragon
Yolande de Dreux
Yolande de Dreux, queen of Scotland
Yoland de Valois
Ysabel (la commanderesse)
Ysabelle de l'Espine [Ysabel]
Ysabiau (la ferpière) [Ysabel]
Ysabel de la Heuse
Ysabel (la meresse)
Ysabiau (la nourrice) [Ysabel]
Zabelia

GERMANY

Adelheid of Burgundy, Holy Roman Empress [Adelaide]
Adelheid of Germany, abbess of Quedlinburg [Adelaide]
Adelheid of Savoy [Adelaide]
Adelheid of Vohburg [Adelaide]
Agnes Bernauer
Agnes Broumattin
Agnes of Dedo
Agnes of Germany
Agnes of Hapsburg, queen of Hungary
Agnes of Meissen
Agnes of Poitou, Holy Roman Empress
Agnes of Saarbrücken
Agnes von Staufen
Angelberga
Anne, princess of Bohemia
Barbara von Brandenburg
Barbara of Cilly, Holy Roman Empress
Barbara Gwichtmacherin
Beatrice of Burgundy
Beatrice of Falkenstein
Beatrice (of France), duchess of Haute-Lorraine
Beatrice of Swabia, queen of Castile
Beatrice of Viennois, countess of Albon
Bertha of Sulzbach
Bertha of Susa
Bertha of Swabia
Bertha of Swabia, duchess of Lorraine
Bertheida
Bianca Maria Sforza
Blanche, princess of England
Brunetta
Katherine Husenboltz [Catherine]
Katherine Rebestoeckyn [Catherine]
Christina (of Gandersheim)
Christina of Stommeln [Christine]
Clara Gatterstedt [Clare]
Clara Hätzerlin [Clare]
Claricia of Augsburg
Clementia of Zähringen
Constance of Aragon, queen of Hungary
Constance of Hohenstaufen
Constance of Sicily, Holy Roman Empress
Cunigund of Luxembourg, Holy Roman Empress (St.) [Cunigunde]
Kunigunda of Nuremberg [Cunigunde]
Cunegunde of Swabia [Cunigunde]
Cunigunda of Swabia, queen of Bohemia [Cunigunde]
Diemud of Wessobrun
Diemudis of Wessobrun [Diemud]
Doda
Dorothy of Montau
Eadburg of Mercia
Edith of England, queen of Germany
Eilika of Saxony
Elizabeth of Austria
Elizabeth of Bohemia
Elizabeth of Goerlitz
Elizabeth of Hungary (St.)
Elizabeth of Pomerania
Elizabeth of Schönau (St.)
Else von Ortemberg
Emma, queen of Germany
Ermengarde, Holy Roman Empress
Ermengard (of Italy), Holy Roman Empress (Ermengarde)
Ermengard, duchess of Lombardy, queen of Provence (Ermengarde)
Ermengarde (of St. Adrian)
Euphemia of Arnstein, queen of Norway
Eufemia (of Mecklenburg) [Euphemia]
Eupraxia of Kiev, Holy Roman Empress
Friderun (of Germany)
Fygen van Berchem
Gerberga of Bavaria
Gerberga of Saxony, queen of France
Gertrude of Babenberg

Gertrude of Bavaria
Gertrude of Hackeborn
Gertrude von Helfta
Gertrude of Meissen
Gertrud of Merano (Gertrude)
Gertrude of Saxony, duchess of Bavaria
Gertrude of Saxony, countess of Holland
Gisela
Gisela of Bavaria, queen of Hungary
Gisela of Kerzenbroeck
Gisela of Swabia, queen of Germany
Godila (of Walbeck)
Guda (of Germany)
Gunnhild of Denmark, queen of Germany
Hatheburg
Hathui (of Germany)
Hathumoda of Gandersheim
Hedwig of Bavaria
Hedwig of Silesia (St.)
Herrad von Landsberg
Hildegard
Hildegarde of Bingen (St.)
Hroswitha of Gandersheim
Ida of Boulogne
Ida of Swabia
Imma of Saxony
Ingeltrude
Irene Angela, Holy Roman Empress
Isabeau of Bavaria [Isabelle]
Isabella of England, Holy Roman Empress [Isabelle]
Judith, duchess of Bavaria
Judith of Bavaria, Holy Roman Empress
Judith of Bavaria, duchess of Swabia
Judith of Flanders
Judith (of Germany)
Judith of Schweinfurt
Jutta of Sponheim
Liutberga (St.)
Liutgard of Germany
Margaret of Babenberg
Margaret of Bavaria
Margaret of Bavaria
Margaret of Brabant, Holy Roman Empress
Margaretha Cartheuserin [Margaret]
Margaret Ebner
Margaret of Hainault, duchess of Burgundy
Margaret of Hainault, Holy Roman Empress
Margaret Maultasch
Marguerite of Naples [Margaret]
Marguerite Scheppers [Margaret]
Margaret (of Sicily)
Marie de Brabant, Holy Roman Empress [Mary]
Maria, queen of Hungary [Mary]
Matilda of England, duchess of Bavaria
Matilda of England, Holy Roman Empress
Matilda of Essen
Matilda, queen of Germany
Matilda of Quedlinburg
Matilda of Rottenburg
Mechtild von Hackeborn
Mechtild of Magdeburg
Oda
Relindis of Hohenburg
Richardis
Richardis von Stade
Richenza of Nordheim, Holy Roman Empress
Richilde of Autun
Rotrude
Sabina von Steinbach
Sara (of Wurzburg) [Sarah]
Serlin
Sewis van Berchem
Sibylla of Acerra [Sibyl]
Sophia of Gandersheim
Svanhild of Essen
Taddea Visconti
Tenxwind of Andernach
Theoda of Mainz
Theophano of Byzantium, Holy Roman Empress
Theutberga, queen of Lotharingia
Tryngen Ime Hove
Ulricha de Foschua
Uta of Niedermünster
Waldrada
Waldrada (of Arles)
Wulfhild of Saxony
Ydette of Metz
Yolande (of Jerusalem), Holy Roman Empress

GREECE

Catherine de Valois
Charlotte of Lusignan
Constance of Hohenstaufen
Irene, empress of Byzantium
Irene Lascaris, empress of Byzantium
Isabel of Achaia
Matilda of Hainault
Morphia of Melitene
Theodora, empress of Byzantium

GREENLAND
Gudrid (of Greenland)

HUNGARY
Agatha (of Hungary)
Agnes of Hapsburg, queen of Hungary
Anastasia of Kiev
Anne de Châtillon
Barbara of Cilly, Holy Roman Empress
Beatrice of Aragon
Christina (of Hungary) [Christine]
Clemence of Hungary
Constance of Aragon, queen of Hungary
Constance (of Hungary)
Kunigunda of Hungary [Cunigunde]
Elizabeth of Bosnia
Elizabeth of Hungary (St.)
Elizabeth of Luxembourg
Elizabeth of Poland, queen of Hungary
Evfimia of Kiev [Euphemia]
Gertrud of Merano [Gertrude]
Gisela of Bavaria, queen of Hungary
Helene Kotanner
Jadwiga of Hungary
Judith (of Germany)
Margaret of France, queen of Hungary
Margaret of Hungary
Margaret, queen of Scotland (St.)
Maria, queen of Hungary [Mary]
Yolande of Hungary, queen of Aragon

ICELAND
Aud "the Deep-minded"
Freydis of Norway
Gudrid (of Greenland)
Ingunn (of Iceland)
Kristin (of Iceland)

IRELAND
Affreca of Man, countess of Ulster
Alice Kyteler
Anne Mortimer
Annota Lange
Aud "the Deep-minded"
Basilia de Clare
Cecily Neville, duchess of York [Cecilia]
Dervorgilla (O'Ruairc)
Elizabeth de Burgh
Elizabeth de Burgo, queen of Scotland
Elizabeth de Clare
Elizabeth le Veel
Eva of Brounestown
Eva MacMurrough
Gormflath (of Ireland)
Helen Galrussyn
Isabella de Clare [Isabelle]
Joan de Genville [Jean]
Maud de Brose [Matilda]
Ota (of Norway)
Petronilla of Meath
Rose O'Connor
Saiv Kavanagh
Sarah of Meath
Syssoh Galrussyn

ISRAEL
Adelaide of Savona
Agnes of Courtenay
Alice of Jerusalem, princess of Antioch
Catherine de Courteney
Hodierna of Jerusalem
Isabella of Jerusalem [Isabelle]
Maria Comnena, queen of Jerusalem [Mary]
Mélisende, queen of Jerusalem
Morphia of Melitene
Philippa of Champagne
Sibylla of Jerusalem [Sibyl]
Theodora Comnena, queen of Jerusalem
Yolande (of Jerusalem), Holy Roman Empress

ITALY
Abella of Salerno
Adelheid of Burgundy, Holy Roman Empress [Adelaide]
Adelaide of Savona
Adelheid of Savoy [Adelaide]
Adelasia of Torres, queen of Sardinia
Adriana del Mila
Ageltrudis (of Spoleto)
Agnese Arizonelli [Agnes]
Agnes of Hapsburg, queen of Hungary
Agnese del Maino [Agnes]
Agnes of Meran
Agnes da Montepulciano (St.)
Agnes of Poitou, Holy Roman Empress
Alberada of Buonalbergo
Alda of Arles
Alesandra Gilani [Alessandra]
Alessandra Strozzi
Alfonsina Orsini
Amalberga
Angela Borgia

Angela of Foligno
Angela Merici (St.)
Angela Nogarola
Angelberga
Angelica del Lama
Anne de Lusignan
Anne of Savoy, empress of Byzantium
Anna Sforza [Anne]
Antonia Daniello
Antonia Uccello
Barbara Arrenti
Barbara von Brandenburg
Barbera Ragnoni [Barbara]
Battista da Montefeltro
Battista Sforza
Beatrice of Aragon
Beatrice Candia
Beatrice di Correggio
Beatrice d'Este
Beatriz Galindo [Beatrice]
Beatrice Portinari
Beatrice of Provence
Beatrice of Rethel, queen of Sicily
Beatrice, marchioness of Tuscany
Bertha of Avenay
Bertha of Italy
Bertha of Susa
Bertha of Tuscany
Bertha of Tuscany
Bertilla
Bethlem of Greci
Bianca of Savoy
Bianca Giovanna Sforza
Bianca Maria Sforza
Bianca Maria Visconti
Blanche of Anjou, queen of Aragon
Blanche of Montferrat, duchess of Savoy
Blanche of Navarre
Bonne de Berry [Bona]
Bonne de Bourbon, countess of Savoy [Bona]
Bona of Savoy
Bridget of Sweden (St.)
Carlotta d'Aragona
Cassandra Fedele
Catherine of Austria
Catherine of Bologna
Caterina Caldiera [Catherine]
Caterina Cornaro, queen of Cyprus [Catherine]
Catherine de Courteney
Caterina of Florence [Catherine]
Catherine of Genoa
Catherine of Pallanza
Catherine of Sebastopol
Catherine Sforza
Catherine of Siena (St.)
Catherine de Valois
Caterina Visconti [Catherine]
Cavolaja of Florence
Cecilia Gallerani
Cecilia Gonzaga
Cecile de Turenne [Cecilia]
Charlotte of Lusignan
Charlotte of Savoy
Chiara Gonzaga
Christine de Pisan
Clare of Assisi
Clare of Montefalco (St.)
Clarissa Orsini [Claricia]
Constance, queen of Aragon
Constance of Aragon, queen of Hungary
Costanza of Aragon, queen of Sicily
Costanza Calenda [Constance]
Constance of Hohenstaufen
Constance of Sicily, Holy Roman Empress
Costanza Varano [Constance]
Contessina de'Bardi
Delphine of Languedoc
Donella of Bologne
Dorotea Bocchi [Dorothy]
Dorotea Caracciolo [Dorothy]
Dorotea Gonzaga [Dorothy]
Drusiana (Sforza)
Eadburg of Mercia
Leonora of Aragon, duchess of Ferrara [Eleanor]
Eleanora di Arborea [Eleanor]
Leonor of Sicily, queen of Aragon [Eleanor]
Elisabetta Gonzaga [Elizabeth]
Elvira of Castile, queen of Sicily
Emilia Pia
Emma (of Apulia)
Emma of Italy, queen of France
Ermengard (of Italy), Holy Roman Empress [Ermengarde]
Ermengarde (of Ivrea)
Ermengard, duchess of Lombardy, queen of Provence [Ermengarde]
Ermengard (of S. Salvatore)
Eupraxia of Kiev, Holy Roman Empress
Fiametta
Fiametta Adimari
Frances of Rome (St.)
Francesca Bentivoglio

Francesca da Rimini
Francesca de Romana
Fressenda (de Hauteville)
Gabrina Albetti
Ginevra (Datini)
Ginevra d'Este
Ginevra Nogarola
Gisela (of France)
Guglielma (of Milan)
Guilia Farnese
Gunnhild of Denmark, queen of Germany
Helena (Guiscard) [Helen]
Illuminato Bembo
Ingeltrude
Ippolita Sforza
Irene Angela, Holy Roman Empress
Isabella of Aragon, duchess of Milan [Isabelle]
Isabella of England, Holy Roman Empress [Isabelle]
Isabella d'Este [Isabelle]
Isabelle of France, duchess of Milan
Isabel of Lorraine [Isabelle]
Isotta degli Atti
Isotta Nogarola
Jacoba (of Passau)
Jacobina (medica)
Joanna of Aragon, queen of Naples [Jean]
Joanna of England, queen of Sicily [Jean]
Jeanne de Laval [Jean]
Joanna I, queen of Naples [Jean]
Joanna II, queen of Naples [Jean]
Judith of Évreux
Juliana Falconieri (St.)
Laura Cereta
Leonetta (medica)
Lisa Strozzi
Lucia Brocadelli
Lucia Marliani
Lucrezia d'Alagno
Lucrezia Borgia
Lucrezia Crivelli
Lucrezia Donati
Lucrezia d'Este
Lucrezia de'Medici
Lucrezia Tornabuoni
Maddalena Bonsignori [Madeleine]
Maddalena de'Medici [Madeleine]
Maddalena Scrovegni [Madeleine]
Margherita [Margaret]
Margaret Aldobrandeschi
Margaret of Bavaria
Margaret of Brabant, Holy Roman Empress
Margaret of Citta di Castello
Margaret of Cortona (St.)
Margherita Datini [Margaret]
Marguerite of Naples [Margaret]
Margaret of Navarre, queen of Sicily
Marguerite Saluzzio [Margaret]
Margaret (of Sicily)
Margherita di Trento
Marie of Brittany, duchess of Anjou [Mary]
Maria (la medica) [Mary]
Marie of Montpellier [Mary]
Maria of Sicily [Mary]
Marie of Valois [Mary]
Marozia of Rome
Matilda of Hainault, princess of Achaia
Matilda of Sicily, countess of Alife
Matilda of Tuscany
Mayfreda de Pirovano
Mercuriade of Salerno
Nannina de'Medici
Novella d'Andrea
Onorata Rodiana
Otta of S. Salvatore
Parisina Malatesta
Perna
Pierina de Bugatis
Rebecca Guarna
Regina della Scala
Richenza of Nordheim, Holy Roman Empress
Rosalia of Palermo (St.)
Rose of Viterbo (St.)
Roza
Rozala of Lombardy
Sancia d'Aragona
Sancia of Majorca
Sibylle of Acerra [Sibyl]
Sibillina Biscossi [Sibyl]
Sybil of Conversano [Sibyl]
Sichelgaita of Salerno
Simonetta Cattaneo
Sophia, princess of Moscow
Stephania (of Rome)
Taddea Visconti
Teodorina (Cibo)
Theodora of Rome
Trotula of Salerno
Umiliana dei Cherchi (St.)
Umilita of Faenza
Valentine Visconti, queen of Cyprus
Valentine Visconti, duchess of Orléans

Vanozza Catanei
Violante Visconti
Virdimura of Sicily
Waldrada (of Arles)
Willa
Willa of Tuscany, queen of Italy
Yolande of Aragon
Yolande (of Jerusalem), Holy Roman Empress
Yolande of Montferrat
Zita of Lucca (St.)

LEBANON

Cecilia of France
Hodierna of Jerusalem
Isabella of Jerusalem [Isabelle]

LITHUANIA

Elena of Moscow
Jadwiga of Hungary

LUXEMBOURG

Bona of Luxembourg
Cunigund of Luxembourg, Holy Roman Empress (St.) [Cunigunde]
Elizabeth of Bohemia
Elizabeth of Goerlitz
Elizabeth of Luxembourg
Elizabeth of Pomerania
Jacquetta of Luxembourg
Margaret of Brabant, Holy Roman Empress
Marie of Bohemia [Mary]

NETHERLANDS

Ada of Scotland, countess of Holland
Beatrice of Nazareth
Bertha of Holland
Eleanor of England, countess of Guelders
Eleanora of Vermandois
Elizabeth, princess of England
Elizabeth of Goerlitz
Gertrude van Öosten
Gertrude of Saxony, countess of Holland
Ida of Boulogne
Isabelle of Achaia
Jacqueline of Hainault
Jeanne de Valois, countess of Hainault [Jean]
Lydwine of Schiedam
Margaret of Alsace
Margaret of Austria
Margaret of Hainault, Holy Roman Empress
Mary of Gelders, queen of Scotland
Matilda of Lancaster, duchess of Zealand
Philippa de Dammartin
Philippa of Hainault
Richilde, countess of Flanders

NORWAY

Aasta Grönske
Aelfgifu of Northampton
Asa, queen of Agdir
Astrid of Norway
Astrid of Sweden
Blanche of Namur
Christina of Norway [Christine]
Elizabeth of Kiev
Euphemia of Arnstein, queen of Norway
Freydis of Norway
Gudrid (of Greenland)
Gunhild of Denmark, queen of Norway
Ingeborg of Denmark, queen of Norway
Ingebjorg of Norway [Ingeborg]
Ingeborg of Norway
Ingibiorg, queen of Scotland [Ingeborg]
Ingerid of Sweden
Isabella Bruce [Isabelle]
Malfrid of Kiev, queen of Norway, queen of Denmark
Margaret of Denmark
Margaret, queen of Norway
Margaret, "the Maid of Norway"
Margaret of Norway, queen of Scotland
Margaret of Scotland, queen of Norway
Margaret of Sweden, queen of Norway
Margaret of Sweden, queen of Norway
Ota (of Norway)
Philippa of England
Ragnhild of Denmark
Ragnhild (of Ringerike)
Thora of Norway
Thyra of Denmark

POLAND

Anne, princess of Bohemia
Dubravka of Bohemia
Elena of Moscow
Elizabeth of Austria
Elizabeth of Bosnia
Elizabeth of Luxembourg
Elizabeth of Poland, queen of Hungary
Elizabeth of Pomerania
Hedwig of Silesia (St.)

PORTUGAL

RUSSIA

SCOTLAND

Matilda of Northumberland, queen of Scotland
Matilda of Scotland
Sibilla (of England) [Sibyl]
Strathearn (countess of)
Yolande de Dreux, queen of Scotland

SPAIN

Agnes, countess of Aix
Agnes of Navarre
Aurembaix, countess of Urgel
Beatrice of Aragon
Beatrice of Castile
Beatrice of Castile, queen of Portugal
Beatriz Galindo [Beatrice]
Beatrice de Guzman
Beatrix of Portugal, queen of Castile [Beatrice]
Beatrice of Swabia, queen of Castile
Berengaria of Navarre, queen of England
Berenguela of Castile
Blanche of Anjou, queen of Aragon
Blanche of Aragon
Blanche of Artois
Blanche of Bourbon
Blanche of Castile, queen of France
Blanche of France
Blanche of Navarre
Blanche of Navarre, countess of Champagne
Katharine of Aragon [Catherine]
Catherine of Lancaster
Catherine of Navarre
Constance, queen of Aragon
Constance of Aragon, queen of Hungary
Costanza of Aragon, queen of Sicily [Constance]
Constance of Castile, queen of France
Constance of Castile, duchess of Lancaster
Constance of France, queen of Castile
Constance of Hohenstaufen
Douce (II) of Barcelona
Douce (III) of Provence
Leonor of Albuquerque [Eleanor]
Leonor of Aragon, queen of Castile [Eleanor]
Leonor of Aragon, queen of Navarre [Eleanor]
Leonor of Aragon, queen of Portugal [Eleanor]
Leonor of Aragon, countess of Toulouse [Eleanor]
Leonor of Castile, queen of Aragon [Eleanor]
Leonor of Castile, queen of Aragon [Eleanor]
Eleanor of Castile, queen of England
Leonor of Castile, queen of Navarre [Eleanor]
Eleanor of England, queen of Castile
Leonor de Guzman [Eleanor]
Leonor Lopez [Eleanor]
Leonor of Portugal, queen of Aragon [Eleanor]
Leonor of Sicily, queen of Aragon [Eleanor]
Elisenda de Moncada, queen of Aragon
Elizabeth of Portugal (St.)
Elvira of Castile
Elvira of Castile, queen of Sicily
Elvira of Leon
Ende
Ermessend of Carcassonne, countess of Barcelona
Esclarmunda de Foix, queen of Majorca
Florencia Pinar
Ines de Castro
Isabel of Aragon, princess of France [Isabelle]
Isabella of Aragon, queen of Portugal [Isabelle]
Isabel de Borgia [Isabelle]
Isabella, queen of Castile and Aragon [Isabelle]
Isabel of Castile, duchess of York [Isabelle]
Isabella of France, queen of Navarre [Isabelle]
Juana of Aragon, queen of Castile [Jean]
Joanna of Aragon, queen of Naples [Jean]
Juana of Castile [Jean]
Jeanne de Dammartin, queen of Castile [Jean]
Juana Enriquez, queen of Aragon [Jean]
Jeanne of France, queen of Navarre [Jean]
Juana Manuel, queen of Castile [Jean]
Joan of Navarre, queen of England [Jean]
Juana of Portugal [Jean]
Margaret of Austria
Marguerite de Bourbon, queen of Navarre [Margaret]
Margaret of Navarre, queen of Sicily
Margarita de Prades [Margaret]
Matha d'Armagnac (Martha)
Maria of Aragon, queen of Portugal [Mary]

Maria of Castile [Mary]
Maria Enriquez [Mary]
Maria de Luna [Mary]
Maria de Malla [Mary]
Maria de Molina [Mary]
Marie of Montpellier [Mary]
Marie of Navarre [Mary]
Maria Padilla [Mary]
Maria of Portugal [Mary]
Maria of Sicily [Mary]
Maria of Vivar [Mary]
Petronilla, queen of Aragon
Petronille of Comminges
Phillippia, countess of Poitou [Philippa]
Sancha of Castile [Sancia]
Sancha, queen of Leon and Castile [Sancia]
Sancia of Majorca
Sibilia de Forcia [Sibyl]
Subh of Cordoba
Tarub (of Cordoba)
Teresa de Cartagena [Theresa]
Theresa of Castile
Teresa de Entenza [Theresa]
Theresa of Portugal, queen of Leon (St.)
Toda, queen of Navarre
Urraca, queen of Castile
Urraca of Castile, queen of Portugal
Urraca Gonzalez
Urraca of Portugal
Ximena Diaz
Ximena, queen of Leon
Yolande of Aragon
Yolande of Hungary, queen of Aragon
Zaida of Seville

SWEDEN

Astrid of Sweden
Blanche of Namur
Bridget of Sweden (St.)
Catherine of Sweden (St.)
Christina of Sweden [Christine]
Eufemia (of Mecklenburg) [Euphemia]
Ingebjorg of Norway [Ingeborg]
Ingeborg of Norway
Ingegarde of Sweden
Ingerid of Sweden
Margaret of Denmark
Margaret of Sweden, queen of Norway
Margaret of Sweden, queen of Norway
Philippa of England
Sigrid, queen of Sweden
Thyra of Denmark

SWITZERLAND

Angelberga
Anne de Lusignan
Bonne de Bourbon, countess of Savoy
Cornelie van Wulfskerke
Dorothea Hindremstein
Else of Meersburg
Jeannette Charles
Marguerite Scheppers [Margaret]
Theutberga, queen of Lotharingia

TURKEY

Agnes of Courtenay
Agnes of France
Alice of Jerusalem, princess of Antioch
Anne de Châtillon
Cecilia of France
Constance of Antioch
Constance of France
Constance of Hohenstaufen
Emma FitzOsbern, countess of Norfolk
Irene Lascaris, empress of Byzantium
Philippa of Antioch

WALES

Anne Stafford
Basilia de Clare
Ealdgyth (of Merica)
Eleanora de Montfort [Eleanor]
Elizabeth, princess of England
Gwenllian (of Wales)
Gwenllian (of Wales)
Isabella de Fortibus [Isabelle]
Joan of England, princess of Gwynedd [Jean]
Maud de Braose [Matilda]
Myfanwy (Tudor)
Nesta

BIOGRAPHICAL CATEGORIES

ABBESSES

includes prioresses, superiors, etc.

Adelheid of Germany, abbess of Quedlinburg [Adelaide]
Adelaide of Roumainmoutier
Agnes, countess of Aix
Agnes Desjardins
Agnes of Hapsburg, queen of Hungary
Agnes d'Harcourt
Agnes of Meissen
Agnes da Montepulciano (St.)
Alice Henley
Alix de Mâcon [Alice]
Amalberga
Beatrice of Nazareth
Bertha of Avenay
Bertha of Italy
Bethlem of Greci
Blanche of Portugal
Catherine of Bologna (St.)
Katherine de la Pole [Catherine]
Katherine of Sutton [Catherine]
Cecilia of Flanders
Christina (of Hungary) [Christine]
Christina of Markyate [Christine]
Clare of Montefalco (St.)
Kunigunde of Goss [Cunigunde]
Cwenthryth of Mercia
Cyenthryth, queen of Mercia
Diemuod of Nonnberg [Diemud]
Eadgifu of Lominster
Ebba
Ela, countess of Salisbury
Ermengard (of S. Salvatore)
Ermentrude of Jouarre
Euphemia of Wherwell
Friderun (of Germany)
Gerberga of Bavaria
Gertrude of Hackeborn
Gisla of Lorraine
Hathumoda of Gandersheim
Heloise of Argenteuil
Herrad von Landsberg
Hersende (of Fontevrault)
Hildegarde (of France)
Hildegarde of Bingen (St.)
Huguette du Hamel
Ianka of Kiev
Ida of Nivelles
Illuminato Bembo
Jeanne de Valois, countess of Hainault [Jean]
Juliana of Cornillon
Jutta of Sponheim
Lucia Brocadelli
Lutgard of Aywières (St.) [Liutgard]
Marguerite d'Oingt [Margaret]
Margarita de Prades [Margaret]
Margaret Wavere
Margaret Worthham
Margery de Honylane
Margery Twynyho
Mary of Blois
Maria Enriquez [Mary]
Marie de France [Mary]
Matilda of Anjou
Matilda of Essen
Matilda of Quedlinburg
Oda
Osburga of Coventry (St.)
Otta of S. Salvatore
Petronille of Fontevrault
Relindis of Hohenburg
Richardis

Richardis von Stade
Rothild of Chelles
Sancha of Portugal (St.) [Sancia]
Sophia of Gandersheim
Svanhild of Essen
Tenxwind of Andernach
Thomasine Dinham
Umilita of Faenza
Uta of Niedermünster
Wulfhilda of Barking (St.)
Wulfthryth, queen of England (St.)

ABDUCTION

Adelheid of Burgundy, Holy Roman Empress [Adelaide]
Adelheid of Germany, abbess of Quedlinburg [Adelaide]
Agnes atte Holte
Alice Burle
Alice Denecoumbe
Alice Lacy, countess of Lancaster
Alice atte March
Alice Stanford
Asa, queen of Agdir
Bertha of Swabia
Borte
Catherine de Thouars
Châtellerault (countess of)
Constance of France, countess of Toulouse
Dervorgilla (O'Ruairc)
Dorotea Caracciolo [Dorothy]
Eadgifu of England, queen of France
Eadgifu of Lominster
Eleanora de Montfort [Eleanor]
Elizabeth de Clare
Ida of Boulogne
Isabel of Vermandois, countess of Leicester [Isabelle]
Judith of Schweinfurt
Lucia Brocadelli
Maria, queen of Hungary [Mary]
Maria of Sicily [Mary]
Marjorie, countess of Carrick [Margery]
Nesta
Oelun
Ragnhild (of Ringerike)
Rogneda of Polotsk
Rose Savage
Theodora Comnena, queen of Jerusalem
Wulfhilda of Barking (St.)
Yolande de Valois

ADULTERY

includes bigamy, fornication, clerical marriages, etc.

Also see: MISTRESSES; WOMEN OF EASY VIRTUE.

Aelfgifu of Northampton
Aelfthryth
Agnes of France
Agnes of Meran
Alexandra Crowe [Alessandra]
Alys of France [Alice]
Angelberga
Anne of York, duchess of Exeter
Anne-Marie de Georgel
Beatrice Brounying
Beatrice de Guzman
Beatrice Puttock
Beatrice Sharpe
Blanche of Burgundy
Blanche of Portugal
Bona of Luxembourg
Katherine Swynford [Catherine]
Charlotte (de Valois)
Constance of York, countess of Gloucester
Eadburg of Mercia
Leonor Teles, queen of Portugal [Eleanor]
Elena Baroun
Elizabeth of Lancaster
Emma of Italy, queen of France
Evfimia of Kiev [Euphemia]
Euphrosyne of Byzantium
Eupraxia of Kiev, Holy Roman Empress
Fiametta
Francesca da Rimini
Grazida Lizier
Hatheburg
Heloise of Argenteuil
Huguette du Hamel
Ingeltrude
Isabeau of Bavaria [Isabelle]
Isabella of France, queen of England [Isabelle]
Jacqueline of Hainault
Jeanne of Burgundy, queen of France [Jean]
Joan of Kent [Jean]
Judith of Bavaria, Holy Roman Empress
Judith, queen of England
Loba de Pueinautier
Lucrezia Donati
Margaret Aldobrandeschi
Margaret of Babenberg
Margaret of Burgundy

Margaret Maultasch
Margaret of Navarre, queen of Sicily
Margarita de Prades [Margaret]
Margherita di Trento [Margaret]
Margaret Wavere
Marozia of Rome
Mélisende, queen of Jerusalem
Mengarde Buscalh
Parisina Malatesta
Philippa of Antioch
Richardis
Rotrude
Sancia d'Aragona
Tanglost
Theresa of Castile
Theutberga, queen of Lotharingia
Urraca, queen of Castile
Vanozza Catanei
Zoe the Porphyrogenita

ALEWIVES

includes brewers/sellers of ale and wine dealers

Also see: MERCHANTS; TAVERNERS.

Agnes de Broughton
Agnes Kateline
Alice atte Harpe
Alice de Lye
Anès (la cervoisière) [Anne]
Beatrice Brounying
Beatriz (la buffretière) [Beatrice]
Katherine Boteler [Catherine]
Cristina Blake [Christine]
Edith Paumer
Eleana Baroun
Elisia Hundesdich
Fabrisse Rives
Isabella Hodere [Isabelle]
Jane Harold
Johanna Beauflour [Jean]
Joan Everard [Jean]
Marguerite Joli [Margaret]
Margery Kempe
Matilda Yonge
Petronilla Turk
Rose Nosterfeld
Sarra (of Broughton) [Sarah]

Alms see: CHARITY.

ANCHORESSES

includes recluses

Alix la Bourgolle [Alice]
Anna Palmer [Anne]
Annora de Braose
Catherine of Pallanza
Catherine of Siena (St.)
Childlove (de Worth)
Christina of Markyate [Christine]
Colette of Corbie
Dorothy of Montau
Eadburg of Mercia
Eva of Saint-Martin
Julian of Norwich
Jutta of Sponheim
Liutberga (St.)
Loretta de Braose
Matilda of Leicester
Rosalia of Palermo (St.)
Sibillina Biscossi (Sibyl)
Umilita of Faenza

ANTINOMIAN

includes a variety of antinomian heresies

Also see: HERETICS.

Guglielma (of Milan)
Jeanne Dabenton [Jean]
Margherita di Trento [Margaret]
Mayfreda de Pirovano
Prous Bonetta

APOTHECARIES

growers/sellers of kitchen and/or medicinal herbs and spices

Also see: MEDICINE.

Adelie l'Erbière [Adele]
Colette la Moynesse
Emeline (la poréeresse)
Isabeau (apotiqueresse) [Isabelle]
Isabelle de Ferièves
Marguerite Saluzzio [Margaret]
Margot Pipelarde
Nicole (l'erbière) [Nichole]
Pérronnele (l'espicière) [Pérronelle]
Rebecca Guarna

APPAREL

craftswomen who made dresses, hose, hats, shoes, and a variety of accessory items

Also see: CLOTHWORKERS; SILKWORK.

Alice la Wymplere
Alison la Jourdain
Ameline (la cordoanière)
Ameline (la couturière)

Aveline (la chapelière)
Denise (la sainturière)
Edeline (la paonnière)
Ellen Sage
Else von Ortemberg
Eudeline (la baudréere)
Genevieve (la paonnière)
Guiote Serre
Henriette la Patriarche
Jacqueline (la saacière)
Jehanne (la boutonnière) [Jean]
Jehanne (la loirrière) [Jean]
Jehanne Poufille [Jean]
Maheut (la chapelière) [Mahaut]
Margot (la gantière)
Nicole (la boursière) [Nichole]
Susane (la coiffière)

APPRENTICES

includes mistresses of apprentices

Also see: EMPLOYERS.

Agnes Brundyssch
Agnes Cook
Alice Seford
Katherine Dore [Catherine]
Elizabeth Moring
Elisabeth Scepens [Elizabeth]
Emma Hatfield
Emma Turk
Fygen van Berchem
Isabel Gobbe [Isabelle]
Joan Woulbarowe
Matilda Yonge
Perrette la Maugarnie
Poncette Aubry
Roesia de Borford
Sara of Saint-Gilles [Sarah]
Sewis van Berchem
Tryngen Ime Hove

Architecture see: BUILDERS.

ART PATRONS

Also see: PATRONS OF LITERATURE.

Aelflaed
Agnes of Burgundy, duchess of Bourbon
Anne de Châtillon
Beatrice d'Este
Bianca Maria Visconti
Blanche of France
Blanche of Navarre, queen of France
Bona of Luxembourg
Caterina Cornaro, queen of Cyprus [Catherine]
Catherine of France, queen of England
Charlotte of Savoy
Eleanor of Aquitaine
Leonora of Aragon, duchess of Ferrara [Eleanor]
Eleanor of Provence, queen of England
Elisabetta Gonzaga [Elizabeth]
Elizabeth of Poland, queen of Hungary
Gisela of Bavaria, queen of Hungary
Godgifu, lady of Mercia
Isabeau of Bavaria [Isabelle]
Isabel Despenser, countess of Warwick [Isabelle]
Isabella d'Este [Isabelle]
Jeanne de Boulogne, queen of France [Jean]
Jeanne de Bourbon, queen of France [Jean]
Jeanne of Burgundy, queen of France [Jean]
Jeanne de Dammartin, queen of Castile [Jean]
Jeanne d'Évreux, queen of France [Jean]
Lucrezia Borgia
Lucrezia de'Medici
Lucrezia Tornabuoni
Mahaut of Artois
Margaret of Austria
Margaret Beaufort
Margaret of Flanders, duchess of Burgundy
Margaret of France, queen of England
Maria of Castile [Mary]
Maria Enriquez [Mary]
Matilda of Boulogne, queen of Portugal
Matilda of Essen
Mélisende, queen of Jerusalem
Michelle of France
Philippa of Lancaster, queen of Portugal
Sophia, princess of Moscow
Tamara, queen of Georgia
Theophano of Byzantium, Holy Roman Empress
Uta of Niedermünster

ARTISTIC CLOTHWORK

includes tapestry weavers and embroiderers of all types

Also see: CLOTHWORKERS; SILKWORK.

Aelflaed
Agnes of Meissen

Aaeles (la tapicière) [Alice]
Asa, queen of Agdir
Bertha de Sens, countess of Vienne
Christina of Markyate [Christine]
Clare of Assisi
Colette (of Paris)
Kunigunde of Goss [Cunigunde]
Edith of Wessex, queen of England
Eleanor of Castile, queen of England
Elizabeth Stokton
Ermengard (of Italy), Holy Roman Empress
Ermentrude of Orléans
Guillemette (la tapicière)
Jehanne Gaultière [Jean]
Jehanne (la tapicière) [Jean]
Judith of Bavaria, Holy Roman Empress
Liutberga (St.)
Mabel of Bury St. Edmunds
Margaret Neville, countess of Oxford
Matilda of Flanders
Matilda of Quedlinburg
Maura of Troyes (St.)
Roesia de Borford

ARTISTS

includes painters, sculptors, illuminators, etc.

Agnes of Meissen
Aalis (l'ymaginière) [Alice]
Anastaise of Paris [Anastasia]
Antonia Uccello
Barbara Gwichtmacherin
Barbera Ragnoni [Barbara]
Catherine of Bologna (St.)
Clara Gatterstedt [Clare]
Clara Hätzerlin [Clare]
Claricia of Augsburg
Cornelie van Wulfskerke
Kunigunda of Nuremberg [Cunigunde]
Diemudis of Wessobrun [Diemud]
Donella of Bologne
Elisabeth Scepens [Elizabeth]
Ende
Ermengarde (of St. Adrian)
Gisela of Kerzenbroeck
Guda (of Germany)
Herrad von Landsberg
Mabel of Bury St. Edmunds
Margaretha van Eyck [Margaret]
Marguerite Scheppers [Margaret]
Onorata Rodiana
Philippa of Coimbra
Sabina von Steinbach
Sainte (la paintre)

ASTRONOMY

Gisela
Philippa of Lancaster, queen of Portugal
Relindis of Hohenburg
Tiphaine Raguel [Tiffania]

Bakers see: PROVISIONING.

BANKING

includes women who minted coins, lent money, borrowed money, or were involved in exchequer or treasury affairs

Alice Perrers
Anastasia of Kiev
Angelberga
Anne de Châtillon
Anna Dalassena [Anne]
Anna Harbatova [Anne]
Avice Gardebois
Bertha of Swabia, duchess of Lorraine
Blanche of Castile, queen of France
Bona of Savoy
Contessina de'Bardi
Cyenthryth, queen of Mercia
Delphine of Languedoc
Dorothy of Strygl
Eleanor of Aquitaine
Elizabeth of Goerlitz
Emma of Normandy
Ermentrude of Jouarre
Foria (of Vermandois)
Goda la Gablere
Gytha of Denmark
Isabella d'Este [Isabelle]
Isabella de Fortibus [Isabelle]
Isabella of France, queen of England [Isabelle]
Isabella de Toppesham [Isabelle]
Margaret de Botreaux, lady Hungerford
Margaret of Hainault, Holy Roman Empress
Mariota Convers
Olga, princess of Kiev (St.)
Vanozza Catanei

BARBERS

hairdressers and medical practitioners of the barbering craft—treating wounds, etc.

Also see: MEDICINE.

Aalis (la barbière) [Alice]
Aveline (la barbière)

BATHHOUSE

owners, operators, workers, and customer

BEGUINES

BEQUESTS

women who wrote wills or were beneficiaries; some of the extant wills include itemized lists of personal effects

Also see: ESTATE

Petronilla Turk
Quintine van den Zande
Roesia de Borford
Sarah Stroby
Ulricha de Foschua
Walgrave (lady)
Wynflaed

Bigamy see: ADULTERY.

BOOK OWNERS

Also see: PATRONS OF LITERATURE; WRITERS.

Agnes of Anjou
Agnes Forster
Alice Chaucer, duchess of Suffolk
Anne of Bohemia, queen of England
Anne of Brittany, queen of France
Anna Sforza [Anne]
Anne Shirley
Anne of Woodstock
Blanche of Navarre, queen of France
Bona of Luxembourg
Bonne de Berry [Bona]
Catherine of Burgundy, duchess of Austria
Cecily Neville, duchess of York [Cecilia]
Charlotte of Savoy
Clarissa Orsini [Claricia]
Clemence of Hungary
Constance of York, countess of Gloucester
Cunigund of Luxembourg, Holy Roman Empress (St.) [Cunigunde]
Eleanor de Bohun, duchess of Gloucester
Elisabetta Gonzaga [Elizabeth]
Ellen Dalok
Gerberga of Saxony, queen of France
Gisela (of France)
Gisela of Swabia, queen of Germany
Ippolita Sforza
Isabeau of Bavaria [Isabelle]
Isabel, lady Bourchier [Isabelle]
Isabella d'Este [Isabelle]
Isabelle of France, duchess of Milan
Isabella of France, queen of Navarre [Isabelle]
Isotta Nogarola
Joan Beaufort, countess of Westmoreland [Jean]
Jeanne de Bourbon, queen of France [Jean]
Jeanne of Burgundy, queen of France [Jean]
Jeanne d'Évreux, queen of France [Jean]
Judith of Flanders
Louise of Savoy
Lucrezia Borgia
Mahaut of Artois
Margaret of Anjou
Margaret de Bohun, countess of Devon
Margaret of Brabant, countess of Flanders
Margaret of Burgundy
Margaret of Flanders, duchess of Burgundy
Margaret Lacy
Marguerite of Provence, queen of France [Margaret]
Margaret, queen of Scotland (St.)
Marie de Berry [Mary]
Marie de Brabant, queen of France [Mary]
Marie of Cleves [Mary]
Mary of St. Pol
Matilda of Essen
Matilda of Rottenburg
Matilda of Tuscany
Mélisende, queen of Jerusalem
Philippa of Coimbra
Philippa of Hainault
Valentine Visconti, duchess of Orléans
Wynflaed
Yolande of Aragon
Yolande de Valois

BOOKMAKING

includes scribes, producers, ink dealers, parchmenters, etc.

Also see: ARTISTS; WRITERS.

Anastaise of Paris [Anastasia]
Barbara Gwichtmacherin
Christine de Pisan
Clara Hätzerlin
Claricia of Augsburg
Clemence of Barking
Colette (of Paris)
Cornelie van Wulfskerke
Coustance (la parcheminière)
Kunigunda of Nuremberg [Cunigunde]
Diemuod of Nonnberg [Diemud]
Diemud of Wessobrun
Diemudis of Wessobrun [Diemud]
Donella of Bologne
Eleanor of Castile, queen of England
Elisabeth Scepens [Elizabeth]
Ende
Ermengarde (of St. Adrian)
Gisela of Kerzenbroeck
Guda (of Germany)
Herrad von Landsberg

CHILDBIRTH

predominantly women who died in or immediately following childbirth

Also see: MEDICINES; MIDWIVES.

Agnes of Meran
Agnes Sorel
Anna Sforza [Anne]
Beatrice d'Este
Beatrice of Rethel, queen of Sicily
Beatrice de Vesci
Bonne of Artois [Bona]
Clementia, countess of Flanders
Constance of Castile, queen of France
Constance of Sicily, Holy Roman Empress
Costanza Varano [Constance]
Eleanora de Montfort [Eleanor]
Elizabeth Berkeley, countess of Warwick
Elizabeth of York, queen of England
Eudocia Baiane, empress of Byzantium
Gertrude of Saxony, duchess of Bavaria
Gundreda (of Warenne)
Isabel of Aragon, princess of France [Isabelle]
Isabella of Aragon, queen of Portugal [Isabelle]
Isabella of England, Holy Roman Empress [Isabelle]
Isabella of France, queen of England [Isabelle]
Isabelle of France, duchess of Milan [Isabelle]
Isabella of Hainault, queen of France [Isabelle]
Isabel Neville [Isabelle]
Isabel of Vermandois, countess of Leicester [Isabelle]
Jadwiga of Hungary
Jeanne de Bourbon, queen of France [Jean]
Joanna of England, queen of Sicily [Jean]
Lucrezia Borgia
Margaret of Austria
Margaret of Scotland, queen of Norway
Marjory Bruce [Margery]
Marie of Bohemia [Mary]
Mary de Bohun
Marie of Navarre [Mary]
Richilde of Autun
Sybil of Conversano
Teresa de Entenza [Theresa]
Yolande (of Jerusalem), Holy Roman Empress
Zaida of Seville

CHILDCARE

women who became guardians, foster mothers, etc. also includes women who abused or neglected children

Also see: SERVANTS.

Adriana del Mila
Aelfthryth
Agnes Paston
Alice la Wymplere
Angele de la Barthe [Angela]
Anne, princess of Bohemia
Anne of Caux
Anne Devereux
Astrid of Norway
Avice la Wymplere
Bianca Maria Sforza
Blanche of Laurac
Brunetta
Catherine de Courteney
Katharine Grandison [Catherine]
Catherine de l'Isle Bouchard
Katherine de la Pole [Catherine]
Katherine Swynford [Catherine]
Christina (of Hungary) [Christine]
Clemence Sillone
Coucy (lady de)
Dhuoda
Dionysia de Mountchesny
Drahomira
Leonor of Albuquerque [Eleanor]
Elizabeth of Hungary (St.)
Elizabeth of Portugal (St.)
Elvira of Castile
Gertrude of Hackeborn
Helwise of Nevers, countess of Évreux
Ida de Portunhale
Isabel Romée [Isabelle]
Jeanne de Dammartin, queen of Castile [Jean]
Jeanne Pouponne [Jean]
Jutta of Sponheim
Louise of Savoy
Lucrezia Borgia
Lucrezia de'Medici
Ludmila (of Bohemia)
Mabel Rich
Margaret of Austria
Margaret of Citta di Castello
Margherita Datini [Margaret]
Margaret of Denmark
Margaret Marshall
Margaret Paston

Margaret Worthham
Maria of Castile [Mary]
Marie of Champagne, countess of Flanders [Mary]
Maria de Luna [Mary]
Mengarde Buscalh
Peronne Loessart
Philippa of Hainault
Relindis of Hohenburg
Sancia d'Aragona
Thomasine Dinham
Valentine Visconti, duchess of Orléans
Willa of Tuscany, queen of Italy
Ydain of Lorraine
Yolande of Aragon

CLOTHWORKERS

includes dealers in raw materials, and workers in all facets and types of clothmaking—except silk

Also see: APPAREL; ARTISTIC CLOTHWORK; SILKWORK.

Aaeles (la tapicière) [Alice]
Alison la Jourdain
Anne of Bohemia, queen of England
Anees de Quinkere
Katherine l'Avise [Catherine]
Katherine of Sutton [Catherine]
Colette (of Paris)
Elizabeth Kirkeby
Elizabeth Moring
Guillemette (la tapicière)
Hélissent (la ferpière)
Hodierne (la cerencerresse)
Huitace (la lanière)
Jehanne Gaultière [Jean]
Jeanne Laisne [Jean]
Jehanne Lecointe [Jean]
Jehanne (la tapicière) [Jean]
Juliana Roos
Kateline de Coster
Mahaut of Artois
Maheut (la feutrière) [Mahaut]
Marguerite la Bonne Estranée [Margaret]
Marguerite (la chanevacière) [Margaret]
Milessent (la cerenceresse)
Perrette la Maugarnie
Philippa of Hainault
Poncette Aubry
Raouline la Malingré
Roesia de Borford
Sewis van Berchem
Thyphainne (la toière) [Tiffania]
Tryngen Ime Hove
Wynflaed
Ysabelle d l'Espine [Ysabel]

Courts see: ECCLESIASTICAL COURTS; LEGAL ACTIVITY; MANORS; and ORDEALS.

Crafts see: OCCUPATIONS; and individual crafts.

CRUSADES

participants and supporters; and wives of Crusaders

Also see: SOLDIERS.

Agnes of France
Alix of France, countess of Blois and Chartres
Alice of Jerusalem, princess of Antioch
Alice de Montmorency
Berengaria of Navarre, queen of England
Bertha of Sulzbach
Cecilia of France
Eleanor of Aquitaine
Eleanor of Castile, queen of England
Eleanor de Montfort, countess of Leicester
Elvira of Castile
Emma FitzOsbern, countess of Norfolk
Faydide of Millau, countess of Toulouse
Godevere of Toëni
Hersende (of France)
Hildegarde of Bingen (St.)
Irene Angela, Holy Roman Empress
Isabel of Aragon, princess of France [Isabelle]
Isabelle of France
Isabella of France, queen of England [Isabelle]
Joan of England, countess of Gloucester [Jean]
Joanna of England, queen of Sicily [Jean]
Jeanne of Toulouse [Jean]
Margaret, countess of Flanders
Marguerite of Provence, queen of France [Margaret]
Marie of Champagne, countess of Flanders [Mary]
Mélisende, queen of Jerusalem
Richilde, countess of Flanders
Sybille of Anjou, countess of Flanders

DANCE

amateurs and/or professionals; also includes patrons

Anne Neville, queen of England
Beatrice di Correggio
Beatrice d'Este

Beaugrant (madame de)
Elisabetta Gonzaga [Elizabeth]
Ippolita Sforza
Isabella d'Este [Isabelle]
Isabel of Lorraine [Isabelle]
Jeanne de Boulogne, duchess of Berry [Jean]
Lucrezia Borgia
Margaret of Scotland
Marie of Bourbon [Mary]
Marie of Cleves [Mary]
Marie d'Orléans [Mary]
Maud Makejoy (Matilda)
Or (madame d')
Valentine Visconti, duchess of Orléans
Yolande de Dreux, queen of Scotland

DIVORCE

includes separations, annulments, broken betrothals, etc.

Adelaide of Anjou
Azalais de Rocamartina [Adelaide]
Adelaide of Savona
Adelheid of Vohburg [Adelaide]
Adelasia of Torres, queen of Sardinia
Aelfgifu
Aelflaed
Agnes, countess of Aix
Agnes of Anjou
Agnes of Courtenay
Agnes of Meran
Agnes of Navarre
Alberada of Buonalbergo
Alison la Jourdain
Almodis (II) de La Marche, countess of Barcelona
Alys of France [Alice]
Angelberga
Anne Holland
Anne of York, duchess of Exeter
Ansgard
Berenguela of Castile
Bertha of Chartres
Bertha of Holland
Bertha of Susa
Bertha of Swabia
Bertrade de Montfort, queen of France
Blanche of Aragon
Blanche of Bourbon
Blanche of Burgundy
Katharine of Aragon [Catherine]
Clementia of Zähringen
Constance of Brittany
Constance of France, countess of Toulouse
Dorotea Gonzaga [Dorothy]
Douce (III) of Provence
Eleanor of Aquitaine
Leonor of Castile, queen of Aragon [Eleanor]
Leonor of Castile, queen of Aragon [Eleanor]
Leonor of Castile, queen of Navarre [Eleanor]
Eleanor Cobham
Eleanor Talbot
Leonor Teles, queen of Portugal [Eleanor]
Elizabeth of Lancaster
Ermengarde of Anjou, duchess of Brittany
Estrith of Denmark
Eudoxia Comnena
Gormflath (of Ireland)
Hatheburg
Hawise of Gloucester
Ingeborg of Denmark, queen of France
Ingibiorg, queen of Scotland (Ingeborg)
Ingeltrude
Irene Ducas, empress of Byzantium
Isabelle of Angoulême, queen of England
Isabella de Despenser, countess of Arundel [Isabelle]
Isabella of England, countess of Bedford [Isabelle]
Isabella of Hainault, queen of France [Isabelle]
Isabella of Jerusalem [Isabelle]
Jacqueline of Hainault
Juana of Castile [Jean]
Joan of England, queen of Scotland [Jean]
Joan of England, queen of Scotland [Jean]
Jeanne of France, duchess of Orléans [Jean]
Joan of Kent [Jean]
Judith, queen of England
Lucienne of Rochefort
Lucrezia d'Alagno
Lucrezia Borgia
Lucy atte Lee
Malfrid of Kiev, queen of Norway, queen of Denmark
Margaret Aldobrandeschi
Margaret of Babenberg
Margaret Beaufort
Margaret, countess of Flanders
Margaret of Logy
Margaret Maultasch

Marguerite de Turenne [Margaret]
Mary of Blois
Marie of Montpellier [Mary]
Matilda of Boulogne, queen of Portugal
Matilda of England, Holy Roman Empress
Matilda of Tuscany
Northilda
Odeline
Petronilla of Aquitaine, countess of Vermandois
Philippa de Coucy
Richardis
Rozala of Lombardy
Sancia d'Aragona
Sybille of Anjou, countess of Flanders [Sibyl]
Sybille de Château-Porcien [Sibyl]
Tamara, queen of Georgia
Theodora, empress of Byzantium
Theophano, empress of Byzantium
Theresa of Portugal, queen of Leon (St.)
Theutberga, queen of Lotharingia
Thyra of Denmark
Urraca, queen of Castile
Urraca of Portugal
Waldrada
Waldrada (of Arles
Wulfthryth, queen of England (St.)
Zoe Carbounopsina

DOCTORS/EMPIRICS

licensed and non-licensed physicians, including women who practiced on battlefields, those who specialized in optometry, obstetrics, etc.

For other specialized practices see: MEDICINE.

Agnes Avesot
Agnes of Huntingdon
Alice Shedyngton
Ameline (la miresse)
Antoinette de Bellegarde
Antonia Daniello
Beatrice Candia
Belota (the Jew)
Bertrande of Avignon
Brunetta
Caterina of Florence [Catherine]
Clarice of Rotomago [Claricia]
Costanza Calenda [Constance]
Denise de Partenay
Dorothea Hindremstein [Dorothy]
Gilette of Narbonne
Haoys (la meresse)
Heloys (la miergesse)
Helvidis
Henriette de Craus
Hersende (of France)
Isabiau la mergesse [Isabelle]
Jacoba Felicie
Jacoba (of Passau)
Jacobina (medica)
Jeanne Clarisse [Jean]
Jeanne "Conversa" [Jean]
Jeanne de Cusey [Jean]
Jeanne Villain{Jean]
Jeannette Camus
Leonetta (medica)
Marguerite of Naples [Margaret]
Marguerite Saluzzio [Margaret]
Margery of Hales
Marie de Blansy [Mary]
Maria (la Medica) [Mary]
Marie (la meresse) [Mary]
Perna
Phelippe (la miergesse) [Philippa]
Rebecca Guarna
Richeut (la meresse)
Sarre (la mirgesse) [Sarah]
Sara of Saint-Gilles [Sarah]
Sara (of Wurzburg) [Sarah
Serlin
Trotula of Salerno
Ulricha de Foschua
Virdimura of Sicily
Ysabel (la meresse)

DOWRY/DOWER

women who brought important dowries, or who tied up disposition of large dower lands

Ada of Warenne
Adelaide of Savona
Adele of Champagne, queen of France
Adela of France [Adele]
Aelfthryth of Wessex
Affreca of Man, countess of Ulster
Agnes Cook (le Keu)
Agnes FitzJohn
Agnes of France
Agnes von Staufen
Alice Lacy, countess of Lancaster
Angelberga
Anne, princess of Byzantium
Anne de Many, countess of Pembroke
Anna Sforza [Anne]
Avis Wade

Basilia de Clare
Beatrice of Burgundy
Beatrice of Portugal
Beatrix of Portugal, queen of Castile [Beatrice]
Beatrice of Viennois, countess of Albon
Beatrice de Warenne
Berengaria of Navarre, queen of England
Bianca Maria Sforza
Blanche of Anjou, queen of Aragon
Blanche of Bourbon
Blanche of Namur
Borte
Katherine Neville [Catherine]
Cecily FitzJohn [Cecilia]
Cecily Neville [Cecilia]
Chiara Gonzaga
Constance of France, countess of Toulouse
Constance of Hohenstaufen
Contessina de'Bardi
Eadgifu of England, queen of France
Ealdgyth (of Mercia)
Eleanor of Castile, queen of England
Eleanor of England, queen of Castile
Elizabeth, lady Abergavenny
Elizabeth Holland
Ermengarde de Beaumont, queen of Scotland
Ermengarde (of Burgundy)
Eva MacMurrough
Frederun of Lorraine, queen of France
Gerberga of Saxony, queen of France
Ginevra (Datini)
Gisela of Swabia, queen of Germany
Hatheburg
Ingeborg of Denmark, queen of France
Isabella of France, queen of England [Isabelle]
Isabella of France, queen of England [Isabelle]
Isabelle of France, duchess of Milan
Isabella of Hainault, queen of France [Isabelle]
Jeanne d'Artois [Jean]
Joan de Bar, countess of Surrey [Jean]
Joan of England, countess of Gloucester [Jean]
Joan FitzAlan, lady Bergavenny [Jean]
Joan Holland, duchess of Brittany [Jean]
Jeanne Laisne [Jean]
Joan of Navarre, queen of England [Jean]
Judith of Bavaria, duchess of Swabia
Lucrezia Borgia
Marguerite de Bourbon [Margaret]
Margaret of Burgundy
Margaret of England, queen of Scotland
Margaret of France, queen of Hungary
Margaret of Hainault, duchess of Burgundy
Margaret of Norway, queen of Scotland
Margaret of Sweden, queen of Norway
Margery Paston
Mary of England
Marie of France, duchess of Brabant [Mary]
Marie of Navarre [Mary]
Marie, countess of Ponthieu and Aumale [Mary]
Mary of St. Pol
Matilda of Anjou
Matilda of England, Holy Roman Empress
Matilda of France
Maud Francis [Matilda]
Matilda, queen of Germany
Matilda of Sicily, countess of Alife
Michelle of France
Nannina de'Medici
Philippa de Dammartin
Philippa of Hainault
Roiantken
Rozala of Lombardy
Sancha of Castile [Sancia]
Sybille of Anjou, countess of Flanders [Sibyl]
Sybil of Conversano [Sibyl]
Thyra of Denmark
Violante Visconti
Waldrada (of Arles)

DRAMA

actresses, spectators, playwrights, patronesses, etc.

Anne Neville, queen of England
Katherine of Sutton [Catherine]
Hildegarde of Bingen (St.)
Hroswitha of Gandersheim
Isabella d'Este [Isabelle]

Dressmakers see: APPAREL.

DWARVES

includes owners of dwarves

Barbara von Brandenburg
Beaugrant (madame de)
Margaret of York
Marie of Burgundy [Mary]
Or (madame d')

ECCLESIASTICAL COURTS

includes Inquisition courts

Agnese Arizonelli [Agnes]
Agnes Francou
Agnes Knetchur
Alice Kyteler
Angele de la Barthe [Angela]
Anne de Many, countess of Pembroke
Anna Palmer [Anne]
Beatrice d'Estellin
Beatrice of Planisolles
Beatrice Sharpe
Catherine Delort
Katherine Dertford [Catherine]
Catharine Pykring [Catherine]
Catherine Royer
Clarice of Rotomago [Claricia]
Deniselle Grenières
Ellen Dalok
Grazida Lizier
Guillemette Benet
Hauviette (of Domremy)
Hawise Mone
Ida de Portunhale
Isabella, queen of Castile and Aragon [Isabelle]
Isabella de Despenser, countess of Arundel [Isabelle]
Isabel Romée [Isabelle]
Isabellette of Épinal
Joan of Arc (St.) [Jean]
Jeannette Charles
Margaret Elyott
Margaret Porete
Margherita di Trento [Margaret]
Margery Baxter
Margery Kempe
Maria (la Medica) [Mary]
Matilda of Leicester
Mengarde Buscalh
Northilda
Peronne Loessart
Perrine Martin
Petronilla of Meath
Prous Bonetta
Tanglost
Theoda of Mainz

EDUCATED

women who received some education but were not scholars

Also see: SCHOLARS.

Adelaide de Porcairques
Adele, countess of Blois and Chartres
Adelicia of Louvain, queen of England
Adriana del Mila
Agnes of Anjou
Agnes of Burgundy, duchess of Bourbon
Agnes Forster
Agnes of Hapsburg, queen of Hungary
Agnes Paston
Agnes of Poitou, Holy Roman Empress
Alessandra Strozzi
Alice Chaucer, duchess of Suffolk
Alice Henley
Anne Beauchamp, countess of Warwick
Anne of Brittany, queen of France
Anna Comnena [Anne]
Anne of Kiev
Anne Shirley
Antoinette de Villequier
Antonia Daniello
Barbara von Brandenburg
Beatrice of Aragon
Beatrice of Burgundy
Beatrice di Correggio
Beatrice d'Este
Beatrice of Nazareth
Beatrice Portinari
Bertha of Sulzbach
Bianca Maria Visconti
Blanche of Castile, queen of France
Blanche, princess of England
Blanche of France
Blanche of Lancaster
Blanche of Namur
Blanche of Navarre, queen of France
Katharine of Aragon [Catherine]
Catherine of Bugundy, duchess of Austria
Catherine of France, queen of England
Katherine Riche [Catherine]
Clara Hätzerlin
Claricia of Augsburg
Clarissa Orsini [Claricia]
Costanza Calenda [Constance]
Constance (FitzGilbert)
Cunigund of Luxembourg, Holy Roman Empress (St.) [Cunigunde]
Dhuoda
Diemudis of Wessobrun [Diemud]
Dorotea Gonzaga [Dorothy]
Douceline (St.)
Eadburga of Winchester (St.)
Eadgyth (of England) (St.)
Edith of Wessex, queen of England

Eleanor of Aquitaine
Leonora of Aragon, duchess of Ferrara [Eleanor]
Eleanor de Montfort, countess of Leicester
Eleanora de Montfort [Eleanor]
Eleanor Stuart, duchess of Austria
Elisabetta Gonzaga [Elizabeth]
Elizabeth Woodville
Emilia Pia
Ermengarde of Anjou, duchess of Brittany
Euphemia of Arnstein, queen of Norway
Eva of Saint-Martin
Evfosinia of Polotsk
Fiametta
Florencia Pinar
Francesca de Romana
Ginevra (Datini)
Gisela
Gisela of Swabia, queen of Germany
Guilia Farnese
Gundrada
Gwenllian (of Wales)
Hathumoda of Gandersheim
Hawise Mone
Hedwig of Silesia (St.)
Heloise of Argenteuil
Herrad von Landsberg
Hroswitha of Gandersheim
Ianka of Kiev
Ida of Nivelles
Idonea
Ippolita Sforza
Irene Ducas, empress of Byzantium
Isabella of Aragon, duchess of Milan [Isabelle]
Isabella, queen of Castile and Aragon [Isabelle]
Isabella of England, countess of Bedford [Isabelle]
Isabella d'Este [Isabelle]
Isabelle of France
Isabella of France, queen of England [Isabelle]
Isabella of France, queen of Navarre [Isabelle]
Isabelle of France, duchess of Milan
Isabella of Portugal [Isabelle]
Isotta degli Atti
Jane Shore
Jane Stonor
Juana of Aragon, queen of Castile [Jean]
Jeanne of Burgundy, queen of France [Jean]
Jeanne of Burgundy, queen of France [Jean]
Jeanne of France, duchess of Brittany [Jean]
Joanna I, queen of Naples [Jean]
Judith of Bavaria, Holy Roman Empress
Judith, queen of England
Judith (of Germany)
Judith of Schweinfurt
Juliana of Cornillon
Julian of Norwich [Juliana]
Jutta of Sponheim
Kasia (of Byzantium)
Lisa Strozzi
Liutberga (St.)
Louise of Savoy
Lucia Brocadelli
Lucrezia Borgia
Lucrezia d'Este
Lucrezia de'Medici
Maddalena de'Medici [Madeleine]
Margaret of Austria
Margaret Beaufort
Margaret de Bohun, countess of Devon
Margaret of Burgundy
Margaretha Cartheuserin [Margaret]
Margherita Datini [Margaret]
Margaret of Denmark
Margaret of Flanders, duchess of Burgundy
Margaret of Hainault, duchess of Burgundy
Marguerite d'Oingt [Margaret]
Marguerite of Naples [Margaret]
Margaret Paston
Margaret Porete
Margaret Rocliffe
Marguerite Saluzzio [Margaret]
Margaret of Scotland
Margaret Wake
Margaret Worthham
Marie de Berry [Mary]
Mary of Blois
Marie of Burgundy [Mary]
Marie de France [Mary]
Marie of France, countess of Champagne [Mary]
Mary of Scotland, countess of Boulogne
Matilda of Anjou
Matilda of England, duchess of Bavaria
Matilda of England, Holy Roman Empress
Matilda of Essen
Matilda of Flanders
Matilda, queen of Germany

Matilda of Scotland
Matilda of Tuscany
Mechtild of Magdeburg
Mélisende, queen of Jerusalem
Mercuriade of Salerno
Michelle of France
Nannina de'Medici
Péronnelle d'Armentières [Pérronelle]
Petronille of Comminges
Philippa of England
Philippa of Hainault
Philippa of Lancaster, queen of Portugal
Pregente of Melun
Relindis of Hohenburg
Richardis von Stade
Rotrude
Sibylla of Jerusalem [Sibyl]
Simonetta Cattaneo
Sophia, princess of Moscow
Tamara, queen of Georgia
Theodora Comnena
Theophano of Byzantium, Holy Roman Empress
Tiphaine Raguel [Tiffania]
Valentine Visconti, duchess of Orléans
Vanozza Catanei
Ydain of Lorraine

Embroiderers see: ARTISTIC CLOTHWORK.

EMPLOYERS

includes female employees

Also see: APPRENTICES. RECOMMANDRESSES.

Agnes Wombe
Alice de Wylesdone
Beatrice of Planisolles
Elizabeth Moring
Gunnora de Stratford
Joan Buckland [Jean]
Jeanne Clarisse [Jean]
Joan Hunt [Jean]
Johanna Travers [Jean]
Margaret Stoke
Margery Haynes
Maria de Malla [Mary]

Envoys see: NEGOTIATORS.

ESTATE

women who owned, inherited, or bought large amounts of land

Also see: LAND/PROPERTY; MANAGERS.

Adelaide of Anjou
Adelaide of Roumainmoutier
Adelasia of Torres, queen of Sardinia
Adela of Flanders, queen of Denmark [Adele]
Adelicia of Louvain, queen of England
Aelips de Beauchamp
Aethelflaed of Damerham
Agnes of Germany
Agnes de Monceaux
Agnes Paston
Agnes Sorel
Alda of Arles
Alix of Brittany [Alice]
Alice de Bryene
Alix of Champagne [Alice]
Alice Drayton
Alice Kyteler
Alice Lacy, countess of Lancaster
Alix de Mâcon [Alice]
Alice Montacute
Alice Montagu, countess of Salisbury
Alice de Montfort
Alice de Montmorency
Alice Perrers
Almodis (II) de La Marche, countess of Barcelona
Almodis (III) of Toulouse
Almodis (IV), countess of La Marche
Amice de Clare [Amicia]
Amicia de Gael, countess of Leicester
Amicia of Gloucester
Amicia of Leicester
Anne Beauchamp, countess of Warwick
Anne of Beaujeu
Anne of Brittany, queen of France
Anne Holland
Anne Mortimer
Anne of Woodstock
Anne of York, duchess of Exeter
Annora de Braose
Aurembaix, countess of Urgel
Aveline de Forz, countess of Aumale
Baddlesmere (lady)
Beatrice of Provence
Beatrice, marchioness of Tuscany
Beatrice de Vesci
Beatrice of Viennois, countess of Albon
Beatrice de Warenne
Bertha of Swabia
Bethoc of Scotland
Bianca Maria Visconti
Blanche of Artois

Blanche of Lancaster
Blanche of Navarre
Blanche of Ponthieu
Blanche of Portugal
Catherine of Austria
Catherine of Bugundy, duchess of Austria
Catherine de Courteney
Catherine of Navarre
Katherine Neville [Catherine]
Catherine de Thouars
Caterina Visconti [Catherine]
Cecilia of France
Cecilia Gallerani
Châtellerault (countess of)
Clementia, countess of Flanders
Clementia of Zähringen
Constance, queen of Aragon
Costanza of Aragon, queen of Sicily [Constance]
Constance of Castile, duchess of Lancaster
Constance of Sicily, Holy Roman Empress
Contessina de'Bardi
Coucy (lady de)
Cunigunda of Swabia, queen of Bohemia
Devorguilla of Galloway
Dionysia de Mountchesny
Douce (I) of Provence
Douce (III) of Provence
Edith of Wessex, queen of England
Eilika of Saxony
Ela, countess of Salisbury
Leonor of Aragon, queen of Navarre [Eleanor]
Eleanor Beauchamp, duchess of Somerset
Eleanor de Bohun, duchess of Gloucester
Eleanor de Clare
Eleanor of England, countess of Bar
Leonor of Sicily, queen of Aragon [Eleanor]
Eleanora of Vermandois [Eleanor]
Eleanor West
Elizabeth Badlesmere
Elizabeth Berkeley, countess of Warwick
Elizabeth Bourchier
Elizabeth de Burgh
Elizabeth de Clare
Elizabeth Howard, countess of Oxford
Elizabeth of Goerlitz
Elizabeth of Luxembourg
Elizabeth Say
Elizabeth, lady Scales
Elizabeth le Veel
Elizabeth of York, duchess of Suffolk
Emma FitzOsbern, countess of Norfolk
Ermengard (of Italy), Holy Roman Empress
Ermentrude of Orléans
Eufemia (of Mecklenburg) [Euphemia]
Friderun (of Germany)
Garsenda de Forcalquier
Gertrude of Babenberg
Gertrude of Flanders, duchess of Lorraine
Gertrude of Meissen
Gertrude of Saxony, duchess of Bavaria
Gertrude of Saxony, countess of Holland
Gisela
Gisla of Lorraine
Godgifu (of England)
Hawise of Gloucester
Hélene de Chambes [Helen]
Ida of Boulogne
Ida of Swabia
Imma of Saxony
Ingeborg of Denmark, queen of Norway
Ingeltrude
Isabelle of Achaia
Isabella of Aragon, duchess of Milan [Isabelle]
Isabella de Clare [Isabelle]
Isabel Despenser, countess of Warwick [Isabelle]
Isabella of England, countess of Bedford [Isabelle]
Isabelle of France
Isabella of Jerusalem [Isabelle]
Isabella Marshall [Isabelle]
Isabelle de Melun
Isabel Mowbray, lady Berkeley [Isabelle]
Isabel Neville [Isabelle]
Isabel of Vermandois, countess of Leicester [Isabelle]
Isabella of Vermandois, countess of Flanders [Isabelle]
Isabelle de Vescy
Jacqueline of Hainault
Jeanne d'Artois [Jean]
Joan Beaufort, queen of Scotland [Jean]
Jeanne de Boulogne, queen of France [Jean]
Jeanne de Bourbon [Jean]
Jeanne de Dammartin, queen of Castile [Jean]
Joan Fauconberg [Jean]
Jeanne of France, queen of Navarre [Jean]
Joan de Genville [Jean]
Joan Holland, duchess of Brittany [Jean]

Joan Lenelonde [Jean]
Joan de Munchensi [Jean]
Jeanne of Navarre, queen of France [Jean]
Jeanne of Toulouse [Jean]
Juliana de Leybourne, countess of Huntingdon
Lesceline, countess of Eu
Liutgard of Vermandois
Lucia Marliani
Margaret Aldobrandeschi
Margaret of Alsace
Margaret de Audley, lady Stafford
Margaret of Babenberg
Margaret Beaufort
Margaret de Braose
Margaret de Clare
Margaret of Flanders, duchess of Burgundy
Margaret of Hainault, Holy Roman Empress
Margaret of Leicester
Margaret of Maine
Margaret Marshall
Margaret Neville, countess of Oxford
Marguerite of Provence, queen of France [Margaret]
Margaret Wake
Margaret of York
Marjorie, countess of Carrick [Margery]
Mary of Blois
Mary de Bohun
Marie de Brabant, Holy Roman Empress [Mary]
Marie of Burgundy [Mary]
Maria, queen of Hungary [Mary]
Marie of Montpellier [Mary]
Marie d'Orléans [Mary]
Marie, countess of Ponthieu and Aumale [Mary]
Mary of St. Pol
Maria of Sicily [Mary]
Matilda of Boulogne, queen of Portugal
Maud de Braose [Matilda]
Maud Francis [Matilda]
Matilda of Hainault, princess of Achaia
Matilda of Lancaster, duchess of Zealand
Matilda de Lucy
Matilda of Northumberland, queen of Scotland
Matilda of Tuscany
Maud de Vere, countess of Oxford [Matilda]
Nichola de la Hay [Nichole]
Olga, princess of Kiev (St.)
Petronilla, queen of Aragon
Petronilla of Grandmesnil, countess of Leicester
Philippa of Champagne
Philippa of Clarence
Philippa de Coucy
Regina della Scala
Richenza of Nordheim, Holy Roman Empress
Roiantken
Saiv Kavanagh
Sancia d'Aragona
Sibylla of Jerusalem [Sibyl]
Sybil de Lacy [Sibyl]
Sigrid, queen of Sweden
Sophia of Gandersheim
Stephania (of Rome)
Teresa de Entenza [Theresa]
Wulfhild of Saxony
Wynflaed
Ximena Diaz
Ximena, queen of Leon
Yolande de Dreux
Yolande de Dreux, queen of Scotland
Yolande (of Jerusalem), Holy Roman Empress

Estate administrators see: MANAGERS.

Executions see: PUNISHMENTS.

Fishmongers see: PROVISIONING.

GAMES

includes bowling, chess, tennis, etc.
Also see: HUNTING.

Catherine of Burgundy, duchess of Austria
Eleanor of Castile, queen of England
Elizabeth, lady Scales
Elizabeth Woodville
Juliana (Cordwaner)
Mahaut of Artois
Margaret of Flanders, duchess of Burgundy
Margot de Hainault

GEMS/JEWELRY

includes uses, importance of, owners of, makers/sellers, etc.
Also see: BANKING; GOLDSMITHS.

Alice Perrers
Anastasia of Kiev
Beatrice of Provence
Hildegarde of Bingen (St.)
Isabella d'Este [Isabelle]

Lucia Marliani
Margerie de Haustede [Margery]
Mariota Convers
Roesia de Borford
Wynflaed

GENEALOGY

women whose major importance (so far as we have been able to discover) was their titles or their place in important family lines

Ada of Scotland, countess of Holland
Adelaide of Tours
Adela of France [Adele]
Adela of France [Adele]
Agnes Chaucer
Agnes of Dedo
Agnes d'Évreux, countess of Montfort
Aénor of Châtellerault
Agatha (of Hungary)
Agnes of Germany
Alda of Arles
Alix of Brittany [Alice]
Alice Montagu, countess of Salisbury
Almodis (I) of Limoges
Amicia de Gael, countess of Leicester
Amicia of Gloucester
Amicia of Leicester
Anne Mortimer
Anne Stafford
Anne of York
Arlette (of Normandy)
Beatrice of Castile, queen of Portugal
Beatrice of England
Beatrice of Rethel, queen of Sicily
Beatrice of Swabia, queen of Castile
Bertha
Bertha of Tuscany
Bethoc of Scotland
Carlotta d'Aragona
Catherine of Burgundy
Catherine of France
Catherine Percy, countess of Kent
Katherine Woodville [Catherine]
Katharine of York [Catherine]
Cecile de Béziers
Cecily Bonville [Cecilia]
Cecily FitzJohn [Cecilia]
Cecily of York [Cecilia]
Christina of Sweden [Christine]
Constance of Aragon, queen of Hungary
Costanza of Aragon, queen of Sicily [Constance]
Constance (of Hungary)
Constance of Normandy
Cunegunde of Swabia
Douce (II) of Barcelona
Eadgyfu of England, queen of Burgundy and Provence
Eadhild of Wessex
Ecgwyna
Edith Swan-neck
Leonor of Aragon, queen of Castile [Eleanor]
Eleanor of England, countess of Bar
Eleanor of Lancaster
Eleanor Neville, lady Lumley
Eleanor Neville, countess of Northumberland
Eleanor Neville, lady Stanley
Elizabeth Berkeley, countess of Warwick
Elizabeth Bryene
Elizabeth de Burgh
Elizabeth de Burgo, queen of Scotland
Elizabeth, princess of England
Elizabeth Howard, countess of Oxford
Elizabeth Paston
Elizabeth Percy, countess of Westmoreland
Elizabeth Stapilton
Elvira of Castile, queen of Sicily
Emma (of Apulia)
Emma FitzOsbern, countess of Norfolk
Ermengarde, Holy Roman Empress
Eufemia (of Mecklenburg) [Euphemia]
Fressenda (de Hauteville)
Gertrude of Bavaria
Gertrud of Meran [Gertrude]
Ginevra d'Este
Gisela (of France)
Godgifu (of England)
Gunnhild of Denmark, queen of Germany
Gwenllian (of Wales)
Gyda of England
Hathui (of Germany)
Hildegard
Ingegarde of Sweden, princess of Kiev
Isabel Beaumont
Isabella Marshall [Isabelle]
Isabel of Savoy
Jeanne d'Armagnac
Joan of England, countess of Gloucester [Jean]
Liutgard of Germany
Liutgard of Vermandois
Madeleine Valois
Mahaut de Brabant
Mahout de Châtillon

Margaret of Alsace
Margaret de Audley, lady Stafford
Margaret of Bavaria
Margaret of Bavaria
Marguerite de Bourbon [Margaret]
Margaret of England, duchess of Brabant
Margaret of England, countess of Pembroke
Margaret of Leicester
Margaret Neville
Margaret (of Sicily)
Mary of Scotland, countess of Boulogne
Marie of Valois [Mary]
Maria of Vivar [Mary]
Maud Chaworth
Maud Clifford, countess of Cambridge [Matilda]
Matilda of Lancaster
Nesta
Philippa of Clarence
Philippa Mortimer
Ragnhild of Denmark
Rose O'Connor
Saiv Kavanagh
Taddea Visconti
Willa
Wulfhild of Saxony
Yolande of Anjou
Yolande of Hungary, queen of Aragon

GOLDSMITHS

Also see: GEMS/JEWELRY.
Katherine Rebestoeckyn [Catherine]
Elizabeth Kirkeby
Erembourc de Braières
Marote (de Douai)

Governesses see: CHILDCARE; SERVANTS; TEACHERS.

HANDICAPPED

blind, deaf, lame, etc., women—and the treatment of

Also see: MEDICINE.
Dorotea Gonzaga [Dorothy]
Joan Fauconberg [Jean]
Jeanne of France, duchess of Orléans [Jean]
Lutgard of Aywières (St.) [Liutgard]
Margaret of Citta di Castello
Mechtild of Magdeburg
Sibillina Biscossi [Sibyl]
Sophia, princess of Moscow
Teresa de Cartagena [Theresa]
Zita of Lucca (St.)

Hat makers see: APPAREL.
Hawking see: HUNTING.
Herbwives see: APOTHECARIES.

HERETICS

includes women who were involved in vague, iconoclastic, or unidentifiable heresies; and some who fought against heresies

Also see: ANTINOMIAN; CATHARS; HUSSITES; LOLLARDS; WALDENSIANS; WITCHCRAFT.
Agnes Francou
Beatrice of Planisolles
Bloemardine
Constance of Arles, queen of France
Deniselle Grenières
Drahomira
Fabrisse Rives
Guglielma (of Milan)
Guillemette Benet
Henriette de Craus
Joan of Arc (St.) [Jean]
Margaret Porete
Margherita di Trento [Margaret]
Margery Kempe
Mayfreda de Pirovano
Mengarde Buscalh
Sancia of Majorca
Theoda of Mainz

Hucksters see: MERCHANTS.

HUNTING

women who were knowledgeable about, or participants in, hunting and hawking

Barbara von Brandenburg
Beatrice d'Este
Katherine Swynford [Catherine]
Eleanor of Castile, queen of England
Elisabetta Gonzaga [Elizabeth]
Elizabeth of Lancaster
Isabella d'Este [Isabelle]
Isabella of France, queen of England [Isabelle]
Juliana Berners
Margaret of Anjou
Marie of Burgundy [Mary]
Philippa of Lancaster, queen of Portugal

HUSSITES

Also see: HERETICS.
Anna of Mochov [Anne]
Barbara of Cilly, Holy Roman Empress

Catherine of Vraba
Sophia, queen of Bohemia

ILLEGITIMACY

Alison Dumay
Antigone (of Gloucester)
Beatrice of Castile
Beatrice de Guzman
Beatrice of Portugal
Beatrix of Portugal, queen of Castile [Beatrice]
Bertha of Tuscany
Bianca Giovanna Sforza
Bianca Maria Visconti
Catherine Sforza
Charlotte (de Valois)
Constance of Castile, duchess of Lancaster
Constance of Hohenstaufen
Drusiana (Sforza)
Eadgyth (of England) (St.)
Elvira of Castile
Ginevra (Datini)
Gisla of Lorraine
Gyda of England
Huguette du Hamel
Isabel of Castile, duchess of York [Isabelle]
Joan Beaufort, countess of Westmoreland [Jean]
Juana of Castile [Jean]
Joan of England, princess of Gwynedd [Jean]
Juliana (Bonaventure)
Lucrezia Borgia
Lucrezia d'Este
Marie of France, duchess of Brabant [Mary]
Sancia d'Aragona
Sibilla (of England) [Sibyl]
Teodorina (Cibo)
Theresa of Castile
Valentine Visconti, queen of Cyprus
Waldrada (of Arles)

Illuminators see: ARTISTS; BOOKMAKING.

INNKEEPERS

Denyse la Normande [Denise]
Isabella de Toppesham [Isabelle]
Quintine van den Zande
Vanozza Catanei

Inquisition see: ECCLESIASTICAL COURTS.

INSANITY

sufferers from; treatment of; caretakers; etc.

Abella of Salerno
Angele de la Barthe [Angela]
Beatrice of Monyons
Ermengarde of Anjou, duchess of Brittany
Juana of Aragon, queen of Castile [Jean]
Jeanne de Bourbon, queen of France [Jean]
Joan Fauconberg [Jean]
Jeanne de Montfort [Jean]
Jeanne Potier [Jean]
Marie de Blansy [Mary]
Odette de Champdivers
Valentine Visconti, duchess of Orléans

Jewelry makers see: GEMS/JEWELRY.

JEWS

also includes women who had an effect on Jewish communities

Antonia Daniello
Belota (the Jew)
Blanche of Castile, queen of France
Brunetta
Catherine of Lancaster
Foria (of Vermandois)
Isabella of Aragon, queen of Portugal [Isabelle]
Isabella, queen of Castile and Aragon [Isabelle]
Perna
Sarre (la mirgesse) [Sarah]
Sara of Saint-Gilles [Sarah]
Sara (of Wurzburg) [Sarah]
Serlin
Slymina Fort
Virdimura of Sicily

LAND/PROPERTY

includes lower-and middle-class women who owned and/or managed urban or rural property

Also see: ESTATE; MANAGERS.

Agnes Brid
Agnes de Broughton
Agnes Forster
Agnes of Huntingdon
Agnes Kateline
Agnes Molton
Agnes Russell
Alessandra Strozzi
Alice Bokerel

Alice Hulle
Alice de Lincoln
Alice atte March
Alice of Rallingbury
Aaeles (la tapicière) [Alice]
Alice la Wymplere
Alison la Jourdain
Alison la Métaille
Anés (la cervoisière) [Anne]
Avis Wade
Basilia Maderman
Beatrice la Welsshe
Bourgot de Noir
Katherine l'Avise [Catherine]
Katherine Boteler [Catherine]
Catherine de Bruyères
Katherine Riche [Catherine]
Catherine Royer
Cavolaja of Florence
Denise (la barbière)
Denise (la sainturière)
Denise la Vileyn
Dionisia de Wodemerstham
Elizabeth, lady Avergavenny
Eudeline (la barbière)
Geneviève (la paonnière)
Gile (la mâconne)
Goda la Gablere
Gunnora de Stratford
Haoys (la meresse)
Huitace (la lanière)
Idonea le Hukestere
Isabelle Hodere [Isabelle]
Jacqueline Machecoue
Johanna Beauflour [Jean]
Jehanne (la boutonnière) [Jean]
Jeanne Dupré [Jean]
Jehanne (la fouacière) [Jean]
Jehanne Gaultière [Jean]
Joan Grene [Jean]
Joan Hunt [Jean]
Jehanne Lecointe [Jean]
Jeanne Saignant [Jean]
Jehanne (la tapicière) [Jean]
Johanna Travers [Jean]
Juliana Hauteyn
Lucrezia Crivelli
Lucy atte Lee
Maheut (la feutrière) [Mahaut]
Marguerite la Bonne Estranée [Margaret]
Marguerite (la chanevacière) [Margaret]
Marguerite (la cordière) [Margaret]
Marguerite Joli [Margaret]
Margaret Stoke
Margery (of Frocestor)
Margery Haynes
Margery de Honylane
Margery Kempe
Margery Paston
Margot (la Grosse)
Marion la Dentue
Maria de Malla [Mary]
Marie (la mareschale) [Mary]
Marie (la meresse) [Mary]
Matilda de Burgham
Matilda Yonge
Nicole (la saunière) [Nichole]
Perrette la Hance
Pérronnele (l'espicière) [Pérronelle]
Petronilla of Teye
Petronilla Turk
Quintine van den Zande
Raouline la Malingré
Richolda
Roesia de Borford
Sarah Stroby
Sara (of Wurzburg) [Sarah]
Sedillon Rossignol
Sewis van Berchem
Slymina Fort
Susane (la coiffière)
Thyphainne (la toière) [Tiffania]
Tryngen Ime Hove
Ulricha de Foschua
Vanozza Catanei
Ysabel de la Heuse
Ysabel (la meresse)
Ysabiau (la nourrice)

LAUNDRESSES

Also see: SERVANTS.

Massiota (la Lavendere)
Pérronnele (la lavendière) [Pérronelle]

LEGAL ACTIVITY

active participants in the legal system—holding manor courts, serving as attorney or executrix, giving judgements, enacting laws, bringing suit, etc.

Adelaide of Maurienne, queen of France
Aelips de Beauchamp
Ageltrudis (of Spoleto)
Agnes Brid
Agnes de Bury
Agnes Forster
Agnes Molton

Alice de Bryene
Alice Cantebrugge
Alice Chaucer, duchess of Suffolk
Alice Denecoumbe
Alice Perrers
Alice Shedyngton
Almodis (II) de La Marche, countess of Barcelona
Almodis (IV), countess of La Marche
Amalberga
Anastasia Spychefat
Angelica del Lama
Aud "the Deep-minded"
Avice Gardebois
Barbara Arrenti
Basilia Maderman
Beatrice d'Estellin
Beatrice de Warenne
Bertheida
Bethlem of Greci
Catherine d'Artois
Catherine Royer
Catherine Sforza
Catherine de Thouars
Katharine Vaux [Catherine]
Cecilia le Boteler
Cecily Chaumpaigne
Constance of Arles, queen of France
Coucy (lady de)
Denise la Vileyn
Douce (I) of Provence
Eleanor of Aquitaine
Eleanora di Arborea [Eleanor]
Eleanor Beauchamp, duchess of Somerset
Elizabeth de Clare
Elizabeth Kirkeby
Elizabeth Quintin
Emma Hatfield
Ermengarde of Anjou, duchess of Brittany
Ermengarde, viscountess of Narbonne
Ermessend of Carcassonne, countess of Barcelona
Hauviette (of Domremy)
Idonea le Hukestere
Irene, empress of Byzantium
Isabella, queen of Castile and Aragon [Isabelle]
Isabella de Fortibus [Isabelle]
Isabella Hodere [Isabelle]
Isabel Mowbray, lady Berkeley [Isabelle]
Isabel Romée [Isabelle]
Isabelle de Vescy
Isabellette of Épinal
Jacquetta of Luxembourg
Jane Stonor
Joan FitzAlan [Jean]
Joan Hart [Jean]
Joan Hunt [Jean]
Jeanne de Latilly [Jean]
Johanna (of London) [Jean]
Joan de Munchensi [Jean]
Johanna Wolsy [Jean]
Joan Woulbarowe [Jean]
Juliana Roos
Maddalena Bonsignori [Madeleine]
Mahaut of Artois
Margaret de Botreaux, lady Hungerford
Margaret Elyott
Margaret of France, queen of Hungary
Margaret of Logy
Margaret Paston
Margaret Stoke
Margaret Worthham
Margery de Honylane
Margery Russell
Marie de Brabant, queen of France [Mary]
Mary of St. Pol
Matilda of France
Matilda of Tuscany
Maud de Vere, countess of Oxford [Matilda]
Northilda
Perna
Peronne Loessart
Perette la Maugarnie
Petronille of Fontevrault [Petronilla]
Petronilla of Grandmesnil, countess of Leicester
Petronilla of Teye
Petronilla Turk
Philippa of Hainault
Poncette Aubry
Richilde, countess of Flanders
Roesia de Borford
Rose Savage
Saiv Kavanagh
Sewis van Berchem
Sybille of Anjou, countess of Flanders [Sibyl]
Thomasine Dinham
Tryngen Ime Hove
Valentine Visconti, duchess of Orléans
Virdimura of Sicily
Walgrave (lady)
Zoe the Porphyrogenita

LEPROSY

victims of; and women who cared for lepers

Also see: Medicine.

Agnes of Courtenay
Constance of Brittany
Eleanor of England, countess of Guelders
Hedwig of Silesia (St.)
Mary of Oignies
Mélisende of Jerusalem

LESS-AFFLUENT

townswomen who were apparently at the lower end of the urban socio-economic scale

Adelie l'Erbière [Adele]
Agnes Deyntee
Agnes (of Holbourne)
Agnes Rokingeham
Agnes Sigily
Alice Staundon
Alice (of Stratford)
Aalis (l'ymaginière) [Alice]
Alison (la nourrice)
Ameline (la bouchière)
Ameline (la couturière)
Amice la Plomere [Amicia]
Anès (la taupière) [Anne]
Ascelinne (la deicière)
Beatrice Bassett
Beatriz (la buffretière) [Beatrice]
Bietrix (la metresse) [Beatrice]
Katherine (l'attachière) [Catherine]
Coustance (la parcheminière)
Cristiana la Flaoners
Denisette de Periers
Edeline (la barbière)
Edeline (la paonnière)
Edelot (la fourmagière)
Emeline (la poréeresse)
Emeline (la ventrière)
Erembourc (la florière)
Erembourc (la potière)
Eudeline (la baudréere)
Felise (la pastéere)
File (la barbière)
Heaulmière (la belle)
Hélissent (la ferpière)
Heloys (l'uilière)
Heloyson (la nourrice)
Hodierne (la cerencerresse)
Jacqueline (la saacière)
Jehanne (la cristalière) [Jean]
Jehanne (la loirrière) [Jean]
Jehanne (la verrière) [Jean]
Jeannette du Fossé
Jourdenete (la nourrice)
Juliane (la potière) [Juliana]
Mabile (la regratière)
Maheut (la chapelière) [Mahaut]
Maheut (la pescheresse) [Mahaut]
Marguerite (la savonnière) [Margaret]
Martha (of Paris)
Marie d'Atainvile [Mary]
Marie (la barbière) [Mary]
Marie (la fanière) [Mary]
Massiota (la Lavendere)
Maud Makejoy [Matilda]
Michièle (la ventrière)
Milessent (la cerenceresse)
Nicole (la boursière) [Nichole]
Nicole (l'erbière) [Nichole]
Nicole (l'esperonnière) [Nichole]
Pentecouste (la fruitière)
Pérronnele (la lavendière) [Pérronelle]
Pérronele (la nourrice) [Pérronelle]
Phelipote (la fritière)
Phelippe (la miergesse) [Phillipa]
Richeut (la meresse)
Sainte (la paintre)
Sedile (la fournière)
Typhainne (la blazennière) [Tiffania]
Tyfainne (mestresse de l'école) [Tiffania]
Ysabelle de l'Espine [Ysabel]
Ysabiau (la ferpière) [Ysabel]
Ysabelet la Blanche

Liege-lords see: MANAGERS.

LOLLARDS

Also see: HERETICS.

Alice Dexter
Anna Palmer [Anne]
Katherine Dertford [Catherine]
Hawise Mone
Joan of Kent [Jean]
Margery Baxter
Matilda of Leicester

MANAGERS

liege-lords; women who administered large estates

Also see: ESTATE; LAND/PROPERTY; REGENTS.

Adelheid of Germany, abbess of Quedlinburg [Adelaide]
Adelaide of Roumainmoutier

Agnes of Courtenay
Agnes, countess of Dunbar
Agnes Paston
Agnes de Sechelles
Alessandra Strozzi
Alice de Bryene
Alice Chaucer, duchess of Suffolk
Alice Knyvet
Almodis (IV), countess of La Marche
Amalberga
Anne Devereux
Aud "the Deep-minded"
Baddlesmere (lady)
Beatrice, marchioness of Tuscany
Bertha of Avenay
Bethlem of Greci
Blanche of Laurac
Blanche of Ponthieu
Catherine d'Artois
Colette of Corbie
Constance of France, countess of Toulouse
Contessina de'Bardi
Cwenthryth of Mercia
Dhuoda
Eleanor of Castile, queen of England
Eleanor de Montfort, countess of Leicester
Eleanor Neville, countess of Northumberland
Elizabeth Bourchier
Elizabeth de Burgh
Elizabeth de Clare
Elisabetta Gonzaga [Elizabeth]
Ermengard (of S. Salvatore)
Ermentrude of Jouarre
Esclarmonde de Foix
Friderun (of Germany)
Gerberga of Bavaria
Hersende (of Fontevrault)
Ippolita Sforza
Isabella d'Este [Isabelle]
Isabella de Fortibus [Isabelle]
Isabel Mowbray, lady Berkeley [Isabelle]
Isabel Plumpton [Isabelle]
Jane Stonor
Joan Buckland [Jean]
Joan of England, countess of Gloucester [Jean]
Joan FitzAlan [Jean]
Joan FitzAlan, lady Begavenny [Jean]
Joan of Kent [Jean]
Jeanne de Valois [Jean]
Juliana de Leybourne, countess of Huntingdon
Kristin (of Iceland)
Lesceline, countess of Eu
Liutberga (St.)
Lucrezia Tornabuoni
Mabel of Bellême
Margaret Beauchamp, countess of Shrewsbury
Margaret de Bohun, countess of Devon
Margaret de Botreaux, lady Hungerford
Marguerite de Clisson [Margaret]
Margherita Datini [Margaret]
Margaret of France, countess of Flanders
Margaret Holland
Margaret Lacy
Margaret Marshall
Margaret Paston
Margery de Honylane
Margery Twynyho
Matha d'Armagnac [Martha]
Martha Boretsky
Marie de Berry [Mary]
Mary of St. Pol
Matilda of France
Matilda of Lancaster
Maud de Vere, countess of Oxford [Matilda]
Otta of S. Salvatore
Petronille of Comminges [Petronilla]
Petronille of Fontevrault [Petronilla]
Petronilla of Grandmesnil, countess of Leicester
Philippa de Dammartin
Philippe de Moncada
Regina della Scala
Roiantken
Sybille de Château-Porcien [Sibyl]
Sophia of Gandersheim
Svanhild of Essen
Tiphaine Raguel [Tiffania]

MANORS

includes peasant women (bondswomen and free women); predominantly women whose existence is documented only in local, village, manorial records—usually court rolls

Agnes Brid
Agnes de Broughton
Agnes Kateline
Agnes Page
Agnes Sadler
Agnes Thomas
Alice Barley
Alice Hulle

Alice of Rallingbury
Alson Potkyn
Avis Wade
Beatrice Brounying
Beatrice d'Estellin
Beatrice Puttock
Katherine Boteler [Catherine]
Cecilia le Boteler
Eleanor de Wendale
Elena Baroun
Hauviette (of Domremy)
Isabel Romée [Isabelle]
Isabellette of Épinal
Joan of Arc (St.) [Jean]
Joan Everard [Jean]
Lucy atte Lee
Margery (of Frocestor)
Margery of Hales
Margery Haynes
Peronne Loessart
Petronilla of Teye
Sarra (of Broughton) [Sarah]
Masons see: BUILDERS.

MEDICINE

includes medical assistants, lecturers, hospital builders, those women who were especially known for medical knowledge, etc.

For specific ailments see: CHILDBIRTH; HANDICAPPED; INSANITY; LEPROSY; PLAGUE.

For specific medical practitioners see: APOTHECARIES; BARBERS; DOCTORS/EMPIRICS; MIDWIVES; NURSES; SURGEONS.

Abella of Salerno
Agnes da Montepulciano (St.)
Alesandra Gilani [Alessandra]
Alix of Brittany [Alice]
Anne, princess of Bohemia
Anna Comnena [Anne]
Beatriz Galindo [Beatrice]
Beatrice of Savoy, countess of Provence
Bertha of Sulzbach
Bertrande of Avignon
Bridget of Sweden
Catherine of Bologna (St.)
Caterina of Florence [Catherine]
Catherine of Genoa
Catherine Sforza
Catherine of Siena (St.)
Christine Swath
Clementia, countess of Flanders
Dorotea Bocchi [Dorothy]
Eleanor of Aquitaine
Elizabeth of Poland, queen of Hungary
Elizabeth of Portugal (St.)
Esclarmonde de Foix
Euphemia of Wherwell
Frances of Rome (St.)
Guigone de Salins
Hedwig of Silesia (St.)
Hersende (of Fontevrault)
Hildegarde of Bingen (St.)
Hroswitha of Gandersheim
Huguette Balarin
Irene Lascaris, empress of Byzantium
Isabella, queen of Castile and Aragon [Isabelle]
Juliana Falconieri (St.)
Laurette de Saint-Valéry
Lydwine of Schiedam
Maddalena Bonsignori [Madeleine]
Mahaut of Artois
Margaret of Austria
Margaret of Cortona (St.)
Margaret, queen of Scotland (St.)
Maria Enriquez [Mary]
Mary of Gelders, queen of Scotland
Mary of Oignies
Matilda of Quedlinburg
Matilda of Scotland
Mélisende, queen of Jerusalem
Mercuriade of Salerno
Péronnele (l'espicière) [Pérronelle]
Philippa of Hainault
Sichelgaita of Salerno
Toda, queen of Navarre
Urraca of Castile, queen of Portugal
Yolande of Aragon

MERCHANTS

small businesses, hucksters, unknown, or vague, craft affiliations; and a variety of miscellaneous trades that included few female participants

Agnes Asser
Agnes Broumattin
Agnes de Bury
Agnes Chaucer
Agnes Mundene
Agnes Sigily
Alessandra Strozzi
Alice Bokerel
Alice Cantebrugge
Alice Chester
Aelis (la poissonière) [Alice]

Alice (of Stratford)
Ameline (la cordoanière)
Amice la Plomere [Amicia]
Anés (la gueinnière) [Anne]
Ascelinne (la deicière)
Basilia Maderman
Bourgot de Noir
Katerine (l'attachière) [Catherine]
Catherine de Bruyères
Katherine Husenboltz [Catherine]
Cavolaja of Florence
Colette la Moynesse
Denise (la sainturière)
Denisette de Periers
Elizabeth, lady Abergavenny
Elizabeth Croke
Elizabeth Kirkeby
Elisabeth Scepens [Elizabeth]
Ellen Sage
Erembourc de Braières
Erembourc (la florière)
Estienne (la gravelière)
Geneviève (la paonnière)
Gunnora de Stratford
Haouys (la poulaillière)
Heaulmière (la belle)
Heloys (l'uilière)
Huitace (la lanière)
Idonea le Hukestere
Isabella de Fortibus [Isabelle]
Isabella Hodere [Isabelle]
Isabel Norman [Isabelle]
Jacqueline Machecoue
Jane Harold
Jehanne (la bouchière) [Jean]
Jehanne (la cristalière) [Jean]
Jehanne (la fouacière) [Jean]
Jehanne Lecointe [Jean]
Joanna Rowley [Jean]
Johanna Travers [Jean]
Jehanne (la verrière) [Jean]
Kateline de Coster
Mabel of Bury St. Edmunds
Maheut (la feutrière) [Mahaut]
Marguerite (l'avenière) [Margaret]
Marguerite (la chanevacière) [Margaret]
Marguerite (la cordière) [Margaret]
Marguerite (la savonnière) [Maqrgaret]
Margery Haynes
Margery Kempe
Margery Russell
Mariota Convers
Martha Boretsky
Marie (la fanière) [Mary]
Maria de Malla [Mary]
Maud Francis [Matilda]
Matilda Yonge
Nicole (l'esperonnière) [Nichole]
Nicole (la saunière) [Nichole]
Olga, princess of Kiev (St.)
Pérronnele (l'espicière) [Pérronelle]
Petronilla of Grandmesnil, countess of Leicester
Petronilla Turk
Roesia de Borford
Sanche Snoth [Sancia]
Sarah Stroby
Sewis van Berchem
Susane (la coiffière)
Tryngen Ime Hove
Typhainne (la blazennière) [Tiffania]
Vanozza Catanei
Ysabelle de l'Espine [Ysabel]
Ysabiau (la ferpière) [Ysabel]
Ysabelet la Blanche

MIDWIVES

Also see: CHILDBIRTH; DOCTORS/EMPRIRICS; MEDICINE.

Elizabeth, lady Scrope
Emeline (la ventrière)
Margaret Cobbe
Michièle (la ventrière)
Peretta Peronne [Perrette]
Trotula of Salerno

Miniaturists see: ARTISTS; BOOKMAKING.

MINING

women who owned mines, or who worked in or around the mining business

Estienne (la gravelière)
Odeline

MISCREANTS

Also see: MURDER; PRISONS; PUNISHMENTS.

Agnes Avesot
Agnes de Broughton
Agnes de Bury
Agnes Deyntee
Agnes Irlond
Agnes Mundene
Agnes Page
Agnes Thomas
Agnes Wombe

Alexandra Crowe [Alessandra]
Alice Barley
Alice atte Harpe
Alice de Lincoln
Alice de Lye
Alice Shether
Ameline (la miresse)
Antoinette de Bellegarde
Beatrice Bassett
Beatrice Puttock
Beatrice la Welsshe
Brunetta
Catharine Pykring [Catherine]
Cristina Blake [Christine]
Christine Swath
Claude des Armoises
Denise de Partenay
Eleanor de Wendale
Elena Baroun
Gytha of Denmark
Huguette du Hamel
Ida de Portunhale
Isabella de Toppesham [Isabelle]
Jacoba Felicie
Jane Harold
Joan, lady Beauchamp [Jean]
Jeanne "Conversa" [Jean]
Jeanne de Cusey [Jean]
Joan Grene [Jean]
Jeanne de Latilly [Jean]
Jeanne de Valois [Jean]
Jeannette Camus
Judith (of Germany)
Juliana Roos
Margaret Wavere
Marguerite de Ypres [Margaret]
Margery Paston
Mariota Convers
Massiota (la Lavendere)
Matilda of Flanders
Peretta Peronne [Perrette]
Poncette Aubry
Rose Nosterfeld

MISTRESSES

Also see: ADULTERY; PROSTITUTES; WOMEN OF EASY VIRTUE.

Agnese del Maino [Agnes]
Agnes Sorel
Alice Perrers
Alison Dumay
Antoinette de Villequier
Arlette (of Normandy)
Aurembaix, countess of Urgel
Bertha
Bezole
Katherine Swynford [Catherine]
Cecilia Gallerani
Châtellerault (countess of)
Cyenthryth, queen of Mercia
Doda
Ecgwyna
Edith Swan-neck
Leonor de Guzman [Eleanor]
Elizabeth Lucy
Felise Reynard
Guilia Farnese
Gunnor (of Denmark)
Guyette Durand
Ines de Castro
Isotta degli Atti
Jane Shore
Jeanne de Divion [Jean]
Joan Hart [Jean]
Jeanne de Milières [Jean]
Lucia Marliani
Lucrezia d'Alagno
Lucrezia Crivelli
Margherita [Margaret]
Margaret of Cortona (St.)
Margery (of Calais)
Maria de Padilla [Mary]
Nesta
Odette de Champdivers
Richilde of Autun
Rosamund Clifford
Roza
Sclerena (of Byzantium)
Sibilia de Forcia [Sibyl]
Subh of Cordoba
Tarub (of Cordoba)
Theodora Comnena
Theodora Comnena, queen of Jerusalem
Theodora of Rome
Thora of Norway
Vanozza Catanei
Waldrada
Zoe Carbounopsina

MODELS

women used as images/models in art and/or literature

Aasta Grönske
Azalais de Rocamartina [Adelaide]
Adelaide of Toulouse
Adele, countess of Blois and Chartres

Aelfthryth
Aethelflaed, lady of the Mercians
Agnes of Burgundy, duchess of Bourbon
Agnes Desjardins
Agnes of Hapsburg, queen of Hungary
Agnes de Launcreona
Agnes da Montepulciano (St.)
Agnes of Navarre
Agnes Sorel
Agnes von Staufen
Alesandra Gilani [Alessandra]
Alix la Bourgolle [Alice]
Alice Chaucer, duchess of Suffolk
Alice Drayton
Alys of France [Alice]
Alice Lacy, countess of Lancaster
Alice de Montfort
Alice Perrers
Alison (of Port-Royal)
Almucs de Castelnau
Ambroise de Lore
Anastaise of Paris [Anastasia]
Anne of Beaujeu
Anne of Bohemia, queen of England
Anna Dalassena [Anne]
Anna of Mochov [Anne]
Anne Mowbray
Anne Neville, queen of England
Antoinette de Villequier
Asa, queen of Agdir
Astrid (of Denmark)
Astrid of Norway
Aubrée d'Ivry
Aud "the Deep-minded"
Barbara von Brandenburg
Barbara of Cilly, Holy Roman Empress
Battista Sforza
Beatrice di Correggio
Beatrice Portinari
Bertha
Bertrade de Montfort, queen of France
Bianca Giovanna Sforza
Blanche of Burgundy
Blanche of Castile, queen of France
Blanche of Lancaster
Blanche of Montferrat, duchess of Savoy
Blanche of Portugal
Bonne of Armagnac
Bonne of Artois
Catherine of Bologna (St.)
Catherine de Bruyères
Caterina Cornaro, queen of Cyprus [Catherine]
Catherine of France, queen of England
Katharine Grandison [Catherine]
Katherine Neville [Catherine]
Katherine Riche [Catherine]
Catherine of Sweden (St.)
Katherine Swynford [Catherine]
Catherine de Vausselles
Cecilia of Flanders
Cecilia Gallerani
Cecile de Turenne [Cecilia]
Charlotte of Savoy
Christina of Markyate [Christine]
Christina of St. Trond [Christine]
Christina of Stommeln [Christine]
Clementia, countess of Flanders
Constance of Arles, queen of France
Constance of Hohenstaufen
Cunigund of Luxembourg, Holy Roman Empress (St.) [Cunigunde]
Cwenthryth of Mercia
Cyenthryth, queen of Mercia
Diemudis of Wessobrun [Diemud]
Dorotea Gonzaga [Dorothy]
Dorothy of Montau
Drahomira
Eadburg of Mercia
Eadgyth (of England) (St.)
Ebba
Edith of England, queen of Germany
Edith Swan-neck
Edith of Wessex, queen of England
Eleanor of Aquitaine
Leonor of Aragon, countess of Toulouse [Eleanor]
Eleanor de Bohun, duchess of Gloucester
Eleanor of Castile, queen of England
Eleanor Cobham
Eleanor of England, queen of Castile
Eleanor de Montfort, countess of Leicester
Eleanor Talbot
Elisabetta Gonzaga [Elizabeth]
Elizabeth Higgins
Elizabeth of Hungary (St.)
Elizabeth of Luxembourg
Elizabeth of Schönau (St.)
Elizabeth of York, queen of England
Emilia Pia
Emma, queen of Germany
Emma of Normandy
Ermengarde of Anjou, duchess of Brittany
Ermengarde (of Ivrea)
Ermengarde, viscountess of Narbonne
Ermentrude of Orléans

Eudoxia Comnena [Eudocia]
Eudocia Ingerina, empress of Byzantium
Eudocia Macrembolitissa, empress of Byzantium
Euphemia of Arnstein, queen of Norway
Euphemia of Wherwell
Eupraxia of Kiev, Holy Roman Empress
Fiametta
Francesca da Rimini
Freydis of Norway
Garsenda de Forcalquier
Gerberga of Bavaria
Gertrude van Öosten
Gertrude of Saxony, duchess of Bavaria
Gilette of Narbonne
Ginevra (Datini)
Gisela
Gisela of Bavaria, queen of Hungary
Gisela of Swabia, queen of Germany
Godgifu, lady of Mercia
Gruoch, queen of Scotland
Gudrid (of Greenland)
Guigone de Salins
Guillemette (la tapicière)
Gundreda (of Warenne)
Gunnhild of Denmark, queen of Germany
Gunhild of Denmark, queen of Norway
Hathumoda of Gandersheim
Heaulmière (la belle)
Hedwig of Bavaria
Helena (Guiscard) [Helen]
Heloise of Argenteuil
Helwise of Nevers, countess of Évreux
Herrad von Landsberg
Huguette du Hamel
Ida of Swabia
Ines de Castro
Ingunn (of Iceland)
Ippolita Sforza
Irene, empress of Byzantium
Irene Ducas, empress of Byzantium
Irene Lascaris, empress of Byzantium
Isabella of Aragon, duchess of Milan [Isabelle]
Isabeau of Bavaria [Isabelle]
Isabelle of Bourbon
Isabel Despenser, countess of Warwick [Isabelle]
Isabella d'Este [Isabelle]
Isabelle of France
Isabella of France, queen of England [Isabelle]
Isabella of Hainault, queen of France [Isabelle]
Isabel of Lorraine [Isabelle]
Isabel de Montfort [Isabelle]
Isabella of Portugal [Isabelle]
Isotta degli Atti
Isotta Nogarola
Ivetta of Huy
Jacqueline Machecoue
Jane Shore
Joan of Arc (St.) [Jean]
Joan Beaufort, queen of Scotland [Jean]
Jeanne de Belleville [Jean]
Jeanne de Boulogne, duchess of Berry [Jean]
Jeanne de Boulogne, queen of France [Jean]
Jeanne de Bourbon, queen of France [Jean]
Jehanne de Bretagne [Jean]
Jeanne of Burgundy, queen of France [Jean]
Juana of Castile [Jean]
Juana Enriquez, queen of Aragon [Jean]
Jeanne d'Évreux, queen of France [Jean]
Joan Hart [Jean]
Joan of Kent [Jean]
Jeanne Laisne [Jean]
Jeanne de Laval [Jean]
Juana Manuel, queen of Castile [Jean]
Jeanne de Milières [Jean]
Jeanne de Montfort [Jean]
Joanna I, queen of Naples [Jean]
Jeanne de Penthièvre [Jean]
Juana of Portugal [Jean]
Judith of Bavaria, Holy Roman Empress
Kasia (of Byzantium)
Laura
Lesceline, countess of Eu
Liutberga (St.)
Lutgard of Aywières (St.) [Liutgard]
Loba de Pueinautier
Louise of Savoy
Lucrezia d'Alagno
Lucrezia Borgia
Lucrezia Crivelli
Lucrezia Donati
Lucrezia d'Este
Lucrezia Tornabuoni
Ludmila (of Bohemia)
Lydwine of Schiedam
Mabel of Bellême
Mabel Rich
Maddalena Scrovegni [Madeleine]
Margaret of Anjou
Margaret of Burgundy

Margaret of France, queen of Hungary
Margaret of Hainault, duchess of Burgundy
Marguerite Joli [Margaret]
Margaret of Logy
Margaret of Maine
Margaret Neville, countess of Oxford
Margaret Rocliffe
Margarida de Roussillon [Margaret]
Marguerite de Turenne [Margaret]
Margaret of York
Margaret of Ypres
Margery (of Calais)
Marjorie, countess of Carrick [Margery]
Margery Paston
Margot (la Grosse)
Margot de Hainault
Marion la Dentue
Marozia of Rome
Martha Boretsky
Marthe (of Paris) [Martha]
Marie de Berry [Mary]
Marie of Bourbon [Mary]
Marie of Burgundy [Mary]
Marie of Cleves [Mary]
Marie of France, countess of Champagne [Mary]
Mary of Oignies
Marie d'Orléans [Mary]
Marie, countess of Ponthieu and Aumale [Mary]
Maria of Vivar [Mary]
Matilda of England, duchess of Bavaria
Matilda of England, Holy Roman Empress
Matilda of Flanders
Matilda, queen of Germany
Maud Lovell, lady Arundel [Matilda]
Matilda of Quedlinburg
Matilda of Rottenburg
Matilda of Scotland
Matilda of Tuscany
Maura of Troyes (St.)
Mechtild von Hackeborn
Mélisende, queen of Jerusalem
Myfanwy (Tudor)
Novella d'Andrea
Odeline
Olga, princess of Kiev (St.)
Onorata Rodiana
Ota (of Norway)
Parisina Malatesta
Péronnelle d'Armentières [Pérronelle]
Petronilla of Aquitaine, countess of Vermandois
Philippa of Antioch
Philippa de Coucy
Philippa of Hainault
Philippa of Lancaster, queen of Portugal
Philippe de Moncada [Philippa]
Philippa Mortimer
Philippa Roet
Ragnhild (of Ringerike)
Regina della Scala
Richardis von Stade
Richenza of Nordheim, Holy Roman Empress
Rogneda of Polotsk
Rosalia of Palermo (St.)
Rosamund Clifford
Rose of Viterbo (St.)
Rotrude
Roza
Rozala of Lombardy
Sancia d'Aragona
Sanchia of Provence [Sancia]
Sclerena (of Byzantium)
Sybil of Conversano [Sibyl]
Sichelgaita of Salerno
Sigrid, queen of Sweden
Simone of Byzantium
Simonetta Cattaneo
Sophia, princess of Moscow
Stephania (of Rome)
Strathearn (countess of)
Tamara, queen of Georgia
Teodorina (Cibo)
Theodora Comnena
Theodora of Rome
Theophano, empress of Byzantium
Theresa of Castile
Theresa of Portugal, countess of Flanders
Theutberga, queen of Lotharingia
Thyra of Denmark
Tibors d'Omelas
Tiphaine Raguel [Tiffania]
Trotula of Salerno
Turakina
Urraca, queen of Castile
Violante Visconti
Waldrada
Walgrave (lady)
Willa of Tuscany, queen of Italy
Ximena Diaz
Ydain of Lorraine
Yolande de Dreux, queen of Scotland

Money changers see: BANKING.

MURDER

includes victims, murderers, and those accused of murder

Adela of Flanders, queen of Denmark [Adele]
Aelfthryth
Agnes Sorel
Alice de Clare
Alison Dumay
Almodis (II) de La Marche, countess of Barcelona
Anastasia Spychefat
Ankarette Twynyho
Asa, queen of Agdir
Aubrée d'Ivry
Bertilla
Blanche of Aragon
Bonne de Bourbon, countess of Savoy [Bona]
Catherine Sforza
Cecilia le Boteler
Cecilia Rygeway
Charlotte (de Valois)
Christine Swath
Constance of Arles, queen of France
Cwenthryth of Mercia
Cyenthryth, queen of Mercia
Drahomira
Eadburg of Mercia
Ebba
Edith of Wessex, queen of England
Leonor of Aragon, queen of Navarre [Eleanor]
Leonor of Castile, queen of Aragon [Eleanor]
Leonor de Guzman [Eleanor]
Elizabeth of Bosnia
Francesca Bentivoglio
Francesca da Rimini
Gerberga (of Toulouse)
Gertrude of Meissen
Gertrud of Meran [Gertrude]
Ginevra d'Este
Giralda de Laurac
Gunhild of Denmark, queen of Norway
Ines de Castro
Ingeborg of Norway
Ingerid of Sweden
Isabella of Jerusalem [Isabelle]
Isabel Neville [Isabelle]
Isotta degli Atti
Jeanne of Burgundy, queen of France [Jean]
Juana Enriquez, queen of Aragon [Jean]
Joanna I, queen of Naples [Jean]
Juliana (Cordwaner)
Lucia Tasseburgh
Lucrezia Borgia
Ludmila (of Bohemia)
Mabel of Bellême
Margaret Aldobrandeschi
Margaret of Brabant, countess of Flanders
Margaret of Sweden, queen of Norway
Marozia of Rome
Mary of Antioch
Marie de Brabant, queen of France [Mary]
Maria Comnena, princess of Byzantium [Mary]
Maria Enriquez [Mary]
Maria of Portugal [Mary]
Maud de Braose [Matilda]
Onorata Rodiana
Parisina Malatesta
Richolda
Rogneda of Polotsk
Sigrid, queen of Sweden
Stephania (of Rome)
Tanglost
Tarub (of Cordoba)
Theophano, empress of Byzantium
Zoe the Porphyrogenita

MUSIC

composers, singers, patronesses, musicians

Agnes Butler
Beatrice de Dia
Beatrice d'Este
Catherine of Bologna (St.)
Caterina Cornaro, queen of Cyprus [Catherine]
Cecilia Gallerani
Charlotte of Savoy
Clara Hätzerlin
Constance of Castile, duchess of Lancaster
Eleanor of England, queen of Castile
Elisabetta Gonzaga [Elizabeth]
Hadewijch
Herrad von Landsberg
Hildegarde of Bingen (St.)
Ianka of Kiev
Isabeau of Bavaria [Isabelle]
Isabelle d'Este [Isabelle]
Judith of Bavaria, Holy Roman Empress
Liutberga (St.)
Lucrezia Borgia

Lucrezia Tornabuoni
Mahaut of Artois
Margaret of Flanders, duchess of Burgundy
Margaret of France, queen of England
Margaret of Scotland
Margaret, queen of Scotland (St.)
Marie of Burgundy [Mary]
Matilda of Scotland
Mechtild von Hackeborn
Noel (of France)
Parisina Malatesta
Pearl in the Egg
Péronnelle d'Armentières [Pérronelle]
Valentine Visconti, duchess of Orléans

MYSTICS

visionaries, psychics, seers, etc.

Agnes da Montepulciano (St.)
Angela of Foligno
Beatrice of Nazareth
Bloemardine
Bridget of Sweden (St.)
Catherine of Genoa (St.)
Catherine de la Rochelle
Catherine of Siena (St.)
Christina of Markyate [Christine]
Christina of St. Trond [Christine]
Christina of Stommeln [Christine]
Clare of Montefalco (St.)
Colette of Corbie (St.)
Dorothy of Montau
Douceline (St.)
Elizabeth of Schönau (St.)
Euphemia of Wherwell
Frances of Rome (St.)
Gertrude of Hackeborn
Gertrude von Helfta
Gertrude van Öosten
Guglielma (of Milan)
Hadewijch
Hedwig of Silesia (St.)
Hildegarde of Bingen (St.)
Joan of Arc (St.) [Jean]
Juliana of Cornillon
Julian of Norwich [Juliana]
Jutta of Sponheim
Liutberga (St.)
Lutgard of Aywières (St.) [Liutgard]
Lucia Brocadelli
Lydwine of Schiedam
Margaret of Cortona (St.)
Margaret Ebner
Marguerite d'Oingt [Margaret]
Margaret Porete
Margery Kempe
Marie d'Avignon [Mary]
Mary of Oignies
Matilda, queen of Germany
Mechtild von Hackeborn
Mechtild of Magdeburg
Ota (of Norway)
Ragnhild (of Ringerike)
Theoda of Mainz
Umiliana dei Cherchi (St.)
Wulfhilda of Barking (St.)

NEGOTIATORS

marriage arrangers, political envoys, treaty negotiators, etc.

Adelaide (Capet), queen of France
Adelheid of Savoy [Adelaide]
Adele, countess of Blois and Chartres
Aethelflaed, lady of the Mercians
Agnes of Anjou
Agnes of Courtenay
Agnes of Hapsburg, queen of Hungary
Agnes of Saarbrücken
Alix de Vergy, duchess of Burgundy [Alice]
Angelberga
Anne of Beaujeu
Anne of Burgundy, duchess of Bedford
Anna Dalassena [Anne]
Anne de Lusignan
Anne Neville, duchess of Buckingham
Anne of York, duchess of Exeter
Astrid of Sweden
Barbara von Brandenburg
Beatrice d'Este
Beatrice (of France), duchess of Haute-Lorraine
Beatrice of Savoy, countess of Provence
Berenguela of Castile
Bertha of Swabia, duchess of Lorraine
Bertha of Tuscany
Bianca of Savoy
Blanche of Anjou, queen of Aragon
Blanche of Artois
Blanche of Castile, queen of France
Blanche of Montferrat, duchess of Savoy
Blanche of Navarre, countess of Champagne
Blanche of Navarre, queen of France
Blanche of Ponthieu
Catherine of France, queen of England
Catherine of Navarre

Caterina Visconti [Catherine]
Cecily Neville, duchess of York [Cecilia]
Clarissa Orsini [Claricia]
Colette of Corbie
Cunigund of Luxembourg, Holy Roman Empress (St.) [Cunigunde]
Delphine of Languedoc
Eadgifu of England, queen of France
Edith of Wessex, queen of England
Leonor of Albuquerque [Eleanor]
Eleanor of Aquitaine
Eleanora de Montfort [Eleanor]
Elizabeth of Bosnia
Elizabeth Croke
Elizabeth, princess of England
Elizabeth of Poland, queen of Hungary
Elizabeth of Pomerania
Elizabeth of Portugal (St.)
Elizabeth Talbot
Elizabeth Woodville
Elizabeth of York, queen of England
Emma of France
Ermengarde de Beaumont, queen of Scotland
Ermengard, duchess of Lombardy, queen of Provence
Euphrosyne of Byzantium
Gerberga of Saxony, queen of France
Gisela of Swabia, queen of Germany
Gormflath (of Ireland)
Isabeau of Bavaria [Isabelle]
Isabella of France, queen of England [Isabelle]
Isabel of Lorraine [Isabelle]
Isabella of Portugal [Isabelle]
Isotta degli Atti
Jacquetta of Luxembourg
Jadwiga of Hungary
Joan of England, princess of Gwynedd [Jean]
Jeanne d'Évreux, queen of France [Jean]
Joan of Kent [Jean]
Jeanne de Penthièvre [Jean]
Jeanne de Valois, countess of Hainault [Jean]
Kateline de Coster
Lucrezia Tornabuoni
Margaret of Anjou
Margaret of Austria
Margaret of Brabant, Holy Roman Empress
Margaret de Clare
Marguerite de Clisson [Margaret]
Margaret of Cortona (St.)
Margaret of Denmark
Margaret of Flanders, duchess of Burgundy
Margaret of France, countess of Flanders
Margaret of York
Martha Boretsky
Marie of Bohemia [Mary]
Maria of Castile [Mary]
Maria Comnena, queen of Jerusalem [Mary]
Matilda of Boulogne, queen of England
Matilda of England, Holy Roman Empress
Matilda of Savoy
Matilda of Tuscany
Mélisende, queen of Jerusalem
Morphia of Melitene
Petronille of Comminges
Philippa of England
Philippa of Hainault
Philippa of Lancaster, queen of Portugal
Richenza of Nordheim, Holy Roman Empress
Sibylla of Jerusalem [Sibyl]
Subh of Cordoba
Theophano of Byzantium, Holy Roman Empress
Theresa of Portugal, countess of Flanders
Toda, queen of Navarre
Turakina
Yolande of Aragon
Yolande de Valois

NUNS

also includes canonesses
Also see: ABBESSES; ANCHORESSES; BEGUINES; RELIGIEUSES.
Agnes of Bohemia
Agnes Butler
Alice Romayn
Alison (of Port-Royal)
Barbara Gwichtmacherin
Beatrice of Castile
Beatrice of Monyons
Bertha
Catherine of Sweden (St.)
Cecilia Gonzaga
Christina (of Gandersheim)
Clare of Assisi
Clara Gatterstedt [Clare]
Clemence of Barking
Cornelie van Wulfskerke
Kunigunda of Nuremberg [Cunigunde]

Diemud of Wessobrun
Diemudis of Wessobrun [Diemud]
Dulcia de Bosqueto
Eadburga of Winchester (St.)
Eadgyth (of England) (St.)
Elena Taillour
Elvira of Leon
Ermengarde (of St. Adrina)
Eupraxia of Kiev, Holy Roman Empress
Evfosinia of Polotsk
Gerberga (of Toulouse)
Gertrude von Helfta
Gisela
Gisela of Kerzenbroeck
Goda la Gablere
Guda (of Germany)
Gwenllian (of Wales)
Hroswitha of Gandersheim
Idonea
Jeanne de Crespi [Jean]
Joanna of England, queen of Sicily [Jean]
Jeanne Potier [Jean]
Margaretha Cartheuserin [Margaret]
Margaret Ebner
Margaret of England (St.)
Margaret of Hungary
Mary of Blois
Mechtild von Hackeborn
Mechtild of Magdeburg
Philippine de Porcellet
Sancha of Portugal (St.) [Sancia]
Simone of Byzantium
Teresa de Cartagena [Theresa]
Theresa of Portugal, queen of Leon (St.)
Zoe Carbounopsina

NURSES

Agnes, countess of Aix
Agnes of Bohemia
Agnes Francou
Alison (la nourrice)
Anne, princess of Bohemia
Anne of Caux
Clemence Sillone
Eleanor of Castile, queen of England
Elizabeth of Hungary (St.)
Hedwig of Silesia (St.)
Heloyson (la nourrice)
Jeanne Pouponne [Jean]
Joan Waring [Jean]
Jourdenete (la nourrice)
Laurette de Saint-Valéry
Margaret Cobbe
Pérronele (la nourrice) [Pérronelle]
Ysabiau (la nourrice)

Occupations

For medical occupations see: MEDICINE.
For educators see: TEACHERS.
Many women—coopers, hucksters, florists, fur dealers, etc.—are found under the catch-all term: MERCHANTS.
For specific crafts see: ALEWIVES; APPAREL; APPRENTICES; BANKING; BATHHOUSE; BOOKMAKING; BUILDERS; CANDLE MAKERS; CLOTHWORKERS; EMPLOYERS; GEMS/JEWELRY; GOLDSMITHS; INNKEEPERS; LAUNDRESSES; MINING; POTTERS; PROVISIONING; RECOMMANDRESSES; SERVANTS; SHIPPING; SILKWORK; TANNERS; TAVERNERS.

ORDEALS

women involved in trials by ordeal or battle

Agnes (of Norfolk)
Cunigund of Luxembourg, Holy Roman Empress (St.) [Cunigunde]
Emma of Normandy
Galiena (of Norfolk)
Margaret of Sweden, queen of Norway
Margery of Hales
Matilda of Scotland
Richardis
Theutberga, queen of Lotharingia

ORPHANS

Agnes atte Holte
Alice atte March
Angela Merici (St.)
Anne, princess of Bohemia
Constance of Sicily, Holy Roman Empress
Leonor of Albuquerque [Eleanor]
Gwenllian (of Wales)
Irene Lascaris, empress of Byzantium
Jeanne de Boulogne, duchess of Berry [Jean]
Joan Fauconberg [Jean]
Jeanne of Flanders [Jean]
Jeanne of France, queen of Navarre [Jean]
Johanna Hadham [Jean]
Joan of Kent [Jean]
Jeanne Paynel [Jean]
Margaret of Citta di Castello
Margaret, countess of Flanders

Maria of Sicily [Mary]
Petronille of Comminges
Sibillina Biscossi
Sophia, princess of Moscow
Yolande de Dreux
Painters see: ARTISTS.

PATRONS OF LITERATURE

Also see: BOOK OWNERS.
Azalais de Rocamartina [Adelaide]
Adelaide of Toulouse
Adele, countess of Blois and Chartres
Adelicia of Louvain, queen of England
Agnes of Poitou, Holy Roman Empress
Alix of France, countess of Blois and Chartres [Alice]
Alice Henley
Alice Perrers
Almucs de Castelnau
Anne of Bohemia, queen of England
Anne of Brittany, queen of France
Anne Shirley
Battista Sforza
Beatrice of Burgundy
Beatrice d'Este
Beatrice of Savoy, countess of Provence
Bertha of Sulzbach
Bona of Luxembourg
Caterina Cornaro, queen of Cyprus [Catherine]
Cecilia of Flanders
Charlotte of Savoy
Constance (FitzGilbert)
Costanza Varano [Constance]
Dionysia de Mountchesny
Edith of Wessex, queen of England
Eleanor of Aquitaine
Leonora of Aragon, duchess of Ferrara [Eleanor]
Leonor of Aragon, countess of Toulouse [Eleanor]
Eleanor of Castile, queen of England
Eleanor of England, queen of Castile
Leonor of Lancastre [Eleanor]
Eleanor of Provence, queen of England
Elisabetta Gonzaga [Elizabeth]
Emilia Pia
Emma of Normandy
Ermengarde, viscountess of Narbonne
Eudoxia Comnena [Eudocia]
Euphemia of Arnstein, queen of Norway
Garsenda de Forcalquier
Giralda de Laurac
Gisela of Swabia, queen of Germany
Gunhild of Denmark, queen of Norway
Irene Ducas, empress of Byzantium
Irene Lascaris, empress of Byzantium
Isabeau of Bavaria [Isabelle]
Isabel, lady Bourchier [Isabelle]
Isabella d'Este [Isabelle]
Isabella of Portugal [Isabelle]
Isabella of Vermandois, countess of Flanders [Isabelle]
Jeanne of Burgundy, queen of France [Jean]
Jeanne of Navarre, queen of France [Jean]
Jeanne de Valois, countess of Hainault [Jean]
Judith of Bavaria, Holy Roman Empress
Judith (of Germany)
Loba de Pueinautier
Lucrezia Borgia
Lucrezia Tornabuoni
Margaret Beaufort
Margaret of Flanders, duchess of Burgundy
Margaret Lacy
Marguerite of Provence, queen of France [Margaret]
Margarida de Roussillon [Margaret]
Margaret of Scotland
Marguerite de Turenne [Margaret]
Margaret of York
Margery Twynyho
Marie de Berry [Mary]
Marie de Brabant, queen of France [Mary]
Maria of Castile [Mary]
Marie of Champagne, countess of Flanders [Mary]
Marie of France, countess of Champagne [Mary]
Marie, countess of Ponthieu and Aumale [Mary]
Marie de Ventadour [Mary]
Matilda of England, duchess of Bavaria
Matilda of England, Holy Roman Empress
Matilda of Quedlinburg
Matilda of Rottenburg
Matilda of Scotland
Matilda of Sicily, countess of Alife
Mélisende, queen of Jerusalem
Petronille of Fontevrault
Philippa of Hainault
Philippa of Lancaster, queen of Portugal
Tamara, queen of Georgia
Theodora Comnena

Theophano of Byzantium, Holy Roman Empress
Tibors d'Omelas

PAWNS

women used by others as political/financial pawns in treaties, alliances, marriages, etc.

Adelaide of Anjou
Adelaide, queen of France
Adelheid of Germany, abbess of Quedlinburg [Adelaide]
Adelheid of Vohburg [Adelaide]
Aelfthryth of Wessex
Aethelswith of Wessex, queen of Mercia
Affreca of Man, countess of Ulster
Agnes of France
Agnes of Germany
Agnes of Navarre
Alda of Arles
Alfonsina Orsini
Alys of France [Alice]
Anne of Brittany, queen of France
Anne of Burgundy, duchess of Bedford
Anne, princess of Byzantium
Anne Holland
Anne Mowbray
Anne Neville, queen of England
Anne Paston
Antigone (of Gloucester)
Astrid of Sweden
Aveline de Forz, countess of Aumale
Basilia de Clare
Bayalun
Beatrice of Falkenstein
Beatrix of Portugal, queen of Castile [Beatrice]
Beatrice of Provence
Beatrice, marchioness of Tuscany
Bertha of Sulzbach
Bertha of Susa
Bertilla
Bianca Giovanna Sforza
Bianca Maria Sforza
Blanche of Aragon
Blanche of Bourbon
Blanche, princess of England
Bonne of Armagnac
Katharine of Aragon [Catherine]
Catherine of Austria
Catherine of Austria
Catherine of Burgundy
Catherine of Burgundy, duchess of Austria
Caterina Cornaro, queen of Cyprus [Catherine]
Catherine of France
Catherine of France, queen of England
Katherine Neville [Catherine]
Catherine de Thouars
Katherine Woodville [Catherine]
Katharine of York [Catherine]
Cecily of York [Cecilia]
Charlotte d'Albret
Chiara Gonzaga
Clementia of Zähringen
Constance of Brittany
Constance of Castile, duchess of Lancaster
Constance of Hohenstaufen
Constance of Sicily, Holy Roman Empress
Cunegunde of Swabia
Dhuoda
Dorotea Gonzaga [Dorothy]
Douce (III) of Provence
Drusiana (Sforza)
Dubravka of Bohemia
Eadgyfu of England, queen of Burgundy and Provence
Ela, countess of Salisbury
Leonor of Aragon, queen of Castile [Eleanor]
Eleanor of Brittany
Leonor of Castile, queen of Aragon [Eleanor]
Leonor of Castile, queen of Navarre [Eleanor]
Eleanor of England, countess of Bar
Eleanor of England, countess of Guelders
Eleanora de Montfort [Eleanor]
Elena of Moscow
Elisenda de Moncada, queen of Aragon
Elizabeth of Kiev
Elizabeth of York, queen of England
Ermengarde de Beaumont, queen of Scotland
Estrith of Denmark
Eudocia Baiane, empress of Byzantium
Eudocia of Decapolis, empress of Byzantium
Eudocia Ingerina, empress of Byzantium
Eudocia Macrembolitissa, empress of Byzantium
Eupraxia of Kiev, Holy Roman Empress
Eva MacMurrough
Francesca Bentivoglio
Gertrude of Babenberg
Godila (of Walbeck)

Gwenllian (of Wales)
Hathui (of Germany)
Helene de Chambes [Helen]
Helena (Guiscard) [Helen]
Ida of Swabia
Ingeborg of Norway
Isabelle of Achaia
Isabella of Aragon, duchess of Milan [Isabelle]
Isabella Bruce [Isabelle]
Isabel of Castile, duchess of York [Isabelle]
Isabella de Clare [Isabelle]
Isabella of England, Holy Roman Empress [Isabelle]
Isabella of France, queen of England [Isabelle]
Isabelle of France, duchess of Milan
Isabella of Jerusalem [Isabelle]
Jeanne d'Artois [Jean]
Joan Beaufort, queen of Scotland [Jean]
Joan of England (of Woodstock) [Jean]
Joan of England, princess of Gwynedd [Jean]
Joan of England, queen of Scotland [Jean]
Joan of England, queen of Scotland [Jean]
Joan Fauconberg [Jean]
Jeanne of France, queen of Navarre [Jean]
Joanna I, queen of Naples [Jean]
Joan of Navarre, queen of England [Jean]
Jeanne Paynel [Jean]
Lucienne of Rochefort
Lucrezia Borgia
Maddalena de'Medici [Madeleine]
Malfrid of Kiev, queen of Norway, queen of Denmark
Margaret of Austria
Margaret of Babenberg
Margaret of Maine
Margaret, "the Maid of Norway"
Margaret, queen of Norway
Margarita de Prades [Margaret]
Margaret of Scotland
Margaret of Sweden, queen of Norway
Maria of Aragon, queen of Portugal [Mary]
Mary of Blois
Mary of England
Marie of France, duchess of Brabant [Mary]
Maria Lacapena [Mary]
Marie of Montpellier [Mary]
Marie of Navarre [Mary]
Maria of Portugal [Mary]
Mary of Scotland
Maria of Sicily [Mary]
Matilda of Anjou
Matilda of England, Holy Roman Empress
Matilda of France
Matilda of Hainault, princess of Achaia
Matilda de Lucy
Nannina de'Medici
Petronilla, queen of Aragon
Rose O'Connor
Rozala of Lombardy
Simone of Byzantium
Subh of Cordoba
Teodorina (Cibo)
Theodora Comnena
Theophano, empress of Byzantium
Theresa of Portugal, queen of Leon (St.)
Theutberga, queen of Lotharingia
Thyra of Denmark
Urraca Gonzalez
Violante Visconti
Ximena Diaz
Yolande de Dreux
Yolande (of Jerusalem), Holy Roman Empress
Zoe the Porphyrogenita

Peasants see: MANORS.

PILGRIMS

Agnes Paston
Agnes of Poitou, Holy Roman Empress
Angela of Foligno
Bridget of Sweden (St.)
Catherine of Sweden (St.)
Constance of Castile, queen of France
Eadburg of Mercia
Elizabeth of Portugal (St.)
Elizabeth Talbot
Ermengarde of Anjou, duchess of Brittany
Ermentrude of Jouarre
Isabeau of Bavaria [Isabelle]
Isabella of France, queen of England [Isabelle]
Ivetta of Huy
Judith, duchess of Bavaria
Judith of Flanders
Margaret of England (St.)
Margaret of Logy
Margaret Paston
Margery Kempe
Theophano of Byzantium, Holy Roman Empress

PLAGUE

victims of; doctors during, etc.

Ambroise de Lore
Annabella Drummond, queen of Scotland
Anne of Bohemia, queen of England
Anne of Burgundy, duchess of Bedford
Blanche of Lancaster
Bona of Luxembourg
Catherine of Austria
Catherine of Genoa
Leonor of Portugal, queen of Aragon [Eleanor]
Elizabeth of Bohemia
Fiametta
Gunnhild of Denmark, queen of Germany
Huguette Balarin
Jacoba (of Passau)
Jeanne of Burgundy, queen of France [Jean]
Joan of England (of Woodstock) [Jean]
Laura
Margaret of Brabant, Holy Roman Empress
Margaret of Denmark
Margaret Paston
Marie of Champagne, countess of Flanders
Matilda of Lancaster, duchess of Zealand
Philippa of Lancaster, queen of Portugal
Rosalia of Palermo (St.)

Playwrights see: DRAMA; WRITERS.

POETS/TROUBADOURS

includes patronesses of

Also see: PATRONS OF LITERATURES; WRITERS.

Adelaide de Porcairques
Azalais de Rocamartina [Adelaide]
Adelaide of Toulouse
Alice de Montfort
Almucs de Castelnau
Beatrice de Dia
Castelloza of Provence
Clara d'Anduza [Clare]
Douce (III) of Provence
Ermengarde, viscountess of Narbonne
Eudoxia Comnena [Eudocia]
Florencia Pinar
Garsenda de Forcalquier
Guillelma de Rosers
Iseut de Capio
Jeanne Filleul [Jean]
Lombarda
Margaret of Scotland
Marie de France [Mary]
Marie of France, countess of Champagne [Mary]
Marie de Ventadour [Mary]
Tibors d'Omelas

POLITICS

active participants, or catalysts, in political actions

Also see: NEGOTIATORS; REGENTS; RULERS.

Aasta Grönske
Adelheid of Burgundy, Holy Roman Empress [Adelaide]
Adelaide, queen of France
Adelheid of Germany, abbess of Quedlinburg [Adelaide]
Adelheid of Savoy [Adelaide]
Aelfgifu
Aelfthryth
Agnes of Courtenay
Agnes of Hapsburg, queen of Hungary
Agnese del Maino [Agnes]
Agnes of Navarre
Agnes Sorel
Agrippina of Moscow
Alfonsina Orsini
Alice Chaucer, duchess of Suffolk
Alice of Jerusalem, princess of Antioch
Alice Lacy, countess of Lancaster
Alice Perrers
Amice de Clare [Amicia]
Anne Beauchamp, countess of Warwick
Anne of Brittany, queen of France
Anna Comnena [Anne]
Anne de Lusignan
Antoinette de Villequier
Astrid (of Denmark)
Astrid of Sweden
Aud "the Deep-minded"
Barbara of Cilly, Holy Roman Empress
Basilia de Clare
Battista da Montefeltro
Beatrice d'Este
Beatrice de Guzman
Beatrix of Portugal, queen of Castile [Beatrice]
Beatrice of Savoy, countess of Provence
Berenguela of Castile
Bertha of Sulzbach
Bertha of Tuscany
Bertrade de Montfort, queen of France
Bianca Maria Visconti

Bianca of Savoy
Blanche of Anjou, queen of Aragon
Blanche of France
Blanche of Montferrat, duchess of Savoy
Bona of Savoy
Bridget of Sweden (St.)
Catherine of Siena (St.)
Cecily Neville, duchess of York [Cecilia]
Charlotte of Lusignan
Christina of Norway [Christine]
Christine de Pisan
Clare of Assisi
Colette of Corbie
Constance of Arles, queen of France
Constance of Castile, duchess of Lancaster
Constance of France, queen of Castile
Constance of York, countess of Gloucester
Kunigunda of Hungary [Cunigunde]
Cunigund of Luxembourg, Holy Roman Empress (St.) [Cunigunde]
Eadgifu of England, queen of France
Eadgifu of Kent, queen of England
Edith of England, queen of Germany
Edith of Wessex, queen of England
Eleanor of Aquitaine
Leonor of Aragon, queen of Portugal [Eleanor]
Eleanor Beauchamp, duchess of Somerset
Leonor of Castile, queen of Aragon [Eleanor]
Leonor of Lancastre [Eleanor]
Leonor Lopez [Eleanor]
Leonor of Sicily, queen of Aragon [Eleanor]
Elena of Moscow
Elizabeth of Austria
Elizabeth of Kiev
Elizabeth of Luxembourg
Elizabeth of Poland, queen of Hungary
Elizabeth of Portugal (St.)
Elizabeth Say
Elizabeth Woodville
Elizabeth of York, duchess of Suffolk
Emma, queen of Germany
Emma of Normandy
Ermengarde (of Burgundy)
Ermengarde (of Ivrea)
Ermengard, duchess of Lombardy, queen of Provence [Ermengarde]
Ermentrude of Jouarre
Gertrude of Babenberg
Gertrude of Flanders, duchess of Lorraine
Gertrude of Meissen
Gisela of Bavaria, queen of Hungary
Gisela of Swabia, queen of Germany
Gisla of Lorraine
Gormflath (of Ireland)
Gundrada
Gunhild of Denmark, queen of Norway
Gunnor (of Denmark)
Hedwig of Bavaria
Helene Kotanner
Helen Lacapena, empress of Byzantium
Hildegarde of Bingen (St.)
Hildegarde (of France)
Huguette Balarin
Idonea
Ingeborg of Denmark, queen of France
Ingeltrude
Ingerid of Sweden
Ippolita Sforza
Irene Angela, Holy Roman Empress
Irene Ducas, empress of Byzantium
Isabelle of Angoulême, queen of England
Isabella of Aragon, duchess of Milan [Isabelle]
Isabeau of Bavaria [Isabelle]
Isabelle of Bourbon
Isabella, countess of Buchan [Isabelle]
Isabel of Castile, duchess of York [Isabelle]
Isabella de Fortibus [Isabelle]
Joan Beaufort, queen of Scotland [Jean]
Joan Beaufort, countess of Westmoreland [Jean]
Jeanne de Belleville [Jean]
Jeanne of Burgundy, queen of France [Jean]
Jeanne of Burgundy, queen of France [Jean]
Juana Enriquez, queen of Aragon [Jean]
Joan FitzAlan [Jean]
Jeanne of France, duchess of Brittany [Jean]
Jeanne de Montfort [Jean]
Jeanne de Penthièvre [Jean]
Jeanne de Valois [Jean]
Jeanne de Valois, countess of Hainault [Jean]
Judith, duchess of Bavaria
Judith of Bavaria, Holy Roman Empress
Judith (of Germany)
Loretta de Braose
Louise of Savoy
Lucia Marliani
Lucrezia de'Medici
Lucrezia Tornabuoni

Ludmila (of Bohemia)
Mahaut of Artois
Margaret Beauchamp, countess of Salisbury
Margaret Beaufort
Margaret de Braose
Margaret of France, countess of Flanders
Margaret of Maine
Margaret Marshall
Margaret Maultasch
Marguerite of Provence, queen of France [Margaret]
Margaret Wake
Margaret of York
Marozia of Rome
Marie d'Avignon [Mary]
Mary of Blois
Marie de Brabant, queen of France [Mary]
Marie of Brittany, duchess of Anjou [Mary]
Marie of Cleves [Mary]
Maria Comnena, princess of Byzantium [Mary]
Maria Comnena, queen of Jerusalem [Mary]
Marie de Coucy, queen of Scotland [Mary]
Maria Lacapena [Mary]
Maria de Padilla [Mary]
Mary of St. Pol
Maud de Braose [Matilda]
Matilda of England, Holy Roman Empress
Matilda, queen of Germany
Matilda of Scotland
Matilda of Sicily, countess of Alife
Matilda of Tuscany
Mélisende, queen of Jerusalem
Morphia of Melitene
Otta of S. Salvatore
Philippa of Lancaster, queen of Portugal
Richardis
Richilde of Autun
Rose of Viterbo (St.)
Rothild of Chelles
Sancha of Castile
Sybille of Anjou, countess of Flanders [Sibyl]
Sibilia de Forcia [Sibyl]
Sichelgaita of Salerno
Sigrid, queen of Sweden
Sophia of Gandersheim
Sophia, princess of Moscow
Strathearn (countess of)
Tarub (of Cordoba)
Theodora of Rome
Urraca of Portugal
Waldrada (of Arles)
Willa of Tuscany, queen of Italy
Ximena, queen of Leon
Yolande of Hungary, queen of Aragon
Yolande de Valois

POPES

supporters of, and those who were related to, or had dealings with, the papacy

Adelheid of Burgundy, Holy Roman Empress [Adelaide]
Adelheid of Savoy [Adelaide]
Adelaide of Toulouse
Adelasia of Torres, queen of Sardinia
Adele of Champagne, queen of France
Adriana del Mila
Ageltrudis (of Spoleto)
Agnes of Anjou
Agnes of Bohemia
Agnes of Meran
Agnes of Poitou, Holy Roman Empress
Alice Perrers
Angelberga
Anna Dalassena [Anne]
Anne of Kiev
Anne of Savoy, empress of Byzantium
Barbara von Brandenburg
Beatrice de Guzman
Beatrice, marchioness of Tuscany
Berengaria of Navarre, queen of England
Bertha of Chartres
Bertha of Susa
Bertrade de Montfort, queen of France
Blanche of Castile, queen of France
Blanche of Navarre, countess of Champagne
Bona of Savoy
Bridget of Sweden (St.)
Catherine de Courteney
Catherine Sforza
Catherine of Siena (St.)
Catherine of Sweden (St.)
Cecile de Turenne [Cecilia]
Charlotte d'Albret
Christina of Markyate [Christine]
Claude des Armoises
Colette of Corbie (St.)
Constance, queen of Aragon
Constance of France
Constance of France, queen of Castile
Constance of Sicily, Holy Roman Empress
Cunigund of Luxembourg, Holy Roman Empress (St.) [Cunigunde]

Dubravka of Bohemia
Eleanor of Aquitaine
Leonor of Aragon, countess of Toulouse [Eleanor]
Elisabetta Gonzaga [Elizabeth]
Elizabeth of Poland, queen of Hungary
Elizabeth of Portugal (St.)
Ermengarde of Anjou, duchess of Brittany
Ermengard, duchess of Lombardy, queen of Provence [Ermengarde]
Ermengarde, viscountess of Narbonne
Ermengard (of S. Salvatore) [Ermengarde]
Eupraxia of Kiev, Holy Roman Empress
Eva of Saint-Martin
Gisela of Swabia, queen of Germany
Guilia Farnese
Ingeborg of Denmark, queen of France
Ingeltrude
Ippolita Sforza
Irene, empress of Byzantium
Isabel de Borgia [Isabelle]
Isabella, queen of Castile and Aragon [Isabelle]
Isabella d'Este [Isabelle]
Jacqueline of Hainault
Jeanne de Belleville [Jean]
Joan of Kent [Jean]
Joanna I, queen of Naples [Jean]
Judith, queen of England
Lucrezia d'Alagno
Lucrezia Borgia
Lucrezia de'Medici
Maddalena de'Medici [Madeleine]
Mahaut de Brabant
Margaret Aldobrandeschi
Margaret, countess of Flanders
Margaret of Logy
Margaret Maultasch
Marozia of Rome
Maria of Castile [Mary]
Maria Enriquez [Mary]
Marie of Montpellier [Mary]
Matilda of England, Holy Roman Empress
Matilda of Scotland
Matilda of Tuscany
Mayfreda de Pirovano
Petronille of Fontevrault
Richardis
Richenza of Nordheim, Holy Roman Empress
Richilde of Autun
Roesia de Borford
Sancia d'Aragona
Sancia of Majorca
Sophia of Gandersheim
Sophia, princess of Moscow
Stephania (of Rome)
Teodorina (Cibo)
Theodora of Rome
Theophano of Byzantium, Holy Roman Empress
Theresa of Portugal, queen of Leon (St.)
Theutberga, queen of Lotharingia
Urraca of Portugal
Vanozza Catanei
Waldrada

POTTERS

Alison la Métaille
Erembourc (la potière)
Juliane (la potière)

Poulterers see: PROVISIONING.

PREACHERS

women who preached, and those who wrote sermons or aided male preachers

Bloemardine
Catherine of Vraba
Esclarmonde de Foix
Liutberga (St.)
Margaret of Cortona (St.)
Margherita di Trento [Margaret]
Mary of Oignies
Matilda Maresflete
Rose of Viterbo (St.)
Theoda of Mainz
Umilita of Faenza

Prioresses see: ABBESSES.

PRISONS

inmates, jailers, and women who were confined, held captive, or imprisoned in any type of facility

Also see: PUNISHMENTS.

Adelheid of Burgundy, Holy Roman Empress [Adelaide]
Agnes de Bury
Agnes Forster
Agnes Irlond
Agnes Mundene
Agnes de Sechelles
Alice atte Harpe
Alice Lacy, countess of Lancaster
Anna Palmer [Anne]
Annora de Braose
Baddlesmere (lady)

Barbara of Cilly, Holy Roman Empress
Beatrice of Burgundy
Beatrice (of France), duchess of Haute-Lorraine
Beatrice, marchioness of Tuscany
Blanche of Aragon
Blanche of Bourbon
Catherine Sforza
Katharine Vaux [Catherine]
Cecilia Rygeway
Cristina Blake [Christine]
Crystene Houghton [Christine]
Christine Swath
Constance of Brittany
Constance of France
Constance of Sicily, Holy Roman Empress
Leonor of Albuquerque [Eleanor]
Eleanor of Aquitaine
Eleanor of Brittany
Eleanor Cobham
Leonor de Guzman [Eleanor]
Leonor Lopez [Eleanor]
Eleanora de Montfort [Eleanor]
Leonor of Sicily, queen of Aragon [Eleanor]
Elizabeth of Bohemia
Elizabeth of Bosnia
Elizabeth de Burgo, queen of Scotland
Elizabeth de Clare
Elizabeth of York, duchess of Suffolk
Guillemette Benet
Ingeborg of Denmark, queen of France
Isabella, countess of Buchan [Isabelle]
Isabel Mowbray, lady Berkeley [Isabelle]
Isabella de Toppesham [Isabelle]
Jane Shore
Juana of Aragon, queen of Castile [Jean]
Joan of Arc (St.) [Jean]
Joan Beaufort, queen of Scotland [Jean]
Jeanne of Burgundy, queen of France [Jean]
Joan de Genville [Jean]
Joan Lenelonde [Jean]
Joan of Navarre, queen of England [Jean]
Jeanne Paynel [Jean]
Jeanne de Valois [Jean]
Margaret of Anjou
Margaret of Brabant, countess of Flanders
Margaret of Burgundy
Marguerite de Clisson [Margaret]
Margaret of Navarre, queen of Sicily
Marjory Bruce [Margery]
Mariota Convers
Marozia of Rome
Martha Boretsky
Marie of Brittany [Mary]
Maria, queen of Hungary [Mary]
Maria (la Medica) [Mary]
Maud de Braose [Matilda]
Matilda of Hainault, princess of Achaia
Maud Lovell, lady Arundel [Matilda]
Matilda of Tuscany
Peretta Peronne [Perrette]
Philippa of Hainault
Richilde, countess of Flanders
Richolda
Sancia d'Aragona
Sibylla of Acerra [Sibyl]
Sibilia de Forcia [Sibyl]
Strathearn (countess of)
Tanglost
Theophano, empress of Byzantium
Theresa of Castile
Theutberga, queen of Lotharingia
Willa of Tuscany, queen of Italy
Yolande de Valois
Zoe the Porphyrogenita

PROSTITUTES

also includes procurers and owners/workers at whorehouses

Also see: ADULTERY; MISTRESSES; WOMEN OF EASY VIRTUE.

Agnes (of Holbourne)
Alice Donbely
Alice de Lincoln
Alice Tredewedowe
Alison la Jourdain
Anna Harbatova [Anne]
Casotte Cristal
Crystene Houghton [Christine]
Dorothy of Strygl
Dulcia Trye
Elizabeth Judela
Elizabeth Moring
Heaulmiere (la belle)
Huguette du Hamel
Jehanne de Bretagne [Jean]
Joan Grene [Jean]
Joan Hunt [Jean]
Johanna (of London) [Jean]
Jeanne Saignant
Jeannette la Petite
Margot de la Barre
Margot (la Grosse)
Marion la Dentue

Notekina Hoggenhore
Perrine Martin
Ysabelet la Blanche

PROVISIONING

includes: bakers (and regratresses); butchers; cabbage sellers; dairy (and dairy products); fishmongers; fruit sellers; pastry; and poultry sellers.

Also see: ALEWIVES; INNKEEPERS; TAVERNERS.

Agnes Deyntee
Aelis (la poissonière) [Alice]
Alice Staundon
Ameline (la bouchière)
Berte (la tartrière)
Cavolaja of Florence
Colette la Moynesse
Cristiana la Flaoners
Edelot (la fourmagière)
Eleanor de Wendale
Elena Baroun
Emma Turk
Felise (la pastéere)
Haouys (la poulaillière)
Isabel Gobbe [Isabelle]
Jacqueline Machecoue
Jehanne (la bouchière) [Jean]
Jehanne (la fouacière) [Jean]
Mabile (la regratière)
Maheut (la pescheresse) [Mahaut]
Marguerite (l'avenière) [Margaret]
Margaret Stoke
Nicole (la saunière) [Nichole]
Pentecouste (la fruitière)
Phelipote (la fritière)
Sedile (la fournière)
Thomasse (la talemelière)

PUNISHMENTS

includes excommunication; execution; flogging; ostracism; pillory; spanking; stocks; etc.

Also see: PRISONS.

Agnes Bernauer
Agnes Deyntee
Agnes Sadler
Alice Shether
Angele de la Barthe [Angela]
Ankarette Twynyho
Anne-Marie de Georgel
Beatrice Puttock
Beatrice Sharpe
Belota (the Jew)
Catherine Delort
Catharine Pykring [Catherine]
Cecilia Rygeway
Crystene Houghton [Christine]
Clarice of Rotomago [Claricia]
Clementia, countess of Flanders
Corba de Péreille
Deniselle Grenières
Dionysia Baldewyne
Eleanor Cobham
Elena Baroun
Elizabeth Judela
Elizabeth Moring
Gabrina Albetti
Guillemette Benet
Henriette de Craus
Jacoba Felicie
Joan of Arc (St.) [Jean]
Jehanne de Brigue [Jean]
Jeanne Dabenton [Jean]
Jeanne de Divion [Jean]
Jeannette Camus
Jeannette la Petite
Lucia Tasseburgh
Macete de Ruilly
Margaret Porete
Margherita di Trento [Margaret]
Marjery Jourdemain [Margery]
Margery Paston
Margot de la Barre
Marie de Blansy [Mary]
Maria (la Medica) [Mary]
Mayfreda de Pirovano
Perrine Martin
Petronilla of Meath
Prous Bonetta
Rose Savage
Theoda of Mainz

QUEENS

predominantly includes women who were not politically active consorts; or those who are not often remembered as rulers

Also see: REGENTS; RULERS.

Aasta Grönske
Adelaide of Savona
Adelasia of Torres, queen of Sardinia
Adela of Flanders, queen of Denmark [Adele]
Adelicia of Louvain, queen of England
Aethelflaed of Damerham
Ageltrudis (of Spoleto)
Agnes of France

Alix of Champagne, queen of Cyprus [Alice]
Anastasia of Kiev
Annabella Drummond, queen of Scotland
Anne de Châtillon
Anne Neville, queen of England
Bayalun
Beatrice of Aragon
Beatrice of Falkenstein
Beatrice of Provence
Beatrice of Rethel, queen of Sicily
Beatrice of Swabia, queen of Castile
Berengaria of Navarre, queen of England
Bertha of Chartres
Bertha of Holland
Bertha of Susa
Blanche of France
Blanche of Navarre
Catherine de Valois
Clemence of Hungary
Costanza of Aragon, queen of Sicily [Constance]
Constance of Castile, queen of France
Constance of Hohenstaufen
Cunegunde of Swabia
Cunigunda of Swabia, queen of Bohemia
Douce (II) of Barcelona
Eadburg of Mercia
Ealdgyth (of Mercia)
Leonor of Aragon, queen of Castile [Eleanor]
Leonor of Aragon, queen of Navarre [Eleanor]
Leonor of Castile, queen of Navarre [Eleanor]
Leonor of Portugal, queen of Aragon [Eleanor]
Elizabeth of Austria
Elizabeth de Burgo, queen of Scotland
Elizabeth of Pomerania
Elvira of Castile, queen of Sicily
Emma, queen of Germany
Ermengarde de Beaumont, queen of Scotland
Ermengarde, Holy Roman Empress
Esclarmunda de Foix, queen of Majorca
Eudocia Baiane, empress of Byzantium
Eudocia of Decapolis, empress of Byzantium
Eudocia Ingerina, empress of Byzantium
Evfimia of Kiev [Euphemia]
Frederun of Lorraine, queen of France
Gertrude of Bavaria
Gertrud of Meran [Gertrude]
Gruoch, queen of Scotland
Gyda of England
Ines de Castro
Ingerid of Sweden
Ingibiorg, queen of Scotland
Isabella Bruce [Isabelle]
Isabella of England, Holy Roman Empress [Isabelle]
Isabella of France, queen of England [Isabelle]
Isabella of France, queen of Navarre [Isabelle]
Isabella of Hainault, queen of France [Isabelle]
Isabella of Jerusalem [Isabelle]
Juana of Aragon, queen of Castile [Jean]
Jeanne de Boulogne, queen of France [Jean]
Joan of England, queen of Scotland [Jean]
Joan of England, queen of Scotland [Jean]
Joanna of England, queen of Sicily [Jean]
Jeanne of France, queen of Navarre [Jean]
Jeanne de Laval [Jean]
Juana Manuel, queen of Castile [Jean]
Juana of Portugal [Jean]
Margaret of Babenberg
Margaret of England, queen of Scotland
Margaret of France, queen of England
Margaret of France, queen of Hungary
Margaret "the Maid of Norway"
Margaret, queen of Norway
Margaret of Norway, queen of Scotland
Margarita de Prades [Margaret]
Margaret of Scotland, queen of Norway
Margaret of Sweden, queen of Norway
Margaret of Sweden, queen of Norway
Marie of Anjou [Mary]
Maria of Aragon, queen of Portugal [Mary]
Marie of Bohemia [Mary]
Marie of Brittany, duchess of Anjou [Mary]
Marie de Coucy, queen of Scotland [Mary]
Mary of Kiev
Maria Lacapena [Mary]
Marie of Navarre [Mary]
Maria of Portugal [Mary]
Matilda of Northumberland, queen of Scotland
Matilda of Savoy
Phillippia, countess of Poitou [Philippa]
Ragnhild of Denmark

RAPE

REBELLIONS

leaders of/participants in/victims of grass roots rebellions, palace coups, etc. Also see: SQUABBLES.

Recluses see: ANCHORESSES.

RECOMMANDRESSES

"employment agents" for servants

REGENTS

Also see: MANAGERS; POLITICS; QUEENS; RULERS.

Alice of Jerusalem, princess of Antioch
Alix de Vergy, duchess of Burgundy [Alice]
Almodis (III) of Toulouse
Almucs de Castelnau
Angelberga
Anne of Beaujeu
Anna Dalassena [Anne]
Anne of Kiev
Anne of Savoy, empress of Byzantium
Asa, queen of Agdir
Battista Sforza
Beatrice (of France), duchess of Haute-Lorraine
Berenguela of Castile
Bertha of Swabia, duchess of Lorraine
Bertha of Tuscany
Bianca Maria Visconti
Blanche of Artois
Blanche of Castile, queen of France
Blanche of Montferrat, duchess of Savoy
Blanche of Navarre
Blanche of Navarre, countess of Champagne
Bonne de Bourbon, countess of Savoy [Bona]
Bona of Savoy
Catherine of Lancaster
Catherine Sforza
Catherine de Valois
Caterina Visconti [Catherine]
Constance of Antioch
Constance, queen of Aragon
Constance of France
Constance of Sicily, Holy Roman Empress
Cunigund of Luxembourg, Holy Roman Empress (St.) [Cunigunde]
Eleanor of Aquitaine
Leonora of Aragon, duchess of Ferrara [Eleanor]
Leonor of Aragon, queen of Portugal [Eleanor]
Eleanor of England, countess of Guelders
Leonor of Lancastre [Eleanor]
Leonor of Sicily, queen of Aragon [Eleanor]
Leonor Teles, queen of Portugal [Eleanor]
Elizabeth of Bosnia
Elvira of Leon
Emma of Italy, queen of France
Ermengarde of Anjou, duchess of Brittany
Ermengarde (of Ivrea)
Ermengard, duchess of Lombardy, queen of Provence
Ermessend of Carcassonne, countess of Barcelona
Eudocia Macrembolitissa, empress of Byzantium
Francesca Bentivoglio
Garsenda de Forcalquier
Gerberga of Saxony, queen of France
Gertrude of Saxony, duchess of Bavaria
Gisela of Swabia, queen of Germany
Godila (of Walbeck)
Helen Lacapena, empress of Byzantium
Hodierna of Jerusalem
Ingeborg of Denmark, queen of Norway
Ingebjorg of Norway [Ingeborg]
Irene, empress of Byzantium
Isabeau of Bavaria [Isabelle]
Isabella of France, queen of England [Isabelle]
Isabel of Lorraine [Isabelle]
Isabella of Portugal [Isabelle]
Isotta degli Atti
Joanna of Aragon, queen of Naples [Jean]
Joan Beaufort, queen of Scotland [Jean]
Jeanne of Burgundy, queen of France [Jean]
Joan of Navarre, queen of England [Jean]
Louise of Savoy
Lucrezia Borgia
Margaret of Austria
Marguerite de Bourbon, queen of Navarre [Margaret]
Margaret of Denmark
Margaret of Flanders, duchess of Burgundy
Marguerite of Lorraine [Margaret]
Margaret of Navarre, queen of Sicily
Mary of Antioch
Marie of Brittany, duchess of Anjou
Marie of Cleves [Mary]
Maria Comnena, queen of Jerusalem [Mary]
Maria Enriquez [Mary]
Marie of France, countess of Champagne [Mary]
Mary of Gelders, queen of Scotland
Maria de Luna [Mary]
Maria de Molina [Mary]
Matilda of Boulogne, queen of England
Matilda of England, duchess of Bavaria
Matilda of Flanders
Matilda of Hainault, princess of Achaia
Matilda of Quedlinburg
Mélisende, queen of Jerusalem

RELICS

women who owned, collected, or donated relics of saints—also includes women whose own relics were particularly valued

Also see: RELIGIOUS PATRONS; SAINTS.

RELIGIEUSES

catch-all term for women who entered, were sent to, or retired at religious houses, but who did not usually take vows

Also see: ABBESSES; ANCHORESSES; BEGUINES; NUNS.

Elizabeth of Portugal (St.)
Ende
Ermengarde of Anjou, duchess of Brittany
Eudoxia Comnena [Eudocia]
Euphrosyne of Byzantium
Frances of Rome (St.)
Garsenda de Forcalquier
Gisla of Lorraine
Godgifu, lady of Mercia
Gundrada
Hatheburg
Ingeborg of Denmark, queen of France
Irene, empress of Byzantium
Irene Ducas, empress of Byzantium
Isabelle of Angoulême, queen of England
Isabelle of France
Isabella of France, queen of England [Isabelle]
Isabel de Montfort [Isabelle]
Isabella of Portugal [Isabelle]
Isotta Nogarola
Ivetta of Huy
Joan Beaufort, countess of Westmoreland [Jean]
Juana of Castile [Jean]
Judith, duchess of Bavaria
Judith of Bavaria, Holy Roman Empress
Judith, queen of England
Judith of Flanders
Judith of Schweinfurt
Juliana Falconieri (St.)
Kasia (of Byzantium)
Lesceline, countess of Eu
Liutberga (St.)
Lucrezia Borgia
Mabel Rich
Margaret of Babenberg
Margaret of Citta di Castello
Margaret of Denmark
Marguerite of Lorraine [Margaret]
Marguerite Scheppers [Margaret]
Margaret of Ypres
Margery Kempe
Marozia of Rome
Mary de Bohun
Mary of Oignies
Mary of St. Pol
Matilda, queen of Germany
Matilda of Scotland
Odette de Champdivers
Petronille of Comminges
Phillippia, countess of Poitou [Philippa]
Rosamund Clifford
Rose of Viterbo (St.)
Rotrude
Sancha of Castile [Sancia]
Sancia of Majorca
Theodora Comnena, queen of Jerusalem
Theodora of Paphlagonia
Theodora the Porphyrogenita
Theophano, empress of Byzantium
Theophano, empress of Byzantium
Theutberga, queen of Lotharingia
Waldrada

RELIGIOUS PATRONS

founders/patronesses of religious institutions—including abbeys, chantries, hospitals, monasteries, schools, etc.—also includes those who started religious orders

Also see: CHARITY.

Adelheid of Burgundy, Holy Roman Empress [Adelaide]
Adelaide (Capet), queen of France
Adelaide of Maurienne, queen of France
Adelaide of Roumainmoutier
Adelaide of Savona
Adelaide of Tours
Aelflaed
Aelfthryth
Aelfthryth of Wessex
Aethelflaed of Damerham
Aethelflaed, lady of the Mercians
Aethelswith of Wessex, queen of Mercia
Affreca of Man, countess of Ulster
Agnes, countess of Aix
Agnes of Anjou
Agnes of Bohemia
Agnes de Condet
Agnes FitzJohn
Agnes Molton
Alberada of Buonalbergo
Alix of France, countess of Blois and Chartres [Alice]
Alice Chester
Alix de Vergy, duchess of Burgundy
Almodis (II) de La Marche, countess of Barcelona
Almodis (IV), countess of La Marche
Angela Merici (St.)
Angelberga
Anne, princess of Bohemia
Anne of Burgundy, duchess of Bedford
Anne, princess of Byzantium
Anne of Kiev
Anne de Many, countess of Pembroke

Lesceline, countess of Eu
Loretta de Braose
Lucrezia de'Medici
Ludmila (of Bohemia)
Mabel of Bellême
Mahaut of Artois
Margaret of Anjou
Margaret Beaufort
Margaret de Botreaux, lady Hungerford
Margaret de Braose
Margaret of Denmark
Margaret, countess of Flanders
Margaret of France, queen of England
Margaret of Hainault, Holy Roman Empress
Marguerite Joli [Margaret]
Margaret Marshall
Margaret of Navarre, queen of Sicily
Margaret, queen of Scotland (St.)
Margaret of Sweden, queen of Norway
Martha Boretsky
Marie of Anjou [Mary]
Marie de Brabant, Holy Roman Empress [Mary]
Maria of Castile [Mary]
Maria Enriquez [Mary]
Mary of Gelders, queen of Scotland
Marie of Navarre [Mary]
Mary of St. Pol
Matilda of Boulogne, queen of Portugal
Matilda of England, Holy Roman Empress
Matilda of Essen
Matilda of Flanders
Matilda of France
Matilda, queen of Germany
Matilda of Scotland
Matilda of Tuscany
Mélisende, queen of Jerusalem
Oda
Odeline
Olga, princess of Kiev (St.)
Petronille of Comminges
Philippa of Coimbra
Philippa of England
Philippa of Hainault
Richardis
Roiantken
Sancha of Castile [Sancia]
Sancia of Majorca
Sancha of Portugal (St.) [Sancia]
Sclerena (of Byzantium)
Sophia, queen of Bohemia
Sophia, princess of Moscow
Svanhild of Essen
Theodora of Paphlagonia
Theresa of Portugal, queen of Leon (St.)
Umilita of Faenza
Urraca of Castile, queen of Portugal
Urraca of Portugal
Valentine Visconti, duchess of Orléans
Vanozza Catanei
Wulfhilda of Barking (St.)
Wynflaed
Zabelia

RULERS

women who governed as partners with their husbands, and those who ruled large or important areas alone

Also see: QUEENS; REGENTS.

Adelaide (Capet), queen of France
Adelaide of Maurienne, queen of France
Adelheid of Savoy [Adelaide]
Aelfthryth
Aethelflaed, lady of the Mercians
Aethelswith of Wessex, queen of Mercia
Agnes of France
Almodis (II) de La Marche, countess of Barcelona
Angelberga
Anne de Lusignan
Aurembaix, countess of Urgel
Barbara of Cily, Holy Roman Empress
Bertha de Sens, countess of Vienne
Blanche of Castile, queen of France
Caterina Cornaro, queen of Cyprus [Catherine]
Catherine of Navarre
Catherine Sforza
Charlotte of Lusignan
Constance of Aragon, queen of Hungary
Constance of Brittany
Costanza Varano [Constance]
Cyenthryth, queen of Mercia
Eleanor of Aquitaine
Eleanora di Arborea [Eleanor]
Elizabeth of Bohemia
Emma of France
Ermengarde, viscountess of Narbonne
Gunhild of Denmark, queen of Norway
Helwise of Nevers, countess of Évreux
Irene, empress of Byzantium
Isabelle of Achaia
Isabella, queen of Castile and Aragon [Isabelle]
Isabella d'Este [Isabelle]
Jadwiga of Hungary

SAINTS

also includes popular saints, some who have now been dropped from offiical lists, and a few who were beatified

SCHOLARS

women who devoted themselves to learning and scholarship

Also see: EDUCATED; WRITERS.

Hildegarde of Bingen (St.)
Irene Lascaris, empress of Byzantium
Isotta Nogarola
Laura Cereta
Lucrezia Tornabuoni
Maddalena Bonsignori [Madeleine]
Maddalena Scrovegni [Madeleine]
Mechtild von Hackeborn
Novella d'Andrea
Theodora Comnena, queen of Jerusalem

Scribes see: BOOKMAKING; WRITERS.

Sculptors see: ARTISTS.
includes women patrons and those who had effigies made of/for themselves
Also see: ART PATRONS.

SERVANTS

includes the gamut of childcare and serving positions, from women who were lower-class maids to those who were ladies-in-waiting to queens
Also see: CHILDCARE.; EMPLOYERS.

Agnes Avesot
Agnes d'Harcourt
Agnes Knetchur
Agnes de Launcreona
Agnes de Monceaux
Alexandra Crowe [Alessandra]
Alice Shedyngton
Angela Borgia
Ankarette Twynyho
Anne of Caux
Anna of Mochov [Anne]
Beatriz Galindo [Beatrice]
Carlotta d'Aragona
Katherine Swynford [Catherine]
Katharine Vaux [Catherine]
Cecily Bonville [Cecilia]
Clemence Sillone
Coucy (lady de)
Delphine of Languedoc
Dionisia de Wodemerstham
Doda
Eleanor de Clare
Eleanor Cobham
Leonor Lopez [Eleanor]
Alienor de Poitiers [Eleanor]
Elizabeth Croke
Elizabeth, lady Scales
Elizabeth, lady Scrope
Elizabeth Talbot
Elizabeth Woodville
Elizabeth of York, duchess of Suffolk
Gertrude van Öosten
Ingunn (of Iceland)
Isabelle de Vescy
Jeanne de Boulogne, duchess of Berry [Jean]
Jeanne Filleul [Jean]
Johanna (of London) [Jean]
Jeanne Pouponne [Jean]
Joan Waring [Jean]
Joan la Whycchere [Jean]
Liutberga (St.)
Lucrezia Crivelli
Margaret of Citta di Castello
Margaret Cobbe
Margaret of Hungary
Margaret Page
Margerie de Haustede [Margery]
Mary Hervey
Matilda de Burgham
Maura de Troyes (St.)
Nicola de la Hay [Nichole]
Or (madame d']
Philippa Roet
Pregente of Melun
Sarra (of Broughton) [Sarah]
Sibillina Biscossi
Zita of Lucca (St.)

SHIPPING

includes long-distance traders, explorers, pirates, ship owners, investors, slave traders, and pioneers

Alice Chester
Alice Horsford
Asa, queen of Agdir
Aud "the Deep-minded"
Catherine of Sebastopol
Cecily Neville, duchess of York [Cecilia]
Elizabeth Kirkeby
Elizabeth Stokton
Freydis of Norway
Fygen van Berchem
Gudrid (of Greenland)
Gunnora de Stratford
Ingeborg of Denmark, queen of Norway
Isabella, queen of Castile and Aragon [Isabelle]
Isabel Norman [Isabelle]
Joanna Rowley [Jean]
Johanna Travers [Jean]
Margaret of Denmark
Margery Russell
Maria de Malla

SILKWORK

also includes makers of small silk items—belts, handkerchiefs, etc.

Also see: APPAREL; ARTISTIC CLOTHWORK; CLOTHWORKERS.

SLAVES

female slaves and owners

SOLDIERS

includes women who defended their own lands or castiles, as well as women who fought in Crusades, etc.

Also see: CRUSADES; POLITICS; REBELLIONS.

Joan of Arc (St.) [Jean]
Jeanne de Belleville [Jean]
Joanna of England, queen of Sicily [Jean]
Jeanne of France, duchess of Brittany [Jean]
Jeanne Laisne [Jean]
Jeanne de Montfort [Jean]
Jeanne Paynel [Jean]
Joan Pelham [Jean]
Jeanne de Penthièvre [Jean]
Judith of Évreux
Mabel of Bellême
Mahaut of Artois
Margaret Aldobrandeschi
Margaret of Anjou
Marguerite de Clisson [Margaret]
Margaret of Denmark
Margaret Paston
Marguerite of Provence, queen of France [Margaret]
Martha Boretsky
Marie of Brittany, duchess of Anjou [Mary]
Maria of Castile [Mary]
Mary of Gelders, queen of Scotland
Maria de Luna [Mary]
Matilda of Boulogne, queen of England
Matilda of England, Holy Roman Empress
Matilda of France
Matilda of Quedlinburg
Matilda of Tuscany
Nicola de la Hay [Nichole]
Olga, princess of Kiev (St.)
Onorata Rodiana
Philippa of Hainault
Richenza of Nordheim, Holy Roman Empress
Richilde, countess of Flanders
Sancha of Castile
Sibylla of Acerra [Sibyl]
Sybille of Anjou, countess of Flanders [Sibyl]
Sibylla of Jerusalem [Sibyl]
Sichelgaita of Salerno
Tamara, queen of Georgia
Theodora of Paphlagonia
Theresa of Castile
Thora of Norway
Toda, queen of Navarre
Turakina
Urraca, queen of Castile
Valentine Visconti, duchess of Orléans
Willa of Tuscany, queen of Italy
Ximena Diaz
Yolande of Aragon
Zoe Carbounopsina

Spicers see: APOTHECARIES.

SPIES

Also see: NEGOTIATORS; POLITICS.

Antoinette de Villequier
Astrid (of Denmark)
Bertha of Tuscany
Casotte Cristal
Christina of Norway [Christine]
Mary of Blois
Marie of Cleves [Mary]
Maria Comnena, princess of Byzantium [Mary]
Mary of Scotland
Strathearn (countess of)

SQUABBLES

women who started or continued family feuds, political strife, and/or inheritance fights

Also see: POLITICS; REBELLIONS.

Adelaide, queen of France
Adele of Champagne, queen of France
Aelfgifu of Northampton
Alix of Champagne, queen of Cyprus [Alice]
Alice Kyteler
Alice Lacy, countess of Lancaster
Alice de Montfort
Alice of Rallingbury
Almodis (IV), countess of La Marche
Amice de Clare [Amicia]
Ansgard
Aubree d'Ivry
Aurembaix, countess of Urgel
Beatrice (of France, duchess of Haute-Lorraine
Beatrice of Savoy, countess of Provence
Bertha of Avenay
Bertha of Swabia, duchess of Lorraine
Bertheida
Bertrade de Montfort, queen of France
Blanche of Navarre, countess of Champagne
Bonne de Berry [Bona]
Bonne de Bourbon, countess of Savoy [Bona]
Cecily Neville [Cecilia]
Charlotte of Lusignan
Constance of Arles, queen of France
Cyenthryth, queen of Mercia
Devorgilla (O'Ruairc)
Douce (III) of Provence

SUPERSTITIONS

SURGEONS

MIDWIVES; MEDICINE.

Antoinette de Bellegarde
Francesca de Romana
Guillemette du Luys
Jacobina (medica)
Jeanne d'Auxerre [Jean]
Jeanne de Cusey [Jean]
Marguerite de Ypres [Margaret]
Mercuriade of Salerno
Peretta Peronne [Perrette]

TANNERS

Elisia Hundesdich
Marie d'Atainvile [Mary]

Tapestry makers see: ARTISTIC CLOTHWORK.

TAVERNERS

owners, managers, and/or workers
Also see: ALEWIVES; INNKEEPERS.

Agnes Desjardins
Agnes Rokingeham
Alice Bokerel
Cristina Rokingeham [Christine]
Elizabeth Higgins
Joan Everard [Jean]
Marguerite Joli [Margaret]
Perrette la Toutaine
Sarah Stroby

TEACHERS

also includes governesses, tutors, lecturers, mothers who taught their children, etc.

Abella of Salerno
Adriana del Mila
Alesandra Gilani [Alessandra]
Alice Drayton
Angela Merici (St.)
Barbara Arrenti
Battista da Montefeltro
Bietrix (la metresse) [Beatrice]
Beatriz Galindo [Beatrice]
Bianca Maria Visconti
Blanche of Castile, queen of France
Catherine of Austria
Katherine Swynford [Catherine]
Catherine de Valois
Christina (of Hungary) [Christine]
Christine de Pisan
Clarissa Orsini [Claricia]
Costanza Calenda [Constance]
Coucy (lady de)
Denisette de Nérel
Dhuoda
Dionysia de Mountchesny
Dorotea Bocchi [Dorothy]
Drahomira
Elizabeth Scolemaystres
Elen Skolmastre [Ellen]
Esclarmonde de Foix
Evfosinia of Polotsk
Gerberga of Bavaria
Gertrude of Hackeborn
Gisela of Swabia, queen of Germany
Hathumoda of Gandersheim
Hawise Mone
Helena (Guiscard) [Helen]
Hersende (of Fontevrault)
Ianka of Kiev
Ingunn (of Iceland)
Isabella, queen of Castile and Aragon [Isabelle]
Isabella of Portugal [Isabelle]
Isabel Romée [Isabelle]
Judith of Bavaria, Holy Roman Empress
Jutta of Sponheim
Laura Cereta
Liutberga (St.)
Lucrezia Tornabuoni
Ludmila (of Bohemia)
Maddalena Bonsignori [Madeleine]
Margaret Beaufort
Margaret de Botreaux, lady Hungerford
Margaret of Denmark
Margaret of Flanders, duchess of Burgundy
Margaret Worthham
Mary Hervey
Mary of Oignies
Matilda of Flanders
Matilda Maresflete
Mechtild von Hackeborn
Mercuriade of Salerno
Novella d'Andrea
Oelun
Péronnelle d'Armentières [Péronelle]
Philippa of Lancaster, queen of Portugal
Relindis of Hohenburg
Sarre (la mirgesse) [Sarah]
Sara of Saint-Gilles [Sarah]
Sersive la Berangière
Theophano of Byzantium, Holy Roman Empress
Thomasine Dinham
Tyfainne (mestresse de l'ecole) [Tiffania]

TOURNAMENTS

participants, models, hostesses, etc.

UNIVERSITY

includes women who attended, lectured at, or founded universities

UNMARRIED

single, adult women—the majority of whom were neither nuns nor widows (some of these women later married, but they accomplished more before their marriages)

Also see: NUNS; WIDOWS.

VIRGINITY

women who were forced into chastity, as well as those who took vows of chastity; also include importance of, proponents of, and more than ordinarily diligent protectors of virginity

Also see: UNMARRIED.

Agnes Butler
Alice Lacy, countess of Lancaster
Alison (of Port-Royal)
Anne of Burgundy, duchess of Bedford
Catherine of Siena (St.)
Cecilia Gonzaga
Christina of Markyate [Christine]
Clare of Assisi
Colette of Corbie (St.)
Delphine of Languedoc
Douceline (St.)
Ebba
Eleanor de Montfort, countess of Leicester
Elisabetta Gonzaga [Elizabeth]
Frances of Rome (St.)
Hatheburg
Isabelle of France
Joan of Arc (St.) [Jean]
Jeanne Potier [Jean]
Lucia Brocadelli
Margaret of Babenberg
Margaret of Hungary
Marie d'Avignon [Mary]
Mary of Oignies
Onorata Rodiana
Richardis
Wulfhilda of Barking (St.)
Yolande of Aragon
Zita of Lucca (St.)
Zoe the Porphyrogenita

WALDENSIANS

Also see: HERETICS.

Agnes Francou
Zabelia

Wetnurses see: CHILDCARE; NURSES; SERVANTS.

Whorehouse see: PROSTITUTES.

WIDOWS

because every other woman could fall in this category, we have largely restricted it to women who accomplished something as widows—or women whose experiences as widows serve to illustrate typical opportunities and hardships faced by medieval widows

Ada of Warenne
Adelaide (Capet), queen of France
Adelaide, queen of France
Adelheid of Savoy [Adelaide]
Adelicia of Louvain, queen of England
Adriana del Mila
Aelfthryth
Aethelflaed of Damerham
Aethelflaed, lady of the Mercians
Affreca of Man, countess of Ulster
Ageltrudis (of Spoleto)
Agnes of Anjou
Agnes Brid
Agnes of Burgundy, duchess of Bourbon
Agnes of Courtenay
Agnes Forster
Agnes of France
Agnes of France
Agnes of Hapsburg, queen of Hungary
Agnes Kateline
Agnes of Poitou, Holy Roman Empress
Alessandra Strozzi
Alice de Bryene
Alice Chaucer, duchess of Suffolk
Alice Chester
Alice de Clare
Alice Denecoumbe
Alice Horsford
Alice Hulle
Alice of Jerusalem, princess of Antioch
Alice Kyteler
Alice Lacy, countess of Lancaster
Alix de Mâcon [Alice]
Alice of Rallingbury
Alix de Vergy, duchess of Burgundy [Alice]
Almodis (III) of Toulouse
Amice de Clare [Amicia]
Angela of Foligno
Angelberga
Angelica del Lama
Anne Beauchamp, countess of Warwick
Anna Comnena [Anne]
Anna Dalassena [Anne]
Anne Devereux
Anne de Many, countess of Pembroke
Anees de Quinkere [Anne]
Anne of Savoy, empress of Byzantium
Anne of Woodstock
Annora de Braose
Astrid of Norway

Gunhild of Denmark, queen of Norway
Gunnor (of Denmark)
Gytha of Denmark
Hedwig of Bavaria
Hildegarde (of France)
Ida of Boulogne
Ingeborg of Denmark, queen of Norway
Ingebjorg of Norway [Ingeborg]
Ingerid of Sweden
Irene, empress of Byzantium
Irene Ducas, empress of Byzantium
Isabelle of Achaia
Isabelle of Angoulême, queen of England
Isabel de Borgia [Isabelle]
Isabella Bruce [Isabelle]
Isabella de Fortibus [Isabelle]
Isabella of France, queen of England [Isabelle]
Isabella Hodere [Isabelle]
Isabel of Vermandois, countess of Leicester [Isabelle]
Isotta degli Atti
Ivetta of Huy
Jacqueline Machecoue
Jane Stonor
Juana of Aragon, queen of Castile [Jean]
Joanna of Aragon, queen of Naples [Jean]
Johanna Beauflour [Jean]
Joan Beaufort, queen of Scotland [Jean]
Joan Beaufort, countess of Westmoreland [Jean]
Jeanne de Belleville [Jean]
Joan Buckland [Jean]
Jeanne de Dammartin, queen of Castile [Jean]
Joanna of England, queen of Sicily [Jean]
Joan Fauconberg [Jean]
Joan FitzAlan [Jean]
Joan of Kent [Jean]
Joan de Munchensi [Jean]
Joanna II, queen of Naples [Jean]
Joan of Navarre, queen of England [Jean]
Jeanne de Penthièvre [Jean]
Joanna Rowley [Jean]
Jeanne de Valois, countess of Hainault [Jean]
Judith, duchess of Bavaria
Judith, queen of England
Judith of Flanders
Judith (of Germany)
Kateline de Coster
Lesceline, countess of Eu
Loretta de Braose
Louise of Savoy
Ludmila (of Bohemia)
Maddalena Scrovegni [Madeleine]
Mahaut Artois
Mahaut de Brabant
Margaret of Austria
Margaret of Babenberg
Margaret Beaufort
Margaret de Bohun, countess of Devon
Margaret de Botreaux, lady Hungerford
Marguerite de Bourbon, queen of Navarre [Margaret]
Marguerite de Clisson [Margaret]
Margherita Datini [Margaret]
Margaret of Denmark
Margaret of France, queen of England
Margaret of Hainault, Holy Roman Empress
Marguerite Joli [Margaret]
Margaret Lacy
Marguerite of Lorraine [Margaret]
Margaret Marshall
Margaret of Navarre, queen of Sicily
Margaret Paston
Margaret of Sweden, queen of Norway
Margaret of York
Marjorie, countess of Carrick [Margery]
Margery (of Frocestor)
Margery Haynes
Margery Russell
Marote (de Douai)
Marozia of Rome
Martha Boretsky
Mary of Antioch
Marie de Berry [Mary]
Marie de Brabant, Holy Roman Empress [Mary]
Marie of Brittany, duchess of Anjou [Mary]
Marie of Cleves [Mary]
Marie de Coucy, queen of Scotland [Mary]
Maria Enriquez [Mary]
Mary of Gelders, queen of Scotland
Maria de Malla [Mary]
Maria de Molina [Mary]
Mary of St. Pol
Mary of Scotland
Matilda of Anjou
Matilda of England, Holy Roman Empress
Maud Francis [Matilda]
Matilda, queen of Germany
Matilda of Hainault, princess of Achaia
Maud Lovell, lady Arundel [Matilda]
Matilda of Tuscany

Matilda Yonge
Mélisende, queen of Jerusalem
Oelun
Olga, princess of Kiev (St.)
Petronilla of Grnadmesnil, countess of Leicester
Petronilla of Teye
Quintine van den Zande
Richenza of Nordheim, Holy Roman Empress
Richilde of Autun
Richilde, countess of Flanders
Roesia de Borford
Sancha of Castile [Sancia]
Sancia of Majorca
Sara of Saint-Gilles [Sarah]
Sarah Stroby
Sibylla of Acerra [Sibyl]
Sybille of Anjou, countess of Flanders [Sibyl]
Sibilia de Forcia [Sibyl]
Sichelgaita of Salerno
Sigrid, queen of Sweden
Sophia, queen of Bohemia
Stephania (of Rome)
Theophano, empress of Byzantium
Theophano of Byzantium, Holy Roman Empress
Theresa of Castile
Thyra of Denmark
Toda, queen of Navarre
Turakina
Umiliana dei Cherchi (St.)
Urraca, queen of Castile
Urraca Gonzalez
Valentine Visconti, duchess of Orléans
Violante Visconti
Waldrada (of Arles)
Walgrave (lady)
Wynflaed
Ximena Diaz
Yolande de Dreux, queen of Scotland
Yolande de Valois
Zoe Carbounopsina

Wills see: BEQUESTS.

Wine dealers see: ALEWIVES; TAVERNERS.

WITCHCRAFT

includes women who were accused of practicing all types of magic, and those about whom superstitions were built

Also see: ECCLESIASTICAL COURTS; HERETICS; SUPERSTITIONS.

Agnese Arizonelli [Agnes]
Agnes Bernauer
Agnes (of Norfolk)
Alice Kyteler
Alice Perrers
Angele de la Barthe [Angela]
Anne-Marie de Georgel
Annota Lange
Armande Robert
Catherine Delort
Cwenthryth of Mercia
Dionysia Baldewyne
Dorothea Hindremstein [Dorothy]
Eleanor of Aquitaine
Eleanor Cobham
Ellen Dalok
Else of Meersburg
Eva of Brounestown
Gabrina Albetti
Galiena (of Norfolk)
Gerberga (of Toulouse)
Gunhild of Denmark, queen of Norway
Helen Galrussyn
Henriette de Craus
Isabelle de Ferièves
Jacquetta of Luxembourg
Jane Shore
Joan of Arc (St.) [Jean]
Joan, lady Beauchamp
Jeanne of Burgundy, queen of France [Jean]
Jehanne de Brigue [Jean]
Jeanne de Latilly
Joan of Navarre, queen of England [Jean]
Jeanne Potier [Jean]
Jeanne Villain [Jean]
Johanna Wolsy [Jean]
Jeannette Charles
Judith of Bavaria, Holy Roman Empress
Macete de Ruilly
Mahaut of Artois
Margaret Lindsay
Margery of Hales
Marjery Jourdemain [Margery]
Margot de la Barre
Marie de Blansy [Mary]
Maria (la Medica) [Mary]
Matheline Fauré
Paule Viguier
Peretta Peronne [Perrette]
Petronilla of Meath
Pierina de Bugatis
Pierrille Roland

Rosamund Clifford
Sarah of Meath
Sibilia de Forci [Sibyl]
Syssoh Galrussyn
Tanglost
Valentine Visconti, duchess of Orléans
Waldrada
Ydette of Metz

WOMEN OF EASY VIRTUE

women who were not professional prostitutes or mistresses

Also see: ADULTERY; MISTRESSES; PROSTITUTES.

Agnes Butler
Agnes Desjardins
Agnes Knetchur
Agnes de Launcreona
Alice (Poplar)
Angela Borgia
Beatrice of Planisolles
Bertilla
Bona of Savoy
Catherine of France, queen of England
Catherine de l'Isle Bouchard
Catherine Sforza
Catherine de Vausselles
Caterina Visconti [Catherine]
Cecile de Turenne [Cecilia]
Clara d'Anduza [Clare]
Kunigunda of Hungary [Cunigunde]
Cwenthryth of Mercia
Devorgilla (O'Ruairc)
Dorotea Caracciolo [Dorothy]
Eleanor of Aquitaine
Eleanor Cobham
Elizabeth Higgins
Ermengarde (of Ivrea)
Eudocia Ingerina, empress of Byzantium
Gormflath (of Ireland)
Guillelma de Rosers
Guillemette (la tapicière)
Helen Lacapena, empress of Byzantium
Ingeborg of Denmark, queen of Norway
Ingebjorg of Norway [Ingeborg]
Isabella of Vermandois, countess of Flanders [Isabelle]
Joan, lady Beauchamp [Jean]
Joanna II, queen of Naples [Jean]
Juana of Portugal [Jean]
Macete de Ruilly
Margarida de Roussillon [Margaret]
Marguerite de Turenne [Margaret]
Marthe (of Paris) [Martha]
Mary of Antioch
Mary of Gelders, queen of Scotland
Péronnelle d'Armentières [Pérronelle]
Sybille de Château-Porcien [Sibyl]
Simonetta Cattaneo
Stephania (of Rome)
Subh of Cordoba
Theophano, empress of Byzantium
Willa of Tuscany, queen of Italy

WRITERS

includes women who wrote several extant letters, as well as females who wrote or dictated biographies, etiquette books, history, law, medicine, theology, etc.

Also see: POETS/TROUBADOURS; SCHOLARS.

Abella of Salerno
Adele of Champagne, queen of France
Agnes d'Harcourt
Agnes of Meissen
Alessandra Strozzi
Alix of Brittany [Alice]
Alice Drayton
Almodis (II) de La Marche, countess of Barcelona
Angela of Foligno
Angela Nogarola
Anne Beauchamp, countess of Warwick
Anna Comnena [Anne]
Anne Paston
Anne Shirley
Ava of Melk
Barbara Arrenti
Beatrice of Burgundy
Beatrice of England
Beatrice of Nazareth
Bertha of Avenay
Bridget of Sweden (St.)
Cassandra Fedele
Caterina Caldiera [Catherine]
Catherine of Genoa (St.)
Catherine of Lancaster
Catherine of Siena (St.)
Katherine of Sutton [Catherine]
Cecilia of Flanders
Cecilia Gallerani
Cecilia Gonzaga
Chiara Gonzaga
Christina of Markyate [Christine]
Christine de Pisan
Clarissa Orsini [Claricia]
Clemence of Barking

Constance (FitzGilbert)
Costanza Varano [Constance]
Contessina de'Bardi
Dhuoda
Diemuod of Nonnberg [Diemud)
Diemudis of Wessobrun [Diemud]
Douceline (St.)
Leonora of Aragon, duchess of Ferrara [Eleanor]
Eleanor of Brittany
Eleanor de Clare
Leonor Lopez [Eleanor]
Eleanora de Montfort [Eleanor]
Eleanor de Montfort, countess of Leicester
Aliénor de Poitiers [Eleanor]
Eleeanor of Provence, queen of England
Eleanor Stuart, duchess of Austria
Elizabeth Croke
Elizabeth Howard, countess of Oxford
Elizabeth Paston
Elizabeth of Schönau (St.)
Elizabeth of York, queen of England
Fiametta Adimari
Gertrude von Helfta
Ginevra Nogarola
Gisela of Kerzenbroeck
Guilia Farnese
Hadewijch
Helene Kotanner
Heloise of Argenteuil
Herrad von Landsberg
Hildegarde of Bingen (St.)
Hroswitha of Gandersheim
Illuminato Bembo
Isabelle of Angoulême, queen of England
Isabella of Aragon, duchess of Milan [Isabelle)
Isabella d'Este [Isabelle]
Isabella of France, queen of England [Isabelle]
Isabel Mowbray, lady Berkeley [Isabelle]
Isabel Plumpton [Isabelle]
Isotta Nogarola
Jane Stonor
Juana of Aragon, queen of Castile [Jean]
Joan Beaufort, countess of Westmoreland [Jean]
Jeanne Dabenton [Jean]
Joan of England, princess of Gwynedd [Jean]
Joan FitzAlan [Jean]
Joan of Kent [Jean]
Juliana Berners
Juliana of Cornillon
Julian of Norwich [Juliana]
Kasia (of Byzantium)
Kristin (of Iceland)
Laura Cereta
Lucrezia Borgia
Lucrezia de'Medici
Lucrezia Tornabuoni
Lutgard of Aywières (St.) [Liutgard]
Maddalena Bonsignori [Madeleine]
Maddalena de'Medici [Madeleine]
Maddalena Scrovegni [Madeleine]
Margaret of Anjou
Margaret Beaufort
Margaret de Bohun, countess of Devon
Margaret de Botreaux, lady Hungerford
Marguerite de Bourbon, queen of Navarre [Margaret]
Margaretha Cartheuserin [Margaret]
Margherita Datini [Margaret]
Margaret Ebner
Margaret of England, queen of Scotland
Marguerite of Naples [Margaret]
Marguerite d'Oingt [Margaret]
Margaret Paston
Margaret Porete
Marguerite of Provence, queen of France [Margaret]
Margaret Wake
Margery Kempe
Margery Paston
Matha d'Armagnac [Martha]
Marie of Anjou [Mary]
Mary of Blois
Marie of Cleves [Mary]
Marie de France [Mary]
Matilda of England, Holy Roman Empress
Matilda of Scotland
Mechtild von Hackeborn
Mechtild of Magdeburg
Mercuriade of Salerno
Nannina de'Medici
Péronnelle d'Armentières [Pérronelle]
Philippa of Lancaster, queen of Portugal
Philippine de Porcellet
Pregente of Melun
Rebecca Guarna
Richardis von Stade
Tenxwind of Andernach
Teresa de Cartagena [Theresa]
Trotula of Salerno
Umilita of Faenza
Vanozza Catanei
Yolande of Aragon

Cross Reference

by Last Names, Titles, Estates, Regions and Cities

Abergavenny
Elizabeth, lady Abergavenny
Isabel Despenser, countess of Warwick [Isabelle]
Joan FitzAlan, lady Bergavenny [Jean]

Acerra
Sibylla of Acerra [Sibyl]

Achaia
Catherine de Valois
Isabelle of Achaia
Matilda of Hainault, princess of Achaia

Acre
Joan of England, countess of Gloucester [Jean]
Marie de Coucy [Mary]

Adimari
Fiametta Adimari

Adorna
Catherine of Genoa (St.)

Adrianople
Agnes of France

Agda
Ermessend of Carcassonne, countess of Barcelona

Agdir
Asa, queen of Agdir

Aix
Agnes, countess of Aix

Alagno
Lucrezia d'Alagno

Albemarle
See—Aumale

Albetti
Gabrina Albetti

Albi
Adelaide of Toulouse

Albon
Beatrice de Dia
Beatrice of Viennois, countess of Albon

Albret
Catherine of Navarre
Charlotte d'Albret

Albuquerque
Leonor of Albuquerque [Eleanor]

Aldobrandeschi
Margaret Aldobrandeschi

Alençon
Marguerite of Lorraine [Margaret]

Alife
Matilda of Sicily, countess of Alife

Alnwick
Beatrice de Vesci

Alsace
Eleanora of Vermandois [Eleanor]
Ermengard (of Italy), Holy Roman Empress [Ermengarde]
Gertrude of Flanders, duchess of Lorraine
Helvidis
Isabella of Vermandois, countess of Flanders [Isabelle]
Margaret of Alsace
Sybille of Anjou, countess of Flanders [Sibyl]

Amancier
Antigone (of Gloucester)

Amesbury
Eleanor of Provence, queen of England

Amiens
Laurette de Saint-Valèry

Andelau
Richardis

Andernach
Tenxwind of Andernach

Andrea
Novella d'Andrea

Andrechs
Agnes of Dedo
Agnes of Meran
Gertrud of Meran [Gertrude]
Hedwig of Silesia (St.)

Anduza
Clara d'Anduza [Clare]

Angela
Irene Angela, Holy Roman Empress

Angia
See—Angela

Angoulême
Isabelle of Angoulême, queen of England
Isabelle of France, queen of England
Louise of Savoy
Tibors d'Omelas
Yolande de Dreux

Anjou
Adelaide of Anjou
Adelaide of Tours
Agnes of Anjou
Beatrice of Provence
Bertrade de Montfort, queen of France
Blanche of Anjou
Catherine of Austria
Katharine Vaux [Catherine]
Elizabeth of Bosnia
Elizabeth of Poland, queen of Hungary
Ermengarde of Anjou, duchess of Brittany
Isabelle of Achaia
Isabel of Lorraine [Isabelle]
Jadwiga of Hungary
Jeanne de Laval [Jean]
Joanna I, queen of Naples [Jean]
Joanna II, queen of Naples [Jean]
Margaret of Anjou
Margaret of Maine
Marie of Anjou [Mary]
Marie of Bourbon [Mary]
Marie of Brittany, duchess of Anjou [Mary]
Maria, queen of Hungary [Mary]
Matilda of Anjou
Matilda of England, Holy Roman Empress
Mélisende, queen of Jerusalem
Sybille of Anjou, countess of Flanders [Sibyl]
Yolande of Anjou
Yolande of Aragon

Antioch
Alice of Jerusalem, princess of Antioch
Anne de Châtillon
Cecilia of France
Constance of Antioch
Constance of France
Emma (of Apulia)
Mary of Antioch
Philippa of Antioch

Antwerp
Adelicia of Louvain, queen of England

Apulia
Alberada of Buonalbergo
Emma (of Apulia)
Fressenda (de Hauteville)
Irene Angela, Holy Roman Empress
Sichelgaita of Salerno

Aquino
Fiametta

Aquitaine
Adelaide (Capet), queen of France
Aénor of Châtellerault
Agnes of Anjou
Agnes of Poitou, Holy Roman Empress
Châtellerault, countess of
Dhouda
Eleanor of Aquitaine
Ermengarde of Anjou, duchess of Brittany
Petronilla of Aquitaine, countess of Vermandois
Phillippia, countess of Poitou [Philippa]

Aragon
Aurembaix, countess of Urgel
Beatrice of Aragon, queen of Hungary
Blanche of Anjou, queen of Aragon
Blanche of Aragon
Blanche of France
Blanche of Navarre
Carlotta d'Aragona
Katharine of Aragon [Catherine]
Constance, queen of Aragon
Constance of Aragon, queen of Hungary
Costanza of Aragon, queen of Sicily [Constance]
Constance of Hohenstaufen
Douce (III) of Provence
Leonor of Albuquerque [Eleanor]
Leonor of Aragon, queen of Castile [Eleanor]
Leonora of Aragon, duchess of Ferrara [Eleanor]
Leonor of Aragon, queen of Navarre [Eleanor]
Leonor of Aragon, queen of Portugal [Eleanor]
Leonor of Aragon, countess of Toulouse [Eleanor]
Leonor of Castile, queen of Aragon [Eleanor]
Leonor of Castile, queen of Aragon [Eleanor]
Leonor of Portugal, queen of Aragon [Eleanor]
Leonor of Sicily [Eleanor]
Elisenda de Moncada, queen of Aragon
Elizabeth of Portugal (St.)
Eudoxia Comnena [Eudocia]
Garsenda de Forcalquier
Ippolita Sforza
Isabel of Aragon, princess of France [Isabelle]
Isabella of Aragon, duchess of Milan [Isabelle]
Isabella of Aragon, queen of Portugal [Isabelle]
Isabella, queen of Castile and Aragon [Isabelle]
Juana of Aragon, queen of Castile [Jean]
Joanna of Aragon, queen of Naples [Jean]
Juana Enriquez, queen of Aragon [Jean]
Lucrezia Borgia
Lucrezia d'Alagno
Margaret of Austria
Margarita de Prades [Margaret]
Matha d'Armagnac (Martha)
Maria of Aragon, queen of Portugal [Mary]
Maria of Castile [Mary]
Maria Enriquez [Mary]
Maria de Luna [Mary]
Marie of Montpellier [Mary]
Marie of Navarre [Mary]
Maria of Sicily [Mary]
Petronilla, queen of Aragon
Petronille of Comminges [Petronilla]
Phillippia, countess of Poitou [Philippa]
Sancia d'Aragona
Sancha of Castile [Sancia]
Sibilia de Forcia [Sibyl]
Teresa de Entenza [Theresa]
Urraca, queen of Castile
Yolande of Aragon
Yolande of Hungary

Arborea
Eleanora di Arborea [Eleanor]

Arc
Joan of Arc (St.) [Jean]

Jeanne de Divion [Jean]
Mahaut of Artois
Margot Pipelarde
Marote (de Douai)

Argenteuil
Heloise of Argenteuil

Argyrus
Zoe the Porphyrogenita

Ardinghelli
Lucrezia Donati

Arizonelli
Agnese Arizonelli [Agnes]

Arles
Adelaide of Anjou
Alda of Arles
Almodis (II) de La Marche, countess of Barcelona
Bertha of Chartres
Bertha of Swabia
Bertha of Tuscany
Bertha of Tuscany
Bezole
Constance of Arles, queen of France
Roza
Waldrada (of Arles)

Armagh
Ota (of Norway)

Armagnac
Bonne of Armagnac [Bona]
Bonne de Berry [Bona]
Jeanne d'Armagnac
Matha d'Armagnac (Martha)

Armentières
Péronnelle d'Armentières [Pérronelle]

Armoises
Claudes des Armoises

Arnstein
Euphemia of Arnstein, queen of Norway
Eufemia (of Mecklenburg) [Euphemia]

Arran
Mary of Scotland

Arras
Deniselle Grenières

Arrenti
Barbara Arrenti

Artevelde
Kateline de Coster

Artois
Adelaide of Tours
Blanche of Artois
Blanche of Burgundy
Bonne of Artois [Bona]
Catherine d'Artois
Isabelle de Ferièves
Jeanne d'Artois [Jean]
Jeanne of Burgundy, queen of France [Jean]
Jeanne de Divion [Jean]
Jeanne de Valois [Jean]
Mahaut of Artois
Mahaut de Brabant
Marguerite (la barbière) [Margaret]
Margaret of France, countess of Flanders
Marie de Berry [Mary]
Noel (of France)
Pérronele (l'espicière) [Pérronelle]

Arundel
Adelicia of Louvain, queen of England
Beatrice of Portugal
Eleanor of Lancaster
Elizabeth Holland
Isabella de Despenser, countess of Arundel [Isabelle]
Joan FitzAlan [Jean]
Joan FitzAlan, lady Bergavenny [Jean]
Maud Lovell, lady Arundel [Matilda]
Philippa Mortimer

Ascania
Eilika of Saxony

Asolo
Caterina Cornaro, queen of Cyprus [Catherine]

Asser
Agnes Asser

Assisi
Clare of Assisi

Atainville
Marie d'Atainville

Athens
Irene, empress of Byzantium
Isabelle of Achaia
Matilda of Hainault, princess of Achaia

Atholl
Mary of Scotland (Atholl)

Attechapel
Agnes Chaucer

Atti
Isotta degli Atti

Attigny
Northilda

Aubigny
Adelicia of Louvain, queen of England

Aubrey
Maud Francis [Matilda]

Aubry
Poncette Aubry

Audele
See—Audley

Audley
Margaret de Audley, lady Stafford
Margaret de Clare

Augsburg
Clara Hätzerlin [Clare]
Claricia of Augsburg
Hedwig of Bavaria

Aumale
Agnes de Monceaux
Aveline de Forz, countess of Aumale
Blanche of Ponthieu
Catherine d'Artois
Isabella de Fortibus [Isabelle]
Jeanne de Dammartin, queen of Castile [Jean]
Marie, countess of Ponthieu and Aumale [Mary]

Autun
Richilde of Autun

Auvergne
Castelloza of Provence
Hildegarde (of France)
Jeanne de Boulogne, duchess of Berry [Jean]
Jeanne de Boulogne, queen of France [Jean]

Auxerre
Adelaide of Tours
Jeanne d'Auxerre [Jean]

Avalon
Emma of France

Avenay
Bertha of Avenay
Theutberga, queen of Lotharingia

Avesnes
Isabelle of Achaia
Margaret, countess of Flanders
Matilda of Hainault, princess of Achaia

Avesot
Agnes Avesot

Avignon
Bertrande of Avignon
Laura
Marie d'Avignon [Mary]

Avis
Leonor Teles, queen of Portugal [Eleanor]

Avise
Katherine l'Avise [Catherine]

Aywières
Lutgard of Aywières (St.) [Liutgard]

Babenberg
Gertrude of Babenberg
Margaret of Babenberg
Theodora Comnena

Backster
Margery Baxter

Baden
Gertrude of Babenberg

Badenoch
Margaret Wake

Baddlesmere
Baddlesmere (lady)
Elizabeth Badlesmere
Maud de Vere, countess of Oxford [Matilda]

Badlesmere
See—Baddlesmere

Baiane
Eudocia Baiane, empress of Byzantium

Bailliol
Devorguilla of Galloway

Balarin
Huguette Balarin

Baldewyne
Dionysia Baldewyne

Ballenstedt
Eilika of Saxony

Bar
Councy (lady de)
Eleanor of England, countess of Bar
Joan de Bar, countess of Surrey [Jean]

Barbaro
Caterina Visconti [Catherine]

Barcelona
Almodis (II) de La Marche, countess of Barcelona
Constance, queen of Aragon
Constance of Aragon, queen of Hungary
Douce (I) of Provence
Douce (II) of Barcelona
Ermessend of Carcassonne, countess of Barcelona
Maria de Malla [Mary]
Maria of Vivar [Mary]
Petronilla, queen of Aragon
Theresa of Portugal, queen of Leon (St.)

Bardi
Beatrice Portinari
Contessina de'Bardi

Bardolf
Beatrice de Warenne

Bari
Beatrice d'Este
Isabella of Aragon, duchess of Milan [Isabelle]

Barking
Katherine of Barking [Catherine]
Katherine de la Pole [Catherine]
Clemence of Barking
Wulfhilda of Barking (St.)

Barley
Alice Barley

Barnet
Alice of Rallingbury

Baroun
Elena Baroun

Barre
Margot de la Barre

Barres
Alice de Montmorency
Amicia of Leicester

Barthe
Angéle de la Barthe [Angela]

Basque
Ximena, queen of Leon

Bassanello
Adriana del Mila

Bassett
Beatrice Bassett
Elizabeth, lady Abergavenny

Bassum
Richardis von Stade

Bavaria
Adelheid of Germany, abbess of Quedlinburg [Adelaide]
Agnes Bernauer
Agnes of Poitou, Holy Roman Empress
Agnes von Staufen
Blanche, princess of England
Clementia of Zähringen
Cunegunde of Swabia
Diemud of Wessobrun
Diemudis of Wessobrun [Diemud]
Elizabeth of Bohemia
Elizabeth of Goerlitz
Gerberga of Bavaria
Gertrude of Bavaria
Gertrude of Saxony
Gisela of Bavaria, queen of Hungary
Hedwig of Bavaria
Hroswitha of Gandersheim
Ida of Swabia
Isabeau of Bavaria [Isabelle]
Judith, duchess of Bavaria
Judith of Bavaria, Holy Roman Empress
Judith of Bavaria, duchess of Swabia
Judith of Flanders
Margaret of Bavaria
Margaret of Bavaria
Margaret of Hainault
Margaret of Hainault, Holy Roman Empress
Margaret Maultasch
Matilda of England, duchess of Bavaria
Matilda of Lancaster, duchess of Zealand
Matilda of Tuscany
Taddea Visconti
Uta of Niedermünster
Wulfhild of Saxony

Baxter
Margery Baxter

Bayeux
Aubrée d'Ivry

Beauchamp
Aelips de Beauchamp
Anne Beauchamp, countess of Warwick
Cecily Neville [Cecilia]
Eleanor Beauchamp, duchess of Somerset
Elizabeth Berkeley, countess of Warwick
Isabel Despenser, countess of Warwick [Isabelle]
Joan, lady Beauchamp [Jean]
Joan FitzAlan, lady Bergavenny [Jean]
Margaret Beauchamp, countess of Shrewsbury

Beauflour
Johanna Beauflour [Jean]

Beaufort
Eleanor Beauchamp, duchess of Somerset
Joan Beaufort, queen of Scotland [Jean]
Joan Beaufort, countess of Westmoreland [Jean]
Margaret Beaufort
Margaret Holland

Beaugrant
Beaugrant (Madame de)

Beaujeu
Anne of Beaujeu

Beaumont
Amicia de Gael, countess of Leicester
Amicia of Leicester
Katherine Neville [Catherine]
Eleanor of Lancaster
Eleanora of Vermandois [Eleanor]
Ermengarde de Beaumont, queen of Scotland
Felise Reynard
Isabel Beaumont
Isabel of Vermandois, countess of Leicester [Isabelle]
Isabelle de Vescy
Loretta de Braose
Margaret of Leicester, countess of Winchester
Petronilla of Grandmesnil, countess of Leicester

Beaune
Guigone de Salins

Beauté
Agnes Sorel

Beauvais
Jeanne Laisne [Jean]

Bedford
Agnes Wombe
Anne of Burgundy, duchess of Bedford
Katherine Woodville [Catherine]
Isabella of England, countess of Bedford [Isabelle]
Jacquetta of Luxembourg

Bellegarde
Antoinette de Bellegarde

Bellême
Almodis (IV), countess of La Marche
Mabel of Bellême

Belleville
Jeanne de Belleville [Jean]

Bellière
Tiphaine Raguel [Tiffania]

Belper
Avis Wade

Bembo
Illuminato Bembo

Benet
Guillemette Benet

Benevento
Ageltrudis (of Spoleto)
Bethlem of Greci

Benincasa
Catherine of Siena (St.)

Bentivoglio
Francesca Bentivoglio
Lucrezia d'Este

Berchem
Fygen van Berchem
Sewis van Berchem

Bergamini
Cecilia Gallerani

Bergavenny
Joan FitzAlan, lady Bergavenny [Jean]

Berkeley
Elizabeth Berkeley, countess of Warwick
Isabel Mowbray, lady Berkeley [Isabelle]
Margaret Beauchamp, countess of Shrewsbury

Berkshire
Childlove (de Worth)

Bermondsey Abbey
Catherine of France, queen of England

Bernauer
Agnes Bernauer

Berners
Juliana Berners

Berry
Agnes Paston
Bonne de Berry [Bona]
Jeanne d'Armagnac
Jeanne de Boulogne, duchess of Berry [Jean]
Jeanne of France, duchess of Orlèans [Jean]
Marie de Berry [Mary]

Bertone
Alice Hulle

Berwick
Isabella, countess of Buchan [Isabelle]
Joan Fauconberg [Jean]

Berwyk
See—Berwick

Betson
Katherine Riche [Catherine]

Béziers
Adelaide of Toulouse
Cecile de Béziers
Ermessend of Carcassonne, countess of Barcelona

Bigorre
Alice de Montfort
Petronille of Comminges

Billung
Eilika of Saxony
Wulfhild of Saxony

Bingen
Hildegarde of Bingen (St.)

Bisceglia
Lucrezia Borgia

Biscossi
Sibillina Biscossi [Sibyl]

Blanche
Ysabelet la Blanche

Blake
Cristina Blake [Christine]

Blansy
Marie de Blansy [Mary]

Blois
Adele, countess of Blois and Chartres
Adele of Champagne, queen of France
Alix of Brittany [Alice]
Alix of France, countess of Blois and Chartres [Alice]
Bertha of Chartres (Bertha of Blois)
Ermengarde (of Burgundy)
Jeanne de Penthièvre [Jean]
Liutgard of Vermandois
Marguerite de Clisson [Margaret]
Marie de Berry [Mary]
Mary of Blois
Marie of Brittany, duchess of Anjou [Mary]
Matilda of Boulogne, queen of England

Blount
Anne Neville, duchess of Buckingham
Juliana de Leybourne, countess of Huntingdon

Blund
Alice Kyteler

Bocchi
Dorotea Bocchi [Dorothy]

Bohun
Eleanor de Bohun, duchess of Gloucester
Elizabeth Badlesmere
Elizabeth, princess of England
Joan FitzAlan [Jean]
Margaret de Bohun, countess of Devon
Mary de Bohun

Bokenham
Alice Knyvet

Bokerel
Alice Bokerel

Bolingbroke
Mary Hervey
Mary de Bohun

Bologna
Alesandra Gilani [Alessandra]
Barbara Arrenti
Catherine of Bologna (St.)
Donella of Boulogne
Dorotea Bocchi [Dorothy]
Francesca Bentivoglio
Illuminato Bembo
Jacobina (medica)
Lucrezia d'Este
Maddalena Bonsignori [Madeleine]
Novella d'Andrea

Bonaventure
Juliana (Bonaventure)

Bonrepos
Margarita de Prades [Margaret]

Bonsignori
Maddalena Bonsignori [Madeleine]

Bonville
Cecily Bonville [Cecilia]

Brabant
Beatrice of Nazareth
Bonne de Bourbon, countess of Savoy [Bona]
Elizabeth of Goerlitz
Jacqueline of Hainault
Mahaut de Brabant
Margaret of Brabant, countess of Flanders
Margaret of Brabant, Holy Roman Empress
Margaret of England, duchess of Brabant
Margaret of Flanders, duchess of Burgundy
Marie de Brabant, queen of France [Mary]
Marie de Brabant, Holy Roman Empress [Mary]
Marie of France [Mary]

Branchesle
Alice Bokerel

Brandenburg
Barbara von Brandenburg
Margaret Maultasch
Maria, queen of Hungary [Mary]

Branus
Agnes of France

Braose
Annora de Braose
Loretta de Braose
Margaret de Braose
Maud de Braose [Matilda]

Brefni
Dervorgilla (O'Ruairc)

Brescia
Amalberga
Angela Merici (St.)
Ginevra Nogorola
Laura Cereta
Maria (la Medica) [Mary]
Otta of S. Salvatore

Bresse
Louise of Savoy
Marguerite de Bourbon [Margaret]

Brews
Margery Paston (Brews)

Brézé
Charlotte (de Valois)

Bricquebec
Jeanne Paynel [Jean]

Brid
Agnes Brid

Brienne
Isabelle de Vescy
Marie de Coucy, queen of Scotland [Mary]
Philippa of Champagne
Yolande (of Jerusalem), Holy Roman Empress

Brigue
Jehanne de Brigue [Jean]

Brindisi
Sybil of Conversano [Sibyl]

Briouze
See—Braose

Brittany
Alix of Brittany [Alice]
Alix of Brittany [Alice]
Anne of Brittany, queen of France
Antoinette de Villequier
Beatrice of England
Constance of Brittany
Constance of Normandy
Eleanor of Brittany
Emma FitzOsbern, countess of Norfolk
Ermengarde of Anjou, duchess of Brittany
Jeanne de Belleville [Jean]
Jehanne de Bretagne [Jean]
Jeanne of France, duchess of Brittany [Jean]
Joan Holland, duchess of Brittany [Jean]
Jeanne de Montfort [Jean]
Joan of Navarre, queen of England [Jean]
Jeanne de Penthièvre [Jean]
Marguerite de Clisson [Margaret]
Marie of Brittany, duchess of Anjou [Mary]

Mary of England
Marie of France [Mary]
Roiantken
Yolande of Aragon
Yolande de Dreux

Brocadelli
Lucia Brocadelli

Brotherton
Alice Montacute
Margaret Marshall

Broughton
Agnes de Broughton
Agnes Kateline
Agnes Page
Beatrice Brounying
Katherine Boteler [Catherine]
Eleanor de Wendale
Joan Everard [Jean]
Sarra (of Broughton) [Sarah]

Broumattin
Agnes Broumattin

Brounestown
Eva of Brounestown

Brounying
Beatrice Brounying

Bruce
Elizabeth de Burgo, queen of Scotland
Isabella Bruce [Isabelle]
Joan of England, queen of Scotland [Jean]
Marjorie, countess of Carrick [Margery]
Marjory Bruce [Margery]

Bruges
Clemence Sillone
Elisabeth Scepens [Elizabeth]
Emma of Normandy
Jeanne Pouponne [Jean]
Margaretha van Eyck [Margaret]
Marie of Burgundy [Mary]

Brundyssch
Agnes Brundyssch

Brunham
Margery Kempe

Brunhausen
Oda

Brunswick
Gertrude of Meissen
Gisela of Swabia, queen of Germany
Joanna I, queen of Naples [Jean]
Marie de Brabant, Holy Roman Empress [Mary]
Matilda of England, duchess of Bavaria
Richenza of Nordheim

Brus
See—Bruce

Brussels
Bloemardine
Gertrude of Flanders, duchess of Lorraine

Bruyères
Catherine de Bruyères

Bryene
Alice de Bryene
Elizabeth Bryene

Bryennius
Anna Comnena [Anne]

Buchan
Isabella, countess of Buchan [Isabelle]
Strathearn (countess of)

Buckingham
Anne Neville, duchess of Buckingham
Anne Stafford
Katherine Woodville [Catherine]
Margaret Beaufort

Buckland
Joan Buckland [Jean]

Bucknall
Godgifu, lady of Mercia

Bugatis
Pierina de Bugatis

Buonalbergo
Alberada of Buonalbergo

Bures
Alice de Bryene

Burford
Roesia de Borford

Burgh
Beatrice de Warenne
Elizabeth de Burgh
Elizabeth de Burgo, queen of Scotland
Elizabeth de Clare
Hawise of Gloucester
Matilda of Lancaster

Burgham
Matilda de Burgham

Burgo
Elizabeth de Burgo, queen of Scotland

Burgos
Urraca Gonzalez

Burgundy
Adelheid of Burgundy, Holy Roman Empress [Adelaide]
Adelaide of Romainmoutier
Agnes of Anjou
Agnes of Burgundy, duchess of Bourbon
Agnes of France
Alix de Vergy, duchess of Burgundy [Alice]
Anne of Burgundy, duchess of Bedford
Beatrice of Burgundy
Beatrice of Vienne, countess of Albon
Beaugrant (Madame de)
Bertha of Chartres
Bertha of Swabia
Blanche of Burgundy
Bonne of Artois [Bona]
Catherine of Burgundy
Catherine of Burgundy, duchess of Austria
Catherine of France
Clementia, countess of Flanders
Colette of Corbie
Constance of France, queen of Castile
Eadgyfu of England, queen of Burgundy and Provence
Aliénor de Poitiers [Eleanor]
Emma of France
Ermengarde (of Burgundy)
Guigone de Salins
Isabelle of Bourbon
Isabella of Portugal [Isabelle]
Jacqueline of Hainault
Juana of Aragon, queen of Castile [Jean]
Jeanne de Boulogne, queen of France [Jean]
Jeanne of Burgundy, queen of France [Jean]
Jeanne of Burgundy, queen of France [Jean]
Mahaut of Artois
Margaret of Austria
Margaret of Burgundy
Margaret of Burgundy
Margaret of Flanders, duchess of Burgundy
Margaret of Hainault
Margaret of York
Marie of Burgundy [Mary]
Matilda of France
Matilda of Hainault, princess of Achaia
Michelle of France
Or (Madame d')
Theresa of Castile
Yolande de Valois

Burlatz
Adelaide of Toulouse

Burle
Alice Burle

Bury
Agnes de Bury

Bury St. Edmunds
Mabel of Bury St. Edmunds

Buscalh
Mengarde Buscalh

Butler
Agnes Butler
Eleanor Talbot
Saiv Kavanagh

Buxhall
Maud Francis [Matilda]

Carcassonne
Adelaide of Toulouse
Ermessend of Carcassonne, countess of Barcelona

Cardigan
Nesta

Carrick
Annabella Drummond, queen of Scotland
Marjorie, countess of Carrick [Margery]

Carrillo
Leonor Lopez [Eleanor]

Cartagena
Teresa de Cartagena [Theresa]

Cartheuserin
Margaretha Cartheuserin [Margaret]

Cashio
Lucy atte Lee

Castel
Christine de Pisan

Castelnau
Almucs de Castelnau

Castile
Beatrice of Castile
Beatrice of Castile, queen of Portugal
Beatriz Galindo [Beatrice]
Beatrice de Guzman
Beatrix of Portugal, queen of Castile [Beatrice]
Beatrice of Swabia, queen of Castile
Berenguela of Castile
Blanche of Aragon
Blanche of Bourbon
Blanche of Castile, queen of France
Blanche of France
Blanche of Navarre
Catherine of Lancaster
Constance of Castile, queen of France
Constance of Castile, duchess of Lancaster
Constance of France, queen of Castile
Leonor of Aragon, queen of Castile [Eleanor]
Leonor of Aragon, queen of Portugal [Eleanor]
Leonor of Castile, queen of Aragon [Eleanor]
Leonor of Castile, queen of Aragon [Eleanor]
Eleanor of Castile, queen of England
Leonor of Castile, queen of Navarre [Eleanor]
Eleanor of England, queen of Castile
Leonor de Guzman [Eleanor]
Leonor Lopez [Eleanor]
Elvira of Castile
Ines de Castro
Isabella of Aragon, queen of Portugal [Isabelle]
Isabella, queen of Castile and Aragon [Isabelle]
Isabel of Castile, duchess of York [Isabelle]
Juana of Aragon, queen of Castile [Jean]
Juana of Castile [Jean]
Jeanne de Dammartin, queen of Castile [Jean]
Juana Manuel, queen of Castile [Jean]
Juana of Portugal [Jean]
Margaret of Austria
Maria of Castile [Mary]
Maria de Molina [Mary]
Maria de Padilla [Mary]
Maria of Portugal [Mary]
Sancha of Castile [Sancia]
Sancha, queen of Leon and Castile [Sancia]
Theresa of Castile
Urraca, queen of Castile
Urraca of Castile, queen of Portugal
Urraca Gonzalez
Ximena Diaz
Zaida of Seville

Castro
Ines de Castro

Catalonia
Philippe de Moncada

Catanei
Vanozza Catanei

Catania
Virdimura of Sicily

Catesby
Margaret Wavere

Cattaneo
Simonetta Cattaneo

Caux
Anne of Caux

Caylar
Garsenda de Forcalquier

Cely
Joan Hart [Jean]
Margery (of Calais)

Cerda
Blanche of France

Cereta
Laura Cereta

Chalon-sur-Saône
Gerberga (of Toulouse)
Jeanne d'Auxerre [Jean]

Chamars
Henriette de Craus

Chambes
Helene de Chambes [Helen]

Champagne
Adele, countess of Blois and Chartres
Adele of Champagne, queen of France
Alix of Champagne, queen of Cyprus [Alice]
Blanche of Artois
Blanche of Navarre, countess of Champagne
Constance of France
Hersende (of Fontevrault)
Hersende (of France)
Isabella of Jerusalem [Isabelle]
Jeanne of France, queen of Navarre [Jean]
Jeanne de Navarre, queen of France [Jean]
Marguerite de Bourgon, queen of Navarre [Margaret]
Marie of Champagne, countess of Flanders [Mary]
Marie of France, countess of Champagne [Mary]
Péronnelle d'Armentiéres [Pérronelle]
Petronilla of Aquitaine, countess of Vermandois
Philippa of Champagne

Champdivers
Odette de Champdivers

Charlemagne
Bertha
Eadburg of Mercia
Gisela
Gundrada
Hildegard
Rotrude

Charles
Jeannette Charles

Charolais
Catherine of France
Isabelle of Bourbon

Chartley
Anne Devereux

Chartres
Adele, countess of Blois and Chartres
Alix of France, countess of Blois and Chartres [Alice]
Bertha of Chartres
Liutgard of Vermandois

Château-Porcien
Sybille de Château-Porcien [Sibyl]

Châtellerault
Aénor de Châtellerault
Châtellerault (countess of)

Châtillon
Agnes de Sechelles
Alix of Brittany, countess of Blois [Alice]
Anne de Châtillon
Blanche of France
Constance of Antioch
Mahaut de Brabant

Mahaut de Châtillon
Mary of St. Pol, countess of Pembroke

Chaucer
Agnes Chaucer
Alice Chaucer, countess of Suffolk
Philippa Roet

Chaworth
Maud Chaworth

Chelles
Ermentrude of Orléans
Rothild of Chelles
Rotrude

Cherchi
Umiliana dei Cherchi (St.)

Cheshire
Joan FitzAlan, countess of Hereford and Essex [Jean]

Cheshunt
Elizabeth Say

Chester
Alice Chester
Constance of Brittany
Ealdgyth (of Mercia)
Gundreda (of Warenne)
Margaret Lacy, countess of Lincoln

Cheville
Petronille of Fontevrault

Cibo
Maddalena de'Medici [Madeleine]
Teodorina (Cibo)

Cilly
Barbara of Cilly, Holy Roman Empress

Citta di Castello
Margaret of Citta di Castello

Clare
Alice de Clare
Amice de Clare [Amicia]
Amicia of Gloucester
Baddlesmere (lady)
Basilia de Clare
Eleanor de Clare
Eva MacMurrough
Isabella de Clare [Isabelle]
Joan of England, countess of Gloucester [Jean]
Margaret de Clare

Clarence
Ankarette Twynyho
Elizabeth de Burgh
Isabel Neville (Isabella)
Margaret Holland
Philippa of Clarence
Violante Visconti

Clarisse
Agnes Avesot
Jeanne Clarisse

Clerkenwell
Dionisia de Wodemerstham
Elena Taillour

Clermont
Jeanne de Bourbon [Jean]
Marie de Berry [Mary]
Marie, countess of Ponthieu and Aumale [Mary]

Cleves
Marie of Cleves [Mary]

Clifford
Agnes de Condet
Elizabeth Percy, countess of Westmoreland
Maud Clifford, countess of Cambridge [Matilda]
Rosamund Clifford

Clifton
Eleanor West

Clinton
Juliana de Leybourne, countess of Huntingdon

Clisson
Jeanne de Belleville [Jean]
Marguerite de Clisson [Margaret]

Yolande of Montferrat
Zoe the Porphyrogenita

Contarini
Caterina Caldiera [Catherine]

Conteville
Arlette (of Normandy)
Blanche of Ponthieu, countess of Aumale

Convers
Mariota Convers

Conversano
Sybil of Conversano [Sibyl]

Cook
Agnes Cook
Agnes Cook (le Keu)

Copton
Agnes Chaucer

Corbeny
Frederun of Lorraine, queen of France

Corbie
Colette of Corbie
Gundrada

Cordier
Jehanne de Brigue [Jean]

Cordoba
Leonor Lopez [Eleanor]
Subh of Cordoba
Tarub (of Cordoba)
Toda, queen of Navarre

Cordwaner
Juliana (Cordwaner)

Cornaro
Caterina Cornaro, queen of Cyprus [Catherine]

Cornillon
Juliana of Cornillon

Cornwall
Beatrice of Falkenstein
Elizabeth of Lancaster, duchess of Exeter
Isabella Marshall [Isabelle]
Sanchia of Provence [Sancia]

Cornworthy
Margaret Worthham
Thomasine Dinham

Correggio
Beatrice di Correggio

Cortona
Margaret of Cortona (St.)

Corvinus
Beatrice of Aragon, queen of Hungary

Coster
Kateline de Coster

Coucy
Catherine of Austria
Coucy (lady de)
Isabella of England, countess of Bedford [Isabelle]
Marie de Coucy [Mary]
Philippa de Coucy
Sybille de Château-Porcien [Sibyl]

Coudun
Agnes Sorel

Courcy
Affreca of Man, countess of Ulster

Courtenay
See—Courteney

Courteney
Agnes of Courtenay
Catherine de Courteney
Catherine de Valois
Katharine of York [Catherine]
Margaret de Bohun, countess of Devon
Marie de Brabant, Holy Roman Empress [Mary]

Courtrai
Kateline de Coster

Coventry
Godgifu, lady of Mercia
Margery Russell
Osburga of Coventry (St.)

Craon
Petronille of Fontevrault

Craus
Henriette de Craus

Crema
Dorotea Caracciolo [Dorothy]

Cremona
Onorata Rodiana

Crépy
Anne of Kiev
Isabel of Vermandois, countess of Leicester [Isabelle]

Crespi
Jeanne de Crespi [Jean]

Cristal
Casotte Cristal

Crivelli
Lucrezia Crivelli

Croke
Elizabeth Croke

Crowe
Alexandra Crowe

Cunha
Leonor Teles [Eleanor]

Curthose
Margaret of Maine
Sybil of Conversano [Sibyl]

Cusey
Jeanne de Cusey [Jean]

Dabenton
Jeanne Dabenton [Jean]

Dalassena
Anna Dalassena [Anne]

Dalok
Ellen Dalok

Damerham
Aethelflaed of Damerham

Damery
Elizabeth de Clare

Dammartin
Ida of Boulogne
Jeanne de Dammartin, queen of Castile [Jean]
Marie de Brabant, Holy Roman Empress [Mary]
Marie, countess of Ponthieu and Aumale [Mary]
Matilda of Boulogne, queen of Portugal
Philippa de Dammartin

Dampierre
Margaret, countess of Flanders

Daniello
Antonia Daniello

Dati
Margherita [Margaret]

Datini
Ginevra (Datini)
Margherita Datini [Margaret]

Dauphine
Felise Reynard

Decapolis
Eudocia of Decapolis, empress of Byzantium

Dedo
Agnes of Dedo

Delft
Gertrude van Öosten

Delort
Catherine Delort

Denecoumbe
Alice Denecoumbe

Dentue
Marion la Dentue

Derby (and Derbyshire)
Anne Shirley
Avis Wade
Margaret Beaufort
Matilda de Burgham

Dertford
Katherine Dertford [Catherine]

Desjardins
Agnes Desjardins

Despenser
Constance of York, countess of Gloucester
Eleanor de Clare
Eleanor Neville, countess of Northumberland
Isabella de Despenser, countess of Arundel [Isabelle]
Isabel Despenser, countess of Warwick [Isabelle]

Devereux
Anne Devereux

Devon (and Devonshire)
Amice de Clare [Amicia]
Katharine of York [Catherine]
Isabella de Fortibus [Isabelle]
Margaret de Bohun, countess of Devon
Thomasine Dinham

Dexter
Alice Dexter

Deyntee
Agnes Deyntee

Dia
Beatrice de Dia

Diaz
Maria of Vivar [Mary]
Ximena Diaz

Didymoticus
Agnes of France

Dijon
Jeanne de Cusey [Jean]
Jeanne Saignant [Jean]
Jeannette Camus

Dinham
Thomasine Dinham

Diogenes
Eudocia Macrembolitissa, empress of Byzantium

Disibodenberg
Hildegarde of Bingen (St.)
Jutta of Sponheim

Divion
Jeanne de Divion [Jean]

Dobrogneva
Mary of Kiev

Domremy
Beatrice d'Estellin
Hauviette (of Domremy)
Isabel Romée [Isabelle]
Isabellette of Épinal
Joan of Arc (St.) [Jean]

Donati
Lucrezia Donati

Donbely
Alice Donbely

Dore
Katherine Dore [Catherine]

Espine
Ysabelle de l'Espine [Ysabel]

Essen
Matilda of Essen
Sophia of Gandersheim
Svanhild of Essen

Essex
Eleanor de Bohun, duchess of Gloucester
Isabel, lady Bourchier [Isabelle]
Joan FitzAlan [Jean]
Mary de Bohun
Petronilla of Teye

Este
Angela Borgia
Anna Sforza [Anne]
Beatrice di Correggio
Beatrice d'Este
Leonora of Aragon, duchess of Ferrara [Eleanor]
Ginevra d'Este
Isabella d'Este [Isabelle]
Lucrezia Borgia
Lucrezia d'Este
Parisina Malatesta

Estellin
Beatrice d'Estellin

Estouteville
Ambroise de Lore
Jeanne Paynel [Jean]

Esvers
Katherine l'Avise [Catherine]

Étampes
Marie d'Orlèans [Mary]

Eu
Anne of Woodstock
Bonne of Artois [Bona]
Isabelle de Melun
Jeanne d'Artois [Jean]
Lesceline, countess of Eu
Marie de Berry [Mary]

Everard
Joan Everard [Jean]

Evesham
Godgifu, lady of Mercia

Évreux
Agnes d'Évreux, countess of Montfort
Agnes of Navarre, countess of Foix
Blanche of Navarre, queen of France
Helwise of Nevers, countess of Évreux
Jeanne d'Évreux, queen of France [Jean]
Jeanne of France, queen of Navarre [Jean]
Judith of Évreux
Marie of Navarre, queen of Aragon [Mary]

Exeter
Anne Holland
Anne of York, duchess of Exeter
Beatrice (of Portugal)
Dionysia Baldewyne
Elizabeth of Lancaster

Eyck
See—Van Eyck

Faenza
Francesca Bentivoglio
Umilita of Faenza

Falaise
Arlette (of Normandy)

Falconieri
Juliana Falconieri (St.)

Falkenstein
Beatrice of Falkenstein
Kunigunda of Hungary [Cunigunde]

Fanhope
Elizabeth of Lancaster

Fannere
Cristiana la Flaoners

Fano
Perna

Farnese
Guilia Farnese

Fauconberg
Joan Fauconberg [Jean]

Fauré
Matheline Fauré

Fedele
Cassandra Fedele

Felicie
Jacoba Felicie

Ferièves
Isabelle de Ferièves

Ferrara
Angela Borgia
Anna Sforza [Anne]
Beatrice di Correggio
Beatrice d'Este
Leonora of Aragon, duchess of Ferrara [Eleanor]
Ginevra d'Este
Isabella d'Este [Isabelle]
Lucia Brocadelli
Lucrezia d'Este
Parisina Malatesta

Ferrers
Anne Devereux
Elizabeth Woodville
Isabel Mowbray, lady Berkeley [Isabelle]
Joan Beaufort, countess of Westmoreland [Jean]

Fieschi
Catherine of Genoa (St.)

Fife
Isabella, countess of Buchan [Isabelle]

Filleul
Jeanne Filleul [Jean]

FitzAlan
Elizabeth Holland
Joan FitzAlan [Jean]
Joan FitzAlan, lady Bergavenny [Jean]
Marjory Bruce [Margery]

FitzGerald
Basilia de Clare

FitzGilbert
Alice de Clare
Basilia de Clare
Constance (FitzGilbert)
Eva MacMurrough

FitzJohn
Agnes FitzJohn
Beatrice de Vesci
Cecily FitzJohn [Cecilia]
Sybil de Lacy [Sibyl]

FitzOsbern
Emma FitzOsbern, countess of Norfolk

Flaoners
Cristiana la Flaoners

Florence
Alesandra Gilani [Alessandra]
Alessandra Strozzi
Alfonsina Orsini
Angelica del Lama
Antonia Daniello
Beatrice Portinari
Caterina of Florence [Catherine]
Cavolaja of Florence
Clarissa Orsini [Claricia]
Contessina de'Bardi
Jacoba (of Passau)
Juliana Falconieri (St.)
Lucrezia Donati
Lucrezia de'Medici
Lucrezia Tornabuoni
Maddalena de'Medici [Madeleine]
Margherita [Margaret]
Nannina de'Medici
Simonetta Cattaneo
Umiliana dei Cherchi (St.)
Umilita of Faenza

Foix
Agnes of Navarre
Catherine of Navarre
Cecile de Béziers

Leonor of Aragon, queen of Navarrre [Eleanor]
Esclarmonde de Foix
Esclaramunda de Foix, queen of Majorca
Jeanne de Boulogne, duchess of Berry [Jean]
Madeleine Valois
Marie d'Orlèans [Mary]
Philippe of Moncada [Philippa]
Zabelia

Foligno
Angela of Foligno

Fontaines
Laurette de Saint-Valèry

Fontevrault
Agnes, countess of Aix
Bertrade de Montfort, queen of France
Eleanor of Aquitaine
Ermengarde of Anjou, duchess of Brittany
Hersende (of Fontevrault)
Isabelle of Angoulême, queen of England
Joanna of England, queen of Sicily [Jean]
Matilda of Anjou
Petronille of Fontevrault
Phillippia, countess of Poitou [Philippa]

Forcalquier
Garsenda de Forcalquier

Forcia
Sibilia de Forcia [Sibyl]

Forez
Jeanne de Bourbon [Jean]

Forli
Catherine Sforza

Forster
Agnes Forster

Fort
Slymina Fort

Fortibus
Isabella de Fortibus [Isabelle]

Forz
Aveline de Forz, countess of Aumale
Isabella de Fortibus [Isabelle]

Foschua
Ulricha de Foschua

Fossé
Jeannette du Fossé

Francis
Maud Francis [Matilda]

Franconia
Agnes of Germany
Liutgard of Germany

Francou
Agnes Francou

Franken
Hedwig of Silesia (St.)

Frankfurt-am-Main
Marguerite of Naples [Margaret]
Serlin

Fraunceys
Maud Francis [Matilda]

Fraye
Walgrave (lady)

Freiburg
Matilda of Rottenburg

Freyne
Alice Lacy, countess of Lancaster

Frioul
Gisela (of France)

Frise
Bertha of Holland

Friuli
Gisela (of France)
Waldrada (of Arles)

Frocester
Margery of Frocestor

Fychan
Myfanwy (Tudor)

Gablere
Goda la Gablere

Gael
Amicia de Gael, countess of Leicester
Emma FitzOsbern, countess of Norfolk

Gaetani
Margaret Aldobrandeschi

Galicia
Gertrude of Babenberg
Urraca of Portugal

Galindo
Beatriz Galindo [Beatrice]

Gallerani
Cecilia Gallerani

Galloway
Devorguilla of Galloway

Galrussyn
Helen Galrussyn
Syssoh Galrussyn

Gambara
Ginevra Nogarola

Gandersheim
Gerberga of Bavaria
Christina (of Gandersheim)
Hathumoda of Gandersheim
Hroswitha of Gandersheim
Oda
Sophia of Gandersheim

Gandia
Constance, queen of Aragon
Maria Enriquez [Mary]

Gardebois
Avice Gardebois

Gascony
Eleanor of England, queen of Castile

Gatterstedt
Clara Gatterstedt [Clare]

Gaultière
Jehanne Gaultière [Jean]

Gaveston
Margaret de Clare

Gelderland
Eleanor of England, countess of Guelders
Ida of Boulogne
Mary of Gelders, queen of Scotland
Philippa de Dammartin

Gelders
See—Gelderland

Geneva
Jeannette Charles

Genoa
Catherine of Genoa (St.)
Teodorina (Cibo)

Genville
Joan de Genville [Jean]

Georgel
Anne-Marie de Georgel

Georgia
Tamara, queen of Georgia

Gerona
Ermessend of Carcassonne, countess of Barcelona
Matha d'Armagnac (Martha)

Gévaudan
Adelaide of Anjou
Douce (I) of Provence

Ghent
Aelfthryth of Wessex
Anees de Quinkere [Anne]
Jacqueline of Hainault
Kateline de Coster
Quintine van den Zande

Gilani
Alesandra Gilani [Alessandra]

Gille
Ingerid of Sweden

Glandévès
Delphine of Languedoc

Gloucester
Amicia of Gloucester
Anne Neville, queen of England
Anne of Woodstock
Antigone (of Gloucester)
Constance of York, countess of Gloucester
Eleanor de Bohun, duchess of Gloucester
Eleanor de Clare
Eleanor Cobham
Hawise of Gloucester
Isabel Despenser, countess of Warwick [Isabelle]
Isabella Marshall [Isabelle]
Jacqueline of Hainault
Joan of England, countess of Gloucester [Jean]
Margaret de Audley, lady Stafford
Margaret de Clare
Marjery Jourdemain [Margery]

Gobbe
Isabel Gobbe [Isabelle]

Godstow
Alice Henley
Margery Twynyho
Rosamund Clifford

Godwineson
Judith of Flanders

Goerlitz
Elizabeth of Goerlitz

Golden Horde
Bayalun
Turakina

Gonzaga
Barbara von Brandenburg
Cecilia Gonzaga
Chiara Gonzaga
Dorotea Gonzaga [Dorothy]
Elisabetta Gonzaga [Elizabeth]
Isabella d'Este [Isabelle]
Margaret of Bavaria

Gonzalez
Urraca Gonzalez, queen of Leon

Gorzano
Leonetta (medica)

Goseck
Eilika of Saxony

Goss
Kunigunde of Goss [Cunigunde]

Grandison
Katharine Grandison [Catherine]

Grandmesnil
Petronilla of Grandmesnil, countess of Leicester

Greci
Bethlem of Greci

Grene
Joan Grene [Jean]

Grenières
Deniselle Grenières

Grenoble
Guyette Durand

Grey
Anne Holland
Antigone (of Gloucester)
Catherine Percy, countess of Kent
Cecily Bonville [Cecilia]

Elizabeth Woodville

Grönske
Aasta Grönske

Gross
Kunigunde of Goss [Cunigunde]

Gruffydd
Eleanora de Montfort, princess of Wales [Eleanor]
Gwenllian (of Wales)

Guader
Emma FitzOsbern, countess of Norfolk

Guarna
Rebecca Guarna

Guelders and Gueldres
See—Gelderland

Guesclin
Tiphaine Raguel [Tiffania]

Guillebaud
Agnes, countess of Aix

Guiscard
Alberada of Buonalbergo
Emma (of Apulia)
Fressenda (de Hauteville)
Helena Guiscard [Helen]
Sichelgaita of Salerno

Guyenne
Agnes of Poitou, Holy Roman Empress
Charlotte d'Albret
Margaret of Burgundy

Guzman
Beatrice de Guzman
Leonor de Guzman [Eleanor]

Gwichtmacherin
Barbara Gwichtmacherin

Gwynedd
Joan of England, princess of Gwynedd [Jean]

Hachette
Jeanne Laisne [Jean]

Hackeborn
Gertrude of Hackeborn
Mechtild von Hackeborn

Hadham
Johanna Hadham [Jean]

Hainault
Eleanora of Vermandois [Eleanor]
Isabelle of Achaia
Isabella of Hainault, queen of France [Isabelle]
Jacqueline of Hainault
Jeanne de Valois, countess of Hainault [Jean]
Margaret of Alsace
Margaret, countess of Flanders
Margaret of Hainault
Margaret of Hainault, Holy Roman Empress
Margot de Hainault
Matilda of Hainault, princess of Achaia
Philippa of Hainault
Richilde, countess of Flanders

Hales
Agnes Brid
Margery of Hales

Halland
Ingebjorg of Norway [Ingeborg]

Halywell
Alice Romayn

Hambuie
Jeanne Paynel [Jean]

Hamel
Huguette du Hamel

Hamilton
Mary of Scotland

Hampshire
Eleanor West
Euphemia of Wherwell

Hance
Perrette la Hance

Hapsburg
Agnes of Hapsburg, queen of Hungary
Catherine of Austria
Elizabeth of Luxembourg
Marie of Valois [Mary]

Harbatova
Anna Harbatova

Harcourt
Agnes d'Harcourt
Blanche of Ponthieu

Harington
Cecily Bonville [Cecilia]

Harold
Jane Harold

Harpe
Alice atte Harpe

Hart
Joan Hart [Jean]

Hastings
Anne de Many, countess of Pembroke
Anne Stafford
Joan de Munchensi [Jean]
Juliana de Leybourne, countess of Huntingdon
Margaret of England, countess of Pembroke
Philippa Mortimer, countess of Arundel

Hatfield
Emma Hatfield

Hätzerlin
Clara Hätzerlin [Clare]

Haustede
Margerie de Haustede [Margery]

Haute-Lorraine
Beatrice (of France), duchess of Haute-Lorraine

Hauteville
Fressenda (de Hauteville)

Hauteyn
Juliana Hauteyn

Hay
Nicola de la Hay [Nichole]

Haynes
Margery Haynes

Heaulmière
See—Heaumière

Heaumière
Heaulmière (la belle)

Helfta
Gertrude of Hackeborn
Gertrude von Helfta
Mechtild von Hackeborn
Mechtild of Magdeburg

Henley
Alice Henley

Herbert
Anne Devereux
Anne Stafford

Hereford (and Herefordshire)
Agnes Knetchur
Alice Hulle
Cecily FitzJohn [Cecilia]
Eadgifu of Lominster
Eleanor de Bohun, duchess of Glouceste
Elizabeth, princess of England
Elizabeth Say
Emma FitzOsbern, countess of Norfolk
Godgifu (of England)
Joan FitzAlan [Jean]
Margaret de Bohun, countess of Devon
Mary de Bohun

Hertford
Joan of England, countess of Gloucester [Jean]
Lucy atte Lee

Hervey
Mary Hervey

Heuse
Ysabel de la Heuse

Higgins
Elizabeth Higgins

Hindremstein
Dorothea Hindremstein [Dorothy]

Hodere
Isabella Hodere [Isabelle]

Hoggenhore
Notekina Hoggenhore

Hohenburg
Relindis of Hohenburg

Hohenstaufen
Agnes of Germany
Agnes von Staufen
Beatrice of Sulzbach
Beatrice of Swabia, queen of Castile
Constance of Hohenstaufen
Cunigunda of Swabia, queen of Bohemia

Hohenzollern
Barbara von Brandenburg

Holar
Ingunn (of Iceland)

Holbourne
Agnes (of Holbourne)

Holderness
Amice de Clare [Amicia]

Holland
Ada of Scotland, countess of Holland
Anne Holland
Anne of York, duchess of Exeter
Beatrice (of Portugal)
Bertha of Holland
Elizabeth, princess of England
Elizabeth Holland
Elizabeth of Lancaster
Gertrude of Saxony, countess of Holland
Isabelle of Achaia
Jacqueline of Hainault
Joan Holland, duchess of Brittany [Jean]
Joan of Kent [Jean]
Jeanne de Valois, countess of Hainault [Jean]
Margaret Holland

Holte
Agnes atte Holte

Honylane
Margery de Honylane

Horsford
Alice Horsford

Horn
Isabella Hodere [Isabelle]

Horton
Alice Drayton

Houghton
Crystene Houghton [Christine]

Hove
Tryngen Ime Hove

Howard
Anne of York
Elizabeth Howard, countess of Oxford

Hulle
Alice Hulle

Hundesdich
Elisia Hundesdich

Hungerford
Margaret de Botreaux, lady Hungerford

Hunt
Joan Hunt [Jean]

Huntingdon (and Huntingdonshire)
Ada of Warenne
Agnes of Huntingdon
Anne Stafford

Beatrice of Portugal
Elizabeth of Lancaster
Juliana de Leybourne, countess of Huntingdon
Matilda of Northumberland, queen of Scotland

Hurepel
Agnes of Meran
Matilda of Boulogne, queen of Portugal

Husenboltz
Katherine Husenboltz [Catherine]

Huy
Ivetta of Huy

Ibelin
Maria Comnena, queen of Jerusalem [Mary]

Idole
Marion la Dentue

Iffley
Annota de Braose

Imola
Catherine Sforza

Ingerina
Eudocia Ingerina, empress of Byzantium

Inverneath
Joan Beaufort, queen of Scotland [Jean]

Irlond
Agnes Irlond

Isle Bouchard
Catherine de l'Isle Bouchard

Isle Jordan
Esclarmonde de Foix

Ivrea
Adelheid of Burgundy, Holy Roman Empress
Ermengarde (of Ivrea)
Willa of Tuscany, queen of Italy

Ivry
Ambroise de Lore
Aubrée d'Ivry

Jasomirgott
Gertrude of Saxony, duchess of Bavaria
Theodora Comnena

Jerusalem
Adelaide of Savona
Agnes of Courtenay
Alice of Jerusalem, princess of Antioch
Hodierna of Jerusalem
Isabella of Jerusalem [Isabelle]
Maria Comnena, queen of Jerusalem [Mary]
Mélisende, queen of Jerusalem
Morphia of Melitene
Sibylla of Jerusalem [Sibyl]
Theodora Comnena, queen of Jerusalem
Yolande (of Jerusalem), Holy Roman Empress
Yolande of Anjou

Joli
Marguerite Joli [Margaret]

Jordan
Faydide of Millau, countess of Toulouse

Jouarre
Ermentrude of Jouarre

Jourdain
Alison la Jourdain

Jourdemain
Marjery Jourdemain [Margery]

Judela
Elizabeth Judela

Jurdane
Marjery Jourdemain [Margery]

Jutland
Ragnhild of Denmark

Kapler
Catherine of Vraba

Karlsefni
Gudrid (of Greenland)

Kassa
Elizabeth of Poland, queen of Hungary

Kateline
Agnes Kateline

Katlenburg
Gertrude of Meissen

Kavanagh
Elizabeth le Veel
Saiv Kavanagh

Kemnade
Friderun (of Germany)

Kempe
Margery Kempe

Kendal
Joan Fauconberg [Jean]

Kent
Katharine Grandison [Catherine]
Catherine Percy, countess of Kent
Constance of York, countess of Gloucester
Dionysia de Mountchesny
Eadgifu of Kent, queen of England
Elizabeth Holland
Joan Fauconberg [Jean]
Joan of Kent [Jean]
Loretta de Braose
Margaret Holland
Margaret Wake
Roesia de Borford

Kerzenbroeck
Gisela of Kerzenbroeck

Keu
Agnes Cook (le Keu)

Kiev
Anastasia of Kiev
Anne, princess of Byzantium
Anne of Kiev
Christina of Sweden [Christine]
Elizabeth of Kiev
Evfimia of Kiev [Euphemia]
Eupraxia of Kiev, Holy Roman Empress
Gyda of England
Ianka of Kiev
Ingegarde of Sweden
Malfrid of Kiev, queen of Norway, queen of Denmark
Mary of Kiev
Olga, princess of Kiev (St.)
Rogneda of Polotsk

Kirkeby
Elizabeth Kirkeby

Kilconquhar
Marjorie, countess of Carrick [Margery]

Kildare
Elizabeth le Veel

Knetchur
Agnes Knetchur

Knyvet
Alice Knyvet

Konigsfeld
Agnes of Hapsburg, queen of Hungary

Kotanner
Helene Kotanner

Kreuzberg
Anne, princess of Bohemia
Clara Gatterstedt [Clare]

Kymbe
Cecily of York [Cecilia]

Kyteler
Alice Kyteler

Lacapena
Helen Lacapena, empress of Byzantium
Maria Lacapena [Mary]

Lacy
Agnes FitzJohn

Alice Lacy, countess of Lancaster
Cecily FitzJohn [Cecilia]
Joan de Genville [Jean]
Margaret de Braose
Margaret Lacy
Rose O'Connor
Sybil de Lacy [Sibyl]

Lagleize
Beatrice de Planisolles

Laisne
Jeanne Laisne [Jean]

Lama
Angelica del Lama

La Marche
Almodis (I) of Limoges
Almodis (II) de La Marche, countess of Barcelona
Almodis (IV), countess of La Marche
Blanche of Burgundy
Isabelle of Angoulême, queen of England
Yolande de Dreux

Lambercourt
Aelips de Beauchamp

Lambert
Jane Shore

Lampett
Julian of Norwich

Lancaster
Alexandra Crowe [Alessandra]
Alice Lacy
Almodis (IV), countess of La Marche
Aveline de Forz, countess of Aumale
Blanche of Artois
Blanche of Lancaster
Catherine of Lancaster
Katherine Swynford [Catherine]
Constance of Castile, duchess of Lancaster
Eleanor of Lancaster
Elizabeth of Lancaster
Isabel Beaumont
Margaret Holland
Maud Chaworth
Matilda of Lancaster
Matilda of Lancaster, duchess of Zealand
Philippa of Lancaster, queen of Portugal

Lancastre
Leonor of Lancastre [Eleanor]

Landsberg
Herrad von Landsberg

Lange
Annota Lange

Langley
Isabel of Castile, duchess of York [Isabelle]

Languedoc
Delphine of Languedoc

Lanzol
Angela Borgia

Laon
Eadgifu of England, queen of France
Emma of France
Gerberga of Saxony, queen of France
Hildegarde (of France)

La Ramée
Ida of Nivelles

La Rochelle
Catherine de La Rochelle

Lascaris
Irene Lascaris, empress of Byzantium

Las Huelgas
Blanche of Portugal
Eleanor of England, queen of Castile
Leonor of Castile, queen of Aragon [Eleanor]

Latilly
Jeanne de Latilly [Jean]

La Tremoille
Jeanne de Boulogne, duchess of Berry [Jean]

Anna Palmer [Anne]
Katherine Dertford [Catherine]
Godgifu, lady of Mercia
Margaret Lacy
Matilda Maresflete
Nicola de la Hay [Nichole]

Lindsay
Margaret Lindsay

Lisbon
Joanna Rowley [Jean]

Lisieux
Lesceline, countess of Eu

Lizier
Grazida Lizier

Lodi
Violante Visconti

Loessart
Peronne Loessart

Logy
Annabella Drummond, queen of Scotland
Margaret of Logy

Lombardy
Adelheid of Burgundy, Holy Roman Empress [Adelaide]
Ageltrudis (of Spoleto)
Agnese Arizonelli [Agnes]
Ermengard, duchess of Lombardy, queen of Provence [Ermengarde]
Marozia of Rome
Rozala of Lombardy

Lominster
Eadgifu of Lominster

London
Agnes Asser
Agnes Brundyssch
Agnes de Bury
Agnes Chaucer
Agnes Cook
Agnes Cook (le Keu)
Agnes Deyntee
Agnes Forster
Agnes (of Holbourne)
Agnes atte Holte
Agnes Irlond
Agnes Molton
Agnes Mundene
Agnes Pickerell
Agnes Rokingeham
Agnes Russell
Agnes Sigily
Agnes Wombe
Alice Bokerel
Alice Burle
Alice Cantebrugge
Alice Chester
Alice Denecoumbe
Alice Donbely
Alice atte Harpe
Alice Horsford
Alice de Lincoln
Alice atte March
Alice Romayn
Alice Seford
Alice Shether
Alice Stanford
Alice Staundon
Alice Tredewedowe
Alice de Wylesdone
Alice la Wymplere
Amice la Plomere [Amicia]
Anne Neville, duchess of Buckingham
Anna Palmer [Anne]
Avice Gardebois
Avice la Wymplere
Basilia Maderman
Beatrice Bassett
Beatrice la Welsshe
Katherine Dore [Catherine]
Katherine Riche [Catherine]
Cecily Chaumpaigne [Cecilia]
Cristina Blake [Christine]
Crystene Houghton [Christine]
Christina of Markyate [Christine]
Cristina Rokingeham [Christine]
Christine Swath
Cristiana la Flaoners
Denise la Vileyn
Dionysia Bottele (Dionisia)
Dionisia de Wodemerstham
Dulcia Trye
Edith Paumer
Elena Taillour
Elisia Hundesdich
Elizabeth, lady Abergavenny

Elizabeth Croke
Elizabeth Higgins
Elizabeth Judela
Elizabeth Kirkeby
Elizabeth Moring
Elizabeth Scolemaystres
Elizabeth Stokton
Ellen Sage
Emma Hatfield
Emma Turk
Goda la Gablere
Gunnora de Stratford
Idonea le Hukestere
Isabel Gobbe [Isabelle]
Isabella Hodere [Isabelle]
Isabel Norman [Isabelle]
Isabella de Toppesham [Isabelle]
Jane Harold
Jane Shore
Jane Stonor
Johanna Beauflour [Jean]
Joan Grene [Jean]
Johanna Hadham [Jean]
Joan Hunt [Jean]
Joan Lenelonde [Jean]
Johanna (of London) [Jean]
Joanna Rowley [Jean]
Johanna Travers [Jean]
Johanna Wolsy [Jean]
Joan Woulbarowe [Jean]
Juliana (Bonaventure)
Juliana (Cordwaner)
Juliana Hauteyn
Juliana Roos
Margaret de Clare
Margaret Elyott
Margaret Page
Margaret Stoke
Margery de Honylane
Marjery Jourdemain [Margery]
Mariota Convers
Massiota (la Lavendere)
Matilda de Burgham
Maud Francis [Matilda]
Matilda Yonge
Notekina Hoggenhore
Petronilla Turk
Richolda
Roesia de Borford
Rose Nosterfeld
Sanche Snoth
Sarah Stroby
Slymina Fort

Longchamp
Agnes d'Harcourt
Isabelle of France
Jeanne de Crespi [Jean]
Marguerite Joli [Margaret]

Longsword
Ela, countess of Salisbury

Lopez
Leonor Lopez [Eleanor]

Lore
Ambroise de Lore

Lorraine
Alison Dumay
Beatrice (of France), duchess of Haute-Lorraine
Beatrice, marchioness of Tuscany
Bertha of Swabia, duchess of Lorraine
Emma of Italy, queen of France
Gertrude of Flanders, duchess of Lorraine
Gisla of Lorraine
Godevere of Toëni
Isabel of Lorraine [Isabelle]
Liutgard of Germany
Margaret of Bavaria
Marguerite of Lorraine [Margaret]
Matilda of Tuscany
Sybille of Château-Porcien [Sibyl]
Ydain of Lorraine
Yolande of Anjou

Lorvao
Blanche of Portugal
Sancha of Portugal (St.) [Sancia]
Theresa of Portugal, queen of Leon (St.)

Lotharingia
Bertha of Tuscany
Gerberga of Saxony, queen of France
Matilda, queen of Germany
Richilde of Autun
Rothild of Chelles
Theutberga, queen of Lotharingia
Waldrada

Lothier
Mahaut de Brabant

Louvain
Adelicia of Louvain, queen of England
Gertrude of Flanders, duchess of Lorraine
Marie de Brabant, Holy Roman Empress [Mary]

Lovell
Elizabeth Bryene
Maud Lovell, lady Arundel [Matilda]

Lucca
Zita of Lucca (St.)

Lucerne
Dorothea Hindremstein [Dorothy]
Else of Meersburg

Lucy
Elizabeth Lucy
Matilda de Lucy

Lumley
Eleanor Neville, lady Lumley

Luna
Maria Enriquez [Mary]
Maria de Luna [Mary]

Lusignan
Alix of Champagne, queen of Cyprus [Alice]
Almodis (II) de La Marche, countess of Barcelona
Anne de Lusignan
Charlotte of Lusignan
Isabelle of Angoulême, queen of England
Isabella of Jerusalem [Isabelle]
Joan of England, queen of Scotland [Jean]
Sibylla of Jerusalem [Sibyl]
Yolande de Dreux

Luys
Guillemette du Luys

Lye
Alice de Lye

Lynn
Margery Kempe

Lyons
Casotte Cristal
Huguette Balarin
Marguerite d'Oingt [Margaret]
Matilda of France

Machecou
Jacqueline Machecoue

Macinghi
Alessandra Strozzi

MacMurrough
Dervorgilla (O'Ruairc)
Eva MacMurrough

Mâcon
Alix de Mâcon [Alice]

Macrembolitissa
Eudocia Macrembolitissa, empress of Byzantium

Maderman
Basilia Maderman

Madrid
Beatriz Galindo [Beatrice]

Magdeburg
Catherine of Austria
Mechtild of Magdeburg

Maignelais
Antoinette de Villequier

Maine
Ermengarde de Beaumont, queen of Scotland
Mabel of Bellême
Margaret of Maine
Rothild of Chelles
Sybille of Anjou, countess of Flanders [Sibyl]

Maino
Agnese del Maino [Agnes]

Mainz
Teoda of Mainz

Majorca
Esclaramunda de Foix, queen of Majorca
Joanna I, queen of Naples [Jean]
Maria de Malla [Mary]
Sancia of Majorca

Makejoy
Maud Makejoy [Matilda]

Malatesta
Battista da Montefeltro
Dorotea Caracciolo [Dorothy]
Francesca da Rimini
Ginevra d'Este
Isotta degli Atti
Parisina Malatesta

Male
Margaret of Brabant, countess of Flanders
Margaret of France, countess of Flanders

Malingré
Raouline la Malingré

Malla
Maria de Malla [Mary]

Man
Affreca of Man, countess of Ulster

Mandeville
Hawise of Gloucester

Manfredi
Francesca Bentivoglio

Maniace
Margaret of Navarre, queen of Sicily

Mantes
Godgifu (of England)
Odeline

Mantua
Barbara von Brandenburg
Cecilia Gonzaga
Chiara Gonzaga
Dorotea Gonzaga [Dorothy]
Elisabetta Gonzaga [Elizabeth]
Isabella d'Este [Isabelle]
Margaret of Bavaria
Vanozza Catanei

Manuel
Juana Manuel, queen of Castile [Jean]

Many
Anne de Many, countess of Pembroke

Marasch
Agnes of Courtenay

Marburg
Elizabeth of Hungary (St.)

March
Agnes, countess of Dunbar
Alice atte March
Anne Mortimer
Philippa Mortimer
Philippa of Clarence

Marche
See—La Marche

Marcigny
Adele, countess of Blois and Chartres

Maresflete
Matilda Maresflete

Mareuil
Agnes de Sechelles

Marienwerder
Dorothy of Montau

Markyate
Christina of Markyate [Christine]

Marle
Odeline

Marliani
Lucia Marliani

Marseilles
Azalais de Rocamartina [Adelaide]
Douceline (St.)

Marie of Montpellier [Mary]
Philippine de Porcellet
Sara of Saint-Gilles [Sarah]

Marshal
See—Marshall

Marshall
Eleanor de Montfort, countess of Leicester
Isabella de Clare [Isabelle]
Isabella Marshall [Isabelle]
Margaret Marshall

Martel
Margaret of Maine

Martin
Perrine Martin

Maubisson
Alix de Mâcon [Alice]

Mauclerc
Alix of Brittany [Alice]
Yolande de Dreux

Maugarnie
Perrette la Maugarnie

Maultasch
Margaret Maultasch

Mauny
Margaret Marshall

Maurienne
Adelaide of Maurienne, queen of France
Adelheid of Savoy [Adelaide]
Bertha of Susa
Jeanne of Flanders [Jean]
Matilda of Savoy

Mauteby
Margaret Paston

Mayenne
Cecily FitzJohn [Cecilia]

Meath
Gormflath (of Ireland)
Joan de Genville [Jean]
Ota (of Norway)
Petronilla of Meath
Rose O'Connor
Sarah of Meath

Meaux
Adela of France [Adele]
Eadgifu of England, queen of France

Mecklenburg
Eufemia (of Mecklenburg) [Euphemia]

Medici
Alfonsina Orsini
Clarissa Orsini [Claricia]
Contessina de'Bardi
Lucrezia Donati
Lucrezia de'Medici
Lucrezia Tornabuoni
Maddalena de'Medici [Madeleine]
Nannina de'Medici
Simonetta Cattaneo

Medingen
Margaret Ebner

Meersburg
Else of Meersburg

Meffraye
Perrine Martin

Meissen
Agnes of Meissen
Gertrude of Meissen
Margaret (of Sicily)

Melgeuil
Almodis (III) of Toulouse

Melitene
Morphia of Melitene

Melk
Anastasia of Kiev
Ava of Melk

Mellifont
Dervorgilla (O'Ruairc)

Melun
Alix de Mâcon [Alice]
Isabelle de Melun
Liutgard of Vermandois
Pregente of Melun

Melzo
Lucia Marliani

Meneses
Leonor Teles, queen of Portugal [Eleanor]

Meran
Agnes of Dedo
Agnes of Meran
Gertrud of Meran [Gertrude]
Hedwig of Silesia (St.)

Merceyra
Catherine Merceyra

Mercia
Aethelflaed, lady of the Mercians
Aethelswith of Wessex, queen of Mercia
Cwenthryth of Mercia
Cyenthryth, queen of Mercia
Eadburg of Mercia
Ealdgyth (of Mercia)
Ecgwyna
Godgifu, lady of Mercia

Merici
Angela Merici (St.)

Merseburg
Hatheburg

Métaille
Alison la Métaille

Meteola
Margaret of Citta di Castello

Metz
Ydette of Metz

Meulan
Isabel of Vermandois, countess of Leicester [Isabelle]

Mila
Adriana del Mila

Milan
Agnese Visconti [Agnes]
Anna Sforza [Anne]
Beatrice d'Este
Bianca Giovanna Sforza
Bianca Maria Sforza
Bianca Maria Visconti
Bona of Savoy
Catherine of Pallanza
Catherine Sforza
Caterina Visconti [Catherine]
Cecilia Gallerani
Drusiana (Sforza)
Guglielma (of Milan)
Ippolita Sforza
Isabella of Aragon, duchess of Milan [Isabelle]
Isabelle of France, duchess of Milan
Lucia Brocadelli
Lucia Marliani
Lucrezia Crivelli
Mayfreda de Pirovano
Pierina de Bugatis
Roza
Valentine Visconti, duchess of Orléans

Milières
Jeanne de Milières [Jean]

Millau
Faydide of Millau, countess of Toulouse

Miloutin
Simone of Byzantium

Mochov
Anna of Mochov [Anne]

Moens
Anees de Quinkere [Anne]

Moleyns
Margaret de Botreaux, lady Hungerford

Molina
Maria de Molina [Mary]

Molton
Agnes Molton

Moncada
Elisenda de Moncada, queen of Aragon
Philippe de Moncada

Monceaux
Agnes de Monceaux

Mone
Hawise Mone

Monferrato
See—Montferrat

Mongolia (and Mongols)
Borte
Oelun
Turakina

Monmouth
Rose O'Connor

Monomachus
Sclerena (of Byzantium)
Zoe the Porphyrogenita

Montacute
Alice Chaucer, duchess of Suffolk
Alice Montacute
Alice Montagu, countess of Salisbury
Katharine Grandison [Catherine]
Maud Francis [Matilda]

Montagu
Alice Montacute
Alice Montagu, countess of Salisbury
Katharine Grandison [Catherine]
Joan of Kent [Jean]

Montaillou
Agnes Francou
Beatrice of Planisolles
Fabrisse Rives
Grazida Lizier
Guillemette Benet
Mengarde Buscalh

Montargis
Eleanor de Montfort, countess of Leicester
Eleanora de Montfort [Eleanor]

Montau
Dorothy of Montau

Montefalco
Clare of Montefalco (St.)

Montefeltro
Battista da Montefeltro
Battista Sforza
Elisabetta Gonzaga [Elizabeth]
Emilia Pia

Montepulciano
Agnes da Montepulciano (St.)

Montferrat
Blanche of Montferrat, duchess of Savoy
Isabella of Jerusalem [Isabelle]
Maria Comnena, princess of Byzantium [Mary]
Sibylla of Jerusalem [Sibyl]
Violante Visconti
Yolande of Montferrat

Montfort
Agnes d'Évreux, countess of Montfort
Alice de Montfort
Alice de Montmorency
Amicia de Gael, countess of Leicester
Amicia of Leicester
Bertrade de Montfort, queen of France
Eleanor de Montfort, countess of Leicester
Eleanora de Montfort [Eleanor]
Isabel de Montfort (Isabella)
Joan Holland, duchess of Brittany [Jean]
Jeanne de Montfort [Jean]
Margaret Aldobrandeschi
Mary of England
Yolande de Dreux, queen of Scotland

Montgomery
Almodis (IV), countess of La Marche
Elizabeth Say
Mabel of Bellême

Monthermer
Joan of England, countess of Gloucester [Jean]

Montmartre
Adelaide of Maurienne, queen of France
Agnes Desjardins

Montmorency
Adelaide of Maurienne, queen of France
Alice de Montmorency
Marie, countess of Ponthieu and Aumale [Mary]

Montpellier
Adelaide de Porcairques
Eudoxia Comnena [Eudocia]
Marie of Montpellier [Mary]

Montpensier
Chiara Gonzaga

Montreal
Giralda de Laurac

Montreuil
Rozala of Lombardy

Montsegur
Corba de Péreille
Escalrmonde de Foix

Montsoreau
Helene de Chambes [Helen]

Monyons
Beatrice of Monyons

Moon
Hawise Mone

Moravia
Margaret Maultasch

Moray
Agnes, countess of Dunbar

Moring
Elizabeth Moring

Mortimer
Anne Mortimer
Annora de Braose
Elizabeth Badlesmere
Joan de Genville [Jean]
Philippa of Clarence
Philippa Mortimer

Moscow
Agrippina of Moscow
Elena of Moscow
Martha Boretsky
Sophia, princess of Moscow

Mosset
Margarida de Roussillon [Margaret]

Mountchesny
Dionysia de Mountchesny
Joan de Munchensi [Jean]

Mountjoy
Anne Neville, duchess of Buckingham

Mowbray
Anne Mowbray
Katherine Neville [Catherine]
Elizabeth Talbot
Isabel Mowbray, lady Berkeley [Isabelle]
Margaret Marshall

Moynesse
Colette la Moynesse

Munchanesi
Agnes FitzJohn

Munchensy (i)
See—Mountchesny

Mundene
Agnes Mundene

Munich
Ulricha de Foschua

Münster
Bertheida

Namur
Blanche of Namur, queen of Norway and Sweden
Marie of France [Mary]
Sybille de Château-Porcien [Sibyl]

Nancy
Alison Dumay

Naples
Beatrice of Aragon
Beatrice of Provence
Blanche of Anjou, queen of Aragon
Carlotta d'Aragona
Catherine of Austria
Costanza Calenda [Constance]
Delphine of Languedoc
Dorotea Caracciolo [Dorothy]
Leonora of Aragon, duchess of Ferrara [Eleanor]
Elizabeth of Poland, queen of Hungary
Fiametta
Ippolita Sforza
Isabelle of Achaia
Isabella of Aragon, duchess of Milan [Isabelle]
Isabel of Lorraine [Isabelle]
Joanna of Aragon, queen of Naples [Jean]
Joanna I, queen of Naples [Jean]
Joanna II, queen of Naples [Jean]
Marguerite of Naples [Margaret]
Marie of Brittany, duchess of Anjou [Mary]
Maria of Castile [Mary]
Matilda of Hainault, princess of Achaia
Sancia d'Aragona
Sancia of Majorca

Narbonne
Ermengarde, viscountess of Narbonne
Gilette of Narbonne
Marie d'Orléans [Mary]

Narni
Lucia Brocadelli

Navarre
Agnes of Navarre
Berengaria of Navarre, queen of England
Blanche of Aragon
Blanche of Artois
Blanche of Navarre
Blanche of Navarre, countess of Champagne
Blanche of Navarre, queen of France
Blanche of Ponthieu
Catherine of Navarre
Leonor of Aragon, queen of Navarre [Eleanor]
Leonor of Castile, queen of Navarre [Eleanor]
Isabella of France, queen of Navarre [Isabelle]
Jeanne of France, queen of Navarre [Jean]
Joan of Navarre, queen of England [Jean]
Jeanne de Navarre, queen of France [Jean]
Marguerite de Bourbon, queen of Navarre [Margaret]
Margaret of Navarre, queen of Sicily
Marie of Navarre [Mary]
Toda, queen of Navarre
Urraca Gonzalez

Naylor
Elizabeth, lady Abergavenny

Nazareth
Beatrice of Nazareth

Nérac
Charlotte d'Albret, duchess of Valence

Nérel
Denisette de Nérel

Neumarkt
Anne, princess of Bohemia

Neustria
Emma of France

Nevers
Bonne of Artois [Bona]
Eleanora of Vermandois [Eleanor]
Helwise of Nevers, countess of Évreux
Jeanne de Montfort [Jean]
Margaret of France, countess of Flanders
Margaret of Hainault, duchess of Burgundy

Neville
Alice Montagu, countess of Salisbury
Anne Beauchamp, countess of Warwick

Margaret Lindsay
Margaret Neville
Matilda de Lucy
Matilda of Northumberland, queen of Scotland

Northumbria
Ebba

Northwell
Agnes Chaucer

Norwich
Alice Chaucer, countess of Suffolk
Emma FitzOsbern, countess of Norfolk
Julian of Norwich [Juliana]
Lucia Tasseburgh
Margery Baxter
Philippa of Hainault, queen of England

Nosterfeld
Rose Nosterfeld

Notre Dame of Argentueil
Adelaide (Capet)

Notre Dame du Lys
Alix de Mâcon [Alice]

Noves
Laura

Novgorod
Christina of Sweden [Christine]
Malfrid of Kiev, queen of Norway, queen of Denmark
Martha Boretsky

Nuremberg
Barbara Gwichtmacherin
Kunigunda of Nuremberg [Cunigunde]
Margaretha Cartheuserin [Margaret]

O'Connor
Rose O'Connor

Ödenburg
Helene Kotanner

Ofrestad
Astrid of Norway

Oignies
Mary of Oignies

Oingt
Marguerite d'Oingt [Margaret]

Omelas
Tibors d'Omelas

Öosten
Gertrude van Öosten

Oporto
Theresa of Castile

Or
Or (Madame d')

Orange
Beatrice de Dia
Tibors d'Omelas

Oria
Eleanora di Arborea [Eleanor]

Orkneys
Gunhild of Denmark, queen of Norway
Ingibiorg, queen of Scotland [Ingeborg]

Orléans
Anne of Brittany, queen of France
Bonne of Armagnac [Bona]
Ermentrude of Orléans
Isabella of France, queen of England [Isabelle]
Jeanne of France, duchess of Orléans (Jeanne)
Marie of Cleves [Mary]
Marie d'Orléans [Mary]
Valentine Visconti, duchess of Orléans

Ormond
Saiv Kavanagh

O'Rourke
See—O'Ruairc

Orsini
Adriana del Mila
Alfonsina Orsini

Clarissa Orsini [Claricia]
Guilia Farnese
Margaret Aldobrandeschi

Ortemberg
Else von Ortemberg

O'Ruairc
Dervorgilla (O'Ruairc)

Oslo
Ingeborg of Norway

Osnabruck
Gisela of Kerzenbroeck

Ostrevant
Eleanora of Vermandois [Eleanor]

Ourem
Leonor Teles [Eleanor]

Outlaw
Alice Kyteler

Outremer
Eadgifu of England, queen of France
Gerberga of Saxony, queen of France
Matilda of France

Oxford (and Oxfordshire)
Agnes de Launcreona
Alice Drayton
Alice Henley
Devorguilla of Galloway
Elizabeth Howard, countess of Oxford
Elizabeth of York, duchess of Suffolk
Joan, lady Beauchamp [Jean]
Margaret Neville, countess of Oxford
Maud de Vere, countess of Oxford [Matilda]
Philippa de Coucy

Padilla
Maria de Padilla [Mary]

Padua
Laura Cereta
Leonetta (medica)
Maddalena Scrovegni [Madeleine]

Page
Agnes Page
Margaret Page

Paleologa (and Paleologus)
Anne of Savoy, empress of Byzantium
Sophia, princess of Moscow

Palermo
Rosalia of Palermo (St.)

Palestrina
Stephania (of Rome)

Pallanza
Catherine of Pallanza

Palmer
Anna Palmer [Anne]

Pamiers
Esclarmonde de Foix

Pantepoptes
Anna Dalassena [Anne]

Paphlagonia
Theodora of Paphlagonia

Paris
Adelie (l'erbière) [Adele]
Agnes Desjardins
Aalis (la barbière) [Alice]
Alix la Bourgolle [Alice]
Aales (la chandelière) [Alice]
Aelis (la poissonière) [Alice]
Aaeles (la tapicière) [Alice]
Aalis (l'ymaginière) [Alice]
Alison la Jourdain
Alison la Métaille
Alison (la nourrice)
Alison (of Port-Royal)
Ambroise de Lore
Ameline (la bouchière)
Ameline (la cordoanière)
Ameline (la couturière)
Ameline (la miresse)
Anastaise (of Paris) [Anastasia]
Anès (la cervoisière) [Anne]
Anès (la gueinnière) [Anne]

Anès (la taupière) [Anne]
Asceline (la deicière)
Aveline (la barbière)
Aveline (la chapelière)
Aveline (l'estuverresse)
Beatriz (la buffretière) [Beatrice]
Beatrice (of France), duchess of Haute-Lorraine
Bietrix (la metresse) [Beatrice]
Belota (the Jew)
Berte (la tartrière)
Bourgot de Noir
Cateline (of Paris)
Katerine (l'attachière) [Catherine]
Katherine l'Avise [Catherine]
Catherine de Bruyères
Catherine de Vausselles
Claude des Armoises
Colette la Moynesse
Colette (of Paris)
Coustance (la parcheminière)
Denise (la barbière)
Denyse la Normande [Denise]
Denise de Partenay
Denise (la sainturière)
Denisette de Nérel
Denisette de Periers
Eadhild of Wessex
Edeline (la barbière)
Edeline (la paonnière)
Edelot (la fourmagière)
Emeline (la poréeresse)
Emeline (la ventrière)
Erembourc de Braieres
Erembourc (la florière)
Erembourc (la potière)
Estienne (la gravelière)
Eudeline (la barbière)
Eudeline (la baudreere)
Felise (la pastéere)
Geneviève (la paonnière)
Gile (la barbière)
Gile (la mâconne)
Guillemette (la tapicière)
Guiote Serre
Haoys (la meresse)
Haouys (la poulaillière)
Hathui (of Germany)
Heaulmière (la belle)
Hélissent (la ferpière)
Heloys (la miergesse)
Heloys (l'uilière)
Heloyson (la nourrice)
Henriette la Patriarche
Hodierne (la cerencerresse)
Huguette du Hamel
Huitace (la lanière)
Isabeau (apotiqueresse) [Isabelle]
Isabiau (la mergesse) [Isabelle]
Jacoba Felicie
Jacqueline Machecoue
Jacqueline (la saacière)
Jehanne (la bouchière) [Jean]
Jehanne (la boutonnière) [Jean]
Jehanne de Bretagne [Jean]
Jeanne Clarisse [Jean]
Jeanne Conversa [Jean]
Jehanne (la cristalière) [Jean]
Jeanne de Divion [Jean]
Jeanne Dupré [Jean]
Jehanne (la fouacière) [Jean]
Jehanne Gaultière [Jean]
Jehanne Lecointe [Jean]
Jehanne (la loirrière) [Jean]
Jeanne de Milières [Jean]
Jehanne Poufille [Jean]
Jehanne (la tapicière) [Jean]
Jehanne (la verrière) [Jean]
Jeannette du Fossé
Jeannette la Petite
Jourdenete (nourrice)
Juliane (la potière) [Juliana]
Mabile (la regratière) [Mabel]
Macete de Ruilly
Maheut (la chapelière) [Mahaut]
Maheut (la feutrière) [Mahaut]
Maheut (la pescheresse) [Mahaut]
Marguerite (l'avenière) [Margaret]
Marguerite la Bonne Estranée [Margaret]
Marguerite (la chanevacière) [Margaret]
Marguerite (la cordière) [Margaret]
Marguerite Joli [Margaret]
Marguerite (la savonnière) [Margaret]
Marguerite de Ypres [Margaret]
Margot de la Barre
Margot (la gantière)
Margot (la Grosse)
Margot de Hainault
Marion la Dentue
Martha (of Paris)
Martha (of Paris)
Marie d'Atainville [Mary]
Marie (la barbière) [Mary]
Marie de Blansy [Mary]
Marie (la fanière) [Mary]
Marie (la mareschale) [Mary]

Marie (la meresse) [Mary]
Michiele (la ventrière) (Michelle)
Milessent (la cerenceresse)
Nicole (la boursière) [Nichole]
Nicole (l'erbière) [Nichole]
Nicole (l'esperonnière) [Nichole]
Nicole (la saunière) [Nichole]
Pentecouste (la fruitière)
Perrette la Hance
Perrette la Maugarnie
Peretta Peronne [Perrette]
Perrette la Toutaine
Pérronnele (l'espicière) [Pérronelle]
Pérronnele (la lavendière) [Pérronelle]
Pérronele (la nourrice) [Pérronelle]
Phelipote (la fritière)
Phelippe (la miergesse) [Philippa]
Raouline la Malingré
Richeut (la meresse)
Sainte (la paintre)
Sarre (la mirgesse) [Sarah]
Sedile (la fournière)
Sedillon Rossignol
Sersive la Berangière
Susane (la coiffière)
Thomasse (la talemelière)
Typhainne (la blazennière) [Tiffania]
Tyfainne (mestresse de l'école) [Tiffania]
Thyphainne (la toière) [Tiffania]
Ysabel (la commanderesse)
Ysabelle de l'Espine [Ysabel]
Ysabiau (la ferpière) [Ysabel]
Ysabel de la Heuse
Ysabel (la meresse)
Ysabiau (la nourrice) [Ysabel]
Ysabelet la Blanche

Parnel
Petronilla of Grandmesnil, countess of Leicester

Partenay
Denise de Partenay

Pas-de-Calais
Marguerite (la barbière) [Margaret]

Passau
Jacoba (of Passau)

Paston
Agnes Paston
Anne Paston
Elizabeth Paston
Margaret Paston
Margery Paston
Margery Paston

Patriarche
Henriette la Patriarche

Paumer
Edith Paumer

Pavia
Adelheid of Burgundy, Holy Roman Empress [Adelaide]
Agnese del Maino [Agnes]
Roza
Sibillina Biscossi [Sibyl]
Violante Visconti

Paynel
Jeanne Paynel [Jean]

Peiralada
Margarida de Roussillon [Margaret]

Pelham
Joan Pelham [Jean]

Pembroke
Anne Devereux
Anne de Many, countess of Pembroke
Katherine Woodville [Catherine]
Dionysia de Mountchesny
Eleanor de Montfort, countess of Leicester
Eva MacMurrough
Isabella de Clare [Isabelle]
Joan de Munchensi [Jean]
Margaret of England, countess of Pembroke
Mary of St. Pol
Nesta
Philippa Mortimer

Penthièvre
Jeanne de Penthièvre [Jean]
Marguerite de Clisson [Margaret]
Yolande de Dreux

Percy
Catherine Percy, countess of Kent
Eleanor Neville, countess of Northumberland
Elizabeth Percy, countess of Westmoreland
Margaret Neville
Matilda de Lucy

Péreille
Corba de Péreille

Peres
Theresa of Castile

Periers
Denisette de Periers

Peronne
Peretta Peronne [Perrette]

Perpignan
Beatrice of Monyons
Esclaramunda de Foix, queen of Majorca
Margarida de Roussillon [Margaret]

Perrers
Alice Perrers

Pesaro
Battista da Montefeltro
Battista Sforza
Costanza Varano [Constance]
Lucrezia Borgia

Petite
Jeannette la Petite

Pevensey
Joan Pelham [Jean]

Philip
Alice Chaucer, duchess of Suffolk

Phocas
Theophano, empress of Byzantium

Pia
Emilia Pia

Piacenza
Angelberga

Pickerell
Agnes Pickerell

Piedmont
Marguerite Saluzzio [Margaret]
Matilda of Savoy

Pilon
Jeanne Laisne [Jean]

Pinar
Florencia Pinar

Pipelarde
Margot Pipelarde

Pirovano
Mayfreda de Pirovano

Pisan (Pizan)
Christine de Pisan

Plaitz
Elizabeth Howard, countess of Oxford

Planisolles
Beatrice of Planisolles

Plantagenet
Isabel, lady Bourchier [Isabelle]
Joan of England, queen of Scotland [Jean]
Joan of Kent [Jean]
Matilda of England, Holy Roman Empress

Plomere
Amice la Plomere [Amicia]

Plouy-Domquer
Aelips de Beauchamp

Plumpton
Elizabeth Stapilton
Isabel Plumpton
Margaret Rocliffe

Poer
Alice Kyteler

Poitiers
Beatrice de Dia
Constance of Antioch
Alienor de Poitiers [Eleanor]
Ermengarde of Anjou, duchess of Brittany
Gundrada
Jeanne of Burgundy, queen of France [Jean]
Jeanne of Toulouse [Jean]
Mary of Antioch

Poitou
Aénor of Châtellerault
Agnes of Anjou
Agnes of Poitou, Holy Roman Empress
Alix of Brittany [Alice]
Eleanor of Aquitaine
Ermengarde of Anjou, duchess of Brittany
Phillippia, countess of Poitou [Philippa]

Pole
Alice Chaucer, duchess of Suffolk
Katherine de la Pole [Catherine]
Elizabeth of York, duchess of Suffolk
Jane Stonor
Margaret Beaufort

Polenta
Francesca da Rimini

Poletins
Marguerite d'Oingt [Margaret]

Polotsk
Evfosinia of Polotsk
Rogneda of Polotsk

Pomerania
Elizabeth of Pomerania
Philippa of England, queen of Norway, Denmark, and Sweden

Ponthieu
Alys of France [Alice]
Blanche of Ponthieu
Catherine d'Artois
Frederun of Lorraine, queen of France
Jeanne de Dammartin, queen of Castile [Jean]
Marie, countess of Ponthieu and Aumale [Mary]
Philippa de Dammartin

Ponthoiles
Catherine d'Artois

Ponziano
Frances of Rome (St.)

Poplar
Alice (Poplar)

Porcairques
Adelaide de Porcairques

Porcellet
Philippine de Porcellet

Porete
Margaret Porete

Porphyrogenita
Theodora the Porphyrogenita
Zoe the Porphyrogenita

Portinari
Beatrice Portinari

Port-Royal
Alison (of Port-Royal)
Huguette du Hamel

Portunhale
Ida de Portunhale

Posadnitsa
Martha Boretsky

Potier
Jeanne Potier [Jean]

Potkyn
Alson Potkyn

Poufille
Jehanne Poufille [Jean]

Pouponne
Jeanne Pouponne [Jean]

Poville
Adela of Flanders, queen of Denmark [Adele]

Powys
Antigone (of Gloucester)

Poynings
Elizabeth Paston

Prague
Agnes of Bohemia
Anna Harbatova [Anne]
Anna of Mochov [Anne]
Dorothy of Strygl
Elizabeth of Bohemia

Prato
Ginevra (Datini)
Margherita Datini [Margaret]

Procena
Agnes da Montepulciano (St.)

Provence
Almodis (II) de La Marche, countess of Barcelona
Almucs de Castelnau
Beatrice of Burgundy, Holy Roman Empress
Beatrice de Dia
Beatrice of Provence
Beatrice of Savoy, countess of Provence
Bertha of Tuscany
Castelloza of Provence
Katharine Vaux [Catherine]
Clara d'Anduza [Clare]
Delphine of Languedoc
Douce (I) of Provence
Douce (III) of Provence
Douceline (St.)
Eadgyfu of England, queen of Burgundy and Provence
Leonor of Aragon, countess of Toulouse [Eleanor]
Eleanor of Provence, queen of England
Ermengard, duchess of Lombardy, queen of Provence
Faydide of Millau, countess of Toulouse
Garsenda de Forcalquier
Iseut de Capio
Joanna I, queen of Naples [Jean]
Lombarda
Marguerite of Provence, queen of France [Margaret]
Marozia of Rome
Richilde of Autun
Sanchia of Provence [Sancia]

Pueinautier
Loba de Pueinautier

Puttock
Beatrice Puttock

Pykring
Catharine Pykring [Catherine]

Quedlinburg
Adelheid of Germany, abbess of Quedlinburg [Adelaide]
Agnes of Meissen
Eupraxia of Kiev, Holy Roman Empress
Matilda, queen of Germany
Matilda of Quedlinburg

Quenci
See—Quincy

Quincy
Basilia de Clare
Margaret Lacy
Margaret of Leicester

Quinkere
Anees de Quinkere [Anne]

Quintin
Elizabeth Quintin

Rabockenges
Marie of Cleves [Mary]

Raby
Eleanor Neville, lady Lumley
Margaret Neville

Raglan
Anne Devereux

Ragnoni
Barbera Ragnoni [Barbara]

Raguel
Tiphaine Raguel [Tiffania]

Rais
Catherine de Thouars
Jeanne Paynel [Jean]

Rallingbury
Alice of Rallingbury

Ramée
See—La Ramée

Rameru
Philippa of Champagne

Ramirez
Margaret of Navarre, queen of Sicily

Ramleh
Agnes of Courtenay

Ravenel
Tiphaine Raguel [Tiffania]

Ravenna
Francesca da Rimini

Reagh
Saiv Kavvanagh

Rebestoeckyn
Katherine Rebestoeckyn [Catherine]

Redon
Roiantken

Redvers
Amice de Clare [Amicia]
Isabella de Fortibus [Isabelle]

Regensburg
Gerberga of Bavaria

Reggio
Gabrina Albetti
Maddalena Scrovegni [Madeleine]

Reims
Northilda

Remiremont
Waldrada

Rethel
Beatrice of Rethel, queen of Sicily
Elizabeth of Goerlitz

Reynard
Felise Reynard

Rhodes
Charlotte of Lusignan

Riasan
Agrippina of Moscow

Rich
Mabel Rich

Riche
Katherine Riche [Catherine]
Elizabeth Croke

Richemont
Margaret of Burgundy

Richmond
Blanche of Lancaster
Joan Holland,, duchess of Brittany [Jean]
Margaret Beaufort

Rimini
Francesca da Rimini
Ginevra d'Este
Isotta degli Atti
Parisina Malatesta

Ringerike
Aasta Grönske
Ragnhild (of Ringerike)

Rivers
Katherine Woodville [Catherine]
Elizabeth, lady Scales
Elizabeth Woodville
Jacquetta of Luxembourg

Robert
Armande Robert

Robine
Marie d'Avignon [Mary]

Robsart
Elizabeth Bourchier

Rocamartina
Azalais de Rocamartina [Adelaide]

Rochefort
Amicia of Leicester
Lucienne of Rochefort

Rochelle
See—La Rochelle

Rocliffe
Margaret Rocliffe

Rodiana
Onorata Rodiana

Roet
Katherine Swynford [Catherine]
Philippa Roet

Rokingeham
Agnes Rokingeham
Cristina Rokingeham [Christine]

Roland
Pierrille Roland

Rolin
Guigone de Salins

Romainmoutier
Adelaide of Romainmoutier

Romana
Francesca de Romana

Romans
Agnes of Hapsburg, queen of Hungary
Beatrice of Falkenstein

Romayn
Alice Romayn
Juliana Hauteyn
Roesia de Borford

Rome
Ageltrudis (of Spoleto)
Agnes of Poitou, Holy Roman Empress
Alda of Arles
Alfonsina Orsini
Cecile de Turenne [Cecilia]
Charlotte of Lusignan
Clarissa Orsini [Claricia]
Claude des Armoises
Eadburg of Mercia
Frances of Rome (St.)
Guilia Farnese
Judith of Flanders
Lucrezia Borgia
Lucrezia Tornabuoni
Margaret Aldobrandeschi
Marozia of Rome
Sancia d'Aragona
Stephania (of Rome)
Theodora of Rome
Vanozza Catanei

Romée
Isabel Romée [Isabelle]

Romley
Agnes Sadler

Romsey
Christina of Hungary [Christine]
Mary of Blois
Mary of Scotland (Atholl)
Matilda of Scotland

Roos
Juliana Roos

Rosers
Guillelma de Rosers

Rossignol
Sedillon Rossignol

Rothenburg
Gertrude of Bavaria

Rotomago
Clarice of Rotomago [Claricia]

Rottenburg
Matilda of Rottenburg

Rouen
Clarice of Rotomago [Claricia]
Gunnor (of Denmark)
Lesceline, countess of Eu
Peretta Peronne [Perrette]

Rougiers
Guillelma de Rosers

Roussillon
Bertha de Sens, comtesse de Vienne
Margarida de Roussillon [Margaret]

Rouvres
Jeanne de Boulogne, queen of France [Jean]
Margaret of Flanders, duchess of Burgundy

Rowley
Joanna Rowley [Jean]

Royer
Catherine Royer

Rucellai
Nannina de'Medici

Ruilly
Macete de Ruilly

Rulle
Gisela of Kerzenbroeck

Rupertsberg
Hildegarde of Bingen (St.)
Richardis von Stade

Russell
Agnes Russell
Margery Russell

Ruthin
Catherine Percy, countess of Kent

Ryche
See—Riche

Rygeway
Cecilia Rygeway

Saarbrücken
Agnes of Saarbrücken

Sabran
Delphine of Languedoc

Sacomburs
Isabel Plumpton [Isabelle]

Sade
Laura

Sadler
Agnes Sadler

Sage
Ellen Sage

Saignant
Jeanne Saignant [Jean]

St. Adrian
Ermengarde (of St. Adrian)

St. Albans
Anastasia Spychefat

St. Gilles
Cecilia of France
Sara of Saint-Gilles [Sarah]

Saint-Gilles
See—St. Gilles

St. John
Philippa Mortimer

St. Leger
Anne of York, duchess of Exeter

Saint-Martin
Eva of Saint-Martin

St. Michael's
Agnes Butler

St. Pol
Jacquetta of Luxembourg
Mary of St. Pol

St. Quentin
Eleanora of Vermandois [Eleanor]

St. Riquier
Bertha

S. Salvatore
Amalberga
Bertha of Italy
Ermengard (of Italy), Holy Roman Empress [Ermengarde]
Ermengard (of S.. Salvatore) [Ermengarde]
Otta of S. Salvatore

St. Trond
Christina of St. Trond [Christine]
Lutgard of Aywières (St.) [Liutgard]

St. Valéry
Laurette de Saint-Valéry
Maud de Braose [Matilda]

Salamanca
Beatriz Galindo [Beatrice]

Salerno
Abella of Salerno
Alberada of Buonalbergo
Costanza Calenda [Constance]
Francesca de Romana
Marguerite of Naples [Margaret]
Mercuriade of Salerno
Rebecca Guarna
Sichelgaita of Salerno
Trotula of Salerno

Salins
Guigone de Salins

Salisbury
Alice Chaucer, duchess of Suffolk
Alice Montagu, countess of Salisbury
Katharine Grandison [Catherine]
Cecily Neville [Cecilia]
Ela, countess of Salisbury
Eleanor Neville, lady Stanley
Joan of Kent [Jean]
Margaret Neville, countess of Oxford
Maud Francis [Matilda]

Saluzzio
Marguerite Saluzzio [Margaret]

Salviati
Lucrezia de'Medici

Sancto Paulo
See—St. Pol

Sandringham
Elizabeth, lady Scales

San Severino
Bianca Giovanna Sforza

Sardinia
Adelasia of Torres, queen of Sardinia
Eleanora di Arborea [Eleanor]

Saumar
Jeanne de Laval [Jean]

Sauve Benité
Margaret of England (St.)

Savage
Rose Savage

Savona
Adelaide of Savona

Savoy
Adelheid of Savoy [Adelaide]
Anne de Lusignan
Anne of Savoy, empress of Byzantium
Beatrice of Savoy, countess of Provence
Bertha of Susa
Bianca of Savoy
Blanche of Montferrat, duchess of Savoy
Bonne de Berry [Bona]
Bonne de Bourbon, countess of Savoy [Bona]
Bona of Savoy
Charlotte of Lusignan
Charlotte of Savoy
Isabelle of Achaia
Isabel of Savoy
Louise of Savoy
Margaret of Austria
Marguerite de Bourbon [Margaret]
Matilda of Savoy
Yolande de Valois

Saxony
Adelheid of Burgundy, Holy Roman Empress [Adelaide]
Agnes von Staufen
Beatrice of Swabia, queen of Castile
Christina (of Gandersheim)
Clementia of Zahringen
Cunigund of Luxembourg, Holy Roman Empress (St.) [Cunigunde]
Edith of England, queen of Germany
Eilika of Saxony
Gerberga of Saxony, queen of France
Gertrude of Bavaria
Gertrude of Flanders, duchess of Lorraine
Gertrude of Saxony
Gertrude of Saxony, countess of Holland
Hathumoda of Gandersheim
Imma of Saxony
Judith of Bavaria, duchess of Swabia
Liutberga (St.)
Matilda of England, duchess of Bavaria
Matilda, queen of Germany
Oda
Richenza of Nordheim, Holy Roman Empress
Wulfhild of Saxony

Say
Elizabeth Say

Scala
Regina della Scala

Scales
Elizabeth, lady Scales

Scepens
Elisabeth Scepens [Elizabeth]

Scheppers
Marguerite Scheppers [Margaret]

Schiedam
Lydwine of Schiedam

Schiffi
Clare of Assisi

Schönau
Elizabeth of Schönau (St.)

Schweinfurt
Judith of Schweinfurt

Scolemaystres
Elizabeth Scolemaystres

Scrope
Elizabeth, lady Scrope

Scrovegni
Maddalena Scrovegni [Madeleine]

Seagrave
Margaret Marshall

Sebastopol
Catherine of Sebastopol

Sechelles
Agnes de Sechelles

Seford
Alice Seford

Segrave
See—Seagrave

Sempringham
Gwenllian (of Wales)

Senlis
Judith, queen of England
Matilda of Northumberland, queen of Scotland

Sens
Bertha de Sens, countess of Vienne

Septimania
Dhuoda
Gerberga (of Toulouse)

Serbia
Simone of Byzantium

Serina
Laura Cereta

Serré
Guiote Serré

Seville
Elizabeth Kirkeby
Zaida of Seville

Sforza
Agnese del Maino [Agnes]
Anna Sforza [Anne]
Battista Sforza
Beatrice di Correggio
Beatrice d'Este
Bianca Giovanna Sforza
Bianca Maria Sforza, Holy Roman Empress
Bianca Maria Visconti
Bona of Savoy, duchess of Milan
Catherine Sforza
Costanza Varano [Constance]
Drusiana (Sforza)
Ippolita Sforza
Isabella of Aragon, duchess of Milan [Isabelle]
Lucia Marliani
Lucrezia Borgia
Lucrezia Crivelli

Shaftesbury
Marie de France [Mary]

Sharpe
Beatrice Sharpe

Shedyngton
Alice Shedyngton

Shench
Joan Lenelonde [Jean]

Shether
Alice Shether

Shirley
Anne Shirley

Shore
Jane Shore

Shrewsbury
Alice de Lye
Eleanor Talbot
Elizabeth Talbot
Margaret Beauchamp, countess of Shrewbury

Sicily
Adelaide of Savona
Beatrice of Provence
Beatrice of Rethel, queen of Sicily
Blanche of Anjou, queen of Aragon
Blanche of Navarre
Constance, queen of Aragon
Costanza of Aragon, queen of Sicily [Constance]
Constance of Sicily, Holy Roman Empress
Leonor of Sicily [Eleanor]
Elvira of Castile
Emma (of Apulia)
Fressenda (de Hauteville)
Helena (Guiscard) [Helen]
Isabelle of Achaia
Isabel of Lorraine [Isabelle]
Joanna of Aragon, queen of Naples [Jean]
Joanna of England, queen of Sicily [Jean]
Joanna I, queen of Naples [Jean]
Judith of Évreux
Margaret of Navarre, queen of Sicily
Margaret (of Sicily)
Marie of Brittany, duchess of Anjou [Mary]
Maria de Luna [Mary]

Maria of Sicily, countess of Alife [Mary]
Sibylla of Acerra [Sibyl]
Sybil of Conversano [Sibyl]
Sichelgaita of Salerno
Virdimura of Sicily
Yolande of Anjou
Yolande of Aragon

Sidon
Agnes of Courtenay

Siena
Catherine of Siena (St.)
Margaret Aldobrandeschi

Sigily
Agnes Sigily

Sijena
Sancha of Castile [Sancia]

Silesia
Anne, princess of Bohemia
Hedwig of Silesia (St.)

Sillone
Clemence Sillone

Simiane
Almucs de Castelnau

Sion
Cornelie van Wulfskerke
Marguerite Scheppers [Margaret]

Skolemastre
Elen Skolemastre [Ellen]

Slupsk
Elizabeth of Pomerania

Snoth
Sanche Snoth [Sancia]

Soissons
Adela of France [Adele]
Alix of Champagne, queen of Cyprus [Alice]
Liutgard of Vermandois

Somerset
Ankarette Twynyho
Eleanor Beauchamp, duchess of Somerset
Joan Beaufort, queen of Scotland [Jean]
Margaret Beaufort
Margaret Holland

Soreau
See—Sorel

Sorel
Agnes Sorel
Antoinette de Villequier
Charlotte (de Valois)

Spires
Agnes of Saarbrücken

Spoleto
Ageltrudis (of Spoleto)
Marozia of Rome

Sponheim
Jutta of Sponheim

Spychefat
Anastasia Spychefat

Squillace
Sancia d'Aragona

Stade
Richardis von Stade

Stafford
Anne Neville, duchess of Buckingham
Anne Stafford
Anne of Woodstock
Katherine Woodville [Catherine]
Eleanor de Bohun, duchess of Gloucester
Elizabeth Bourchier
Margaret de Audley, lady Stafford
Margaret Beaufort
Matilda of Lancaster, duchess of Zealand
Maud Lovell, lady Arundel [Matilda]

Stamford
Agnes Butler

Stanford
Alice Stanford

Stanley
Eleanor Neville, lady Stanley
Margaret Beaufort

Stapilton
Elizabeth Stapilton

Staufen
See—Von Staufen

Staundon
Alice Staundon

Staunesby
Alice atte March

Steinbach
Sabina von Steinbach

Stewart
See—Stuart

Stirling
Joan Beaufort, queen of Scotland [Jean]

Stoke
Margaret Stoke

Stokker
Elizabeth, lady Abergavenny

Stokton
Elizabeth Stokton

Stommeln
Christina of Stommeln [Christine]

Stone
Crystene Houghton [Christine]

Stonor
Alice Drayton
Katherine Riche [Catherine]
Elizabeth Croke
Jane Stonor

Strangways
Katherine Neville, duchess of Norfolk [Catherine]

Strasbourg
Agnes Broumattin
Katherine Husenboltz [Catherine]
Katherine Rebestoeckyn [Catherine]
Else von Ortemburg

Strassburg
Sabina von Steinbach

Stratford
Alice (of Stratford)
Gunnora de Stratford

Strathearn
Strathearn (countess of)

Striguil
Eva MacMurrough
Isabella de Clare [Isabelle]

Stroby
Sarah Stroby

Strozzi
Alessandra Strozzi
Lisa Strozzi

Strygl
Dorothy of Strygl

Stuart
Eleanor Stuart
Joan Beaufort, queen of Scotland [Jean]
Margaret of Scotland
Marjory Bruce [Margery]

Substantion
Almodis (III) of Toulouse

Suffolk
Alice de Bryene
Alice Chaucer, duchess of Suffolk
Katherine de la Pole [Catherine]
Elizabeth of York, duchess of Suffolk
Jane Stonor
Margaret Beaufort

Sulzbach
Bertha of Sulzbach

Supplinburg
Gertrude of Saxony
Richenza of Nordheim, Holy Roman Empress

Surrey
Alice Lacy, countess of Lancaster
Anne of York
Isabel of Vermandois, countess of Leicester [Isabelle]
Joan de Bar, countess of Surrey [Jean]
Roesia de Borford

Susa
Adelheid of Savoy [Adelaide]
Bertha of Susa

Sussex
Roesia de Borford

Sutton
Katherine of Sutton [Catherine]

Swabia
Adelheid of Savoy [Adelaide]
Agnes of Germany
Agnes of Saarbrücken
Beatrice of Swabia, queen of Castile
Bertha of Swabia
Bertha of Swabia, duchess of Lorraine
Constance, queen of Aragon
Kunigunda of Hungary [Cunigunde]
Cunegunde of Swabia [Cunigunde]
Cunigunda of Swabia, queen of Bohemia [Cunigunde]
Edith of England, queen of Germany
Gisela of Swabia, queen of Germany
Hedwig of Bavaria
Ida of Swabia
Irene Angela, Holy Roman Empress
Judith of Bavaria, duchess of Swabia

Swath
Christine Swath

Swynford
Katherine Swynford [Catherine]

Syonne
Hauviette (of Domremy)

Taillefer
Beatrice of Viennois, countess of Albon

Taillour
Elena Taillour

Talbot
Eleanor Talbot
Elizabeth Talbot
Margaret Beauchamp, countess of Shrewsbury

Talvas
Mabel of Bellême

Tankerville
Antigone (of Gloucester)

Tarantaise
Adelheid of Savoy [Adelaide]
Bertha of Susa

Taranto
Catherine de Valois
Constance of France
Joanna I, queen of Naples [Jean]

Tasseburgh
Lucia Tasseburgh

Taunton
Elen Skolemastre [Ellen]

Teles
Leonor Teles [Eleanor]

Teye
Petronilla of Teye

Thiembronne
Aelips de Beauchamp

Thessalonica
Yolande of Montferrat

Thomas
Agnes Thomas

Thorp
Isabel Plumpton [Isabelle]

Thouars
Alix of Brittany [Alice]
Catherine de Thouars
Constance of Brittany
Jeanne d'Artois [Jean]

Thuringia
Elizabeth of Hungary (St.)

Tiffauges
Catherine de Thouars

Tiptoft
Cecily Neville [Cecilia]

Tirel
Alice de Clare

Tirlemont
Beatrice of Nazareth

Tisnov
Cunigunda of Swabia, queen of Bohemia [Cunigunde]

Toëni
Godevere of Toëni
Isabel de Montfort (Isabella)

Tongern
Lutgard of Aywières (St.) [Liutgard]

Tonnere
Catherine de l'Isle Bouchard

Toppesham
Isabella de Toppesham [Isabelle]

Tornabuoni
Lucrezia Tornabuoni

Toron
Isabella of Jerusalem [Isabelle]

Torres
Adelasia of Torres, queen of Sardinia

Tosny
Godevere of Toëni

Toulouse
Adelaide of Toulouse
Almodis (II) de La Marche, countess of Barcelona
Almodis (III) of Toulouse
Angéle de la Barthe [Angela]
Anne-Marie de Georgel
Beatrice of Vienne, countess of Albon
Bertha of Tuscany
Catherine Delort
Constance of Arles, queen of France
Constance of France, countess of Toulouse
Douce (III) of Provence
Leonor of Aragon, countess of Toulouse [Eleanor]
Elvira of Castile
Ermengarde, viscountess of Narbonne
Faydide of Millau, countess of Toulouse
Gerberga (of Toulouse)
Joanna of England, queen of Sicily [Jean]
Jeanne of Toulouse [Jean]
Lombarda
Phillippia, countess of Poitou [Philippa]
Urraca, queen of Castile

Touraine
Jacqueline of Hainault

Tours
Adelaide of Tours
Adele, countess of Blois and Chartres
Bertha de Sens, countess of Vienne
Ermengard (of Italy), Holy Roman Empress
Liutgard of Vermandois

Toutaine
Perrette la Toutaine

Trastamara
Leonor of Castile, queen of Navarre [Eleanor]
Leonor de Guzman [Eleanor]
Juana Manuel, queen of Castile [Jean]

Elizabeth de Burgo, queen of Scotland
Matilda of Lancaster
Ota (of Norway)
Philippa of Clarence, countess of Meath

Umfraville
Matilda de Lucy

Unchair
Péronnelle d'Armentières [Pérronelle]

Urbino
Battista da Montefeltro
Battista Sforza
Elisabetta Gonzaga [Elizabeth]
Emilia Pia

Urgel
Aurembaix, countess of Urgel
Teresa de Entenza [Theresa]

Usodimare
Teodorina (Cibo)

Ussel
Jeanne de Bourbon [Jean]

Ussher
Johanna Hadham [Jean]

Vadstena
Blanche of Namur
Bridget of Sweden (St.)
Catherine of Sweden (St.)

Valence
Charlotte d'Albret
Dionysia de Mountchesny
Joan de Munchensi [Jean]
Mary of St. Pol

Valencia
Ximena Diaz

Valenciennes
Richilde, countess of Flanders

Valle
Alice Kyteler

Valois
Anne of Kiev
Blanche of France
Blanche of Navarre, queen of France
Catherine de Courteney
Catherine of France
Catherine of France, queen of England
Catherine de Valois
Charlotte (de Valois)
Eleanora of Vermandois
Isabelle of France, duchess of Milan
Isabella of France, queen of Navarre [Isabelle]
Isabel of Savoy
Jeanne of Burgundy, queen of France [Jean]
Jeanne de Divion [Jean]
Jeanne of France, duchess of Orléans [Jean]
Jeanne de Valois [Jean]
Jeanne de Valois, countess of Hainault [Jean]
Madeleine Valois
Mahaut de Châtillon
Marie of Valois [Mary]
Michelle of France
Yolande de Valois

Van Beijeren
Jacqueline of Hainault

Van Eyck
Margaretha van Eyck [Margaret]

Varano
Costanza Varano [Constance]

Vaucouleur
Catherine Royer

Vaudemont
Yolande of Anjou

Vausselles
Catherine de Vausselles

Vaux
Katharine Vaux [Catherine]

Veel
Elizabeth le Veel

Venice
Beatrice Candia
Cassandra Fedele
Caterina Caldiera [Catherine]
Caterina Cornaro, queen of Cyprus [Catherine]
Illuminato Bembo
Maddalena Scrovegni [Madeleine]
Waldrada (of Arles)

Venisy
Philippa of Champagne

Ventadour
Marguerite de Turenne [Margaret]
Marie de Ventadour [Mary]

Verdon
Elizabeth de Clare

Verdun
Emma of Italy, queen of France

Vere
Agnes de Launcreona
Elizabeth Howard, countess of Oxford
Margaret Neville, countess of Oxford
Maud de Vere, countess of Oxford [Matilda]
Philippa de Coucy

Vergy
Alix de Vergy, duchess of Burgundy [Alice]

Vermandois
Adela of France [Adele]
Eadgifu of England, queen of France
Eleanora of Vermandois [Eleanor]
Foria (of Vermandois)
Isabella of Vermandois, countess of Flanders [Isabelle]
Isabel of Vermandois, countess of Leicester [Isabelle]
Liutgard of Vermandois
Petronilla of Aquitaine, countess of Vermandois

Verona
Ginevra Nogarola
Isotta Nogarola

Vesci
Beatrice de Vesci
Isabelle de Vescy

Vescy
See—Vesci

Vespucci
Simonetta Cattaneo

Vestfold
Aasta Grönske
Asa, queen of Agdir

Vexin
Godgifu (of England)

Viana
Blanche of Navarre
Catherine of Navarre
Madeleine Valois

Vicenza
Caterina Visconti [Catherine]
Regina della Scala

Vienne
Alix de Mâcon [Alice]
Beatrice of Viennois, countess of Albon
Bertha de Sens, countess of Vienne
Ermengard, duchess of Lombardy, queen of Provence
Matilda of France

Viennois
Beatrice of Viennois, countess of Albon

Vigri
Catherine of Bologna (St.)

Viguier
Paule Viguier

Vik
Astrid of Norway
Ota (of Norway)

Vikings
Aethelflaed of Damerham
Aethelswith of Wessex, queen of Mercia

Aud "the Deep-Minded"
Ebba
Ota (of Norway)

Vileyn
Denise la Vileyn

Villain
Jeanne Villain [Jean]

Villehardouin
Isabelle of Achaia
Matilda of Hainault, princess of Achaia

Villena
Juana Manuel, queen of Castile [Jean]

Villequier
Antoinette de Villequier

Vimeu
Jeanne d'Artois [Jean]

Vinland
Freydis of Norway
Gudrid (of Greenland)

Visconti
Agnese Visconti [Agnes]
Bianca Maria Visconti
Bianca of Savoy
Caterina Visconti [Catherine]
Isabelle of France, duchess of Milan [Isabelle]
Regina della Scala
Taddea Visconti
Valentine Visconti, queen of Cyprus
Valentine Visconti, duchess of Orléans
Violante Visconti

Viseu
Leonor of Lancastre [Eleanor]

Viterbo
Lucia Brocadelli
Rose of Viterbo (St.)

Vivar
Maria of Vivar [Mary]
Ximena Diaz

Vohburg
Adelheid of Vohburg [Adelaide]

Von Staufen
Agnes von Staufen

Vouthon
Isabel Romée [Isabelle]

Vraba
Catherine of Vraba

Vreden
Adelheid of Germany, abbess of Quedlinburg [Adelaide]

Wade
Avis Wade

Wake
Margaret Wake

Walbeck
Godila (of Walbeck)

Walgrave
Walgrave (lady)

Warboys
Beatrice Puttock
Elena Baroun

Ware
Petronilla of Grandmesnil

Warenne
Ada of Warenne
Alice Lacy, countess of Lancaster
Beatrice de Warenne
Beatrice of Portugal
Gundreda (of Warenne)
Isabel of Vermandois, countess of Leicester [Isabelle]
Joan de Bar, countess of Surrey [Jean]

Waring
Joan Waring [Jean]

Wimpler
Alice la Wymplere
Avice la Wymplere

Winchester
Eadburga of Winchester (St.)
Emma of Normandy
Margaret of Leicester

Windsor
Alice Perrers
Nesta

Wingfield
Katherine Woodville [Catherine]

Wistow
Elena Baroun

Wodemerstham
Dionisia de Wodemerstham

Wolsy
Johanna Wolsy [Jean]

Wombe
Agnes Wombe

Woodstock
Anne of Woodstock
Eleanor de Bohun, duchess of Gloucester
Joan of England [Jean]
Margaret Wake, countess of Kent

Woodville
Katherine Neville [Catherine]
Katherine Woodville [Catherine]
Cecily of York [Cecilia]
Elizabeth, lady Scales
Elizabeth Woodville
Jacquetta of Luxembourg

Worcester (and Worcestershire)
Cecily Neville [Cecilia]
Margery of Hales

Wormegay
Beatrice de Warenne

Worth
Childlove (de Worth)

Worthham
Margaret Worthham

Woulbarowe
Joan Woulbarowe [Jean]

Wulfskerke
Cornelie van Wulfskerke

Wurzburg
Sara (of Wurzburg) [Sarah]

Wylesdone
Alice de Wylesdone

Wymplere
See—Wimpler

Yelverton
Anne Paston

Yonge
Matilda Yonge

York
Anne Mowbray
Anne of York
Anne of York, duchess of Exeter
Katharine of York [Catherine]
Cecily Neville, duchess of York [Cecilia]
Cecily of York [Cecilia]
Constance of York, countess of Gloucester
Elizabeth Woodville
Elizabeth of York, queen of England
Elizabeth of York, duchess of Suffolk
Gunhild of Denmark, queen of Norway
Isabel, lady Bourchier [Isabelle]
Isabel of Castile [Isabelle]
Isabella de Fortibus [Isabelle]
Margaret of York

Ypres
Margaret of Ypres
Marguerite de Ypres [Margaret]

Abbreviations

for Sources

A.S.	Acta Sanctorum
C.P.	Complete Peerage
D.B.F.	Dictionnaire de Biographie Française
D.N.B.	Dictionary of National Biography
Nuisance	London Assize of Nuisance

Sources

Without Authors

Acta Sanctorum. By J. Bollandus and G. Henschenius. Editio Novissima. Ed. by J. Carnandet et al. Paris, 1863.

Book of the Divine Consolation of the Blessed Angela of Foligno. London and New York, 1909.

Cahiers de Civilisation Médiévale Xe–XIIe Siècles: Bibliographie. Poitiers, 1958 to date.

Calendar of Documents Relating to Scotland. Ed. by Joseph Bain. Edinburgh, 1881–88.

Calendar of Letter-Books of the City of London: A,C, and L. Ed. by R.R. Sharpe. London, 1899 (A), 1901 (C), 1912 (L).

Calendar of Plea and Memoranda Rolls, 1323–1364. (I). Ed. by A.H. Thomas. Cambridge, 1926.

Calendar of Plea and Memoranda Rolls, 1364–1381. (II) Ed. by A.H. Thomas. Cambridge, 1929.

Calendar of Plea and Memoranda Rolls, 1458–1482. (VI) Ed. by Philip E. Jones. Cambridge, 1951.

Calendar of Wills Proved and Enrolled in the Court of Husting, London. 2 vols. (A.D. 1258–1688). Ed. by R.R. Sharpe. London, 1889 and 1890.

Calendar of the Close Rolls preserved in the Public Record Office, 1272–1485. Prepared by W.H. Stevenson, A.B. Hinds, and W.H. Bird. London, 1892–1954.

Cambridge Medieval History. Vols. II, III, IV, V, and VII. Ed. by H.M. Gwatkin, J.R. Tanner, et al. Cambridge and London, 1913–1936.

Carolingian Chronicles. "Royal Frankish Annals" and Nithard's "Histories." Trans. by Bernhard Walter Scholz with Barbara Rogers. Ann Arbor, 1970.

Cely Letters, 1472–1488. Ed. by Alison Hanham. Early English Text Society, #273. London and Toronto, 1975.

Chronicles of the Crusades. Ed. by Elizabeth Hallam. New York, 1989.

Complete Peerage of England, Scotland, Ireland, Great Britain, and the United Kingdom. Ed. by Vicary Gibbs et al. London, 1910–1959.

Comptes du Domaine de la Ville de Paris, 1424–1457. Histoire Générale de Paris Series. V. I. Ed. by A. Vidier, L. le Grand, and P. Dupieux. Paris, 1948.

Coronation of Elizabeth Wydeville. Set forth from a 15th Century Manuscript by George Smith. London, 1935.

The Defiant Muse: Feminist Poems from the Middle Ages to the Present. New York, 1986.

The Defiant Muse: German Feminist Poets from the Middle Ages to the Present. Swarthmore, 1986.

The Defiant Muse: Hispanic Poems from the Middle Ages to the Present. Swarthmore, 1986.

Dialogue of Saint Catherine of Siena. Translation and introduction by Suzanne Noffke. New York, 1980.

Dichtüngen der Frau Ava. New York, 1986.

Dictionary of National Biography to 1900. Ed. by Sir Leslie Stephen and Sir Sidney Lee. 22 vols. Oxford, 1967 (rpt).

Dictionary of the Middle Ages. Joseph R. Strayer, editor-in-chief. New York, 1982–1989.

Dictionnaire de Biographie Française. Under the direction of J. Balteau, M. Barroux, and M. Prevost. Paris, 1933.

Dictionnaire de Spiritualité, Ascetique et Mystique, Doctrine et Histoire. 15 vols. to date. Paris, 1932 to date.

Exercises of St. Gertrude, Virgin and Abbess of the Order of St. Benedict. London, 1877.

Fifty Earliest English Wills in the Court of Probate, London. Ed. by F.J. Furnivall. London, 1882.

Gesta Stephani: The Deeds of Stephen. Trans. by K.R. Potter. Edinburgh and London, 1955.

Hours of Jeanne d'Évreux. New York, 1957.

Household Book of Dame Alice de Bryene of Acton Hall, Suffolk, Sept. 1412–Sept. 1413. Trans. by M.K. Dale and ed. by V.B. Redstone. Ipswich, 1931.

Household Book of Queen Isabella of England, for the fifth regnal year of Edward II, 8th July 1311 to 7th July 1312. Edmonton, Alberta, 1971.

International Medieval Biliography. Leeds, 1968 to date.

Julian of Norwich: Showings. Ed. and trans. by Edmund Colledge and James Walsh. New York, 1978.

Legend and Writings of St. Clare of Assisi. New York, 1953.

Letters of Abelard and Heloise. Trans. by Betty Radice. London, 1974.

Letters of Queen Margaret of Anjou. Ed. by Cecil Monro. Westminster, 1863.

Liber Albus. Ed. by Henry T. Riley. London, 1859.

Life and Sayings of St. Catherine of Genoa. Trans. and ed. by Paul Garvin. Staten Island, New York, 1964.

London Assize of Nuisance, 1301–1431: A Calendar. Ed. by Helena M. Chew and William Kellaway. London Record Society, 1973.

London Eyre of 1244. Ed. by Helena M. Chew and Martin Weinbaum. London Record Society, 1976.

London Eyre of 1276. Ed. by Martin Weinbaum. London Record Society, 1976.

Manners and Household Expenses in the Thirteenth and Fifteenth Century. Ed. by H.T. Turner. London, 1841.

New Catholic Encyclopedia. 15 vols. and 3 supls. New York, 1967; Washington, DC, 1974, 1979; Palatine, 1989.

Online Computer Library Center. (database of more than 6,000 libraries).

Oxford Book of Late Medieval Verse and Prose. Ed. by Douglas Gray. Oxford, 1985.

Oxford Illustrated History of Medieval Europe. Ed. by George Holmes. Oxford, 1988.

Paston Letters and Papers of the Fifteenth Century. Ed. by Norman Davis. Oxford, 1976.

Plumpton Correspondence. Ed. and intro. by Thomas Stapleton. London, 1839.

Research Libraries Information Network. (Online union catalog of major American research libraries).

Revelations of Mechtild de Magdeburg ("*The Flowing Light of the Godhead.*") Trans. by Lucy Menzies. London and New York, 1953.

Revue d'Histoire, Ecclésiastique Bibliographie. Louvain, 1900 to date.

Rule of the Holy Virgin: S. Clare. London, 1975.

Scalacronica. Sir Thomas Gray of Heton. Ed. by Joseph Stephenson. Maitland Club, 1836.

Select Cases in the Court of King's Bench under Edward I. Vol. I. Ed. by G.O. Sayles. Selden Society, v. 55. London, 1936.

Select Pleas of the Crown. Vol. I, 1200–1225. Selden Society. London, 1888.

Short Relation of the Life, Virtues, and Miracles of S. Elizabeth, called the Peacemaker, queen of Portugal. Antoine Arnauld, le franc discours. London, 1975.

St. Catherine of Siena as Seen in Her Letters (*Letters of Catherine Benincasa*). Trans. and ed. by Vida D. Scudder. New York and London, 1906.

Stonor Letters and Papers, 1290–1483. Ed. by Charles L. Kingsford. Vols. I and II. London, 1919.

Studies on Women Abstracts. Abdingdon, 1983 to date.

Translations and Reprints from the Original Sources of European History. Philadelphia, 1898.

Vita Sanctae Coletae (*1381–1447*). Brill, 1982.

Women Studies Abstracts. Rush, 1972 to date.

Sources

With Authors

Abate, G. S. *Rosa di Viterbo, terziana francescana. Fonti storiche della vita e loro revisione critica.* Rome, 1952.

Abels, Richard and Harrison, Ellen. "The Participation of Women in Languedocian Catharism." *Medieval Studies* 41 (1979), 215–251.

Abram, A. *English Life and Manners in the Later Middle Ages.* New York, 1913.

________. "Women Traders in Medieval London." *Economic Journal* (June 1916), 276–285.

Abulafia, David. "Catalan Merchants and the Western Mediteranean, 1236–1300: Studies in the Notarial Acts of Barcelona and Sicily." *Viator: Medieval and Renaissance Studies,* 16 (1985), 209–242.

Ady, Cecilia. *The Bentivoglio of Bologna: A Study in Depotism.* London, 1937.

________. *A History of Milan Under the Sforza.* New York, 1907.

Albanes, J. H., ed. and trans. *La Vie de Douceline, fondatrice des Beguines de Marseilles.* Marseilles, 1879.

Allan, A. Stewart. "Historical Notices of the Family of Margaret of Logy." *Transactions of the Royal Historical Society,* VII, ed. by Charles Rogers. (London, 1878), 330–361.

Altamira, Rafael. *History of Spain.* Trans. by Muna Lee. New York, 1949.

Ancelet-Hustache, Jeanne. *Mechtilde de Magedebourg 1207–1282.* Paris, 1926.

Anderson, Bonnie S. and Judith P. Zinsser. *A History of their Own: Women in Europe from Prehistory to the Present,* Vol. 1. New York, 1988.

Anderson, Marjorie. "Blanche, Duchess of Lancaster." *Modern Philology* 45 (Feb. 1948), 152–159.

Andersson, Ingvar. *History of Sweden.* Trans. by Carolyn Hannay. New York, 1968.

Anselme de Sainte-Marie, Pierre de Guibors. *Histoire généologique et chronologique de la maison royale de France.* Paris, 1968.

Appleby, John Tate. *John, King of England.* New York, 1959.

Armitage-Smith, Sydney. *John of Gaunt.* London, 1964 (orig. edit. 1904).

Aston, Margaret. "Lollard Women Priests?" *Journal of Ecclesiastical History* 31 (1980), 444–451.

Atkinson, Clarissa W. *Mystic and Pilgrim: The Book and the World of Margery Kempe.* Ithaca and London, 1983.

Attwater, Donald. *A Dictionary of Saints.* New York, 1938.

Aubert, Marcel. "The Decorative and Industrial Arts." *The Legacy of the Middle Ages,* ed. by C.G.Crump and E.F.Jacob (1962), 123–145.

Ault, Warren O. *Open Field Farming in Medieval England: A Study of Village By-Laws.* London and New York, 1972.

Ayerbe-Chaux, Reinaldo. "Las Memorias de Dona Leonor Lopez de Cordoba." *Journal of Hispanic Philology* 2, #1 (Autumn, 1977), 11–33.

Bachmann, Donna G. and Sherry Piland, eds. *Women Artists: An Historical, Contemporary, and Feminist Bibliography.* Metuchen, NJ, 1978.

Baker, Derek. "A Nursery of Saints: St. Margaret of Scotland Reconsidered." *Medieval Women,* ed. by Derek Baker (1978), 119–142.

________. ed. *Medieval Women.* Oxford, 1978.

Baldwin, John W. *The Government of Philip Augustus: Foundations of French Royal Power in the Middle Ages.* Berkeley, Los Angeles, London, 1986.

Bannister, A.T., ed. *A Transcript of the Red Book.* Camden Miscellany. vol. XV. Camden, 3rd ser., vol XLI (London, 1929).

Barbé, Louis A. *Margaret of Scotland and the Dauphin Louis.* London, 1917.

Barber, Richard and Juliet Barker. *Tournaments: Jousts, Chivalry, and Pageants in the Middle Ages.* New York, 1989.

Barlow, Frank. *Edward the Confessor.* Berkeley and Los Angeles, 1970.

________. *The Feudal Kingdoms of England, 1042–1216.* London, New York, Toronto, 1955.

________. *Thomas Becket.* Berkeley and Los Angeles, 1986.

Barraclough, Geoffrey. *The Origins of Modern Germany.* Oxford, 1966.

Barron, Caroline. "The Lords of the Manor." *The Making of Britain,* ed. by L.M. Smith (1985), 101–117.

Barrow, G.W.S. *Feudal Britain: The Completion of the Medieval Kingdoms, 1066–1314.* London, 1956 (rpt. 1967).

________. *Robert Bruce and the Community and Realm of Scotland.* London, 1965.

Barstow, Anne L. *Joan of Arc: Heretic, Mystic, Shaman.* Lewiston, NY, 1986.

Barthélemy, Dominique. "Kinship." *A History of Private Life,* vol. 2. Ed. by G. Duby (1988), 85–155.

Baskin, Judith R. "Jewish Women in the Middle Ages." *Jewish Women in Historical Perspective,* ed. by Judith Baskin (1991), 1–26.

Batelli, Guido, ed. *La leggenda della beata Umiliana de' Cerchi.* Florence, 1932.

Bates, David. *Normandy Before 1066.* New York, 1982.

Bedos Rezak, Brigitte. "Women, Seals and Power in Medieval France, 1150–1350." *Women and Power in the Middle Ages,* ed. by M. Erler and M. Kowaleski (1988), 61–82.

Bell, Mary. *A Short History of the Papacy.* London, 1921.

Bell, Susan Groag. "Medieval Women Book Owners: Arbiters of Lay Piety and Ambassadors of Culture." *Women and Power in the Middle Ages,* ed. by M. Erler and M. Kowaleski (1988), 149–187.

Bellamy, John. *Crime and Public Order in England in the Later Middle Ages.* London and Toronto, 1973.

Belleval, Réne de. *Les Fiefs et les Seigneuries du Ponthieu et du Vimeu.* Paris and Brionne, 1975.

Belloncí, Maria. "Beatrice and Isabella d'Este." *The Italian Renaissance,* by J.H. Plumb (Boston, 1961), 284–301.

Bendiner, Elmer. *The Rise and Fall of Paradise.* New York, 1983.

Benes, Vaclav L. and Norman J.G. Pounds. *Poland.* New York, 1970.

Bennett, Henry S. *Life on the English Manor: A Study of Peasant Conditions, 1150–1400.* Cambridge, 1967.

Bennett, Judith M. "Public Power and Authority in the Medieval English Countryside." *Women and Power in the Middle Ages,* ed. by M. Erler and M. Kowaleski (1988), 18–36.

________. *Sisters and Workers in the Middle Ages.* Chicago, 1989.

________. *Women in the Medieval English Countryside.* New York and Oxford, 1987.

Bennett, Michael J. " 'Good Lords' and 'Kingmakers', The Stanleys of Lathom in English Politics, 1385–1485." *History Today,* 31 (July 1981), 12–17.

Benton, John F. "The Court of Champagne as a Literary Center." *Speculum,* 36, #4 (1961), 551–591.

________. "Philip the Fair and the Jour of Troyes." *Studies in Medieval and Renaissance History,* 6 (1969), 279–344.

Bernardo, Aldo. "Petrarch's Laura: The Convolutions of a Humanistic Mind." *The Role of Women in the Middle Ages,* ed. by R. T. Morewedge (1975), 65–89.

Berners, Dame Juliana. *The Book of St. Albans.* First printed 1496. Facsimile reprint: New York, 1966.

Berrigan, Joseph. "The Tuscan Visionary: Saint Catherine of Siena." *Medieval Women Writers,* ed. by K. Wilson (1984), 252–268.

Bertrand, Réne. *La France de Blanche de Castile.* Paris, 1977.

Berzeviczy, A. *Beatrice of Aragon, reine de Hongrie.* 2 vols. Paris, 1911/12.

Biles, Martha. "The Indominitable Belle: Eleanor of Provence." *Seven Studies in Medieval History.* Jackson, Miss., 1983, 113–131.

Bingham, Caroline. *The Crowned Lions: The Early Plantagenet Kings.* London, 1978.

Bishop, Jane. "Bishops as Marital Advisors in the Ninth Century." *Women of the Medieval World,* ed. by Wemple and Kirshner (1985), 54–84.

Bishop, Morris. *The Middle Ages.* New York, 1970.

________. "Petrarch." *The Italian Renaissance,* by J.H. Plumb (Boston, 1961), 160–175.

Bisson, Thomas N. *The Medieval Crown of Aragon: A Short History.* Oxford, 1986.

Blair, Peter Hunter. *An Introduction to Anglo-Saxon England.* Cambridge, 1966.

Blok, Petrus Johannes. *History of the People of the Netherlands.* New York and London, v. 1, 1898; v. 2, 1907.

Blumenfeld-Kosinski, Renate. "Christine de Pizan and the Misogynistic Tradition." *Romanic Review,* 82, #3 (May 1990), 279–292.

Boase, T.S.R. "Mortality, Judgment, and Remembrance." *The Flowering of the Middle Ages,* ed. by Joan Evans (1976), 203–244.

Bogin, Meg. *The Women Troubadours.* New York, 1976.

Bolton, Brenda M. "Mulieres Sanctae." *Women in Medieval Society,* ed. by Susan Stuard, (1976), 141–158.

________. "Vitae Matrum: A Further Aspect of the Frauenfrage." *Medieval Women,* ed. by Derek Baker (1978), 253–273.

Bonfante, Larissa, ed. and trans. *The Plays of Hrotswitha of Gandersheim.* New York, 1975.

Bonner, Anthony, trans. *The Complete Works of François Villon.* New York, 1960.

________, ed. *Songs of the Troubadours.* New York, 1972.

Bonzi da Genova, Umile. *S. Caterina Fieschi Adorni.* 2 vols. Turin, 1961–62.

Borderie, Arthur le Moyne de la. *Histoire de Bretagne.* 6 vols. Rennes, Paris, 1899.

Bornstein, Diane. "Military Manuals in Fifteenth Century England." *Medieval Studies,* 37 (1975), 469–477.

Boswell, John. *Christianity, Social Tolerance and Homosexuality.* Chicago and London, 1980.

________. *The Kindness of Strangers: The Abandonment of Children in Western Europe from Late Antiquity to the Renaissance.* New York, 1988.

Boulding, Elise. *The Underside of History: A View of Women Through Time.* Boulder, Colorado, 1976.

Bourassin, Emmanuel. *Jeanne d'Arc.* Paris, 1977.

Bourchier, Sir John, trans. *The Chronicle of Froissart.* London, 1901–1903.

Boutière, J. and A.H. Schutz. *Biographies des Troubadours.* Paris, 1973.

Boyd, Catherine. *A Cistercian Nunnery in Italy in the Thirteenth Century: The Story of Rifreddo Saluzzo, 1220–1300.* Cambridge, 1943.

Boyesen, Hjalmar H. *The Story of Norway.* New York, 1887.

Braddy, Haldeen. "Chaucer, Alice Perrers and Cecily Chaumpaigne." *Speculum,* 52, #4 (October 1977), 906–911.

________. "Chaucer and Dame Alice Perrers." *Speculum,* 21, #1 (January 1946), 222–228.

Bradley, Ritamary. "Julian of Norwich: Writer and Mystic." *An Introduction to the Medieval Mystics of Europe,* ed. by P.E. Szarmach. Albany, NY, 1984, 195–216.

Branca, Vittore. *Boccacio: The Man and His Works.* New York, 1976.

Branner, Robert. "Manuscript-Makers in Mid-Thirteenth Century Paris." *Art Bulletin,* XLVIII (1966), 65–67.

Braswell, Laurel. "St. Edburga of Winchester: A Study of her Cult, a.d. 950–1500." *Medieval Studies,* vol. 33 (1971), 292–333.

Braswell, Mary Flowers. *The Medieval Sinner: Characterization and Confession in the Literature of the English Middle Ages.* London and Toronto, 1983.

________. "Sin, the Lady, and the Law: The English Noblewoman in the Late Middle Ages." *Medievalia et Humanistica,* n.s. #14 (1986), 81–100.

Braunstein, Philippe. "Toward Intimacy: The Fourteenth and Fifteenth Centuries." *A History of Private Life,* vol. 2. ed. by G. Duby (1988), 535–630.

Breisach, Ernst. *Caterina Sforza, a Renaissance Virago.* Chicago, 1967.

Bréquigny, Louis George Oudart-Feudrix de, ed. *Lettres de Rois, Reines, et Autres Personnages des Cours de France et Angleterre.* 2 vols. Paris, 1839.

Brewer, Derek. *Chaucer in His Time.* London, 1963.

Bridenthal, Renate and Claudia Koonz, eds. *Becoming Visible: Women in European History.* Boston, 1977. [Note: there is also a 1987 edition; however, page numbers may differ.]

Bridge, Antony. *The Crusades.* New York, 1982.

Brinton, Selwyn. *The Gonzaga—Lords of Mantua.* London, 1927.

Brion, Marcel. *Blanche de Castile, femme de Louis VIII, mere de Saint Louis.* Paris, 1939.

________. *Catherine Cornaro, reine de Chypre.* Paris, 1945.

________. *The Medici: A Great Florentine Family.* Trans. by Heather and Gilles Cremonesi. New York, 1969.

Britton, Edward. *The Community of the Vill.* Toronto, 1977.

Brooke Rosalind B. and Christopher N.L. Brooke. "St. Clare." *Medieval Women,* ed. by Derek Baker (1978), 275–287.

Brooke, Christopher. *From Alfred to Henry III, 871–1272.* Edinburgh, 1961.

Brown, Elizabeth A.R. "Eleanor of Aquitaine: Parent, Queen, and Duchess." *Eleanor of Aquitaine, Patron and Politician,* ed. by William W. Kibler (1976), 9–39.

Brown, Peter Hume. *History of Scotland.* Vol. I. Cambridge, 1909.

Brown, R. Allen. *The Normans and the Norman Conquest.* New York, 1969.

Brucker, Gene A. *Renaissance Florence.* Berkeley and Los Angeles, 1983.

Brugman, John (ed. A. de Meijer). *Iohannis Brugman O.F.M. Vita Alme Virginis Lidwine.* Groningen, 1963.

Brundage, James A. *Law, Sex and Christian Society in Medieval Europe.* Chicago, 1987.

________. "Prostitution in Medieval Canon Law." *Sisters and Workers in the Middle Ages,* ed. by J.M. Bennett et al (1989), 79–99.

Brusher, Joseph S. *Popes through the Ages.* Princeton, 1959.

Bryant, Arthur. *The Age of Chivalry.* Garden City, NY, 1963.

Bryant, Gwendolyn. "The French Heretic Beguine: Marguerite Porete." *Medieval Women Writers,* ed. by K. Wilson (1984), 204–226.

Bryce, James. *The Holy Roman Empire.* New York, 1961.

Buckler, Georgina. *Anna Comnena: A Study.* London, 1968.

Bukdahl, Jørgen et al, eds. *Scandinavia Past and Present.* Vol. I. *From the Viking Age to Absolute Monarchy.* Arnkrone, Denmark, 1959.

Bullough, D.A. and R. L. Storey, eds. *The Study of Medieval Records.* Oxford, 1971.

Bullough, Vern L. "Medieval Medical and Scientific Views of Women." *Viator: Medieval and Renaissance Studies,* 4 (1973), 485–501.

________. "Medieval Medical and Scientific Views of Women." *Sex, Society, and History,* (New York 1976), 43–59.

________. and James Brundage. *Sexual Practices and the Medieval Church.* Buffalo, 1982.

Burbidge, Frederick Bliss. *Old Coventry and Lady Godiva.* Birmingham, 1952.

Butler, *Lives . . .* (see Thurston, Herbert).

Butler, Pierce. *Women of Medieval France.* Philadelphia, 1907.

Butt, Ronald. *A History of Parliament: The Middle Ages.* London, 1989.

Bynum, Caroline Walker. *Fragmentation and Redemption: Essays on Gender and the Human Body.* New York and Cambridge, 1991.

________. *Holy Feast and Holy Fast: The Religious Significance of Food to Medieval Women.* Berkeley, 1987.

________. *Jesus as Mother: Studies in the Spirituality of the High Middle Ages.* Berkeley, 1982.

Byock, Jesse L. *Medieval Iceland: Society, Sagas, and Power.* Berkeley and Los Angeles, 1988.

Cabaniss, Allen. *Judith Augusta: A Daughter-in-law of Charlemagne, and other Essays.* New York, 1974.

Calmette, Joseph. *The Golden Age of Burgundy.* Trans. by Doreen Weightman. New York, 1963.

Cames, Géraud. *Allégories et symboles dans l'Hortus deliciarum.* Leiden, 1971.

Campbell, James, ed. *The Anglo-Saxons.* Ithaca, NY, 1982.

Campbell, Miles W. "Queen Emma and Aelfgifu of Northampton: Canute the Great's Women." *Medieval Scandinavia,* 4 (1971), 66–79.

Caraman, Philip. *St. Angela; the life of Angela of Merici, foundress of the Ursulines (1474–1540).* London, 1963.

Carr, Anne Marie Weyl. "Women Artists in the Middle Ages." *Feminist Art Journal,* 5, #1 (Spring 1976), 5–9.

Carroll, Berenice A., ed. *Liberating Women's History: Theoretical and Critical Essays.* Urbana, Chicago, and London, 1976.

Cartellieri, Otto. *The Court of Burgundy.* New York, 1972 (orig. publ. 1929).

Cartwright, Julia. *Beatrice d'Este, Duchess of Milan, 1475–1497.* London and New York, 1926 (first publ. 1899). [Note: dated but informative.]

________. *Isabella d'Este, Marchioness of Mantua.* 2 vols. London, 1903. [Note: see above.]

Carus-Wilson, E.M. "The Overseas Trade of Bristol." *Studies in English Trade in the Fifteenth Century,* ed. by Power and Postan (1933), 183–246.

Casey, Kathleen. "The Cheshire Cat: Reconstructing the Experience of Medieval Women." *Liberating Women's History: Theoretical and Critical Essays,* ed. by Berenice A. Carroll (1976), 224–249.

Castillon, H. *Histoire du Comté de Foix.* Toulouse, 1852. [Note: chatty but interesting.]

Castries, Duc de. *The Lives of the Kings and Queens of France.* New York, 1979.

Catherine (St. Catherine of Genoa). *Treatise on Purgatory and the Dialogue.* Trans. by Charles Balfour and Helen D. Irvine. London, 1946.

Cazel, F.A., Jr. and Sidney Painter. "The Marriage of Isabelle of Angoulême." *English Historical Review,* 63, #246 (1948), 83–89.

Cereta, Laura. *Laurae Ceretai Epistolae.* Ed. by J.F. Tomasini. Padua, 1640.

Chamberlin, E.R. *The Count of Virtue: Giangaleazzo Visconti, Duke of Milan.* London, 1965.

________. *The Fall of the House of Borgia.* New York, 1974.

________. *The World of the Italian Renaissance: Italy c. 1268–1559.* London, 1982.

Chambers, E.K. *The Mediaeval Stage.* 2 vols. London, 1967 (first publ. 1903).

Chambers, James. *The Norman Kings.* London, 1981.

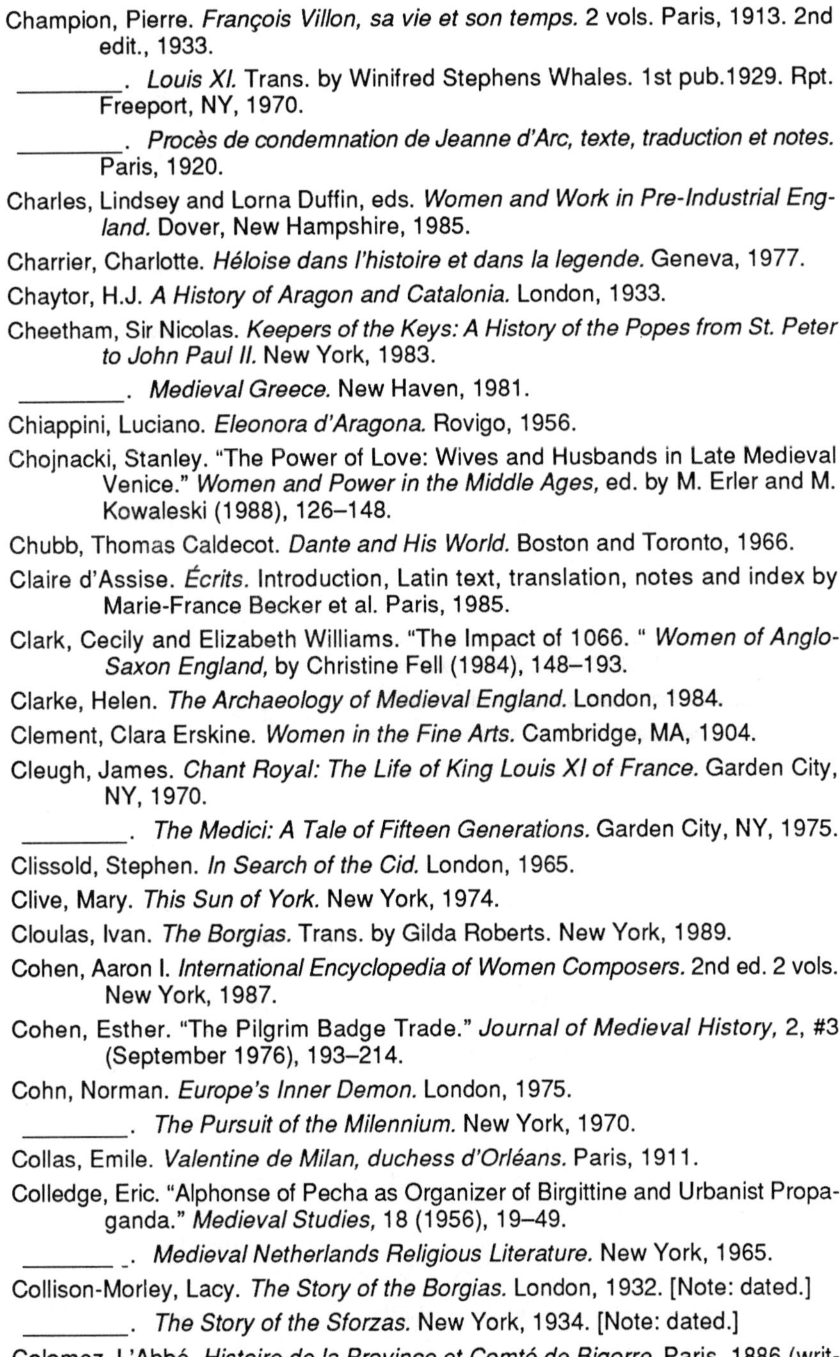

Champion, Pierre. *François Villon, sa vie et son temps.* 2 vols. Paris, 1913. 2nd edit., 1933.

________. *Louis XI.* Trans. by Winifred Stephens Whales. 1st pub.1929. Rpt. Freeport, NY, 1970.

________. *Procès de condemnation de Jeanne d'Arc, texte, traduction et notes.* Paris, 1920.

Charles, Lindsey and Lorna Duffin, eds. *Women and Work in Pre-Industrial England.* Dover, New Hampshire, 1985.

Charrier, Charlotte. *Héloise dans l'histoire et dans la legende.* Geneva, 1977.

Chaytor, H.J. *A History of Aragon and Catalonia.* London, 1933.

Cheetham, Sir Nicolas. *Keepers of the Keys: A History of the Popes from St. Peter to John Paul II.* New York, 1983.

________. *Medieval Greece.* New Haven, 1981.

Chiappini, Luciano. *Eleonora d'Aragona.* Rovigo, 1956.

Chojnacki, Stanley. "The Power of Love: Wives and Husbands in Late Medieval Venice." *Women and Power in the Middle Ages,* ed. by M. Erler and M. Kowaleski (1988), 126–148.

Chubb, Thomas Caldecot. *Dante and His World.* Boston and Toronto, 1966.

Claire d'Assise. *Écrits.* Introduction, Latin text, translation, notes and index by Marie-France Becker et al. Paris, 1985.

Clark, Cecily and Elizabeth Williams. "The Impact of 1066. " *Women of Anglo-Saxon England,* by Christine Fell (1984), 148–193.

Clarke, Helen. *The Archaeology of Medieval England.* London, 1984.

Clement, Clara Erskine. *Women in the Fine Arts.* Cambridge, MA, 1904.

Cleugh, James. *Chant Royal: The Life of King Louis XI of France.* Garden City, NY, 1970.

________. *The Medici: A Tale of Fifteen Generations.* Garden City, NY, 1975.

Clissold, Stephen. *In Search of the Cid.* London, 1965.

Clive, Mary. *This Sun of York.* New York, 1974.

Cloulas, Ivan. *The Borgias.* Trans. by Gilda Roberts. New York, 1989.

Cohen, Aaron I. *International Encyclopedia of Women Composers.* 2nd ed. 2 vols. New York, 1987.

Cohen, Esther. "The Pilgrim Badge Trade." *Journal of Medieval History,* 2, #3 (September 1976), 193–214.

Cohn, Norman. *Europe's Inner Demon.* London, 1975.

________. *The Pursuit of the Milennium.* New York, 1970.

Collas, Emile. *Valentine de Milan, duchess d'Orléans.* Paris, 1911.

Colledge, Eric. "Alphonse of Pecha as Organizer of Birgittine and Urbanist Propaganda." *Medieval Studies,* 18 (1956), 19–49.

________. *Medieval Netherlands Religious Literature.* New York, 1965.

Collison-Morley, Lacy. *The Story of the Borgias.* London, 1932. [Note: dated.]

________. *The Story of the Sforzas.* New York, 1934. [Note: dated.]

Colomez, L'Abbé. *Histoire de la Province et Comté de Bigorre.* Paris, 1886 (written around 1735).

Commynes, Philippe de. *The Memoirs of Philippe de Commynes.* 2 vols. Ed. by Samuel Kinser; trans. by Isabelle Cazeaux. Columbia, 1969.

Comnena, Anna. *The Alexiad.* Trans. by E.R.A. Sewter. New York, 1969 (rep. 1979).

Contamine, Philippe. "Peasant Hearth to Papal Palace: The Fourteenth and Fifteenth Centuries." *A History of Private Life,* Vol. 2. Ed. by G. Duby (1988), 425–505.

Cope, Christopher. *Phoenix Frustrated; the Lost Kingdom of Burgundy.* New York, 1987.

Coryn, Marjorie. *House of Orleans.* New York, 1936.

Cotton, Nancy. *Women Playwrights in England, c.1363–1750.* London and Toronto, 1980.

Coulton, G.G. *Life in the Middle Ages.* 4 vols. Cambridge, 1930 (orig. publ. 1910).

Cox, Eugene L. *The Eagles of Savoy.* Princeton, 1974.

Craig, Hardin. *English Religious Drama of the Middle Ages.* Oxford, 1955.

Crawford, Francis Marion. *The Rulers of the South.* New York, 1900. [Note: old but still useful.]

Creighton, M. *A History of the Papacy.* Vol. IV. London, 1923.

Crombie, A.C. *Medieval and Early Modern Science.* New York, 1959.

Cronin, Vincent. *The Flowering of the Renaissance.* New York, 1969.

Cross, Claire. "'Great Reasoners in Scripture': The Activities of Women Lollards 1380–1530." *Medieval Women,* ed. by Derek Baker (1978), 359–379.

Crowe, J.A. and G.B. Cavalcaselle. *The Early Flemish Painters: Notices of their Lives and Work.* London, 1872, 2nd. edit.

Cruikshank, A.P.J., ed. and trans. *The Book of the Visions and Instructions of Blessed Angela of Foligno.* New York, 1903.

Crump, C.G. and E.F. Jacob, eds. *The Legacy of the Middle Ages.* Oxford, 1962 (orig. publ., 1926).

Curtis, Edmund. *A History of Ireland.* London, 1936 (rpt. 1968).

________. *A History of Medieval Ireland from 1086 to 1513.* New York, 1968.

________. *Roger of Sicily and the Normans in Lower Italy.* New York, 1912.

Cuthbert, R.P. *A Tuscan Penitent. The Life and Legend of St. Margaret of Cortona.* London, 1907.

Cutler, Kenneth E. "Edith, Queen of England, 1045–1066." *Medieval Studies,* 35 (1973), 222–231.

Daichman, Graciela S. *Wayward Nuns in Medieval Literature.* Syracuse, NY, 1986.

Dale, Marion K. "The London Silkwomen of the Fifteenth Century." *Economic History Review,* 4 (1933), 324–335.

Daniel-Rops, Henry. *The Church in the Dark Ages.* Trans. by Audrey Butler. London and New York, 1963.

Davies, Norman. *God's Playground: A History of Poland.* Vol I. New York, 1982.

Davis, Elizabeth Gould. *The First Sex.* New York, 1971.

Davis, G.R.C. *Medieval Cartularies of Great Britain; a Short Catalogue.* London, 1958.

Day, John. "On the Status of Women in Medieval Sardinia." *Women of the Medieval World,* ed. by J. Kirshner and S. Wemple (1985), 304–316.

De Feo, Italo. *Giovanna d'Angio regina di Napoli.* Naples, 1968.

De Robeck, Nesta. *St. Clare of Assisi.* Milwaukee, 1951.

Dean, Ruth J. "Elisabeth, Abbess of Schönau, and Roger of Ford." *Modern Philogy,* 41 (1944), 209–220.

________. "Manuscripts of St. Elisabeth of Schönau in England." *Modern Language Review,* 32 (1937), 62–67.

Decaux, Alain. *Histoire des Françaises I: La Soumission.* Paris, 1972.

Delaney, John J. *Dictionary of Saints.* New York, 1980.

Dembinska, Maria. "A Polish Princess—Empress of Spain and Countess of Provence in the 12th Century." *Frauen in Spätantike und Fruhmittelalter,* ed. by Werner Affledt et al (Sigmaringen, 1990), 283–290.

Denholm-Young, Noel. "The Yorkshire Estates of Isabella de Fortibus." *Yorkshire Archaeological Journal,* 31 (1934), 389–420.

Denieul-Cormier, Anne. *Wise and Foolish Kings: The First House of Valois, 1328–1498.* Garden City, NY, 1980. [Note: opinionated, no footnotes, not the best source.]

Derry, Thomas Kingston. *A History of Scandinavia.* Minneapolis, 1979.

Desclot, Bernat (tr. by F.L. Critchlow). *Chronicle of the Reign of King Pedro III of Aragon. Part I. A.D. 1134–1275.* Princeton, 1934.

Destefanis, Abel. *Louis XII et Jeanne de France.* Avignon, 1975.

Deyermond, Alan. "El Convento de Dolencias: The Works of Teresa de Cartagena." *Journal of Hispanic Philology,* Vol. I, #1 (Autumn, 1976), 19–29.

Dezert, G. Desdevises du. *Don Carlos d'Aragon, Prince de Viane.* Paris, 1889. [Note: an old, but reliable source.]

Dhuoda. *Le Manuel de Dhuoda (843): L'Education Carolingienne.* Paris, 1887.

________. *Manuel pour mon fils.* Ed. and trans. by P. Riché. Paris, 1975.

Didier, J.C. "Elisabeth de Schönau." *Dictionaire d'histoire et de geographique ecclésiastiques,* 15 (1963), 221–224.

Diehl, Charles. *Byzantine Empresses.* Trans. by Harold Bell and Theresa de Kerpely. New York, 1963.

Dos Passos, John. *The Portugal Story: Three Centuries of Exploration and Discovery.* New York, 1969.

Douglas, David C. *The Norman Fate: 1100–1154.* Berkeley and Los Angeles, 1976.

________. *William the Conqueror: The Norman Impact Upon England.* Berkeley and Los Angeles, 1966.

Drinker, Sophie. *Music and Women; the Story of Women in Their Relation to Music.* New York, 1948.

Dronke, Peter. "The Provençal Trobairitz: Castelloza." *Medieval Women Writers,* ed. by K. Wilson (1984), 131–152.

________. *Women Writers of the Middle Ages.* Cambridge, 1984.

Duby, Georges. *The Knight, the Lady, and the Priest: The Making of Modern Marriage in Medieval France.* Trans. by Barbara Bray. New York, 1983.

________. *Medieval Marriage: Two Models from Twelfth Century France.* Baltimore, 1978.

________, ed. and author. *A History of Private Life.* Vol. 2: *Revelations of the Medieval World.* Trans. by Arthur Goldhammer. Cambridge, MA and London, 1988.

Duckett, Eleanor S. *Carolingian Portraits: A Study in the Ninth Century.* Ann Arbor, 1962.

________. *Death and Life in the Tenth Century.* Ann Arbor, 1967.

Duff, Nora. *Matilda of Tuscany, la gran donna d'Italia.* London, 1909. [Note: dated but informative.]

Duhamelet, Geneviève. *S. Elzéar et la bienheureuse Delphine.* Paris, 1944.

Dumont, Georges Henri. *Histoire de la Belgique.* Paris, 1977.

Dunbabin, Jean. *France in the Making: 843–1180.* Oxford, 1985.

Duncan, Archibald A.M. *Scotland: The Making of the Kingdom.* Edinburgh, 1975.

Dupouy, Auguste. *Histoire de Bretagne.* Paris, 1932.

Duraffour, A., P. Gardette, and P. Durdilly (eds.) *Les Oeuvres de Marguerite d' Oingt.* Paris, 1965.

Durtelle de Saint-Sauveur, Edmond. *Histoire de Bretagne: Des origines à nos jours.* Rennes, 1957.

Duvernoy, Jean. *Inquisition à Pamiers, Interrogatoiries de Jacques Fournier Évêque de Pamiers (1318–1325).* Toulouse, 1966.

Eckenstein, Lina. *Woman Under Monasticism.* Cambridge, 1896. [Note: an old, but still useful source.]

Edwards, Robert and Stephen Spector, eds. *The Old Daunce: Love, Friendship and Desire in the Medieval World.* Albany, 1990.

Effinger, John R. *Women of the Romance Countries.* Philadelphia, 1907. [Note: an older, not very scholarly source.]

Egan, Margarita (trans. and ed.) *The Vidas of the Troubadours.* New York and London, 1984.

Elkins, Sharon K. *Holy Women of Twelfth-Century England.* Chapel Hill and London, 1988.

Emden, Alfred Brotherton. *A Biographical Register of the University of Oxford to A.D. 1500.* Oxford, 1957–59.

Ennen, Edith. *The Medieval Woman.* Trans. by Edmund Jephcott. Oxford, 1989.

Erickson, Carolly and Kathleen Casey. "Women in the Middle Ages: A Working Bibliography." *Mediaeval Studies,* 37 (1975), 340–359.

Erlanger, Philippe. *Margaret of Anjou; Queen of England.* Trans. by E. Hyams. Coral Gables, Florida, 1970.

Erler, Mary and Kowaleski, Maryanne, eds. *Women and Power in the Middle Ages.* Athens and London, 1988.

Ernouf, Le Baron. *Histoire de Waldrade, de Lother II, et de Leurs Descendants.* Paris, 1858. [Note: an old, not very scholarly source.]

Esposito, M. "La vie de sainte Vulfilde par Goscelin de Cantorbery." *Analecta Bollandiana,* xxxii (1913), 10–26.

Evans, Joan, ed. *The Flowering of the Middle Ages.* New York, 1976.

Evergates, Theodore. "The Chancery Archives of the Counts of Champagne: Codicology and History of the Cartulary-Registers." *Viator: Medieval and Renaissance Studies,* 16 (1985), 159–180.

Ewen, Cecil Henry. *Witchcraft and Demonianism.* London, 1970.

Facinger, Marion F. "A Study of Medieval Queenship: Capetian France, 987–1237." *Studies in Medieval and Renaissance History,* 5 (1968), 3–48.

Farmer, David Hugh. *Oxford Dictionary of Saints.* Oxford, 1978.

Farmer, Sharon. "Persuasive Voices: Clerical Images of Medieval Wives." *Speculum,* 61, #3 (1986), 517–543.

Farreras, Joaquim, Wolff, Philippe, et al. *Histoire de la Catalogne.* Toulouse, 1982.

Favier, Jean. *Les Contribuables Parisiens à la Fin de la Guerre de Cent Ans: Les Rôles d'Impôt de 1421, 1423, and 1438.* Geneva, 1970.

Fawtier, Robert. *The Capetian Kings of France: Monarchy and Nation (987–1328).* Trans. by Lionel Butler and R.J. Adam. London and New York, 1960.

________. *Les Oeuvres de Sainte Catherine de Sienne.* II. Paris, 1930.

________. *Sainte Catherine de Sienne.* I. *Sources Hagiographiques.* Rome, 1921.

Fedele, Cassandra. *Cassandrae Fidelis Venetae: Epistolae et Orationes.* Ed. by J.F. Tomasini. Padua, 1636.

Fell, Christine, with C. Clark and E. Williams. *Women in Anglo-Saxon England and the Impact of 1066.* Bloomington, 1984. Fell, 1–147, Clark and Williams, 148–193.

Ferguson, Wallace F. and Geoffrey Bruun. *Survey of European Civilization.* Boston, 1936.

Ferrante, Joan M. "The Education of Women in the Middle Ages in Theory, Fact, and Fantasy." *Beyond Their Sex,* ed. by Patricia Labalme, (1980), 9–42.

________. "The French Courtly Poet: Marie de France." *Medieval Women Writers,* ed. by K. Wilson (1984), 64–89.

________. "Public Postures and Private Manuevers: Roles Medieval Women Play." *Women and Power in the Middle Ages,* ed. by M. Erler and M. Kowaleski (1988), 213–229.

________. *Women as Image in Medieval Literature.* New York and London, 1975.

________ and R.W. Hannings, eds. *The Lais of Marie de France.* New York, 1978.

Ferré, M.J. "Les Principales Dates de la Vie d'Angéle de Foligno." *Revue d'histoire franciscaine,* 2 (1925), 21–34.

________. *La Spiritualité de Sainte Angéle de Foligno.* Paris, 1927.

Fine, Elsa Honig. *Women and Art: A History of Women Painters and Sculptors from the Renaissance to the Twentieth Century.* Montclair, NJ, 1962.

Fines, J. "Studies in the Lollard Heresy." Phd. Thesis, University of Sheffield, 1964.

Finucane, Ronald C. *Soldiers of the Faith: Crusaders and Moslems at War.* New York, 1983.

Fisher, Herbert. *The Medieval Empire.* 2 vols. London, 1898. [Note: an old source which does include women.]

Fitzgibbon, Constantine. *The Irish in Ireland.* New York, 1983.

Fletcher, Richard. *The Quest for El Cid.* New York, 1990.

Florinski, Michael T. *Russia: A Short History.* London, 1969.

Forester, Thomas, trans. *Ecclesiastical History of Ordericus Vitalis,* vols. 1–4. London, 1853–1856.

Forster, Ann M. *The Good Duchess: Joan of France (1464–1505).* London, 1950.

Fossier, Robert. *Peasant Life in the Medieval West.* Trans. by Juliet Vale. Oxford and New York, 1988.

Fowler, Kenneth. *Age of Plantagenets and Valois.* New York, 1967.

Fox, John. *A Literary History of France: The Middle Ages.* London and New York, 1974.

Frager, Marcel. *Marie d'Anjou, femme de Charles, 1404–1463.* Paris, 1948.

Franceschini, G. "Battista Montefeltre Malatesta, Signora di Pesaro." *Studia Oliveriana,* 6 (1958), 7–43.

Frank, Roberta. "Marriage in Twelfth and Thirteenth Century Iceland." *Viator: Medieval and Renaissance Studies,* 4 (1973), 473–484.

Frederiksen, Elke, ed. *Women Writers of Germany, Austria, and Switzerland: An Annotated Bio-Bibliographical Guide.* Westport, CT, 1989.

Freeman, Michelle. "The Power of Sisterhood: Marie de France's 'Le Fresne'." *Women and Power in the Middle Ages,* ed. by M. Erler and M. Kowaleski (1988), 250–264.

Frey, Linda, Marsha Frey, & Joanne Schneider, eds. *Women in Western European History: A Select Chronological, Geographical, and Topical Bibliography.* Vol. 1, *The Middle Ages* (1982), 215–351.

Friedenwald, Harry. "Jewish Doctoresses in the Middle Ages." *The Jews and Medicine: Essays.* Baltimore, 1944. Chap. 13, 217–220.

________. *The Jews and Medicine: Essays.* Baltimore, 1944.

Fries, Maureen. "Margery Kempe." *An Introduction to the Medieval Mystics of Europe,* ed. by P.E. Szarmach. Albany, N.Y., 1984, 217–235.

Froissart, Sir John. *Chronicles of England, France, Spain.* Trans. by Thomas Johnes. Revised edit., 2 vols. New York and London, 1901.

Fryde, Natalie. *The Tyranny and Fall of Edward II, 1321–1326.* Cambridge, 1979.

Fügedi, Erik. *Castle and Society in Medieval Hungary (1000–1457).* Budapest, 1986.

Fuhrmann, Horst. *Germany in the High Middle Ages, c. 1050–1200.* Trans. by Timothy Reuter. Cambridge, 1986.

Fusero, Clemente. *The Borgias.* Trans. by Peter Green. New York, 1972 (orig. publ. Italy, 1966).

Ganshof, F.L. *The Carolingians and the Frankish Monarchy.* Trans. by Janet Sondheimer. Ithaca, N.Y., 1971.

Gardiner, Dorothy K. *English Girlhood at School: A Study of Women's Education through Twelve Centuries.* London, 1929.

Gardner, Edmund G. *Dukes and Poets in Ferrara.* New York, 1903.

Gardner, John. *The Life and Times of Chaucer.* New York, 1977.

Gardner, Monica Mary. *Queen Jadwiga of Poland.* Dublin, 1944.

Garner, John Leslie. *Caesar Borgia: A Study of the Renaissance.* New York, 1912.

Gasquet, Abbot Francis Aidan. *English Monastic Life.* Freeport, NY, 1971 (1st print., 1904).

Géraud, Hercule. "Ingeburge de Danemark, reine de France, 1193–1236." *Bibliothèque de l'École des chartes* 6 (1844) 3–27, 93–118.

________. *Paris Sous Phillippe le Bel. Le Rôle de la Taille.* Paris, 1837.

Gies, Frances. *The Knight in History.* New York, 1984.

________ and Joseph. *Merchants and Moneymen: The Commercial Revolution, 1000–1500.* New York, 1972.

________ and Joseph. *Women in the Middle Ages.* New York, 1978.

Gillingham, John Bennett. *Richard the Lionheart.* New York, 1978.

Gilson, Étienne. *Heloise and Abelard.* Trans. by L.K. Shook. Chicago, 1951.

Given-Wilson, Chris. *The English Nobility in the Later Middle Ages: The Fourteenth Century Political Community.* London and New York, 1987.

Glover, Janet R. *The Story of Scotland.* New York, 1959.

Gold, Penny Schine. *The Lady and the Virgin.* Chicago, 1985.

Goodich, Michael. "Ancilla Dei: The Servant as Saint in the Late Middle Ages." *Women of the Medieval World,* ed. by Wemple and Kirshner (1985), 119–136.

________. "The Contours of Female Piety in Later Medieval Hagiography." *Church History,* 50, #1 (1981), 20–32.

Goodman, A.E. "The Piety of John Brunham's Daughter, of Lynn." *Medieval Women,* ed. by Derek Baker (1978), 347–358.

Goodman, Anthony. *The Wars of the Roses: Military Activity and English Society,* 1452–97. London and Boston, 1981.

Goulianos, Joan, ed. *By a Woman Writt; Literature from Six Centuries by and about Women.* Indianapolis, 1973.

Gout, R., trans. *La Vie de Ste. Douceline.* Paris, 1927.

Grandeau, Yann. *Jeanne insultée: Procés en Diffamation.* Paris, 1973.

Gransden, Antonia. "The Alleged Rape by Edward III of the Countess of Salisbury." *English Historical Review,* 87 # 343 (April 1972), 333–344.

Grayeff, Felix. *Joan of Arc: Legends and Truth.* London, 1978.

Green, M.A.E. *Letters of Royal and Illustrious Ladies of Great Britain.* Vol. I. London, 1846.

Green, Monica. "Women's Medical Practice and Health Care in Medieval Europe." *Sisters and Workers in the Middle Ages,* ed. by J.M. Bennett et al (1989), 39–78.

Greer, Germaine. *The Obstacle Race; the Fortune of Women Painters and their Work.* New York, 1979.

Griffiths, Ralph A. "The Trial of Eleanor Cobham: an Episode in the Fall of Duke Humphrey of Gloucester." *Bulletin of the John Rylands Library,* 51 #2 (1969), 381–399.

________. "Queen Katherine of Valois and a missing statute of the Realm." *Law Quarterly Review,* 93 (1977), 248–58.

________ and Roger S. Thomas. *The Making of the Tudor Dynasty.* New York, 1985.

Guérout, Jean. "Le monastère a l'époque Carolingiene." *L'Abbaye Royale Notre Dame de Jouarre.* Ed. by W. Chaussey et al. Vol. 1. Paris, 1961.

Guilloreau, L. "Aliénor de Bretagne, quelques détails relatifs à sa captivité." *La Revue de Bretagne,* 1907.

Gundersheimer, Werner L. "Women, Learning, and Power: Eleonora of Aragon and the Court of Ferrara." *Beyond their Sex,* ed. by Patricia Labalme (1980), 43–65.

Haight, Anne L., ed. *Hrotswitha of Gandersheim: Her Life, Times, and Works, and a Comprehensive Bibliography.* New York, 1965.

Haines, Roy Martin. *The Church and Politics in Fourteenth-Century England; The Career of Adam Orleton, c. 1275–1345.* Cambridge, 1978.

Hair, P.E.H., comp. *Before the Bawdy Court.* London and New York, 1972.

Halecki, Oskar. *A History of Poland.* Trans. by M. Gardner and M. Corbridge-Patkaniowska. New York, 1943 (rpt. 1966).

Hallam, Elizabeth M., ed. *Four Gothic Kings.* New York, 1987.

________., ed. *The Plantagenet Chronicles.* New York, 1986.

Halligan, Theresa A., ed. *Booke of Gostlye Grace of Mechtild of Hackeborn.* Toronto, 1979.

Hamilton, Bernard. "Women in the Crusader States: The Queens of Jerusalem, 1100–1190." *Medieval Women,* ed. by Derek Baker (1978), 143–174.

Hampe, Karl. *Germany under the Salian and Hohenstaufen Emperors.* Trans. by Ralph Bennett. Totowa, NJ, 1973.

Hanawalt, Barbara A. "The Female Felon in Fourteenth Century England." *Viator: Medieval and Renaissance Studies,* 5 (1974): 253–268.

________. "The Female Felon in Fourteenth Century England." *Women in Medieval Society,* Ed. by Susan M. Stuard (1976), 143–174.

________. "Fur Collar Crime: The Pattern of Crime among the Fourteenth Century English Nobility." *Journal of Social History,* 8 (Summer 1975): 1–17.

________. "Golden Ages for the History of Medieval English Women." *Women in Medieval History and Historiography,* ed. by S.M. Stuard (1987), 1–24.

________. *The Ties that Bound: Peasant Families in Medieval England.* Oxford, 1986.

________., ed. *Women and Work in Pre-Industrial Europe.* Bloomington, Indiana, 1986.

Hansen, Elaine Tuttle. "The Powers of Silence: The Case of the Clerk's Griselda." *Women and Power in the Middle Ages,* ed. by M. Erler and M. Kowaleski (1988), 230–249.

Hanson-Smith, Elizabeth. "A Woman's View of Courtly Love: The Findern Anthology." *Journal of Women's Studies in Literature,* 1, #3 (Summer, 1979), 179–194.

Hardy, Blanche Christabel. *Philippa of Hainault and Her Times.* London, 1910.

Harksen, Sibylle. *Women in the Middle Ages.* New York, 1975.

Harrsen, Meta. *Cursus Sanctae Mariae.* New York, 1937.

Harvey, Nancy Lenz. *Elizabeth of York: The Mother of Henry VIII.* New York, 1973.

Haskell, Ann S. "The Paston Women on Marriage in Fifteenth-Century England." *Viator: Medieval and Renaissance Studies,* 4 (1973), 459–471.

Haskins, Charles Homer. *The Normans in European History.* New York, 1959 (1st print. 1915).

Haverkamp, Alfred. *Medieval Germany 1056–1273.* Trans. by Helga Braun and Richard Mortimer. Oxford, 1988.

Hazlitt, W. Carew. *The Coinage of the European Continent.* Chicago, 1974.

Heer, Frederick. *The Holy Roman Empire.* Trans. by J. Sondheimer. New York, 1968.

________. *The Medieval World: Europe, 1100–1500.* New York, 1962.

Heinrich, Sister Mary Pia. *The Canonesses and Education in the Early Middle Ages.* Washington, D.C., 1924.

Henderson, Ernest H. *A Short History of Germany.* Vol. I. New York, 1916.

Henry, Sondra and Emily Taitz. *Written Out of History: Our Jewish Foremothers.* Fresh Meadows, NY, 1983.

Henshaw, Millet. "The Attitude of the Church Toward the Stage at the End of the Middle Ages." *Medievalia et Humanistica,* 7 (1952), 3–17.

Herlihy, David. "Medieval Children." *Essays on Medieval Civilization,* ed. by Lackner and Philp (1978), 109–142.

________. *Medieval Households.* Cambridge, MA, 1985.

________. *Opera Muliebria: Women and Work in Medieval Europe.* New York, 1990.

Herrade de Landsberg. *Hortus Deliciarum.* Ed. by A. Straub and G. Keller. Strasbourg, 1899.

Hildegard, Saint. *Scivias.* Trans. by Bruce Hozeski. Santa Fe, NM, 1986.

Hill, George. A *History of Cyprus.* 4 vols. Cambridge, 1940–52.

Hillgarth, J.N. *The Spanish Kingdoms, 1250–1516.* Vol. 1. Oxford, 1976.

Hillgarth, Mary, trans. *Pere III of Catalonia (Pedro IV of Aragon), Chronicle.* Toronto, 1980.

Hilton, Rodney H. *The English Peasantry in the Later Middle Ages.* Oxford, 1975.

Hindley, Geoffrey. *England in the Age of Caxton.* New York, 1979.

Hinton, David A. *Alfred's Kingdom: Wessex and the South, 800–1500.* London, 1977.

Hodgkin, R.H. *A History of the Anglo-Saxons.* V. II. Oxford, 1935.

Hogan, M. Patricia. "Medieval Villany: A Study in the Meaning and Control of Crime in an English Village." *Studies in Medieval and Renaissance History,* n.s. vol. 2. Ed. by Evans and Unger (1979), 121–215.

Hohler, Christopher. "Court Life in Peace and War." *The Flowering of the Middle Ages,* ed. by Joan Evans (1976), 133–178.

Holdsworth, Christopher J. "Christina of Markyate." *Medieval Women,* ed. by Derek Baker (1978), 185–204.

Hollaender, A.E. and W. Kellaway, eds. "Aliens in and around London in the Fifteenth Century." *Studies in London History Presented to P.E. Jones.* London, 1969.

Hollister, C.W. "The Anglo-Norman Succession." *Journal of Medieval History,* 1, #1 (April, 1975), 19–42.

________. *Medieval Europe: A Short History.* Sixth edition, New York, 1990.

________ et al. *Medieval Europe: A Short Sourcebook.* New York, 1982.

Holmes, George. *Florence, Rome, and the Origins of the Renaissance.* Oxford, 1986.

________. *The Later Middle Ages, 1272–1485.* New York, 1962.

Holweck, Frederick George. *A Biographical Dictionary of Saints.* St. Louis and London, 1924.

Homans, George C. *English Villages of the Thirteenth Century.* Cambridge, MA, 1941.

Hommel, Luc. *Marguerite d'York: ou la duchess Junon.* Paris, 1959.

Hook, Judith. *Lorenzo de' Medici.* London, 1984.

Howard, John. "The German Mystic: Mechtild of Magdeburg." *Medieval Women Writers,* ed. by K. Wilson (1984), 153–185.

Howell, Cicely. *Land, Family, and Inheritance in Transition.* Cambridge, 1983.

Howell, Martha C. "Citizenship and Gender: Women's Political Status in Northern Medieval Cities." *Women and Power in the Middle Ages,* ed. by M. Erler and M. Kowaleski (1988), 37–60.

________, with S. Wemple and D. Kaiser. "A Documented Presence: Medieval Women in Germanic Historiography." *Women in Medieval History and Historiography,* ed. by S.M. Stuard (1987), 101–131.

________. *Women, Production, and Patriarchy in Late Medieval Cities.* Chicago, 1986.

Huddy, Mrs. Mary E. *Matilda, Countess of Tuscany.* London, 1906. [Note: still useful.]

Hügel, Friedrich freiherr von. *The Mystical Element of Religion as Studied by St. Caterina of Genoa and her Friends.* London and New York, 1923.

Hughes, Diane Owen. "Earrings for Circumcision: Distinction and Purification in the Italian Renaissance City." *Persons in Groups,* ed. by R.C. Trexler (1985), 155–177.

________. "Invisible Madonnas? The Italian Historiographical Tradition and the Women of Medieval Italy." *Women in Medieval History and Historiography,* ed. by S.M. Stuard (1987), 25–57.

Hughes, Muriel J. "The Library of Philip the Bold." *Journal of Medieval History,* 4, #2 (June 1978), 145–188.

________. *Women Healers in Medieval Life and Literature.* New York, 1968.

Huizinga, John. *The Waning of the Middle Ages: A Study of the Forms of Life, Thought, and Art in France and the Netherlands in the XIVth and XVth Centuries.* New York, 1954.

Hurd-Mead, Kate Campbell. *A History of Women in Medicine.* Haddam, CT, 1938.

Hutchison, Harold F. *King Henry V.* New York, 1967.

Hutton, Diane. "Women in Fourteenth Century Shrewsbury." *Women and Work in Pre-Industrial England,* ed. by Charles and Duffin (1985), 83–99.

Huysman, Joris Karl. *St. Lydwine de Schiedam.* Paris, 1901.

Hyatte, Reginald, trans. *Laughter for the Devil: The Trials of Gilles de Rais, Companion-in-arms of Joan of Arc.* Cranbury, NJ, 1984.

Ide, Arthur Frederick. *Women: A Synopsis.* Mesquite, TX, 1983.

Iongh, Jane de. *Margaret of Austria, Regent of the Netherlands.* Trans. by M.D. Herter-Norton. New York, 1953.

Jackson, Gabriel. *The Making of Medieval Spain.* New York, 1972.

Jacob, E.F. "The Book of St. Albans." *Bulletin of the John Rylands Library,* 28, #1 (March, 1944), 99–118.

________. *The Fifteenth Century, 1399–1485.* Oxford, 1961.

Jacquart, D. *Le Milieu Médical en France du XIIe au XIV Siècle.* Geneva and Paris, 1981.

James, Edward. *The Origins of France: From Clovis to the Capetians, 500–1000.* New York, 1982.

Jamison, D.F. *The Life and Times of Bertrand du Guesclin: A History of the Fourteenth Century.* 2 vols. Charleston, 1864.

Jamison, Evelyn M. "The Abbess Bethlem of Santa Maria di Porta Somma and the Barons of the Terra Beneventana." *Oxford Essays in Medieval History Presented to H.E. Salter,* New York, 1968 (1st publ. 1934).

Jany, N. "Women Painters in Belgium and in Holland." *Women Painters of the World,* ed. by Walter Sparrow (1976), 253–302.

Jarman, Rosemary Hawley. *Crispin's Day: The Glory of Agincourt.* Boston and Toronto, 1979.

Javierre Mur, Aurea L. "Matha de Armanyach, Duquesa de Gerona (1373–1378)." *Boletín de la Real Academia de la Historia Madrid,* 96 (Jan.–Mar.1930), 107–247.

Jenkins, Romilly. *Byzantium; the Imperial Centuries AD 610–1071.* New York, 1966.

Jenkinson, Hilary. "Mary de Sancto Paulo, Foundress of Pembroke College, Cambridge." *Archaeologia,* LXVI (1915), 401–446.

Johnson, Marion. *The Borgias.* New York, 1981.

Johnson, P.A. *Duke Richard of York: 1411–1460.* Oxford, 1988.

Johnson, Penelope D. *Equal in Monastic Profession: Religious Women in Medieval France.* Chicago, 1991.

________. *Prayer, Patronage and Power: The Abbey of la Trinité, Vendôme, 1032–1187.* New York and London, 1981.

Johnstone, Hilda. "Poor-Relief in the Royal Households of Thirteenth Century England." *Speculum,* 4 (1929), 149–167.

Joly, Edmond. *Le Cantique de Vitrail.* Paris, 1934.

Jones, Catherine. "The English Mystic: Julian of Norwich." *Medieval Women Writers,* ed. by K. Wilson (1984), 269–296.

Jones, Gwyn. *A History of the Vikings.* London, 1968.

Jones, Michael. *The Creation of Brittany: A Late Medieval State.* London and Ronceverte, 1988.

________. *Ducal Brittany, 1364–1399: Relations with England and France During the Reign of Duke John IV.* London, 1970.

Jones, P.J. *The Malatesta of Rimini and the Papal State.* Cambridge, 1974.

Jordan, William Chester. "Jews on Top: Women and the Availibility of Consumption Loans in Northern France in the Mid Thirteenth Century." *Journal of Jewish Studies,* 29, #1 (Spring 1978), 39–56.

________. *Louis IX and the Challenge of the Crusade: A Study in Rulership.* Princeton, NJ, 1979.

José, Marie. *La Maison de Savoie.* Paris, V. I, 1956; V. II and III, 1962.

Jourdain, Charles. "Memoire sur l'education des femmes au Moyen Âge." *Excursions historiques et philosophiques à travers le Moyen Âge,* Paris, 1888; Frankfurt, 1966. 463–510.

Jusserand, J.J. *English Wayfaring Life in the Middle Ages.* Trans. by L.T. Smith. New York, 1950 (orig. publ. 1929).

Kanner, Barbara, ed. *Women of England: From Anglo-Saxon Times to the Present: Interpretative Essays.* Camden, CT, 1979.

Kantorowicz, Ernst. *Frederick the Second, 1194–1250.* London, 1931.

Karacsonyi, J. *The Life of King St. Stephen.* Budapest, 1904.

Karras, Ruth Mazo. "The Regulation of Brothels in Later Medieval England." *Sisters and Workers inthe Middle Ages,* ed. by J.M. Bennett et al (1989), 100–134.

Kashnitz, Rainer. "The Gospel Book of Abbess Svanhild of Essen in the John Rylands Library." *Bulletin of the John Rylands Library,* 53, #1 (Autumn 1970), 122–166.

Kay, George F. *Lady of the Sun: The Life and Times of Alice Perrers.* New York, 1966. [Note: a popular biography.]

Kelleher, Patrick J. *The Holy Crown of Hungary.* Rome, 1951.

Kelly, Amy. *Eleanor of Aquitaine and the Four Kings.* Cambridge, MA, 1950.

Kelly, H.A. "Canonical Implications of Richard III's Plan to Marry his Niece." *Traditio,* 23 (1967), 269–311.

Kelly, Joan. "Early Feminist Theory and the Querelle des Femmes." *Women, History and Theory: The Essays of Joan Kelly,* (1984), 65–109.

________. *Women, History, and Theory: The Essays of Joan Kelly.* Chicago and London, 1984.

[also see Kelly-Gadol below.]

Kelly, John Norman Davidson. *The Oxford Dictionary of Popes.* New York, 1986.

Kelly-Gadol, Joan. *Bibliography in the History of European Women.* 5th Edition. Bronxville, NY, 1982.

________. "Did Women Have a Renaissance?" *Becoming Visible: Women in European History,* ed. by Bridenthal and Koonz (1977), 137–164.

Kempe, Margery. *The Book of Margery Kempe.* Trans. by W. Butler Bowdon. London, 1936.

Kendall, Paul Murray. *Louis XI.* New York, 1971.

________. *Yorkist Age.* New York, 1962.

Kennan, Elizabeth. "Innocent III and the First Political Crusade: A Comment on the Limitations of Papal Power." *Traditio,* 27 (1971), 231–249.

Kibler, William, W., ed. *Eleanor of Aquitaine, Patron and Politician.* Austin, TX, 1976.

Kidson, Peter. *The Medieval World.* New York and Toronto, 1967.

Kieckhefer, Richard. *European Witch Trials; Their Foundation in Popular and Learned Culture, 1300–1500.* Berkeley and Los Angeles, 1976.

King, Margaret L. "Book-Lined Cells: Women and Humanism in the Early Italian Renaissance." *Beyond Their Sex: Learned Women of the European Past,* ed. by Patricia Labalme (1980), 66–90.

________. "Goddess and Captive." *Medievalia et Humanistica.* n.s. #10 (1981): 103–127.

________. "The Religious Retreat of Isotta Nogarola (1418–1466): Sexism and its Consequences in the Fifteenth Century." *Signs,* 3 (1978), 807–22.

________. "Thwarted Ambitions: Six Learned Women of the Italian Renaissance." *Soundings,* 59 (1976), 280–304.

________ and Albert Rabil, Jr., eds. *Her Immaculate Hand: Selected Works by and About the Women Humanists of Quattrocento Italy.* Binghamton, NY, 1983.

Kirschner, Julius and Suzanne Wemple, eds. *Women of the Medieval World: Essays in Honor of John H. Mundy.* Oxford and New York, 1985.

Kittredge, George Lyman. *Witchcraft in Old and New England.* Cambridge, MA, 1929.

Klaits, Joseph. *Servants of Satan: The Age of the Witch Hunts.* Bloomington, 1985.

Klapisch-Zuber, Christiane. "The Cruel Mother: Maternity, Widowhood and Dowry in Florence in the Fourteenth and Fifteenth Centuries." *Women, Family and Ritual in Renaissance Italy* (1985), 117–131.

Klassen, John Martin. *The Nobility and the Making of the Hussite Revolution.* New York, 1978.

Kluchevsky, V.O. *A History of Russia.* Trans. by C.J. Hogarth. New York, 1960.

Knowles, David. *Thomas Becket.* Stanford, California, 1971.

Kosztolnyik, Z.J. *Five Eleventh Century Hungarian Kings: Their Policies and their Relations with Rome.* New York, 1981.

________. *From Coloman The Learned to Béla III (1095–1196).* New York, 1987.

Kraemer, Ross S. "The Conversion of Women to Ascetic Forms of Christianity." *Sisters and Workers in the Middle Ages,* ed. by J.M. Bennett et al (1989), 198–207.

Kraft, Kent. "The German Visionary: Hildegard of Bingen." *Medieval Women Writers,* ed. by K. Wilson (1984), 109–130.

Kristeller, Oskar. "Learned Women of Early Modern Italy: Humanists and University Scholars." *Beyond their Sex: Learned Women of the European Past,* ed. by Patricia H. Labalme (1980), 102–114.

Kuehn, Thomas. "Cum Consensu Mundualdi: Legal Guardianship of Women in Quattrocento Florence." *Viator: Medieval and Renaissance Studies,* 13 (1982), 309–333.

Labalme, Patricia H., ed. *Beyond Their Sex: Learned Women of the European Past.* New York, 1980.

Labarge, Margaret Wade. *A Baronial Household of the Thirteenth Century.* London, 1965.

________. *Simon de Montfort.* London, 1962.

________. *A Small Sound of the Trumpet: Women in Medieval Life.* Boston and London, 1986.

Lacarra, J.M. and Anton Gonzales. "Les Testaments de la Reine Marie de Montpellier." *Annales du Midi,* 90 (1978), 105–120.

Lacey, Kay E. "Women and Work in Fourteenth and Fifteenth Century London." *Women and Work in Pre-Industrial England,* ed. by Charles and Duffin (1985), 24–82.

Ladurie, Emmanuel Le Roy. *Montaillou: The Promised Land of Error.* New York, 1978.

Lagorio, Valerie M. "The Medieval Continental Women Mystics: An Introduction." *An Introduction to the Medieval Mystics of Europe,* ed. by P.E. Szarmach (1984), 161–193.

Lambert, Malcolm. *Medieval Heresy: Popular Movements from Bogomil to Hus.* New York, 1977.

Lancaster, R. Kent. "Artists, Suppliers and Clerks: The Human Factors in the Art Patronage of King Henry III." *Journal of the Warburg and Courtauld Institutes,* XXXV (1972), 81–107.

Larsen, Karen. *History of Norway.* Princeton, 1948.

Latten, C. "Isabelle de Portugal, duchess de Bourgogne et Comtess de Flandre." *Revue de Litterature Comparés,* vol. XVIII, 1938.

Le Patourel, John. *Feudal Empires: Norman and Plantagenet.* London, 1984.

Lea, Henry C. *History of the Inquisition of the Middle Ages.* Vols. II and III. New York, 1922.

________. *Materials Toward a History of Witchcraft.* Vol. I. Ed. by A.C. Howland. Philadelphia, 1939.

Lee, Patricia-Ann. "Reflections of Power: Margaret of Anjou and the Dark Side of Queenship." *Renaissance Quarterly,* 39 (1986), 183–217.

Leff, Gordon. *Heresy in the Later Middle Ages.* Vol. I and II. New York, 1967.

Legge, M. Dominica, ed. *Anglo-Norman Letters and Petitions.* Oxford, 1941.

Lehmann, A. *Le Rôle de la Femme dans l'Histoire de France au Moyen Âge.* Paris, 1952.

Lehugeur, Paul. *Histoire de Philippe le Long, roi de France (1316–1322).* Paris, 1897.

Lejeune, Rita. "La Femme dans les litteratures Française et Occitane du XI au XIII Siècle." *Cahiers de Civilisation Medieval,* 20, #2–3 (April–September 1977), 201–217.

Leroy, Beatrice. *La Navarre au Moyen Âge.* Paris, 1984.

Lesourd, Paul. *La Lorraine, le Barrois, les Trois Éveches dans l'histoire de la France et, demain, de l'Europe.* Paris, 1966.

Leuschner, Joachim. *Germany in the Late Middle Ages.* Amsterdam, New York, and Oxford, 1980.

Leveque, Paul-Jacques. *Agnes Sorel and Her Legend.* Trans. by J.E. Schloder. Tours, 1970.

Levin, Carole and Jeanie Watson, eds. *Ambiguous Realities: Women in the Middle Ages and Renaissance.* Detroit, 1987.

Lewis, Archibald R. *The Development of Southern French and Catalan Society, 718–1050.* Austin, TX, 1965.

Lewis, D.B Wyndham. *François Villon.* New York, 1928.

________. *King Spider.* New York, 1929.

Lewis, Frank R. "Beatrice of Falkenburg, the Third Wife of Richard of Cornwall." *English Historical Review,* 52, #206 (April 1937), 279–282.

Lewis, N.B. "The Anniversary Service for Blanche, Duchess of Lancaster, 12th September 1374." *Bulletin of the John Rylands Library,* 21, #1 (April 1937), 176–192.

Leyser, K.J. *Medieval Germany and Its Neighbors, 900–1250.* London, 1982.

________. *Rule and Conflict in an Early Medieval Society: Ottonian Saxony.* Bloomington, Ind. 1979.

Lipinska, Melanie. *Histoire des Femmes Médicins.* Paris, 1900.

Livermore, H.V. *A History of Portugal.* Cambridge, 1947.

________. *A New History of Portugal.* Cambridge, 1976.

Lloyd, Alan. *The Maligned Monarch: A Life of King John of England.* New York, 1972.

Lloyd, John Edward. *A History of Wales from the Earliest Times to the Edwardian Conquest.* Third Edition. New York, 1948 (first published in 1911). [Note: an old source which does include women.]

Loengard, Janet Senderowitz. "Of the Gift of her Husband: English Dower and Its Consequences in the Year 1200." *Women of the Medieval World,* ed. by J. Kirshner and S. Wemple (1985), 215–255.

Lowell, Francis C. *Joan of Arc.* Boston, 1896.

Lucas, Angela M. *Women in the Middle Ages: Religion, Marriage and Letters.* New York, 1983.

Lutzow, Count von. *Bohemia: An Historical Sketch.* London, 1939.

________. *The Hussite Wars.* London and New York, 1914.

Lyonne, René. *Jeanne d'Arc, legende et histoire.* Nancy, 1973.

Macinghi negli Strozzi, Alessandra. *Lettere di una gentildonna fiorentina del secolo XV ai figliuoli esuli.* Ed. by C. Guasti. Florence, 1877.

Mackenney, Richard. "Towns and Trade." *The Making of Britain,* ed. by Lesley M. Smith (1985), 119–134.

Mackie, J.D. *History of Scotland.* Baltimore, 1964.

Mackie, Robert Laird. *Short History of Scotland.* Ed. by G. Donaldson. New York, 1963.

Maguire, Yvonne. *Women of the Medici.* London, 1927.

Marchand, James. "The Frankish Mother: Dhuoda." *Medieval Women Writers,* ed. by K. Wilson (1984), 1–29.

Marek, George R. *The Bed and the Throne: The Life of Isabella d'Este.* New York, 1976.

Margolis, Nadia. *Joan of Arc in History, Literature, and Film: A Select Annotated Bibliography.* New York, 1990.

Markale, Jean. *Aliénore d'Aquitaine reine de France, puis d'Angleterre, dame des troubadours et des bardes bretons.* Paris, 1979.

Marks, Claude. *Pilgrims, Heretics and Lovers: A Medieval Journey.* New York, 1975.

Martin, C. Trice. "Clerical Life in the Fifteenth Century, as Illustrated by Proceedings of the Court of Chancery." *Archaeologia,* LX (1907), 374–6.

Martines, Lauro. "A Way of Looking at Women in Renaissance Florence." *Journal of Medieval and Renaissance Studies,* 4, #1 (Spring 1974), 15–28.

Martinière, J. de la. "Une falsification de document au commencement du XIIe siècle." *Moyen Âge,* 2 ser. 17 (1911), 1–45.

Mason-Hohl, Elizabeth. "Trotula: Eleventh Century Gynecologist." *Medical Woman's Journal,* 47 (Dec. 1940), 349–356.

Mate, Mavis. "Profit and Productivity on the Estates of Isabella de Forz." *Economic History Review,* 2nd. ser., 33, #3 (August 1980), 326–334.

Matthews, William. "The Wife of Bath and All Her Sect." *Viator: Medieval and Renaissance Studies,* 6 (1975), 413–444.

Mauriac, Francois. *St. Margaret of Cortona.* Trans. by Bernard Frechtman. New York, 1948.

Maurice, C. Edmund. *Story of Bohemia.* New York, 1896. [Note: old, but still useful.]

May, W. "The Confessions of Prous Boneta, Heretic and Heresiarch." *Essays in Medieval Life and Thought,* ed. by J. Mundy et al (1965), 3–30.

Mayer, Dorothy M. *The Great Regent: Louise of Savoy, 1476–1531.* New York, 1966.

McCall, Andrew. *The Medieval Underworld.* London, 1979.

McDonnell, Ernest W. *The Beguines and Beghards in Medieval Culture.* New York, 1969.

McFarlane, K.B. *The Nobility of Later Medieval England.* Oxford, 1973.

McKitterick, Rosamund. *The Frankish Kingdoms under the Carolingians, 751–897.* London, 1983.

McLaughlin, Eleanor. "Women, Power, and the Pursuit of Holiness." *Women of Spirit: Female Leadership in the Jewish and Christian Traditions,* ed. by R. Ruether and E. McLaughlin (1979), 99–130.

McLaughlin, Mary Martin. "Creating and Recreating Communities of Women: The Case of Corpus Domini, Ferrara, 1406–1452." *Sisters and Workers in the Middle Ages,* ed. by J.M. Bennett et al (1989), 261–288.

McNabb, Vincent Joseph. *St. Elizabeth of Portugal.* New York, 1937.

McNamara, Jo Ann, and Suzanne F. Wemple. "Marriage and Divorce in the Frankish Kingdom." *Women in Medieval Society,* ed. by Susan M. Stuard (1976), 95–124.

________. "The Power of Women through the Family in Medieval Europe, 500–1100." *Women and Power in the Middle Ages,* ed. by Erler and Kowaleski (1988), 83–101.

________. "Sanctity and Power: The Dual Pursuit of Medieval Women." *Becoming Visible: Women in European History,* ed. by Bridenthal and Koonz (1977), 90–118.

Meade, Marion. *Eleanor of Aquitaine: A Biography.* New York, 1977.

Merriman, Roger. *The Rise of the Spanish Empire.* Vol. I, New York, 1918.

Mertes, Kate. *The English Noble Household 1250–1600: Good Governance and Politic Rule.* Oxford and New York, 1988.

Meyer, Edith Patterson. *First Lady of the Renaissance: A Biography of Isabella d'Este.* Boston, 1970.

Michaëlsson, Karl. *Le Livre de la taille de Paris l'an de grace* 1313. Stockholm, 1962.

Mickel, Emmanuel. *Marie de France.* Boston, 1974.

________. "A Reconsideration of the Lais of Marie de France." *Speculum,* 46 (January 1971), 39–65.

Miller, Townsend. *The Castles and the Crown: Spain, 1451–1555.* New York, 1963.

Miron, E.L. *The Queens of Aragon: Their Lives and Times.* Port Washington, NY, 1970.

Mirot, L. *Isabelle de France, reine d'Angleterre, comtesse d'Angoulême, duchess d'Orléans.* Paris, 1905.

Molinari, P. *Julian of Norwich, the Teachings of a Fourteenth-Century Mystic.* London, 1958.

Mongour, Paul. *Sainte Marguerite de la Seauve: Son Histoire et Sa Legende.* Paris, 1954.

Monica, Sister M. *Angela Merici and Her Teaching Idea.* New York, 1927.

Montalemberg, Charles Forbes René de Tryon, comte. *L'Histoire de Elisabeth de Hongrie, duchesse de Thuringe.* Paris, 1930.

More, Thomas. *The History of Richard III and Selections from the English and Latin Poems.* Ed. by R. Sylvester. New Haven, 1976.

Morewedge, Rosemarie T., ed. *The Role of Women in the Middle Ages.* Albany, 1975.

Morrall, John B. *The Medieval Imprint: The Founding of the Western European Tradition.* New York, 1967.

Morson, John. "The English Cistercians and the Bestiary." *Bulletin of the John Rylands Library,* 39, #1 (Sept. 1956), 146–170.

Motley, John Lothrop. *The Rise of the Dutch Republics.* Vol. I, New York and London, 1909.

Moulin, Jeanine, ed. *La Poésie féminine du XII au XIX siècle.* Paris, 1966.

Mozans, H.J. *Woman in Science.* Cambridge, MA, 1974 (orig. publ. 1913).

Muckle, J.T. "The Personal Letters Between Abelard and Heloise." *Medieval Studies,* 15 (1953), 47–94.

Muir, Lynette R. *Literature and Society in Medieval France: The Mirror and the Image 1100–1500.* London, 1985.

Muir, Richard. *The English Village.* New York, 1980.

Munsterberg, Hugo. *A History of Women Artists.* New York, 1975.

Muré, Jean-Marie de la. *Histoire des ducs de Bourbon et des comtes de Forez.* Ed. by R. Chantelauze. 4 vols. Paris, 1860–1897.

Musset, Lucien. *Les Peuples Scandinaves au Moyen Âge.* Paris, 1951.

Musto, Ronald G. "Queen Sancia of Naples (1286–1345) and the Spiritual Franciscans." *Women of the Medieval World,* ed. by Kirshner and Wemple (1985), 179–214.

Myers, A.R. "The Captivity of a Royal Witch: The Household Account of Queen Joan of Navarre, 1419–1421." *Bulletin of the John Rylands Library,* 24 (October 1940), 263–284.

________. "The Household of Queen Elizabeth Woodville, 1466–7." *Bulletin of the John Rylands Library,* 50 (1967–1968): 207–235.

________. "The Household of Queen Margaret of Anjou, 1452–1453." *Bulletin of the John Rylands Library,* 40, #1 (September 1957): 79–113.

Nagy, Kazmer. *St. Margaret of Scotland.* Glasgow, 1973.

Neel, Carol. "The Origins of the Beguines." *Sisters and Workers in the Middle Ages,* ed. by J.M. Bennett et al (1989), 240–260.

Nelson, Janet L. *Politics and Ritual in Early Medieval Europe.* London and Ronceverte, WV, 1986.

Newman, Barbara. *Sister of Wisdom: St. Hildegard's Theology of the Feminine.* Berkeley, 1987.

Nicholas, David. *The Domestic Life of a Medieval City: Women, Children and the Family in Fourteenth Century Ghent.* Lincoln and London, 1985.

Nichols, John and Lillian Shanks, eds. *Distant Echoes: Medieval Religious Women.* Kalamazoo, MI, 1984.

________. *Peace Weavers: Medieval Religious Women.* Kalamazoo, MI, 1987.

Nichols, Stephen G., Jr. "The Medieval Lyric and Its Public." *Medievalia et Humanistica,* 2nd ser. #3 (1972), 133–153.

Nicholson, Ranald. *Scotland: The Later Middle Ages.* Edinburgh, 1974.

Nogarola, Isotta. *Isotae Nogarolae Veronesis opera quae supersunt omnia.* Ed. by E. Abel, 2 vols. Vienna and Budapest, 1886.

Norwich, John Julius. *History of Venice.* New York, 1982.

________. *The Kingdom in the Sun, 1130–1194.* London, 1976.

________. *The Normans in the South, 1016–1130.* London, 1967.

Nowell, Charles Edward. *History of Portugal.* New York, 1952.

O'Callaghan, Joseph F. *A History of Medieval Spain.* Ithaca and London, 1975.

O'Faolain, Julia. *Not in God's Image: Women in History from the Greeks to the Victorians.* London, 1973.

Oakley, Stewart. *A Short History of Denmark.* New York and Washington, 1972.

Obrist, Barbara. "The Swedish Visionary: Saint Bridget." *Medieval Women Writers,* ed. by K. Wilson (1984), 227–251.

Odegaard, Charles E. "The Empress Engelberge," *Speculum* 26 (1951), 77–103.

Ogilvie, Marilyn. *Women in Science: Antiquity Through the Nineteenth Century: A Biographical Dictionary with Annotated Bibliography.* Cambridge, MA, 1986.

Oliveira Martins, Joaquim de. *History of Iberian Civilization.* Trans. by Aubrey F. G. Bell. New York, 1969 (orig. publ. 1930).

Origo, Iris. "The Domestic Enemy: The Eastern Slaves in Tuscany in the Fourteenth and Fifteenth Century." *Speculum,* 30, #3 (July 1955), 321–366.

Orme, Nicholas. *Education in the West of England, 1066–1548.* Exeter, 1976.

________. *English Schools in the Middle Ages.* London, 1973.

Orpen, Goddard Henry. *Ireland Under the Normans, 1169–1216.* Vols. I and II. London, 1968 (1st publ. 1911).

Osborne, James van Wyck. *The Greatest Norman Conquest.* New York, 1937.

Otis, Leah Lydia. "Prostitution and Repentance in Late Medieval Perpignan." *Women of the Medieval World,* ed. by Kirshner and Wemple (1985), 137–160.

________. *Prostitution in Medieval Society: The History of an Urban Institution in Languedoc.* Chicago, 1985.

Otway-Ruthven, A.J. *A History of Medieval Ireland.* New York, 1980.

Owen, Dorothy M. "White Annays and Others." *Medieval Women,* ed. by Derek Baker (1978), 331–346.

Paden, William D., ed. *The Voice of the Trobairitz: Perspectives on the Women Troubadours.* Philadelphia, 1989.

Page, R.I. *Life in Anglo-Saxon England.* London and New York, 1970.

Pain, Nesta. *Empress Matilda; Uncrowned Queen of England.* London, 1978.

Palmer, J.J.N. "England, France, the Papacy and the Flemish Succession." *Journal of Medieval History,* 2, #4 (Dec. 1976), 339–364.

Palmer, Robert C. *County Courts of Medieval England, 1150–1350.* Princeton, 1982.

Pamlényi, Ervin, ed. *A History of Hungary.* London, 1975.

Parbury, Kathleen. *Women of Grace: A Biographical Dictionary of British Women Saints, Martyrs, and Reformers.* Stocksfield, Eng., 1985.

Pares, Bernard. *A History of Russia.* New York, 1949.

Paris, Mathew. *Chronicles of Matthew Paris: Monastic Life in the Thirteenth Century.* Ed. by Richard Vaughan. New York, 1986.

Paris, Paulin. "Livres de Jehanne d'Évreux." *Bulletin du Bibliophile,* (1838), 492–494.

Parker, Rozsika and Griselda Pollack. *Old Mistresses: Women, Art, and Ideology.* New York, 1981.

Parsons, John Carmi, ed. *The Court and Household of Eleanor of Castile in 1290.* Toronto, 1977.

Partner, Peter. *The Lands of St. Peter: The Papal State in the Middle Ages and Early Renaissance.* Berkeley and Los Angeles, 1972.

Pasolini, Pier Desiderio. *Catherine Sforza.* Trans. by Paul Sylvester. Chicago and New York, 1898. [Note: old but still useful.]

Paul, James Balfour, Sir. *The Scots Peerage.* Edinburgh, 1904–14. Rpt. 1976.

Payne, Robert. *The Dream and the Tomb: A History of the Crusades.* New York, 1984.

Pelicier, Paul. *Essai sur le gouvernement de la dame de Beaujeu, 1483–1491.* Chartres, 1882. [Note: old but informative.]

Pernoud, Régine. *Blanche of Castile.* Trans. by Henry Noel. London, 1975.

________. *Eleanor of Aquitaine.* Trans. by Peter Wiles. New York, 1967/8.

________. *La femme au temps des Cathédrales.* Paris, 1984.

________. *Héloise et Abelard.* Paris, 1980.

________. *Joan of Arc, by Herself and Her Witnesses.* Trans. by Edward Hyams. London, 1964.

________. *The Retrial of Joan of Arc; the Evidence at the Trial for her Rehabilitation, 1450–1456.* Trans. by J.M. Cohen. London, 1955.

Peters, Edward. *Europe: The World of the Middle Ages.* Englewood Cliffs, NJ, 1977.

Petersen, Karen and J.J. Wilson. *Women Artists: Recognition and Reappraisal from the Early Middle Ages to the Twentieth Century.* New York, 1976.

Petroff, Elizabeth A. *Medieval Women's Visionary Literature.* New York and Oxford, 1986.

Petteys, Chris et al. *Dictionary of Women Artists: An International Dictionary of Women Artists Born Before 1900.* Boston, 1985.

Philippe, Robert. *Agnes Sorel.* Poitiers, 1983.

Phillips, Tom, trans. and illus. *Dante's Inferno: The First Part of the Divine Comedy of Dante Alighieri.* London, 1985.

Pinnow, Herman. *History of Germany.* Trans. by M. R. Brailsford. Freeport, N.Y., 1970 (orig. publ. 1929).

Pirenne, Henri. *Histoire de Belgique.* Vol. II. Brussels, 1922.

Pisan (Pizan), Christine de. *The Book of the City of Ladies.* Trans. by Jeffrey Richards. New York, 1982.

Pool, Jeannie G. *Women in Music History: A Research Guide.* Ansonia Station, N.Y., 1977.

Porète, Marguerite. *Le Miroir des Simples Âmes.* Ed. by R. Guarnieri. Rome, 1961.

Post, John. "The King's Peace." *The Making of Britain,* ed. by Lesley M. Smith (1985), 149–162.

Poupardin, René. *Le Royaume de Bourgogne (888–1038): Étude sur les origines du royaume d'Arles.* Paris, 1907. Rpt. Geneva, 1974.

Power, Eileen. *Medieval English Nunneries.* Cambridge, 1922.

________. *Medieval Women.* Cambridge, 1975.

________. "The Position of Women." *The Legacy of the Middle Ages,* ed. by C.G. Crump and E.F. Jacob (1962), 401–435.

Powicke, Sir Frederick M. *The Christian Life in the Middle Ages and Other Essays.* Oxford, 1935.

Powicke, Sir Frederick M. "Loretta, countess of Leicester." *The Christian Life in the Middle Ages. . . .* , pp 147–168.

________. *The Thirteenth Century: 1216–1307.* 2nd edition. Oxford, 1962.

Prescott, Orville. *Princes of the Renaissance.* New York, 1969.

Prestwich, Michael. *Edward I.* Berkeley and Los Angeles, 1988,

________. "Isabella de Vescy and the Custody of Bamburgh Castle." *Bulletin of the Instiitute of Historical Research,* 44 (Nov. 1971), 148–152.

Previte-Orton, C.W. *Outlines of Medieval History.* New York, 1965.

________. *The Shorter Medieval History.* Vol. I. Cambridge, 1952.

Provost, William. "The English Religious Enthusiast: Margery Kempe." *Medieval Women Writers,* ed. by K. Wilson (1984), 297–319.

Putnam, Samuel. *Marguerite of Navarre.* New York, 1935. [Note: not especially scholarly.]

Rabil, A., Jr. *Laura Cereta: Quattrocento Humanists.* Binghampton, NY, 1981.

Radice, Betty. "The French Scholar-Lover: Heloise." *Medieval Women Writers,* ed. by K. Wilson (1984), 90–108.

Ragg, Laura M. *The Women Artists of Bologna.* London, 1907.

Ranke-Heinemann, Uta. *Eunuchs for Heaven: The Catholic Church and Sexuality.* Trans. by John Brownjohn. London, 1990.

Rawcliffe, Carol. *The Staffords, Earls of Stafford and Dukes of Buckingham.* Cambridge, 1979.

Razi, Zvi. "Family, Land, and the Village Community in Later Medieval England." *Past and Present,* #93 (Nov. 1981), 3–36.

Reddaway, W.F. et al, eds. *The Cambridge History of Poland.* Vol. I. Cambridge, 1950.

Rees, David. *The Son of Prophecy: Henry Tudor's Road to Bosworth.* London, 1985.

Reilly, Bernard F. *The Kingdom of Leon-Castilla under Queen Urraca, 1109–1126.* Princeton, 1982.

Richard, Jules Marie. "Les Livres de Mahaut, Comtesse d'Artois et de Bourgogne, 1302–1329." *Revue des Questions Historiques,* 40 (1886), 135–41.

________. *Une Petite-niece de saint Louis: Mahaut Comtesse d'Artois et de Bourgogne.* 1887. Rpt. Geneva, 1975/76.

Richards, Jeffrey. *Sex, Dissidence, and Damnation: Minority Groups in the Middle Ages.* London and New York, 1991.

Richardson, H.G. "The Letters and Charters of Eleanor of Aquitaine." *English Historical Review,* 74, #291 (April 1959), 193–213.

________. "The Marriage and Coronation of Isabelle of Angoulême." *English Historical Review,* 61, #241 (1946), 289–314.

Riché, Pierre. *Les Carolingiens: Une Famille qui fit l'Europe.* Poitiers, 1983.

Richter, Michael. *Medieval Ireland: The Enduring Tradition.* Trans. by Brian Stone and Adrian Keogh. New York, 1988.

Riley, Henry Thomas. *Memorials of London and London Life in the 13th, 14th and 15th Centuries.* London, 1868.

Ritchie, Neil. "Bohemund, Prince of Antioch." *History Today,* 28, #5 (May, 1978), 293–303.

Robathan, Dorothy M. "A Fifteenth-Century Bluestocking." *Medievalia et Humanistica,* 2 (1944), 106–111.

Robbins, Rossell Hope. *Encyclopedia of Witchcraft and Demonology.* New York, 1959.

Roberts, Phyllis B. "Stephen Langton's 'Sermo de Virginibus'." *Women of the Medieval World,* ed. by J. Kirshner and S. Wemple (1985), 103–118.

Robertson, D.W., Jr. *Chaucer's London.* New York, 1968.

Robinson, James Hardy. *Readings in European History.* Vol. I. Boston, 1904.

Roche, Thomas William Edgar. *Philippa: Dona Filipa of Portugal.* London, Chicester, Phillimore, 1971.

Rokseth, Yvonne. "Les Femmes musiciennes du XII au XIV siècle." *Romania,* 61 (October 1935), 464–480.

Roncière, Charles de La. "Tuscan Notables on the Eve of the Renaissance." *A History of Private Life,* Vol. 2. ed. by G. Duby (1988), 157–309.

Rose, Mary Beth. *Women in the Middle Ages and Renaissance.* Syracuse, NY, 1986.

Rosenthal, Joel T. *Medieval Women and the Sources of Medieval History.* Athens, GA, 1990.

________. *Nobles and the Noble Life, 1295–1500.* London, 1976.

________. *The Purchase of Paradise: Gift Giving and the Aristocracy, 1307–1485.* London, 1972.

Ross, Charles Derek. "The Household Account of Elizabeth Berkeley, countess of Warwick, 1420–1." *Transactions of the Bristol and Gloucester Archeological Society,* 70 (1951), 81–105.

________. *Wars of the Roses, a Concise History.* London, 1976.

Rossiaud, Jacques. *Medieval Prostitution.* Trans. by Lydia G. Cochrane. New York, 1988.

Rowland, Beryl., ed. and trans. *Medieval Woman's Guide to Health: The First English Gynaecological Handbook.* London, 1981.

Rubin, Stanley. *Medieval English Medicine.* London, 1974.

Ruether, Rosemary and Eleanor McLaughlin, eds. *Women of Spirit: Female Leadership in the Jewish and Christian Traditions.* New York, 1979.

Runciman, Sir Stephen. "The Empress Irene the Athenian." *Medieval Women,* ed. by Derek Baker (1978), 101–118.

________. *The Sicilian Vespers.* Cambridge, 1958.

Russell, Jeffrey B. *Dissent and Reform in the Early Middle Ages.* Berkeley, 1965.

________. *A History of Witchcraft: Sorcerers, Heretics, and Pagans.* London, 1980.

________. *Witchcraft in the Middle Ages.* Ithaca and London, 1972.

Ryder, Alan. *The Kingdom of Naples Under Alfonso the Magnanimous: The Making of a Modern State.* Oxford, 1976.

Sachs, Hannelore. *The Renaissance Woman.* New York, 1971.

Salisbury, Joyce E. *Medieval Sexuality: A Research Guide.* New York, 1990.

Salzman, L.F. *English Life in the Middle Ages.* London, 1966.

Sanborn, Helen J. *Anne of Brittany; The Story of a Duchess and Twice-crowned Queen.* Boston, 1917.

Santy, Sernin. *La Comtesse de Die, sa vie, ses oeuvres completes, les fetes données en son honneur, avec tous les documents.* Paris, 1893. [Note: an old but informative source].

Sassier, Yves. *Hugues Capet.* Paris, 1987.

Saxl, Fritz. *Illustrated Medieval Encyclopedias,* II: *The Christian Transformation. Lectures.* London, 1957.

Scherman, Katharine. *Daughter of Fire: A Portrait of Iceland.* Boston and Toronto, 1976.

________. *The Flowering of Ireland: Saints, Scholars, and Kings.* Boston and Toronto, 1981.

Schoenfeld, Hermann. *Women of the Teutonic Nations.* Philadelphia, 1907. [Note: not very scholarly, but fairly accurate.]

Schulenburg, Jane Tibbetts. "Female Sanctity: Public and Private Roles, ca. 500–1100." *Women and Power in the Middle Ages,* ed. by M. Erler and M. Kowalewski (1988), 102–125.

________. "The Heroics of Virginity." *Women in the Middle Ages and Renaissance,* ed. by Mary Beth Rose (1986), 29–72.

________. "Women's Monastic Communities, 500–1100: Patterns of Expansion and Decline." *Sisters and Workers in the Middle Ages,* ed. by J.M. Bennett et al (1989), 208–239.

Scofield, Cora L. *The Life and Reign of Edward the Fourth.* 2 vols. London, 1923.

Scott, Franklin D. *Sweden: The Nation's History.* Carbondale and Edwardsville, 1988.

Scott, Ronald McNair. *Robert Bruce: King of Scotland.* London, 1982.

Scott, Walter Sidney. *Jeanne d'Arc: Her Life, Her Death and the Myth.* New York, 1974.

Sermoise, Pierre de. *Jeanne d'Arc et la Mandragore: Les Drogues et l'Inquisition.* Monaco, 1983.

Seward, Desmond. *The Hundred Years War: The English in France, 1337–1453.* New York, 1978.

Shahar, Shulamith. *The Fourth Estate: A History of Women in the Middle Ages.* London and New York, 1983.

Sheehan, Michael M. *The Will in Medieval England; from the Conversion of the Anglo-Saxons to the End of the Thirteenth Century.* Toronto, 1963.

Sherman, Claire Richter. "The Queen in Charles V's Coronation Book: Jeanne de Bourbon and the 'Ordo ad reginam benedicendam'." *Viator: Medieval and Renaissance Studies,* 8 (1977), 255–298.

Shirley, Janet. *A Parisian Journal, 1405–1449.* Oxford, 1968.

Shneidman, J. Lee. *The Rise of the Aragonese-Catalan Empire, 1200–1350.* Vols. I and II. New York, 1970.

Sienaert, E. *Les Lais de Marie de France.* Paris, 1978.

Simon, Kate. *A Renaissance Tapestry: The Gonzaga of Mantua.* New York, 1988.

Sismondi, J.C.L. Simonde de. *The French under the Merovingians and the Carolingians.* Trans. by William Bellington. Rpt. New York, 1976.

Sivéry, Gérard. *Marguerite de Provence: Une Reine au Temps des Cathédrales.* Paris, 1987.

Sizeranne, Robert de la. *Beatrice d'Este and Her Court.* Trans. by N. Fleming. London and New York, 1926.

Slatkin, Wendy. *Women Artists in History: From Antiquity to the 20th Century.* Englewood Cliffs, NJ, 1985.

Smith, Denis Mack. *A History of Sicily: Medieval Sicily, 800–1713.* (Vol. II). London, 1968.

Smith, Jacqueline. "Robert of Arbrissel: Procurator Mulierum." *Medieval Women,* ed. by Derek Baker (1978), 175–184.

Smith, Rhea Marsh. *Spain: A Modern History.* Ann Arbor, Mich., 1965.

Snow, Joseph. "The Spanish Love Poet: Florencia Pinar." *Medieval Women Writers,* ed. by K. Wilson (1984), 320–332.

Solente, Suzanne. *Christine de Pisan.* Paris, 1969.

Somerset, Anne. *Ladies-in-Waiting.* New York, 1984.

Southern, R.W. *The Making of the Middle Ages.* London, 1967.

Sparrow, Walter Shaw. "Women Painters in Italy since the Fifteenth Century." *Women Painters of the World,* Reissued New York (1976), 21–56.

________. *Women Painters of the World.* Orig. publ. London, 1905. Reissued, New York, 1976.

Spuler, Bertold. *History of the Mongols Based on Eastern and Western Accounts of the Thirteenth and Fourteenth Centuries.* Trans. by Helga and Stuart Drummond. New York, 1988 (orig. 1972).

St. Aubyn, Giles. *Year of Three Kings: 1483.* New York, 1983.

Stafford, Pauline. "King's Wife in Wessex." *Past and Present,* 91 (1981), 3–27.

________. *Queens, Concubines, and Dowagers: The King's Wife in the Early Middle Ages.* Athens, GA, 1983.

________. "Sons and Mothers: Family Politics in the Early Middle Ages." *Medieval Women,* ed. by Derek Baker (1978), 79–100.

Staley, John Edgcumbe. *The Guilds of Florence.* New York, 1967 (1st publ. 1906).

Stenton, F.M. *Anglo-Saxon England.* Oxford, 1943.

Stephens, G.R. "The Early Life of Joan Makepiece." *Speculum,* 20, #1 (January 1945), 300–309.

Stephens, H. Morse. *The Story of Portugal.* New York, 1891.

Stephenson, Carl. *Mediaeval History from the Second to the Sixteenth Centuries.* Ed. and rev. by Bryce Lyon. New York, 1962 (4th edit.). Orig. publ. 1935.

Stolpe, Sven. *The Maid of Orleans.* London, 1956.

Strayer, Joseph R. *The Albigensian Crusades.* New York, 1971.

Strickland, Agnes. *Lives of the Queens of England.* London, 1840. [Note: old yet still useful.]

Stuard, Susan M. "Fashion's Captives: Medieval Women in French Historiography." *Women in Medieval History and Historiography,* ed. by S. M. Stuard (1987), 59–80.

________. "A New Dimension? American Scholars Contribute their Perspective." *Women in Medieval History and Historiography,* ed. by S. M. Stuard (1987), 81–99.

________. "Women in Charter and Statute Law: Medieval Ragusa/Dubrovnik." *Women in Medieval Society,* ed. by Susan M. Stuard (1976), 199–207.

________, ed. *Women in Medieval History and Historiography.* Philadelphia, 1987.

________, ed. *Women in Medieval Society.* Philadelphia, 1976.

Stubbs, William. *Germany in the Early Middle Ages, 476–1250.* Ed. by Arthur Hassall. New York, 1969 (1st publ. 1908). [Note: old but quite useful.]

________. *Germany in the Later Middle Ages, 1200–1500.* Ed. by Arthur Hassall. New York, 1969 (1st publ. 1908). [See note above.]

Sturcken, H.T. "The Unconsummated Marriage of Jaime of Aragon and Leonor of Castile (Oct. 1319)." *Journal of Medieval History,* 5 (1979), 185–201.

Summers, Montague. *The Geography of Witchcraft.* New York, 1970.

Sumption, Jonathan. *The Albigensian Crusade.* London and Boston, 1978.

Szarmach, Paul E., ed. *An Introduction to the Medieval Mystics of Europe.* Albany, NY, 1984.

Talbot, C.H., ed. and trans. *The Life of Christina of Markyate: A Twelfth Century Recluse.* Oxford, 1959.

________ and E.A. Hammond. *The Medical Practitioners in Medieval England: A Biographical Register.* London, 1965.

Tanner, Norman P., ed. *Heresy Trials in the Diocese of Norwich.* London, 1977.

Thièbaux, Marcelle, trans. and ed. *The Writings of Medieval Women.* New York and London, 1987.

Thomas, Keith. *Religion and the Decline of Magic.* London, 1971.

Thompson, James Westfall. *Feudal Germany.* Vols. I and II. New York, 1962 (1st publ. 1928).

________. *The Literacy of the Laity in the Middle Ages.* New York, 1960.

Thomson, John A. *The Later Lollards, 1414–1520.* London, 1965.

Thorndike, Lynn. *A History of Magic and Experimental Science.* Vols. III and IV: 14th and 15th centuries. New York, 1934.

Thrupp, Sylvia. *The Merchant Class of Medieval London.* Chicago, 1948.

Thurston, Herbert, S.J. and Donald Attwater, ed. *Butler's Lives of the Saints.* Vols. 1–4. New York, 1956.

Tierney, Brian and Sidney Painter. *Western Europe in the Middle Ages, 300–1475.* 4th ed. New York, 1983.

Toumanoff, Prince Cyril. "On the Relationship between the Founder of the Empire of Trebizond and the Georgian Queen Thamar." *Speculum,* 15 (1940), 299–312.

Tout, T.F. "A Mediaeval Burglary." *Bulletin of the John Rylands Library,* 2, #4 (Oct.–Dec. 1915), 348–369.

Trevelyan, Janet Penrose. *Short History of the Italian People.* New York, 1956.

Trotula. *The Diseases of Women.* Trans. by Elizabeth Mason-Hohl. Los Angeles, 1940.

Tuchman, Barbara W. *A Distant Mirror: The Calamitous Fourteenth Century.* New York, 1978.

Tuck, Anthony. *Richard II and the English Nobility.* New York, 1974. [Note: not an especially scholarly source.]

Turgot, trans. by Alan O. Anderson. "Life of Queen Margaret." *Early Sources of Scottish History, A.D. 500–1286.* Vol. 2 (Edinburgh, 1922).

Tyerman, Christopher. *England and the Crusades, 1095–1588.* Chicago and London, 1988.

Uitz, Erika. *Women in the Medieval Towns and Cities: The Legend of Good Women.* Mount Kisco, NY, 1990.

Uminski, Sigmund H. *The Royal Beggar: The Story of St. Elizabeth of Hungary.* New York, 1971.

Vale, Malcolm G.A. *Charles VII.* Berkeley and Los Angeles, 1974.

Vallet, M. *Histoire de Charles VII.* Vol. II. Paris, 1865.

Valous, Guy de. *Le Patriciat Lyonnais aux XIII et XIV Siècles.* Paris, 1973.

Vambery, Arminius. *Hungary: In Ancient, Mediaeval, and Modern Times.* New York, rep. 1972.

Van Cleve, Thomas Curtis. *The Emperor Frederick II of Hohenstaufen: Immutator Mundi.* Oxford, 1972.

Vanderauwera, Ria. "The Brabant Mystic: Hadewijch." *Medieval Women Writers,* ed. by K. Wilson (1984), 186–203.

Vauchez, André. "Charité et Pauvreté chez sainte Elisabeth de Thuringe." *Études sur l'Histoire de la Pauvreté,* ed. by Michel Mollat, vol. 1 (Paris, 1974), 163–173.

Vaughan, Richard. *John the Fearless: The Growth of Burgundian Power.* London, 1966.

________. *Philip the Bold: The Formation of the Burgundian State.* Cambridge, MA, 1962.

Vercauteren, F. "Les Médecins dans les principautés de la Belgique et du Nord de France du viiie au xiiie siècle." *Moyen Âge,* 57 (1951), 61–92.

Verdon, Jean. "Recherches sur les monastères feminins dans la France du Sud aux ixe–xie siècles." *Annales du Midi,* 88 (1976), 117–38.

________. "Les Sources de l'histoire de la Femme en Occident aux xe–xiiie siècles." *Cahiers de Civilisation Medievale,* Vol. 20, #2–3 (April–Sept. 1977), 219–251.

Verheyen, Egon. *The Paintings in the Studiolo of Isabella d'Este at Mantua.* New York, 1971.

Vernadsky, George. *Kievan Russia.* Vol. II of *History of Russia.* New Haven, 1948.

________. *The Mongols and Russia.* Vol. III of *History of Russia.* New Haven, 1953.

________. *Russia at the Dawn of the Modern Age.* Vol. IV of *History of Russia.* New Haven, 1959.

Vitalis, Orderic. *The Ecclesiastical History of Orderic Vitalis.* Trans. and ed. by M. Chibnall. Oxford, 1969. Vols. I–IV.

Volpato, Antonio. "Between Prophetesses and Doctor Saints: Catherine of Siena." *Women and Men in Spiritual Culture, XIV–XVII Centuries,* ed. Elisja Schulte van Kesses, 149–61. The Hague, 1986.

Wainwright, F.T. "Aethelflaed, Lady of the Mercians." *The Anglo-Saxons,* ed. by Peter Clemoes (London, 1959), 53–69.

Wakefield, Walter L. *Heresy, Crusade, and Inquisition in Southern France 1100–1250.* Berkeley and Los Angeles, 1974.

Warlop, E. *The Flemish Nobility Before 1300.* Kortrijk, 1975–1976.

Warren, Ann K. *Anchorites and their Patrons in Medieval England.* Berkeley, 1985.

Warren, W.L. *Henry II.* Berkeley and Los Angeles, 1973.

Waugh, Scott L. "Marriage, Class and Royal Lordship in England under Henry III." *Viator: Medieval and Renaissance Studies,* 16 (1985), 181–208.

Weisheipl, James A. *Friar Thomas d'Aquino; his life, thought, and work.* Garden City, NY, 1974.

Weiss, Michael. "The Castellan; the Early Career of Hubert de Burgh." *Viator: Medieval and Renaissance Studies,* 5 (1974), 235–252.

Wemple, Suzanne. "S. Salvatore/S. Guilia: A Case Study in the Endowment and Patronage of a Major Female Monastery in Northern Italy." *Women of the Medieval World,* ed. by Wemple and Kirschner, (1985), 85–102.

________. *Women in Frankish Society: Marriage and the Cloister, 500–800.* Philadelphia, 1981.

Wensky, Margret. "Women's Guilds in Cologne in the Later Middle Ages." *Journal of European Economic History,* 11, #3 (1982), 631–650.

Wentersdorf, Karl P. "The Clandestine Marriages of the Fair Maid of Kent." *Journal of Medieval History,* 5 (1979), 203–231.

Werveke, H. Van. "Industrial Growth in the Middle Ages: The Cloth Industry in Flanders." *Economic History Review,* 2nd. ser., vol. VI, #3 (1954), 237–245.

Wessley, Stephen. "Female Imagery: A Clue to the Role of Joachim's Order of Fiore." *Women of the Medieval World,* ed. by Kirshner and Wemple (1985), 161–178.

________. "The Thirteenth Century Guglielmites: Salvation through Women." *Medieval Women,* ed. by Derek Baker (1978), 289–304.

Westphal-Wihl, Sarah. "The Ladies Tournament: Marriage, Sex, and Honor in Thirteenth Century Germany." *Sisters and Workers in the Middle Ages,* ed. by J.M. Bennett et al (1989), 162–189.

Whitelock, Dorothy, ed. and trans. *Anglo-Saxon Wills.* Cambridge, 1930.

Wickersheimer, E. ed. *Dictionnaire Biographique des médicins en France au Moyen Âge.* 2 vols. Rpt. Geneva, 1979. Pp. 1–417= v.1; Pp. 418–867= v. 2.

Willard, Charity Cannon. "A Fifteenth Century View of Women's Role in Medieval Society: Christine de Pizan's 'Livre des Trois Vertus'." *The Role of Women in the Middle Ages,* ed. by R.T. Morewedge (1975), 90–120.

________. "The Franco-Italian Professional Writer: Christine de Pizan." *Medieval Women Writers,* ed. by K. Wilson (1984), 333–363.

________. "Isabel of Portugal and the French Translation of the Triunfo de las Donas." *Revue belge de philologie et d'histoire,* 43 (1965), 961–969.

Williamson, David. *Debrett's Kings and Queens of Britain.* Exeter and London, 1986.

Wilson, Katharina M., ed. *Medieval Women Writers.* Athens, GA, 1984.

________. "The Saxon Canoness: Hrotsvit of Gandersheim." *Medieval Women Writers,* ed. by K. Wilson (1984), 30–63.

Wimsatt, James I. "Beatrice as a Figure for Mary." *Traditio,* 33 (1977), 402–414.

Windeatt, B.A. "Julian of Norwich and her Audience." *Review of English Studies,* new ser. 28 (1977), 1–17.

Winston, Richard. *Thomas Becket.* New York, 1967.

Wolf, Leonard. *Bluebeard; the Life and Crimes of Gilles de Rais.* New York, 1980.

Wolff, Robert Lee. "Baldwin of Flanders and Hainaut, First Latin Emperor of Constantinople: His Life, Death, and Resurrection, 1172–1225." *Speculum,* 27 (July 1952), 281–299.

Wood, Charles T. "Queens, Queans and Kingship: An Inquiry into Theories of Royal Legitimacy in Late Medieval England and France." *Order and Innovation in the Middle Ages,* ed. by Jordan et al (1976), 385–400.

Wood, Michael. *In Search of the Dark Ages.* New York, 1987.

Wright, C.E. *The Cultivation of Saga in Anglo-Saxon England.* Edinburgh, 1939.

Wright, F.A., trans. and intro. *The Works of Liutprand of Cremona.* New York, 1930.

Wright, Thomas, ed. *A Contemporary Narrative of the proceedings against Dame Alice Kyteler, prosecuted for sorcery in 1324, by Richard de Ledrede, bishop of Ossory.* London: Camden Society, 1843.

Wrightman, W.E. *The Lacy Family in England and Normandy, 1066–1194.* Oxford, 1966.

Wylie, James Hamilton. *History of England under Henry the Fourth.* London, 1969.

Young, Karl. *The Drama of the Medieval Church.* 2 vols. Oxford, 1933.

Yriarte, Charles. *Rimini: Études sur les lettres et les arts a la cour des Malatesta.* Paris, 1882. [Note: very complete, but old, opinionated and chatty.]

Zarnecki, George. "The Contributions of the Orders." *The Flowering of the Middle Ages,* ed. by Joan Evans (1976), 41–80.

Zum Brunn, Emile and Georgette Epiney-Burgard, eds. *Women Mystics in Medieval Europe.* New York, 1989.